TWENTIETH CENTURY CHINA

20TH CENTURY

CHINA

THIRD EDITION

By O. EDMUND CLUBB

NEW YORK

COLUMBIA UNIVERSITY PRESS

O. Edmund Clubb was the U.S. Consul General in Peking when Sino-American diplomatic and consular relations were broken off in 1950. Since retiring from the State Department after twenty years' service in Asia, he has lectured on Chinese history at Columbia, Cornell, and other universities.

Biog.
DS
774
.C57
1978

Columbia University Press
New York   Guildford, Surrey

Copyright © 1978 Columbia University Press

First edition 1964
Second edition 1972
Third edition 1978

Library of Congress Cataloging in Publication Data

Clubb, Oliver Edmund, 1901–
    20th century China.

    Bibliography: p.
    1. China—History—1900–   I. Title.
DS774.C57   1978   951.04   77–18991
ISBN 0–231–04518–2
ISBN 0–231–04519–0 pbk.
9 8 7 6 5 4 3 2

To Mariann

PREFACE

THE SUBJECT of twentieth century China is vast, extending as it does from the imperial era, through the transitional Republican period, and into the Communist stage of Chinese history. China's domestic affairs during that period were exceedingly complex. In the Republican era particularly, a number of self-contained separate regimes, under warlord rule, made their own minor local histories without more than casual relationship to what was happening in Peking—the putative center of the country's government. Contemporary Chinese accounts were as partisan as the politics, making for much conflict of testimony: Sun Yat-sen's version of events would be found notably different from that offered by a warlord regime at Peking, for example, and Nationalist history diverges substantially from that written by the Communists with whom the Nationalists wrestled from 1927 to 1949. This sector of China's modern history has been sadly neglected in many major aspects by scholars and is characterized by large patches of terra incognita and other elements which are still controversial. The present, Communist, stage of China's historical progression is being subjected to the most intensive research by American scholars, but here we see a process of change that defies final determinations.

This book finds its first warrant in the very circumstance that there is an acknowledged growing need, in the West, for fuller understanding of twentieth century China. The full telling would take many volumes, and within the compass of one book much must necessarily be omitted—even of the important. This volume is a political history, a bird's-eye survey aimed at tracing the main course of the developments that led to the final collapse of the dynastic principle, the abortive experiment in republicanism, and the final resort to a Sinicized communism as the presumed solution for China's tremendous problems. And, as Chinese history would warn us, the subject is of prime importance. The Chinese now count easily one fourth of the human race, and they are a great nation in terms of cultural and political accomplishment. Unified by the iron rule of Mao Tse-tung and his fellow Communists, driven by the urge to regain a position of dominance in Asia, China shows a clear potential for playing once more, as on numerous occasions during its two thousand years of existence, a major role in the making of history.

This is a matter of great concern to the United States, which, in mid-century, with the advent of the Communists to power, abandoned its traditional China policy and embarked upon a radically different approach. Whether the present policy constitutes a fruitful strategy for dealing with the new China will be proved in the latter part of this century. The Asian situation of which China is the storm center is one of both great complexity and great instability, and it is impossible to foresee the situation as it will exist at the year 2000. It is nevertheless logical to assume that the history of the decades that have gone before suggest some of the possible future trends. And this is to be said: the dangers involved in being wrong about China today are vastly greater than they were at the time of the Battle of Manila Bay.

I express my deep thanks to Dr. Richard C. Howard and Prof. A. Doak Barnett, who kindly read, respectively, Parts I and II and Part III of the manuscript and made many helpful suggestions. I am indebted to Mr. Lu Kuang-huan for his courtesy in providing me with the Chinese characters adorning the face of the book cover, comprising the translation of "Twentieth Century China" into the Chinese language. I acknowledge further the generosity of various persons who have supplied photographs used to illustrate the work. The photograph of Dr. Sun Yat-sen comes from the work by Paul Linebarger, *Sun Yat-sen and the Chinese Republic* (New York, Century, 1925); that of Tuan Ch'i-jui is from B. L. Putnam Weale, *The Fight for the Republic in China* (New York, Dodd, Mead, 1917). I am grateful, too, to my son, Dr. Oliver E. Clubb, Jr., for helpful editorial criticism. For both valuable criticism and assistance with the typing and other matters related to the preparation of the manuscript, I am deeply indebted to my wife Mariann.

I express my thanks to the Harvard University Press for authorization to use, as a basis for the redrawn maps showing the borders of China at various periods of its development, certain maps contained in the work by Albert Herrmann, *Historical and Commercial Atlas of China* (Cambridge, 1935). I acknowledge likewise the courtesy of Avrahm Yarmolinsky for permitting me to quote a long passage from the work he translated from the original Russian and edited, *The Memoirs of Count Witte* (New York, Doubleday, 1921).

September, 1963   O. EDMUND CLUBB

PREFACE TO SECOND EDITION

As the first edition of this book came off the press, in 1964, China saw the beginnings of a "cultural revolution" which in due course came to full flowering as the Great Proletarian Cultural Revolution. This new edition has been designed in main to encompass that historic episode, and to bring the account down to October, 1971, when Communist China won entry into the United Nations. After a half century of existence, the Chinese Communist Party had brought China to a new stage in both its domestic condition and its foreign affairs. In the end, at the point where the revolutionary leadership of 1921–71 prepares to leave the stage of history, I have endeavored to set forth some salient features of "Mao's China," as seen today. China will change with the passing of Mao and his remaining Old Comrades; but the China of the future will still bear their imprint.

January, 1972   O. EDMUND CLUBB

PREFACE TO THIRD EDITION

IMPLEMENTATION of the Maoist doctrine of "uninterrupted revolution" resulted effectively in the institutionalization of political instability, and disorder, in the People's Republic of China. Injection of the "class struggle" into the Party leadership structure during the course of the Great Proletarian Cultural Revolution exacerbated the trend toward factionalism within the ruling hierarchy proper. The purge in seriatim of close associates of Mao Tse-tung, such as Liu Shao-ch'i and Teng Hsiao-p'ing, and circumstances surrounding the death and political disgrace of Lin Piao in 1971, demonstrated that there was indeed no secure refuge from Mao's arbitrary assaults other than a strong defensive faction. The logical operation of Maoism thus rendered highly unlikely an orderly succession to power upon Mao's passing: in the conflict between the (radical) Maoist "revolutionary line" and the (moderate) "bourgeois revisionist line" one faction or the other would be subjected to coup and purge, and both factions knew it. Chairman Mao had himself laid the groundwork for a power struggle.

Events in the years 1971–76 bore out the logical expectation of trouble. Premier Chou En-lai at the Fourth National People's Congress of January, 1975 made a final valiant effort to provide for an orderly succession, but his death one year later provided the occasion for a fresh coup by the Maoists against alleged "capitalist-roaders" within the leadership. That the Maoists' tactics had, however, acted over the years to strengthen the opposition was shown when Mao died in September, 1976—and Party and Army leaders, waiting upon no further purges by the radical faction, struck swiftly and decisively at the radical leadership in turn. Successful in their coup, the organization men then undertook the reorientation of basic national policies and the reordering of the national priorities.

This, then, is the rationale for bringing out a new edition of *Twentieth Century China* at this time. The revised work includes a record of the chief events marking the end of the Maoist era, and depicts new trends discernible at the beginning of the post-Mao stage of China's twentieth-century development, with the story brought down to the Eleventh Party Congress of August, 1977, which marked consolidation of the new leadership in power.

February, 1978   O. EDMUND CLUBB

CONTENTS

MAPS

ILLUSTRATIONS

following page 80

INTRODUCTION: "CONFUCIAN" CHINA

AT THE END of the thirteenth century, when Marco Polo told Europe what he had seen during his seventeen years in China, he was met with incredulity and derision. But by the eighteenth century Europe had come to believe not only Marco Polo's tales but also that China had evolved a perfect form of government. A hundred years later the Western nations undertook to break down the Middle Kingdom's exclusionism and to bring to China the "benefits" of Occidental trade and religion. As the century neared its end, the powers thought they saw China disintegrating, and some reached out to possess themselves of rich fragments. At the beginning of the present century, the United States assumed the role of China's protector, with the moral obligation of assuring that China might have unimpeded opportunity to develop its own modern political institutions. After fifty years, however, the United States abandoned the overidealized picture of its involuntary protégé. It adopted a diametrically opposed policy toward China and set about building another Great Wall of exclusionism to replace the one that had been so laboriously torn down—this time to keep China "contained" in isolation.

The violent oscillations in Western evaluation over the years indicate that China has been, and remains, as it was in Marco Polo's time, the unknown, the uncomprehended—and the unbelievable. But it behooves the Occident to study modern China assiduously. The present Chinese revolution unfolding before our eyes may radically change the course of human history.

In order to understand the China of today, one must take into
account its geographical environment, its long and turbulent history, and many influences from its political and social traditions.

FROM FEUDALISM TO EMPIRE

China possessed, according to the Confucians, a Golden Age
when social organization and government were perfect. But this
was only a legend that attempted to describe conditions existing
two millennia before Confucius lived. At the beginning of recorded
history there was no "Middle Kingdom," no "China," but only a
large number of feudal city-states ruled by autocrats. If, as the legend holds, they had once lived at peace with one another in accordance with the dictates of high moral principles, it is a fact that in
Confucius' time the order of the day was dissension between these
feudal states and misery within them.

In this period the Hundred Schools of Philosophy debated the
relation of Man to the Universe and of Man to Society. Confucianism, emerging in this milieu, sought to sanction the existing feudal
system, but at the same time to refine it, by recalling to the hard-
bitten feudal autocrats the Golden Age of the third millennium B.C.
and the worthy examples of governmental conduct provided in that
far-off period by the sage-kings Yao, Shun, and Yü. Confucianism
constituted a vain attempt to restore what had never existed—
government by virtue and merit. As a political philosophy, it stood
in middle ground, flanked on one extreme by the full-fledged altruism of the Mohists who offered universal love as the prime governing force in the world, and on the other by mankind's first philosophical totalitarianism, the thought of the Legalist School. Other
philosophers offered an infinite variety of systems.

The distinguishing feature of the Chou era was the gulf existing
between the Hundred (feudal) Clans and "the little folk," characterized by the saying "Ritual does not extend as far down as the
people, nor the penal code as far up as the nobility." The over-all
picture presented by the end of the feudal era is indicated by its
common designation, the period of the Warring States. Confucianism, at the time of Confucius, was notably ineffectual.

Today China is a vast conglomerate of deserts, mountains, high
plateaus, and rich river valleys; two thousand years ago the brawl-
ing feudal states held much less territory. Most of the domains were
located in river valleys, and all of them were within the area that

eventually became China proper. Fertile land was of narrowly limited extent: it was bounded by arid regions, interrupted by mountainous areas, and often afflicted by floods. China was no natural paradise.

Peoples of other blood lived to the south, west, and north. The feudal states were in a more advanced stage of cultural development than their crude neighbors. But if one factor making for conflict among the feudal states in their central position was the impact of vigorous barbarian tribes on their periphery, an even greater factor was sharply increasing population pressures on the available agricultural land. Disorders grew as the peasant serfs were overloaded with ever heavier taxes and herded into the nobles' armies. It was a period of social disintegration.

The Warring States, in a fratricidal conflict that lasted 250 years, destroyed the feudal system of which they were a part. A highly centralized empire succeeded. It was not Confucianism that brought about the change, but the harsh, terribly logical philosophy of the Legalists, whose advocates guided the victorious Ch'in ruler to establish, for the first time, an empire—China. The Confucianists and followers of various other philosophical creeds got short shrift: Ch'in Shih Huang-ti (the First Emperor of Ch'in) burned all works of opposition philosophies that could be found, and buried a goodly number of scholars, to demonstrate that he would brook no further contention. The Hundred Schools of Philosophy had been able to exist by reason of the very anarchy of the times. When the anarchy ceased, free political discussion also ended.

Thus, in the third century B.C., China abandoned feudalism in favor of imperialism. Not immediately, but before the beginning of the Christian era, the autocracy proceeded to retrieve the philosophy of Confucius, adapted it to the uses of empire even though it had been framed originally for the feudal system, and established a rigid social and bureaucratic hierarchy on the basis of that transformed "Confucianism." The essence of the doctrine was the concept that the political system was a part of the cosmic system and as unchanging, and that the social system's Truth was both eternal and of universal application. It provided for enlightened rule by a moral, ethical ruler—the emperor, Son of Heaven. The five human relationships of Confucianism, binding the subject in obedience to the ruler and defining other social ties, provided moral sanction for the hierarchy by which the empire was ruled.

This order of things did not in practice prevent social convulsions.

The concept, circulated abroad in the seventeenth and eighteenth centuries especially, was that of a people who were essentially quiet and peace-loving by virtue of the Chinese philosophical system. The Chinese, however, were not born Confucian but were fitted into that mold for certain purposes. The truth is that Confucianism no more kept China away from violence than the Christian religion brought peace to Christendom. Indeed, China has a history that yields to none in bloodshed.

CHINESE AND THE "BARBARIANS"

A study of China's wars helps to a fuller understanding of China. Many of those wars were fought, naturally enough, against the "barbarians" on the country's periphery. The Chinese regarded all peoples other than themselves as "barbarians," and the wars against these non-Chinese were waged unceasingly. With the fortunes of war the boundaries of the Chinese empire alternately expanded and contracted. As expansion of the boundaries dominated the cycles, so through the centuries China has grown in size to match its growth in power as a nation.

This power was made manifest when China was unified, and a unified China was always expansionist, inclined to demand that weaker neighboring peoples accept vassal status and pay tribute or, abruptly, simply to flood over the "barbarians" and absorb them. The ethics of Confucianism contained no proscription of such expansionism at the expense of "barbarians." Indeed, Confucianism embodied the idea of universal empire. The country's frontiers were regarded as expansible.

When the nation's power ebbed, however, the non-Chinese periphery tended to break away, usually because the Chinese were engaged in civil strife. Their domestic wars tended to be far bloodier and more debilitating than those waged abroad. In the two millennia of dynastic history, the empire split into fragments on a number of occasions. At times, parts of purely Chinese territory were ruled by small alien peoples, by uncouth "barbarians" like the Toba Tatars, the Kidani, or the Jurchen. At other times China was unified, as in the Han, T'ang, and Ming dynasties. Only two alien peoples succeeded in establishing their rule over China as a whole, the Mongols and the Manchus. It is nevertheless noteworthy that these two numerically insignificant peoples expanded the boundaries of the Chinese Empire to their greatest extent.

History records twenty-five dynasties for two millennia; twenty-five times the ruling house was ousted from power. Although complex, the history of these dynasties shows a pattern of certain constants, most notable among which are (1) ethnocentrism, manifesting itself in a strong sense of cultural superiority; and, collaterally, (2) a demand that other nations approach China not as equals but as inferiors; and, consequently, (3) an inherent urge to impose China's will on peripheral nations by force of arms, in conquest. Steeped in the concept of hierarchy, the Chinese naturally regarded relations with other peoples as being between superior and inferior —with China the superior.

THE DOMESTIC STRUCTURE

This was the external manifestation of China's nationhood. It clearly provided for change, for what might be called an ever-expanding political universe. Domestically, the situation was very different. The Chinese state system by no means worked ideally. The violent social storms that periodically swept over the land were evidence of a malfunctioning of Confucianism as it had been institutionalized for purposes of government.

The domestic pattern was one of hierarchy, of social stratification, of established rites and procedures, including those governing tenure of both political position and land. In theory, the peasant's son could become prime minister. In practice, his parents first had to find money for an education that would enable him to pass the extraordinarily difficult civil service examinations, then he had to wait years for an appointment, and perhaps in the end he would have dispensed large bribes to numerous eunuchs standing in the path to high preferment. Patently, the greater opportunity was offered to a son of the land-holding gentry class.

Agriculture was the dominant economic activity and main source of revenue, but there was a fundamental maladjustment in the country's Confucian system of land tenure: the cultivator was at a disadvantage before the tax collector and the usurer. In theory, the system permitted the peasant to buy more good earth from a landlord, if he could gather together the money; but, with equal legitimacy, it also permitted the landlord to acquire the final bits of land of starving peasants. Since the landlord was much the stronger, there was a distinct tendency for agricultural lands to become concentrated in ever fewer hands.

The peasants were ordinarily unable to recover control of lost lands by legitimate means. When their want and misery became sufficiently painful, they often took to banditry, and sometimes under strong leaders they formed revolutionary armies in order to overthrow a dynasty and despoil the landowners through a redistribution of the land. In this way two peasants even became founders of new dynasties, the Han and the Ming. But the essential relationship of peasant to governor and landlord did not change.

Another grave weakness of the Confucian system was manifested at the very heart of government: the emperor, who, for the proper working of the political system, was called upon to be a moral man as well as the omniscient and omnipotent Son of Heaven, in real life was often all too human. In the emperor's palace, instead of ineffable wisdom, there was frequently deep ignorance of prevailing conditions in the empire, and a pervasive corruption fostered by wilful concubines and evil eunuchs. The Hsia and Shang lines had ended, according to the Confucian interpretation, owing in good measure to the deep-laid vices of the last rulers. But the viciousness did not disappear when Confucianism became the basis of the state: it made for bad government at the top and maladministration throughout, causing oppression of the "little people." Corruption was an incurable cancer in the Confucian body politic.

WAXING AND WANING OF EMPIRE

It was within this framework that China, "the Middle Kingdom," piled up its rich history. The Occident called the vigorous nation "Chinese," presumably after the Ch'in dynasty that created the empire, but in their own language they call themselves "men of the Middle Kingdom" (*chung kuo jen*)—or often, especially under the present Communist order, "men of Han."

For it was the Han dynasty that began the expansion of the Chinese authority from the minor base that had been the Ch'in dominion. The Han rulers projected Chinese rule right into Central Asia, where, for a brief time, it touched the Roman Empire. Because of domestic disorders, the Han dynasty crumbled after 400 years. The Middle Kingdom lost its power in non-Chinese Central Asia, and even the Chinese part of the empire broke up into several contending kingdoms. But the division did not result in destruction of the imperial principle. Each regional ruler viewed himself as the legitimate successor to the unified imperial power.

Force, not Confucian reason, ended the division. Reunification came with the Sui dynasty, over three and a half centuries after the fall of the Han. The T'ang dynasty followed (618–907 A.D.). In early T'ang times, China was self-confident and tolerant in its foreign relations, hospitable to influences from India, Central Asia, and elsewhere. Arab ships traded by sea, Buddhism and Nestorian Christianity came overland; and, at the same time, Chinese culture flowered and scattered rich fruits into other areas of East Asia, particularly Japan and Korea.

Whereas the Han dynasty had collapsed by reason of inner rot, the T'ang fell chiefly because of the devastating, long-term effects of a great rebellion launched by an ambitious general, the favorite of the imperial concubine Yang Kuei Fei. The T'ang armies had earlier thrust part way into Central Asia, but they, too, were now forced to relinquish their hold on non-Chinese lands and peoples. The empire shrank, then shattered into pieces once more. It was to be a thousand years, except for the brief period of Mongol rule, before "Chinese" authority in Central Asia was restored by the Manchus.

The successor Sung dynasty never achieved a full restoration of the empire as it had existed in the T'ang era. Chinese culture was now brought to perhaps its greatest height, but not so Chinese political power. It was left to the conquering Mongols to give the "Chinese" empire, in a short space of eighty years, dimensions greater than it ever possessed before—or since.

The conqueror Mongols, like the T'ang Chinese, were hospitable to foreign visitors and foreign contacts. One of the criticisms that the Confucians made of Mongol rule was, in fact, that the Mongols made extensive use of aliens as administrators instead of relying exclusively upon the corps of Chinese scholar-officials, so ready and willing to serve. But no need was felt in either T'ang or Mongol times to introduce foreign political concepts into China, since the Chinese ideology was manifestly so superior, in the eyes of both the Chinese and the Asian "barbarian," to any alternative system.

The Mongol rule in China collapsed chiefly by reason of schisms that developed between various descendents of Genghis Khan's clan who ruled different parts of an empire extending from Korea and China to Lithuania and Persia and from the Siberian steppes on the north to India. The succeeding Ming dynasty was again Chinese, and it was also weak. The empire contracted again, until it was once more bounded on the land side by the Great Wall that

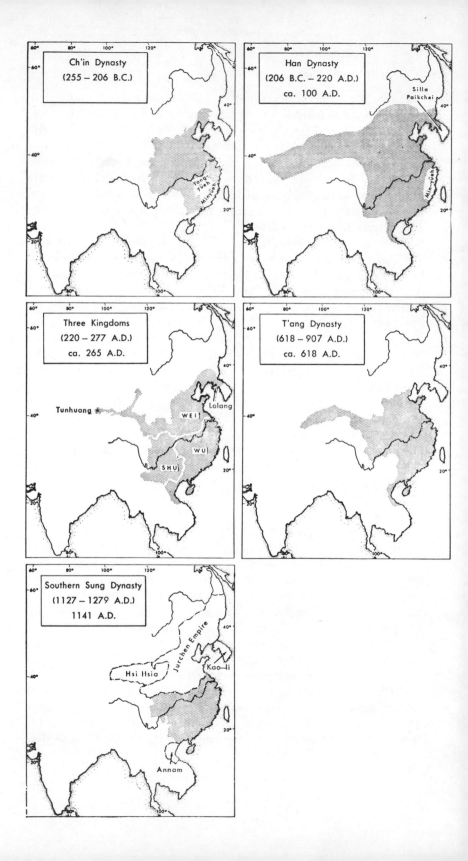

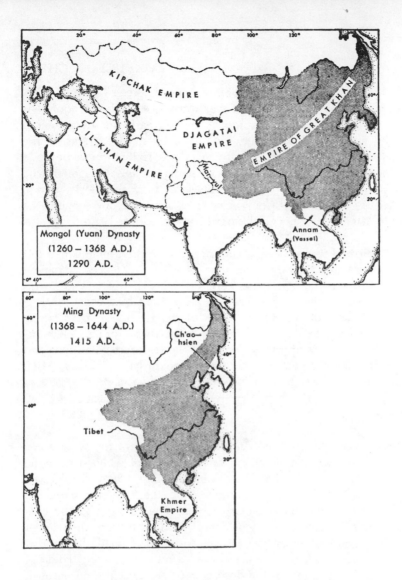

Mongol (Yuan) Dynasty
(1260 – 1368 A.D.)
1290 A.D.

Ming Dynasty
(1368 – 1644 A.D.)
1415 A.D.

CHINA UNDER SUCCESSIVE DYNASTIES

The Expansion and Contraction of Empire

The Chinese Empire, running through twenty-five dynasties, was not a geographical constant but, instead, from time to time, expanded, changed shape, or contracted, reflecting a variety of influences. In particular, internal union tended to make the nation both strong and expansive; domestic dissension, making for national weakness (and upon occasion actual division), and sometimes the pressures of strong "barbarians," tended contrariwise to bring about the breaking off of non-Chinese elements on the periphery, with consequent shrinkage of the empire. China's boundaries were not immutable but instead reflected national strength or weakness. And the imperial urge persists today.

Based on Albert Herrmann, *Historical and Commercial Atlas of China* (Cambridge, Mass., Harvard University Press, 1935).

had been completed by Ch'in Shih Huang-ti fifteen hundred years earlier. But now a new element was introduced into the equation: with the coming of the Portuguese by sea early in the sixteenth century and, less than a hundred years later, the arrival of the Russian Cossacks in East Asia by overland routes, there began a prolonged siege of China by white seafarers and landsmen who were prepared neither to admit Chinese cultural superiority nor to follow the established Confucian rules of intercourse with the Middle Kingdom. They did not come as tribute-bearers but as equals.

The spiritual wounds of the experience with the Mongols had left the Chinese inordinately suspicious of alien influences. Japanese piracy, early in the Ming era, kept the wounds open. The Portuguese, by similar plunder and rapine along the China coast, quickly confirmed some of the deeper fears of the Chinese. There began to grow, alongside the ignorance of what these foreign elements represented, a deep apprehension as to the seafarers' intentions and good faith. Concerned for the Confucian order of things, Ming China tried to close the door on the new influences.

THE MANCHUS

History was quick to give an element of warrant for Ming fears, while still denying the effectiveness of a policy of seclusion. Taking advantage of the fact that there were feckless Chinese rulers on the Dragon Throne, a minor Tungusi tribe, the Manchus, came out of the northeast to conquer giant China. The country, in the configuration familiar to us today, is actually the creation of the warrior Manchus. The vast expansion was not in terms of fertile land, however, but was made up mainly of the semi-arid grazing lands of Mongolia and Dzungaria, the deserts and widely scattered oases of Eastern Turkestan, and the lofty Tibetan plateau. In China proper, vast sections were either mountainous or semi-arid and hardly suitable for agriculture. During the Ming period the population of China had begun to show a marked increase. The pressure of population on the land was therefore certain to grow—and so was peasant misery.

Despite the fact that the empire had expanded during two millenia, the problem of land tenure took on critical dimensions in the late dynastic period. Whereas China's population had fluctuated narrowly between fifty and sixty million during the Ming dynasty (1368–1644), it had reached nearly three hundred million at the

beginning of the nineteenth century. The increase was no evidence
of an inherent capacity of the country to provide livelihood for ever
more Chinese. Instead, it reflected the Draconian peace maintained
by the Manchu conquerors and a substantial, if still limited, increase in productive capacity because of the introduction of the
sweet potato from the Occident.

The hard fact was that the Chinese population always expanded
to the margin of subsistence, that is, to the limits of the food supply.
And each time that the food supply was temporarily reduced in
some part of the country by flood, drought, locusts, or the ravages
of warfare, thousands starved to death. The Chinese countryside
was a very different world from that of the urbane, glittering, and
well-fed capital—and that countryside was generally outside the
field of vision of the admiring and somewhat covetous West. For
the great mass of the Chinese people China was a land of recurrent
dearth and famine.

At the end of the eighteenth century, peasant distress once more
took the form of violent insurrection. The White Lotus Rebellion,
lasting from 1796 to 1803, was anti-Manchu in its manifestation,
but it was born of the growing imbalance between population and
food supply. The movement had been put down with difficulty.
The crisis was passed, but the augury remained.

THE BREAKDOWN OF EXCLUSIONISM

It was at this very time that the white seafarers were becoming
more insistent in their demand that, as a matter of right, they
should be permitted to trade freely with China and have their diplomatic representatives reside in Peking. Since it was also the period
of expansive Protestant evangelism, Christian missionaries soon
joined forces with mercantilism to knock at the door of the Middle
Kingdom.

But Confucian China refused to deal with non-Chinese on a basis
of equality. It had no "foreign relations" as such, for it continued
to view all countries and nations as being inferior and intrinsically
subordinate to China. Non-Chinese affairs were handled, under the
Manchus, by either the Li Fan Yuan (Court for the Governance of
the Borderlands) or the Board of Rites (which prescribed the
amount of tribute to be paid by neighboring princes and the procedure for its delivery). China's only system of peacetime foreign
relations was its tributary system.

China's Closed Door was finally broken down by the sea powers

—Britain, the United States, and France. As a result of the Opium War of 1839–42 between Britain and China, the victorious British, by the 1842 Treaty of Nanking, forced the opening of five China ports to trade and Peking's agreement to specific low import tariffs. In a supplementary treaty signed the following year, the British introduced the "most-favored-nation" clause, by which British subjects were to enjoy all privileges that China might thereafter grant to any other nation.

In the 1844 Treaty of Wanghia, the United States expanded upon the preceding British agreements and established extraterritorial jurisdiction in both civil and criminal cases for American citizens in China. Shortly afterward the French signed a treaty of their own, which, in addition, gave Catholic missionaries the right to construct churches in the treaty ports. The foundation for a century of relations between the Western seafarers and imperial China had been laid. Extraterritoriality, the most-favored-nation clause, and Western insistence upon the principles of freedom of trade, of evangelism, and of residence—all would contribute substantially through the years to the build-up of Occidental positions in China. These factors would progressively contribute as well to the growth of Chinese resentments against the oppression of the "unequal treaty" system and to the undermining of the dynastic authority.

Even that partial opening of China's door to foreign economic and ideological influences was quick to affect both the country's economy and Chinese thinking. The morbid opium trade had introduced a cancerous growth into the nation and was gradually infecting vital parts of the Chinese government. The impact of cheap foreign textiles, brought in under an import tariff pegged low by the first treaties, began to break down the country's autarchic village economy. And whereas the bureaucracy's limited imagination envisaged only firearms and ships, and some knowledge of geography and languages, as Western contributions of possible use to China, potentially rebellious elements of the nation were in due course attracted to various alien political concepts.

THE T'AIP'ING REBELLION

The nature of the danger that the West's political influence held for the Manchu rule was soon made manifest. Anti-Manchu sentiment was exacerbated by widespread economic distress. In mid-century, from 1850 to 1864, the country was racked by a new upheaval, the T'aip'ing Rebellion. This revolutionary movement, built upon the widespread unrest of the depressed peasantry, differed from previous popular insurrections in that it incorporated distinctly Western elements: its leader, Hung Hsiu-ch'uan, characterized himself as the younger brother of Jesus and formulated a revolutionary ideology that was a Chinese version of Protestant Christianity.

The T'aip'ings proposed not only to overthrow the Manchu rule; they intended also to achieve a social revolution. Driven by Hung's messianic creed, the rebels aimed at improving the status of women, opposed the opium traffic, and introduced communal economic organization. They also embarked upon a reform of land tenure in order to achieve a better balance between the agricultural population and available arable lands and thus won support from the discontented Chinese peasantry.

The times patently demanded social and economic change. Social revolution nearly sufficed as a motive force for the T'aip'ings: their armies came within sight of Peking. But the movement incorporated basic weaknesses of both leadership and ideology and, moreover, collided with the interests of the foreign powers. By military actions undertaken against China between 1857 and 1860, the British and the French had won new political and commercial concessions from the Manchu Court. And the Americans, through a treaty signed at the same time and through operation of the most-favored-nation clause, had won the same privileges for their merchants and missionaries and the right of residence for their diplomatic envoy at Peking. Having now a big stake in the continued existence of the Manchu rule, the British, the French, and the Americans alike turned to support it. The Manchu government, on its part, in 1861 established a Tsung Li Ko Kuo Shih Wu Yamen (Office in General Charge of Affairs Concerning All [Foreign] Nations), commonly termed the Tsungli Yamen—China's first Office of Foreign Affairs. The "barbarians" had wrung from China the grudging acknowledgment of their political equality.

Chinese generals, of whom the most outstanding was Tseng Kuo-fan, had in the meantime begun to get the upper hand over the rebels. In 1864, after fifteen years of struggle and the expenditure of some twenty million lives, the great Chinese peasant uprising collapsed. The blood-letting and final failure of the T'aip'ing Rebellion caused the postponement of major social change in China for nearly a full century. The Western sea powers, for their part, had evolved a "cooperative policy" the better to further their aim of maintenance of the newly won "treaty rights."

RELATIONS WITH TSARIST RUSSIA

Substantial political gains had also been won in the 1857–60 period by an imperialist power not associated with the "cooperative policy"—Tsarist Russia. Russia's relations with China dated back to Mongol times, and China's first treaty ties with a European power were with Russia. The treaties of Nerchinsk and Kiakhta, signed in 1689 and 1727, had fixed the boundaries between the domains of the Tsar and the Manchu emperor in East Asia. They had incidentally provided points of reference for the expansion of the Russian Empire. Russian envoys had reached Peking while the representatives of the sea powers were still struggling fruitlessly to get through the gate at Canton, but they had failed to achieve a regularization (in the Occidental sense) of Russo-Chinese diplomatic relations. Nevertheless, there had been direct political contacts and a limited overland trade between the two countries for over three centuries, so that Russia stood in a distinctly different relationship to China, as evidenced by the aforementioned treaties, than did the sea powers.

Rivalries among the Occidentals, and especially between Britain and Russia, played their part. From the start of the nineteenth century, Russia had been in conflict with Britain in the Black Sea region, Persia, and Central Asia. Britain had developed fears of Russian designs on India. The Crimean War (1853–56) increased the tensions between the two powers. Consequently, Russia, the great Eurasian land power, did not associate itself with the "cooperative policy" of the three sea powers. Its Far Eastern policy in mid-century was instead designed to offset British imperial power in particular and to strengthen the Russian position in the Pacific region—where expanding empires were converging. As the Manchu vigor visibly declined, Russia acted energetically to consolidate its sovereign rule over Northeast Asia.

The Anglo-French military pressure of 1857–60 gave the Russians a major opportunity to advance their East Asian interests. China, desirous of obtaining an effective counterweight to the Anglo-French importunities, availed itself of Russia's offer to mediate between the Manchu Throne and the allies; and Sino-Russian treaties signed in 1858 and 1860 combined to give Russia, as a *quid pro quo,* title to the territory on the left bank of the Amur and east of the Ussuri River. This territory, lightly populated by Tungusi tribes, was of little immediate economic value, but it substantially buttressed the Russian Empire's Far Eastern frontier. The Russian domain now half enveloped Manchuria, the land of the Manchus, and its southeastern tip bordered on Korea. The town the Russians established as their base on the Pacific frontage was significantly named Vladivostok, "Ruler of the East."

EMERGING JAPAN

The year 1860 can be taken as a critical turning point for Manchu power. The proven debility of the Chinese empire constituted a standing invitation to the covetousness of foreign powers. Japan, wrenched out of its own exclusionism, joined in the East Asian power struggle by moving against Formosa and Korea, China's vassal, in the 1870s. It levered China out of its claim to suzerainty over the Ryukyu Islands and annexed the Bonins. Other empire builders went into action. In the 1880s, the French waged a new war against China in order to win control over Annam, another Manchu vassal state; farther west, the British pushed back Manchu claims to suzerainty and extended their control over Burma.

In 1894, China and Japan went to war over Korea. Japan had come a long way since combined American and Russian pressure in the mid-nineteenth century had broken down the barriers Japanese feudal lords had erected against the outside world. And the Empire of the Rising Sun easily defeated the armed forces of the Middle Kingdom, by land and by sea, within a few short months after the Japanese declaration of war on August 1. By the April, 1895, Treaty of Shimonoseki that ended the war Japan gained title to Formosa and the Pescadores and recognition of the independence (from Chinese authority) of Korea. The peace treaty also included provision for new commercial privileges and payment of an indemnity to Japan.

By a new commercial treaty Japan also wrung from China the coveted most-favored-nation clause. It had not been invited to participate in the Western powers' councils, but, by so handily beating giant China, it had won a prominent position in the arena previously dominated by the Westerners. The results of the Sino-Japanese War truly signified the end of an era for East Asia.

The immediate consequences of the Sino-Japanese War in China's foreign relations were disastrous for the Manchu rule. The disclosure of the nation's—and the dynasty's—inherent weakness made it appear that "The Breakup of China" (as one contemporary book was entitled) was imminent. The powers avidly eyed valuable fragments, toned down the "cooperative policy," and jostled each other in a scramble for large shares of the spoils. There ensued that struggle for territorial concessions, leaseholds, "nonalienation" commitments, and spheres of influence that came to be called "the Battle for Concessions." From 1896 to 1898, Russia, Germany, Britain, France, and Japan, exploiting the Japanese victory, acquired substantially increased political and economic holdings in China. Japan's sphere of influence was established in Fukien and, of course, "independent" Korea. The United States, heavily engaged in the Spanish-American War, came into the picture too late to share in the prizes, had it so desired.

The Spanish-American War had brought American "manifest destiny" to the Western Pacific, with the result that Americans thereafter would look upon China with new eyes. Brooks Adams, in his book *America's Economic Supremacy,* defined the issue as follows:

By 1870 the most tempting regions of the earth had been occupied, for the Anglo-Saxons had reached the Pacific. . . . The last step of the advance was taken in the war with Spain. Then the Americans crossed the Pacific, and the two great branches of the Anglo-Saxon race met on the coast of China, having girdled the earth.

In the favored line, running from east to west, all the choicest territory had been occupied, besides most of what is accessible in the southern hemisphere. Eastern Asia now appears, without much doubt, to be the only district likely soon to be able to absorb any great increase of manufactures, and accordingly, Eastern Asia is the prize for which all the energetic nations are grasping.[1]

In the Orient Japanese leaders saw the danger that the disintegration of China would bear for Japan. Viscount Ishii quoted an old Chinese phrase to make a point: "As the teeth are exposed to the cold when the lips are gone, so would Japan be exposed to tragic developments if China's territory were lost." At this time was born the conviction that, for national survival, Japan had to extend its authority to the mainland.

In Chinese eyes the prestige of the Manchu rule had been in steep decline since mid-century. The defeat at the hands of the Japanese and the new infringements of China's political sovereignty and territorial integrity deeply stirred the nation. Nationalistic feelings were whipped into violent motion, and the country's thinkers addressed themselves actively to the exigent problem of finding means to restore the empire's once great power.

From the Opium War up to 1860 the Manchu Court and the mandarinate had refused to face up to the meaning of the new forces in play. There was a real, and vast, ignorance of the Occident, resulting in much ineptness in dealings with the Westerners. Persistent recourse to evasion and procrastination in diplomatic relations, and countermeasures adopted by foreign powers, led to an exacerbation of antiforeignism.

After the 1860 treaties of Tientsin, the meaning of the various shifts in the balance of power between the forces maneuvering in the West Pacific area grew upon Chinese thinkers. As in Japan, Chinese officials and scholars in the T'ung Chih reign (1862–75) undertook a "restoration." The Peking government purchased some guns and naval vessels abroad, set up arsenals, and engaged in the construction of Western-style ships. Increased attention was given to the study of Western geography and even of foreign languages.

But all the changes undertaken, or envisaged, thus far were based upon the concept that "Chinese knowledge is the theme, Western knowledge is for [practical] use." Reforms were still strictly conceived within the rigid framework of the Confucian tradition. The innate conservatism of the Confucian system still ruled. There was no perceptible move toward the exploration, not to mention adoption, of concepts of social change and economic progress. In particular, even the most radical of the innovators continued to cleave to the principle that agriculture was the basis of the nation's livelihood and of state revenue. No thinkers of the period drew upon the indelible lessons of the T'aip'ing Rebellion for their inspiration. They sought instead to employ some of the trappings of Western power against the Westerners themselves in a process of "self-strengthening."

ATTEMPTED REFORM

Only in 1898 did there come to the Throne a realization that the measures of "reform" thus far undertaken did not suffice to serve

even the limited aim in view and that the nation's very existence
was at stake. In response to the urgings of a group led by the
Confucian innovator K'ang Yu-wei, the Emperor Kuang Hsu decided on sweeping reforms in China's ancient structure. June, 1898,
marked the beginning of a series of edicts directing modernization
of the bureaucracy, revision of the educational system that produced the country's bureaucrats, the modernization of agriculture
and other changes in the nation's economy, the introduction of both
an annual budget and Western forms of military drill, and a variety
of other innovations. Spurred on by a sense of urgency, the reformers pushed for a fundamental renovation of the established order
of things.

The dynastic structure had been showing unmistakable signs of
debility, and drastic measures were called for. But reform, in a
system that by definition was philosophically perfect, where forms
and practices had the strong sanction of custom reaching back two
thousand years, was hardly to be viewed as a simple matter: transition for Chinese society's great mass from an antique to a vastly
different "modern" form was bound to be an arduous process. Reform in the heart of government was especially difficult.

The decrees envisaged, among other things, the abolition of sinecures and the removal of conservative officials from office. They
constituted a frontal assault upon the cherished privileges of the
ruling Manchu house and upon the vested interests of the upper-
level bureaucracy. The chances for victory by such a campaign
were small. The benighted but determined supporters of the *status
quo* mobilized their forces, rallying around Kuang Hsu's aunt, the
obscurantist Empress Dowager Tz'u Hsi. The Emperor moved to
meet the threat, but the forces headed by the Empress Dowager
were too strong for him. Tz'u Hsi struck, incarcerated the Emperor,
effected the execution of six of the leading reformers (K'ang Yu-wei
and some others escaped, to fight another day), and promptly un-
did the reforms of the "Hundred Days." The Emperor's reform
spirit was replaced by a bigoted xenophobia, and the Peking government reverted to the traditional use of subterfuge and the obvious device of trying to play off one power against another in the
sphere of foreign affairs. The Manchus had fumbled their last
chance to save the dynasty by reform of the system from the top.

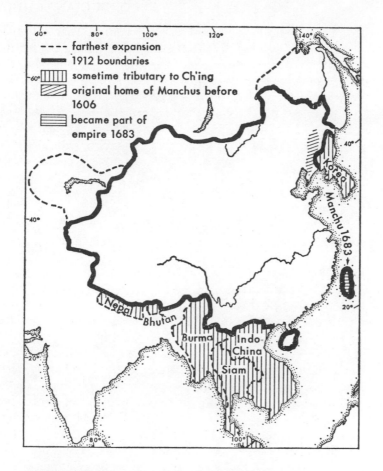

THE EMPIRE AT THE TIME OF THE
MANCHU (CH'ING) DYNASTY (1644–1912)

Based on Albert Herrmann, *Historical and Commercial Atlas
of China* (Cambridge, Mass., Harvard University Press, 1935).

PART I

COLLAPSE OF THE CONFUCIAN ORDER

1 DECAY OF THE DYNASTIC PRINCIPLE

THE YEAR 1900 marked a fundamental shift in the world balance of power. The process of colonization that had resulted in an expansion of Western empires in the Orient had reached its peak. The Western empire builders were now pressing on the last independent entities of the East. The question was whether there should be accommodation or conflict. The answer seemed clear: a frontal clash was impending—not only with weak Oriental states but among powers competing for imperial advantage.

Sir Halford Mackinder, in a far-sighted discussion of "The Geographical Pivot of History" before the Royal Geographic Society in 1904, held that the era of four centuries of European expansion against nearly negligible political resistance was ending. The empty spaces of the world had been filled, and the closed political system of the past would govern in the future. Thereafter, "every explosion of social forces, instead of being dissipated in a surrounding circuit of unknown space and barbarian chaos, will be sharply re-echoed from the far side of the globe, and weak elements in the political and economic organism of the world will be shattered in consequence."

A conflict among the "crowded" powers was clearly developing in East Asia. The United States, Russia, and Japan had measurably advanced their positions there. Construction of the Trans-Siberian Railway had begun in 1891, and the Russian thrust eastward had gained momentum after China and Russia had bound themselves by the Li-Lobanov alliance of 1896 to mutual support in opposition to any aggression by Japan against Russian East Asia, China, or Korea. In 1898, the United States annexed the Philippines, thus projecting its "manifest destiny" into the West Pacific. Washington thereafter shifted its policy in China, diverging from the cooperative policy of the preceding forty years.

Powerful forces had been at work both within China and between China and steadily encroaching elements of Western civilization. In 1900 those forces manifested themselves in the Boxer Rebellion. The curtain was rising on the death agony of the dynasty and the end of an imperial era that had lasted over two millennia.

THE BEGINNING OF THE END: THE BOXER REBELLION

The situation in China had undergone a fundamental change after the failure of the reform effort of 1898: the political balance of power having swung sharply toward political reaction, those who had favored reform were pushed toward revolution. This development occurred against a familiar pattern of popular distress. By the end of 1898 northern Kiangsu Province had experienced two bad crop years, and the result was famine, unrest, and banditry, which spread to Anhwei and Shantung. In the fall of 1898 Shantung suffered disastrous floods that affected about 2,500 square miles of territory with a population of one to one and a half million people. In the spring of 1899, with the deepening of the famine, children sold in northern Kiangsu for 50 to 1,000 copper cash each. The secret sect known as the Big Swords became active, and, after three missionaries were involved in disturbances in Shantung, the movement of discontent focused on foreigners.

Rumors spread that foreigners had been driven from Peking, and antiforeignism grew with the news. Looting of missionary properties added fuel to the flames. Governor Yü Hsien of Shantung tolerated the disturbances, and it soon became clear that he was probably a Big Sword member himself. The situation worsened with transfer of leadership from the traditionally peasant Big Swords to a secret society which became known as the Boxers and with adoption by the Boxers, in 1899, of the slogan "Support the Manchus, annihilate the foreigners." After protests from the foreign legations in Peking, official instructions were issued to protect the missionaries—but those instructions were accompanied by secret orders to the contrary. The antiforeign movement had received the blessing of the Throne.

In a secret edict of November 21, Empress Dowager Tz'u Hsi informed her viceroys: "Our Empire is now laboring under great difficulties which are becoming daily more serious. The various powers cast upon us looks of tiger-like voracity, hustling each other in their endeavors to be the first to seize upon our innermost territories." She directed that they stand fast in resistance to the foreign aggression.

Tz'u Hsi embodied the strength, and the fatal weaknesses, of the last half century of the Manchu era. Born Yehonala, she became the imperial concubine of the Emperor Hsien Feng, and after the Emperor's death in 1861 her son had become the Emperor T'ung Chih. She and the Empress Consort were made empresses dowager by an early edict issued in the name of the infant ruler, and, with the help of Prince Kung, Hsien Feng's brother, they overthrew the established regency and won the palladium of authority.

As Empress Dowager Tz'u Hsi, Yehonala then undertook to concentrate power in her own hands. When the Emperor T'ung Chih died in 1875, officially of smallpox but probably by reason of dissolute excesses encouraged by Tz'u Hsi, the latter imposed her will on the court and in violation of the established rules of succession had her infant nephew selected for the throne. T'ung Chih's widowed consort, sensing her probable fate, thereupon committed suicide. In 1881 the other Empress Dowager, Tz'u An, suddenly died. Rumor had it that she had been poisoned. In 1884, having long harbored a hatred of Prince Kung for his role in the execution of a favorite eunuch, Tz'u Hsi had that experienced statesman stripped of all his posts. Her autocratic authority had now been fully consolidated.

The Manchu throne commanded the services of some able and wise advisers. Prince Kung had contributed in large measure to the careful conduct of China's foreign affairs from 1860 to 1884. Tseng Kuo-fan, the sober Chang Chih-tung (Liang Kwang viceroy), and the skillful Li Hung-chang, were able to—and upon occasion did—provide sage advice on the administration of affairs of state.

But Tz'u Hsi effectively replaced the spirit of Prince Kung by her own bigotry in China's affairs. A vicious new favorite eunuch, Li Lien-ying, both pandered to Tz'u Hsi's vices and cultivated her native bent toward misrule. The Empress Dowager's corrupt nature made her incapable of providing the leadership required of the Manchu rule in those years of change. When the first superficial innovations undertaken by the government failed to win substantial gains in the foreign field particularly, her innate conservatism, and that of her sycophantic associates, was strengthened.

In 1889, after marrying a niece to her nephew the Emperor Kuang Hsu, who had now reached his majority, Tz'u Hsi gave up her regency and retired to the Summer Palace on the outskirts of Peking. She clearly expected the young Emperor, under the less-than-benevolent surveillance of her niece, to continue the general policies she had laid down. She had acknowledged the need of some modernization—but would limit reforms to the modest measures of "self-strengthening" supported by Li Hung-chang, Chang Chih-tung, and other moderates, during the 1880s and 1890s. When Kuang Hsu in 1898, heeding impatient innovators spurred by a sense of national urgency, embarked upon his radical reform program and projected it so far as to threaten Tz'u Hsi's own position, however, she wrenched him from power. A plan to murder Kuang Hsu and put the son of Prince Tuan on the throne leaked out, and the expressed opposition of both foreign diplomats and powerful viceroys deflected the scheme. But Tz'u Hsi kept her nephew prisoner and effectively ruled in his stead. With the Empress Dowager again at the helm, the Chinese ship of state was now heading directly into the storm.

Tz'u Hsi was right in feeling that the various powers were jostling each other to obtain additional concessions and privileges in China, but she was profoundly wrong in viewing the Boxers as an effective instrument of response. The antiforeign movement had spread by the end of 1899 from Shantung into Chihli, Shansi, and also southern Manchuria. But the Boxers were committed by Tz'u Hsi's clever manipulations to the defense of the dynasty and thus, unlike the T'aip'ings, could find no support in broad peasant resentments. The Boxers had their chief backing in court circles, where Tz'u Hsi eagerly hearkened to the advice of Chief Eunuch Li Lien-ying and Prince Tuan—who hated the foreigners for their "interference" in the plan for replacing Kuang Hsu by his son—and dreamed of expelling the foreign influence from China by use of a rabble whose chief strength was a superstitious belief in the efficacy of magic practices in battle.

In late 1899, after the killing of a number of Chinese Christians and the widespread burning of churches in Shantung, the legations at Peking succeeded in getting the removal of Yü Hsien from that province. He was replaced as Shantung governor by

Yuan Shih-k'ai, who saw clearly that his career would not be served by cession of his authority to the like of the Boxers. Yuan proceeded to demonstrate, by example, that the Boxers' magic fell far short of making them invulnerable to bullets as they claimed. He suppressed the movement in his province—and went on to expand his army. Yü Hsien, made governor of Shansi, continued to permit the Boxers to run wild under his jurisdiction, with the result that in the end more foreign missionaries were killed in Shansi than in any other province.

The Western sea powers united once more in cooperative action. On January 18, 1900, the American, British, French, and German Ministers sent identic notes to the Tsungli Yamen in which, referring to the current violence directed against their missionaries, they demanded (in the language of the American note) "speedy suppression of these rioters [Boxers and Big Swords], the restoration of order, the punishment of the criminals and the derelict officials, and prompt compensation for the property destroyed." [1] The nonparticipation of the Russian and Japanese envoys in those joint *démarches* was noteworthy: Russia and Japan, in line with their own policies, were retaining freedom of action.

But the die was cast. The Empress Dowager, heeding both her own xenophobic urges and the malevolent advice of court figures such as Prince Tuan and Grand Eunuch Li Lien-ying, decided to combine the power of the Boxers with the strength of the imperial armies and drive the foreigners from the country. She had support in other armed forces than those of the Boxers. Tung Fu-hsiang, commanding a force of hard-fighting Moslem soldiery from Kansu stationed just outside Peking, was as antiforeign as Tz'u Hsi. On June 11, Tung's troops killed a secretary of the Japanese legation; two days later, the Boxers were invited into Peking and promptly joined Tung's forces in rapine and pillage. Then, on June 20, there came the murder of the German Minister, Baron von Kettler, and the Manchu Government's declaration of war on the foreign powers. The "siege of the legations," which were only lightly defended, now began.

The Manchu Court had committed its crowning folly. Eight powers organized an international force, reduced the Taku forts, and occupied Tientsin. They were tardier in undertaking the relief of the legations, and the desultory siege there was prolonged, but on August 14 the international army, including Japanese and Russian contingents, captured the capital—in time to save the foreign community from the general massacre that had been ordered by Tz'u Hsi.

The Empress Dowager fled in disguise to avoid capture by the hated foreigners. She took the captive Emperor with her, and, accompanied by Grand Eunuch Li Lien-ying, kept going until she reached Sian (Changan), the ancient capital in China's Northwest. Kuang Hsu's favorite consort, the Pearl Concubine, had suggested that the Emperor be left behind to negotiate peace—and Tz'u Hsi had her thrown down a well.

The disorders did not spread. Powerful viceroys, such as Li Hung-chang at Canton (where he had been consigned in disgrace in 1899) and Chang Chih-tung at Wuchang, kept order in South and Central China. Military leaders now made short work of the shattered remnants of the Boxers, and the Boxer Protocol of 1901 brought an end to the matter by providing for punishments and indemnities, the razing of the Taku forts, the establishment of an autonomous extraterritorial legation quarter in Peking, and the right of foreign troops to maintain open communications between Peking and the sea.

In 1899 the American Secretary of State, John Hay, had dispatched a note to six powers aimed at obtaining their agreement for maintenance of the Open Door of commercial opportunity in China. The responses had expressed approval in varying terms, generally stipulating that the rule had to apply to all for acceptance. Although the Russian reply was distinctly equivocal, Secretary Hay had chosen to assume general agreement on his principle and had informed the interested chancelleries accordingly.

At the height of the 1900 Boxer troubles, Hay sent out another note, this time to eleven countries, stating that

the policy of the Government of the United States is to seek a solution which may bring about permanent safety and peace to China, preserve Chinese territorial and administrative entity, protect all rights guaranteed to friendly powers by treaty and international law, and safeguard for the world the principle of equal and impartial trade with all parts of the Chinese Empire.[2]

Even as the Hay note was dispatched (July 3), joint armed intervention by the eight powers was in course. The Department of State purported at the time to understand that there had been general acceptance of the American position, but the wish was patently father to the thought. In hard fact, the Hay notes had no substantial effect on the course of future events. Once the Boxer crisis was past, schisms in the ranks of the powers reappeared, deeper than ever. China was saved from dismemberment at that time not by the admonitions of the American Secretary of State but by the very competition between the powers for the spoils: the conflicting designs and jealousies of Britain, France, Germany, Italy, the United States, Russia, and Japan tended to offset each other. But the clashing ambitions remained—and continued to batter at the collapsing dynasty.

Peking's joining of battle in 1900 with the greatly superior Occident was a political and military error of first magnitude. Nevertheless, even subsequent recognition of the error failed to convince the Chinese people that their cause was not just. The native forces of dissatisfaction that had erupted in the Boxer rebellion were still alive. Diverted from the channel of antiforeignism, they now threw themselves against the decaying Manchu power.

TWILIGHT OF THE DYNASTY

For the time being, however, the shifts in the balance of power in domestic politics were overshadowed by developments in the field of foreign relations. When the Boxer disorders had spread to Manchuria, Russia had sent in troops to occupy the whole area. A Sino-Russian agreement of late 1900 gave Russia broad powers of control in South Manchuria. St. Petersburg modified its stance under pressure from the powers, but the Japanese and British both took alarm at this new evidence of imperialistic hunger.

The Japanese, who had faced Russian competition in Korea ever since the Sino-Japanese War, were seeking ways to strengthen their international position. They approached St. Petersburg with the aim of obtaining a profitable alliance in that quarter, only to be ignored. The British, however, had by now become disillusioned with the ability of China to recover its imperial vigor and were looking for a new counterweight in the Far Eastern balance of power. In this instance British and Japanese interests coincided, and on January 30, 1902, the two countries signed a treaty of alliance. Japan was now protected against flank attacks by third powers as it sought a resolution of the conflict with Russia.

The Russian forces sent into Manchuria at the time of the Boxer Rebellion were still there. After the signing of the Anglo-Japanese treaty of alliance, China and Russia reached an agreement for withdrawal of the Russian troops. But the formulation of Russian Far Eastern policy was effectively in the hands of the adventurer and court favorite, Bezobrazov, who dominated the policy of the weak-willed Tsar, Nicholas II. There was, consequently, procrastination and delay in the withdrawal. In July, 1903, the arrogant and in-experienced Admiral Evgeni I. Alexieff was made Far Eastern Viceroy, and the potential for political disaster was compounded.

The relatively modern-minded Russian statesman Sergei I. Witte, in a report of that same month, gave an estimate of the over-all Far Eastern situation that doubtless reflected a prominent school of Russian strategic thought:

Rapid ways of communication have drawn the yellow races into the whirlpool of international intercourse. Beginning with the middle of the last century, industrial overproduction and the colonization urge directed the eager attention of Europe and America to the vast dormant countries of the Far East. . . . Given the technical and military superiority of the Westerners, it is not difficult to forecast the outcome of the conflict for those native states. Only those countries will survive which, like Japan, will have speedily acquired those achievements of European culture that are necessary for self-defense; the more inert countries will fall a prey to the powerful invaders and will be divided up between them.

Such is the essence of the Far Eastern problem. Accordingly the problem of each country concerned is to obtain as large a share as possible of the outlived Oriental states, especially of the Chinese Colossus. Russia, both geographically and historically, has the undisputed right to the lion's share of the expected prey. The elemental movement of the Russian people eastward began under Ivan the Terrible. Continuing ever since, it has lately stopped with the occupation of the Kwantung Peninsula. Obviously, neither this territory nor Manchuria can be Russia's final goal. Given our enormous frontier line with China and our exceptionally favorable situation, the absorption by Russia of a considerable portion of the Chinese Empire is only a question of time, unless China succeeds in protecting itself. But our chief aim is to see that this absorption shall take place naturally, without seizing territory, in order to avoid a premature division of China by the Powers concerned, which would deprive Russia of China's most desirable province.[3]

That "most desirable province" was, of course, Manchuria. Japan saw that too, and the conflict of interests led inevitably to collision. A Russo-Japanese treaty of 1898, the so-called Nishi-Rosen treaty, had provided for joint recognition of Korea's independence and noninterference by either signatory. But Russia still interfered. Japan, after the Boxer Rebellion, had proposed the division of Korea at the 38th parallel into Russian and Japanese spheres of influence. This was rejected by St. Petersburg. In 1903, after the

Anglo-Japanese alliance, there were new exchanges of Russian and Japanese proposals. In that year the Chinese Eastern Railway was completed, giving Russia through rail connections from Vladivostok to St. Petersburg. The Court was pursuing the aims outlined by Witte but disregarded his prescription of caution. The negotiations finally terminated fruitlessly on February 5, 1904; on February 8, the Russo-Japanese War began with a surprise attack by Vice Admiral Togo Heihachiro on the Russian squadron in the harbor of Port Arthur.

The war on land was fought in Manchuria, but Russia's Chinese ally was not engaged for all of the provisions of the 1896 alliance, and Manchuria was viewed as "neutral." The Russians had on the spot, including railway guards and the Vladivostok and Port Arthur garrisons, some 80,000 troops; the Japanese first-line army counted 270,000 men. The Japanese had 200,000 reserves, whereas the Russian reserves were practically unlimited. But the Russians could bring up their reserves only along the thin line of the single-track Trans-Siberian Railway, at the maximum of 30,000 men a month.

Russia suffered a serious loss in its top command when the Russian flagship "Petropavlovsk" was blown up by a mine on April 13: Admiral Stepan O. Makarov, the able naval commander for the Far Eastern fleet, went down with his vessel. The Port Arthur squadron thereafter remained cautiously in port, and Togo had nothing to do but keep guard and try—unsuccessfully, as it turned out—to catch the Vladivostok squadron.

The long, tortuous build-up of the Russian army began, with the Japanese racing against time. The Manchurian hostilities pitted Generals Kuroki and Oyama against General Aleksei N. Kuropatkin. The first important land battle was fought at the Yalu River. There the Russian battle plan was thrown out of joint by the quixotism of a local commander who refused to obey Kuropatkin's orders to make a tactical withdrawal on the grounds that it was not customary for a Knight of the Order of St. George to retreat. The Russians consequently lost one third of the force engaged. Again, as in the Sino-Japanese War, a major battle was fought in the Liaoyang sector, causing the main Russian forces to retreat to Mukden. The Japanese, who for months had blockaded Port Arthur from the sea, at the end of July began to besiege that fortified position with their ground forces. On January 2, 1905, Port Arthur surrendered to the enemy.

The fall of Port Arthur marked a turning point in the war. In

October, while the fort still held, a Russian fleet under Admiral Zinovi P. Rozhdestvenski had left the Baltic for the Far East. In February and March, hard on the heels of Port Arthur's capitulation, the great Battle of Mukden was fought, with slightly over 300,000 men engaged on each side. The Russians were again defeated, with losses of nearly 100,000 compared with Japanese casualties of some 40,000–50,000; but they successfully withdrew the remainder of their forces to the north.

In March, following the defeats at Port Arthur and Mukden, the Tsarist Government dispatched naval reinforcements under the command of Rear Admiral Nebogatov to join Rozhdestvenski. The two fleets effected a rendezvous at Camranh Bay, off Indo-China, and on May 17 the combined force—a heterogeneous collection of thirty-six vessels (including twelve battleships)—sailed north. Would it proceed east of the Japanese archipelago to Vladivostok or by the more direct route? On May 27, correctly anticipating the Russian decision to take the direct route, Togo met the Russian armada with his fleet in the Tsushima Strait, and in the ensuing engagement thirty-two of the Russian ships, with their complements, were destroyed.

In Manchuria, the Russians were continuing to reinforce their army, whereas the Japanese had practically exhausted their trained reserves. The Russian field commanders, confident of final victory, desired to continue the struggle. But the Russian Revolution of 1905 had begun in January, and the Tsushima defeat stirred up further animosity against the Tsarist Government. In early June, with disorders spreading at home and defeats in the field weighing heavily upon the Russian effort on the foreign front, Nicholas II accepted President Theodore Roosevelt's offer of mediation. The peace conference was held on American soil, at Portsmouth, New Hampshire, with Roosevelt exercising his good offices. In September the Russo-Japanese War was brought to an end by the Treaty of Portsmouth. Southern Sakhalin and the Liaotung Peninsula were ceded to Japan; Korea was identified as being within the Japanese sphere of influence; and the Russians agreed to evacuate Manchuria. International rivalries in China were now entering a new stage.

The Russo-Japanese War had a powerful impact on China. There, too, changes had been in course. Tz'u Hsi, accompanied by Grand Eunuch Li Lien-ying and prisoner Kuang Hsu, had in 1902 returned from Sian to Peking in a somewhat chastened mood. She appreciated to a degree, at long last, the need for reform. The Court's capacity for effectively embarking upon the way of change, however, had been seriously reduced. Prince Kung had died in 1898. In fine disregard of the circumstance that the Empress Dowager had held him in retirement with his abilities unused from 1884 to 1894, he was canonized as "The Loyal," but his experienced and steadying hand on the State's helm was gone. Li Hung-chang had died, doubtless with a heavily laden heart, two months to the day after signing the Boxer Protocol of September, 1901. Chang Chih-tung and another great viceroy, Liu K'un-yi, still lived and, in response to an early command from the Empress Dowager, jointly submitted to the Throne three memorials setting forth a program for the reform of the educational and civil-service examination systems, the administrative organization, and the military system. But in October of that same year, 1902, Liu K'un-yi died. Grand Eunuch Li Lien-ying lived on, restored to full favor and power. And with the disappearance of so many of the older generation, the star of another man—Yuan Shih-k'ai—was rapidly rising.

Yuan Shih-k'ai had been raised to prominence in the first instance as a protégé of Li Hung-chang. In 1882, when the Court had become alarmed at the growing threat to its suzerainty over Korea, Li had dispatched a contingent of troops there. Yuan Shih-k'ai was on the commanding general's staff. With successful action by the Chinese forces in Korea, imperial rewards flowed to the subordinate officers. Yuan became chief of staff of the Chinese garrison.

In that capacity he was involved in a clash with Japanese guard troops in December, 1884, when pro-Japanese Koreans had attempted a *coup d'état*. Following the burning of the Japanese Legation and the forced flight of the Japanese Minister, Japan sent a naval force to the scene. War threatened but was warded off, for the time being, by a *modus vivendi* negotiated by Li Hung-chang in April, 1885. Yuan became Commissioner of Trade at Seoul and promptly assumed for himself both the functions and title of Imperial Resident.

When war with Japan threatened again in the summer of 1894, Yuan Shih-k'ai submitted his resignation, but it was rejected. Yuan was smitten then by "illness" and thus succeeded in getting back to China before the war broke out. He was sent to Manchuria to help with the service of supply to the Chinese troops and there witnessed the shattering defeat of some of the country's best forces. Back in Peking in 1895, he won the patronage of the Manchu Jung Lu, commander in chief of the army, and was put in charge of training a new, modern army corps. His work in that connection impressed Jung Lu favorably. In 1898 Yuan was able to consolidate his position. Approached by an emissary of the Emperor Kuang Hsu with the proposition that he should take action to neutralize the conservative forces rising in opposition to the reforms being launched, Yuan disclosed the matter to Jung Lu, who promptly informed Tz'u Hsi, and the Emperor's cause was finished.

Because of his part in this, Yuan Shih-k'ai was naturally *persona grata* with the Empress Dowager. He was also in the favor of Grand Eunuch Li Lien-ying. When Li Hung-chang died in 1901, Yuan succeeded him as Chihli Viceroy and "Peiyang Great Official" (North China Trade Commissioner), that is, he was given charge of military and political matters, including foreign affairs, in the metropolitan province. In accordance with the Chang-Liu reform proposals, Yuan undertook in 1902 to expand Chihli's small modernized military force. In December, 1903, he was made Assistant Commissioner of the newly established Army Reorganization Council, charged with creating a model army. His chief of staff was a man who would eventually rise to the peak of power in China, his sworn brother Hsu Shih-ch'ang. His new army, which by 1905 would comprise six divisions, came to be called the Peiyang Army; the divisional commanders, all selected from among Yuan's personal protégés, in due course were to form the nucleus of a powerful clique, the Peiyang Party.

Reforms had been undertaken in the civil as well as the military sector. An imperial edict spurred education by directing the creation of new schools and the introduction of Western subjects into the curricula. The Peking University, established by imperial order, had been the only one of Kuang Hsu's 1898 reforms allowed to remain. Now its work was being supplemented. There began a notable expansion of education by both the government and foreign missionary organizations.

New schools, publishing houses, and newspapers, were putting strange doctrines into circulation—doctrines that were quite heretical by existing Confucian standards. The Throne abolished the classical examination system in 1905, and the "new learning" became the royal road to a political or scholarly career. The Russian Revolution of 1905 had a minor impact on Chinese revolutionary thought, which theretofore had been in large measure nationalistic and directed at political change within the Confucian system and at the expulsion of the Manchus from power. But it was the Japanese victory over imperial Russia in that same year that gave the greatest stimulus to Chinese thinking regarding ways of achieving national strength through internal reforms. Chinese youth, seeking answers to the questions that had begun to burn in their minds, went abroad to study in increasing numbers. While hundreds proceeded to Europe and the United States, thousands went to Japan. There were 500 Chinese students in Japan in 1902, 8,000 in 1905, and 13,000 in 1906. When the United States remitted part of its share of the Boxer indemnity in 1908, the funds were used for the establishment of Tsinghua College in Peking. But Japan had become the gathering place for fervid young nationalists beginning to think along revolutionary lines.

Among the leaders were two of the reformers of 1898, K'ang Yu-wei and his disciple Liang Ch'i-ch'ao. Essentially, they were still "reformers." K'ang's thought in particular remained basically unchanged: he desired to see the establishment of a constitutional monarchy, but aimed first at support of monarchism, and formed a Society for Protection of the Emperor. Liang Ch'i-ch'ao founded a newspaper in Yokohama, the *Hsin Min Ts'ung Pao* (New People's Miscellany), to propagate his ideas on ways of creating a new culture through the study of the strong points of other nations. "Only if we can make something new every day can we find the means to keep the old complete." A loyalist like K'ang, he, too, proposed no more than the transformation of the existing order into a constitutional monarchy.

Other Chinese in Japan of a more revolutionary bent were led by Hu Han-min, Wang Ching-wei, Sung Chiao-jen, and Sun Yat-sen. In 1903 Hu Han-min had briefly attended the Kobun Normal School, which provided special facilities for Chinese students, and had become associated with the revolutionary students Huang Hsing and Yang Tu. Wang Ching-wei had come to Japan as a student sent by Nanyang University. Sung Chiao-jen was editor of a revolutionary periodical. Huang, Hu, Wang, and Sung became the chief political associates of Sun Yat-sen. Sun, possessed of both the fire of nationalism and a deep drive to leadership, provided the focus.

Born near Macao in 1866, Sun represented an older generation. In 1894 he had organized the revolutionary Hsing Chung Hui (China Renaissance Society) in Honolulu. In Canton in 1895 he had been involved in an abortive uprising and had subsequently gone abroad again—only to be kidnapped by the Chinese Legation in London. His life was saved by the intervention of Sir James Cantlie, whom he had come to know while studying medicine at Hong Kong.

Sun's experiences pushed him along ever more radical ways. In Tokyo, in 1905, he was the prime mover in the organization of the T'ung Meng Hui (Alliance Society), a combination of his Hsing Chung Hui with two minor revolutionary parties. The T'ung Meng Hui had four aims: expulsion of the Manchus; restoration of a Chinese national state; establishment of a republic; and equalization of land ownership, with the value increment going to the nation.

From the start, Sun clashed with Liang Ch'i-ch'ao, setting the land tenure issue and the "people's livelihood" against Liang's conservatism. The single-tax concept embodied in the fourth point of the 1905 T'ung Meng Hui manifesto was in line with this thinking, and so was the further statement of the organization's aims: "Besides the driving out of the barbarian dynasty and the restoration of China, it is necessary also to change the national polity and the people's livelihood. And though there are a myriad ways and means to achieve this goal, the essential spirit that runs through them all is freedom, equality and fraternity." Sung Chiao-jen's periodical was transformed into the party's paper, *Min Pao* (People's Newspaper), standing in opposition to Liang's journal. Hu Han-min and Wang Ching-wei were the chief theoretical writers for the *Min Pao* and developed much of the party's revolutionary thought. The Chinese student element in Japan drifted steadily away from the moderation of the monarchists K'ang Yu-wei and Liang Ch'i-ch'ao toward the radicalism offered by Sun Yat-sen and his associates.

In 1907, however, the Japanese government was confronted with protests from the Manchu Throne regarding the revolutionary activity being fomented on Japanese soil. Sun Yat-sen was given a modest cash sum and invited to move elsewhere. He went to Indo-China. The *Min Pao* was left behind, to be finally closed by the Japanese authorities in October, 1908, after three years of existence. By that time, however, it had widely implanted the seeds of nationalism in a whole generation of Chinese students, the T'ung Meng Hui had developed a wide membership within China itself, and a revolutionary group was groping its way toward leadership.

THE CHINESE REVOLUTION OF 1911

Changes in the Confucian political system had proceeded much more slowly than in either international relations or political thinking. In 1902 the Manchu Court had undertaken revision of the ancient legal code and in 1905 sent a mission abroad to study foreign parliamentary systems. In 1906 there was promise of the introduction of parliamentary government; and in August, 1908, the promise was made more categorical: parliamentary government would be introduced in nine years.

Events were crowding on the heels of the decaying dynasty. In 1907 Yuan Shih-k'ai had been appointed president of the Board of Foreign Affairs and concurrently Grand Councilor. He was thus separated from his military authority. In 1908 he became Senior Guardian of the Heir Apparent. That the Heir Apparent occupied an important role in Manchu planning was evident. The Emperor Kuang Hsu died on November 14, 1908, and the following day death ended the long, disastrous rule of Tz'u Hsi herself. It was suspected that the vindictive Tz'u Hsi, who had been ailing, had cold-bloodedly arranged for the Emperor to die before her. Prominent at her official funeral a year later, and perhaps the only real mourner present, was Grand Eunuch Li Lien-ying.

Tz'u Hsi had provided for the succession by arranging that the childless Kuang Hsu should be succeeded by his nephew, the three-year-old P'u Yi. P'u Yi ascended the Manchu Throne as the Emperor Hsuan T'ung. His father, Prince Ch'un (Kuang Hsu's brother), was named regent. There was one more important shift in the balance of internal power. Prince Ch'un had reputedly been asked by Kuang Hsu on his deathbed that Yuan Shih-k'ai be executed for his 1898 betrayal of the Emperor's reform effort. The Regent was not made of heroic stuff, and so the execution did not take place. Nevertheless, in January, 1909, Prince Ch'un announced that Yuan Shih-k'ai was suffering from a foot ailment—and Yuan was graciously permitted to retire to nurse his illness.

In October, 1909, one of the last of the elder statesmen, Chang Chih-tung, died. Hardly any of the top men of the older generation were left to help steady the Manchu rule. Provincial assemblies, viewed as precursors of national parliamentary government, were convened in the same year. Their functions were limited to debating proposals submitted to them, but they became focuses for discontents and centers of political agitation. They promptly demanded an earlier convocation of the promised national assembly. In October, 1910, the Provisional National Assembly was actually convened, with one half of the delegates elected, and the rest appointed by the Throne.

For the Manchu government the convocation of a national assembly was no more than a dying gesture. The Court was racked by the jealousies and intrigues of political figures, women, and eunuchs—a common occurrence at the last stages of Chinese dynasties. With only an infant, the Emperor Hsuan T'ung, on the Throne, the imperial scepter trembled uncertainly in Prince Ch'un's hands.

The international climate contributed to a notable worsening of the Chinese domestic situation. Theodore Roosevelt had mediated in the Russo-Japanese imbroglio with the conviction, expressed in a letter of June, 1905, that "our future history will be more determined by our position on the Pacific facing China, than by our position on the Atlantic facing Europe." For all of its diplomatic support of Japan, however, the United States did not benefit from the changed balance of power in East Asia. In a switch presaging new complications, Japan moved into Russia's place as chief foreign contender for power in Northeast Asia. In 1905 the Anglo-Japanese Alliance of 1902 was renewed. American-Japanese relations were strained the following year by California's application of discriminatory regulations against Japanese school children. Then, by a secret convention of July 30, 1907, the former enemies Japan and Russia agreed to divide Manchuria into Japanese and Russian spheres of influence; in addition, Russia undertook not to obstruct the further development of Japan's political relations with Korea, while Japan recognized Russia's "special interests" in Outer Mongolia.

With that neat apportioning of dominions, the United States found itself effectively frozen out of Manchuria and Korea. In December, 1909, Secretary of State Knox made what was in the circumstances a hopeless gambit: he proposed the internationalization of Manchuria's railways. The move caused the two parties concerned to draw closer together for the protection of their interests. Russia and Japan selected July 4, 1910, as the day to sign a new secret convention, further defining their respective spheres of interest in Manchuria and providing in minatory terms that "in case these special interests should be threatened the two High Contracting Parties shall agree on the measures to be taken in regard to common action or the support to be accorded for the protection and defence of these interests." [4]

In that same year Japan annexed Korea outright, blandly ignoring a seemingly pertinent provision of the American-Korean treaty of 1882: "If other Powers deal unjustly or oppressively with either Government, the other will exert their good offices, on being informed of the case, to bring about an amicable settlement, thus showing their friendly feelings." The United States Government, "on being informed of the case," made no move. The Russo-Japanese entente regarding China and Korea had proved its effectiveness.

At the same time the Western powers helped, by various acts, substantially to weaken the Manchu Dynasty. They continued to exact concessions to build railways in various sections of China, and they pressed loans on the harassed Manchu government to finance railway construction—with interest arrangements highly profitable to the foreign lenders. British, French, and German banks organized a combine to handle such loans; strongly supported by the Taft administration, an American group was able to elbow its way into the combine, and the four-power Consortium was born.

However, the foreign influence embroiled the unstable domestic situation. Minister of Communications Sheng Hsuan-huai was notoriously corrupt; and prominent members of the imperial household wrangled for their share of the commission on government loans. In 1910 China's Provisional National Assembly provided a major forum for the voicing of popular resentments, including strong opposition to the foreign railway loans. That opposition was especially strong in Szechwan Province, where local interests desired to engage in any railway construction for their own profit and had undertaken financing of part of a projected Canton-Hankow-Chengtu Railway, the so-called Hukuang project.

The wishes of local entrepreneurs were understandable, but such an approach to railway building soon proved uneconomic. In early 1911, the central government decided to undertake the construction instead. Chief authority resided in the hands of Minister of Communications Sheng Hsuan-huai, and one consequence was to provide the four Consortium powers with opportunities denied to Chinese competitors. In April, 1911, the Consortium powers practically forced the Manchu Court to accept a loan of £10 million for construction of the Canton-Hankow and Hankow-Chungking lines. The Hukuang loan proved a powder keg. The government's proposal to compensate Szechwan investors not for the amount subscribed but only for actual expenditures on railway construction set off the explosion. Protests were made, workmen struck and shops closed, students stopped attending classes, and societies were formed for "protection of the railroads."

That same April, after months of intensive preparation, the T'ung

Meng Hui attempted a major uprising at Canton. This was the so-called Huang Hua Kang (Yellow Flowers Hill) revolt. It was intended to spark an anti-Manchu revolution, but it failed utterly, and Chinese revolutionary history commemorates the "Seventy-two Martyrs" who died on that occasion. The event doubtless advanced the insurrectionist cause to some extent. But when the revolution actually came, it was in a manner and form largely outside T'ung Meng Hui plans.

In September the Szechwan Military Governor, Chao Erh-feng, arrested some agitators. When a crowd appeared before the provincial government office to demand their release, guards opened fire and killed some forty persons. Chao then petitioned the Throne to abandon the proposed nationalization of the Canton-Hankow-Chengtu Railway. But ex-viceroy Tuan Fang, the powerful new superintendent of the line, took issue with Chao in another memorial to the Throne and was appointed Acting Viceroy of Szechwan with authority to overcome Szechwan's resistance. He started out for the unruly province at the head of a military force.

Meanwhile, at Wuhan, comprising the three middle-Yangtze towns of Wuchang, Hankow, and Hanyang, the authorities got wind of a plot for a military uprising and began to round up suspects. On October 9, a bomb exploded in the Russian Concession at Hankow. That night another explosion occurred in the Military Governor's offices, and two military training officers were executed on the spot. Although the scheduled date for the projected uprising was still a week off, since action had started, the plotters went ahead. On October 10, in Wuchang, a Chinese soldier killed his commanding officer, and the Revolution began.

The military rebels won early success at Wuchang. They placed a reluctant colonel, Li Yuan-hung, in command and proceeded to occupy Hankow and Hanyang, which had an arsenal.

The regime sensed the gravity of the trouble and on October 14 appointed Yuan Shih-k'ai to the post of Hukuang Viceroy and charged him with suppressing the revolt. Yuan replied that his ailing foot still troubled him. Then began the time-consuming process of bargaining with Yuan for his valuable services. It was only after he had been appointed Imperial Commissioner in charge of all China's armed forces that, on October 22, he formally assumed the Hukuang post.

At that time the Peiyang Army comprised the best military units of China. The force was, in the main, Yuan Shih-k'ai's own creation;

and its foremost commanders owed their advancement, and consequently their personal allegiance, to him. Yuan ordered two of his ablest commanders, Feng Kuo-chang and Tuan Ch'i-jui, into action in the Wuhan sector, and, after a brisk fight, they defeated the revolutionary troops commanded by Li Yuan-hung and Huang Hsing (who had by now joined the struggle) and recaptured first Hankow and then, on October 27, Hanyang. In early November, Yuan was named Premier of the Provisional Parliament.

The demonstration of the prowess of the Peiyang Army had satisfactorily established Yuan's bargaining position—which was his chief purpose. The imperial armies thereafter remained motionless. In South and West China, province after province declared its independence of Manchu rule, and the Manchu garrisons were slaughtered. Szechwan was among the revolting provinces. Tuan Fang was murdered by his own men while still en route to Chengtu, and not long afterwards Chao Erh-feng also was killed.

On December 6 Prince Ch'un retired as Imperial Regent, and the following day Empress Dowager Lung Yü gave Yuan full powers to negotiate a settlement with the rebels. This was exactly what the Machiavellian Yuan wanted. He had already formed a new Cabinet composed of his own followers. To the position of Minister of Posts and Communications he had appointed a man who had served him loyally since their first meeting in Korea in 1883, T'ang Shao-yi. Yuan now made T'ang head of an official delegation to go to Hankow to negotiate peace with the rebels, who in the meantime had declared a republican government with Li Yuan-hung and Huang Hsing Generalissimo and Deputy Generalissimo, respectively.

Secret negotiations between Yuan and the rebels had actually begun even before he assumed the Hukuang post, and they continued. Yuan had been charged with saving the dynasty, but he aimed instead at his own rise to power. There was as yet no unity of purpose among the rebellious provinces, but the revolutionaries led by Li Yuan-hung and Huang Hsing joined with a group at Shanghai to set up a provisional government at Nanking. In December T'ang's delegation moved to Shanghai and began negotiations with a delegation representing the revolutionary forces and headed by Wu T'ing-fang. Behind the scenes Yuan's confidential agents kept busy, bargaining with military and political figures, gathering support—for Yuan.

The two official delegations began their formal deliberations on December 18. On December 20 the confidential negotiators, also meeting in Shanghai, reached a secret agreement providing for the exit of the Manchus. It included, among other items, the provisions (1) that a republican form of government be established; (2) that the Emperor and the imperial family be given favorable treatment; and (3) that the man who overthrew the Manchus should become China's first President.[5]

There now were two problems to be resolved: what Chinese leader should become President, and how the Manchus should be finally ousted from legal authority. The first matter was settled without great difficulty. Sun Yat-sen, who was in the United States when the Revolution began, did not reach Shanghai until December 25. On December 29 he was elected Provisional President of China; on January 1 he formally assumed that post at Nanking. But there was no blinking the fact that Yuan Shih-k'ai controlled the effective military power. Even before assumption of the post, Sun had assured Yuan that his action was to be only temporary; on January 15 he formally stated that, when the Manchus abdicated and Yuan declared his support of the Republic, he (Sun) would resign.

Yuan Shih-k'ai, therefore, faced no major obstacle from that direction. Because of the positions he occupied, however, he was technically committed to the support of the dynasty. This obstacle was easily overcome; his agents' efforts had been energetic and fruitful. Chinese diplomats abroad sent in a joint telegram demanding the Manchu abdication. And on January 19, 1912, three of Yuan's Cabinet members presented a joint memorial stating that it was impossible to maintain the monarchical system and requesting Empress Dowager Lung Yü to come to a decision. Two days later an imperial conference was convened to consider the matter of abdication. On January 27, the day the Empress Dowager made Yuan Shih-k'ai a marquis in recognition of his service, forty-seven military leaders, with the name of Yuan's faithful lieutenant Tuan Ch'i-jui heading the list, issued a telegram requesting Manchu abdication and the proclamation of a Republic.

The Manchu dynasts, lost in ignorant bewilderment before the storm beating upon them, weakened by corruption and inefficiency, had reached their term. On February 12, 1912, the ruling house abdicated the Chinese Throne, the Empress Dowager Lung Yü signing the abdication document in the name of the child Emperor Hsuan T'ung. This document conveyed authority to Yuan Shih-k'ai in the following words:

Let Yuan Shih-k'ai organize with full powers a provisional republican government, and confer with the Republican Army as to methods of union, thus assuring peace to the people and tranquility to the Empire, and forming one Great Republic of China by the union as heretofore of the five peoples, namely, Manchus, Chinese, Mongols, Mohammedans, and Tibetans, together with their territory in its integrity.

That part of the charge adjuring the succession regime to unify the five peoples as "one Great Republic of China" would never be forgotten, over the years, by the Chinese leaders who followed. It was notable, however, that even in 1912 important segments of Mongol, Tibetan, and Mohammedan (Turki) territory lay outside the boundaries of the Manchu Empire. The Chinese Republic thus inherited a traditional urge to reassert its authority over certain peripheral areas that, if once held in some way or other by Chinese conquerors, had by now fallen under other authority. This circumstance was to make for grave clashes in the future.

TRANSITION

Yuan Shih-k'ai's succession to power was assured when the Emperor Hsuan T'ung upon abdication transferred all authority to him. But even before the abdication, Yuan held commitments from powerful Chinese civil and military officials and from various T'ung Meng Hui leaders, including Sun Yat-sen. Once the abdication was an accomplished fact, Sun retired in Yuan's favor, and on February 15, 1912, the Provisional National Assembly at Nanking elected Yuan Provisional President of China. A few days later, Li Yuan-hung was made Vice President.

It had been less a political revolution than a massive *coup d'état* arranged by that master of ceremonies, Yuan Shih-k'ai. His own maneuvers had tipped the balance against the Manchu power. But the problem of discovering "methods of union" in discussion with the revolutionaries remained to be solved.

By initial commitment to the revolutionaries, Yuan was charged with moving the capital from Peking to Nanking, the site of the provisional government. Ts'ai Yuan-p'ei, a member of the T'ung Meng Hui, led a South China delegation to Peking for the purpose of accompanying Yuan with due ceremony to the new seat of government. Ts'ai was ably supported by Wang Ching-wei, who had captured national attention in 1910 by an attempt on the Regent's life, and Sung Chiao-jen, the able and imaginative revolutionary who had led the party during Sun Yat-sen's extended absence from China. But Yuan easily sloughed off his obligation: he staged troop disorders that, overflowing into the delegation's place of residence, caused the negotiators to flee to the safety of the privileged Legation Quarter. Similar performances were staged in other important North China centers, with "unruly" troops in each case opposing the proposed removal to the South. In due course, the delegation reported that removal at that time was inadvisable.

So it was at Peking that Yuan Shih-k'ai was formally installed, on March 10, as Provisional President of the new Republic. Sun Yat-sen bequeathed to Yuan a tentative pattern for republican government. The Senate at Nanking, still in existence, on March 11 proclaimed a Provisional Constitution. It provided for a cabinet form of government, with a bicameral parliament, headed by a president and vice president. The president was commander in chief of the nation's armed forces and exercised the power of appointment of high civil and military officials. His appointment of cabinet ministers and diplomatic envoys was subject, however, to approval by the parliament.

The parliament was given the authority to approve declarations of war, the negotiation of peace, and treaties generally. Finally, it was the parliament, which was to be convened within ten months of the proclamation of the Provisional Constitution, that would decide upon a permanent constitution. In short, the president's powers were limited; it was the premier who was to be the effective head of government. That intent could hardly suit Yuan's autocratic aspirations and was soon to prove a burning issue.

Sun Yat-sen remained for the time being in Nanking. It was not he who became Yuan's first premier, but American-educated T'ang Shao-yi. T'ang had only recently joined the T'ung Meng Hui. Yet he nominally represented the revolutionary element and, after his appointment, proceeded to Nanking to consult with Sun Yat-sen and Huang Hsing regarding the composition of the new Cabinet.

The beginnings seemed auspicious. T'ang won approval for a Cabinet that included academician Ts'ai Yuan-p'ei as Minister of Education, Ch'en Ch'i-mei as Minister of Industry and Commerce, and Sung Chiao-jen as Minister of Agriculture and Forestry. But it was also notable that Yuan's men controlled key power posts: Tuan Ch'i-jui, one of Yuan's most trusted military captains, was Minister of War; and strong henchman Chao Ping-chün was Minister of the Interior. The appointment of China's first Cabinet completed the paper formalities. The Nanking government decided to remove to Peking. The Republican era had begun. But Ch'en Ch'i-mei's refusal to proceed to the capital to take up his ministership might have been interpreted as a bad omen.

The new government faced an immediate problem of formidable dimensions: its treasury was practically empty. The governmental insolvency was naturally directly related to the question of power. Legally the country was unified under an acknowledged central Chinese rule, but in actual fact Peking was unable to provide funds to the provinces for the conduct of government. The end of the dynasty found Chinese military men in control in most of the provinces, and they commanded a total of some eight hundred thousand troops. Some of the top militarists, such as Feng Kuo-chang and Tuan Ch'i-jui, were Yuan's own men. Others, such as Ch'en Ch'i-mei at Shanghai, Hu Han-min in Kwangtung, and Li Lieh-chün in Kiangsi, were of the revolutionary party. And there were others still, like Yang Tseng-hsin in Sinkiang and Chang Tso-lin in Manchuria, who had risen in power incidental to the revolution and might be expected to manifest a thirst for independent power—this had frequently happened after the fall of earlier dynasties.

Yuan endeavored to make a virtue of his cramped necessity by investing the provincial military leaders in their posts with the title of *tutuh,* or military governor. In exchange for the title, and the position of semi-independence that went with it, the various *tutuh* were expected to maintain themselves without too exigent demands on the central government for funds to meet military or civil expenses. The practical effect of this move was, naturally, to strengthen the inherent tendency of the militarists to indulge in empire-building of their own.

To meet the exigencies of finance, Yuan Shih-k'ai found it most expedient to look abroad. He was in a favorable position. The alien Manchus had vacated the seat of power, but there had nevertheless been no revolution in either economic or foreign affairs. All of Yuan's past indicated that, since he was conservative at heart and governed by inordinate ambition, it was not likely that he would be the innovator of sweeping change in China. The manner in which he inaugurated his government served to confirm this impression and could only please those foreign powers concerned with the preservation of treaty rights and special privileges. They could be expected to prove receptive to Yuan's requests for the means to help him remain in power. Even as money questions connected with railway construction had aggravated the revolutionary trend in the pre-1911 period, loans were now to become once more a major issue in domestic politics.

Developments in that field were not long in appearing. Even in February, Yuan had begun negotiations with the foreign banking consortium, now expanded by the inclusion of Japanese and Russian interests, for a loan. Two days after his inauguration he obtained an advance of cash from the six-power consortium, and a promise of more—in exchange for a commitment giving the banking group a firm option on a "comprehensive loan for general reorganization purposes." When, six days later, Premier T'ang Shao-yi borrowed more money from an Anglo-Belgian syndicate, the consortium protested, and Yuan lightly disavowed the action of his premier. The issue of whether president or premier wielded superior power was thus brought to the fore. T'ang was committed to the concept that the presidential powers were limited and the premier was the responsible head of government. After the initial clash over authority to administer finances, however, Yuan continued to override T'ang's authority. In June, seizing upon the relatively minor issue of Yuan's reversal of his own commitment to make one Wang Chih-hsiang, candidate of the revolutionaries, *tutuh* of Chihli Province, T'ang resigned the post of premier and departed from Peking without even saying goodbye to the man he had served loyally for nearly three decades. His cabinet ministers resigned with him.

The chief function of the new Cabinet—formed in July, 1912, with Lu Cheng-hsiang as premier—was, as Yuan saw it, the sanctioning of the so-called Reorganization Loan. A brief hitch occurred in August when Yuan engineered the assassination of General Chang Chen-wu, one of the revolutionaries who had participated in the Wuchang uprising. The revolutionaries were angered. At Yuan's invitation, Sun Yat-sen and General Huang Hsing went to Peking to discuss the matter. Yuan succeeded in mollifying Sun by placing him in charge of the nation's railway construction—for which there were no funds.

Abetted by competition among the powers, the matter of the Reorganization Loan went forward. The rivalry for concessions and the American bid for preeminence among the rivals had combined to devitalize the sea powers' "cooperative policy." On the very day of the Manchu abdication, American Minister W. J. Calhoun described the existing state of affairs in a dispatch to the Secretary of State:

I have the honor to report that the international situation here is critical, at times very strained. . . .

All of the powers are more or less suspicious of the Americans. They seem to think we have some exclusive or personal policy in mind; that our professions of altruism are a mere blind; and that we hope or intend, somehow or somewhere, to secure an advantage, either in prestige or in substance, in which the rest will have no share. . . . It was all right so long as we released indemnities, educated Chinese youth at home, and sent missionaries to China. But when we rather forcibly injected ourselves into the Hukuang [railway] loan, tried to neutralize the Manchurian railways, proposed to build the Chinchow-Aigun railway [in Manchuria], and finally negotiated a preliminary contract for the currency loan, we were then and are now believed to entertain an active and aggressive policy, which is competitive if not hostile to all other foreign interests in China.[6]

During the last four decades of the nineteenth century the United States had followed the "cooperative policy" of establishing and maintaining joint positions with France and Britain vis-à-vis China. From the acquisition of the Philippines in 1898 onward, and particularly with the Hay notes of 1899 and 1900, the American policy was to tend increasingly toward unilateral action. Given the existence of the Anglo-Japanese and Franco-Russian alliances, the American inclination was understandable. But it was to make for a growing isolation of the United States in the West Pacific.

The international rivalry reported by Minister Calhoun had been evident in the negotiation of the Reorganization Loan. Between August and the end of 1912, there had been various efforts to float loans, but it was Yuan's Reorganization Loan that was finally negotiated. Although the loan was for $125 million, it was discounted 16 percent—which meant that the Government received only $105 million. Of that amount, over $50 million went to pay outstanding and pending central government and provincial obligations, $27.5 million was allotted for the Government's current expenses from April to September of 1913, and $10 million was allocated to reorganization of the salt gabelle—the only element of "reorganization" to which the loan was actually applied. And by law the approval of Parliament had still to be obtained.

Yuan turned to combat unfavorable developments on the domestic stage. In the early fall of 1912, the T'ung Meng Hui had been transformed into the Kuomintang (Nationalist Party), with Sung

Chiao-jen as prime mover. Whereas the group had functioned in Manchu times as a conspiratorial organization, it now operated as a legitimate political party. So successful was Sung that, in the elections held at the end of 1912 and beginning of 1913, the Kuomintang won 269 seats in the House and 123 in the Senate; the Republicans, led by Li Yuan-hung and Wu T'ing-fang, won only 120 and 53 seats respectively. By now Sung was the *de facto* leader of the Kuomintang. Sun Yat-sen, the Party's titular director general, evinced little interest in parliamentary politics, and in late 1912 made another trip to Japan, this time for the purpose of furthering his plans for China's railway development. Sung Chiao-jen became chairman of the Party executive committee.

If Sung Chiao-jen looked toward the advent of representative government, Yuan Shih-k'ai did not. He viewed the Kuomintang program, which was based upon the three general concepts of nationalism, democracy, and "the people's livelihood," as dangerous radicalism. Nor did the Kuomintang men regard Yuan with any less distaste: they knew an autocrat when they saw one.

Yuan forced the issue by the customary measure: he caused the assassination of Sung Chiao-jen at Shanghai, just as Sung was preparing to return to Peking and the scene of political battle. The revolutionary group was deeply stirred. Sun Yat-sen returned from Japan, and there was much coming and going of politicians. Discontent with Yuan Shih-k'ai's rule was taking on dangerous proportions. As a conservative bulwark against republicanism, Yuan had the sympathy of the powers, most of whom were imperial in form and outlook. But it was still to be proved that Yuan was the "strong man" he had set himself up to be and that he could weld the Chinese people into a nation.

President Woodrow Wilson's administration, taking office in the spring of 1913, had found the Reorganization Loan so unsavory that it forced the American bankers to withdraw from the consortium in March, the month Sung Chiao-jen was killed. Toward the end of April Yuan Shih-k'ai, confronted with Parliament's obstinacy, simply by-passed that body and had the Premier and two of his ministers sign the agreement. These signatures sufficed for the consortium.

Yuan's first major test now occurred. On May 5 Parliament voted a resolution finding the loan agreement illegal because it lacked prior parliamentary approval. The Kuomintang had led the opposition, and Kuomintang military men responded in the field. Sun

Yat-sen and Li Lieh-chün, the Kiangsi *tutuh,* schemed to effect the overthrow of Yuan's rule by military force. Yuan undertook swift countermoves. In early June he replaced three provincial *tutuh* for allegedly supporting the Kuomintang and opposing the Reorganization Loan. Among those dismissed were Hu Han-min of Kwangtung and Li Lieh-chün of Kiangsi. Yuan also dispatched three armies to the Yangtze region to support his policies.

In July Li Lieh-chün declared Kiangsi independent and began to move troops. At a military conference in Nanking, Huang Hsing and his followers decided to join with Kiangsi against Yuan, with Huang Hsing to be commander in chief of the allied forces. Ch'en Ch'i-mei at Shanghai and other provincial leaders declared in favor of the rebels, and the Second Revolution began with military engagement in mid-July.

The revolt had been poorly conceived and badly coordinated from the first. Kuomintang dignitaries Wang Ching-wei and Ts'ai Yuan-p'ei had opposed the move. Huang Hsing had been reluctant to challenge Yuan Shih-k'ai in the beginning and performed indifferently in his role as commander in chief. Liang Ch'i-ch'ao and his followers supported President Yuan. Yuan commanded both superior arms and, with Reorganization Loan funds in hand, more money—with which he proceeded to buy over various potential rebel supporters. The Second Revolution collapsed within two months.

There were several immediate results. The Kuomintang camp lost control of six provinces; among those defeated were Ch'en Chiung-ming in Kwangtung, and T'an Yen-k'ai in Hunan. And the victory over the opposition increased the tensions among Yuan's own generals, relieved as they were of the necessity of keeping an eye on the "outsiders." Finally, the usefulness to Yuan of parliamentary forms had been reduced.

On October 6 Yuan was formally elected to the office he held, with the opposition conspicuous by its absence. This was a mark of his domestic victory. International approval was soon to follow. Early in July, 1912, the United States had sounded out the governments concerned on recognition of the new regime and had found them unwilling to undertake the matter so soon. In view of the apparent instability of Yuan's regime, they proposed to proceed deliberately. In due course Brazil and Peru gave recognition, and the United States finally refused to wait any longer on the powers for the formalization of relations. On May 2, 1913, just as the

Second Revolution was about to begin, the American Minister at Peking delivered to Yuan President Wilson's message of recognition: "I extend, in the name of my Government and of my people, a greetings of welcome to the new China thus entering into the family of nations." The twelve foreign governments that had refused to join the United States in its move waited until after Yuan's election and then, by identic notes, extended recognition in time for his formal inauguration on October 10, 1913, as Republican China's first president.

The Premier at this time was an able and liberal man, Hsiung Hsi-ling. But Hsiung had only one real supporter in his Cabinet, Liang Ch'i-ch'ao. Liang had long since broken with the monarchism of his old mentor, K'ang Yu-wei, and was a leading figure in the Chin Pu Tang (Progressive Party). He, however, commanded no such force as would have been needed to face up to Yuan's power. Most of the other Cabinet members, led by Minister of War Tuan Ch'i-jui, were Yuan's men.

With the Reorganization Loan in hand, confirmed as President by Parliament, and enjoying formal recognition by the powers, Yuan had little remaining need for the trappings of republican government. In November he declared the Kuomintang illegal and ousted the party's representatives from Parliament, and on January 10, 1914, he dissolved Parliament itself. Hsiung Hsi-ling soon afterwards resigned as Premier, and Liang Ch'i-ch'ao followed him out of government.

Yuan then began to rule by fiat. The major quarrel between Yuan and Parliament had centered on the issue of whether Parliament or the presidency should be the main seat of power. With Parliament dissolved, the way was clear for Yuan to settle that issue in his own favor. His American "constitutional adviser," Professor Frank J. Goodnow of Columbia University, proved a handy if unwitting instrument to that end. The Revised Provisional Constitution promulgated May 1, 1914, which had been drafted in good part by Goodnow and a Japanese colleague, Dr. N. Ariga, reframed the government and substantially strengthened the powers of the president. The American Minister reported to the Secretary of State: "The powers now centralized in the hands of the President are extraordinarily great." Yuan had won the first round against republicanism. He next turned to the task of obtaining full legitimization of his autocratic authority.

2 THE REVOLUTION THAT FAILED

THE ISSUE facing China in 1914 was whether the Revolution of 1911 could be brought to fruition. The government needed a new legitimacy. The proscription of the political Opposition, and the substitution of one Constitution for another, clearly fell far short of meeting the requirements in that regard. There was as yet no question of fundamental social reforms, for the 1911 movement had not been a mass upheaval of protest. Nevertheless, the progressive nationalism to which the Revolution gave expression required, at the bare minimum, a reassertion of China's nationhood against foreign would-be aggressors and the elimination of autocratic absolutism in domestic affairs. If partly implicit, those had been the basic aims of the revolutionaries.

President Yuan Shih-k'ai's troubles were far from ended. The Reorganization Loan had been exhausted in April; other foreign loans followed, but at ever larger discounts. Moreover, the impact of the First World War, which began in August, was at once felt in the Far East. Japan, as the treaty ally of Great Britain, was quick to live up to obligations that promised rich rewards for little effort, entered the war against Germany in August and proceeded promptly to occupy not only those parts of Shantung that constituted the German concession but more besides. Peking protested feebly, but Yuan stood in need of more funds, and also of Japanese support for another planned venture. The Japanese readily consolidated their position in Shantung and went on to occupy the Marshall, Caroline, and Mariana islands, which Germany had bought earlier from Spain.

In the field of foreign affairs Yuan Shih-k'ai started with an initial handicap: the powers were not yet ready to have China rise out of its position of international inferiority—particularly if that meant China's sloughing off the trammels of the "unequal treaties." The war situation favored further Japanese advance, and the Japanese ever since the 1868 Restoration had shown themselves alert to take advantage of opportunities offered in the international sphere. On January 18, 1915, the Japanese Minister at Peking, Hioki Eki, presented to Yuan Shih-k'ai personally what came to be known as the Twenty-one Demands.

The Demands were far-reaching. Divided into five groups, they effectively envisaged China's subordination to Japan's will. They provided for the confirmation of Japan's new-won gains in Shantung; the grant of special privileges and concessions in Manchuria; joint Sino-Japanese control of the Hanyehp'ing mining and metallurgical enterprise in the middle-Yangtze valley; a commitment of nonalienation to another power of any harbor, bay, or island on the coast of China; and, as the fifth group, railway concessions, the employment of Japanese advisers in financial, political, military, and police matters, and a virtual veto power over the use of non-Japanese foreign capital for mines and other works in Fukien Province.

Minister Hioki had enjoined Yuan to maintain strict secrecy, but word of the Demands soon leaked out. However, Japan and Great Britain were allied against Germany in a war which, at that point, was of desperate gravity on the Western front. Russia was also engaged in that war. Obviously none of the belligerent powers was going to save the situation for China. That left the United States—but it too was preoccupied with the war in Europe. Secretary of State William Jennings Bryan was content merely to pronounce what came to be called the "nonrecognition doctrine." The United States Government solemnly declared that it would not recognize any agreements that might contravene the Open Door Policy or China's integrity.

The declaration had no teeth in it, and Japan, of course, ignored it. The Chinese meanwhile had been stalling. On May 7, however, Minister Hioki delivered an ultimatum requiring Chinese acceptance of all demands except those in the fifth group, which, Hioki said, the Japanese Government "will undertake to detach . . . from the present negotiations and discuss separately in the future." Yuan capitulated the following day, and China signed the agreement on May 25.

The battle of Tsushima in 1905 had marked Japan's advent into the competition in East Asia. By annexing Korea in 1910, the Japanese had taken a giant step toward the creation of a mainland empire. Japan's actions of 1914–15 signalized the notable reduction of stature of Western sea power in Asian waters. Asia was indeed entering a new era.

Yuan had three strong reasons for not resisting the Japanese Demands to the breaking point. Two of them were obvious: first, he needed money; second, the Sino-Japanese War of 1894–95 had taught him that Japan was a foe too dangerous to challenge. The third reason, however, had only thus far been hinted at: Yuan Shih-k'ai planned to become Emperor of China. In September, 1914, Yuan had announced his decision to adhere to Confucian precepts; and on December 23, when all the celestial signs were right, he had performed the ceremony of worshipping Heaven at the Altar of Heaven south of the old Tatar City's walls, with certain changes "appropriate to republicanism." *But by the Confucian rites only the Emperor was permitted to worship Heaven.*

In June, 1915, after accepting the Twenty-one Demands, President Yuan established five ranks of nobility, with which he proposed to reward deserving civil and military officials. Professor Goodnow, back in Peking on a visit in July, was asked by Yuan to prepare a memorandum on the respective merits of the republican and monarchical forms of government, with particular reference to existing conditions in China. In the memorandum he drew up, he wrote: "It is of course not susceptible of doubt that a monarchy is better suited than a republic to China." Goodnow qualified his statement by laying down the following prerequisites for restoration of a monarchy: the move should not be taken against the wishes of either the Chinese people *or* the powers; there should be clear provision made for the development of constitutional rule in such an imperial China. Goodnow also endeavored to divest himself of any personal responsibility for the ultimate decision: "Whether the conditions which have been set forth as necessary for such a change from republic to monarchy as has been suggested are present, must of course be determined by those who both know that country and are responsible for its future development." [1]

When the memorandum was published, Yuan's agents strove to give a semblance of reality to the claim that there was a ground swell of popular opinion in favor of the President's ascending the Dragon Throne. In August a number of his supporters formed a group called the Ch'ou An Hui (Peace Planning Society), and military and civil provincial governors were invited to send delegates to Peking to consider the matter of creating a proper political system for China. The issue of legitimacy had become of primary importance. In its first formal meeting of August 23, the Society adopted a resolution favoring the monarchical system. The public campaign for Yuan's becoming Emperor had been launched.

Even in the camp of Yuan Shih-k'ai, signs of disaffection were quick to make their appearance. Various military leaders had initially supported his accession to the throne. But there were notable exceptions. One was Feng Kuo-chang, then *tutuh* of Kiangsu. Another was Yuan's trusted lieutenant, Tuan Ch'i-jui.

Tuan had graduated with the first class of Li Hung-chang's Peiyang Military Academy; as one of Yuan's chief aides in creation of the New Army, he had risen in power with Yuan's ascendancy and thus had become Minister of War. But Tuan had his own ambitions and, as early as 1914, had begun to challenge Yuan's power by usurping military functions previously retained in the President's hands. As a consequence, Yuan curtailed Tuan's power and clinched the matter by causing the transfer of legal authority governing the disputed functions to a new Office of the Generalissimo, the Generalissimo being none other than Yuan himself. The two had clashed, moreover, regarding the authority and activities of Hsu Shu-cheng, Tuan's Vice Minister of War.

Those developments, rather than Yuan's imperial ambitions, held the substance of the dispute. Nevertheless, the plan for restoring the monarchy provided an occasion—and perhaps, in the longer range, an opportunity. Tuan made known his opposition to Yuan's policy and in June retired from office, taking with him Vice Minister of War Hsu Shu-cheng. Yuan went forward with his plan. A new law of October 8 provided for the election of a National Congress of Representatives, empowered to determine the future form of the Chinese state.

Yuan's purpose was by now quite evident. At this juncture, a foreign factor was injected into the picture. It has been alleged that Yuan, when he signed the Twenty-one Demands, received as part compensation a Japanese promise to support his assumption of the throne, but this has not been proven. During the critical negotiations for big stakes, however, the Japanese side had displayed an attitude that Yuan was able easily to *interpret* as approval of his proposal to restore the monarchical system.

At first glance it seemed logical that Japan would approve a discarding of the republican form of government: Japan possessed an imperial structure incorporating many ancient Chinese elements. But deeper motives were influencing events. Japan had already developed an urge to try for mainland empire, and such a program would hardly have been fostered by the establishment of a strongly centralized monarchy in China. In addition, Yuan Shih-k'ai's movement was threatening to stir up such opposition as to endanger the stability of the Chinese central government, and thus of the agreements signed and loans negotiated. So, in October, Japan launched a countermove.

Tokyo, viewing the developments "with grave concern," approached the American, British, and Russian Governments with a proposal for a united *démarche* to stop Yuan's plan. On October 28, 1915, the Japanese, British, and Russian envoys jointly called on the Chinese Foreign Minister to tender their "advice" against the proposed step. France and Italy followed a few days later. Not until November 4 did Washington reply to Japanese and British representations made to it. The American notes contained an identical concluding paragraph:

The American Government is naturally in sympathy with republican institutions, but is of the opinion that any change by the Chinese in their form of government, however radical, is wholly a domestic question and that any sort of interference by the Government of the United States would be, therefore, an invasion of China's sovereignty and would be without justification unless convincing evidence, which is not now in the possession of the United States Government, should show that any foreign interests which it is the privilege of the United States to safeguard would be imperilled.[2]

The move by foreign governments naturally strengthened and crystallized the growing Chinese opposition. Ch'en Ch'i-mei, who had taken refuge in Japan after collapse of the abortive Second Revolution of 1913, was now back in Shanghai. Operating from the sanctuary of the French Concession, he plotted to bring about Yuan's downfall. Yuan had already caused the assassination of two old T'ung Meng Hui leaders; on November 10 Ch'en engineered the assassination of the Shanghai garrison commander, a Yuan appointee.

It took more than an assassination to shake the determination of Yuan Shih-k'ai. He was probably still entirely confident of his destiny, and, in any event, he had gone too far to retreat. The National Congress of Representatives, Yuan's creation, voted unanimously in favor of a restoration of the monarchical system, and the Council of State then invited Yuan to ascend the Dragon Throne. On December 12 Yuan accepted. Investiture was fixed for the following spring.

Various opposition forces now converged. The sentiment in favor of republicanism had apparently taken deep root in China. Yuan's Premier and sworn brother, Hsu Shih-ch'ang, was "taken ill" and left his office. Lu Cheng-hsiang again took up the post. Yuan honored another of his followers, Li Yuan-hung, with the title of Prince Wu Yi, but Li refused the honor. On December 18 Yuan appointed Feng Kuo-chang to be his Chief of General Staff, but Feng continued to suffer from that political "illness" that had therefore kept him from supporting his old chief. Feng nevertheless was well enough to carry on an active correspondence with Liang Ch'i-ch'ao in Peking. Not even K'ang Yu-wei, who held to his original position of support for the Manchu Dynasty, could find merit in Yuan's proposal to occupy the vacant throne.

Further opposition came from the ousted Kuomintang politicians and other republican elements. Sun Yat-sen's following entered the picture. In July, 1914, after the Kuomintang was outlawed, he had reorganized his party in Japan as the secret and conspiratorial Komingtang (Revolutionary Party), with its membership committed to strict allegiance to himself as leader. Huang Hsing and others had objected to Sun's concepts of revolutionary organization and had broken with the group, but Ch'en Ch'i-mei and Hu Han-min continued to serve as Sun's loyal lieutenants.

Among those present in Peking during the summer was Ts'ai O, former *tutuh* of Yunnan. Yuan had transferred Ts'ai to Peking a few years earlier to become a "military adviser," a post where Yuan could keep an eye on him. But Ts'ai was one of Liang Ch'i-ch'ao's former students and had been in contact with him at Peking while Yuan was moving toward the throne. Ts'ai now left Peking secretly, went to Japan, and established contact with the Komingtang.

Liang Ch'i-ch'ao resigned his ministerial post on the grounds of ill health and left the capital ostensibly to obtain treatment in the United States. Upon reaching the safety of a foreign concession in

Tientsin, however, he published an article on "The Strange Problem of the Form of Government," condemning Yuan and his monarchical scheme. Several outstanding members of the Komingtang met in the Philippines under the leadership of Hu Han-min to determine a plan of operations, and afterwards they dispatched various of their comrades to key provinces on anti-Yuan missions. As one of those agents, Li Lieh-chün went to Yunnan. From Japan Ts'ai O also made his way, by an indirect route, to that remote Southwest China province.

On December 25, *tutuh* T'ang Chi-yao, Ts'ai O, and other Yunnan generals declared Yunnan's independence of Peking and their opposition to Yuan Shih-k'ai. They named their rebel force the Hu Kuo Chün (National Protection Army). Ts'ai O advanced against Szechwan at the head of one division. Two other divisions advanced against Hunan and Kwangsi. In a New Year's message, Yuan proclaimed 1916 as the first year of his new dynasty with the reign name Hung Hsien (Great Constitution). He despatched Ts'ao K'un to meet the rebel threat to Szechwan.

Ts'ai O advanced rapidly and on January 20 captured Hsufu in Szechwan on the upper Yangtze. A week later the military men of Kweichow declared that province's independence, and at the beginning of February Yunnan and Kweichow forces entered Hunan. By now Ts'ai O's move was sparking the dry tinder of a nation-wide revolt.

As Ts'ai O's campaign progressed in Szechwan, Yuan reinforced his position desperately. Among his units was the 16th Mixed Brigade, commanded by a burly man destined to become famous on China's battlefields, Feng Yü-hsiang. At the beginning of March, Feng's hard-fighting brigade inflicted a defeat on Ts'ai's force and drove it back.

At this juncture Yuan committed a major error: he removed the militarist Lu Jung-t'ing from the Military Governorship of Kwangsi, giving him instead the thorny honor of being Pacification Commissioner for rebellious Kweichow. This he did to insure that Lu would not act against him, but his move backfired. On March 15 Lu Jung-t'ing and his generals declared Kwangsi independent. Kwangsi's virtual independence of the rest of China was to persist for two full decades and prove of unusual significance in the country's historical development.

Lu Jung-t'ing's move marked the turning of the tide. Yuan called for aid from his old supporters, Hsu Shih-ch'ang, Tuan Ch'i-jui, and Feng Kuo-chang. Their help was qualified: Feng and four other military men jointly recommended that Yuan abandon the idea of becoming Emperor; Hsu Shih-ch'ang proposed that Yuan seek a political settlement with the Yunnan rebels; and Tuan Ch'i-jui, for the moment, refused to do anything.

Yuan thus found himself essentially alone. In January he had been forced to postpone the ceremony of investiture. Now, on March 22, he formally decreed the end of the Hung Hsien Dynasty. Nothing remained to mark the existence of his empire except a large quantity of porcelain manufactured to commemorate the first year of his reign. On that same March 22 Yuan appointed Hsu Shih-ch'ang Premier, and on the following day Tuan Ch'i-jui took up the post of Chief of General Staff that Feng Kuo-chang had refused to occupy.

Thus buttressed, Yuan Shih-k'ai undertook to save the presidency for himself. But there could be no restoration of the authority he had destroyed. More provinces in the south, so recently brought under Yuan's influence, declared their independence of his rule. In Szechwan, Ts'ao K'un's army was crumbling, and, in an ironical reversal of fortunes, Feng Yü-hsiang's 16th Mixed Brigade surrendered to Ts'ai O. In desperation Yuan gave Tuan Ch'i-jui the authority he demanded as a price for his assistance: he appointed him Premier on April 22. Tuan also assumed the post of Minister of War in the new cabinet he formed and put Hsu Shu-cheng in as Vice Minister of War again. From Nanking Feng Kuo-chang now called upon Yuan Shih-k'ai to retire from office. And at this juncture, Sun Yat-sen returned to Shanghai from Japan.

Yuan Shih-k'ai's China broke into pieces. Having declared their independence, T'ang Chi-yao of Yunnan, Lu Jung-t'ing of Kwangsi, and the governors of Kweichow and Kwangtung, on May 8 organized a joint military affairs office at Chaoching in Kwangtung. The following day Sun Yat-sen announced that he would cooperate with all quarters to punish Yuan and thus to show respect to constitutional government. Shensi Province declared its independence the same day. At Shanghai, on the eighteenth, Yuan Shih-k'ai's agents accomplished another political assassination that Yuan undoubtedly ardently desired, that of Ch'en Ch'i-mei. But Yuan was nearing the end of his career. It was too late to stop the movement of revolt against his autocracy by the murder of individual leaders. The independence movement continued relentlessly. Ch'en Huan, Governor of Szechwan, and one of Yuan's most trusted lieutenants, declared that province independent. Hunan Province followed. In Shantung Province, Peking's backyard, revolutionary forces pressed their attacks.

Yuan Shih-k'ai was by this time a sick man—in the Chinese version, "made ill by shame and anger." Frustrated of his life's ambition, he died on June 6, 1916. He had been guilty of three great betrayals—of the Emperor Kuang Hsu, of the dynasty, and of the Republic. For history, those acts would outweigh his demonstrated capacities as military and civil administrator.

Ts'ai O, who had been suffering from tuberculosis even as he led the movement against Yuan, died the following November in Japan, where he had gone for treatment. Ten days before, the staunch revolutionary Huang Hsing had succumbed to the same disease in Shanghai. They were at the time of death thirty-five and forty-four years of age, respectively. But they had both fulfilled their life's mission of advancing the republican cause.

PARLIAMENT, PARTIES, AND POLITICS

The national structure had been badly shattered. Instead of consolidating the republican principle and the central government, Yuan Shih-k'ai had weakened it. Plain power had checked his monarchical ambitions, but the military men who had engaged in opposition were notably less ready than before to recognize the political authority of Peking. All over the country, powerful men stood at the head of armies. The political contest threatened to become military. Obviously much depended upon what happened next in Peking.

Li Yuan-hung, as Vice President, moved into the presidency on the death of Yuan Shih-k'ai. Li seemed to have been fated for frustration. After he had trained for a naval career, his ship had been sunk in an early engagement of the Sino-Japanese War, and he had sat out the rest of the war in Port Arthur. A brigade commander at Wuchang in 1911, he had joined the revolutionaries at the time of the October outbreak, but only upon being dragged out of hiding and threatened with physical violence if he refused to assume leadership. Later, he had gladly ceded place to Huang Hsing as Generalissimo. When elected to the vice presidency under Yuan Shih-k'ai after having served Sun Yat-sen in that post, he had lingered long in his native Hupeh before reluctantly making his way to Peking after the Second Revolution of 1913. Essentially a weak man, under the powerful Yuan Shih-k'ai he had been a mere figurehead—which was, of course, what the astute Yuan had wanted him for.

With Yuan dead, Li was called upon to provide leadership, willy-nilly. He duly set to work restoring the republican system that had existed before Yuan Shih-k'ai undertook reinstitution of the imperial structure. Yuan's Constitution was discarded, and the Provisional Constitution of 1912 resurrected. Parliament returned. The wheels of republicanism appeared to mesh once more—after a fashion. China seemed to have one last chance for agreement on a common program, political unification, and national progress.

Yet the situation could not possibly be as if Yuan had never existed. His influence lived after him, in his Peiyang Party. The Peiyang leaders controlled the country's best armies, while Li Yuan-hung commanded no armed forces owing him personal loyalty. The drama of Li's service under Yuan Shih-k'ai threatened to be re-enacted.

Foremost among the Peiyang men in terms of power was Tuan Ch'i-jui. Like his former chief, Tuan was interested in political power, and, when he returned to the arena in April, 1916, the radically changed situation seemed to offer a major opportunity to advance his personal political fortunes.

As a long-time associate of Yuan Shih-k'ai, Tuan had been at the very heart of the nation's affairs. Holding the posts of Premier and Minister of War at the time of Yuan's death and having wisely refused to have anything to do with Yuan's scheme for the restoration of the monarchy, he was in a position of considerable authority that he patently had no intention of relinquishing. One of the chief instruments of his power was Hsu Shu-cheng.

On Tuan's recommendation Hsu Shu-cheng had been sent by the Imperial Government in 1908 to study in the Japanese Military Officers' Academy. After graduation, Hsu had served as Tuan's chief of staff in military operations against the revolutionaries in 1911—and rose with Tuan upon the creation of the Republic. Tuan trusted him implicitly and depended heavily upon him. Hsu was faithful to Tuan's cause. He was also ruthless, unprincipled, and corrupt.

In the final struggle with Yuan in 1916, Tuan had endeavored to get approval for the appointment of Hsu Shu-cheng to the strategic position of Chief Secretary of Cabinet. Here he failed, Yuan putting in his own man and giving Hsu no more than his former post as

Vice Minister of War. After Tuan was confirmed as Premier under Li Yuan-hung on August 1, 1916, he renewed his effort to get Hsu into the strategic Cabinet post. Li resisted the move but was constrained to bow when Hsu Shih-ch'ang intervened in support of Tuan's request.

Hsu Shu-cheng was consequently brought into a position where he administered major governmental affairs. His concept of government was that the Premier (Tuan) was the fountainhead of power, whereas the President (Li Yuan-hung) had no more than the ceremonial function of affixing his seal of approval to papers placed before him (by Hsu). Moreover, he arrogated to himself, as Chief Secretary, the right to initiate action at Cabinet meetings. He would thus in an important sense be more powerful than the President. A complete reversal of the Yuan Shih-k'ai political doctrine had now taken place—without, however, any real improvement in the political situation.

As might be guessed, Hsu's position was not accepted by Li Yuan-hung. It was his contention that the President had the right to attend Cabinet meetings and set forth his independent position, and, moreover, that he was not legally charged with indorsing measures he disapproved of. The contest began. On its outcome hung the future of representative government in China.

There was a complicating factor. After the death of Yuan Shih-k'ai, Sun Yat-sen undertook to direct national affairs from his Shanghai base as if *he* were the fount of authority. He began issuing orders to various military men, calling upon them to desist from armed actions, and he telegraphed to both Li Yuan-hung and Tuan Ch'i-jui demanding a prompt restoration of parliamentary government. The state of Peking's relations with Sun's camp was demonstrated, however, when Sun's follower T'ang Shao-yi, who had been appointed Minister for Foreign Affairs in Tuan's new Cabinet, was unable to take up his post because of the opposition of Northern military men. But, on August 1, Parliament was reconvened. And at the end of October Feng Kuo-chang was elected to fill the vacant vice presidency. A semblance of political order was restored.

The successes won by various military men who had announced provincial independence had, however, been a heady wine. As there had been strong undercurrents of rivalry in the Peking Government under Li's weak hand, so new challenges were building up in the hinterland where military men had achieved virtual independence of Peking. In recognition of the latter situation, early in July, 1916, the Peking Government changed the designation of the provincial military governors from *tutuh* to *tuchün*. And a listing of the new *tuchün* sufficed to confirm that they were semi-independent military men, often of such stature as to make them potential challengers for political power. Their semi-independent status was strengthened by the requirement, reflecting the penury of the central government, that they support themselves from local revenues. Sun Yat-sen had returned from Japan, but his activities and pronunciamentos clearly were having less effect on the situation than the movements of armed men.

Some of the military leaders had already shown their mettle. T'ang Chi-yao was dominant in Yunnan, Lu Jung-t'ing in Kwangtung and Kwangsi, and both were men of power. In Szechwan, alert to seize upon political opportunities, there were several strong potential challengers; the province would continue in a state of turbulence for a full two decades. Nearer the capital, in Shansi Province, a crafty military man named Yen Hsi-shan had seized power; in Anhwei an older militarist, Chang Hsun, dominated the scene. Both were destined to play major roles.

China's borderlands were also showing a spirit of independence toward the capital. The Mongols in Urga and the Tibetans at Lhasa had eagerly and early submitted to centrifugal forces. In Sinkiang one man, harder than the rest, Yang Tseng-hsin, had made his way to the apex of power in the course of the bloodshed attending the Manchu collapse and was steadily consolidating his authority by dint of his own efforts. He owed nothing to Peking and would be inclined to pay no more than nominal homage. And in Manchuria a sometime bandit, Chang Tso-lin, as Fengtien *tuchün* stood on a level with some of the older military men, ready to challenge them.

T'ang Chi-yao and his colleagues, upon receipt of their appointments as *tuchün*, announced the closure of their Military Affairs Office at Chaoching. Other military men would, for the time being, pay lip service to Peking's authority. But in Peking itself conflicts were not long in taking shape. A clash between Hsu Shu-cheng and Interior Minister Sun Hung-yi developed into a power struggle between Tuan Ch'i-jui and President Li Yuan-hung. Peiyang elder statesman Hsu Shih-ch'ang, called in to mediate, resolved the matter by bringing about the removal of both Hsu and Sun from office.

Yuan's Peiyang Party, without an acknowledged leader, was showing schismatic tendencies. Tuan Ch'i-jui headed a strong Anhwei faction, but the new Vice President, Feng Kuo-chang, found his main strength in the Chihli group. And Hsu Shu-cheng, though now forced to operate behind the scenes, was committed to putting Tuan Ch'i-jui on the pinnacle of power.

Shortly afterward foreign influences began again to play an important role in China's domestic affairs. When the American Government decided to take a stand against Germany's submarine warfare, it urged other states, including China, to do likewise. Tuan Ch'i-jui, looking to the material and political advantages that China could expect to obtain as one of the Allied Powers, was early committed to the American proposition. Peking thus, although far from being affected directly by the depredations of German submarines, on February 9, 1917, sent a note of protest to Germany; then, on March 14, in the absence of a reply to the *démarche*, broke off diplomatic relations.

When the United States entered the war in April, Tuan demanded implementation of his plan to take China into the war also. Li Yuan-hung and Parliament refused their sanction. At the end of April, Tuan convened a conference of *tuchüns*—his own supporters—which duly decided that China should participate in the war. Enjoying the support of Parliament, Li held out and dismissed Tuan as Premier on May 23.

Tuan promptly mobilized some Peiyang generals, and the rebellious faction announced that they proposed to launch a punitive expedition against Peking in order "to enforce respect for the Constitution." More particularly, they demanded that Tuan be restored to power and Parliament dismissed.

Li, without troops of his own, called upon sometime Viceroy Chang Hsun, the powerful Anhwei *tuchün,* to come to the defense of the government. Chang moved troops but, as a condition for his intervention, demanded the dismissal of Parliament. President Li, in no position to bargain, acceded to the demand. Parliament was dissolved on June 13, and Chang Hsun's forces entered Peking a few days later. At this point the United States Government admonished China not to indulge in civil war.

The Articles of Favorable Treatment that were a part of the abdication agreement of 1912 had permitted the boy P'u Yi to retain his title of Manchu (not Chinese) Emperor, and he had been maintaining his royal court in Peking. In addition, the Articles had stipulated that the Emperor should in due course remove his residence to the Summer Palace outside Peking's walls, and, when the Empress Lung Yü died in 1913, Yuan Shih-k'ai had asked compliance with that provision in the agreement. But the Imperial Household Department, heavily overstaffed, scheming, and vice-ridden, used every available strategem to block the move as it would have meant substantial reductions of both personnel and perquisites. P'u Yi remained in the Winter Palace in Peking.

On June 30, events took a dramatic turn: on that date, Chang Hsun announced in a message to the nation that he had requested the Emperor to resume his imperial duties. On July 1, P'u Yi, now eleven years of age, ascended the Throne a second time as the Emperor Hsuan T'ung.

But Chang Hsun had made a capital mistake. He had the support of die-hard monarchists, including the sometime reformer, K'ang Yu-wei, and evidently thought that he had the firm concurrence of leading Peiyang Party personalities. In particular, the Anhwei *tuchün* believed that Anhwei chieftain Tuan Ch'i-jui supported his move—whereas Tuan was actually only using Chang as a cat's-paw to eliminate obstacles on the way to power.

In general, things worked out as Tuan had foreseen. In extremity, Li Yuan-hung on July 2 secretly called upon Tuan Ch'i-jui to resume power as Premier, telegraphed Vice President Feng Kuo-chang (then in Nanking) asking him to assume leadership of the government, and then fled to the safety of the Japanese Legation. Tuan ably exploited Chang Hsun's political weakness and promptly put troops into the field against him. In a brisk fight at Langfang, midway between Tientsin and Peking, Chang's forces were defeated, and the monarchy fell just twelve days after its hasty restoration. Chang Hsun, in turn, fled for refuge to the Legation Quarter, selecting, however, the Dutch Legation.

In mid-July Tuan formally resumed the premiership and the post of Minister of War. Li Yuan-hung, for his part, had had enough. Intimidated by the forbidding frown of Tuan Ch'i-jui, he refused to return to the office of President, turned the office over to Feng Kuo-chang, and took up residence in the Japanese Concession at Tientsin. On August 14, 1917, Tuan at last had his way, and China declared war on the Central Powers. That done, Tuan turned the Ministry of War over to Hsu Shu-cheng.

Tuan Ch'i-jui and Feng Kuo-chang, both being Peiyang Party men, might have been able to achieve teamwork as Premier and

President, had it not been that both wanted to dominate the government. And Feng was in a better position to hold his ground than Li Yuan-hung had been. A Chihli man, he commanded Chihli sympathies. He was, moreover, an abler military politician than Li Yuan-hung. During his tenure in the lower Yangtze provinces, he had built up a network of allegiances that provided a solid base of military support in a critical area. And, when he went to Peking to take over the presidency, he was accompanied by one of his two personal guards divisions.

One Chihli man to be watched was Ts'ao K'un. In February, 1912, as commander of the 3rd Division, he had staged Yuan Shih-k'ai's "mutinies" in Peking for the benefit of the Nanking Provisional Government's delegation and in 1913 had fought Yuan's battle against Ts'ai O in Szechwan. In the summer of 1916, after Yuan's death, he became *tuchün* of Chihli. He had aided Tuan Ch'i-jui against Chang Hsun in the July, 1917, Restoration affair and subsequently received the concurrent post of Chihli civil governor. He was thus in a pivotal position.

The elements of a great power struggle were there, and those involved were immediately confronted with an issue, this time one that fell principally in the field of domestic politics. The issue centered on Parliament. Strictly speaking, one of Li Yuan-hung's final acts should have been to recall the Parliament that he had been forced to dismiss under pressure from Chang Hsun. But Li had never really resumed his office, and Premier Tuan was in standing conflict with Parliament over the war issue. Feng Kuo-chang, the Chihli man, entertained different political views than those of Anhwei chieftain Tuan Ch'i-jui.

Out of this conflict of forces, a new political opposition developed in the Southwest. In early August Sun Yat-sen returned by gunboat to Canton. On August 11 a telegram was sent by Yunnan *tuchün* T'ang Chi-yao, who (1) called for the return of President Li Yuan-hung to office or else his formal resignation to Parliament, (2) demanded the reassembly of the old Parliament, (3) stigmatized as illegal the assumption of office by (high) officials not approved by Parliament and appointed by the President, and (4) proposed the punishment, in accordance with the law, of military men who refused to obey orders. The accusing finger was unmistakably pointed at Tuan Ch'i-jui and his cohorts.

Within days, other military men of the South and Southwest voiced their support of T'ang's stand. Sun Yat-sen called upon the dismissed members of Parliament to join him at Canton. Military men, political leaders such as Wang Ching-wei and T'ang Shao-yi, and deposed members of parliament, gathered at Canton to launch what came to be known as the Movement for Protection of the Constitution.

In the years since his 1914 transformation of the Kuomintang into the Komingtang, Sun had failed to obtain the desired Japanese support for his revolutionary cause, and he had not built the Komingtang into an effective political organization. Japan, for its part, already possessed more useful instruments than Sun—Chang Tso-lin in Manchuria and Hsu Shu-cheng in Peking. Sun's concept of party organization as a one-man dictatorship naturally attracted few strong and ambitious personalities, and the absence of a compelling political ideology was a critical weakness. Sun's Komingtang had consequently sunk deeply into uselessness. When he returned to Canton, it was not as head of a powerful political party.

So, at Canton, as a result of the efforts of a variety of militarists, politicians, and legislators, there was organized what was called the Chinese National Military Government. Since the members of Parliament who had answered Sun's call were fewer than required for a legal quorum, a Special Parliament was established which in due course was built up by elections from among parliamentary alternates. On September 10, 1917, Sun formally assumed the post of Generalissimo of the new regime. Not to be outdone by Peking, the Government on September 26 declared war on Germany. But that was not enough to satisfy the militancy of the Canton group: characterizing the Tuan Ch'i-jui Government as being in rebellion against the Republic, Sun, as Generalissimo, issued orders for a military expedition against Peking.

Under the rule of Yuan Shih-k'ai, there had at least been the outward appearance of centralized rule from Peking. But Yuan's attempt to restore the monarchy had shattered the flimsy facade of legitimacy. Individual military men, having declared their independence of Peking during the rebellion against Yuan's ambitions, clung to their power, and began to reach for more after the establishment of the *tuchün* system. There had been a last slender chance that after Yuan's death government by law instead of government by men would be strengthened as a guiding principle, but the violence done by Tuan Ch'i-jui to constitutionalism now led to the crystallization of regional separatism in China. The legacy that "strong man" Yuan Shih-k'ai had left to China, consolidated by the actions of Tuan Ch'i-jui, was the warlord era. It was to last a full decade, with the major division being between the *tuchün* government at Peking in the North and the "revolutionary" regimes that followed one after the other at Canton in the South.

THE WARLORDS TAKE OVER

The insurrectionary Constitution Protection Army, composed of military forces drawn from South and Southwest China, started out on its march against Peking in September, and fighting began soon after in Hunan. The warfare spread, with Szechwan in particular drawn into the melee. The Northern armies did not achieve the quick success anticipated in Tuan's camp, and the situation became politically complicated when, in mid-November, the Feng Kuo-chang commanders, led by Chihli *tuchün* Ts'ao K'un, issued peace proposals. A pattern for the years to come, a pattern of politico-military maneuver, was being established.

Feng Kuo-chang was in correspondence with the Southern leaders and had wished from the beginning to settle the matter by political means. Tuan proposed to unify China, and to settle the particular issue at hand, by the use of military force. Taking into consideration the failures of the government arms in Hunan and Szechwan, it had to be conceded that President Feng had won the first round. On November 15, two days after the issue of the circular telegram by Feng's commanders, Tuan once more resigned the premiership. Hsu Shu-cheng retired with him—but had no intention of remaining in the political wilderness.

A Chihli man, Wang Shih-chen, took over the post of Premier, and the Feng government went to work at implementation of its own policy of settling the "Southern Question." This intensified a schism in the Northern camp. Prior to the November, 1917, clash of wills, there had been a residual amity between the Anhwei and Chihli groups, existing from the time when the Peiyang Party was a unified whole. After that date, however, Yuan Shih-k'ai's powerful Peiyang organization began to break up into two distinct and antipathetic factions—the Anhwei and Chihli cliques. A real struggle for power now began between the two.

The next round went to the Tuan forces. On December 3 various Northern military leaders and the representatives of others stationed in distant provinces met in conference at Tientsin. Ts'ao K'un himself was present, but it was not a discussion of peace proposals that dominated the gathering. The conference demanded that the government (that is, Feng Kuo-chang) issue appropriate orders for military action against the Southerners, and on December 16 the orders were issued. Ts'ao K'un was to spearhead the attack with an advance in the direction of Hupeh. Blocked by Tuan's party from negotiations, Feng Kuo-chang went to war.

Two days later, Tuan Ch'i-jui was appointed director of the (European) War Participation Board, and Hsu Shu-cheng became Chief of the General Staff. But this did not suffice for the ambitious pair, and Hsu maneuvered to restore his chief to dominant power. In Manchuria Chang Tso-lin had just enhanced his power by getting the appointment of one of his own men as governor of Heilungkiang Province. He was clearly a man of rising fortunes. Hsu went to Mukden, obtained from Chang the loan of some Fengtien forces, and appointed himself their deputy commander. (Chang, of course, remained commander.) Hsu then, in February, 1918, set up his military headquarters near Tientsin.

The War Participation Board, with Tuan at its head, was formally established on March 1, 1918. On March 7 Hsu Shu-cheng and Wang I-t'ang organized the Anfu Club, a political organization devoted to the furtherance of Tuan's political fortunes in the election of the National Assembly scheduled for June. Thereupon Hsu threatened Feng with the use of the Fengtien forces he had borrowed. Feng capitulated, Wang Shih-chen retired from office, and Tuan Ch'i-jui once more resumed the premiership.

Tuan's followers returned to power with him. He was now in a position to dispose of the Southern Question without hindrance from those who yearned for political settlements. The Northern forces had already been deployed. One noteworthy event attending their early movement was the action of Brigade Commander Feng Yü-hsiang in refusing orders on the northern Hunan Front. Tuan ordered the recalcitrant officer removed from command of his 16th Mixed Brigade, but Feng merely moved farther west, out of range of Tuan's avenging authority. In early March Ts'ao K'un's force attacked the positions of the Constitution Protection Army in northern Hunan.

The Southerners abandoned first Yochow and then Changsha. By the end of April Wu P'ei-fu, commanding Ts'ao's old 3rd Division, had occupied Hengchow in southern Hunan. Tuan's strategy seemed to promise victory. At that juncture, however, the machinations of Hsu Shu-cheng bore some bitter fruit. Ts'ao K'un found reason to believe that Hsu was planning to replace him as Chihli *tuchün;* and Wu P'ei-fu felt that his merits had not been accorded appropriate recognition by the Peking authorities.

Military operations stopped, and Tuan's program of military unification of the country came to a halt. While Tuan—and Hsu— negotiated with Ts'ao K'un in an effort to win him back to coopera- tion, during the summer of 1918 3rd Division Commander Wu P'ei-fu bombarded the Peking Government with telegrams demand- ing peace. Relations between Tuan and Ts'ao became increasingly embittered, and the two were irreconcilably alienated. Ts'ao, it appeared, would be a logical challenger for power in the event of a shift in the balance of forces at the capital. On August 30, the Peking government in effect capitulated and informed Wu P'ei-fu that it accepted his proposals for peace.

The balance of power had shifted, but not in favor of Feng Kuo- chang. There were new challengers rising up in the provinces, but within the central government the power was for the most part Tuan's, not the President's. Feng in his turn had become largely a figurehead. Tuan had put together a so-called Legislative Assem- bly and charged it with drafting a new Organic Law to supplant the 1912 act on which the original Parliament had been founded. On August 12, 1918, the "Anfu Parliament," based on Tuan's law and manned mainly by his own followers, met at Peking. On that same day Feng Kuo-chang, his term of office having expired, set forth his aspirations for national peace and unity in a public proclamation and announced that he was retiring from public life. (He died in Peking the following year.) The new Parliament elected Peiyang elder statesman Hsu Shih-ch'ang President of China on Septem- ber 4, and he assumed office on October 10, 1918. On the same day Tuan Ch'i-jui again resigned as Premier.

By this time the significance of developments following upon the death of Yuan Shih-k'ai had become entirely clear: the struggle for succession had severely undermined the central government, and Peking's control over important parts of the country had weakened. Outer Mongolia and Tibet had fallen away, Sinkiang was effectively autonomous, and, in addition, various regions much nearer Peking were defying its authority.

The military men who were competing for national predominance had little time for distant adventures, engaged as they were in a dizzy game of musical chairs around the seat of power in Peking. As they played, in fact, their authority over other parts of the country became ever more circumscribed. Progressively, power was being shifted into the hands of regional warlords.

There was not one pattern, but several, for that usurpation of power. Practically all provinces saw struggles of local interest and importance, but often these were only side shows, of no importance to the main contest between North and South. Developments in some regions, however, did bear a national significance. This was true especially for Sinkiang and for China's Northeast, Manchuria.

In Sinkiang, China's distant "new borderland," Yang Tseng-hsin had grasped power in the turbulent aftermath of the 1911 Revolution. Having voiced allegiance to the Chinese Republic, he had been duly confirmed in the position of *tutuh*. He was concurrently appointed military governor of the Ili Special Region, which, with the Altai and Chuguchak Special Regions, then lay outside the political boundaries of Sinkiang.

Yang's first task was to restore order in Sinkiang and Ili. In Sinkiang proper, the Ko Lao Hui (Brothers and Elders Society), a secret political organization, had carried out a reign of terror following the slaughter of the Manchu garrisons; Yang wiped out the Ko Lao Hui influence by 1914. In the Ili Region the native Turkis had set up an autonomous rule. By political manipulation and selective execution of leaders, Yang reestablished Chinese authority in the region.

But his troubles had not ended. He was faced with financial problems, since Peking had urgent need for its funds close at home and could not support so distant a province as Sinkiang. Yang resorted to independent measures to meet his budgetary requirements. He also moved to bring the three Special Regions progressively under his administration. Peking, which had no one else to turn to when troubles broke out in those regions, authorized him to incorporate them into Sinkiang Province. The last of the three, the Altai Special Region, became a part of Sinkiang in 1919.

By this time Yang was virtually independent of Peking, and he ruled the 660,000 square miles of Sinkiang with due appreciation of the virtue of the ancient Chinese saying "Heaven is high, and the Emperor is far away." Yang Tseng-hsin had indeed been autocratic in his rule; nevertheless, as a semi-autonomous Chinese warlord of intelligence and ability, he had succeeded in blocking the natural Turki urge to take the road to independence when the Middle Kingdom's central power might be weak. In this respect Yang had already made a substantial contribution, not to Peking, but to China. But he was still confronted with the problem of dealing conclusively with turbulent forces flowing into Sinkiang from neighboring Russia.

An even more critical region than Sinkiang was Manchuria. China's Northeast had in the past been the focus for the clash of empires. Its strategic importance had been confirmed by both the Russo-Japanese War and Japan's Twenty-one Demands of 1915. Its resources were vast, its agriculture rich, and, through the investment of both Russian and Japanese capital and energy since early in the century, it was on the way to becoming a powerful economic entity in its own right. It was to China's national interest to hold on to this valuable piece of property. But it was not uncommon for Chinese generals to place their own selfish interests ahead of the nation's. In Manchuria, warlord Chang Tso-lin pursued, above all else, his own ends.

Chang Tso-lin had been energetically consolidating his power in Manchuria ever since the 1911 Revolution. Born in poverty, he had served as a common soldier in the Sino-Japanese War of 1894–95 and, after the war, had turned bandit. In 1903, however, he took advantage of a proffered amnesty and led his followers into regular military service as the garrison force for a market town near Mukden. In that position he amassed considerable wealth, and, when the Russo-Japanese War broke out, he was able, at first, to act as supplier to the Russian forces and, then, when the Japanese began to get the upper hand, to perform the same services for the Imperial Japanese Army.

In the postwar period, with Japanese support, Chang became garrison commander at Mukden itself. After the 1911 Revolution, for services not in the revolutionary cause but in the interests of peace and order, he was appointed commander of the 27th Division. At first he supported Yuan Shih-k'ai's monarchical scheme in 1915–16, but later, when the scheme failed, he forced Fengtien Governor Tuan Chih-kuei (a Yuan man) out of office. In April, 1916, he was appointed Military and Civil Governor of Fengtien Province by the unhappy President.

The following year Chang forced the installation of one of his own followers as governor of Heilungkiang Province. In 1918 he became high inspecting commissioner of the Three Eastern Provinces (Manchuria) and further strengthened his fighting forces. Finally, in 1919, he ousted the incumbent Military Governor in Kirin Province and put his own man in the post. At that point Chang Tso-lin's control of Manchuria's half-million square miles was complete, and his independent power was great. He was in a position to play a role in relation to current international rivalries in that strategic arena— of course, designedly for his own benefit—and in domestic struggles for power "inside the Wall" as well.

Another potential challenge to Peking's authority was to be found in nearby Shansi Province, a natural mountain fortress ruled by Yen Hsi-shan. Yen, a graduate of the Imperial Military Academy at Tokyo and a T'ung Meng Hui man, had been a colonel in the Shansi Army at the time of the Revolution and had undertaken to bring Shansi into the revolutionary camp. After some initial military successes, he was defeated by Ts'ao K'un on the Chihli plain and retreated back into Shansi. He was saved from destruction only by the Manchu abdication and the cessation of hostilities.

Yen had survived and in the process had learned a lesson in craftiness. As a "revolutionary" Yen was made Shansi *tutuh* by Yuan Shih-k'ai and hence became a follower of Yuan instead of Sun Yat-sen. But when Yuan made his bid for the Throne, Yen remained quietly "neutral" on the issue—and his caginess paid off. A golden opportunity arose in July, 1917, at the time of the attempted restoration. Siding with Tuan Ch'i-jui against Chang Hsun at the critical moment, Yen went on with Tuan's tacit consent to oust the Shansi Civil Governor. Yen's control of Shansi was thus complete. He had new ties with Tuan Ch'i-jui, but he had already demonstrated a natural Machiavellianism that warned against any easy assumptions with respect to his long-term loyalties.

The South had still to develop a comparable strength. When the rump Parliament formed the Military Government at Canton in September, 1917, Yunnan *tuchün* T'ang Chi-yao was one of two deputies to Generalissimo Sun Yat-sen. The other deputy was Lu Jung-t'ing, the Kwangsi military man whom Yuan Shih-k'ai had alienated by endeavoring to displace him. Lu had subsequently been appointed *tuchün* of Kwangtung. In early 1917 he became high inspecting commissioner for Kwangtung and Kwangsi. He dominated these two provinces, just as T'ang Chi-yao reigned in Yunnan. Both men voiced nominal allegiance to Sun's leadership, but both were concerned primarily with their own aggrandizement.

The auguries did not favor Sun Yat-sen. Lu Jung-t'ing tolerated rather than supported Sun's preeminence in the Military Government at Canton. Sun's own autocratic bent, coupled with his lack of personal troop strength, made him the obvious target of a political power move. And, in fact, his own Emergency Parliament re-organized the Military Government in May, 1918, and replaced Sun as Generalissimo by a board of seven Directors General, of whom he was only one. Only two of Sun's supporters, T'ang Shao-yi and Wu T'ing-fang, were named to the board with him; the other four members were men who commanded military power, including, of course, T'ang Chi-yao and Lu Jung-t'ing. A Kwangsi militarist, Ts'en Ch'un-hsuan, not Sun, was chairman of the board.

The day after the board was inaugurated Sun Yat-sen departed for Japan, but, in due course, he again took up residence in Shanghai. The domination of the Southern warlords was beyond challenge by the politicians. If there was lack of unity in the North, the same condition prevailed, for the time being, in the South. That contest was temporarily stalemated. Only with respect to the war against the Central Powers was China united.

CHINA IN THE FIRST WORLD WAR

China's entry into the World War had been by a circuitous route. Its war activities were to be more important on the diplomatic front than on the fighting front; and this participation in the power struggle would profoundly affect the subsequent course of events in China. It left an indelible mark on the Peking regime.

Even Yuan Shih-k'ai had wanted to take China into the European War, thinking to elevate China's international standing and to further his own ambitions. As a belligerent, China would sit as an equal on war councils and at a peace conference would have an unparalleled opportunity to rid itself of some of the encumbrances of the "unequal treaties." And Yuan Shih-k'ai, as chief of a belligerent state, would be in a position to ask friendly governments for money and other aid so that China might be strong and "help in the common struggle."

The Western Allies had looked longingly at the large tonnage of German shipping interned in China ports and had found good reasons for wishing China in the war. Thus, after Britain, Russia, and France had joined Japan in advising Yuan Shih-k'ai to drop his plans for becoming Emperor, their ambassadors in Tokyo sounded out the Foreign Office on the matter of getting the Japanese Government to join in persuading China to enter the war against Germany. Foreign Minister Ishii Kikujiro rejected the idea, saying that Japan could regard with equanimity neither the development of a

Chinese army sufficiently strong to participate actively in the war nor the liberation of the economic activities of China's four hundred million people. When the United States Government broke off relations with Germany on February 3, 1917, and urged Peking to do the same, Premier Tuan's regime, in view of its close ties with Japan, requested Tokyo's advice on the course of action it should follow.

A new government was in power in Japan. The Okuma Cabinet, which had taken Japan into the war and imposed the Twenty-one Demands on China, had fallen in October, 1916. Viscount Terauchi Masatake, the new Premier, evolved a "good neighbor" policy with the aim of improving Sino-Japanese relations. There was no suggestion that Japan would renounce the benefits gained through China's acceptance of the Twenty-one Demands; but there would at least be less harshness in evidence. In response to the Chinese request for advice regarding relations with Germany, Tokyo approved acceptance of the American invitation. It did more: in a secret understanding reached with France in March, Japan agreed to exert its influence directly to bring about a break in China's relations with Germany. Tokyo forthwith despatched an "unofficial" delegation to China to further the project.

One of the members of the delegation was Nishihara Kamezo, informally representing Premier Terauchi. While the Chinese Parliament deliberated the matter of breaking off relations with Germany, the delegation negotiated secretly with leaders of Tuan's camp. One of Nishihara's main Chinese contacts was Ts'ao Ju-lin, member of a Foreign Affairs Commission appointed the previous month. Ts'ao had been a student in Japan for five years at the beginning of the century and had established various Japanese ties, including marriage to a Japanese woman. As Vice Minister for Foreign Affairs under Yuan Shih-k'ai, he had handled negotiations with the Japanese regarding the Twenty-one Demands. A monarchist at heart, he had also supported Yuan's bid for the Throne. From 1916 onward Ts'ao had become more closely associated with Tuan and his enterprises. Scheming and unscrupulous, he was a fit companion to Hsu Shu-cheng. The two were behind Tuan's grand strategy to unify China by force. They were likewise in agreement that this could best be accomplished with Japanese aid. Closely associated with them was the new Chinese Minister to Japan, Chang Tsung-hsiang, as well as his predecessor, Lu Tsung-yü.

In those first secret negotiations, Ts'ao reputedly requested a Japanese loan of ¥100 million and advisers to aid China in training a modern army and building up an armaments industry. The schemers succeeded in persuading Li Yuan-hung to take the important step of breaking off relations with Germany in March, but they failed to accomplish their full mission. Tuan's conflict with the President and Parliament over China's entry into the war forced his temporary retirement from the political scene.

After Tuan's return to power, following the collapse of the Chang Hsun restoration attempt of July, and China's declaration of war on Germany in August, the plan went forward without major interruption. The European War, however, had little direct impact on China. Tuan's new army was not ready to fight—not that he ever had any intention of sending that army to Europe—nor did the Allies seriously consider transporting any of China's hundreds of thousands of ordinary fighting men to the European theater.

Nevertheless, Britain and France, in sore need of manpower, had earlier made arrangements with Peking to provide laborers, contracted for five years, to work behind the front in France and elsewhere, and the first group of 8,000 Chinese had reached France in the winter of 1916. With China's entry into the war, the program was stepped up, and by the end of the war about 175,000 Chinese were serving behind the lines in Mesopotamia, Africa, and Europe. The American forces had even borrowed some 10,000 from the French in 1917.

Attached to the Chinese labor corps were some 400 Chinese students serving as interpreters and a number of academicians and welfare workers assisting in the care of the men. The experience gained by these intellectuals in the field of labor organization and their contacts with Western thought were in due course to have an important impact on developments in China. Among the worker-students who served in France during and after the First World War were men who in the future would play important roles in the Chinese Communist Party.

The Tuan Ch'i-jui government's main preoccupation was elsewhere. The Anhwei clique's aim was to strengthen its own position and political influence—and incidentally to feather the private nests of its members. Corruption at the top in Peking naturally facilitated the Japanese program of penetration. The Terauchi Cabinet's policy toward China doubtless reflected, at least in part, the increasing authority in Peking of men such as Tuan Ch'i-jui, Hsu Shu-cheng, and Ts'ao Ju-lin, who could be expected to fit in, if sometimes only for a price, with the Japanese way of thinking.

Immediately after declaring war against Germany, Tuan's government turned again to financial matters and began to negotiate a series of loans, ostensibly for the purpose of supporting the Chinese war effort. The chief agent on the Japanese side was Nishihara, representing Japanese banking interests. Ts'ao Ju-lin represented the Chinese, having been made Minister of Communications in July. A joint Sino-Japanese banking corporation, the Chinese Exchange Bank, was established to facilitate the program. Its general manager was Ts'ao Ju-lin's associate and the sometime Minister to Japan, Lu Tsung-yü.

Two small loans, one for ¥20 million and another for ¥5 million were negotiated in the fall of 1917. There was a temporary interruption in the smooth progress of the project due to Tuan's retirement from the premiership in November, but the undertaking got a new fillip from Hsu Shu-cheng's *coup de main* that brought Tuan back to full authority and the Anfu clique to full flower. The loan-making reached full spate the following spring, after Tuan resumed the premiership and brought Ts'ao Ju-lin in with him as Minister of Finance. Between April and September, 1918, seven new loans were negotiated for a variety of nominal purposes, from improvement of the telegraph administration to the construction of railways, from development of forestry and mining to war participation.

The total amount of the "Nishihara loans" has never been exactly determined, for the successor Chinese National Government disavowed responsibility for the loans and claimed that the records had been lost. The figure fell somewhere between ¥145 million and ¥240 million. Many of the funds obtained had been diverted from the purpose originally intended and all too often had gone to line the pockets of Anfu officials. In return for these loans Japan had won broad concessions with respect to railways, mining, and military cooperation. By secret agreements between the two governments, signed on March 25 and May 16, 1918, some funds were allotted for the training and equipping of the War Participation Army, in exchange for new arrangements (which will be treated below) concerning Manchuria and Mongolia. The loans had also helped finance Peking's current political operations and domestic military campaigns.

The stage was thus set for a fresh political explosion whenever the malodorous enterprise should come to light—not so much because of popular wrath regarding pecuniary corruption as because of the new bartering away of national rights. From 1915 onward China's intellectuals had been groping for new solutions to the nation's problems, with the development of a potential for modern nationalism. Their indignation would be directed with growing force against those they felt had "betrayed the country" to foreign interests.

Because of the exigencies of the war, Britain and France were unable at this period to play major roles in China's affairs. But for Japan, the war offered clear opportunities to advance its interests in China. The United States and Russia also continued to be active in the Chinese scene.

Imperial Russia had long been interested in Outer Mongolia. In 1911 it had rejected an Outer Mongolian request for support in the move toward independence, but in November, 1912, it signed a protocol with the Hutukhtu, the Mongol theocrat, providing for Russian assistance to Outer Mongolia "to maintain the autonomous regime which she has established." In a Sino-Russian declaration on November, 1913, Russia recognized China's suzerainty over Outer Mongolia, but China on its part acknowledged Mongolian autonomy. Russia and China alike agreed to refrain from interference in Mongolia's internal affairs, from despatching armed forces to Mongolia, and from colonization.

In September, 1914, at the outbreak of the European war, on Russian initiative, a conference was convened at Kiakhta, at which China, Russia, and Outer Mongolia were all represented, for the purpose of determining the status of Outer Mongolia. The Mongolian delegation occupied a favorable position, for the Japanese had already occupied Shantung. With the presentation of the Japanese Twenty-one Demands in January, 1915, the balance was tipped even further against the Peking Government. In June a tripartite treaty was signed at Kiakhta in which China effectively confirmed the less formal understanding of 1913. And the treaty provided specifically that Mongolia, although prohibited from negotiating treaties of a political or territorial nature with foreign powers, had the right to conclude commercial agreements with other states.

Japan and Russia had thus won certain concessions from the Yuan Shih-k'ai government during 1915. Conditions, therefore, favored a new understanding between the two imperial powers for their mutual benefit. They had signed secret treaties in 1907, 1910, and 1912, demarcating their respective spheres of interest in Manchuria and Inner Mongolia. In July, 1916, after a full six months of negotiations, Japan and Russia signed a new treaty of alliance. By this document the two nations bound themselves (1) not to participate in "any arrangement or combination" with a third power against the other and (2) to confer on measures of mutual support when the territorial rights or special interests in the Far East of one of them might be menaced by another power.

It was clearly to the United States, not to Germany, that the treaty signatories had directed their attention. This was especially true for Japan, which had so assiduously been expanding its influence by manipulations in Peking, by investment of new capital in light industry in China, and through the development of Sino-Japanese trade. American enterprise, and the American Government, had long been interested in the potentialities of the Chinese market, and the European war offered a good chance to expand trade with China. Sino-American trade had, in fact, increased substantially from 1914 onward. The war had taken Germany, France, and Britain out of the picture, leaving Japan and the United States as the chief competitors for the China market.

The United States was in China as more than trader. Bryan had frowned upon the Twenty-one Demands of 1915, showing Washington's distaste for Japanese policies. There was, moreover, competition over loans to the Chinese Government. During 1916 American financial interests made several loans of roughly $5 million each to the Peking Government; and the Bank of Chicago obtained an option for loans up to $25 million. And in May, 1916, while the Russo-Japanese negotiations for a new treaty were in course, American Minister Paul S. Reinsch obtained a concession for the Siems-Carey Company to construct a network of five railways totaling 1,500 miles in length.

Yuan's Government looked upon this project as one that would enable it to strengthen its political control throughout China; the American firm doubtless viewed the matter as an excellent opportunity for substantial profit; but Japan could only regard the plan as competition with its own undertakings. The Japanese were saved the trouble of protesting the Siems-Carey project: Britain, France, and Russia objected on the grounds that it violated previous guarantees. Significantly, Dr. Reinsch recommended that the Department of State disregard the Russian protest in particular, since "the preoccupation of Europe with the War was the opportune moment for the United States to force the European powers to abandon their spheres."

The Siems-Carey project failed; but this and other American efforts to profit in East Asia from consequences of the European War led Japan to regard the American economic moves as of major importance. Consequently, the Japanese government found it desirable to endeavor to counteract and nullify anticipated American "interference." The 1915 Bryan doctrine of nonrecognition of gains made in violation of the Open Door doctrine and of existing treaties could obviously be canceled out by other, countervailing commitments.

In January and February of 1917, before urging upon the Tuan Ch'i-jui government the desirability of entering the war against Germany, Japan took the precaution of obtaining from Britain, Russia, and France secret assurances of support for its claim to succeed to German rights in both the Shantung Peninsula and the German island archipelagoes north of the equator—the Marshalls, Carolines, and Marianas.

There remained the problem of directly committing the United States. Here Japan had a precedent for its guidance: in December, 1908, in an exchange of notes between Secretary of State Elihu Root and Japanese Ambassador Takahira Kogoro under somewhat similar circumstances, the American side had *in effect* acknowledged that Japan had certain special rights and interests in East Asia. The device could perhaps be made to work again.

Santayana has pointed out that "those who cannot remember the past are condemned to repeat it." On this occasion the United States seemed to forget what had happened before. As if unmindful of both the Hay Doctrine with respect to China and the history of Japanese-American relations, it again committed the blunder of extending a measure of general recognition to the Japanese position in China. This time another Secretary of State, Robert Lansing, and Viscount Ishii, as Japanese special envoy, were involved. In a formal declaration on November 2, 1917, Japan joined with the United States in making the conventional obeisance to the Hay Doctrine; but the United States acknowledged that "territorial propinquity" created special rights and went on to recognize "that Japan had special interests in China, particularly in the part to which her possessions are contiguous."

Secretary of State Lansing was apparently aware of Japan's secret agreements with Britain and France. He did not neglect to manifest the traditional American concern for the commercial Open Door:

The Government of the United States has every confidence in the repeated assurances of the Imperial Japanese Government that while geographical position gives Japan such special interests they have no desire to discriminate against the trade of other nations or to disregard the commercial rights heretofore granted by China in treaties with other powers.[3]

But the "territorial propinquity" principle had a clear applicability to Manchuria, undeniably "contiguous" to Korea, and could be interpreted to refer as well to the Shantung Question.

China's approach to the peace conference was thus prejudiced in advance. And if there was any reason why China as a nation went to war in 1917, it was with the anticipation of gains to be made at the peace table. Its contribution to the war had been limited to the labor forces it had provided—and been paid for. Its expectations of possible profit, however, were not related to the minor role it had played.

The Manchu imperial concubine Yehonala (1835–1908) first became the Empress Hsiao-ch'in and then Empress Dowager Tz'u Hsi. She contrived to place her nephew Tsai-t'ien (1871–1908), on the Throne as the Emperor Teh Tsung, commonly known by his reign title Kuang Hsu. Kuang Hsu manifested more independence of character and mind than might have been expected. His 1898 reform program took on the aspect of rebellion against the Empress Dowager's influence and authority. The failure of his effort advanced the Manchu rule another stage toward its end.

THE EMPRESS DOWAGER TZ'U HSI

THE EMPEROR KUANG HSU

WITHIN THE LEGATION DEFENSES DURING THE BOXER REBELLION

The pressure exerted against China during the nineteenth century to obtain rights of diplomatic intercourse, trade, and evangelism, none of which was desired by the Chinese nation or its rulers, led to the development of a deep-seated antiforeignism. The failure of Kuang Hsu's "Hundred Days of Reform" led automatically to a further building up of frustrations. The Boxer Rebellion was a not unnatural consequence. Empress Dowager Tz'u Hsi tried to harness the movement in order to check the advance of foreign influences in China. The "siege of the legations" epitomized the emotions, and the futilities, of the Boxer episode. Although it failed, the Boxer Rebellion was an indication of the underlying anger of the Chinese nation against infringements of its sovereign rights—and against the threats to its empire.

YUAN SHIH-K'AI

TUAN CH'I-JUI

SUN YAT-SEN

Yuan Shih-k'ai (1859–1916), by arranging through political maneuver for the birth of a Republic at a time when he was charged with protection of the dynasty, played an important role in the Chinese Revolution of 1911. He continued to be moved, however, by the spirit of autocracy. One of those who carried on the tradition was Tuan Ch'i-jui (1864–1936) who, whether as Premier or Chief Executive, continued the effort to unify China. His resort to military force effectively brought about a division of the country that was to persist for years. Sun Yat-sen (1866–1925), called by the Chinese "the Father of the Country," epitomised the anti-autocratic revolutionary spirit of China.

In the Confucian order of things, the peasant represented the earthy productive forces of China. The Confucian scholar-gentleman served society variously as a bureaucrat, teacher, philosopher, and artist; as the embodiment of the Superior Man, he had much the greater prestige. But in the long struggle for power in the changing China of the first half of the twentieth century, revolutionaries finally turned to the peasant as the source of a political power sufficient to overturn the existing order.

SCHOLAR-OFFICIAL
(TUNG HSUN, 1807–92)

Anson Burlingame

SHANTUNG PEASANT

Gerald F. Winfield

HONAN VILLAGE, **1935,** FLOODED BY YELLOW RIVER

O. J. Todd

WESTERN HONAN VILLAGE, **1935,** ENGULFED IN SILT AFTER FLOODING

O. J. Todd

HANKOW STREET, **1931**

Most of the Chinese people live in the rich river valleys and low-lying coastal regions. But some of the rivers have regularly broken out of the man-made controls imposed upon them and raged over the countryside to destroy villages, lives, and crops. The Yellow River especially has so frequently burst its banks, flooded the entire agricultural countryside, and even changed its course on numerous occasions, that it has well earned the cognomen "China's Sorrow." The Yangtze, the country's mightiest river, is better behaved but commands uncontrollable force when unloosed. Floods, droughts, and locusts have added to the normal tribulations of the common people of China.

O. Edmund Clubb

BUSINESS SECTION AFTER "THE RAPE OF NANKING"

China has suffered not only from natural calamities but from the destruction caused by foreign wars. The second Sino-Japanese War of 1937–45 was the worst of China's modern wars. That eight-year-long struggle was marked, in its early stage, by the destructive fighting at Shanghai and, soon afterwards, by the Japanese occupation of the capital city of Nanking. The second event particularly was characterized by exceptional savagery on the part of the victors. The business section of the town was looted and then burned, and the civilian population generally suffered much abuse in "the rape of Nanking."

SUNGARI
RIVER
BRIDGE,
1946

Oliver E. Clubb, Jr.

CANTON
BRIDGE,
1949

Wide World Photos

In its long history China has never suffered as much from the alien invaders as from its own bloody civil wars. The endless struggles of the warlords in the period from 1916 to 1928, the bloody fights between Chiang Kai-shek and his fellow-Nationalists in 1929 and 1930 particularly, and the merciless struggle between the Nationalist regime and the Communist rebels from 1927 to 1949 (with a restless breathing-spell for the period of the War of Resistance) resulted in great loss of life and greater loss of property and national productive capacity. In the military destruction of communication facilities, actions ranged from destruction of the Sungari River bridge in the northeast by the Communists in 1946 to hamper the Nationalists advance in the early stage of the war to the Nationalists' blowing up of bridges at Canton, at the end of 1949, to protect their retreat from the mainland.

The men who led the two great military forces which survived the battles of elimination that had begun with the institution of the Republic represented the Right and Left in China. Chiang Kai-shek (1887–1975) never developed an adequate concept of the importance of men as compared to fire-power. Mao Tse-tung (1893–1976) had a keen sense of the power of the peasant, multiplied 500 million times in China. With the raw material of revolution already present, Mao Tse-tung supplied leadership and organization, and the War of Resistance provided a major revolutionary drive. Chiang Kai-shek is shown in his Formosan refuge, reviewing the troops who, he hopes, will take him back to the mainland he lost. Mao Tse-tung is shown watching his own troops at the moment of their victorious entry into Peiping on January 31, 1949. It is perhaps symbolic that both cars are, quite evidently, American.

CHIANG KAI-SHEK

MAO TSE-TUNG

3 THE BIRTH OF MODERN CHINESE NATIONALISM

CHINA had given clear indication of the high hopes it entertained for obtaining major national benefit by being counted among the victors in the First World War. In the early bargaining period with Minister Reinsch, not only loans but such matters as remission of the Boxer Indemnity were discussed. The negotiations with the Japanese had likewise been designed, at least in part, to advance the Chinese position: Peking hoped to be able to modernize the Chinese military establishment, to rehabilitate the Chinese authority in Manchuria and Outer Mongolia, and, perhaps, to cause a relaxation of pressures from the side of its "ally" Japan. It was evident that China desired to be treated as having come of age in the community of nations.

THE SHANTUNG QUESTION AND THE MAY FOURTH MOVEMENT

First and foremost, China expected to recover all rights and privileges formerly granted under "unequal treaties" to Germany and Austria. In particular, it desired restitution of full sovereignty over Shantung, Germany's "sphere of interest."

The German rights in Shantung, as set forth in the 1898 lease, were limited in time (to ninety-nine years) and in extent. Sovereignty, though waived temporarily in favor of Germany in certain respects, was expressly reserved to China. In all logic, any successor power could enjoy no greater rights than Germany. The original agreement, moreover, provided that Germany might not transfer its leasehold to any other power; abandonment by Germany should legally have led to a reversion of all rights to the sovereign authority, China.

The Twenty-one Demands imposed on Yuan Shih-k'ai's government in 1915, however, had introduced a new element into the legal situation: China had committed itself, by formal treaty, to accept any disposition of German rights in Shantung that might be agreed upon by Germany and Japan. The Chinese protested that the agreement in question, having been imposed on China by force, was not binding. The argument, however, had no validity in international law. The case for the Chinese was no stronger than the political support that they might be able to rally to their cause.

Secretary of State Bryan's 1915 pronouncement had implied that the United States stood on China's side against Japan. President Wilson's Fourteen Points of January, 1918, designed to shape the peace settlement, were imbued with the spirit of international justice. In his "Four Principles" speech of February 11, 1918, he held that all territorial settlements resulting from the war "must be made in the interest and for the benefit of the populations concerned, and not as a part of any mere adjustment or compromise of claims amongst rival States." His "Four Ends" speech of the following July 4 seemed even firmer in its insistence that territorial (and other) questions should be settled "upon the basis of the free acceptance of that settlement by the people immediately concerned." Consequently, it was only natural that China should expect the United States to support, at the peace conference, its claim for restitution of the Shantung Peninsula.

But Japan deemed that its position regarding Shantung had been confirmed by the Sino-Japanese agreements of 1915, the British, French, and Italian agreements of 1917, and the 1917 Lansing-Ishii agreement. They would also have had Russian support, had it not been for the Russian Revolution. The Japanese went with full confidence to the Peace Conference that convened in Paris, in January, 1919. The delegation was headed by Prince Saionji Kinmochi, leading elder statesman and former premier, ably assisted by Baron Makino Shinken. The chief of the Chinese delegation was Lu Cheng-hsiang, who, as Foreign Minister, had signed the treaty incorporating Yuan's surrender to the Twenty-one Demands in 1915. The Chinese delegation also included representatives from the opposition government at Canton. Under the circumstances, it is not surprising that teamwork proved somewhat lacking.

Discussion of the Shantung question began in late January, with the Japanese demanding their prize of war and the Chinese opposing. The Japanese delegation confronted the conference with the secret commitments of Britain, France, and Italy in 1917, and the various secret agreements signed by the Peking Government, including one of September, 1918, wherein Chinese Minister Chang Tsung-hsiang confirmed in a note to the Japanese Foreign Office that his government "gladly" agreed to Japanese proposals for the financing, construction, and "joint" operation of two new railways in Shantung Province, and for the stationing of Japanese troops at Tsingtao and Tsinan. As a consequence of these revelations the Chinese case was prejudiced from the beginning.

In April, while continuing to argue the proposition for the return of Shantung, the Chinese delegation presented two related memoranda. One asserted the Chinese claim for abrogation of the May, 1915, treaty and related agreements with Japan. The other proposed broad general adjustments of the situation in China deriving from the "unequal treaties," as follows: (1) renunciation of spheres of influence or interest; (2) withdrawal of foreign troops and police; (3) withdrawal of foreign post offices and telegraphic agencies; (4) abolition of consular extraterritorial jurisdiction; (5) relinquishment of leased territories; (6) restoration to China of foreign concessions and settlements; and (7) restoration to China of tariff autonomy. The conference rejected the demands of both memoranda as outside its terms of reference.

The Shantung Question was now brought before the Council of Foreign Ministers (including Japan, as one of the Big Five, but not China). The American delegation had been forced into the position of proposing that the former German rights in Shantung should be transferred to the five Great Powers, who would in turn eventually restore them to China. Naturally Japan did not agree, and the British, French, and Italians were committed to support the Japanese claim. The United States, deeply involved in the Siberian intervention along with Britain, France, and Japan, was not in a position to insist too stubbornly. At the last meeting of the Council of Foreign Ministers, on April 30, Wilson, Lloyd George, and Clemenceau —Orlando of Italy having gone home because of the Fiume question, the Council of Five had become a Council of Four—agreed that all former German rights in Shantung should be transferred to Japan. Japan made what it regarded as a concession: Baron Makino declared on behalf of his government that "the policy of Japan is to hand back the Shantung Peninsula in full sovereignty to China retaining only the economic privileges granted to Germany and the right to establish a settlement under the usual conditions at Tsing-tao." Japan asked for no more than the Germans had held.

But the intellectual climate in China was different from that existing at the time of the Twenty-one Demands. Beginning in 1915, new intellectual winds had begun to sweep through the major urban centers. That year Ch'en Tu-hsiu launched a magazine in Shanghai called *Hsin Ch'ing Nien* (New Youth), which he translated as *La Jeunesse*, for he was a student and admirer of French culture and had been strongly influenced by the ideals of the French Revolution. In his first issue, Ch'en, looking at Chinese society and finding it ridden with antiquated and decadent elements, wrote:

We indeed do not know which of our traditional institutions may be fit for survival in the modern world. I would rather see the ruin of our "national quintessence" than have our race of the present and future extinguished because of its unfitness for survival. Alas, the Babylonians are gone; of what use is their civilization to them now? As a Chinese maxim says, "If the skin does not exist, what can the hair adhere to?" The world continually progresses and will not stop. All those who cannot change themselves and keep pace with it are unfit for survival and will be eliminated by the process of natural selection.[1]

Peking University became a center for the new intellectual ferment. At the end of 1916 a new chancellor, Ts'ai Yuan-p'ei, had been appointed. Ts'ai was a Hanlin scholar who had been active in promoting educational change and had served as Minister of Education in T'ang Shao-yi's Cabinet of early 1912. After the assassination of Sung Chiao-jen, he had resided in France for a while, but, with the death of Yuan Shih-k'ai, he had returned to China to resume an active role in the life of his country. As chancellor, he injected a new and invigorating spirit into the Peking University.

Under Ts'ai, Ch'en Tu-hsiu became dean of the University's School of Letters. His influence among the students grew rapidly. In 1917 another Peking University professor, Hu Shih, launched the movement later called the Literary Revolution. His program was simplicity itself: he advocated abandonment of the stilted, compressed, traditional manner of writing handed down by two millennia of scholarly elite and its replacement by a literary style close to the vernacular, so that the common people might more readily gain access to the printed word. Illiteracy as such had still to be dealt with, but Hu Shih proposed to remove at least one of the major barriers to communication. More magazines destined to influence the thinking of Chinese youth began publication, and they employed the new literary style.

This provided the setting for a major event. Ever since the Shantung issue had been raised in January, the articulate public had followed the matter with close and growing interest. The Shantung deal violated the spirit of Wilson's 1918 assurance of a just peace settlement; it also outraged the new feeling of nationalism among China's youth. The decision of the Council of Foreign Ministers caused an explosion in China which came to be known as the May Fourth Movement.

On May 1 Chinese student organizations met and agreed to hold a mass demonstration on May 7, which had been designated a "National Humiliation Day" to commemorate Japan's 1915 ultimatum for acceptance of the Twenty-one Demands. Liaison was established between various schools, with Peking University the center of activity. On May 3 the students held an inflammatory meeting at Peking University and decided to stage a mass parade the next day, instead of May 7, to show dissatisfaction with the Paris decision. Shortly after noon of May 4, some three thousand students, representing thirteen colleges and universities, were assembled. The demonstrators began their march in the face of warnings from local police authorities and proceeded to the Legation Quarter. There they were refused admittance by the Legation Quarter guards and, at the same time, were harassed by Chinese troops. Shouting "To the house of the traitor!" the frustrated students turned to vent their feelings in another direction. (The "traitors" identified in their shouts were Tuan Ch'i-jui, Hsu Shu-cheng, Lu Tsung-yü, Chang Tsung-hsiang, and Ts'ao Ju-lin.) The marchers arrived at the heavily guarded residence of Ts'ao, broke in expecting to find some "traitors," but discovered that their intended prey had escaped. They thereupon set fire to the house. Finding Chang in a neighboring building shortly afterward, they beat him into insensibility. Ts'ao Ju-lin, who had made his escape into the safe Legation Quarter, submitted his resignation the same evening.

The violence of the demonstration had undoubtedly been compounded by the lethargy of the Peking police. They had, however, finally arrested some thirty-two students, one of whom died of injuries three days later. The affair acted as the catalyst for a nationwide movement of protest that had been long in the making. Immediately after May 4 the students began to organize protest demonstrations, strikes, business stoppages, and an anti-Japanese boycott movement. On May 6, a Peking Students' Union was organized, "to facilitate the performance of students' duties and to promote the welfare of the nation." It helped give direction to the protest movement of the intellectuals. Supported by merchants and the lower middle class, the students demanded that the Chinese delegation at Paris be instructed not to sign the peace treaty.

The Tuan government interdicted parades, speeches, and the dissemination of literature, but to no avail. A new mass student demonstration took place in Peking on June 3, and this time a thousand students were arrested. On June 5, demonstrators demanded the dismissal of Ts'ao, Lu, and Chang. The next day the arrested students were released. Four days later the Tuan regime capitulated further by dismissing the three offending officials. The entire Cabinet resigned on June 12.

The time for signing the peace treaty was drawing near, and the Chinese delegation at Paris was without precise instructions. It sought the conference's agreement to its signing with reservations without success. When the Treaty of Versailles was finally signed on June 28, the Chinese delegation, still uninstructed by Peking, resolved its dilemma by simply absenting itself from the meeting. Only on July 10, after having assessed world sympathy for China's position and the strength of the domestic opposition, did the Peking government issue orders authorizing its delegation not to sign the treaty.

In the turbulent events of June, new personalities came to the fore. A powerful thinker who early took a leading role was Peking University librarian Li Ta-chao. Li had quickly come to view the Russian Revolution of 1917 as presaging the dawn of a new era for mankind. But he was a Chinese nationalist, and Asian; and he proposed that a philosophy of "New Asianism" should govern a socialist federation of the Asian continent in juxtaposition to two other federations—one in Europe and one for the Americas. Li was also a voluntarist, believing in man's capacity to create history in socialist form by conscious act of revolutionary will; and he was a populist, in the pattern of the nineteenth century Narodniki of Russia. His urgent advice of 1919 to China's young intellectuals was, "Go to the villages."

A New Village Movement had already been launched, wherein some of Peking's young intellectuals lived communally and did the chores ordinarily performed in Chinese upper-class families by menials. One of the organizers of that movement was Li Ta-chao's student disciple Chang Kuo-tao. Chang would later become prominent as a Communist, but he was for the moment inspired by Russian anarchism. In March, 1919, he and other students had organized a Mass Education Speech Corps. Seized by essentially the same populism that moved Li, they proposed that mass education should be undertaken in order to achieve social reform.

The May Fourth Movement brought numerous other organizations into being; it spurred an upsurge of student activity and thinking that would continue for years. Having discovered the power of "movements," many academicians and students became "activists." New vistas of thought were opening up. One of the magazines established in 1919 was the *Hsin Ch'ao* (New Tide). The title aptly reflected the spirit of the times. New tides were indeed stirring the minds of China's intelligentsia.

The present Chinese Communists view the May Fourth Movement as marking the birth of contemporary revolutionary nationalism in China. It constituted a break with the old-style antiforeignism centered on "sea-devils" and "the hairy ones," and the beginning of a new impulse, modern "anti-imperialism." Although hardly remarked at the time, a new factor was introduced into power relations between the colonial and "semi-colonial" Orient and the Occident. Writing in December, 1918, and purporting to speak for Asian peoples generally, Ch'en Tu-hsiu demanded egalitarianism for humanity, with abandonment by Europe and America of discrimination against the colored races. The First World War was over, and many nations besides China looked to the dawning of a better day. At the peace conference Japan had put forward a demand for "acceptance of the principle of the equality of nations and the just treatment of their nationals." The American delegation had Southern Senators to consider and was, moreover, under pressure from some of its white allies. President Wilson took the initiative in opposition, and the Japanese demand for recognition of the principle of racial equality was rejected. Wilson had gone to Paris armed with his democratic idealism; he was defeated by power politics.

The decisions of Paris had lasting effects on the Far Eastern situation. The Japanese had probably used their proposal as a bargaining gambit in connection with the Shantung Question; it was, nevertheless, based upon a real urge. New political currents were beginning to course through the whole Asian world, and the spirit of Great Power politics that had governed the Big Five at Versailles was in a sense as outdated as the petty self-seeking policies of Tuan Ch'i-jui. The Shantung Question had far-reaching ramifications and significance. And decades later, in mid-century, the racial issue was to loom large in world politics.

THE RUSSIAN REVOLUTION: CHINA AND THE SIBERIAN INTERVENTION

The Russian Revolution of February, 1917, had in one respect been similar to the Chinese Revolution of 1911: it overturned the dynastic order. Otherwise, conditions in the two countries differed broadly. When the war brought the Russian nation to the verge of desperation in 1917, there already existed in Russia a considerable body of thought counseling action along new and even violent lines. The Chinese had attempted to restore the emperor to the throne. In Russia, by contrast, the revolutionaries proposed to change the whole social order. The Russian Revolution was notably more radical than the Chinese Revolution.

Inexperienced and hardly organized, the Bolsheviks had come suddenly to power, and their November coup came quickly under challenge from various groups supporting the Tsar. They were, moreover, brought under pressure by the German armies and forced on March 3, 1918, to sign the harsh Treaty of Brest-Litovsk, which took Russia out of the war. This was followed by Allied intervention at Murmansk and Odessa and Allied support for the White counter-revolutionary forces.

The Russian Revolution had important repercussions in the Far East, particularly in China's borderlands. In Manchuria, General Dmitrii L. Horvath seized the Chinese Eastern Railway in March 1917, immediately after the first, liberal Russian Revolution, proclaimed independence from the revolutionary government at Petrograd, and announced the establishment of an All-Russian Provisional Government at Harbin, with himself as its Director General. He began to administer the railway and to govern the Russian residents in the territory belonging to it as if it were his personal domain.

Horvath achieved little success in his first effort. His actions came under challenge from both the Chinese and Kerensky, and his position was whittled down to that of Commissioner. But the shifting pattern of events in Russia brought fresh developments. Bolshevik agents became active among the military forces that had been assigned by the former Tsarist regime to protect the railway zone, and in December, having won control of the troops, they seized the power over the railway from Horvath.

At this point the foreign powers intervened. At their request the Peking government sent troops (in violation of existing treaty provisions) to support Horvath. Heilungkiang *tuchün* Pao Kuei-ch'ing, a Chang Tso-lin man, disarmed the Red military formations and expelled them and their leaders from Manchuria. Pao then took over the guarding of the railway zone and asserted a degree of Chinese authority over the administration of the railway. On January 11, 1918, the Chinese closed the Manchurian-Russian frontier.

Imperial Japan, with vital interests in Manchuria, was naturally deeply concerned about the possible effects of the Russian Revolution in the Far East. Even before the Treaty of Brest-Litovsk was signed, Tokyo had proposed to the Peking government that the two countries should undertake joint measures against the Bolsheviks in Siberia. On March 25, after the Treaty of Brest-Litovsk had evoked sharp reactions among the Allied Powers, Tokyo and Peking agreed to confer regarding the protection of their common interests and to take joint action regarding the situation in Siberia. On May 16 China and Japan signed a secret Agreement for Military Cooperation, on the basis of which Japan ultimately moved sixty thousand troops into northern Manchuria, Russia's sphere of influence.

In January, 1918, after the expulsion of the Red railway guards from Manchuria, Horvath had begun to recruit White Russian and Mongolian troops, but the Chinese authorities compelled him to disband his force. After the signature of the Sino-Japanese agreement, however, and the dispatch of Japanese forces into northern Manchuria, the situation changed radically. In May Harbin was host to Admiral Alexander V. Kolchak, former commander of the Russian Black Sea Fleet and an important leader of the anti-Bolshevik forces in Siberia. His purpose was to organize, on that "friendly" Chinese soil, a base of support for White operations against the Reds in the East. His chief collaborator in the enterprise was General Horvath—and Horvath in turn was extended financial assistance by the Japanese.

The Cossack atamans Grigori Semenov and Ivan Kalmykov had in March taken the field against the Red forces in the Trans-Baikal region. In July, the month Tsar Nicholas II and his family were executed at Ekaterinburg, Horvath announced the appointment of Semenov as field commander for his reorganized All-Russian Provisional Government. Semenov's mission was to carry on the war against the Bolsheviks in Siberia.

During 1917 Japan, Britain, and France had several times discussed the advisability of sending armed forces into Russia. Toward the end of the year, after the October Revolution, France and Japan became insistent upon intervention in Siberia. Japan was patently more interested but was not in a good position politically, vis-à-vis either Russia or the United States, to take the initiative. The American Government had stubbornly held out against the importunities of its allies to participate in a joint military intervention, but it had also opposed Japan's acting alone as agent of the others. Early in 1918, however, the United States became increasingly worried by Japan's evident intention to take over the Chinese Eastern Railway. The later dispatch of Japanese troops into Manchuria made it evident that a greater American effort would have to be made if the railway, and perhaps Eastern Siberia, were to be kept out of Japanese hands. In June a moderate "All-Siberian" White Russian regime was established at Omsk. On July 17 Washington proposed that the United States, Japan, Britain, and France undertake a joint military expedition, with each to contribute a contingent of seven thousand men, for the express purpose of assisting the movement of Czech troops eastward to Vladivostok.

The Czech force comprised a group of forty to fifty thousand prisoners of war from the Austrian Army who, in March, 1918, on the basis of an agreement between the Bolsheviks and the French Government, had started to make their way to the Western front via the Trans-Siberian Railway and Vladivostok. The Bolshevik authorities had subsequently vacillated regarding the arrangement. By May the Czechs were stretched out along the railway all the way from Kazan to Vladivostok, but they had faced back westward, and Commissar of War Trotsky categorically ordered military action against them. The Czechs had come to constitute a new front against the Bolshevik authority.

The Allies, although divided on how the Czech troops should be transported and utilized, were at least nominally desirous of getting them safely out of Russia. They were also concerned with the fate of munitions shipped originally to Russia for fighting the war against Germany and now stored in large quantities at Murmansk, Odessa, and Vladivostok. Last but not least, they desired to aid the armed resistance against the Bolshevik forces.

The American and Japanese governments, as the two parties

chiefly concerned, finally reached agreement as to the nature of the proposed intervention, and on August 3 they simultaneously issued statements setting forth their official stands. The American statement read:

The United States and Japan are the only powers which are just now in a position to act in Siberia in sufficient force to accomplish even such modest objects as those that have been outlined [to assist the Czech forces, guard military stores, "and to render such aid as may be acceptable to the Russians in the organization of their own self-defense."] The Government of the United States, has, therefore, proposed to the Government of Japan that each of the two governments send a force of a few thousand men to Vladivostok, with the purpose of cooperating as a single force in the occupation of Vladivostok and in safeguarding, so far as it may, the country to the rear of the westward-moving Czechoslovaks; and the Japanese Government has consented.[2]

Japanese, British, and American warships had arrived at Vladivostok the previous year, shortly after the October Revolution. Allied troops began to disembark there soon after the American and Japanese statements were issued. Britain and France sent token contingents; the United States dispatched seven thousand troops under the command of Major General William S. Graves; Japan dispatched some seventy thousand—and it had already established a base of operations in Manchuria, sanctioned by agreements with both local White Russian leaders and the Chinese government.

China's relationship to the matter was guided by special considerations of its own national interests. Its immediate objective was to gain control of the Russian-owned Chinese Eastern Railway. But, in proposing in July to the United States Department of State that China participate in the control of the Chinese Eastern Railway, Chinese Minister Wellington Koo had also argued that Chinese troops should take part in any military expedition to Russia. Such a military action, he said, would be beneficial to China's domestic affairs—and enhance its standing among the powers.

China was finally permitted to play a token role in the Expedition, and certain sections of both the Trans-Siberian and Chinese Eastern Railways were assigned to Chinese troops to guard. This enabled China to play other Allies against the Japanese, who contended that their treaty arrangements with Peking gave them special rights of participation in the guarding of the Chinese Eastern in particular. China was concerned with the intervention in another way: many of its citizens fought with the Cossack forces serving the Japanese. Semenov's so-called "Savage Division," in particular, was made up of Cossacks, Buryat Mongols, and Chinese. On the other side, Chinese and Korean partisan bands gave substantial aid to the Bolsheviks.

The intervention began. It was obvious that Japan possessed a substantial advantage in the power game among the Allies. At the time, Kolchak, with the aid of the Czech Legion, was campaigning against the Bolshevik forces in Siberia. In northern Manchuria, Horvath had made Harbin into a secondary center for anti-Bolshevik activities, and the Japanese were building up "Russian" strength to support their aims. Atamans Semenov and Kalmykov were enlisted directly under Japanese authority. Japanese columns advanced into the Trans-Baikal and Khabarovsk regions, followed by troops of Semenov and Kalmykov. And on November 18 Kolchak seized power from the Omsk government by a *coup d'état* and declared himself Supreme Ruler of Russia. At Harbin Horvath thereupon abolished his All-Russian Provisional Government and threw his full support to the Kolchak regime.

The Allies were far from united as to the nature and amount of aid to be given Kolchak. General Graves's instructions were "not to interfere in the internal affairs of the Russian people." This policy was opposed by both the American Consul General at Irkutsk, Ernest L. Harris, and the head of the Russian Division of the State Department, DeWitt C. Poole, both of whom were ardent supporters of the Kolchak cause. The government at Moscow could thus count heavily upon contention among the Allies, particularly between Japan and the United States. These two powers were already in dispute over control of the Chinese Eastern Railway, with Japan having the advantage. Japan's command of a much larger military contingent in the field and its utilization of White Russian leaders such as Semenov and Kalmykov promised to serve Japanese purposes more adequately than the Graves effort, hampered by policy uncertainties at Washington, would serve American objectives.

One conflict was resolved when an Inter-Allied Railway Agreement of February, 1919, brought both the Chinese Eastern Railway and the Trans-Siberian Railway under control of an Inter-Allied Railway Board. China was represented on the Board. In Manchuria Pao Kuei-ch'ing became Director General of the Chinese Eastern. The railways were thus to be kept out of Japan's hands for the period of the intervention. However, the Agreement was to lapse automatically with the withdrawal from Siberia of the allied forces; the future had yet to be provided for.

Policy at Washington finally shifted in favor of the pro-Kolchak advocates, and on May 26, 1919, the Big Five at Paris sent a communication to Kolchak, first setting forth their policy objectives and then making a proposition:

They [the Allies] are convinced by their experiences of the last twelve months that it is not possible to attain those [policy] ends by dealings with the Soviet Government of Moscow. They are therefore disposed to assist the Government of Admiral Koltchak and his Associates with munitions, supplies and food, to establish themselves as the government of all Russia, provided they received from them definite guarantees that their policy has the same objects in view as that of the Allied and Associated Powers.[3]

But the excesses of the White Russian forces had gradually alienated the people from the Kolchak regime. The troops of Semenov and Kalmykov had become infamous for their rapine and murder, and they were not alone in their atrocities. The collapse of the much-heralded triple offensive of Kolchak and Generals Yudenich and Denikin in the summer of 1919 was followed by Kolchak's retreat from Omsk to Irkutsk.

This was the beginning of the end. Even the Czechs had become disenchanted with Kolchak and some of his foreign allies and now demanded the repatriation that was the nominal aim of the Siberian intervention in the first place. Since they numbered between forty and fifty thousand, a troop strength about one-half that of all the Allies, their decision was of vital significance to the entire enterprise.

In any event, the failure of the 1919 offensive also had disillusioned the Allies with Kolchak's military and political potential. The collaboration came to an ugly end. In November the Kolchak regime collapsed. Kolchak was arrested and delivered over to the Bolshevik authorities by General Janin, the French officer in command of the allied contingent at Irkutsk. On February 7, 1920, at Irkutsk, Admiral Kolchak and several of his chief lieutenants were put to death by a Bolshevik firing squad. Shortly afterward, the American, British, French, and Czech forces withdrew from Siberia, with the last Americans sailing from Vladivostok on April 1. The Japanese troops pulled back to the Maritime Province and Sakhalin. Kalmykov had succeeded in escaping to China but was killed there by the Chinese. Semenov remained for the time being in occupation of Chita: he was, in a sense, an expression of the residual Japanese ambition.

Since the Japanese forces also remained in being, the Bolsheviks on April 6, 1920, established in the disputed zone a so-called Far Eastern Republic, comprising all of south Siberia east of Lake Baikal. Its titular head was Alexander Krasnoshchikov, and it offered so independent a front to the world that it was able to maintain, informally, representatives in Washington; but it lay effectively under Moscow's control. It furnished a base for political maneuvers vis-à-vis the Chinese; but its prime function was to carry on a holding operation against the Japanese in the Maritime Province and Sakhalin, and in Outer Mongolia and Manchuria as well.

The *bouleversement* in Siberia had had prompt repercussions in Manchuria. The Red railway guards had gone, but the Red Army's success against Kolchak sparked a general strike by the Russian railway workers designed to force Horvath to hand administrative authority over to the Soviet Union. Pao Kuei-ch'ing deployed troops to break the strike but at the same time forced Horvath's resignation. Thus, for all practical purposes, control passed entirely into Chinese hands. The action was duly solemnified by an agreement reached on October 2, 1920, between the Chinese Ministry of Communications and the Russo-Asiatic Bank (which, however, possessed no more than a shadow of legal authority to act in the case).

China had lost the contest against its allies at the Paris Peace Conference, but the Siberian intervention had enabled it to make advances against the established Russian position in Manchuria.

THE RUSSIAN REVOLUTION AND CHINA'S BORDERLANDS

While engaged in Siberia, the Japanese had been making full use of their Cossack cohorts on yet another front. At the end of 1918 Tokyo began to evolve a grand scheme for the creation of a Greater Mongolia, to be composed of both Outer and Inner Mongolia, the Barga region (lying west of the Hsingan Mountain range in Manchuria), and Buryat Mongolia (east of Lake Baikal in Russia). Semenov, the Cossack ataman, was to head the new empire. Such a plan, of course, threatened the interests of Russia. Peking could have stomached infringements of Russian interests without difficulty, but, if the plan was implemented, it would also not only preclude any prospect of future restoration of Chinese influence in Outer Mongolia but would mean the alienation of Mongolian lands in China itself.

One of the Chinese leaders involved in the matter was Hsu Shucheng. In October of 1918 he had made a trip to Japan for the ostensible purpose of observing field maneuvers. He had close ties with Chang Tso-lin in Manchuria at the time and almost certainly had strongly supported the March and May agreements between Peking and Tokyo. By virtue of his position in the pro-Japanese Anfu clique, he was intimately concerned with developments in Manchuria and Outer Mongolia.

Strictly speaking, the tripartite agreement of 1915 between China, Russia, and Outer Mongolia still held: China had suzerainty—for what it was worth—over Outer Mongolia, but Outer Mongolia enjoyed autonomy in its domestic affairs, and neither China nor Russia might send troops there. But, with Russia weakened by revolution, the situation had changed. Early in 1919, at Premier Tuan Ch'i-jui's suggestion, Hsu Shu-cheng submitted a plan to the Peking government for "frontier pacification." In June of that year he was appointed Commissioner of Northwestern Frontier Development and Commander-in-Chief of the Northwest Border Defense Force. The latter position was the more important.

A Chinese Resident Commissioner, Ch'en Yi, was already in Urga and had made good progress in the delicate political effort to win the Mongols back to their allegiance to China. In view of the developments in Russia, to which the Outer Mongols had formerly looked for support, Ch'en stood in good way to accomplish his mission if left alone. But Japan's confederates were in the picture; and so was the ruthless Hsu Shu-cheng, much more inclined by nature to use force than political finesse.

Hsu, after having sent an infantry brigade on ahead, arrived at the Mongolian capital in October. He brusquely by-passed the Resident Commissioner and made his proposition direct to the Mongolian Prime Minister: cancel the autonomy granted by the tripartite agreement of 1915. Not surprisingly, the Mongols opposed Hsu's blunt demand. But Hsu had some four thousand troops in Urga, and he gave the Prime Minister an ultimatum requiring acceptance of his terms—now made more harsh—within thirty-six hours. The Mongols capitulated and "presented" Hsu with a petition, announcing their willingness to renounce autonomy and asking that Peking organize a new government of Outer Mongolia.

The petition was signed by various Urga princes and heads of government departments but not by the theocratic ruler of Outer Mongolia, the Hutukhtu. Peking did not view this omission as invalidating the document. On November 22, 1919, President Hsu Shih-ch'ang proclaimed that the petition had been granted, and

Mongolian autonomy was ended. At Peking, the Russian Minister, Prince Kudashev, protested the Chinese action, but he represented the deposed Tsarist regime, not real authority. The cancellation stood.

Hsu Shu-cheng was made High Commissioner to Outer Mongolia and undertook to consolidate his authority by placing Resident Commissioner Ch'en Yi under house arrest, disarming the Mongolian armed forces, transferring the functions of the former autonomous Mongolian government to his office, and putting his own men into the most important posts at Urga. He did not neglect the financial aspect of the matter: he negotiated a loan of $15 million from the Sino-Japanese Exchange Bank (against the usual mortgage of the region's resources). He later obtained another Japanese loan of $20 million, for the ostensible purpose of constructing a railway between Kalgan and Kiakhta. A grateful Chinese government awarded Hsu the Second Order of Merit in February, 1920, and appointed him director of the projected Kalgan-Kiakhta railway.

It was while Hsu was being decorated in Peking that Kolchak was shot at Irkutsk. The death of Kolchak, signifying a radical turn of events in Northeast Asia, had an inevitable impact on Hsu's future. He would not be permitted long to savor his newly won power. His ways of knavery, betrayal, and murder had earned him enemies. Some of his victims did not carry any weight in the final accounting, as, for instance, Resident Commissioner for Mongolia Ch'en Yi. But by political moves apparently aimed at extending his power into Manchuria, Hsu had made an enemy of a warlord who counted, Chang Tso-lin. He had also, by asserting Chinese authority in Outer Mongolia and disposing some of his armed forces along the border to prevent White Russian military incursions, acted counter to the plans of the power which had acted as protector for both him and Chang Tso-lin—Japan.

At Peking, Hsu's new position and power suddenly dissolved in a struggle between the Chihli and Anhwei cliques, with Chang Tso-lin playing a leading role. As a result of the changed situation in Peking, in August, 1920, Ch'en Yi was given enhanced authority in Outer Mongolia with headquarters at Urga. But it was too late to redress the situation. Hsu's actions had alienated the Mongol princes from China, and events in Outer Mongolia, influenced by the shift of power in Siberia, took a new turn.

At Chita, Semenov came under increasing pressure from the forces of the Far Eastern Republic after the establishment of the new regime in April. But the Mongol princes, looking for help from any quarter against Hsu Shu-cheng's rough invasion of their domain and prerogatives, had nevertheless turned to him for military assistance against the Chinese. The Japanese still had the "pan-Mongolia" card to play. Beginning about August, White Russian forces led by Baron von Ungern-Sternberg, a lieutenant of the Japanese protégé Semenov, began to penetrate the borders of Outer Mongolia. In October they launched a general attack on Urga. At about the same time Semenov abandoned his base at Chita.

The Chinese garrison at Urga beat off the initial attack but proved unable to defeat the Cossacks in the field. Ungern, "the mad Baron," recruited disaffected Mongols and in February, 1921, led a joint Cossack-Mongol force to occupy Urga. His political objective, establishment of a pan-Mongolian empire, closely fitted the Japanese pattern. The Hutukhtu was to be the titular monarch, and he, Ungern-Sternberg, was to wield the real power.

High Commissioner Ch'en Yi and the Chinese garrison had fled to the trading town of Maimaicheng near the Mongolian-Russian frontier. From that point, according to the Soviet version, Ch'en Yi called for help not to Peking but to the Red Army. The situation was highly favorable for Russia's intervention, but the Bolsheviks naturally saw no reason to save the Chinese authority in Outer Mongolia. They proceeded instead along conventional revolutionary lines. On March 1 at Kiakhta—on Russian territory—the Mongolian People's Revolutionary Party was formed. On March 13 the Provisional People's Revolutionary Government of Mongolia was established. It requested the intervention of the Red Army, which now responded promptly. By joint action of the Red Army, the armed forces of the Far Eastern Republic, and a newly formed Mongolian People's Revolutionary Army, the forces of Baron von Ungern-Sternberg were defeated and driven from Outer Mongolia. In early July, the provisional Mongolian government moved to Urga, and on July 10 it was transformed into the Mongolian People's Revolutionary Government. Finally, on November 5, 1921, the USSR and Outer Mongolia signed a secret agreement for the establishment of "friendly relations" between the two countries. This treaty made no mention of China or Chinese suzerainty; instead, Moscow recognized the new government at Urga as the sole legal authority of Mongolia. The Mongolian "revolution" had been successful.

In May the Peking Government had given warlord Chang Tso-lin a role to play in the struggle by appointing him High Commissioner for the Mongolian Borderland and charging him with reasserting Chinese rule over Outer Mongolia. It provided him with a sum of 500 thousand yuan (Chinese dollars) to finance the expedition. The sum was hardly worth a great sacrifice, and the developments of July clearly sufficed to make Chang Tso-lin see that the game was not worth the candle. He pocketed the money and devoted his energies to political maneuvers in the Peking area.

During the foregoing events in the Siberia-Manchuria-Mongolia sector, another part of China's borderlands, Sinkiang, had been experiencing revolutionary turbulence. In the face of domestic enemies Yang Tseng-hsin had only partially consolidated his control over Sinkiang when, in 1916, the hard-pressed Tsarist government began to conscript Kazakh and Turki inhabitants of Russian Turkestan in violation of existing agreements exempting Turkestani tribesmen from military service. The result was a revolt, and tens of thousands of refugees, mostly Kazakhs, fled over the Russian frontier into Sinkiang. By February, 1917, Sinkiang harbored some three hundred thousand refugee Russian subjects.

For all of its area, Sinkiang is not a rich land, and its total population in 1917 was probably no more than three million. To provide for an additional three hundred thousand people was not easy. Yang asked Peking for help in negotiating with the Russian Government, got none, and then cooperated directly with the Russian military authorities in order to achieve the repatriation of the refugees. By March, 1919, according to a report he made to Peking, some two hundred thousand Kazakh and Burut Russian subjects had returned home.

Yang's report, however, noted an interruption in the homeward flow of the refugees: the Russian Revolution and the disorders currently raging in neighboring Semireche had made the refugees increasingly reluctant to return. In fact, as Yang composed his message, the stream of refugees was about to be reversed, with tens of thousands fleeing anew into Sinkiang. The White Russian forces in Semireche were under the over-all command of Admiral Kolchak, who was based in Central Siberia. But the Bolsheviks were already on the ascendancy in Semireche. And when Kolchak's power collapsed in late 1919, the counterrevolutionary effort in Russian Turkestan also came to an end.

As the White forces in Semireche broke up, large numbers of

the defeated men withdrew into Sinkiang. Yang Tseng-hsin was able to read clearly the handwriting on the wall, and in May, 1920, he signed the Ili Trade Agreement, governing trade and other relations between Sinkiang and its Russian neighbor and providing for repatriation of Russian military and civilian refugees from Sinkiang. Yang Tseng-hsin subsequently let Red Army units enter Sinkiang to deal with troublesome White units, and the last battle of the Russian civil war on that front was fought in September, 1921, at Sharasume in Sinkiang. The Red Russians won, and Yang Tseng-hsin, his major domestic and foreign troubles over, was able to settle down to a quieter mode of existence, without concern for the unending internecine wars then rocking China proper.

Sinkiang's position had special significance primarily because of the underlying urge of the Turki peoples for independence from Chinese rule and the consequent potential of Sinkiang in Sino-Russian relations. Russia had shown a keen interest in developments in Chinese Turkestan (as the area had been called earlier) ever since Russian and Manchu power had met in Central Asia in the middle of the nineteenth century. The Kazakh and the Turki peoples—Uighurs, Uzbeks, Kirgizi, Tadjiks, and others—lived on *both* sides of a political frontier that had been drawn arbitrarily from north to south through that region. The separatist movements that swept over Russian Turkestan after the 1917 proclamation of the right of minorities to self-determination was proof of the strength of the Turki peoples' aspiration to independence from alien rule. And the trouble experienced by the young Bolshevik power with both Kolchak's followers and Basmachi insurgents had increased rather than diminished Soviet Russia's concern for that region.

Russian interests in Asia had been under attack on four fronts during the hard years that followed the 1918 Treaty of Brest-Litovsk. The government at Moscow, where the Bolsheviks had moved the capital shortly after signing the treaty, had endeavored to protect its interests by political as well as military means. It had tried to make friendly contacts with the *tuchün* government at Peking, using as bait an offer to establish relations on a basis of equality. On July 4, 1918, Foreign Affairs Commissar Chicherin reported to the Congress of Soviets that Soviet Russia was reversing the former Tsarist policy toward China by renouncing special rights and interests. The Bolshevik announcement, though outwardly attractive, had no perceptible effect upon the Peking government.

That regime was dominated by the pro-Japanese Anfu clique and was bound to a hostile policy by the still secret May agreement. Behind the scenes the foreign powers applied pressure on Peking to refrain from entering into relations with the revolutionary regime at Moscow. Peking did not respond to the Bolshevik overture.

In July, 1919, at the height of Chinese disappointment with the Treaty of Versailles, the Russians tried again. Deputy Commissar for Foreign Affairs Leo M. Karakhan addressed a message to both the northern and southern governments in China. He elaborated upon the earlier offer to establish friendly relations and proposed discussions for cancellation of the "unequal treaties" of Tsarist times, together with abrogation of the special rights and privileges derived from them. The message was long delayed in arriving at Peking. When it came, the Chinese were evidently considering making further inroads on former Russian rights and privileges, not to mention the Russian sphere of influence, by force. Tuan's regime let the offer, which was less favorable than the first Russian *démarche,* go without reply.

But, by this time, the tide had turned against Kolchak's power in Siberia, and the failure of that power would be followed by important developments in China proper arising out of Hsu Shu-cheng's Mongolian adventure. A close relationship existed between the power situation in the capital and the character of China's control over its far-flung borderlands.

A HOUSE DIVIDED

The national picture from 1918 to 1928 was one of great complexity. While the Peking government had been engaged in domestic and foreign struggles, important developments had been taking place in South China. There, the organization of the Directorate of Seven in May, 1918, and Sun Yat-sen's precipitate departure for Shanghai, had brought a substantial change in the character of the Military Government. Authority, in the main, had returned to the hands of the warlords.

After Sun's departure, T'ang Chi-yao, the Yunnan militarist, directed his energies chiefly to the implementation of a scheme to dominate the five provinces of Southwest China from his citadel in isolated Yunnan, and he retained only a nominal connection with the Military Government. The Canton regime was left dominated by the two Kwangsi men, Lu Jung-t'ing and Ts'en Ch'un-hsuan, the first an ex-bandit and the other the son of an imperial viceroy.

T'ang Shao-yi and other political followers of Sun still upheld the Military Government; and Sun had a military supporter in the field in the person of Ch'en Chiung-ming. An old T'ung Meng Hui man who had participated in the 1911 and 1913 revolutions, and the 1916 movement against Yuan Shih-k'ai, Ch'en was a proven revolutionary stalwart. Ordered by Sun in early 1918 on an expedition to extend Canton's authority into neighboring Fukien Province, Ch'en was solidly entrenched in Fukien by the end of the year and energetically engaged in building up his military power.

The new Canton regime had kept alive the challenge to Peking by protesting as illegal the Anfu Parliament's election of Hsu Shih-ch'ang in October, 1918, to succeed Feng Kuo-chang as President. The Peking regime ordered its troops to pull back from the fighting front and thus took much of the wind out of Canton's sails. With Peking adopting a pacific attitude, Canton was constrained to talk peace also.

A formal peace conference of delegates from Peking and Canton opened at Shanghai in February, 1919. T'ang Shao-yi again represented the South. The conference dragged on for months and finally broke down on two major points of difference. For one thing, the South demanded the cancellation of the loan deals related to the 1917 Agreement for Military Cooperation. For another, the Peiyang armies, in violation of the tacit truce, continued to advance against the People's Army under Yü Yu-jen in northern Shensi. In August the conference broke up, and another chance of peace had been lost.

The May Fourth Movement of 1919 had had its impact on Sun Yat-sen's thinking. On October 10, adopting Sung Chiao-jen's pattern at long last, he reorganized his conspiratorial and ineffective Komingtang into the Chinese Kuomintang. He went farther: he proposed to establish a constitutional government, to replace the existing Military Government, as a better instrument with which to challenge Peking. Lu Jung-t'ing and Ts'en Ch'un-hsuan stood in his way. But these Kwangsi militarists, powerful as they were, had a major weakness: their alien troops had been too long in Kwangtung as a "guest army" and had worn out their welcome. By the spring of 1920, realizing the increasing restlessness of Kwangtung under the Lu-Ts'en rule, Sun Yat-sen deemed that the time had come to strike. From Shanghai he ordered Ch'en Chiung-ming to attack Canton.

Ch'en did not move: a major development in the North was to take place before he acted. At this time the threat offered by Hsu Shu-cheng's growing power to various important military men had become manifest, and an organized opposition came into being. Chang Tso-lin made an initial move in mid-March with a demand for change in Anfu policies. Anfu chief Tuan Ch'i-jui stood fast, and in April Chihli-Shantung-Honan High Inspecting Commissioner Ts'ao K'un formed an alliance of eight powerful *tuchüns*, Chang Tso-lin and himself included, against the Anfu regime. In May a warning signal was given when the obstreperous division commander, Wu P'ei-fu, issued a circular telegram attacking the Anfu clique in general and Hsu Shu-cheng in particular and began to march north from his station in southern Hunan.

The combine was prepared to bargain. Chang Tso-lin arrived in North China in June for conferences with the other dissident leaders. They decided to demand that Hsu Shu-cheng be dismissed as High Commissioner for the Northwest and that the Anfu Club be disbanded. Chang Tso-lin met with both President Hsu Shih-ch'ang and Tuan Ch'i-jui regarding the matter but failed to win Tuan's agreement to settle the differences in this way.

The issue, therefore, had to be joined publicly. On July 3 Ts'ao K'un, Fengtien *Tuchün* Chang Tso-lin, and Kiangsu *Tuchün* Li Ch'un demanded Hsu Shu-cheng's dismissal from the two posts that had given him his power in Outer Mongolia. President Hsu Shih-ch'ang surrendered, and the following day abolished one post and ousted Hsu from the other.

The dismissal order lacked Tuan's approval. In turn, Tuan and Hsu Shu-cheng now brought pressure on President Hsu. By an order on July 9, Wu P'ei-fu was relieved of command of the 3rd Division and stripped of his rank and honors. On the same day Tuan formed a so-called National Stabilization Army (Ting Kuo Chün), with himself as Commander-in-Chief and Hsu Shu-cheng as both Chief of General Staff and commander of the 5th Route forces. The eight-province alliance headed by Ts'ao K'un and Chang Tso-lin thereupon publicly announced its opposition to Tuan Ch'i-jui as well, charging that Tuan, "for the sake of Hsu Shu-cheng and also for that of the Anfu Party," had declared war on the Chihli forces.

In accordance with standard practice, both sides had deployed their troops even before making the matter a public issue. Fighting in North China began on July 14. In the western sector the

Anfu forces suffered a debacle before the combined attack of the Fengtien army and Chihli forces led by Wu P'ei-fu. The whole Anfu defense collapsed on July 17. Ten days later Peking was found surrounded by Fengtien forces, and on July 28 a presidential mandate was issued, accepting Tuan Ch'i-jui's resignation as Premier, stripping Hsu Shu-cheng of his posts, ordering the arrest of Hsu and nine others as ringleaders of the Anfu clique, and dissolving the Anfu Club.

The power of the Anfu clique had been broken. Owing to the intercession of Ts'ao K'un and Chang Tso-lin, Tuan Ch'i-jui was not listed among the Anfu men ordered arrested, but his political career had been interrupted and he was not to return to power until 1924. Hsu Shu-cheng had taken refuge in the Japanese Legation and later made his way to Shanghai. The man who had made a name for himself out of all this and now commanded the attention of the nation was Wu P'ei-fu.

The upheaval in the North seemed to decide Ch'en Chiung-ming on his line of action. In August, he embarked upon his mission against Canton, arming himself with the political slogan "Kwangtung for the Kwangtungese." He won an easy victory. One town after another fell to the returning Kwangtung forces, and on October 24, 1920, Lu Jung-t'ing and Ts'en Ch'un-hsuan proclaimed the dissolution of the Military Government. Ch'en's armies occupied Canton two days later. Ts'en Ch'un-hsuan made his way to Shanghai and dropped out of the political picture. Lu Jung-t'ing withdrew with the remnants of his armies to his native Kwangsi and there endeavored to revive his fading fortunes.

At the end of November Sun Yat-sen, T'ang Shao-yi, and Wu T'ing-fang arrived in Canton from Shanghai. After lengthy political conferences, an announcement was made on December 29 in the name of the several directors—T'ang Chi-yao included but Lu and Ts'en Ch'un-hsuan, naturally, omitted—stating that the Military Government had resumed functioning. Sun Yat-sen was concurrently Minister of the Interior, but Ch'en Chiung-ming, as Minister of War, Governor of Kwangtung, Commander-in-Chief of the Kwangtung Army, and High Inspecting Commissioner for Kwangtung and Kwangsi, patently commanded great power.

On January 12, 1921, members of the old Parliament met once more at Canton. They did not comprise a quorum, but they nevertheless arrogated to themselves the cloak of legality. Sun worked to add the semblance of legitimacy to his regime. In April he had himself elected Provisional President of China, and on May 5, 1921, he formally assumed the post at Canton.

When Sun took office, he declared his program to be local autonomy, peaceful national unification, the Open Door, and the development of industry. He was prepared, however, to resort to other than peaceful methods for the extension of his power. At the end of May he ordered Ch'en Chiung-ming to lead the Kwangtung armies against Lu Jung-t'ing in Kwangsi. The campaign was entirely successful: the Kwangtung forces occupied the Kwangsi capital, Nanning, in July.

The North now entered the picture. With Tuan Ch'i-jui forced off the stage, the struggle became one between the victors: Chang Tso-lin against Ts'ao K'un and Wu P'ei-fu. The situation obviously favored political maneuvers on the part of ambitious men. Tuan Ch'i-jui, Chang Tso-lin, and Sun Yat-sen negotiated through their respective emissaries—Tuan's was the ubiquitous Hsu Shu-cheng—and finally agreed upon a tripartite collaboration against Ts'ao and Wu. The South was to launch a Northern Expedition, with its armies proceeding via Hunan, to pin down the Wu P'ei-fu forces in Central China and enable Chang Tso-lin to attack the Chihli men in the rear.

Sun ran into an immediate obstacle. His Minister of War, Ch'en Chiung-ming, was dead set against undertaking the long-planned Northern Expedition at that time, proposing instead the establishment of a federation of autonomous provinces. Ch'en's proposition was nominally in line with Sun's own program and was, moreover, one to which a number of important military figures in Southwest and West China adhered. There were admittedly other complicating factors. Ch'en's quick victory over Lu Jung-t'ing had still left Kwangsi in an unsettled condition. T'ang Chi-yao had in February been ousted from Yunnan by a military coup, and his forces were found widely distributed through Kwangsi and Kweichow. But perhaps the greatest complication was the growing ambition of Ch'en Chiung-ming.

When Sun's representatives were unable to change Ch'en's mind, Sun personally went to Ch'en's Nanning headquarters in October to discuss the project with his captain. Ch'en seemed at last to accept his chief's orders and returned to Canton for the ostensible purpose of preparing for the expedition, scheduled for November. Sun set up advance headquarters at Kweilin. He was now in Kwangsi, and Ch'en in Kwangtung.

But Ch'en showed himself increasingly recalcitrant, neglecting in various ways to carry out orders, particularly with respect to Kwangtung's provision of military supplies. The launching of the expedition was delayed for months. Then an act of violence made Ch'en's rebellious attitude more manifest: Sun's trusted follower General Teng K'eng, Chief of Staff and commander of the Kwangtung First Army, who had been given responsibility for making arrangements for the aforementioned supplies, was assassinated at Canton in March, 1922. The circumstances evoked the suspicion, never verified, that Ch'en Chiung-ming had engineered the killing in order to sabotage Sun's plans.

The blow had an immediate effect. Doubtless by reason of his concern for developments at his home base, Sun Yat-sen decided to bring his expeditionary force back into Kwangtung and advance northward through Kiangsi instead of through Hunan. He proceeded to Wuchow, a strategic point on the West River, and in mid-April summoned Ch'en to meet him. Ch'en didn't go; instead he resigned from all his posts.

Sun accepted Ch'en's resignation from all posts but that of Minister of War. He had offered Ch'en an opening for political retreat. Then Sun led his forces to Samshui, which is on the river immediately west of Canton. Ch'en left Canton the same day, taking with him his personal troops, which he deployed defensively around his home town, Waichow, east of Canton. Significantly, however, his supporters in Kwangsi, led by General Yeh Chü, immediately announced that they were bringing *their* troops back from Kwangsi to Canton.

On withdrawing from Canton, Ch'en Chiung-ming had announced a readiness to obey Sun's orders and carry out the duties of Minister of War. Later it became known that Ch'en had already established covert liaison with Ts'ao K'un and Wu P'ei-fu; but at the time Sun believed that the "old revolutionary" could not possibly waver in his basic loyalty. On May 4, Sun, as Generalissimo of his government's land and naval forces, ordered the expeditionary force to advance into Kiangsi. And he proceeded to his field headquarters at Shaokwan in northern Kwangtung.

Sun's army, commanded by Hsu Ch'ung-chih, advanced into southern Kiangsi. But his rear failed him. General Yeh Chü and other Ch'en Chiung-ming subordinates back in Canton demanded the restoration of Ch'en to his original posts. On June 1 Sun returned to his capital and tried still to mollify his old comrade with new concessions. On June 15, however, Yeh Chü demanded that Sun Yat-sen resign as President, as Hsu Shih-ch'ang had just done in the North; and on the following day Yeh Chü staged a revolt that struck at Sun's Canton headquarters.

Sun took refuge on one of his tiny navy's gunboats lying in Canton harbor. He ordered the expeditionary force to return to Canton to quell the revolt. And he sent Wu Chih-hui and Wang Ching-wei, both old revolutionaries, to negotiate with Ch'en. All Sun's efforts were to no avail. Ch'en Chiung-ming would not be reconciled, and the military odds were strongly in his favor. In early August Sun Yat-sen transferred from the gunboat "Yung Feng" to a British ship and sailed for Shanghai. With him was a young officer who had once served in Ch'en Chiung-ming's force, Chiang Kai-shek.

In the meantime, things had gone badly in North China for Sun's allies, Tuan Ch'i-jui and Chang Tso-lin. Chang Tso-lin had moved troops from Manchuria inside the Wall in April, proclaiming that the deployment was designed to unify his rear, and on May 1 he announced that Manchuria was aligning itself with the South-west and would thereafter exercise autonomy (with respect to Peking) in the administration of its affairs.

But the original strategy had called for the South to move long before, in order to create a diversion for the Chihli forces in Central China. Sun's expeditionary force had not even started out by the time Chang Tso-lin's forces were inside the Wall. In April Ts'ao K'un publicly denounced Chang's strategy of unification by mili-tary force, and eight other North China militarists, including Wu P'ei-fu and Feng Yü-hsiang, shortly afterward came out in support of the Chihli Party. The issue was decided in a critical battle fought on May 3 at Changhsintien, a town on the railway line south of Peking. There the Fengtien forces were defeated. Chang Tso-lin retreated with his armies back to Manchuria, and the first Fengtien-Chihli War was over. Chang's autonomy in Manchuria was unshaken, but the grand tripartite alliance for the overthrow of the Chihli regime had failed.

The failure had broader consequences. Wu P'ei-fu, although nominally still subordinate to Ts'ao K'un, by the victory over Chang Tso-lin had become the most powerful political figure in North China. He now moved to expel Hsu Shih-ch'ang from the presi-dential office.

He and Ts'ao summoned the members of the 1913 Parliament

back to Peking, announcing that the 1912 Constitution was again in effect. In accordance with Wu's arrangements, over 150 former members of Parliament gathered in Tientsin and on June 1 announced their resumption of office and proclaimed the dissolution of both the Northern and Southern governments. Sun Ch'uan-fang, High Inspecting Commissioner for Hupeh and Hunan (a Wu P'ei-fu appointee), doubtless acting at Wu's suggestion, had proposed that the northern and southern presidents should simultaneously retire. Hsu Shih-ch'ang read the handwriting on the wall and submitted his resignation on June 2, thus paving the way for Ch'en Chiung-ming's demand, voiced by General Yeh Chü a fortnight later, that Sun Yat-sen do the same at Canton.

Urged to resume office, Li Yuan-hung showed a reluctance that was in all probability more than ritualistic and stipulated as a precondition for his return that the several provinces should renounce their control of armed forces. All the leading military men agreed, obviously without in the least intending to observe the condition. On June 11 Li Yuan-hung took office a second time as President of China. Li supported the principle of federalism. In theory, he was merely taking up his tenure of office where it had been interrupted in 1917. If his position embraced a legal ambiguity, it was nevertheless stronger than Sun's.

In October, 1922, Sun Yat-sen stood at a critical juncture in his political career. Ch'en Chiung-ming had first blocked his Northern Expedition and then wrecked his Canton regime. With the restoration of "constitutional government" and the reconvening of the 1913 Parliament at Peking he had been robbed of his political program. It was not surprising that old-style military men, doubtful political allies in the country's power centers, and worn-out political concepts had proved of no help to him in his bid to power against the *tuchüns*. These elements were not the stuff of which revolutions are made. There were no prospects of success for Sun's revolution as it had been formulated up to that time.

4 REVOLUTIONARIES AGAINST THE WARLORDS

IN THE DECADE extending from the end of the Sino-Japanese War (1895) to the Japanese victory over Russia (1905), Chinese thinking, including the most radical extreme, had been centered on the renovation of the Confucian system. After the impact of the Russo-Japanese War and the Russian Revolution of 1905, sentiment was channeled increasingly toward political revolution. The revolutionaries, however, were moved mainly by simple nationalism: they desired to get rid of a hated alien dynasty. This feeling sprang from deep historical roots in China itself: it did not necessarily reflect foreign ideological influences. The anarchism of Bakunin and Kropotkin had attracted a small, elite following; Marxist ideology was not present.

The 1911 Revolution ousted the alien dynasty, and foreign governments accepted Yuan Shih-k'ai's form of *rule* as an effective continuum of the previous legitimacy. But some observers perceived a possible wider significance in the change. In July, 1912, looking at the Chinese Revolution from the other side of the world, Lenin characterized Sun Yat-sen as a "revolutionary democrat," representative of a class that was on the ascendancy, "a class which, instead of striving to preserve and restore the past in order to safeguard its privileges, hates the past and knows how to discard its deadening decay, which strangles every living thing." Lenin wrote: "The East has finally struck the path of the West . . . new *hundreds and hundreds of millions of people* will henceforth take part in the struggle for the ideals which the West has worked out." [1]

The role of the "revolutionary democrats" was indeed destined to be increasingly important in China. Parliamentary democracy was stillborn, and the aspirations of 1911 had been balked by the growth of warlordism and disunity and a renewal of foreign pressures. Early in the republican period political reaction and alien imperialism were frustrating the moderate hopes of Chinese intellectuals and diverting their thoughts to radical measures.

STIRRING CHINESE NATIONALISM

The Twenty-one Demands of 1915, Yuan's effort of 1916 and return to the dynastic principle, and Chang Hsun's attempted restoration of Hsuan T'ung to the throne in 1917 had spurred thoughtful Chinese to begin to break new ideological ground. In 1917, in particular, the revolutionary spirit was strongly aroused. Ch'en Tu-hsiu, as if reflecting the changed political temper, spoke out more pointedly than before in his magazine *New Youth* in an article devoted to "Present Political Problems of China." The evil aspect of the existing situation, said Ch'en, was that "the military men do not observe the law" and need curbing; they should employ their armed forces in foreign, not domestic, affairs. He set forth three requirements: first, military government should be discarded; second, the concept of unifying China through the influence of one party should be abandoned; and third, a choice should be made between (Chinese) conservatism and (modern) reform, as a matter of national policy.[2] Nevertheless, for a whole generation the three needs listed by Ch'en would continue to be unsatisfied.

President Wilson's Fourteen Points of January, 1918, increased the potency of the heady mixture Chinese youth was imbibing. In 1919 the men who had served with the Chinese labor corps in France and the Middle East began to return home, bringing with them new impressions and ideas. Moreover, after the disappointments of the Paris Peace Conference, Chinese intellectuals began to turn from Western political philosophies and to look elsewhere for answers to the problems that plagued their nation.

Up to this time, Chinese "progressive" thinking had been far from advanced. In 1898 even K'ang Yu-wei's constitutional monarchism had been too radical for the Empress Dowager. With the establishment of the Republic, the revolutionary forces had broken up into jarring sects. In 1913 Liang Ch'i-ch'ao's Progressive Party and the Kuomintang had both stood for Western parliamentarianism, the chief difference between them being that the former had supported Yuan Shih-k'ai's government whereas the latter had opposed it. Yuan had effectively wrecked the Kuomintang, Sun Yat-sen had tried to reconstruct a party from the shattered pieces but had failed; Liang, after the death of Yuan in 1916, had reconstructed the Progressive Party in a grouping known as the Research Clique.

Other groups called themselves "political parties" when Parliament functioned under *tuchün* rule in 1916–17 and 1918–20, but they were artificial contrivances, set up chiefly to give a semblance of constitutionality to the government of straw men ruling by the *tuchüns'* will. The situation of the budding radicals similarly remained fluid and undefined, up to 1919. The Literary Revolution fostered by Ch'en Tu-hsiu and Hu Shih had developed into a New Culture Movement, which opposed Confucianism and advocated Ch'en's "democracy and science." It had given an impetus to thought, but only vaguely indicated new directions. Chinese anarchism, which in 1912 had assumed organizational form, in 1919 took on added momentum, but never became a working revolutionary movement. Some intellectuals had undertaken the study of socialism, but again without serious revolutionary purpose.

Between 1919 and 1921 the American philosopher John Dewey and the British Fabian socialist Bertrand Russell paid visits to China. In a sense, Dewey and Russell both presented viewpoints to counteract an incipient Bolshevik influence. Both made a considerable impression on one wing of the Chinese intellectuals, the middle-of-the-road liberals, including men like Hu Shih, Chiang Monlin, and the guild socialist Chang Tung-sun. Chinese intellectuals to their left, however, were coming under a rival Western influence. Under the impact of the May Fourth Movement, the Chinese intelligentsia in particular became notably anti-imperialistic—and automatically began to diverge from Western liberalism.

In the beginning, the men gathered around Ch'en Tu-hsiu and Li Ta-chao did not constitute a party: they had simply drawn together in a common search for political solutions. Probably in late 1918, Li had organized a Marxist Research Society, but that was essentially an academic enterprise. That fledgling organization was transformed in December, 1919, into a Society for the Study of Socialism, located at Peking University. Membership was drawn from both faculty and student body, and included anarchists and guild socialists as well as Marxists. The internal strains were too great. In March, 1920, when the Karakhan declaration of the year before first became publicly known in China, the Marxists split off to form a Society for the Study of Marxist Theory; about the same time, a Society for the Study of Russia was founded. Again Li Ta-chao was the prime mover in the ventures. Political radicalism had taken a big stride forward.

Another young radical, Mao Tse-tung, had now entered upon the scene. Mao, son of a middle peasant and graduate of the Hunan Normal School, had in 1918 became a library assistant to Li Ta-chao. His thinking, at first bent toward anarchism, soon took on the coloring of the Marxist ideology of the older man. Mao had returned to Hunan in 1919 and, when the May Fourth Movement began, launched a magazine that advocated "democracy and new culture." This and similar enterprises evoked the hostility of Hunan warlord Chang Ching-yao, and in January, 1920, Mao returned to Peking, and drew even closer to Li Ta-chao. For the first time, he read the *Communist Manifesto*.

In its turn after the May Fourth Movement, the Karakhan declaration influenced developments in China. Ignored by the Peking Government, it attracted wide attention among intellectuals, especially since it was in such notable contrast to the imperialistic spirit displayed by the Great Powers at the Paris Peace Conference. And the Bolsheviks undertook to press their advantage. In April, 1920, three members of the Bolshevik Party, G. N. Voitinsky, Yang Ming-chai, and I. K. Mamaev, went to China as representatives of the Far Eastern Secretariat of the Executive Committee of the Comintern. At Peking the delegates met with Li Ta-chao and other men who had been active in the May Fourth Movement. Then, armed with an introduction from Li, they proceeded to Shanghai. The Karakhan declaration had assured them a warm welcome in leftist circles, the area of chief interest to them.

The Comintern representatives sought to give added organization and purpose to the rising tide of Chinese nationalism. At Shanghai Voitinsky met with various liberals, including Sun Yat-sen and other Kuomintang personalities. He undertook to merge three liberal periodicals headed by Ch'en Tu-hsiu, Tai Chi-t'ao, and Chang Tung-sun, respectively, only to have the latter two balk at the proposed association for Marxist ends. In May, 1920, at Shanghai, the first revolutionary Marxist cell was formed. It comprised seven persons, all members of the intelligentsia. Ch'en Tu-hsiu was its leader. This cell was the nucleus of the future Chinese Communist Party. The Marxist group still maintained a measure of collaboration with the middle-of-the-road group. On August 1, 1920, for instance, Hu Shih, Chiang Monlin, and other liberal but nonradical professors joined with Li Ta-chao to issue the "Manifesto of the Struggle for Freedom," demanding certain basic freedoms of speech and publication. In August, also, the Socialist Youth League was established at Shanghai.

The next objective of the Marxist group in Shanghai was the practical work of forming cells elsewhere in China. In September Li Ta-chao established a cell in Peking, and Mao Tse-tung set up another at Changsha in his native Hunan. A cell in Wuhan was organized by Tung Pi-wu, a Hupeh revolutionary who had participated in the Wuchang uprising of 1911. Other cells were formed at Canton and Tsinan. Weekly discussion groups were now organized in the main urban centers—Peking, Canton, Wuhan, Changsha, and, of course, Shanghai. Leftist periodicals began to mushroom. On November 7, 1920, the third anniversary of the Bolshevik Revolution in Russia, the first number of the magazine *Communist* was published in Shanghai.

The Third (Communist) International (Comintern), established in 1919, shortly turned its attention to China, since Moscow was inevitably concerned with the Far East. The Second Comintern Congress, meeting in July and August, 1920, gave expression to the then current thinking of the Bolshevik leadership. Lenin reported that "the foundation of the Soviet movement has been laid all over the East, all over Asia, among all the colonial peoples." The Congress gave its own estimate of the situation: "The breakup of the colonial empire, together with the proletarian revolution in the home country, will overthrow the capitalistic system in Europe." And the Theses of the Congress proposed active Communist support to "revolutionary movements of liberation" in "those states and nationalities where a backward, mainly feudal, patriarchal, or patriarchal-agrarian regime prevails." *The description fitted China exactly.* As a direct result of that Comintern meeting, the First Congress of the Peoples of the East convened at Baku some three weeks later, on August 31. China was among the various potentially revolutionary Asian countries represented. The veteran Bolshevik Grigori E. Zinoviev was chairman. He analyzed the revolutionary situation in the Middle East; but his gaze was upon farther horizons. He said: "The Communist International is convinced that there will hasten under its banner not only the European proletariat but the heavy mass of our reserve, our foot-soldiers—the hundreds of millions of peasants inhabiting Asia, our Near and Far East." [3]

Zinoviev laid down a thesis that has persisted in Soviet doctrine up to the present. Observing that there were four times as many people in Asia as in Europe, he said: "We desire to liberate all peoples, all workers, independent of the color of their skins, independent of whether they show themselves as peoples of white, black or yellow skins." The challenge to the colonial powers had been delivered. Moscow was bidding for the loyalties of colonial and "semi-colonial" peoples.

Numerous young Chinese already aspired to go to Moscow to study. But the continued Japanese occupation of Vladivostok made travel by the direct route difficult. Consequently, the majority of revolutionary students continued to go to Japan; others, like Chou En-lai and Teng Hsiao-p'ing, went to France, and some went to Germany. In January, 1921, however, one Ch'ü Ch'iu-pai, a member of the Peking Marxist cell, went to Moscow as correspondent of the *Ch'en Pao* (Morning Post) to be followed by Liu Shao-ch'i and others of the Shanghai Socialist Youth League. The channel for the transmission of ideology was being widened. The significance of some of these peregrinations could be seen when, in February, 1921, some young Chinese formed a Young China Communist Party at Paris. Among the organizers were men who later became prominent in the Chinese Communist Party—Chou En-lai, Ts'ai Ho-shen (a schoolmate of Mao Tse-tung at the First Hunan Normal School), Wang Jo-fei, Li Li-san, Li Fu-ch'un.

The radical movement continued to develop. In January, 1921, at the same time that Ch'ü Ch'iu-pai went to Moscow, the authorities of the French Concession suppressed Ch'en Tu-hsiu's *New Youth* magazine. The *New Tide* magazine expired. The Marxists were now battling harder against rival groups, especially the liberals on their right. From the time of Voitinsky's first trip, they had liaison with, and were thus able to receive directives from, the Far Eastern Secretariat of the Comintern located at Irkutsk. The time of decision was approaching. Chang T'ai-lei, as representative of the Chinese Marxists, participated in the proceedings of the Third Comintern Congress at Moscow in June, 1921. In that same month the Far Eastern Secretariat gave formal consideration to the matter of organization of a Chinese Communist Party.

Still in June, a Dutch Comintern representative named H. Sneevliet, known by the alias of Maring, arrived in Peking in the company of a representative of the (Red) Trade Unions International (Profintern). After meeting there with Li Ta-chao, they went on to Shanghai where twelve or thirteen delegates, representing a total of fifty-seven Chinese Marxists, gathered in the French Concession to organize a national Communist Party. Ch'en Tu-hsiu, paradoxically enough, did not attend; he had been invited by Ch'en Chiung-ming in early 1921 to reorganize the Kwangtung educational system and was engaged in conspiratorial work at Canton. Li Ta-chao was busy with revolutionary matters at Peking and also did not participate. But among those present were Mao Tse-tung, Tung Pi-wu, Ch'en Kung-po, and Chang Kuo-tao. The Comintern and Profintern representatives were also there.

The group was nearly caught by French Concession police on July 5. It shifted the meeting place to a boat on a lake at Shaohsing and there completed the work of organization and the party program. The Chinese Communist Party was thus formally established, with Ch'en Tu-hsiu as General Secretary. Its official birth date is July 1, 1921. The Chinese left wing looked no longer to the French Revolution for inspiration but to the Russian Revolution. And the Comintern, with its headquarters in Moscow, had established an organizational tie with the rising force of Chinese nationalism.

THE RUSSIANS AND THE FIRST KUOMINTANG-COMMUNIST COALITION

With the shift in the Far Eastern balance of power upon collapse of the Kolchak regime and the end of the Allied intervention in Siberia, China stood to lose more than it could gain from the absence of contacts with the Bolshevik authority. In May, 1920, following closely upon the withdrawal of the Allied expeditionary forces, a Chinese mission headed by General Chang Shih-lin arrived at Verkhneudinsk for discussions with the government of the newly established Far Eastern Republic. Then, after the ousting of the Tuan Ch'i-jui regime, General Chang's mission went on to Moscow, and a representative of the Far Eastern Republic, one Ignatius L. Yurin, proceeded to Peking.

Yurin soon wrung one important concession from the Chinese government. On September 23, 1920, in view of the incontrovertible evidence that the White authority had ended in Russia, Peking revoked the recognition previously accorded to Minister Kudashev and Tsarist consular officers in China. Yurin, nevertheless, was unable to make progress toward his main objective, recovery of control over the Chinese Eastern Railway. The Chinese had the disputed property in their hands and were obviously loath to part with it. Even Yurin's acceptance of various Chinese proposals did not lead to success. Developments in Outer Mongolia intruded into the negotiations at Peking.

The Chang Shih-lin mission likewise proved unfruitful. The 1919 manifesto had been full of promise, but the Chinese at Moscow discovered changes in Russia's intent. This was not surprising. China had not clinched the Russian offer in 1919, and the political situation had altered since then. Russia's position, particularly, was notably stronger than it had been a year before; the position of the Peking government was weaker. On September 27, 1920, Karakhan addressed a second statement of Soviet policy to the Chinese Minister of Foreign Affairs in which he repeated Moscow's voiding of all treaties signed between the Tsarist government and China, with the return to China of the former Russian holdings; but, as for the Chinese Eastern Railway, Karakhan merely proposed that the two countries negotiate a special treaty governing its future.

At the beginning of August, 1921, after the Red Army's intervention in Outer Mongolia, Yurin departed from Peking and did not return. The next mission came directly from Moscow in mid-December and was headed by Alexander K. Paikes. His purpose likewise was the settlement of the Chinese Eastern Railway question and the establishment of normal relations with China. The obstacles remained the same: the situation in Outer Mongolia and the pressures of the powers on the Peking government. The negotiations remained stalemated.

The task of the Russian negotiators was complicated by the opening, in late 1921, of the Washington Conference which had been convened by the United States to discuss Far Eastern questions. China, in accordance with traditional bargaining procedure, would wait to see what was offered at the conference table before making new deals with its neighbor. This approach was all the more firmly indicated because Russia had not been invited. The problems to be considered at the conference were the balance of naval power (principally, of the United States, Great Britain, and Japan) and "Pacific and Far Eastern Questions." Under the latter title, the United States proposed that Siberia as well as China should be discussed.

On July 19 Russian Commissar for Foreign Affairs Chicherin had sent Washington a note via the American Chargé d'Affaires in

Sweden in which he remarked that "the above-mentioned powers declared that they will themselves take into consideration the interests of Russia, without the latter's representation, and reserve the right of inviting eventually a new Russian Government, which should replace the present one, to accede to the decisions and agreements they adopt." Chicherin protested strongly against Russia's exclusion from the proposed conference on Pacific questions, characterized the preference offered to a counterrevolutionary government as "a hostile act," and said that, although the Russian Government was much interested in the matter of disarmament, it would be forced to ignore "decisions reached in which the Russian Government, not being represented, will have no part." Chicherin concluded with a warning: "A policy tending to leave Russia outside the collective decisions of various powers on questions concerning her, far from conducing to the settlement of conflicts at present disturbing the world, can only render them more acute and more complicated." [4]

The protest was ignored. So was a new note of November 2, sent to the United States, Britain, France, Italy, and Japan. When the Washington Conference convened on November 12, 1921, European states such as Italy, Belgium and Portugal were represented, and so too was the Peking *tuchün* Government. Russia, with three quarters of its territory in Asia and bordering on both China and the Pacific Ocean, was not.

At the Conference the United States succeeded in breaking the Anglo-Japanese Alliance and in getting Britain and Japan to agree to a 5-5-3 ratio for capital ships. It won Japan's consent to cancellation of the embarrassing Lansing-Ishii Agreement. Japan and China reached a settlement of the vexatious Shantung question. And the Washington Nine-Power Treaty committed the United States and the other signatories (excepting China) "to provide the fullest and most unembarrassed opportunity to China to develop and maintain for herself an effective and stable government." Moscow, not being represented, was not committed.

At the end of January 1922, while the Washington Conference was still in session, Russia convened a conference of its own in Moscow, the Congress of the Toilers of the Far East. Delegates attended from the Far Eastern countries, including China, Japan, and Korea. Again Zinoviev played an important part in the proceedings and spoke of revolution:

The Comintern inscribed on its banner "World Revolution," and not merely European revolution. The European revolution is only a fraction, a little corner on the map of the world revolution. . . . Even if we achieve victory in Europe, ours will not be a final victory so long as the Far Eastern question remains unsolved, so long as the last reserves of humanity will not be called up and the multi-million masses in the countries whose representatives you are will not be aroused.

In line with this thinking, the manifesto adopted by the Congress was addressed to the peoples of the Far East and ended in a militant statement:

We declare war to the death on the Japanese, American, British, French and all other rapacious world plunderers. We declare war to the death on the mendacious Tuchuns and lackeys of our oppressors in China. We declare war to the death on Japanese imperialism and plutocracy.

We declare war to the death on the hypocritical and thievish American imperialism and the greedy British usurpers.

Out with them from China and Korea, the Pacific Islands, Indo-China and the Dutch Indies! [5]

There was no indication that the assembled diplomats at Washington heeded, or even heard, the Communist challenge. But, paradoxically, Russia had already won something of a victory at the Washington Conference from which it had been barred. The Japanese efforts to support a separatist Russian regime at Vladivostok that would preserve the Maritime Province independent of the Far Eastern Republic had encountered heavy going. In January, the Japanese delegation, under American pressure and doubtless also with an eye to future developments, assumed undertakings for the withdrawal of Japanese troops from Russian soil.

Shortly afterward, on February 12, 1922, the People's Revolutionary Army commanded by one Vassili K. Bluecher won a decisive victory over the White forces in the battle of Volochaev and two days later went on to capture the important center of Khabarovsk. In October the Japanese withdrew from Russia's Maritime Province. Except for the continued Japanese occupation of Northern Sakhalin (which was to continue until 1925), the Anglo-Franco-American-Japanese Siberian intervention that had begun in 1918 was ended. Its mission performed, the Far Eastern Republic went out of existence the following month, and the Union of Soviet Socialist Republics came into being. One of its prime interests was China.

Russian efforts in the field Voitinsky had begun to cultivate were not without fruits. The infant Chinese Communist Party at its Second Congress of July, 1922, decided to join the Comintern. In a manifesto of the month before, it had called for a meeting with the revolutionary elements of the Kuomintang and the revolutionary socialists "to discuss the question of creating a united front for struggle against landlords of the feudal type and against all relics of feudalism." And the larger purpose of the struggle? "This struggle along a broad united front is a war to liberate the Chinese people from a dual yoke—the yoke of foreigners and the yoke of powerful militarists in our country—a war which is just as urgently needed as it is inevitable." [6]

Moscow, through its emissaries, was contributing to China's political ideology—and organization. But there was for the moment less progress in the field of direct diplomacy. Paikes had possessed very little bargaining leverage for his negotiations at Peking while the Washington Conference was in course. Such standing as he originally enjoyed had been speedily undermined. Upon his arrival he had denied the existence of the Russo-Mongolian treaty of November. Publication of the text had left him with little room for maneuver, and even less to say. His mission had been aborted.

In August, 1922, a new mission from Moscow arrived at Peking under the leadership of the able Adolph A. Joffe, one of the chief Bolshevik negotiators at Brest-Litovsk, and Paikes left for home. Like his predecessors, Joffe was charged with settling outstanding questions preparatory to the establishment of diplomatic relations between the Soviet Union and China. Shortly after his arrival, he proposed that negotiations be undertaken on the basis of the Karakhan declarations of 1919 and 1920.

The Chinese Foreign Minister, who was also Acting Premier at this time, was V. K. Wellington Koo, an American-educated diplomat who had represented China at both the Paris and Washington Conferences. Koo demanded that, *before* negotiations begin, the Red Army forces should withdraw from Outer Mongolia and Moscow reaffirm its intention to renounce, without compensation, all Russian rights and interests in the Chinese Eastern Railway. With Peking thus demanding all possible concessions from the Soviet Union in advance of negotiations, not even a beginning was made. In January, 1923, Joffe left Peking for Shanghai.

He went to see Sun Yat-sen, residing in the refuge of a foreign concession. Early in his Canton venture, Sun had sought foreign recognition, and foreign aid. His démarches had all been fruitless. He had made an overture to the United States Government in May, 1921, only to get a sharp rebuff from the Department of State. The American position had not changed substantially after the Washington Conference, as indicated by the instruction addressed by Minister Jacob Gould Schurman to American consular officers in China on June 26, 1922:

The Department [of State] believes that foreign nations should stand as far as possible aloof from internal dissensions in China and accordingly desires that officials of the United States in China adhere to strict impartiality as between the local leaders of political factions in China and that they avoid intervention of any kind between factions or in the plans for the settlement of dissensions.[7]

When the alert Maring had seen that the Kuomintang was a core around which a revolutionary movement could be constructed out of bourgeois nationalism, he had visited Sun Yat-sen in his Kweilin headquarters in December, 1921. Maring proposed to Sun that there should be collaboration between the Kuomintang and the Chinese Communist Party. Nothing concrete had come from that first meeting, because Sun regarded himself as generalissimo of impressive military forces and allied to such powerful figures as Tuan Ch'i-jui and Chang Tso-lin. But good relations between the two parties had been advanced; and when Sun arrived at Shanghai in defeat in August, 1922 (the month Joffe reached Peking) Maring sought him out again and now found him much more receptive to suggestions that the methods of mass propaganda and mass organization be substituted for a simple reliance upon military force. A correspondence was started between Sun and the Soviet envoy at Peking even before the end of August. In early September, Kuomintang leaders met at Shanghai and decided that the party should be reorganized. A manifesto defining the Kuomintang policies, and especially Sun's Principle of Nationalism, in more concrete terms than before was issued on January 1, 1923. Sun was making a new approach.

It was against that background that Adolph Joffe in January, 1923, met with Sun Yat-sen at Shanghai. The two men quickly found it possible to lay the foundation for a broad measure of collaboration between the USSR and the Kuomintang. In a joint statement on January 26, Sun and Joffe agreed that conditions in China were not ripe for the establishment of Communism or the Soviet system, and Joffe set forth the opinion that China's paramount and most urgent problems were "the achievement of national unification and the attainment of full national independence." In the statement Joffe assured Sun: "China has the warmest sympathy of the Russian people and can count on the support of Russia."

Lenin's "Thesis on the National and Colonial Question," as presented to the Second Comintern Congress in 1920, had proposed that Communist parties should undertake "temporary agreements or even alliances" with bourgeois-democratic movements in dependent countries—and China was viewed as being at most "semi-colonial." Owing primarily to Maring's insistence, the Third National Congress of the Chinese Communist Party decided in June, 1923, that "the Kuomintang should be the central force of the national revolution and should assume its leadership." This was in line with the Sun-Joffe agreement. It was also in accord with the larger revolutionary goal. The Chinese Communist Party, by entry into the Comintern, had been accepted into the revolutionary brotherhood. But this newborn party was still very feeble (it numbered only 432 members at the time) and was not viewed as constituting a suitable revolutionary instrument by itself. For the time being, the Kuomintang would have to be the vanguard.

A new shift in the unstable political situation about the time of the Sun-Joffe meeting had once more favored moves by Sun Yat-sen. In mid-January, small dissident Kwangtung forces with major help from Yunnan and Kwangsi armies commanded respectively by Yang Hsi-min and Liu Chen-huan, forced Ch'en Chiung-ming out of Canton. Sun returned to his old revolutionary base in February and on March 2, 1923, once more set up a "general headquarters" with himself as generalissimo.

Shortly afterward, American Minister Jacob Gould Schurman visited Canton, and Sun Yat-sen took the opportunity to make what was to prove a final approach to the West. He called upon the American Minister and proposed that the United States persuade other foreign powers to agree to undertake a joint military intervention in China for a period of five years. Sun's plan envisaged military occupation of all provincial capitals and the employment of large numbers of foreign military and civilian experts for the rehabilitation of both the national and local government. Subsequently elections would be held, and the foreign administrators would train Chinese personnel to succeed them.

Schurman viewed the proposition without enthusiasm. But events were not waiting upon the treaty powers. In June, at Peking, a new military coup forced the flaccid Li Yuan-hung from the presidency. With the Northern militarists again at loggerheads, Sun was presented with a new chance to drive for power.

At this point, the fruits of the Sun-Joffe entente began to be realized. In an interview published in the New York *Times* of July 22, 1923, Sun referred to his alliance with Chang Tso-lin and spoke with growing bitterness of the treaty powers:

General Chang and I have the same enemy, and I will take him—or anybody else who will help me—into the combination to overthrow Peking.

We have lost hope of help from America, England, France or any of the great Powers. The only country that shows any sign of helping us in the south is the Soviet Government of Russia.

In August, in furtherance of the new relationship, Sun sent a politico-military mission to Moscow. It was led by Chiang Kai-shek; another member of the party was Chang T'ai-lei, the Communist head of the Socialist Youth Corps. The Soviets matched the action by sending to China, to be personal adviser to Sun and political adviser to the Kuomintang, one Michael Borodin. He arrived at Peking in September in the company of a new Soviet envoy to the *tuchün* government, Karakhan himself. After a stopover in the capital, Borodin continued his journey, and reached Canton in early October.

In Moscow the Chinese mission investigated party, governmental, and military establishments. Chiang Kai-shek met with Trotsky, Chicherin, Zinoviev, and other Bolshevik leaders. Chang T'ai-lei remained in Moscow, but Chiang returned to China in December, just in time to witness an exhibit of foreign military power.

Sun's Canton regime, in a note of September 9, had demanded that it, instead of Peking, should receive the southwestern provinces' share of the Maritime Customs surplus. The note appears to have been ignored, but Canton was not to be denied so easily. On December 5 Secretary of State Charles E. Hughes reported to President Calvin Coolidge that the situation at Canton "appears seriously to threaten the integrity of the Chinese Maritime Customs." He explained: "The local Canton Government, under the leadership of Sun Yat-sen, and in professed independence of the recognized Government of China, is threatening to seize the Canton Customs House and to collect on its own behalf and for local official purposes the Customs revenue of that port."

Secretary Hughes added that the consensus of the representatives in Peking of the principal interested powers, including the American Minister, was "that there should be a concentration at Canton of the available naval units of the Powers having war vessels on the China station for the purpose of deterring the Canton Government from its threatened course of action." President Coolidge laconically concurred: "I think the naval units should be sent." [8]

The United States joined with Britain, France, Japan, Italy, and Portugal in the naval demonstration at Canton. "The integrity of the Chinese Maritime Customs," as administered under foreign control, was preserved by that reassertion of the powers' "cooperative policy." In a sense, Sun's Canton government had won a degree of "recognition." However, this first official contact between the treaty powers and the revolutionary regime could hardly be considered auspicious. Perhaps because the American naval contingent was the largest, the local propaganda attacks tended to concentrate on the United States. Speaking on December 31, 1923, before the Canton Y.M.C.A., Sun Yat-sen said flatly: "We no longer look to the Western Powers. Our faces are turned toward Russia." A short two years after the powers had convened at Washington to settle among themselves the problems of the Pacific, the ostracized revolutionary power, Soviet Russia, seemed to have stolen a march on them in China.

THE 1924–27 KUOMINTANG-COMMUNIST COALITION

On the basis of advice tendered by Borodin, work on reorganization of the Kuomintang to make it a more effective instrument of revolution was begun in October. The report made by Chiang Kai-shek on his return from Moscow in December gave general support to the reform project, and the Kuomintang was remodeled on the structural pattern of the Communist Party of the Soviet Union. "Democratic centralism" replaced Sun's personal autocracy, and the principle of party dictatorship was adopted. The First Kuomintang Congress convened at Canton in January, 1924.

The platform of the Congress comprised three major policies: (1) alliance with the Soviet Union in foreign affairs; (2) collaboration with the Chinese Communist Party in domestic affairs; and (3) creation of a base among the workers and peasants. The "Declaration" issued by the Congress was heavy with the spirit of "anti-imperialism" with respect to foreign affairs. In domestic affairs, it took a strong stand against the abuses of warlordism; and, with the issue of federalism become moribund after Ts'ao K'un's advent to the presidency, the Kuomintang edged into middle ground between local autonomy and the concentration of power in the central government. Communists were now accepted for individual membership in the Kuomintang, and three, including Li Ta-chao, were elected to the party's new Central Executive Committee. (Mao Tsetung was among six Communists elected reserve members.) The Kuomintang was now provided with a refurbished political machine. There remained the development of its political appeal and the mobilization of a mass revolutionary movement.

The raw materials for a revolution were present in China. The domination of the corrupt, ineffective, and unimaginative central government by a succession of rival warlords had resulted in maladministration of the country's political affairs and almost complete neglect of national economic problems. Bad government at Peking had led to worse government in the countryside. Every petty military satrap was doing his utmost to squeeze more wealth, as well as endless manpower, from the peasantry for the support of his swollen ambitions. Foreign imports, enjoying that "freedom of commercial opportunity" provided by the five percent import duty fixed by treaty, exacerbated the economic distress of the agricultural villages. The Chinese peasantry was more restless than at any time since the Taiping Rebellion. Banditry, always a warning sign of trouble in Chinese politics, was growing. The process of political disintegration had reached an acute stage.

The Kuomintang had never possessed a revolutionary philosophy with mass appeal. This was about to be provided. Sun Yat-sen, under Borodin's inspiration, sharpened and elaborated the original concepts of the Three People's Principles, which heretofore had been only vaguely outlined. The Principles took the form by which they are known today, impregnated with the basic revolutionary drives of "anti-imperialism" and "antifeudalism." These drives, embodied respectively in the Principles of Nationalism and People's Livelihood, would hurl the revolutionary movement against the treaty powers and China's landlords. The third Principle, that of Democracy, had immediate importance only as a handy stick with which to beat a warlord dog; yet, later it would be developed along lines evidently unanticipated by many of the Kuomintang leaders —but not necessarily by their Russian advisers.

The creation of a revolutionary army had first priority. Borodin had brought in some forty Soviet advisers. Soviet arms were promised (the first shipment would arrive in October). A new military academy was established at Whampoa on the outskirts of Canton. Chiang Kai-shek was appointed its head; the Soviet general of the Siberian civil war, Vassili K. Bluecher, became his Chief of Staff under the alias Galen. The able, young, French-educated Communist Chou En-lai was Chiang's deputy political commissar.

The chief political functionary in the Whampoa establishment was the Kuomintang representative, Liao Chung-k'ai. American-born, Liao had been a loyal follower of Sun Yat-sen since the founding of the T'ung Meng Hui in 1905. After the January, 1923, agreement between Sun and Adolph Joffe, Liao had accompanied Joffe to Japan and spent a month there in further discussion of the proposed Kuomintang-USSR relationship. Liao, together with Sun, was largely responsible for the final arrangements and was wholeheartedly committed to the concept of the alliance with Russia.

In North China the squabbling of the warlords continued. Ts'ao K'un achieved the ouster of President Li Yuan-hung in June, 1923, by applying force through two of Wu P'ei-fu's subordinates, one of them being Feng Yü-hsiang. Li left the capital for Tientsin after signing, under pressure, various orders facilitating the transfer of power. Ts'ao K'un, to make the action legal, next bought the votes of five hundred-odd members of Parliament at the rate of five hundred yuan per head; his majority thus assured, he had himself elected President in October. Peking's attention was now turned briefly to international affairs. Karakhan, after his arrival at Peking in September, had skilfully avoided precommitments and proved to be a hard and patient negotiator. With the relatively liberal Wu P'ei-fu the power behind the government, the Peking regime decided to effect a *rapprochement* with Moscow. On May 31, 1924, the two sides signed an agreement that provided for the reestablishment of diplomatic relations between China and Russia, joint administration of the Chinese Eastern Railway pending definitive settlement of the matter at a later conference, Soviet recognition of China's sovereignty over Outer Mongolia, and Soviet renunciation of special rights and privileges obtained through the "unequal treaties." The agreement tended automatically to strengthen the Soviet position in Canton.

Chang Tso-lin was disinclined to accept the new dispensation: after all, the Chinese Eastern Railway ran through "his" territory. But, when Peking's emissaries failed to bring the Manchurian warlord into line, Karakhan sent his lieutenant Nikolai S. Kuznetsov to Mukden and let it be known that the Soviet Government would take such steps as might be necessary to enforce the new agreement regarding the railway. On September 1, war began between a Chang man, Chekiang *tuchün* Lu Yung-hsiang, and one of the Chihli camp, Kiangsu *tuchün* Ch'i Hsieh-yuan. Chang could not risk fighting on two fronts. On September 20 his representatives and Kuznetsov signed a separate agreement reiterating the substance of the Peking treaty.

Chang Tso-lin had promptly announced his support for Lu Yung-hsiang and moved his troops into Jehol. Wu P'ei-fu deployed his forces in opposition. On September 5, from the south, Sun Yat-sen proclaimed his opposition to President Ts'ao and his military supporter Wu P'ei-fu; and, on September 18, he announced the launching of a Northern Expedition to overthrow both the warlords and the foreign imperialism on which they relied. Lu Yung-hsiang was beaten and retired to Japan, but, by the beginning of October, Chang Tso-lin's forces were attacking at Shanhaikuan, a point at the eastern end of the Great Wall.

Wu P'ei-fu was on that front directing the Chihli force's defense. Fighting was at its heaviest when, in mid-October, Third Army Commander Feng Yü-hsiang and Army Commander Hu Ching-yi abandoned their defense positions at Kupeikow, a strategic pass in the Great Wall north of Peking, and moved swiftly on Peking. On October 25, with the collaboration of Garrison Commander Sun Yueh, they occupied government offices and surrounded Ts'ao K'un's residence. They then sent out a message calling for peace.

Ts'ao K'un bowed to the inevitable and issued orders dictated by the mutineers, including one depriving Wu P'ei-fu of his various military posts and appointing him as Director of Land Reclamation in far-away Tsinghai. Ts'ao was then forced in his turn to give up the presidency, and Tuan Ch'i-jui returned to Peking on November 24 to assume the nation's leadership as Provisional Chief Executive. Chang Tso-lin's armies had entered North China, and Chang received new titles confirming his dominant position in Manchuria. Feng Yü-hsiang organized the Kuominchün (People's Army), at first composed of three armies, commanded respectively by himself, Hu Ching-yi, and Sun Yueh. In an era when betrayals were the order of the day, Feng's coup against Wu P'ei-fu in the second Fengtien-Chihli War would be remembered as one of the most outstanding.

Jurisdiction	Ruling Figure or Group
Area under Peking regime	Chihli faction leaders: Ts'ao K'un, Wu P'ei-fu
Manchuria	Commander in Chief of Three Eastern Provinces Chang Tso-lin
Shansi	*Tuchün* Yen Hsi-shan
Chekiang	*Tuchün* Lu Yung-hsiang (Chang Tso-lin man)
Fukien	*Tuchün* Chou Yin-jen
Eastern Kwangtung	Ch'en Chiung-ming
Kwangtung	Sun Yat-sen's Nationalists
Kwangsi	*Tuchün* Lu Jung-t'ing; Shen Hung-ying; Li Tsung-jen
Hunan	Commander in Chief Chao Heng-t'i
Yunnan-Kweichow	Commander in Chief T'ang Chi-yao
Szechwan	Military Affairs Rehabilitation Commissioner Yang Sen (Wu P'ei-fu man); Border Defense Commissioners Liu Ts'un-hou, Liu Hsiang; Liu Ch'eng-hsun
Kansu	*Tuchün* Lu Hung-t'ao
Sinkiang	*Tuchün* Yang Tseng-hsin
Tibet	*De facto* independent, Thirteenth Dalai Lama
Outer Mongolia	*De facto* independent, *Hutukhtu*

CHINA IN THE WARLORD ERA: mid-1924, at the peak of Chihli power, with the Nationalist movement centered at Canton

In the South, meanwhile, Sun's Northern Expedition had made no progress. At that time Sun did not yet even control all of Kwangtung Province. The year 1924, nevertheless, saw an important advance in the fortunes of the Canton regime. In September the Kwangsi military man Li Tsung-jen joined forces with old-style militarist Shen Hung-ying to put an end to the power of Lu Jung-t'ing. The rising Kwangsi group, headed by the three outstanding leaders Li Tsung-jen, Pai Ch'ung-hsi and Huang Shao-hung, next drew closer to Canton, and Sun's headquarters appointed Li to the posts of Kwangsi Pacification Commissioner and commander of the First Kwangsi Army. In January the Kwangsi trio suddenly turned to attack Shen Hung-ying and drove him from the province. The new relationship between Kwangtung and Kwangsi took on major significance.

Events were leading to a more definitive division between Right and Left in China. Sun Yat-sen's "allies," Chang Tso-lin and Tuan Ch'i-jui, were now in control of the nation's capital, and Tuan had announced his intention to convene a "rehabilitation conference" for the adjustment of national affairs. Tuan, Chang, and Feng Yü-hsiang jointly invited Sun to Peking to confer on the organization of a new government.

Always the optimist, and the political opportunist as well, Sun gave the appearance of believing that these three tough politicians were ready to collaborate in bringing about a new political era in China. He started on his journey, traveling via Shanghai and Japan. His attitude toward the sea powers had not mellowed over the past two years. Speaking in Kobe, he said:

Russia symbolizes and practices a "live and let live" policy. Other powers aim at dominating the so-called weak nations. We Asiatics must emancipate Asia and the down-trodden states of Europe and America from European and American oppression. Japan and China must join hands and harmoniously lead the Asiatics to fight for a greater Asiaticism, thus expediting world-peace.[9]

On December 31, 1924, he arrived in Peking for the purpose of conferring with Tuan and other Northerners regarding a political settlement. "I have come especially," he said in a brief statement at the railway station, "to save the country in cooperation with you gentlemen."

Even before Sun had reached Peking, however, Tuan had promulgated a provisional governmental system that showed that he had no intention of granting the Nationalists any share of the central power. And Feng Yü-hsiang, by that time, had become alienated from his erstwhile allies and was sulking in his tent at Kalgan.

It would be interesting, although fruitless, to speculate on what might have happened in China if Sun simply had failed in his mission. The American Legation had observed cryptically that Sun "would find great opposition if he should attempt to return to Canton." But Sun never returned: he died of cancer in Peking on March 12, 1925. Sun, by his death, had been saved as a symbol of China's nationalist revolution.

There was no reconciliation between the warlord order in the North and the revolutionary South. On May 23 the Kuomintang Central Executive Committee at Canton adopted a resolution severing all connection with the Peking Government and proposing that the Party thereafter should devote its efforts toward cooperation with the Soviet Union.

Soon afterward, on May 30, twelve Chinese students were killed when Shanghai International Settlement police, under the command of a British officer, fired on a crowd of demonstrators. The "May Thirtieth incident" resulted in a general boycott of British trade extending to Hong Kong. Antiforeignism was adding fuel to revolutionary fires. Said Soviet adviser Borodin: "We did not make May 30. It was made for us."

The 1925 wave of antiforeignism channeled much popular sympathy to the nationalistic revolutionaries based at Canton, but the Kuomintang—and their Communist auxiliaries—were not able immediately to exploit this potential: they had first to overcome the divisive forces that operated after Sun Yat-sen's death. In the fall of 1924 Sun had appointed his early Yunnan supporter, T'ang Chi-yao, to the post of Deputy Generalissimo. T'ang had not then taken up the appointment, but, when Sun died, he perceived an opportunity to assume the mantle of power. He clearly expected to receive aid from the two "alien" generals who had helped Sun back to power in 1923—Yang Hsi-min, commanding Yunnan troops, and Liu Chen-huan, at the head of the Kwangsi force. On March 17 he proclaimed his assumption of the post of Deputy Generalissimo and started his troops marching toward Canton—via Kwangsi.

Canton supported its new Kwangsi appointees by dispatching troops to help meet the Yunnan warlord's attack. The stakes were high, and the fighting was heavy, with the Yunnan invasion penetrating deep into Kwangsi. But T'ang's Kwangtung supporters were beaten in the vicinity of Canton, and the forces led by Li Tsung-jen, Pai Ch'ung-hsi, and Huang Shao-hung finally ejected the battered remnants of T'ang's armies from Kwangsi. Toward the end of 1925 the Li-Huang control over Kwangsi was consolidated beyond easy challenge. T'ang Chi-yao was no longer a threat. In fact, in February, 1927, two ambitious local military men seized power in Yunnan from *him;* a few months later, he died.

On July 1, 1925, while the Kwangsi-Yunnan struggle was still continuing, the Military Government at Canton was formally transformed into the Nationalist Government of China. Its armed forces became the National Revolutionary Army. The chief claimants to Sun's role of Kuomintang leader, Hu Han-min and Wang Ching-wei, became respectively Chairman and Minister of Communications. Liao Chung-k'ai was Minister of Finance, and Hsu Ch'ung-chih Minister of War.

This did not end the struggle for power. On August 20 Liao Chung-k'ai was assassinated. Hu Han-min's younger brother was implicated, and Hu felt compelled to resign and take a trip abroad. A committee of three, composed of Hsu Ch'ung-chih, Wang Ching-wei, and Chiang Kai-shek, was formed to handle the Government's military affairs in that time of Party crisis. Hsu was soon forced out of office and retired to Shanghai.

Thus it was disclosed that there had been a left and a right wing within the Kuomintang itself, and the departure of Hu Han-min and Hsu Ch'ung-chih signified that the left wing had won. Various conservative members of the Party left Canton and, in November, a number of them met before the coffin of Sun Yat-sen in the Western Hills outside Peking in what came to be called the Western Hills Conference. They passed resolutions denouncing Wang Ching-wei and demanding expulsion of Communists from the Kuomintang, cancellation of Borodin's appointment as Nationalist Government adviser, and abandonment of the policy of alliance with Russia. Canton, pointing out that the right-wingers did not constitute a quorum, declared their resolutions null and void. The Second Kuomintang Conference, held at Canton in January, 1926, ousted the chief dissenters from the party.

The Nationalist movement was meanwhile extending its military control. By two "Eastern expeditions," the first in January and the second in October–November, 1925, the long-standing threat from Ch'en Chiung-ming in eastern Kwangtung was wiped out. Ch'en retired to Hong Kong and never again played a role in national affairs. And in June the unruly forces of Yang Hsi-min and Liu Chen-huan had been liquidated. Canton's power had been consolidated in Kwangtung. Its orientation was to the left.

After the inauguration of the Nationalist Government, negotiations had been undertaken to integrate Kwangsi with Kwangtung under the Nationalist flag. An agreement was reached in January, 1926. The Kwangsi forces became the Seventh Army of the National Revolutionary Army, with Li Tsung-jen as its commander, Pai Ch'ung-hsi chief of staff, and Huang Shao-hung Party representative.

On March 20, 1926, an event occurred that resulted in a further shift of power. Chiang Kai-shek suddenly charged a Communist plot against his authority and, without consulting Government Chairman Wang Ching-wei, declared military law, arrested a number of Communists and labor organizers, and seized control of the gunboat "Chung Shan."

Because of the implications the "Chung Shan" incident bore for his authority, Wang resigned his post and went abroad. Borodin returned to Canton from Urga at the end of April, and demanded a restoration of the *status quo ante,* failing which Soviet aid would stop. Chiang agreed, but on a compromise basis: he undertook to curb the Kuomintang Right in exchange for a counter commitment that Communist activities within the Kuomintang should be circumscribed —and in return also for Borodin's agreement, previously withheld, to support an early launching of the Northern Expedition. In May, Chiang Kai-shek succeeded to Communist T'an P'ing-shan as head of the important Organization Department of the Kuomintang, and Mao Tse-tung lost his position as deputy chief of the Propaganda Department. Thus, with Wang Ching-wei for the time being out of the picture, Chiang had been able to consolidate his own political control at Canton. Finally, on June 5, 1926, he became commander-in-chief of the National Revolutionary Army.

The balance of power within the enemy camp was also shifting. In the summer of 1925 Chang Tso-lin had made a bid to extend his military power to the Yangtze. His move was successful in its first phase, and in mid-June the warlord's son, Chang Hsueh-liang, entered Shanghai at the head of two thousand troops. However, Sun Ch'uan-fang, who had now become *tuchün* of Chekiang in Lu Yung-hsiang's place, undertook a series of political maneuvers which enabled him on October 15 to proclaim himself commander-in-chief of the allied armies of five provinces: Chekiang, Kiangsu, Anhwei, Fukien, and Kiangsi. He then launched his challenge to the invaders of the lower Yangtze region and won the so-called Fengtien-Chekiang War with hardly a shot being fired. At the end of 1925 the five provinces rested securely in his hands.

One reason why Chang Tso-lin had been willing to relax his grasp on the lower Yangtze so meekly was that he was facing a new threat from Feng Yü-hsiang. Feng had entered into a secret pact with one of Chang's chief commanders, Kuo Sung-ling, and the two began a major move against the Manchurian warlord's power. In November, 1925, Feng's Kuominchün attacked in North China, and Kuo led Marshal Chang's own armies against the latter's base at Mukden. Chang was saved, just as his position was becoming desperate, by a Japanese proscription of fighting within twenty kilometers of the South Manchuria Railway zone (which, of course, included Mukden) and the timely arrival of reinforcements from Kirin and Heilungkiang provinces. Kuo Sung-ling was defeated in the field, and he and his wife were captured in flight and summarily executed. Then Chang, allying himself once more with Wu P'ei-fu, turned his attention to the protean Feng Yü-hsiang.

After modest beginnings in 1924, Feng had built the Kuominchün up to a total of 275,000 men, with some of the ablest generals and best-disciplined troops in China. He had, however, extended his power into Inner Mongolia, the northwestern provinces of Shensi and Kansu, and had even taken control of a part of Honan. Consequently, he was found with only a part of his force in position to meet the Fengtien attack; and on his exposed flank was the Shansi of Yen Hsi-shan, who threatened to make common cause with Chang Tso-lin. On January 1, 1926, Feng announced his retirement: he was going to take a trip abroad.

Feng had obtained the services of a Soviet military advisory group in April, 1925—but had given no firm commitment to either the USSR or the Chinese Revolution. He lingered for some three months in Inner Mongolia, then went on to Urga. There, in April (while the Canton crisis was still in course), he met with Borodin; then he proceeded to Moscow, with the aim of obtaining Soviet supplies for his armies.

During his "retirement," his able captains Chang Chih-chiang and Lu Chung-lin guided the destinies of the Kuominchün. By April, they had successfully executed a withdrawal of their forces from the Tientsin-Peking area into Inner Mongolia. But the rear guard stopped and consolidated a strong defensive position at the Nankow Pass in the Great Wall, less than fifty miles from Peking. There the Kuominchün stood fast.

Tuan Ch'i-jui had returned to Peking as chief executive by the sufferance of Chang Tso-lin and Feng Yü-hsiang. He no longer wielded power in his own right. Tuan had compromised himself by dealings with Feng and now was left isolated before the military authority of Chang Tso-lin. On April 20, 1926, he resigned his Peking post and, taking refuge in the Japanese Concession at Tientsin as so many Anfu men had done before him, he turned to the study of Buddhism.

Wu P'ei-fu had, of course, not taken up his appointment as Reclamation Commissioner in Tsinghai. Failing in an attempt to rally his forces and supporters in Central China, in early 1925 he announced his retirement at Yochow in northern Hunan. With the ouster of Feng Yü-hsiang from Chihli Province, however, Wu was able to stage a military comeback. After having established a base in Hupeh in late 1925, in the first half of the next year he went on to extend his influence into Szechwan, wrest Honan from Kuominchün control, and thrust his military authority northward along the Kin-Han Railway almost to Peking. And when, in March, his friend Governor Chao Heng-t'i was forced from office in Hunan by a subordinate, 4th Division Commander T'ang Sheng-chih, Wu helped drive T'ang out of Yochow and Changsha to the southern part of the province.

T'ang had already secretly agreed in January to join the Southern revolutionaries. In May the Nationalists dispatched part of the Fourth Army into Hunan to his support, whereupon Wu invaded the province with four heavy columns. T'ang then took the final step; in early June he formally assumed the post of commander of the Nationalist Eighth Revolutionary Army, comprising his Hunanese forces, with headquarters at Hengchow.

The battle lines had now been drawn between the *tuchüns* and the revolutionary South. The over-all balance of military forces appeared decidedly against the revolutionaries. Chang Tso-lin, Wu P'ei-fu, and Sun Ch'uan-fang together controlled over half a million men; the eight Nationalist armies numbered only about one hundred thousand. But Chang, Wu, and Sun were far from presenting a united front, and the country was weary of the warlord rule. With Chiang Kai-shek as commander-in-chief, the Northern Expedition so long dreamed of by Sun Yat-sen was finally launched on July 9,

1926—into Hunan. Chiang's deputy chief of staff was the Kwangsi man Pai Ch'ung-hsi.

Owing to T'ang's shift and prior Communist work in the countryside, the drive against Wu P'ei-fu proved surprisingly easy. The Nationalists captured Changsha on July 17 and entered Yochow before the end of the month. Prominent Szechwan generals came out in opposition to Wu P'ei-fu on his western flank. After a long siege, the walled town of Wuchang capitulated to the insurgents on October 10, the fifteenth anniversary of the 1911 Revolution. Wu P'ei-fu retreated into Honan Province. The upper Yangtze valley had fallen into Nationalist hands as easily as a ripe apple in the October wind.

The harder fight was against Sun Ch'uan-fang in the lower Yangtze region. Sun, the former Wu subordinate, had been seized by ambitions of his own. He had maintained a "neutral" attitude during the fighting in Hunan, manifestly hoping to be able to exploit to his own advantage a situation where the two adversaries might exhaust each other. In the meantime, he built up his forces in Kiangsi Province on the Hunan flank. For their part, the Nationalists, with their limited forces, were happy to be able to take on one enemy at a time. But they disposed strong forces on the Kiangsi frontiers against the anticipated later occasion.

The fighting in Kiangsi began in September, with neither side taken by surprise. Big battles raged in the northern part of the province, with heavy losses sustained by the Nationalist First and Sixth Revolutionary Armies in the struggle for Nanchang The victory over Wu P'ei-fu permitted the transfer of additional Nationalist forces to the Kiangsi war theater, and Sun's defenses began to weaken. Finally, on November 1, the Nationalists launched a general offensive that led to the occupation of Nanchang on November 7 and the consolidation of the Nationalist victory in Kiangsi Province. In the seventy days the campaign lasted Sun Ch'uan-fang had lost one hundred thousand men.

This defeat marked the beginning of the end of Sun's power in his five-province domain. The Nationalist armies marched into Fukien and Chekiang without great difficulty. On March 22 Chiang's forces captured Shanghai, the operation having been notably facilitated by an uprising of Communist-organized workers inside the city. Two days later they occupied Nanking. There the Nationalist entry into the town was marked by an attack on foreigners, which was stopped only because of vigorous shelling by American and

British gunboats anchored in the Yangtze River. (According to the later Nationalist explanation, the attack was Communist-inspired.)

The Nationalists now held both the central and lower Yangtze valleys. The revolution had moved halfway to Peking.

END OF A REVOLUTION, END OF THE TUCHÜNS

In the meantime the Nationalist Government had moved from Canton to Wuhan and began functioning officially in its middle Yangtze site on January 1, 1927. Here it was dominated by the Kuomintang Left—Minister of Justice Hsu Ch'ien, pro-Soviet Sun Fo (Sun Yat-sen's son by his first marriage), Chiang Kai-shek's military aide and able political agitator Teng Yen-ta, antiforeign Foreign Minister Eugene Ch'en, and Soong Ch'ing-ling (Mme. Sun Yat-sen, Sun's second wife). The power behind the Nationalist throne was the Comintern adviser, Michael Borodin.

It was already becoming manifest that the movement born of the Sun-Joffe agreement of four years earlier bore the potential for developing into a real social revolution. This was especially true as regards China's antiquated agricultural base. The work of Communist political agents in Hunan had already resulted in the organization of some two million peasants into associations. The long discontented peasantry now proceeded (under Communist incitement) first to demand rent reductions and then to rise up against the landlords. In February, 1927, after an inspection trip through Hunan, Mao Tse-tung described the advent of the movement as "a colossal event" and predicted: "In a very short time, in China's central, southern and northern provinces, several hundred million peasants will rise like a tornado or tempest. . . . They will break all trammels that now bind them and rush forward along the road to liberation."

The peasant revolt accorded with the aspirations of the Marxist revolutionaries who took their guidance from the Comintern. But Joffe had in effect assured Sun Yat-sen that Sino-Soviet collaboration would bring about only a "bourgeois nationalist" revolution and not a social upheaval. The "bourgeois nationalists" of the Kuomintang, many of whom had landlord connections, neither anticipated nor desired a peasant "liberation" like the one foreseen by Mao Tse-tung. In the affected countryside areas Nationalist military officers from landlord families began to show opposition to the turbulent peasant movement.

In the industrial center of Hankow, there was further cause for trepidation in right-wing circles. Under the urging of left-wing organizers, labor began to demand higher wages and better working conditions, staged demonstrations and strikes, and even entered upon political action. In early January "spontaneous" popular demonstrations led to the taking over by the Chinese of the British concessions at Hankow and Kiukiang. Lockouts began in foreign-managed enterprises, antiforeign riots at Foochow followed the disorders at Hankow and Kiukiang, and foreign nationals began to evacuate the interior. Foreign warships and troops converged on Shanghai. With the spreading of labor troubles and the dislocation of trade, Chinese property-holders became increasingly alarmed.

There was already an incipient split in the Nationalist leadership. Chiang Kai-shek's closest ties were to conservative elements in the Kuomintang—men like Tai Chi-t'ao, Wu Chih-hui, Chang Ching-chiang (who had given strong financial support to Sun Yat-sen), and Ch'en Kuo-fu, the nephew of his early benefactor, Ch'en Ch'i-mei. He also had close connections with moneyed interests in Shanghai. Chiang had proposed that the Nationalist Government be moved downriver to Nanchang in northern Kiangsi, and he forced the issue. Immediately after his troops occupied Shanghai in March, he arranged to obtain substantial "loans" from the city's powerful financial interests, and thus he was freed from the necessity of further reliance upon the Soviet Union.

Wang Ching-wei arrived back from Europe on April 1, met with Chiang in Shanghai, then left to join the Nationalist Government at Wuhan. Next occurred an intriguing coincidence of events. On April 6 in Peking, with the advance approval of the dean of the foreign diplomatic corps, Chang Tso-lin's police entered the Legation Quarter for the ostensible purpose of searching the premises of the Chinese Eastern Railway and the Dalbank (Far Eastern Bank, also a Russian organization) adjoining the Soviet Embassy compound. With no one concerned making more than a perfunctory protest, the police went on to search the office of the Soviet military attaché and made off with a large quantity of documents and with twenty Chinese found on the premises, including Li Ta-chao. Li Ta-chao and his fellow-revolutionaries were all strangled. The documents showed a direct connection between the USSR and various Chinese revolutionary activities. The first documents were not published until April 19, but the nature of some of them was undoubtedly known in certain official circles before that.

The connection can hardly have been news to Chiang Kai-shek. In any event, six days afterwards, on April 12, Chiang's troops launched a general attack on the Shanghai labor unions and workers' organizations that had so substantially helped the Nationalists take the city. About three hundred Communists, labor leaders, and "radicals" were massacred, among them a number of important Communist leaders. Chiang Kai-shek had placed himself at the head of the Kuomintang right wing.

Tensions between the Kuomintang right and left had increased nearly to the breaking point some time before. The Kuomintang Central Executive Committee could now no longer ignore the gap that had opened up between the Party and its military commander-in-chief. It passed a resolution attributing twelve "crimes" to Chiang and proclaiming that:

Whereas Chiang Kai-shek is found guilty of massacre of the people and oppression of the Party, and
Whereas he deliberately engages himself in reactionary acts and his crimes and outrages are so obvious,
The mandate is hereby issued that the Central Executive Committee has adopted a resolution that Chiang shall be *expelled from the Party and dismissed from all his posts* and that the commanders and soldiers shall effect his arrest and send him to the Central Government for punishment in accordance with the Law against counter-revolutionaries.[10]

On April 18, at Nanking, Chiang Kai-shek organized his own Nationalist Government. Events moved swiftly to a climax. Feng Yü-hsiang had returned to China from Moscow in September, 1926, armed with promises, promptly fulfilled, of Soviet military aid. From this favorable position he had negotiated an agreement with the Nationalists and, on September 17, swore his forces into service of the Revolution. He then awaited the opportune moment, meanwhile reorganizing and re-equipping his Kuominchün.

His big opportunity came the following spring. In May, 1927, the Wuhan government, after hesitating because of the break with Chiang Kai-shek, threw T'ang Sheng-chih's Eighth Army and Chang Fa-k'uei's Fourth Army (the "Ironsides") against Honan Province. There Wu P'ei-fu, evidently fearing the operations of his conservative "ally" Chang Tso-lin as much as the Red revolutionaries from the South, had been unwilling to reach a firm agreement with the Peking regime for joint defense. When the Nationalist armies attacked, therefore, he withdrew his forces into western Honan and left the battle to be fought by Fengtien alone.

The Fengtien forces were led by Chang Hsueh-liang and Chang Tsung-ch'ang. The latter, like Chang Tso-lin an ex-Manchurian bandit, had fought on the Russian side in the Russo-Japanese War. Although not overly endowed with strategic finesse, he was a courageous, swashbuckling fighter. The Nationalists consequently were forced to fight hard and lost heavily. Then, just as the tide was beginning to turn in their favor, Feng Yü-hsiang's armies suddenly debouched through Tungkuan Pass from Shensi and Kansu to occupy strategic points on the western section of the Lunghai Railway. It was an easy victory; and, because of the break between Chiang Kai-shek at Nanking and the Nationalist Government at Wuhan, Feng occupied a pivotal political position.

At Wuhan, on June 1, the Communist Party received new instructions from Stalin (who by then had risen to the controlling position in the USSR), directing that confiscation of the landlords' land should proceed except for land belonging to military officers, that "unreliable" generals should be destroyed and a new army of twenty thousand Communists and fifty thousand peasants and workers be created, and that "new worker and peasant elements" should be brought into the Kuomintang Central Executive Committee. The recently arrived Comintern representative at Wuhan, the Indian M. N. Roy, showed the telegram to Wang Ching-wei, who had returned from Europe at the beginning of April to join the government. The Kuomintang Left thus learned of the Comintern's plans for them.

Both Kuomintang factions now undertook to negotiate with the man who held the balance of power, Feng Yü-hsiang. Feng met first with an impressive Wuhan delegation that included not only the military men T'ang Sheng-chih and Chang Fa-k'uei but also such political leaders as Wang Ching-wei, T'an Yen-k'ai, Teng Yen-ta, Hsu Ch'ien, Sun Fo, and Ku Meng-yü—and the chief Soviet military adviser, Bluecher. The meeting was at Chengchow, which was under Feng's control, and lasted three days. The Wuhan leaders made a major concession to Feng: the troops of T'ang Sheng-chih and Chang Fa-k'uei evacuated in Feng's favor the Honan territory won at such heavy cost; and Wuhan appointed Feng Honan Provincial Chairman. But Feng conceded nothing, and the delegates returned to Wuhan empty-handed.

Feng next traveled east on the railway to Hsuchow, captured a short time before by Nationalist forces, and there met with Chiang Kai-shek. In a three-day meeting from June 19 to 21, agreement was reached, and the two military leaders made a joint announcement to the nation that they and their troops were disciples of the Three People's Principles and would fight to the death to wipe out the instrumentalities of imperialism in China so as to accomplish the revolutionary mission. The real nature of their agreement was better indicated, however, by a telegram sent by Feng to Wuhan recommending that Borodin return home to the Soviet Union and that Wuhan (Leftist) members of the Kuomintang Central Executive Committee should either take trips abroad "for rest" or join (Chiang's) Nationalist Government at Nanking "if they desire." Feng had decided to tip the balance of power in favor of Chiang.

The Comintern Executive Committee, which had stubbornly refused to read the clear meaning of the spring's events in China, at last realized that the situation was desperate. On July 14 it called for another radical change in tactics: the Chinese Communists should remain in the Kuomintang and at the same time prepare the workers for "decisive action," "develop the agrarian revolution," arm the workers and peasants, and, besides all this, "organize a competent fighting illegal party apparatus."

It was much too late. The Wuhan Nationalists, quickly learning of the new instructions to their Communist allies, swung to the Right instead of the Left. They expelled the Chinese Communists from the Kuomintang and undertook a purge. As early as May 21, at Changsha, T'ang Sheng-chih's forces had undertaken repression of radical labor unions and peasant associations. T'ang now took the sword to the revolutionaries generally. The wave of executions that had begun in Shanghai was extended into the Wuhan jurisdiction.

Borodin and other Soviet advisers and a small number of Kuomintang Leftists made their way out of China by various routes. Chinese Communist leaders fled where they could. Communist-led troops fought a series of desperate battles. On August 1 Yeh T'ing, Ho Lung, and Chu Teh led an uprising in Nanchang, held the town a few days, and were forced to flee. They made their way overland, occupied Swatow on the Kwangtung coast, were defeated again, and melted into the countryside. Back in Hunan Province Mao Tse-tung endeavored to organize a peasant insurrection, but without success. The "autumn harvest uprisings" had failed. Throughout Nationalist-held China, the troops of Chiang Kai-shek, T'ang Sheng-chih, and Southwestern military leader Li Chi-shen hunted down the revolutionaries and radicals and destroyed them. The peasant movement was crushed. The Chinese Communist party, which had built its membership up to a strength of nearly 58,000 in 1927, had endeavored to use the Kuomintang Left as a vehicle to power. But that faction of the "vanguard" party had proved far too weak, and ultimately unwilling, to support a rapid advance toward social revolution. Old-fashioned militarism had easily overcome the premature challenge. The current wave of the Chinese Revolution had reached its crest and was now receding.

Meanwhile, the *tuchün's* camp had been the scene of much activity. Under the leadership of Chang Tso-lin as commander-in-chief of the Ankuochün (National Pacification Army), a loose coalition of northern warlords, including Chang Tsung-ch'ang, Sun Ch'uan-fang, Yen Hsi-shan, and—nominally—Wu P'ei-fu, was formed in December, 1926, for joint defense against the Nationalist threat from the south. In May, 1927, however, Yen Hsi-shan adopted an equivocal attitude; and in early June he assumed the post of commander-in-chief of the National Revolutionary Army for the North. This disturbing development, combined with the defeats suffered in May on the Honan and Kiangsu fronts, forced the warlords to make a critical decision—whether to retreat before the Nationalist movement or to stand and fight. At a Fengtien council of war held at Peking in June, the "old faction" led by Heilungkiang *tuchün* Wu Chün-sheng argued in favor of withdrawing the Fengtien armies from North China back to Manchuria in order to keep that rich empire intact. Chang Tso-lin's trusted chief of staff, the ruthless Yang Yü-t'ing, contended instead that an attempt should be made to reach a compromise agreement with Chiang Kai-shek and Yen Hsi-shan for maintenance of the *status quo,* that is, for preserving the existing division of China into spheres of influence.

Yang Yü-t'ing won the day. On June 18, 1927, Chang Tso-lin proclaimed himself Generalissimo of China's Land and Sea Forces. In July he reorganized his armies into seven corps. Sun Ch'uan-fang and Chang Tsung-ch'ang, commanding the First and Second Corps respectively, drove southward from Hsuchow in August and quickly thrust the Nationalist forces back to the Yangtze.

Partly because of these military setbacks and partly because of major differences over future political orientation and alignments, a major split developed inside the Nanking camp. Chiang's First and Seventh Army commanders, Ho Ying-ch'in and Li Tsung-jen, and Chief of Staff Pai Ch'ung-hsi, refused to take further orders from him. Li and Pai now demanded reconciliation with the Kuomintang forces in Wuhan. Confronted by this rebellion against his authority, Chiang gave up his various Nanking posts in August, saying that he held the success of the Kuomintang above all else and was resigning to eliminate dissension. He then proceeded to Japan, stopping off in Shanghai for a long conference with his "chief political adviser," Chang Ching-chiang. With both the Wuhan and Nanking regimes apparently on the verge of dissolution, it seemed that Yang Yü-t'ing's shrewd estimate of the importance of divisive factors in the Nationalist camp might prove right.

Some seventy thousand of Sun Ch'uan-fang's forces, flushed with their easy victory, had meanwhile crossed the Yangtze. But they had thereby committed a fatal strategic error. Nationalist gunboats cut off their line of retreat back across the river, Li Tsung-jen caught them in a pincers movement and some fifty thousand troops were lost. Thus Sun Ch'uan-fang's main strength disappeared and the position of Chang Tsung-ch'ang was correspondingly weakened. Once more Sun and Chang retreated back to Hsuchow.

Noting the opportunity offered by the fluid political situation, the Western Hills group decided to undertake the mediation between the opposing Kuomintang camps demanded by the Li-Pai faction. It achieved a limited success. A new, "united" Nationalist Government was set up in Nanking in September. It contained elements of both the broken Wuhan regime and the Right Kuomintang, but Chiang Kai-shek's name was missing from the roster. The Nationalist ship was still afloat; however, it was without an effective captain. And Chiang's supporters sabotaged efforts of the Western Hills group to consolidate control over the government. The bickering of parochial and ambitious politicians resumed, and in October, faced by a power bid from their erstwhile comrade T'ang Sheng-chih in the Middle Yangtze region, the Nanking forces drove on Wuhan. T'ang retired to Japan. In November a separate regime was again set up in Canton, this time by the joint efforts of Wang Ching-wei, Hu Han-min, and T. V. Soong.

The confusion, so reminiscent of that which had occurred at the end of Yuan Shih-k'ai's rule, reflected the clash of personal ambitions in a situation where the government's legitimacy was under challenge and party discipline had broken down. With the Nationalist camp thus torn by disunity, the road to power was once more opened to a military "strong man." Chiang Kai-shek, weighing the opportunity, emerged from his retirement in Japan and returned to Shanghai. Wang Ching-wei met with him there in early December, and new negotiations began.

Chiang's political maneuvers were facilitated by a startling development at Wang Ching-wei's base in Canton. On December 11 that southern "capital" was the scene of the Leftist uprising known as the Canton Commune. It was staged by a handful of men acting in accord with the desperate line still governing the Chinese Communist Party, as transmitted to Canton by the Comintern agent Heinz Neumann. The Chinese charged with organizing the insurrection was the Communist who had accompanied Chiang Kai-shek on the 1923 trip to Moscow, Chang T'ai-lei. The prevailing conditions could only be described as hopeless from the point of view of the insurgents. As soon as the insurrection began, the forces of Chang Fa-k'uei, Li Chi-shen, and Huang Ch'i-hsiang began to converge on the scene, and on December 15, when the deployment was completed, the uprising was put down in a blood bath. Neumann succeeded in escaping, but five Soviet consular officials were killed by troops that invaded the Soviet consular office. Also killed was Chang T'ai-lei.

The Canton Commune was the last desperate thrust of the Communists and their supporters who had broken with their erstwhile comrades-in-arms at the Yangtze. As one result, the Nanking government, although still far short of possessing national authority, on December 14 ordered the closure of all Soviet consular offices and commercial agencies in the area under its jurisdiction. The train of events introduced by Chang Tso-lin's raid on the Soviet Embassy in April and accelerated by the political breakup at Wuhan had now reached a conclusion that was inherently logical: the Soviet-Nationalist association had begun at Canton, and there it ended.

The political developments of December were accompanied by a significant Nationalist military advance. The Nationalist forces of Feng Yü-hsiang and Ho Ying-ch'in, comprising the Second and First Army Corps, drove against strategic Hsuchow. The First Army Corps succeeded in occupying that point in mid-December, and Chang Tsung-ch'ang's forces retreated farther north into his Shantung base area.

Some of Wang Ching-wei's followers had been involved in the Canton uprising, and his position was consequently notably weakened. Chiang Kai-shek, allied to both the financial moguls of Shanghai and the powerful military forces of Feng Yü-hsiang, was recognized to be the best available catalytic agent. The Kuomintang Second Central Executive Committee, elected at the Congress of 1926, was resurrected as the governing body of the Party and resumed control. Wang Ching-wei, effectively out of the picture, was absent from the critical sessions. Chiang was present, and in January 1928, with his opponents still disunited and his own political fences mended, he recovered his positions as commander-in-chief of the Nationalist Army and chairman of the Kuomintang Central Executive Committee and, in addition, became chairman of the Military Affairs Commission. Once more, a "reorganized" Nationalist Government began to function at Nanking.

There remained the military task of overthrowing the *tuchün* government at Peking. Feng Yü-hsiang, Yen Hsi-shan, and the Kwangsi men Li Tsung-jen and Pai Ch'ung-hsi were once more joined with Chiang in the Nationalist cause. They launched their final drive in April, and by the end of the month the First Army Corps had occupied the Shantung provincial capital, Tsinan. The Japanese, however, had once more landed troops at Tsingtao and moved them on to Tsinan, ostensibly to protect their nationals. At the beginning of May, Nationalist forces clashed with the Japanese and were driven from town.

The Japanese intervention was, in a sense, a final blow at the foundation of Chang Tso-lin's powers. The move had all the appearance of being for the purpose of buttressing up the power of Chang Tso-lin, and the state of Chinese nationalism was such that a move of that order naturally defeated its own purposes. The Japanese, alarmed by the course of events and concerned particularly for the safety of their major sphere of influence, South Manchuria, had earlier warned Chang Tso-lin to withdraw from North China while there was yet time; now, on May 18, through Japanese Minister Yoshizawa at Peking they advised Chang Tso-lin that, if disturbances in North China continued, "the Japanese Government . . . [might] possibly be constrained to take appropriate and effective steps for the maintenance of peace and order in Manchuria." Moreover, "defeated troops or those in pursuit of them" would be prevented from entering Manchuria. And Yoshizawa advised Chang orally not to return to Manchuria.

The meaning of Yoshizawa's warning was clear enough: Chang Tso-lin had waited too long. By this time the old warlord's political and military positions in China were beyond repair. At the end of May the Fengtien forces lost Paoting, a strategic point south of Peking, and orders went out for a general retreat back toward Shanhaikuan and Manchuria. Chang Tso-lin bade farewell to the Peking diplomatic corps on June 1 and on the following day started back to his home base at Mukden. But on June 4, as he was nearing his destination, his private train was blown up. Chang was killed, together with Wu Chün-sheng. Various other prominent persons in Marshal Chang's entourage were injured. Chang Tso-lin was the last of the *tuchüns,* and the Peking *tuchün* government had now passed out of existence.

Later, a discovery was made that was highly significant for the future: the explosion that brought death to "Old Marshal" Chang Tso-lin had been the fruit of a plot by a small group of staff officers of the Japanese Army. The conspiratorial clique proposed that the killing should be the first step in a larger program for the seizure of Manchuria.

On October 10, 1928 the Nationalist Government, undergoing its fourth mutation at Nanking, became the National Government of China. It was the lineal descendent of its Canton prototype and successor to the claimed authority of the defunct Peking Government to speak for all China. If the name was reminiscent of the Canton Nationalist Government, however, the governing mind and spirit were changed in 1928. The Organic Law for the Republic of China as promulgated by the Kuomintang Central Executive Committee on October 4, 1928, provided for a system of one-party "tutelage" by the Kuomintang, that is, a one-party dictatorship of the country's government. And the controlling Kuomintang faction was the right-wing group, heavy with such conservatives as the brothers Ch'en Li-fu and Ch'en Kuo-fu (who between them created the so-called C-C Clique), Tai Chi-t'ao and his colleagues of the Western Hills Conference group, Chiang Kai-shek's military lieutenants, and leading Shanghai financial and commercial figures.

Chiang Kai-shek dominated the Kuomintang at Nanking. Chiang was no liberal, nor was he a political philosopher. Educated in a Japanese military academy, he had come into contact with the Revolution by joining the T'ung Meng Hui in Japan and by playing a minor military role in the service of General Ch'en Ch'i-mei near Shanghai in 1911. But he had made his exit from the political scene in 1913 and engaged in brokerage in Shanghai for nearly a decade. It was during that period that he had established connections with the powerful political and financial figures in Shanghai that were to have so important an influence on his later orientation.

Conservative forces thus dominated the Kuomintang's beginnings at Nanking. But, for want of an adequate conservative philosophy, the Party retained Sun Yat-sen's revolutionary Three People's Prin-

ciples. It was expedient to vow fealty to the Principle of Nationalism, for this was translated as "anti-imperialism," and Chinese conservatives, even as the radicals, stood opposed to spheres of influence, extraterritoriality, and similar alien invasions of China's sovereignty. The autocrats could easily continue to pay reverent lip
service to the Principle of Democracy, for this was now only a
promise for future performance. But there could be no substantial
exposition of the Principle of the People's Livelihood, for in its
essence that Principle required social change; and the propertied
classes, who now were the pillars of the Kuomintang, desired no
such changes in the system of land tenure, or of the unbridled
usury on which agricultural credits were based, as would affect
their rights of ownership and profits. Imaginative and herculean
efforts were patently needed for the making of a new Chinese
society to replace the old. Just as obviously, lip service alone to
progressive principles would not suffice for the task.

By inherent disposition, therefore, the Nanking Government was
fated to become identified with maintenance of the social and economic *status quo* in the same general sense, if not in the same
manner, as was the Empress Dowager's rule after 1898. Chiang Kai-
shek would carry on in the strong-man tradition of Yuan Shih-k'ai,
Tuan Ch'i-jui, and Chang Tso-lin, depending primarily upon military force to make his will obeyed. Trials of his political authority,
however, were not far off. The Nationalist success had been the
victory of not one man, but of many; and the Nationalist revolution
had derived its strength from various influences, not from guns
alone.

PART II

THE NATIONALIST
INTERREGNUM

5 "FIRST PACIFICATION, THEN RESISTANCE"

THE INAUGURATION of the National Government in October, 1928, did not find the whole country under Nanking's undisputed authority. Not only were Outer Mongolia, Tibet, and Sinkiang outside the new regime's jurisdiction; so was Manchuria. Powerful semi-independent militarists occupied individual provinces. True, the "new" militarists were distinguished from the warlords of the *tuchün* era in that now nearly all of them were members of the same party, the Kuomintang (KMT). But this circumstance did not eliminate rivalry from Chinese politics.

The forces of violence and separatism had not yet run their full course. At the time of its establishment the new regime was aware of the problem. Branch political councils were, of necessity, approved to function in Canton, Wuhan, Kaifeng, Mukden, Taiyuan, Peiping (as old Peking had been renamed), and in the three provinces of Szechwan, Yunnan, and Kweichow. This reflected the realities of power in a national situation where various military men, including unreconstructed old-style warlords of West and Northwest China, still ruled their own bailiwicks. Four of those men were destined to play leading national roles in the years ahead. They were Kwangsi general Li Tsung-jen, "Model Governor" Yen Hsi-shan of Shansi, "Christian General" Feng Yü-hsiang, and "Young Marshal" Chang Hsueh-liang of Manchuria.

Nanking's power was thus narrowly circumscribed. Its authority actually extended to only five provinces in the lower Yangtze region. Chiang Kai-shek dominated the Nanking scene as chairman of the State Council and ex officio President of the National Government, chairman of the Standing Committee of the KMT Central Executive Committee, and commander-in-chief of the Nationalist armies. In theory, the military was subordinate to the civil branch of government, but, whether as military man or civilian, Chiang ruled at Nanking. He had assumed the task of leading Nationalist China toward what he conceived to be its goals.

EFFORTS TO UNITE THE MILITARISTS

Chiang Kai-shek was determined to extend and "centralize" his control. This meant, in essence, the elimination of all armed opposition, including potential opposition in the Nationalist camp itself. The military men who had stood shoulder-to-shoulder with Chiang at various times and places in fighting for the Nationalist victory were just as determined to keep a share of power—and even independence—for themselves.

Nanking benefited by an early windfall in Manchuria, so long a focus of international rivalry. When Chang Tso-lin was blown up by the Japanese in June, 1928, the victorious Nationalists inside the Wall did not automatically inherit his Manchurian domain. Nor was the transition achieved without challenge in Manchuria itself. The logical successor to power there would have been either Chang Tso-hsiang, governor of Kirin Province and an old-time associate of Chang Tso-lin, or Chief of Staff Yang Yü-t'ing. They were "strong men." It seemed hardly likely that the succession would pass to Chang Tso-lin's eldest son, Young Marshal Chang Hsueh-liang.

The Young Marshal was not a complete nonentity. After receiving a military education, he had participated in his father's campaigns of the early 1920s for North China and had been one of the three Northern field commanders in the final struggle against the Nationalist armies. But Chang Hsueh-liang was only twenty-seven and, moreover, had acquired the drug habit. He was generally considered no match for the tough warlords of his father's generation.

In the council that met at Mukden to determine Manchuria's future, however, Chang Tso-hsiang refused power and urged Chang Hsueh-liang to assume authority. Yang Yü-t'ing, with his close Japanese ties, would almost certainly have been acceptable to Japan. But Yang as chief of staff bore the blame for the disastrous results of his strategy in North China. Moreover, he was still inside the Wall, supervising the retreat of the Fengtien forces. Thus it was

Chang Hsueh-liang who finally took over control of the Ankuochün and assumed the title of Commander-in-Chief for Peace Preservation in Manchuria.

Chang adhered to the newer nationalistic ideas of the age. He faced an immediate political dilemma: What should be Manchuria's relationship to the Nationalists, and to Japan? As early as July Chang Hsueh-liang indicated to the Nationalist chieftains that he sympathized with their cause and planned to bring Manchuria under the Nationalist flag. But the Japanese concern that Manchuria would be engulfed by the rising tide of nationalism was still unallayed. They warned Chang not to proceed with his intentions.

Chang Hsueh-liang still inclined in Nanking's direction. Tokyo then sent Baron Hayashi Gonsuke to Manchuria, officially to attend warlord Chang Tso-lin's funeral but actually to dissuade Chang Hsueh-liang from taking Manchuria into the Nationalist camp. The ultimate Japanese aim was that Chang should declare Manchuria independent of Nanking; they proposed that he follow, not the Three Principles of Sun Yat-sen, but the ancient Chinese concept of *Wang Tao* (the Way of Kings).

Chang finally agreed not to accede to the Nationalist proposals for three months and broke off negotiations with Nanking's representatives. The matter remained pending until after the National Government was formally established on October 10. At that time the Nationalists hopefully appointed Chang State Councilor and chairman of the Northeastern (Manchurian) Branch Political Council. He voiced his allegiance to Nanking and resumed negotiations.

In December a new factor was introduced into the situation: W. H. Donald, the Australian journalist who in time became known as Donald of China, joined the Young Marshal's entourage as adviser. Working mainly behind the scenes, Donald was to exert a substantial influence on the policies of China for a full decade. He strongly supported Chang Hsueh-liang's nationalistic leanings and the concept of Chinese unification. On December 29, 1928, Chang, in defiance of Japan, hoisted the Nationalist flag over Mukden. Manchuria had chosen the new order.

The choice signified no practical dilution of the Mukden regime's authority. As soon as Chang had declared his allegiance to the National Government, Nanking confirmed him and the other Manchurian officials in the posts they occupied. The power factor had been judiciously served.

Chang himself took early steps to ensure that the power balance should not be disturbed by actions *inside* Manchuria. Two weeks after the change of flags, as if to wipe the slate clean, Chang effected the cold-blooded killing of his father's pro-Japanese aide, General Yang Yü-t'ing, and the powerful Heilungkiang Governor, Ch'ang Yin-huai. In a statement issued on January 11, Chang accused the dead men of having opposed the unification of China and of plotting against the authority of the Manchurian government— that is, himself. It could readily be inferred that the two men had stood for a pro-Japanese policy. Chang's action proved him the true son of his father. Nanking now named him commander-in-chief of the Northeastern Border Defense Army.

The Manchurian coup added greatly to the National Government's prestige. But that first easy victory was not the forerunner of quick submissions to Chiang Kai-shek's control by other Kuomintang stalwarts who had helped him to power. The government still faced the thorny problem of "reorganizing" the country's national military establishment.

At this time poverty-stricken China was burdened by some 2,250,000 troops, compared with about 1,200,000 five years earlier and a maximum of 400,000 in Manchu times. There was an urgent need for reduction of the country's armed forces. This had been recognized in theory by the top military leaders. Chiang Kai-shek, Feng Yü-hsiang, Yen Hsi-shan, and Pai Ch'ung-hsi had discussed the matter at Peking in July of 1928 and had agreed, in principle, that China's future army should comprise fifty to sixty divisions and a complementary gendarmerie of 200,000.

During the succeeding months many pious statements were issued regarding plans to demobilize; but China reached the end of the year more heavily burdened with soldiers than before. After Manchuria had turned Nationalist in December, however, no important non-Nationalist force remained, and the time seemed propitious to attack the problem of demobilization again. A full-dress conference was convened at Nanking in mid-January, 1929, to consider the matter. Most of the top generals who had participated in the victorious Northern Expedition were present. The nominal problem up for consideration was demobilization; but the real issue was that of power. Could Chiang Kai-shek persuade his erstwhile colleagues that authority should be concentrated in the National Government?

Success could have been achieved only by permitting the principal leaders to share in the fruits of victory through an equal voice in government. It quickly became apparent from Chiang Kai-shek's presentation of the agenda to the assembled warriors, however, that he proposed no sharing of power; and that his "demobilization" plans were aimed at dispersal of the commands of other generals and the augmentation of his own forces.

The proposed centralization of power was not basically illogical, but it was an idea that had been long opposed by Party members who argued for a large measure of local autonomy during the transition period. Moreover, it did not reflect contemporary political realities and thus was certain to run into difficulties. Most of China was actually controlled by troops loyal to generals other than Chiang Kai-shek. The Kwangsi forces numbered 230,000. The Second and Third Group Armies led by Feng Yü-hsiang and Yen Hsi-shan totaled 220,000 and 200,000 men, respectively. Chiang Kai-shek's First Group Army and other forces under control of the State Council numbered 420,000.

The conference agreed that the country should be divided into six disbandment areas, five to be centered on Nanking, Wuhan, Loyang, Taiyuan, and Mukden, and Szechwan-Yunnan-Kweichow to be the sixth district. But the "agreement" was only nominal. Long accustomed to semi-independence, the generals were reluctant to surrender the military power on which they depended; political dissension dominated the proceedings. Feng Yü-hsiang suddenly left the conference on February 7. His purpose was to secure Kuominchün control of Shantung Province upon the anticipated evacuation of the Tsinan-Tsingtao rail line by the Japanese forces.

The conference broke up, and the various generals returned to their armies and prepared to resume the old military game that had plagued China since the death of Yuan Shih-k'ai. War was also Chiang Kai-shek's trade. He now began the long, onerous task of endeavoring to unify the country by force of arms. The Third Kuomintang Congress was scheduled for March, but it could not be expected to resolve existing political differences.

The chief immediate challenge to Chiang's power was posed by Kwangsi militarists, led by the powerful quadrumvirate of Pai Ch'ung-hsi, Li Tsung-jen, Li Chi-shen, and Huang Shao-hung. Kwangsi contingents occupied dominant positions in Peiping, Wuhan, and Canton. The distribution of forces betrayed an inner weakness: the Kwangsi military strength was overextended. Moreover, the nominally Kwangsi forces at Peiping were actually Hunan troops taken over from General T'ang Sheng-chih in defeat; and the Wuhan concentration was separated from the Kwangsi base area by Hunan Province, held by a Chiang Kai-shek appointee, General Lu Ti-p'ing.

The Kwangsi leaders were no mean strategists in their own right, and they doubtless saw the weakness of the position, particularly with respect to their natural line of communications through Hunan. On the eve of the Kuomintang Congress, three divisional commanders at Wuhan suddenly attacked Lu, ousted him from power in Hunan, and arbitrarily replaced him with a general of their own choosing.

This was a challenge to Chiang Kai-shek, and events followed in rapid succession. Li Tsung-jen resigned his government posts, thus showing his opposition to Nanking. Feng Yü-hsiang resigned as Minister of War. In the North a sudden coup on March 18–19 wrested control of the Hunanese troops from Pai Ch'ung-hsi and forced him to flee. Li Chi-shen left his Canton headquarters and, his personal safety guaranteed by five outstanding Kuomintang leaders, proceeded to Nanking to attend the Congress and incidentally seek an amicable settlement of "the Hunan affair." On March 21 Chiang Kai-shek had him arrested. Li Tsung-jen sped to Canton and endeavored to enlist the Kwangtung military men in Kwangsi's support. Chiang Kai-shek was already moving troops against Wuhan, and on March 26 Nanking issued a war mandate against the Kwangsi faction. The issue had been joined, as of old, on the field of battle.

It had been anticipated that the Kwangsi forces would put up a strong fight in Central China. But events upset the predictions. The Kwangtung militarists, confounding all expectations, refused to support the Kwangsi group; in the north Feng Yü-hsiang began to move troops, ostensibly to oppose the "rebels." While Generals Li, Huang, and Pai (now arrived in Kwangsi) were adjusting to the shock of the Kwangtung development, the 150,000 men Chiang had concentrated for the campaign went into action against the 120,000 enemy forces in the Wuhan area. In the absence of their top leaders, the Kwangsi generals in the field proved confused and indecisive, a part of their Seventh Army turned over to the government side, and by the end of April Chiang's victory in Central China was complete. The first military victory had been easy.

Meanwhile the Third Kuomintang Congress had tightened Chiang Kai-shek's political control. He could not assume, even with the quick successes in the Manchurian, North China, and Central China arenas, that national unification was imminent. But he was probably confirmed in his estimate that military force offered the answer to the political problem at hand.

The next conflict to develop was between Nanking and Second Group Army commander Feng Yü-hsiang. Feng had been alerted to Chiang's aims, first at the July, 1928, conference at Peking and later by Nanking's holding up funds for the payment of the Second Group Army troops. In February, 1929, when he moved to seize power in Shantung, he thought he was taking what was his by victor's rights. One of his men was, after all, occupying the post of Shantung Provincial Chairman. But his action was also designed to forestall the gradual attrition of his military power.

The maneuvers centered on Shantung were complicated by various local factors, particularly by the impact of the conflict with Kwangsi. As this first conflict neared its end, Feng suddenly ordered his general out of the exposed Shantung salient, concentrated his heavy forces in Honan, and cut rail communications into the province on both the north-south and east-west axes.

Honan was governed at the time by one of Feng's ablest and most trusted generals, Han Fu-chü. The threat to Nanking appeared even more formidable than that posed by the Kwangsi forces so short a while before. In the latter part of May, however, the situation took a dramatic turn when Han Fu-chü, bought over by Chiang Kai-shek, defected from Feng's camp, together with three divisional commanders. The Feng Yü-hsiang machine had received a heavy initial blow.

The Kuominchün field command in Honan passed into the hands of the veteran Sung Che-yuan. In October, with Sung's name heading the list, leading Kuominchün generals addressed a joint telegram to Feng Yü-hsiang and Yen Hsi-shan castigating the policies of the National Government and calling upon the two leaders to rectify the situation. As had happened so often before, announcement of grievances constituted a declaration of war. The Nationalist forces were already in position, and in mid-October the battle was joined on the Honan plain.

Chiang Kai-shek had taken the political precaution of appointing Yen Hsi-shan Deputy Commander of China's land, sea, and air forces. The conferring of this honor would not have helped had the tide run against Chiang, for Yen made no move—perhaps the most that Chiang had expected. The fighting in Honan was heavy and bitter. But the tide of battle finally swung in favor of the Government, partly as the delayed result of Han Fu-chü's betrayal. By the end of November the Kuominchün forces had been driven from the province, and the victory again was Chiang's.

But the victory was not decisive. Feng, who in a decade of in-fighting in North China had shown himself one of the wiliest politi-cal strategists of the era, undertook countermeasures. His Honan campaign had incidentally saved the Kwangsi group from a pos-sibly conclusive defeat by the combined forces of Chiang Kai-shek and Kwangtung, and he could now count on their collaboration. In 1930 he began to mobilize the opposition against Chiang Kai-shek, and it was finally decided in a top-level strategy conference at Peiping to attack Chiang simultaneously with the Second, Third, and Fourth Group Armies, led respectively by Feng, Yen Hsi-shan, and the Kwangsi generals. On May 10 Feng issued orders for a general offensive against the Nanking regime.

The Kwangsi men had been seriously weakened by the 1929 campaign, their and Chang Fa-k'uei's combined command having been reduced to 95,000 men. But their drive from the south was to perform a vital function, and in a boldly conceived move Li Tsung-jen and his captains decided to abandon Kwangsi entirely; by the first part of June they had captured Changsha and Yochow and stood ready to attack Wuhan.

Huang Shao-hung's Fifteenth Army had been charged with trans-port of commissary and munitions and bringing up the rear, but it failed to maintain contact with the main body. He was consequently cut off by an attack of Kwangtung forces from the flank. Li turned his armies back from the Hupeh border to extricate Huang from his perilous position, with the result that the whole expeditionary force suffered a shattering defeat in the vicinity of Hengyang and was eliminated from the campaign against Nanking. The Kwangsi men desperately fought their way back to their home province in an attempt to save something from the disaster.

The Yen-Feng movement had received a body blow. But Wang Ching-wei had arrived on the scene, and the rebellion of the north-ern coalition against what it charged was Chiang's "personal dic-tatorship" continued. The full strength of the Second and Third Group Armies had been thrust into Anhwei and Shantung, and the fighting was heavy.

Meanwhile, the rebels assiduously courted Chang Hsueh-liang

in Manchuria. Chiang courted Chang Hsueh-liang also, even as he had wooed Feng Yü-hsiang in 1927. During the summer of 1930 the contest between the National Government and the northern coalition had reached a stalemate; and Chang Hsueh-liang marked time without indicating which way he would move.

On September 1, 1930, the rebels inaugurated an opposition government in Peiping. Shortly after the formal announcement of the event, however, the Shansi forces were badly beaten in Shantung, where the apostate general Han Fu-chü now fought for the National Government. The coalition was on the verge of collapse and could have been saved only by the intervention of the Manchurian forces.

Chang Hsueh-liang finally reached a decision. He intervened on September 18—as a neutral, in the name of peace and order, and his troops entered North China. The Young Marshal was thus able to dictate the shape of the peace, which consequently found him, and not the Coalition or Chiang Kai-shek, dominating North China.

The situation was highly reminiscent of that in Chang Tso-lin's day. The Kwangsi men could perhaps have been saved from their 1929 defeat by Feng Yü-hsiang, but Feng instead had helped to weaken them—with disastrous consequences for his own 1930 campaign. Feng's climactic effort of 1930 had also suffered from the betrayal at the hands of Han Fu-chü. Feng Yü-hsiang, in the end, had been paid with his own coin, after the pattern of his earlier betrayal of Wu P'ei-fu. The year 1930 marked the end of his old Kuominchün—and of his real political importance. The man who had gained the most was he who had taken what the Chinese call "the fisherman's profit," Chang Hsueh-liang.

The breaking of Feng Yü-hsiang's power and the temporary retirement of Yen Hsi-shan from the political scene had not meant the extension of Nanking's authority so much as the substitution of Young Marshal Chang Hsueh-liang's power for that of the militarists of the northern Coalition. And in South China, Kwangtung and Kwangsi once more entered upon a power combine, and in May, 1931, a new separatist government was established at Canton under the leadership of Wang Ching-wei, Sun Fo, and T'ang Shao-yi. It had the military support of Ch'en Chi-t'ang, Li Tsung-jen, and Chang Fa-k'uei. The country was far from unified under one central control; but in the 1930s greater challenges would overshadow the Kuomintang family quarrels.

Power—or its absence—was a factor in foreign as well as domestic affairs. Ever since the Opium War of 1839–42, China had
occupied a position of legal disability in its relations with the
powers. It was determined to recover full sovereignty.

This feeling was not simply nurtured by the Left or by intellectual circles. The Chinese nation as a whole felt aggrieved by
the "unequal treaties." Even conservatives were ready enough to
be radical in foreign affairs. The Kuomintang right wing, as any
nationalistic group, was determined to hem in, undermine, or otherwise restrict foreign rights and interests in China. Chiang Kai-shek
himself, although he had rejected social revolution, was neither
insensible to the uses of "anti-imperialism" in relations with the
foreign powers nor devoid of nationalistic sentiments.

All Chinese were agreed on the desirability of rehabilitating their
country's power position. All political groups wanted modern armies,
national industrialization, an adequate transportation system, and
a strong national currency. The Chinese generally wished their
country to emerge from a "semi-colonial" status and to attain effective equality in its foreign relations, and they looked to the day
when China would recover its "lost territories" and re-establish itself
as the dominant great power in the Asian sphere. Chiang Kai-shek
was certain to strive, quite as much as *tuchün* Chang Tso-lin before
him, to whittle down the rights and privileges claimed by foreign
powers for their nationals under the unequal treaties.

Nanking was confronted with various arduous tasks in the realm
of foreign affairs: (1) the re-establishment of full national sovereignty, including the recovery of tariff autonomy, the termination
of extra-territoriality, the restoration of sovereign control over foreign concessions in the treaty ports, and the acquisition of the
Manchurian railways then held by the Soviet Union and Japan;
(2) the maintenance of national security, especially vis-à-vis China's
powerful neighbors; (3) the restoration of China's "traditional"
frontiers—interpreted ever since the establishment of the Republic
as being those fixed by the robust Manchu conquerors.

Certain foreign policy devices were available to the Nationalists:
bilateral negotiations, the unilateral application of force, and China's
traditional and oft-used tactic of "using barbarians to control barbarians." Negotiations based upon appeals to reasonableness stood

little chance of proving fruitful. The Nationalists had been remarkably successful, while the Kuomintang-Communist coalition held together, in their frontal attacks on "foreign imperialists," and more particularly on the British. The ancient device of playing one force against another had often been successfully employed in the past against land barbarians, such as the naïve Turki, Mongol, and Tungusi tribes. The question was whether force or guile would prove the more effective against the sophisticated land and sea barbarians of the twentieth century.

One factor favored successful operations in the foreign affairs field: the powers did not stand together in China. The so-called treaty powers, in particular, were divided among themselves. Washington had been quick to move diplomatically after the overthrow of the *tuchün* regime in June, 1928. On July 25 the United States signed a treaty with Nanking regulating tariff relations between the two countries and granting *in principle* China's "complete tariff autonomy" (to remain inoperative with respect to the United States for so long as the nationals of *any* other country might continue importation of goods under the old unequal treaty tariff of five percent). The United States was the first of the great maritime powers to negotiate such a treaty, and it acted alone.

When French Foreign Minister Aristide Briand proposed in mid-August, before the formal inauguration of the National Government on October 10, that the Washington Conference powers confer on the question of recognition of the new Chinese government, Secretary of State Kellogg replied that the United States considered that it had already been recognized—by the signing of the treaty of July 25. There was thus no coordination of policy by the Washington Conference powers on this point. France and Britain recognized the National Government in November. Japan and Italy did not do so until June, 1929, and then they acted jointly with Germany, *not* a Washington Conference power.

The great powers had convened at Washington in 1921 for the express purpose of reconciling to some degree their respective China policies and Pacific Ocean designs; but now the old habit of unilateralism had reappeared.

Under the existing conditions, this development was of great importance. The revolution-minded land power that had been associated with the Chinese nationalist revolution, the Soviet Union, had indeed lost its influence in China for the time being. But the work of the Borodin mission from 1923 to 1927 had been very effective. The USSR's exclusion from the Washington Conference had neither kept Soviet influence out of China nor blocked the establishment of diplomatic relations between Moscow and Peking. That the Comintern venture came a cropper in 1927 gave no assurance that the USSR, an Asian power, would not stage a comeback.

The lack of unity among the Washington Conference powers was especially notable in American-Japanese relations. The Washington Five-Power Treaty was designed to stabilize the naval balance in the Pacific, but the young Oriental sea power was offering an increasing challenge to the American position in China and the West Pacific, and the two countries were perceptibly drifting farther apart on the questions of both naval ratios and China.

Since, in the formulation of its Far Eastern policy, the United States had chosen both to oppose revolutionary Russia and to break up the Anglo-Japanese alliance, sound diplomacy should have dictated a strong effort to coordinate policies with Japan. The chances for coordination between those competing powers were admittedly slight, but even such opportunities as existed were left unexploited in that the United States neglected international consultation in favor of its own sense of expediency. Its unilateral actions in matters involving common interests were to leave a mark on history.

At the end of the 1920s the United States, Japan, the Soviet Union, and not least Great Britain, were all regarded in Chinese eyes as dangerous "imperialist" barbarians to be overcome for China's safety. Emboldened by their victory over the *tuchüns*, the Nationalists promptly gambled on their newly won prestige and, on July 19, 1928, informed Japan that the treaties of 1896 and 1903 had expired and that Japanese nationals in China would henceforth be subject to certain Chinese regulations promulgated two weeks before. Tokyo, on this occasion, replied that, if China proceeded as proposed, the Japanese government would be "obliged to take such measures as they deemed suitable for safeguarding their rights and interests." Chiang Kai-shek, in the light of his clash earlier in the year with the Japanese military at Tsinan, easily perceived the significance of the response. No attempt was made to subject Japanese nationals in China to Chinese law and regulations.

Nanking made some early gains through negotiation. In 1929 the British gave up their concessions at Chinkiang, Amoy, and Weihaiwei; the Belgians turned over their concession at Tientsin. In the same year, also, China successfully abrogated existing treaties with Belgium and Denmark by unilateral action and thus terminated extraterritoriality for the nationals of those countries. And, in a series of treaties signed between 1928 and 1930, Nanking won agreement by the powers concerned to China's exercise of tariff autonomy, and thus sovereign control in this field was re-established in 1930—some ninety years after its abridgement.

Those gains, if minor, were not insubstantial. With respect to the larger issues of spheres of influence and extraterritoriality generally, however, the Nationalists were less successful. The United States had not renounced its extraterritorial rights in the new treaty of 1928; and the attack on Japan's exercise of that particular "special privilege" had failed.

In December, 1929, the National Government tried a general *démarche,* announcing that extraterritoriality in China would end as of January 1, 1930. The great powers refused to budge, and extraterritoriality remained in being. It was only the nationals of the World War losers Germany and Austria, of small countries such as Belgium and Denmark, and of the Soviet Union who did not enjoy that privileged status.

While fighting dissident Nationalists and negotiating on several international fronts, Nanking experimented with direct action elsewhere. It is an accepted rule, under the strategy of "using barbarians to control barbarians," to select an isolated group for destruction. Chiang Kai-shek turned his attention first to the Soviet Union.

Chiang doubtless evaluated the Soviet position on the basis of past performance. The impunity with which Chang Tso-lin had invaded the Soviet Embassy at Peking in April, 1927, and the absence of strong Soviet reaction to Nanking's closing of Soviet consular and commercial establishments in territory under Nationalist control in December of the same year had been reassuring to China's nationalists. An attempted seizure of the Soviet Sungari River fleet by Chang Tso-lin in 1926 had failed; but Chang had been a single *tuchün,* and Manchuria was now part of a "unified," re-invigorated China. It seemed that there were grounds to believe that a fresh advance could be made against Soviet positions without incurring grave danger.

After Chang Hsueh-liang had entered the Nationalist camp in December, 1928, therefore, Nanking turned its attention to that key of empire in Northeast Asia, Manchuria. It aimed now to take possession of the last of Soviet Russia's "special interests" in China, and the Young Marshal was to be the instrumentality. According to Feng Yü-hsiang's later account, Chiang Kai-shek told Chang: "Anyone can beat the Soviet Union." [1]

The Chinese drive began on May 27, 1929, with raids on Soviet consular offices in Manchuria and arrests of Soviet citizens. It reached its logical climax with the seizure, on July 10, of the Chinese Eastern Railway and appurtenances, including the telegraph system, and of Soviet shipping on the Sungari River. The National Government presumably counted on two major factors for success, namely, the desire on Moscow's part to avoid armed conflict with "semi-colonial" China and a readiness of various foreign powers antagonistic to the Soviet Union to support China in case of trouble.

The confidence in continuing Soviet meekness proved ill placed. On July 14, at Moscow, Vice-Commissar for Foreign Affairs Karakhan sent the Chinese chargé d'affaires a virtual ultimatum: while expressing willingness to discuss all outstanding questions, the Soviet government demanded restoration of the *status quo ante*. The Nanking Government, in an obvious delaying action, made counter proposals. The Soviets brushed aside the Chinese "compromise" suggestions and began to move. Moscow withdrew all consular and diplomatic personnel from China and severed rail communications. On October 25 the Nationalists sent a circular communication to all signatories to the Kellogg-Briand Pact, endeavoring to enlist the support of third parties, particularly the United States. Finally, Chang Hsueh-liang deployed some sixty thousand troops against the Soviet border.

General Vassili K. Bluecher, the same Galen who had served as military adviser to Chiang Kai-shek from 1924 to 1927, commanded the Soviet forces in eastern Siberia. On November 17, 1929, the Soviets struck across the western border of Manchuria. Their forces did not exceed one division and thirty planes, but the Chinese armies broke, completely demoralized, and within ten days had retreated beyond the Hsingan range, 150 miles east of their original defense position. The United States came forward to admonish the Soviet Union, which it still had not recognized, to keep the peace.

The Soviet Union had "adhered" to the Kellogg-Briand Pact of 1928, but Moscow rejected a homily that contained no promise that Soviet property would be returned and kept military pressure on Manchuria. Hostilities were terminated by a protocol, signed December 22 at Khabarovsk, in which the Soviet demands were fully met by the Chinese. The Nationalist venture had been a complete failure.

Worse than that, it was an incitement. There was one deeply interested observer, first, of the Nationalist campaign, with its disclosure of expansive long-term objectives; then, of the political inertness of the Western sea powers and of the United States in particular, and, finally, of the neat effectiveness of the Soviet military response. That observer was Japan.

There had been old dreams of a Japanese empire in Asia. At the end of the sixteenth century Hideyoshi had proposed that Japan should proceed via Korea to the conquest of China and the rest of Asia. In the middle nineteenth century Yoshida Shoin, whose influence was profoundly felt by many of the men who became Japan's leaders in the Meiji era, had outlined equally ambitious plans, again envisaging progressive conquest. By the end of the First World War, Japan had actually established control over several useful stepping stones to mainland empire. And the reputed "Tanaka Memorial" of 1927 proposed the conquest of all China, beginning with Manchuria.

The Chinese refused to be reconciled to Japan's enjoyment of a special position in Manchuria, won by imperialistic effort and written into unequal treaties. Japan's sharp rebuff to Nanking in July, 1928, and the stinging defeat suffered by Chang Hsueh-liang and Chiang Kai-shek at the hands of the Soviet Union in 1929 had dampened but did not quench the fires of the new Government's anti-imperialism. The Khabarovsk Protocol was an ever-present warning to the Nationalists that the USSR could not be provoked with impunity. However, they still pursued the tactics, initiated in Chang Tso-lin's day, of harassing Japanese economic and political positions in Manchuria. There would be no repetition of the 1929 error of making forceful seizure; this would be a campaign of attrition.

The Japanese, in their reaction to a series of "incidents" in the Yangtse Valley, Shantung, and Manchuria, had already amply demonstrated a determination to maintain their established treaty position. In this respect their attitude did not differ essentially from that of the other great powers, including the United States. But they were closer to the issue than the other sea powers and were all the more sensitive to threats against their privileged status.

The Japanese were also concerned with the growth of Chinese nationalism. They saw in the upsurge of nationalist feeling that had helped bring the Kuomintang regime to power the potential for the reunification of China under a strong centralized government. And they thought that unification would bring, as all earlier Chinese history indicated, a resurgence of Chinese imperialism, of the traditional Chinese urge toward expansion. Such a force would be exerted against China's periphery and, consequently, against Japanese positions in Northeast Asia.

At this time, moreover, Chinese nationalism contained the latent but virulent element of social revolution, which was viewed as doubling the threat against Japan. Japanese concern with revolution was linked directly to an apprehension of possible trouble from Soviet Russia's direction. The Japanese had met trouble from Russia before; and one of their aims in participating in the Allied intervention of 1918–20 had been to check the eastward advance of revolution. They had viewed with increasing alarm the Soviet consolidation of a strong strategic position in Outer Mongolia. Now they proposed not only to maintain their existing position in Manchuria but to transform Manchuria into a buffer state as much under Japanese domination as Outer Mongolia was under the USSR's.

Japanese feelings during this period were described in a later report of the League of Nations Commission of Inquiry (Lytton Commission):

The likelihood of an alliance between the Communist doctrines in the North [i.e., in the Soviet Union] and the anti-Japanese propaganda of the Kuomintang in the South made the desire to impose between the two a Manchuria which should be free from both increasingly felt in Japan. Japanese misgivings have been still further increased in the last few years by the predominant influence acquired by U.S.S.R. in Outer Mongolia and the growth of Communism in China.[2]

Baron Shidehara Kijuro, then Foreign Minister, was outwardly pursuing a conciliatory policy toward China, in part with the aim of protecting Japanese interests by peaceful measures in so far as possible, but also to build up international good will for Japan. He hoped that a conciliatory policy would prove effective, out of concern for the possible reactions of the two other great naval powers, the United States and Britain. But he could not ignore the upsurge of anti-Japanese sentiment in China and the possibility that he might find it necessary to advocate the use of armed force to safeguard Japan's established rights and interests in Manchuria. In that eventuality, Tokyo would hope to be able to draw upon the reservoir of good will accumulated abroad to get sympathy for Japan's action.

Shidehara and his "peaceful policy" were overwhelmed by events. Powerful opposing forces had been contending for dominance over Japan's grand strategy. The Sino-Soviet imbroglio of 1929 provided an outstanding example of consequences to be anticipated from a radical approach toward the national objective in Northeast Asia. Then came the London Naval Conference of 1930. Japan had participated with the expectation, clearly indicated by Premier Hamaguchi Osachi, that Japan would be accorded a ratio in cruisers and auxiliary craft that would meet what it considered its defense requirements. Owing to combined American and British opposition, that ratio (10:10:7) was not granted—but the Japanese delegation signed the Naval Treaty anyway. That fall Hamaguchi was shot by a fanatical Japanese nationalist. Although it was nine months later that he died of his wounds, the shooting marked the beginning of the end of Japan's conciliatory policy.

The Japanese military began to win dominance over the mainland strategy. This development was facilitated by inadequate coordination within the Japanese government, particularly between the Foreign Office and the Kwantung Army. At this time there was in General Honjo Shigeru's Kwantung Army a group of officers who stood ready to settle "the Manchurian problem" themselves if Tokyo failed to act effectively. The master mind for the project was Colonel Ishihara Kanji, a Kwantung Army staff officer with a high reputation as military strategist. Ishihara exercised strong influence over the Kwantung Army's Chief of Staff, Colonel Itagaki Seishiro. Working in the field directly under Honjo was the able and wily chief of the Kwantung Army's Special Service section, Colonel Doihara Kenji.

Ishihara's plan envisaged the establishment in Manchuria of a separate state in which, as in China, five ethnic groups should live together in harmony. In Ishihara's scheme, however, there were two substitutions, so that the proposed happy family was to comprise Manchus, Mongols, Chinese, Koreans, and Japanese. The National Government at Nanking did not, of course, enter the picture.

Sino-Japanese relations in Manchuria were complex, but they progressed steadily to a climax after Tokyo's first "advice" of 1928 to Chang Hsueh-liang. The decision of the Tokyo government to follow a "positive policy" in order to consolidate the Japanese position in Manchuria probably came not long after the attempted

assassination of Premier Hamaguchi. Now only an excuse was
needed for the Kwantung Army to go into action.

In June, 1931, a certain Captain Nakamura and three companions
were arrested by the Chinese in a restricted military zone of Manchuria. They were in plain clothes and evidently engaged in an
intelligence mission. All four were executed on July 1. The Nakamura case triggered the Japanese strategic decision. On September
18, 1931, one year to the day after Chang Hsueh-liang had intervened in North China on behalf of Chinese nationalism—and his
own ambitions—the Japanese Kwantung Army struck, at Mukden.
Ishihara's plan was being implemented. Hamaguchi had died on
August 26. The "Mukden Incident" of September 18 brought to an
end the Nanking government's attempts to use "anti-imperialism"
as an instrument of foreign policy.

JAPAN AND MANCHURIA, 1931–34

The Japanese invasion of Manchuria sparked a complex series of
maneuvers. The Chinese could hardly be considered defenseless:
Chang Hsueh-liang's Northeastern Frontier Defense Force alone
numbered about four hundred thousand men—and he, even as
other Chinese military men, had been ready enough to throw tens
of thousands of men into China's domestic quarrels. His forces far
outnumbered the invaders. However, when Chang Hsueh-liang
had intervened in North China in 1930, he had done so in force,
moving about one hundred thousand of his best troops inside the
Wall. He had, moreover, built up another large concentration of
Northeastern forces at Chinchow, just outside the Wall.

When the Mukden Incident occurred, Chang Hsueh-liang and
his adviser W. H. Donald were in Peiping. Chang had just engaged
in another civil war, this time against General Shih Yu-san, who
had followed Han Fu-chü over to the Government side in 1929.
Shih Yu-san had been neatly finished off, but Chang's Northeastern
forces were left poorly deployed to meet a foreign thrust.

Even before the Incident, on September 11, Chiang Kai-shek
had instructed Chang Hsueh-liang to be careful to avoid clashing
with the Japanese. When news of the Japanese attack at Mukden
reached Peiping, Chang asked instructions. Chiang's reply determined the policy line: "In order to avoid any enlargement of the
incident, it is necessary resolutely to maintain the principle of

nonresistance." And on September 23 he announced to the nation that China was entrusting its case to the League of Nations.

Chang Hsueh-liang instructed his armed forces accordingly and followed a policy of nonresistance from beginning to end. Donald claimed later to have shared in the formulation of that strategy. But, of course, the decision was made by the Chinese; Chiang Kai-shek and Chang Hsueh-liang would have accepted Donald's advice only if it fitted their own predilections.

Nonresistance might conceivably have worked if the League of Nations had been able, or a third power been willing, to come forward in China's defense. Such was not the case. The League of Nations twice designated time limits for the withdrawal of Japanese troops, but Tokyo ignored the League command. The League debated the use of sanctions, but it was not in a position to take effective action without the support of Japan's chief competitor in the Pacific, the United States, which, of course, was not a member of the League. The United States refused to join in collective action to check the aggression. Briand, who in 1928 had joined Secretary of State Kellogg to sponsor the Pact of Paris, observed to a friend that the American refusal meant the death of the League.

On January 7, 1932, Secretary of State Stimson informed Japan *and* China that the United States did not intend "to recognize any situation, treaty or agreement which [might] be brought about by means contrary to the covenants and obligations of the Pact of Paris." Thus the so-called Stimson Nonrecognition Doctrine was formulated. But it was not a new doctrine: it sprang directly from Bryan's 1915 response to the Twenty-one Demands. For its part, the League of Nations in December appointed a commission of inquiry, the so-called Lytton Commission, to go to Manchuria to delve into the rights and wrongs of the matter and to propose a solution.

Meanwhile the Japanese continued their rapid advance. They had been able quickly to enlist various Chinese military men and politicians in their service and set up puppet provincial governments in two of the Manchurian provinces, Liaoning and Kirin. Then they turned their attention to the largest province, Heilungkiang.

Provincial Chairman Wan Fu-lin, with his best troops, was in North China with Chang Hsueh-liang when the Mukden Incident took place. Wan had left provincial affairs in the hands of his feckless son, Wan Hai-p'eng. Because of the almost complete lack of authority in the province, the Japanese task looked easy.

A complaisant Chinese general, Chang Hai-p'eng, was selected by the Japanese High Command to take power in the name of the new order, and in early October he advanced northwards along the Taonan-Angangchi Railway toward the provincial capital, Tsitsihar. But the garrison commander normally stationed on the Amur River, General Ma Chan-shan, moved to meet the attack, and halted Chang's force at the Nonni River, blowing up the railroad bridge across the river to make his defense position more secure. The Japanese, having financed the railway's construction, had a practical interest in its remaining in operation. They pointed out their concern and demanded that the bridge be repaired within a fixed period of time.

Ma Chan-shan was a direct and engaging man, a plain soldier risen from the ranks, who had never become corrupted by the venality of Chinese power. Under orders not to resist and far from any base of support, in October, 1931, he probably had no plan to launch a campaign against the Kwantung Army. He merely marked time—and undertook no bridge repairs. The Japanese sent their own engineers to repair the bridge, Ma's troops fired on them, and the Japanese armed forces again went into action. Early in November, 1931, a brisk battle took place at the Nonni River which, though far from having the importance that was given it in the Chinese press, nevertheless constituted a creditable performance by Ma Chan-shan's troops.

A few days later Ma's forces were driven back, and the Japanese went on to occupy Tsitsihar, the provincial capital, on November 18. But the nation was exhilarated. As a Chinese commentator put it, "It was General Ma's heroic and stubborn resistance that saved the country from the utter disgrace of cowardice." Ma became "The Hero of the Nonni River Battle." His action did more than save the Chinese honor; it stimulated Chinese "volunteers" to oppose the invaders and their Chinese collaborators in spite of Nanking's policy of nonresistance.

General Li Tu on Ma Chan-shan's eastern flank and General Su Ping-wen in western Manchuria were buttressed by General Ma's stand. But Chang Hsueh-liang, under gentle Japanese pressure, had completely withdrawn his regular forces inside the Great Wall, and Ma Chan-shan and the "volunteers" alike were cut off from both military support and any substantial supply base. Campaigns to collect money and supplies took place in China's bigger towns, but there was no saving the situation. In mid-February, 1932, Ma Chan-shan himself went over to the Japanese side.

And, about the same time, a prominent Manchu also joined the Japanese against the Nationalists. The 1912 Articles of Favorable Treatment had provided for the maintenance in perpetuity, with appropriate rites, of the temples and mausoleums of the Manchu imperial family, the Chinese Republic being responsible for protecting them. In July, 1928, however, shortly after the occupation of Peking by the Nationalists, the imperial tombs near Peking were broken into and looted, and the remains of the great Emperor Ch'ien Lung and Empress Dowager Tz'u Hsi desecrated. P'u Yi, the sometime Manchu Emperor, had been roughly ousted from his palace by Feng Yü-hsiang in 1924 but had not subsequently shown animosity toward the Chinese nation. After 1928, however, his attitude had changed perceptibly.

Thus, the Mukden Incident of September, 1931, found P'u Yi in a more receptive frame of mind than on earlier occasions when approached with schemes for his restoration to the throne. At the beginning of November, Special Service Bureau chief Doihara visited him at his residence in the Japanese Concession at Tientsin with the proposal that he accept an imperial restoration, but in Manchuria. P'u Yi's advisers were divided on the issue, but he finally followed the urging of his minister Cheng Hsiao-hsu, and on November 10, 1931, seven years to the month after he had taken refuge from Feng's men in the Peking Legation Quarter, he boarded a Japanese steamer to return to the land of his ancestors.

The evidence suggests that P'u Yi took that fateful step in expectation of a restoration of the imperial Manchu rule in Manchuria as the "legitimate" rule for all of China. There were certainly those among his followers who expected this to happen. But it did not; evidently the Japanese were not yet ready to go that far. Meeting at Mukden in mid-February, various Chinese and Japanese leaders decided to form a new political entity for Manchuria alone. Manchurian independence was declared on February 18, 1932, and on March 1 the state of Manchoukuo came into being.

Two delegations of "Manchurians" had already called on P'u Yi at Dairen to urge that he head the new state, but they had met with his refusal. His reluctance was ceremonial. Another and more impressive delegation pressed the invitation upon him for the third time, as demanded by tradition. P'u Yi accepted, left immediately for the new capital of Hsinking (Changchun) and on March 9 was formally installed as Chief Executive of Manchoukuo. The ceremony was attended by Japanese military and civilian dignitaries, including, of course, General Honjo. P'u Yi's faithful follower Cheng Hsiao-hsu, poet, calligrapher, and scholar-bureaucrat of the traditional Confucian school, became Premier of the new state. Cheng proposed that his government should follow *Wang Tao*, the ancient Way of Kings so fruitlessly urged on Chang Hsueh-liang by the Japanese. In its modern, Japanese-inspired interpretation, *Wang Tao* was opposed to social radicalism, and to Communism in particular.

The next development was in the ancient Chinese tradition. The Minister of War in the Manchoukuo Government was no other than the Nonni River hero, Ma Chan-shan. Ma had previously been confirmed in the post of Heilungkiang Provincial Chairman by agreement with the Japanese, and so kept his station in Tsitsihar. There, he was finally able to play the card he had kept up his sleeve. On April 1, in the dead of night, General Ma stole out of town with a truck convoy of useful supplies, including a large sum of money. For several days he pretended to be on an inspection trip; but then, on April 12, he issued a long circular telegram explaining his earlier apparent defection to the Japanese, reporting on what he had learned of Japanese plans while acting the role of collaborator, and setting forth his determination to resist to the end.

China's hopes rose again with the news that a Chinese general had hoodwinked the wily foe. The Japanese were temporarily disconcerted. Heavy fighting had begun at Shanghai at the end of January when General Ts'ai T'ing-k'ai of the "alien" 19th Route Army refused to observe Chiang Kai-shek's orders of nonresistance. Chiang's 87th and 88th Divisions had joined General Ts'ai's men, and together they had stopped the Japanese imperial forces in their tracks. Tokyo remained on the defensive before world opinion, and Ma's turnabout also required new military arrangements. The Japanese did not take long to make up their mind. An agreement ending the Shanghai hostilities was signed in May. Having reinforced their Manchurian armies, the Japanese launched a drive in late May against the forces of Ma Chan-shan and cut him off from Li Tu's army farther east.

The Japanese proceeded to consolidate their gains. In a Protocol of Alliance signed on September 15, 1932, Japan recognized Manchoukuo as an independent state "organized in accordance with the free will of its inhabitants"; Manchoukuo, for its part, recognized and agreed to protect existing Japanese rights and interests within its jurisdiction. A further agreement provided that the two states should cooperate for purposes of national security.

The Lytton Commission of the League of Nations did not publish its findings until October 2, and the matter was still to come before the League Council for deliberation. The Japanese did not wait. In November they undertook a final mopping-up campaign to clear Manchuria of all major forces of resistance. Ma Chan-shan on the north, Su Ping-wen on the west, and Li Tu in the northeast—all were shattered. With a few thousand troops whose paltry numbers were the measure of the weakness of the Chinese defense, Su Ping-wen, Ma Chan-shan, and then Li Tu withdrew into the Soviet Union and were disarmed and interned. Nothing remained except some unimportant guerrilla activity. In effect, the Chinese resistance in Manchuria was over. In a move that clearly showed China's disillusionment, Nanking, in December, 1932, resumed regular diplomatic relations with Moscow, after a break of five years.

In early 1933 the Manchurian affair finally came up for formal debate in the League of Nations. The Lytton Commission had produced a finding of joint guilt and proposed what was essentially a compromise solution. China rejected any solution requiring concessions on its part. Japan invoked the factor of national security, saying that it could not "regard with equanimity the 'bolshevization' of China." It expressed special concern as to "the not impossible 'bolshevization'" of Manchuria and Eastern Inner Mongolia (adjacent to Outer Mongolia): "Were those two regions to turn communistic, it would immediately disturb the peace and order of Korea, which in its turn would affect the peace and order of Japan Proper." [3]

Japan indicated clearly that it proposed to purge those two border regions of "communistic elements" for the peace and order of Japan. The appeal to the need to take defensive measures against Bolshevism was, of course, calculated to make Japan's case attractive to the West. Two deep underlying considerations in Japan's national policy went unmentioned: the aim of blocking American economic expansion in East Asia and the determination to keep China disunited in order to facilitate the Japanese mainland advance.

In March, 1933, as a direct result of the League's action on the Manchurian question, Japan withdrew from the world body.

Briand's prediction had begun to come true. The Soviet Union's entry into membership in 1934 did not check the rapid weakening of the League. The Western democracies bent their energies to combatting the depression that had afflicted their respective economies. Germany, Italy, and Japan turned toward conquest.

The occupation of Manchuria was only the initial phase of a broad Japanese program of expansion on the Asian mainland. The establishment of Manchoukuo in March, 1932, had been followed, later in the year, by menacing moves in the direction of Jehol. T'ang Yü-lin, the provincial chairman, was reported ready to defect to the Japanese side. He was a warlord of the old type, fat with the profits of widespread opium cultivation in his province and patently not the stuff of which heroes are made. Japanese feints and blustering, nevertheless, failed to bring him over—possibly because he was under equal threat from his compatriots. And the Chinese spoke confidently of the fight that would be put up for Jehol, where the mountainous terrain strongly favored the defense, if the Japanese dared to attack.

The Chinese pronunciamentos were so much whistling in the dark. On January 1, 1933, the Japanese occupied Shanhaikuan, the chief Great Wall pass between Manchuria and North China, and in February advanced against Jehol with a small force supported nominally by Manchoukuo troops. T'ang Yü-lin was ordered to resist to the last. T. V. Soong flew to Peiping to leave no doubts about the Central Government's determination not to permit another of China's rich provinces to be nipped off by the aggressor. Northern generals met and announced their determination to resist. But T'ang Yü-lin's forces and Heilungkiang ex-Chairman Wan Fu-lin's Third Army melted away before the advancing enemy. Nanking sent neither troops nor planes to the front, and within ten days the Japanese had conquered the province. The capital itself, Chengteh, was taken by a mere handful of Japanese—128 men.

The Chinese debacle was not complete. In their drive westward into Jehol, the Japanese aimed to occupy the strategic passes of the Great Wall on their left flank. The Chairman of Chahar Province, which adjoined Jehol on the West, was the hard-fighting ex-Feng Yü-hsiang man, Sung Che-yuan. When the Kuominchün forces were "reorganized" by Nanking after Chiang Kai-shek's defeat of Feng in 1930, Sung received command of the Twenty-ninth Army, made up of seasoned elements of the Feng forces.

On January 20, 1933, Sung was ordered to participate in the defense of Jehol. Upon arriving at the Great Wall, the Twenty-ninth Army found Wan Fu-lin's forces in precipitate retreat. Nevertheless, they took up a defensive position at Hsifengkow, one of the important passes, in early February. There, and at Lowenyü and Kupeikow farther west, Sung Che-yuan's army gave the Japanese the only fight they experienced in their easy conquest of Jehol.

Outflanked, Sung's forces abandoned Hsifengkow in April and Kupeikow in May, but they continued in the field until the Tangku Truce, signed on May 31, 1933, brought a temporary end to the hostilities. Sung had made a name for himself as "the Hero of Hsifengkow." He now entered upon the stage of national politics.

The easy conquest of Jehol caused profound power shifts in China. Chang Hsueh-liang's political position had deteriorated substantially after the inauguration of Manchoukuo, for he had been made the scapegoat for the results of Nanking's nonresistance policy. Still, he had salvaged 170,000 troops from the debacle and had been appointed Pacification Commissioner and Acting Chairman of the Peiping Branch Military Council. However, when his "powerful" general Wan Fu-lin proved quite incompetent on the fighting front and Jehol was surrendered to the Japanese almost without resistance, it was more than the Young Marshal's debilitated prestige could stand. In March, 1933, under heavy public pressure, he handed over his remaining troops to Chiang Kai-shek and embarked on the politician's traditional "foreign voyage." En route he entered a Shanghai hospital and cured himself of the drug habit—an act that was to be of significance later.

Feng Yü-hsiang briefly re-entered the limelight a short time after Chang Hsueh-liang had bowed out. When the Japanese, flushed with their Jehol victory, occupied the strategic point of Dolonor in eastern Chahar on May 1, 1933, Feng Yü-hsiang emerged from retirement to organize a People's Federated Anti-Japanese Army for the purpose of resisting Japanese aggression. In July the "Army" actually cleared the enemy out of Chahar, Sung Che-yuan's province—and took over political and military control. This brought no rejoicing to the National Government, which had signed the Tangku Truce on May 31 with the hope of avoiding further conflict with the Japanese. Feng's freewheeling activities embarrassed the Nanking policy.

Sung Che-yuan and another former Feng man, Huang Fu, mediated between Nanking and the rebel patriot. The mission was facilitated by the circumstance that other national leaders had not responded to Feng's call to arms. Feng dissolved his Anti-Japanese Army in August and returned to retirement on the sacred mountain, Tai Shan. The Japanese reoccupied Dolonor, the gateway to Chahar.

The Japanese did not consider their mainland adventure ended with the Tangku Truce. That document, with its surrenders to Japanese demands, offered openings for fresh political advances. They began to exploit the possibilities of the situation, first in Hopeh Province and later in Chahar, where the Mongols, long discontented with Chinese rule, now yearned for autonomy. From 1933 to 1936 the Japanese were to be very active in both places.

Japan's Manchurian venture reached a new stage when, on March 1, 1934, Manchoukuo was transformed into an empire. Chief Executive P'u Yi, now twenty-eight years old, rode in a bullet-proof American automobile to a replica of Peking's terraced Temple of Heaven, made obeissance to Heaven, and was enthroned as the Emperor K'ang Teh. It was his third ascension to the throne. But no more than on the two previous occasions was the Emperor a free agent. His Premier, Cheng Hsiao-hsu, seems to have fought hard for his sovereign's authority. But Japanese "advisers" and Japanese power were marshaled behind and around the throne. The Emperor K'ang Teh was only a front man for Japanese imperialism. Manchuria had become the staging-ground for Japan's mainland advance.

In that same year, 1934, however, some winds in East Asia's gathering storm began changing direction.

CHINA DIVIDED AGAINST ITSELF

The institution of the imperial system in Manchuria was only one sign of increasing Japanese resolution regarding China. One month later, in April, 1934, a spokesman of the Japanese Foreign Office in effect proclaimed a protectorate over China. The "Amau Declaration," without even a passing nod at the American Open Door doctrine, frowned upon "any attempt on the part of China to avail herself of the influence of any other country in order to resist Japan" and expressed Japanese opposition to other foreign powers "supplying China with war planes, building airdromes . . . or contracting a loan to provide funds for political uses" in China. The

Declaration arrogated to Japan the right to act as the "guardian of peace and order in eastern Asia."

It was quite clear by that time that Japan planned to impose its will upon China, at least to the extent of neutralizing its strength and "containing" Chinese revolutionary movements. The Amau Declaration, in a sense, was an official announcement of those aims. It was a logical forerunner to Japan's December, 1934, notice of intention to withdraw from the 1922 Washington Naval Limitation Treaty as of December 31, 1936. But the Declaration related chiefly to the developing situation in China.

The situation in China lent itself, as always, to a variety of interpretations. During the 1930s visitors often went away favorably impressed by conditions prevailing in such urban centers as Shanghai and Nanking. In Shanghai, China's biggest port, foreign trade was visibly growing. In Nanking impressive new government buildings were going up; the new capital was patently more "modern" than Peiping, which drowsed in its memories of the distant past. Foreign observers noted what they supposed to be the growing strength of China, and its increased unity. The façade that the port cities presented was deceptive and misleading. Nanking was not China.

Chiang Kai-shek was still strictly adhering to his strategy of offering only political resistance to Japanese moves, while he pursued his aim (harbored by Tuan Ch'i-jui before him) of unifying China by military force. However, the more the Japanese pressed forward, the stronger became the anti-Japanese feeling of the Chinese people. Chiang's two strategies were becoming incompatible. Nanking's foreign policy, instead of fostering national unity, was causing increasing disunity. To discover the true state of China, it was necessary to look beyond the port cities and deep into the hinterland.

Unity—and therefore strength—were in fact so distant as to be out of sight. Outer Mongolia, metamorphosed into the Mongolian People's Republic under the Soviet aegis, showed every sign of remaining independent of China; Tibet remained securely outside Nanking's authority—"beyond the long whip's reach," as the Chinese saying has it. Now Manchuria also lay outside the National Government's jurisdiction, and it comprised China's richest agricultural and industrial area.

Not even the remainder of China was unified. Nanking's authority in Western Inner Mongolia was deteriorating under the impact of developments in Manchuria and Jehol, and as Inner

Mongolia went so North China would tend to go. Sinkiang and individual provinces in West and Northwest China were ruled by semi-independent military men. Finally, South China's opposition to Chiang's regime had again crystallized. Nanking in 1934 was faced with the failure of its strategy. Strongly schismatic forces were at work.

Inner Mongolia. In Inner Mongolia Mongol nationalism was a factor of growing importance. For all of the "self-determination and self-government" that was promised China's minority peoples in Sun Yat-sen's "Principles for National Construction," the National Government had proved no more liberal than the Peking *tuchüns* in their rule of the Mongols. The Nationalist regime, ignoring Mongol objections, on coming to power had promptly made the Special Districts of Western Inner Mongolia into three new provinces, Chahar, Suiyuan and Ningsia. And, in the name of "reclamation," it stepped up the tempo of Chinese colonization of Mongol lands. Mongol delegations visited Nanking in 1928 and 1929 seeking redress but met with failure, and the political and economic condition of the Mongol peoples deteriorated rapidly.

The Japanese occupation of Manchuria, which engulfed three of the six Inner Mongolian Leagues, turned Western Inner Mongolia's entire flank. In the winter of 1932 the ruling tribal prince of the West Sunid Banner in northern Chahar, Teh Wang (Prince Teh), led a Mongol delegation to Nanking to discuss Inner Mongolian affairs—and to propose certain reforms. The delegation returned with empty hands; Nanking's policy remained essentially unchanged.

The Japanese occupation of Jehol and the thrust into eastern Chahar Province heralded new dangers. Given the Nanking Government's proved unwillingness to resist the Japanese advance, the Young Mongols, under the liberal and energetic Teh Wang, undertook to work out their own measures of self-defense.

The Mongols had only a limited choice. The Japanese in March, 1933, coincident with their entry into Jehol, transformed *Eastern* Inner Mongolia into a new political division, with the announced purpose of making it into an autonomous Mongolian part of Manchoukuo. The *Western* Inner Mongolians had no real possibility of achieving an effective independence, for three solid reasons: (1) they could count on no aid from the Mongolian People's Republic and the USSR, since the latter plainly viewed the international situation as one calling for a purely defensive policy; (2)

most of the area they claimed for the Mongol Leagues and Banners was now predominantly Chinese in complexion, and the Chinese governors of the new provinces were no more sympathetic to Mongolian aspirations than was the Central Government itself; and (3) the Japanese military evidently planned to fit the Mongols into a political framework suited to *Japanese* imperial purposes. The Mongol choice was, at best, "autonomy" under the advancing Japanese or an effective Chinese rule.

Prince Teh, besides heading the West Sunid Banner, was deputy chieftain of the Silingol League and supplied most of its leadership. He had a strong supporter in the chief of the Ulanchab League, Yun Wang (Prince Yun), whose nephew was his close friend and follower. In May, 1933, the month the Tangku Truce was signed, Princes Yun and Teh called a small conference of Mongol leaders at Pailingmiao for a preliminary discussion of Inner Mongolia's position. A second meeting followed two months later, and on August 14 the ruling princes of Inner Mongolia informed Nanking that they intended to establish an autonomous Mongolian government.

Nanking was now galvanized into action and in September dispatched a high official, Minister of the Interior Huang Shao-hung, to Kalgan to deal with "the Mongol problem." General Huang found the Mongols unwilling to come to Kalgan, as recognition of his superior authority would have demanded; the Mongols were already holding another conference to consider the shape of the new government. In October Huang went as far as Kweisui, the capital of Suiyuan Province, and endeavored to negotiate from that vantage point with the Mongols at their Pailing-miao headquarters. He made no progress. Finally, with obvious reluctance, he went to Pailingmiao itself and there met with Princes Yun and Teh and other Mongolian leaders. Mohammed, in the end, had gone to the mountain.

The negotiations centered on whether an autonomous Mongolian government should be established, as the Mongols proposed, or whether there should be instead "practical," progressive changes to improve existing arrangements, as suggested by the Chinese. There was an initial agreement, but it was aborted when, in January, 1934, the Kuomintang Central Executive Committee at Nanking passed an act granting the form of what had been agreed upon but omitting the substance. The dispute was resumed, but in changed circumstances. The Japanese had already been in contact with Teh Wang in 1933, and new exchanges had taken place. The Mongols now voiced a strong threat: if Nanking would not accede to their demands, they would be forced to consider aligning themselves with Manchoukuo, where Chief Executive P'u Yi was scheduled to be enthroned as Emperor on March 1.

Nanking canceled the January act, and on February 28, the day before P'u Yi ascended the throne, passed a new one providing for the establishment of an over-all Mongol organ to be called the Mongolian Local Autonomous Political Council. On March 7 Nanking designated Yun Wang to head the Political Council and made Teh Wang director of the Political Affairs Bureau. On April 23 the new Council was formally inaugurated. The Mongols appeared at last to have the substance of what they had determined upon the preceding October.

This did not mean the automatic resolution of Mongolian difficulties. Japanese pressure continued, with the Machiavellian Doihara making a new trip to Inner Mongolia at the end of June. Nanking and the Chinese provincial chieftains of Chahar and Suiyuan, where the Silingol, Ulanchab, and Yeghe-jo Leagues were located, were unimaginative and niggardly in their service of the agreements. The Amau Declaration of April, 1934, had been a clear mark of Japanese intent. The Japanese strategists obviously proposed to weaken further the National Government's control in both Inner Mongolia and North China, where the Tangku Truce had already opened a breach in the Chinese line of defense. There was no veiling the fact that Nanking's ties with an important group of Mongols had been loosened.

Sinkiang. The situation in Sinkiang was, if not typical, at any rate significantly indicative of the trend of developments in China. There the victorious Nationalists had achieved a success when Yang Tseng-hsin, the old *tuchün* who had ruled the province with an iron hand since 1912, had voiced allegiance to the Nanking regime after the overthrow of the Peking Government in June, 1928. But early in July, six days after being invested in office as Nationalist provincial chairman, he was assassinated. The motives of the assassin, an official named Fan Yao-nan, other than some discord with Yang Tseng-hsin and a will to power, will never be fully known, for he and his family and all accomplices were killed within hours by another aspirant to rule in Sinkiang, Chin Shu-jen.

This development started Sinkiang on a long, tortuous course.

Chin Shu-jen was a Yang Tseng-hsin man and was known as an able administrator in subordinate posts under the old *tuchün*. At the time of the July, 1928, coup he was Sinkiang Commissioner of Civil Affairs. He had his ambitions and may have had foreknowledge of the plot to kill General Yang. In any event, he was in a good tactical position to take prompt advantage of Fan Yao-nan's deed, and thus he came to power. Possession was nine points of the law in Sinkiang. Nanking, after some understandable hesitation, confirmed him in the post he had seized.

But Chin proved himself far less capable as Provincial Chairman than as Commissioner for Civil Affairs. He reversed Yang's policy of strict but just rule of Sinkiang's Turki population in favor of one of oppression. The Turki peoples were now confronted with increased tax levies, government monopolization of the province's export trade, and the viciousness of an unbridled Chinese soldiery. Matters came to a head in 1930. When the Hami prince Maqsud Shah died, Chin endeavored to replace the traditional princely rule by a Chinese administration, and went on to foist famine refugees from his native Kansu on Turki farmlands. In February, 1931, pent-up Turki resentment finally exploded into revolt when a Chinese tax-collector abducted a Moslem girl.

China's Northwest was then ruled by hard-fighting Chinese Moslems (Dungans), the Ma Clan. One Ma, who had recently cut a bloody swath through two provinces but had at last been driven into the Kansu panhandle by a combination of opposing generals, was the young Kansu Dungan, Ma Chung-ying. At the invitation of the Turki dissidents, Ma entered the fray in Sinkiang. The revolt took on the aspect of a rebellion.

Ma Chung-ying had already established an unenviable reputation in Northwest China as a killer. Reputedly moved by the counsel of an Istanbul Turk and a Japanese agent in his entourage, he was inspired with dreams of empire. As the Swedish explorer Sven Hedin described him, he was a would-be Tamerlane, and "in conversation with his advisers he calmly worked out a plan for the conquest of the whole world in alliance with Germany, Russia and Turkey." Ma Chung-ying was not a modest man.

In his first foray into the province, Ma was wounded in battle and had to pull back into Kansu. There he received control of four hsien (districts) from one of the generals who had been strafing him so short a time before and was made commander of the 36th

Division by Nanking. So he rested and built up his strength, while some of his followers continued to campaign against Chin Shu-jen in Sinkiang.

One of Chin's field commanders was a Manchurian, Sheng Shih-ts'ai, whose force was partly made up of former White Russian troops recruited by Chin to bolster his regime. In February, 1933, a Ma lieutenant drove to the gates of the provincial capital, Urumchi. The town was saved through the efforts of Sheng's command, but in April a coup led by the White Russian officers forced the corrupt and ineffective Chin Shu-jen from power. The man who succeeded him, with White Russian support, was Sheng Shih-ts'ai.

In May Ma Chung-ying re-entered the Sinkiang arena. Within a month he had achieved control of thirteen hsien, including the important town of Turfan in central Sinkiang. Sheng sent representatives to negotiate with the doughty Dungan; Nanking sent Deputy Chief of General Staff Huang Mu-sung to mediate the quarrel. Sheng caused three important Nanking-appointed officials to be executed in Huang's presence, and General Huang departed without completing his mission. Then Nanking dispatched Foreign Minister Lo Wen-kan to take up the task. Lo made the better effort to bring the warring interests together, but the situation in Sinkiang was beyond Nanking's control, and the Nationalist emissary departed after three weeks of negotiations without having achieved an agreement. The struggle for local power continued, with the Turki elements, who had invited Ma Chung-ying into Sinkiang in the first place, seesawing between the warring Dungan and Chinese groups.

Open warfare was resumed, and the fighting went in favor of Ma Chung-ying. By December the rebel forces were again pressing on Urumchi. In mid-January, at the same time as Ma's allies were advancing from the north and the west, Ma's forces attacked the capital itself. But Sheng Shih-ts'ai had sent a mission to Moscow in December "to strengthen friendly relations." The mission had been successful. When the Dungan attack was on the point of ousting Sheng from power, Soviet cavalry, tanks, and planes intervened, shattered the forces of Ma's allies, and drove Ma's own forces through the T'ien Shan range into South Sinkiang.

The Soviet motive was two-fold. First, the presence on Ma Chung-ying's staff of Turki Kemal Kaya Effendi and the Japanese adviser Onishi Tadashi seems to have convinced the USSR that

Ma's dreams of a Turkic empire bore a long-term threat to the Soviet Union's own Islamic Turkestan and that he was also under a dangerous Japanese influence. Second, as soon became clear, Sheng Shih-ts'ai had agreed to a "sovietization" of Sinkiang along lines more favorable to Soviet national security than anything offered by the unbridled and unpredictable Ma Chung-ying. Even before Ma's January campaign the USSR had permitted the forces of Li Tu and Su Ping-wen, interned after their retreat out of Manchuria, to be "repatriated" into Sinkiang, but that move had not been effective—hence the Soviet intervention. In July, 1934, in a bizarre ending to a colorful career, Ma Chung-ying crossed over the Sinkiang border into the Soviet Union in the company of a Soviet consular official. He never returned.

Sheng Shih-ts'ai had mortgaged his position to the Soviet Union and had made certain commitments relative to the future orientation of the province. He had already demonstrated his inclination to steer clear of ties with Nanking. In view of the developments of the first half of 1934, he would look even more to the making of local arrangements for the furthering of his fortunes. In practice, this meant Sinkiang's dependence upon, and orientation toward, the Soviet Union. The Sinkiang armed forces became the "Anti-Imperialist Army," his political party was named the "Anti-Imperialist Society," and Sinkiang adopted a red flag with a six-pointed star. Nanking's writ did not carry to Sinkiang.

The Canton Regime. Nanking's authority was not much more effective in parts of China proper. In the Northwest Moslems ruled as Nationalist officials, but their loyalty to Nanking was limited, except in the case of Kansu Province, which was now headed by a Nanking man, Chu Shao-liang. Ma Hung-k'uei, who had followed Han Fu-chü over to the Government in 1929, ruled in Ningsia. In Tsinghai the control of Ma Pu-fang and his brother, Ma Pu-ch'ing, was nearly absolute: they paid lip service to Nanking, but their deference did not go much further.

In West China semi-independent militarists, all Nationalists, ruled largely as they pleased. Yunnan was tightly controlled by Lung Yun, a former leader of the Ko Lao Hui and successor in 1928 to the power of T'ang Chi-yao. In neighboring Kweichow General Wang Chia-lieh held sway. But Szechwan, secure behind the forbidden mountain ranges that enclosed its fertile Red Basin, was the prime example of nonconcern with Nanking's rule. Three old-time militarists bickered endlessly among themselves for spheres of influence in northern Szechwan. In the rest of the province the struggle was between Liu Wen-hui and his nephew, Liu Hsiang. The province groaned under the burden of an estimated two hundred thousand troops—none of them under Nanking's control—all hungry for territory on which to feed. Not only was Szechwan beyond Nanking's authority and its laws, but there was not even centralized *local* control.

The active opposition to the Nanking regime still existed in South China. After the Japanese invasion of Manchuria, Hu Hanmin was freed in response to the public demand for national unity, but the Cantonese leaders refused to go to Nanking to discuss reconciliation until granted military control of the Nanking-Shanghai area. Chiang Kai-shek was forced to retire from office a second time in December; the separate Canton government was dissolved, and the Fukienese Nineteenth Route Army took up its station in the Shanghai sector. Wang Ching-wei and Sun Fo returned to Nanking, with Sun assuming the post of President of the Executive Yuan (Premier). Eugene Ch'en came back also, as Foreign Minister.

The National Government under the new leadership proved unable, however, to cope with the fast-moving developments, and Sun Fo found it necessary to beseech Chiang to renounce the retirement into which he had been forced so short a time before, and it was agreed that a triumvirate comprising Chiang, Wang Ching-wei, and Hu Han-min should rule at Nanking. Sun Fo—and Eugene Ch'en—resigned their posts in January, 1932, and left the capital. In a halting fashion the National Government began functioning once more.

The Nationalists had pulled themselves together just in time. Following upon the murder of two Japanese, Japan's armed forces went into action at Shanghai in the latter part of January, and it was then that they were engaged first by the Nineteenth Route Army and next by central government units. The government removed to Loyang, in remote Honan province, and did not return to Nanking until well after the signature of a truce ending the conflict.

New internal difficulties harassed the National Government. T. V. Soong failed to find a place in the new power combine and remained temporarily alienated. Hu Han-min, embittered by his incarceration, refused to leave Canton to take up his post. (He never again returned to Nanking.) Chiang Kai-shek, in the absence of a united opposition, was quickly able to assert his dominance in the Government once again.

A new power crisis developed in the summer of 1932. On August 6 Wang Ching-wei resigned as President of the Executive Yuan, because of differences, he said, between Chang Hsueh-liang and himself regarding the loss of Manchuria. Then Chang Hsueh-liang resigned. On August 9, having failed to change Wang's mind, the whole Cabinet resigned.

At this juncture T. V. Soong returned to the political scene, taking up both the presidency of the Executive Yuan and his former post as Minister of Finance. Wang Ching-wei departed on another of his monotonously frequent trips abroad into self-imposed exile. The year's shifts and maneuverings led to the elimination of Chiang Kai-shek's dangerous political rivals. The net result was so firm a consolidation of his control over the Party and the Government that his authority was never again effectively challenged—in Nanking.

But the Branch Political Council at Canton continued to function independently of Nanking. It was, in effect, the government of the South (although conventionally, because of the formal title of the Branch Political Council, it had come to be termed "the Southwest"). As of mid-1932, the military power behind the Canton regime was made up of the Kwangsi clique, Ch'en Ming-shu and Ts'ai T'ing-k'ai in Fukien, and the Kwangtung generals Ch'en Chi-t'ang and Yü Han-mou. The regime had available a vast, if unconsolidated, political resource—the nation's growing anti-Japanese feeling.

In November, 1933, well after the collapse of Feng Yü-hsiang's effort in the North, Ch'en Ming-shu, Ts'ai T'ing-k'ai, and Li Chi-shen launched a new rebellion, establishing a People's Government in Fukien. The insurgents set forth a liberal domestic platform, and in the field of foreign relations proposed a common front against the Japanese. In the first phase of their program, they called upon the rest of the country to join them in the task of overthrowing the Chiang Kai-shek regime. But the other southerners failed to come to Fukien's aid: with Eugene Chen, sometime Foreign Minister of the Wuhan regime, in charge of the foreign policy of the new government, they sniffed social radicalism. The rebellion was consequently crushed without difficulty by Chiang's forces in January, 1934, and Nationalist control was extended over one more province.

Nanking's authority was now effective in the coastal and down-river provinces of Fukien, Chekiang, Kiangsu, Anhwei, and a part of Kiangsi; it was also dominant in Hunan, Hupeh, Honan, Shensi and Kansu. In total, Nanking's rule in early 1934 reached to about one half of the traditional Eighteen Provinces of China proper. But Chiang Kai-shek's Nanking regime was hemmed in on all sides by inimical forces: the Japanese threatened further advances from the North; the country's West and Far West was ruled by semi-independent satraps jealous of their autonomy; the South offered a standing challenge to the legitimacy of the Nanking dictatorship.

The Nanking rule was faced, at the same time, by a threat from yet another domestic enemy. The social revolutionaries, beaten to earth in 1927, had risen again under the leadership of the Chinese Communist Party and were fighting against the established order on several fronts.

6 THE RESURGENCE OF CHINESE NATIONALISM

AFTER the blood bath of 1927, those Communists who had escaped had either gone underground or fled deep into the countryside. Party membership had plummeted from its peak of 58,000 in April, 1927, to some 10,000 by the end of the year—a mark of the severity of the repressive measures to which the Left had been subjected. Nevertheless, the Party organization, and a hard core of fighting men, had survived. They were in a position to make a fresh bid for power, should the times favor radical solutions. Their problem was to evolve a strategy befitting the social and political conditions of the times.

Political turmoil had persisted. As already remarked, the National Government led by Chiang Kai-shek had attempted, as its first task, to overcome various military men who had helped win the Nationalist victory. If China had been economically strong, if the vast countryside in which most Chinese lived had been stable, and if there had been no foreign foe beating at the gates, such a strategy might have had a chance of success. But these conditions did not in fact exist: the thesis that political unification of the nation should take precedence over both domestic socioeconomic tasks and resistance to foreign aggression contained an inherent weakness that could be readily attacked by bold, imaginative opponents of the regime. The Communists, in particular, sought from the beginning to harness the forces of social revolution, and they would in due course be found aligned again with an even more powerful force —that of a renascent Chinese nationalism.

Agriculture, the foundation of China's economy, had long been deteriorating owing to the pressures of a rapidly growing population on the limited crop-producing area, high rentals and usurious interest rates, and the crushing burden of incessant warfare as manifested in conscription of man-power, warlord taxation, and "special assessments." For a century, cheap low-tariff imports had been exercising a deleterious effect on the village handicrafts industries, so vital a part of agricultural life. China, moreover, was suffering from the effects of the world economic crisis that had begun in 1929: depressed world prices for industrial raw materials and agricultural products hit at the heart of China's export trade— even as at Japan's. On top of this, the loss of Manchuria deprived China, in terms of national production, of thirty percent of its coal, seventy-one percent of its iron ore, twenty-six percent of its developed electric power, and forty-seven percent of its cement.

Rural China, repeating an age-old pattern, had become ripe for revolution. In 1929, the year of the campaign against the Kwangsi forces in Central China and of Feng Yü-hsiang's first rebellion, the year also of the abortive Nationalist clash with the Soviet Union, drought struck nine of China's northern and northwestern provinces, comprising about 340,000 square miles (one eighth of the area of continental United States). The drought—and famine—persisted into 1931.

In 1931 there were an estimated twenty to twenty-five million famine sufferers in those areas, and many others had already died. Those who escaped starvation would reach the end of the drought in a state of beggary, their meager capital exhausted, their utensils sold, houses burned for fuel, even their families disrupted. A Nanking official was quoted in January, 1931, as stating that two million persons had died of famine in Shensi Province alone in the past few years, with thousands of villages become desolate and with four hundred thousand persons sold into slavery.

The dearth had a natural influence on the national market structure. Soaring prices of rice and other food grains made it more difficult still for the hungry citizen to obtain enough food. The national arms establishment, however, continued to mount. A writer in the *Far Eastern Review* estimated that, taking into consideration both soldiers and bandits, some five million armed men were living off the people in China, at a total cost of 3 billion yuan ($1 billion) annually. The National Government itself was spending some 500 million yuan per year on its military establishment. This was not much, as the costs of modern military establishments go, but it constituted eighty to eighty-five percent of the Nanking Government's total revenue.

Moreover, the Nanking military establishment was only one of many; various provincial warlords also maintained their own private armies. Nanking was able to live in the main off customs revenues and bankers' loans; the sundry independent militarists lived off the country. What this meant to the citizen in practical terms may be seen from a contemporary listing of forty-four taxes to which the people of Kansu Province were subjected, resulting (in the descriptive Chinese phrase) in "taking the fat off their fingers:"

acreage tax	land tax
penalty tax	military-aid tax
"purification of countryside" tax	hemp shoe tax
skin overcoat tax	military clothing tax
wheat bran tax	circulation (of money) tax
army mule tax	miscellaneous expenses tax
stocking tax	troop movement tax
soldier reward tax	merchants loan
uniform-alteration tax	cereal-price tax
military expenses tax	house tax
kettle tax	copper tax
change of defence expenses	repair of weapons expenses
repair of defence expenses	hog tax
trestle work tax	public debt
special loan item	temporary expenses
wealthy-house tax	communications tax
kindling-wood tax	flour-shop tax
bedding tax	soldier-enlistment tax
general headquarters loan	extraordinary tax
purchase of equipment tax	road-building expenses
water-mill tax	horse-fodder tax
investigation expenses	additional goods duty

The listed taxes included only those of universal applicability. There were many others besides of special and local character.

Even though there was a shortage of food grains in many areas and high prices prevailed, there was no shortage of opium—and opium prices had dropped. At Hankow opium was sold openly in public shops at a mere 3 yuan an ounce. Of course, it was not only in Szechwan that the peasants were forced to grow opium instead of grain because the militarists taxed land capable of producing opium at a rate that assumed such production. Even where the tax-collector had left something or the perennial warfare had missed some farmlands, an ill-paid, hungry and unruly soldiery often extorted, looted, and killed. Under the multiple burdens imposed on agriculture, ownership of the land was passing progressively from the small landowner to the hands of the landlord-moneylender. The peasant, consequently, was being driven into a state of increasing desperation.

The immediate reflection of deteriorating conditions in China's hinterland was the prevalent banditry. Rebellious or unpaid soldiers, peasants who had lost the struggle against money-lender or the natural environment, unemployed workers or plain ruffians—all alike went to make up the bands that ravaged many areas of China.

The desperate peasantry supplied most of the bandit recruits. Other peasants, not yet reduced to banditry, formed protective societies against the ravages of bandits and soldiers alike. In the past secret societies had often played important roles in popular revolts, and sometimes in the overthrow of dynasties. A typical secret peasant society of the current period was the Red Spears, which became prominent in 1925 when villagers were being conscripted for the *tuchüns'* wars.

The Red Spears' general aims reflected the desires of generations of Chinese peasants—security, peace, freedom from oppression. As insecurity spread, the Red Spears had grown in strength in Central and North China. They were well organized, with departments of military and civil affairs and well-delineated jurisdictions. Discipline was strict, with punishments, including death, imposed upon members for derelictions. In 1930 the membership in Honan Province alone was estimated at about one hundred thousand.

The Red Spears had thus been a force to be reckoned with, and warlords had frequently endeavored to manipulate them for their own selfish purposes. These attempts had been generally unsuccessful, for the Red Spears stood basically opposed to military depredations, as did most other secret peasant societies—"Spears" of other colors, the Ko Lao Hui, Heavenly Gate, Long Hair, Yellow Sand, Big Sword, The Bastards, and so forth. At the end of 1928, an estimated 730,000 peasants had belonged to secret societies in the area north of the Yangtze. In 1929 they had hampered the Kuominchün's campaign in Honan. Feng's troops, not having been paid by Nanking, had been forced to live on the country. Organized to fight exactly that sort of an affliction, the Red Spears had contributed to the Kuominchün's defeat.

This type of secret society was, of course, in the old pattern. But change was in the air. The discontent that finds expression in peasant uprisings needs but a revolutionary ideology to become a real social revolution. The Nationalist revolution's Soviet advisers had from the beginning recognized the value of organizing the peasant masses for revolutionary ends, as evidenced by the documents discovered during the 1927 raid on the Russian Embassy at Peking. And Sun Yat-sen, in his Three People's Principles, had offered a motivating concept for Chinese social revolution.

Distinct from the secret societies, a more modern type of peasant movement had been launched at Haifeng, Kwangtung, in 1921 under the leadership of a revolutionary schoolteacher, P'eng P'ai. Owing to the efforts of Communist organizers working in the Kuomintang-Communist coalition, the South China peasant movement had spread like wildfire to become the powerful revolutionary force of "antifeudalism" that helped the Northern Expedition get so quickly and easily to the Yangtze River. After the 1927 Right-Left split, the latent urge of antifeudalism continued to exist, ready to be utilized by other revolutionaries.

The countryside's revolutionary potential had an urban counterpart. The perennial question of China's industrialization had been largely neglected while the wars were in course. The condition of the ill-fed workers in the industrial centers was a deep source of potential discontent. The social and economic position of China's articulate youth was also a factor in the equation. As long as it was confined to teahouse philosophizing, the Chinese intelligentsia's dissatisfaction with autocratic political rule and a deteriorating national economy was hardly dangerous; but this discontent would be aggravated and perhaps become dangerous if the Chiang regime failed to create an environment providing outlets for the educated talents and aspirations of potential engineers, doctors, economists —and politicians. A disgruntled intelligentsia might decide to offer leadership to the revolutionary forces welling up from the lower strata of Chinese society.

The component elements for a great revolutionary wave were present and visible. When the Confucian governmental principle was abandoned after the 1911 revolution, it was succeeded by no adequate political philosophy. In 1928, likewise, an emasculated Sun Yat-sen-ism was clearly not enough. Chiang Kai-shek's rule faced a fundamental challenge: where the Kuomintang was failing to provide a new philosophy of government, others proposed to do so.

The Chinese intelligentsia, educated along the more radical lines of thought pointed out by Sun Yat-sen, Li Ta-chao, and Ch'en Tu-hsiu, and by Marx, Lenin, and Zinoviev, were bound eventually to oppose the government that based its claim to legitimacy on force alone. Ch'en Tu-hsiu had anathematized warlord rule a decade before, yet Chiang Kai-shek had begun his rule by taking up the sword to settle political questions with other Kuomintang leaders. He was following the road trod by Yuan Shih-k'ai and Tuan Ch'i-jui before him. But any injuries to China's hypersensitive nationalism, any failures to resist "foreign aggression," could only further alienate patriotic intellectuals: "anti-imperialism" was still a major revolutionary drive, to be neither suppressed nor neglected. And the pent-up pressures of antifeudalism threatened to become explosive.

As matters stood, the Left Kuomintang had submitted to the dominance of the right-wing forces led by Chiang Kai-shek; the only political party that might bid for revolutionary leadership was thus, by default, the Chinese Communist Party (CCP). As a result of the 1927 scourge, Party forces had been scattered, with military elements driven in one direction while political elements fled in another. The Party's Central Committee still existed, hidden in a foreign concession in Shanghai. The military forces, after having been pounded at Nanchang, Swatow, and Canton, now moved in small units, fighting for their lives.

The choice before the revolutionaries was whether they should seek support chiefly from the urban proletariat or from the amorphous peasantry. The CCP Central Committee, in Shanghai, was composed chiefly of "urbanites," and the Committee as a whole was, moreover, still governed by Comintern concepts. A revealing index of both the debility and orientation of the Party was that it held its Sixth Party Congress of 1928 in Moscow, where the Sixth Comintern Congress was meeting simultaneously. The Comintern leaders had chided the Chinese Communists for "their" mistakes and went on to forecast a new upsurge in the revolutionary tide. The CCP was assigned the undertaking of "the preparation for and the carrying through of armed insurrection as the sole path to the completion of the bourgeois-democratic revolution and to the overthrow of the power of the imperialists, landlords, and national bourgeoisie —the Kuomintang."

Potential leadership of a tougher brand had meanwhile appeared. In April, 1928, the ragged forces of Chu Teh joined up at Ching-kangshan, in mountainous western Kiangsi, with a small band of men led by Mao Tse-tung; thus the Chinese Red Army came into being. In the fall P'eng Teh-huai arrived with his small force and joined the other two leaders. As reorganized in the spring of 1929, the Red Army counted about ten thousand men, but had only some two thousand rifles. Chu Teh, a graduate of the Yunnan Military Academy who had fought against both the Manchus and would-be Emperor Yuan Shih-k'ai, was Commander-in-Chief; Mao Tse-tung, the sometime library assistant who had been convinced in the spring of 1927 that the peasantry were ripe for rebellion, was Political Commissar.

With its leading members back from the Moscow conclave, the Central Committee still did not join the Red Army in the inhospitable Kiangsi mountains; it remained underground in Shanghai. It also remained under the Comintern influence and was skeptical as to the worth of the Chu-Mao effort to establish a permanent base area.

Mao Tse-tung had his own thoughts on the subject. In a 1928 report to the Second Party Conference of the Hunan-Kiangsi Border Area, he had put his finger on the key to survival: it was possible for a Red Army to survive in the midst of "White" power, he said, because of the unending wars of old warlords and new against each other. Red Army bases should therefore be established in the no man's land of provincial border regions where the ambitions of warlords were in conflict. The revolutionary organization could, in the long run, draw strength from areas where, in the 1924–27 period, great masses of peasants, workers, and soldiers had participated in the revolutionary movement. But for permanence it was essential to build up regular armed forces and stable base areas.

Under attack for his unorthodox revolutionary approach, Mao Tse-tung developed his theme further in a long letter written in January, 1930. He criticized those who disapproved the effort to seize Kiangsi in favor of carrying on simple guerrilla activities in anticipation of a nationwide armed uprising. Comrades suffering from a revolutionary impetuosity tended, he wrote, to overestimate the subjective forces of the revolution and to underestimate the forces of counterrevolution. Such an appraisal would "doubtless lead to the path of adventurism." He agreed that the situation was, in general, a revolutionary one and cited an old Chinese proverb: "A single spark can start a prairie fire." But the situation demanded a preliminary build-up of power:

The laying of the Party's proletarian basis and the establishment of the Party branches in industrial enterprises in key districts are the important organisational tasks of the Party at present; but at the same time the development of struggles in the countryside, the establishment of the Red political power in small areas, and the creation and expansion of the Red Army, are in particular the main conditions for helping the struggle in the cities and accelerating the revolutionary upsurge.[1]

In June, 1930, acting on the Comintern assumption that a new revolutionary tide was rising during which urban centers could be seized by rebel peasant troops acting in conjunction with discontented working masses, a directive along the "Li Li-san line" went out from the Central Committee to the fledgling Red Army: Attack the towns. If the Army met with success, it was assumed that the revolutionary towns would supply the "proletarian hegemony" for the anticipated agrarian revolution.

The "objective" situation at the time was not unfavorable, for Nanking was then engaged in a death struggle with the Northern coalition. *But individual militarists in their separate provincial domains were not.* Chu Teh and Mao Tse-tung stoutly attempted to carry out orders, only to fail disastrously in operations against the strong points Wuhan and Changsha. They took Changsha, but the urban "proletariat" did not rise. Finally, hit by superior military force, the Red Army retired from the field.

But the Communists gained the lesson of experience. Assessing the results of the summer campaign, Chu and Mao concluded that the revolutionary tide was ebbing, not rising, and that they would have to fabricate the revolution from what the peasantry, instead of China's small "urban proletariat," could offer. They broke with the Comintern line. In November, 1930, Li Li-san, who had transmitted Moscow's directives, was found by the Comintern to have been guilty of revolutionary adventurism, and he proceeded to Moscow to have his ways mended.

The Central Committee remained in Shanghai, involved in the serious but somewhat precious problems of formal "leadership." But in the hinterland, under the real leadership of Mao Tse-tung and

Chu Teh, the Chinese Revolution was now oriented resolutely toward the Chinese peasantry.

On the national scene, after the 1930 war against the Northern coalition, the contending factions were without even that mild cement of cohesion which the Japanese invasion of Manchuria was to contribute a year later. Chiang Kai-shek continued to build up his military forces for the struggles he saw ahead. He fully appreciated that the Nationalist victories of 1926–27 had been due in large measure to the modern training given the Revolutionary Army by Soviet military advisers. Those advisers having perforce departed, Chiang had set out to replace them, and he chose Germans. He found no immediate replacement for the able Bluecher in terms of either rank or capacity. Reputedly on the recommendation of American news correspondent Karl von Wiegand, however, Chiang Kai-shek sought the services of Colonel Max Bauer, an associate of General Ludendorff of World War fame. Bauer first arrived in China in December, 1927, at the time of the Canton Commune. He visited Nanking and in due course returned to Germany accompanied by a Chinese military mission headed by Minister of War Ch'en Yi. In November, 1928, he returned, to take up the position of personal adviser to Chiang Kai-shek.

Bauer built up a staff of about forty-five German technicians and went about the work of training and equipping the Chinese National Army along German military lines. He contributed substantially to Chiang's victory over the Kwangsi forces at Wuhan. His end came soon after: he contracted smallpox at Hankow during the campaign and died at Shanghai on May 6, 1929.

But Bauer had laid the foundation. His place as chief of the German military mission was taken by Lieutenant Colonel Hermann Kriebel, the member of the German armistice mission of 1918 who, on bidding farewell to the Allied negotiators, had said: "See you again in twenty years." By 1930 the position of the German military adviser group had been firmly fixed in the Nationalist military establishment, and the work of developing the Government's military might was proceeding steadily. Many of the Germans, like Bauer, were disciples of Ludendorff, and they thus came to be called "Ludendorff's men." Their activities in molding Chiang Kai-shek's army and shaping its strategy received little publicity. But over the years their influence had a great cumulative effect. This was true even in Sino-Japanese relations. At the beginning of the

1930s, however, their role was of immediate significance for its influence on Mao Tse-tung's efforts to organize a peasant rebellion against the Central Government.

WAR WITHIN WAR: THE "BANDIT-SUPPRESSION" CAMPAIGNS

The Red Army's summer campaign of 1930 in the middle Yangtze region aroused the Nationalists to the necessity of eliminating the remaining pockets of rebellion. General Ho Ying-ch'in was made Commander-in-Chief for Bandit-Suppression, and twelve divisions were concentrated for what was viewed as the final mopping-up campaign. On December 10 the Government ordered that Communists and bandits should be suppressed "within three or six months at most." The first bandit-suppression campaign was on.

It failed ingloriously, with Ho Ying-ch'in losing two divisions. The report of a Nationalist brigade commander set forth six reasons for its failure, with the sixth reason supplying the kernel of the story: "The bankrupt condition of the peasantry, unemployment among the artisans and workers, and the general economic distress among the people supply inexhaustible fuel to the growth of Communism." [2]

The second bandit-suppression campaign was launched in February, 1931. Showing no signs of having learned the lessons of the first campaign, the Nationalist high command followed essentially the same strategy as before, in apparent disbelief that conventional procedures could fail against ragged, poorly-armed rebels. The only difference was that Nanking mobilized more troops for the operation. But the Reds were appreciably stronger than they had been six months earlier and made expert use of mobile tactics against the Government's superior forces. The Nationalist drive ground to a halt by June, with the Communist forces again enriched by captured arms and defected Nationalist troops.

Chiang Kai-shek now assumed personal command at Nanchang. An additional one hundred thousand troops were committed to the operation, bringing the total Nationalist force to about three hundred thousand men. Rewards were posted: 50 thousand yuan each for Chu Teh, Mao Tse-tung, and P'eng Teh-Huai alive, 20 thousand yuan each for their heads. On July 1 the third offensive to wipe out the Red rebellion began.

Nanking's military steam roller appeared to proceed without difficulty. On July 31 Reuters carried the news from Nanking: "General

Chiang Kai-shek has officially reported to the Government the capture of all the Communist strong-holds in Kiangsi and states that the Government campaign against the Communists has been successfully completed." The National Government sent a message of congratulation to its victorious commander-in-chief.

But the victory proved less than total. Returned to Nanking, Chiang in mid-August issued new orders for complete eradication of "Red banditry" in Kiangsi by the end of the month. A week later he hurried back to the front and resumed personal command. A critical situation had developed. The Communists, who had avoided decisive actions in the early phase of the campaign, had counterattacked strongly on the Nationalist flank and rear and badly cut up two Nationalist divisions.

The climactic battle of the campaign was fought September 7-9 at Kaohsing, Kiangsi Province. Chiang Kai-shek, once more back in Nanking, confidently reported a major Nationalist success: "The Red bandits having suffered this bitter blow certainly cannot rise up again, and the whole lot can soon be wiped out." It appeared, however, that both sides had suffered heavy losses in the fighting at Kaohsing and that the Reds were still to be "wiped out."

In any event, the Kaohsing engagement marked the end of the third bandit-suppression campaign. At about this juncture, Nanking became distracted by new developments. For one thing, the Canton regime deployed its forces for a march northward through Hunan Province, in a fresh challenge to Nanking. Nanking charged that the dissidents were acting in collusion with the Reds, but the verbal blast stood little chance of halting the military movement.

But when, with the Mukden Incident of September 18, 1931, the Japanese launched their campaign of mainland conquest, a wave of popular disapproval of renewed strife in "a time of national crisis" immediately surged up. This caused the Southerners to pull their forces back. As this latest threat to Chiang's rule faded into the autumn air, Nanking turned from its bandit-suppression campaign with something very like relief, pulled its main forces out of Kiangsi, and left the Communists in control of the south-central part of the province.

The year 1931 had been a hard one for the long-suffering *lao pai hsing* (Old Hundred Names, that is, the common people) in Central China. Besides the bandit-suppression campaigns, the Great Yangtze Flood had spread wide devastation, adding fresh miseries to the burdens borne by China's peasantry. It was Heaven and not the Government that caused heavy rains to fall in all parts of the Yangtze, Han, and Hsiang river basins at the same time, so that the waters, converging upon Wuhan at the confluence of the Yangtze and the Han, became more than could be carried by even the deep, swift-flowing Yangtze or than could be contained by the natural catch basins, the Tungting and Poyang lakes. The waters burst banks and dikes and flooded the entire countryside, destroying villages and crops. The Yangtze waters flowed through the streets of Hankow itself. It was nearly two months before the gorged river channel could drain off the millions of tons of flood waters from the middle Yangtze basin. No one will ever know how many persons died in the flood, but a rough estimate put the figure at approximately two million. And in the wake of the flood came dysentery, cholera, and famine. With the savings of lifetimes washed away, homes destroyed, and families decimated, the potential for social unrest appreciably increased.

In 1931, then, economic conditions had further deteriorated; powerful Nationalist leaders remained in opposition to the Nanking government; Communist rebels, if still not a major threat, also challenged Nanking's authority; and, finally, Japan had launched an attack on China's very sovereignty. It was then that the fateful dichotomy in China's national policy became crystallized. It stemmed from the vital issue: Should China adopt new domestic and foreign policies and, mobilizing its strength, resist the Japanese invaders? Or should the foreign aggressor be appeased while the Nationalists continued to endeavor to suppress by force the growing domestic opposition?

Chiang Kai-shek had in effect made his choice much earlier. For him, attention to enemies at home demanded priority. He feared the wrath of the admittedly powerful Japanese Army; he feared that the loss of domestic right-wing support would give other Nationalist leaders opportunities to advance their respective political fortunes at his expense. He seemingly had no great fear in 1931 of the relatively weak Chinese Communists. Chiang failed to recognize—or to dare gamble on it if he did—the favorable effect that war with Japan would have for consolidation of his rule. Evidently he also failed to appreciate that if he did not harness the forces of unrest, a competing political group might do so. So, he made his choice: "First pacify the country, then oppose the foreign [invader]."

The policy had the weakness of lacking any potential for winning popular support. Chiang's National Government had already effectively repudiated Sun Yat-sen's Principle of the People's Livelihood, and the Chinese Communists were resurrecting the principle in its 1924–27 form of antifeudalism. Thus defined, it would have a lasting and powerful if slow appeal to the poverty-stricken and dispossessed peasants numbering tens of millions. And by adopting a policy of nonresistance to the Japanese, qualified only by the implicit promise that the National Government would fight the foreign invader some day (after China had been "unified"), Chiang Kaishek was letting the powerful drive of nationalism pass by default into the hands of other aspirants to political power.

Chiang's strategy thus ran directly counter to the main political and social currents of the time. The existing conditions were such as had in the past led to popular rebellions. There was an oppressed peasantry, and conditions in the towns were no better. New forces were entering the scene. Western methods of production, introduced in the urban centers, were being grafted on a system of distribution that was a thousand years behind. The result could not be other than disruptive.

The social revolution that had been conceived in the impact of the Occidental industrial culture upon China in the latter part of the nineteenth century, and was born in 1919, had not yet completed its period of development. Only one thing would stop the growing movement of social revolution in China, and that was the bettering of the economic conditions of the population—the application of Sun Yat-sen's Principle of the People's Livelihood. It was impossible to halt the flow of ideas impinging upon the consciousness of the nation. And it was also impossible to limit "national reconstruction" to certain reforms and innovations at the top. A true social revolution had to take place, inevitably, in the great body of the people.

The development that had been interrupted in 1927 had now, five years later, reached a new stage in its progression from the dynastic system to institutions more in conformity with the times. A popular, social revolt against the policies of the Kuomintang had already taken on a clear focus. Six important "soviet" regions had been brought into existence in different parts of China. And on November 7, 1931, the first Chinese Soviet Congress was convened at Juichin, in southern Kiangsi. It adopted a Provisional Constitution and set up a Provisional Soviet Government.

A British newspaper at Hankow commented editorially on the underlying meaning of that event:

In reality it is a very tragic business. From whatever angle one views such a situation one cannot avoid the conclusion that an unhappy people have been driven to the verge of desperation by unmitigated repression and rapacity where they expected, and were fully entitled to, something quite different. It was not armies that brought Canton from the South to the North [in 1926], but the hospitality of a people weary of oppression and hopeful that the promises of better days would be, at least in part, implemented by those who made them as soon as the ruling power became theirs. . . . Never before had an invading army been welcomed by the people and their reward has been that whereas their former masters beat them with whips, since getting rid of them they have had a taste of scorpions. . . . If a Soviet Republic ever becomes a fact, it will be due more to its opponents in the National Government than it will be to the ability or efforts of its supporters either from Soviet Russia or the left wing of the Kuomintang in China.[3]

The same source published the new Provisional Soviet Government's foreign affairs platform. The program proposed the abrogation of all unequal treaties, repudiation of foreign debts, rendition of foreign concessions and leased territories, confiscation of all "imperialist" enterprises located on Chinese soil, and the withdrawal of all foreign armed forces from China. And, the Chinese revolutionaries promised to carry their war against imperialism to the final destruction of *world* imperialism.

The CCP Central Committee was still back in Shanghai. Mao Tse-tung headed the Juichin regime, Chu Teh was People's Commissar for War, chairman of the Revolutionary Military Council, and commander of the Red Army. The Deputy Chairman of the Military Council was Chou En-lai. The revolutionary movement headed by those men was reaching out, through their foreign affairs program, to grasp the power drive of "anti-imperialism." In April, 1932, like a distant defy to the politicians at Nanking, the fledgling Communist regime declared war on Japan.

The National Government remained so heavily engaged in domestic and foreign affairs throughout 1932 that "bandit-suppression" was necessarily left for the most part on the shelf. In April, 1933, when the Japanese forces penetrated the Great Wall and entered Hopei Province, the Chinese people were stirred more deeply, and the national sentiment in favor of resistance to the foreign invader was strengthened. So too, as a corollary, was the popular demand for cessation of civil war for the sake of national unity.

But the National Government intended no permanent relaxation of its efforts at bandit suppression, and, with his position consolidated at Nanking, Chiang Kai-shek launched the fourth bandit-suppression campaign in April, just as the Japanese were breaching the Great Wall. Nanking met the current foreign threat by accepting, in the Tangku Truce of May 31, the Japanese demand for demilitarization of that part of Hopei lying north of the Peiping-Liaoning and Peiping-Suiyuan railways.

Command of the fourth bandit-suppression campaign was in the hands of General Ch'en Ch'eng. Ch'en, like Chiang Kai-shek, was a native of Chekiang Province—and close to Chiang. Nanking had mobilized 250,000 troops for the new drive against the "bandit remnants." The Nineteenth Route Army, the Fukien unit which had fought with distinction against the Japanese at Shanghai the year before, was designated to participate in the action.

Like its predecessors, the new bandit-suppression campaign failed ingloriously. The drive was again focused on Kiangsi Province, where the provisional Soviet government and the main Communist forces were located. Outmaneuvered by the mobile enemy in mountainous terrain, Ch'en Ch'eng in a series of actions lost the equivalent of three divisions, with two divisions of Nanking's better troops entirely wiped out. He was relieved of command, and the campaign ended. The Nineteenth Route Army had proved notably uncooperative in the fighting. The significance of this last circumstance was soon to be discovered.

The Chinese Communists had been highly successful in meeting four bandit-suppression campaigns and had actually grown in strength under the "suppression"—in Hupeh, Hunan, and Szechwan provinces as well as in their Kiangsi base area. A smaller force had won a foothold in Shensi Province. They had made these gains and developed their strength through use of effective intelligence and high mobility in mountainous terrain and by cultivating popular support in their base areas. They had, in short, ably exploited the factors favoring guerrilla warfare.

The Communist position was by no means invulnerable. In establishing their Provisional Government in 1931, the rebels had undertaken commitments beyond their powers. Heavily Leftist, the leadership aspired to move directly to "socialism." The November, 1931, constitution incorporated various Communist dogmas with respect to labor and agriculture that might have had some applicability on a national scale but were poorly fitted to existing conditions in backwoods Kiangsi. The attempt to discover within that region's poverty-stricken agricultural villages the several "social classes" established in orthodox doctrine led to the adoption of highly artificial practices toward both the peasantry and village handicraftsmen. Production was adversely affected as a result, in circumstances where the highest possible output was necessary to sustain the contest with the Nationalist armies.

The Juichin policy hardly met the requirement of putting first things first. Through an excess of radicalism, the provisional Soviet government had alienated an important segment of the local population. The Communists' chief strength had thus far derived from a negative factor. The Nationalists by their political despotism and military ineptitude had themselves contributed substantially toward the creation of a revolutionary situation. But the Communist leadership could not take for granted a continuation of Nationalist military ineptitude. The influence of the German military advisory group was beginning to make itself felt.

Colonel Kriebel had been succeeded as chief German military adviser by Lieutenant General Georg Wetzell. Then, in 1933, after Hitler had come to power in Germany, the famed strategist General Hans von Seeckt went to China at Chiang Kai-shek's invitation, to survey the Nationalist military establishment and the current military situation. Ably seconded by Wetzell, von Seeckt worked out a new strategy for use against the Red Army. Then he went back to Germany—only to return in early 1934 to take over from Wetzell as head of the military advisory group, doubtless with the full approval of Hitler.

The fifth bandit-suppression campaign, which began in October, 1933, where the fourth campaign left off, bore the impress of the German influence. Chiang Kai-shek had adopted a new strategy of encirclement, blockade, and progressive strangulation. A military and economic blockade, buttressed by fortresses and pill boxes, was laid down around the whole Communist area in south central Kiangsi. On the eastern limits, where it lapped over the Kiangsi-Fukien border, the Nineteenth Route Army blocked Communist movement in the direction of the Formosa Strait. All lines of communication between the Red domain and the outside world were heavily guarded, all trading with the "Soviet Republic" was stopped, and the embryo rebel state soon began to feel the pinch in such essential supplies as salt, fats, and medicines.

The Communists made two critical errors in the beginning—one political, the other military. When the group of Nationalist dissidents launched the Fukien Rebellion in November, 1933, and set up a separatist "People's Government," they offered the hand of collaboration to the neighboring "Soviet Government." In the early months of that year, the Communists had three times called for a united front between themselves and other groups against the Nanking regime. When the concrete opportunity now arose, however, they spurned it on the facile grounds that the proffered terms of alliance were unsatisfactory: where other opposition Kuomintang groups found the Fukien rebels too radical in political orientation, the Communists condemned them as "seekers of a third road," and called upon the Fukien "masses" to overthrow them. But when the Fukien revolt was quickly and easily put down by Chiang Kai-shek for lack of support, the Kiangsi Reds found their eastern flank quite uncovered, instead of shielded by a friendly force. Chiang Kai-shek began drawing the iron ring tighter around the central Communist district, always advancing the line of fortifications.

In positional warfare, the mathematical odds were against the Communists. Chiang Kai-shek had mobilized 700,000 troops for this fifth, "decisive" bandit-suppression campaign. The Communists commanded 150,000. And Chiang had vast superiority not only in troop strength but in equipment as well, commanding plenty of artillery—and an air force. In view of the Nationalists' methodical advance, with flanks well guarded and rear buttressed by an interlaced system of strong points, the Communists were faced with two alternatives: to accept heavy sacrifices in a series of positional battles in a hopeless defense of the base area, or to abandon that base area as soon as the effectiveness of the Nationalist tactics became evident and attempt to re-create favorable conditions for the revolutionary movement elsewhere in China. The Red high command chose the former course. The Communists themselves later held that this was their second error, the military one.

The stubborn Communist defense had, of course, an important political function. Abandonment of the Kiangsi central district early in the campaign would have meant undertaking a vast Communist movement of evasion before preparations for retreat had been made; it would have been viewed by the people of Kiangsi and by sympathetic elements elsewhere in the nation as an unwarranted betrayal of the trust that the inhabitants of the Soviet Republic had placed in the Red Army's power to protect them from harsh retribution by Nanking; and, it might have been too early, in the light of developments in Sino-Japanese relations and corresponding reactions in Chinese national sentiment, for the Communists to save themselves by an early escape from the southeastern corner of

China. The delaying action in Kiangsi may have been, after all, the correct strategic choice.

The Red Army fought long and hard, and the fifth bandit-suppression campaign proved a costly operation for the Nationalists. The Juichin government gained time and then faced up to the inevitable. In October, 1934, just one year after the campaign began, some ninety thousand Red troops, divided into five army corps, broke out of the Kiangsi-Fukien base area in which they had been trapped. Marching by different routes and accompanied by a mass of peasants with carrying-poles (their Service of Supply) they started out in search of a refuge.

What followed was an epic in military annals. Fighting against national and provincial forces alike as they marched, they traversed province after province, making their way across the rivers and through the mountains of rugged Western China. They finished their Long March about six thousand miles and one year later when a force of some twenty thousand men led by Mao Tse-tung joined up on October 20, 1935 with ten thousand Communist partisans in Shensi Province in China's Northwest. The Chinese Red Army, if weakened, remained in being. Other Red units would in due course arrive to strengthen Mao's group. And along the line of march, all the way from Kiangsi, there had been left behind not only the many dead but also hard-core cadres who were charged with the task of carrying on the work of the Revolution.

THE SIAN INCIDENT

The National Government could count some incidental profit from the fifth bandit-suppression campaign. As its armies pursued the fleeing Red forces, they established Nanking's authority progressively in Yunnan, Kweichow, and Szechwan provinces. Political opponents suggested that Chiang Kai-shek actually planned to permit the "escape" of the Communist forces in a westerly direction to facilitate the extension of his authority into areas previously beyond Nanking's rule.

In any case, those political gains were balanced by losses elsewhere in China. In Inner Mongolia, particularly, the Autonomous Political Council inaugurated in April, 1934, was soon further alienated from Nanking when promised financial assistance and military equipment were not forthcoming. Colonel Doihara appeared on the scene, bearing gifts and other elements of persuasion as usual. By August, 1934, Teh Wang was openly negotiating with the Japanese. Nationalist agents kidnapped Teh Wang's Chief of Staff, one Han Feng-lin, in Peiping in September and shot him as a Japanese spy. Teh Wang met personally with Chiang Kai-shek in November, when Chiang visited Kweisui in the course of an inspection trip of China's Northwest. They exchanged the usual expressions of loyalty and sympathy; but political developments spoke louder than words. During the following months, Teh Wang gradually established closer and closer ties with the Japanese and Manchoukuo and by the end of 1935 had effectively deserted the Chinese camp.

Teh Wang's shift of allegiance was partly induced by the deterioration of the situation in North China, where the Japanese during 1935 steadily stepped up their efforts of political and economic penetration. In January of that year the Japanese occupied Kuyuan in eastern Chahar on the pretext that it fell properly within Manchoukuo's jurisdiction. There was a new compromise "settlement," but in May a fresh incident led to further Chinese surrenders, incorporated in the so-called Ho-Umetsu agreement of July 6.

Among other things, that agreement provided for the retirement of Hopei Chairman Yü Hsueh-chung and his Fifty-first Army from North China, the withdrawal of Kuomintang elements from Hopei Province, and a general prohibition of anti-Japanese agencies and propaganda. Reputedly also as a result of Japanese pressure, Sung Che-yuan was relieved of his Chahar chairmanship; he became instead Peiping-Tientsin Garrison Commander and Mayor of Peiping. At the end of November Nanking liquidated the Peiping Branch Political Council, which had been headed by Ho Ying-ch'in, and appointed Sung to be Hopei-Chahar Pacification Commissioner, but Sung, still heading the Twenty-ninth Army, declined the appointment.

Sung finally accepted the onerous responsibility of holding the North China situation steady under Japanese pressure, but not until Nanking established a Hopei-Chahar Political Affairs Council with himself as chairman, made him concurrently Hopei Provincial Chairman and Hopei-Chahar Pacification Commissioner, and appointed one of his subordinate generals, Chang Tzu-chung, to be Mayor of Tientsin. Sung needed all the power Nanking would give him. The Japanese by that time had evolved a plan for transformation of the five northernmost provinces of China—Hopei, Chahar, Suiyuan, Shansi and Shantung—into an autonomous area divorced from Nanking's authority.

Chiang Kai-shek was determined to continue with his program of bandit-suppression. A key figure in Chiang's plans was Chang Hsueh-liang, who had returned to China in January, 1934, after a trip to Europe that had taken him to Nazi Germany and Fascist Italy. Chang came back much improved in health and also notably more strongly nationalistic than when he left. Chiang Kai-shek appointed him Deputy Commander-in-Chief for Bandit-Suppression for Honan, Hupeh, and Anhwei, with headquarters at Hankow.

When the Communists retreated into Northwest China, Chang was transferred to that area, with his headquarters at Sian in Shensi Province. There was an empty seat in his council hall, for his adviser, W. H. Donald, had left him in December, 1934, to enter the service of the Generalissimo. An important psychological factor now entered the political equation: both Chang and his Northeastern troops were increasingly concerned with developments in their homeland, Manchuria. It was hardly to be expected, under the circumstances, that they would have their hearts fully in the task of fighting other Chinese.

There was another change in Chiang's military establishment: General von Seeckt had been forced to leave China in March, 1935, because of illness and had been replaced by General Alexander von Falkenhausen. But the basic strategy of giving primacy to the suppression of "domestic disorder" and postponing indefinitely the issue with Japan remained a constant.

The issue of China's domestic and international orientation in 1936 moved toward a climax. After the February military uprising at Tokyo in which several important civilian and military leaders were assassinated, the Japanese government committed itself categorically to a hard line toward China. Speaking before the Diet in May, 1936, Japanese Foreign Minister Arita Hachiro issued a warning: "The Japanese Government is greatly concerned over the inroads of Communist influence in East Asia. In view of the likelihood that Red armies may march northwards at any favorable moment, we are watching developments with particular attention." In June the Southwestern Kuomintang coalition called upon Nanking to mobilize against Japan. Failing to receive the desired response, the Southwestern leaders once more began to move their forces northward toward the Yangtze. They were stopped by Nanking's countering deployment and by the defection of Kwangtung General Yü Han-mou, bought over by Chiang Kai-shek, and of the entire Canton air force.

Yü Han-mou's defection resulted in the collapse of Ch'en Chi-t'ang's Kwangtung military establishment and the extension of the National Government's authority to Canton; the Branch Political Council was dissolved. Hu Han-min, the Council's mainstay, had died in May. Huang Shao-hung had deserted the Kwangsi group and joined the Central Government in 1932. Li Tsung-jen and Pai Ch'ung-hsi were left isolated in Kwangsi Province.

Chiang Kai-shek next proceeded to make military preparations against the Kwangsi group. He sent Huang Shao-hung to negotiate with Huang's former comrades-in-arms. Finally, Li Tsung-jen went to Canton, and there, in a meeting with Chiang, a compromise settlement was reached which left both Li and Pai in Kwangsi, cloaked with titles conferred by Nanking. The South's separatism had lasted for twenty years. Its long opposition to central government policies was now effectively ended. But the *national* movement of opposition to Nanking's policies continued to grow.

Popular dissent became more vocal with the organization at Shanghai, in May, 1936, of the National Salvation League. The organizers were chiefly intellectuals, with some Communist agents also active in the movement. By agitation and propaganda the Association worked to get the Government to abandon civil war and to resist the Japanese.

Political opposition was found even within Chiang Kai-shek's own family. Chiang had a son, Ching-kuo, born of an earlier marriage. In 1925 Chiang had sent Ching-kuo to Moscow to study in the Sun Yat-sen University and the Red Army Academy. After Chiang shifted to an anti-Soviet position in 1927, he ordered his son to return home only to receive a defiant message of refusal and condemnation. In early 1936 Chiang Ching-kuo wrote to his mother from Leningrad to condemn his father again for his politics.

These unfilial manifestations of disapproval did not divert Chiang Kai-shek from his course; neither did the growing opposition to his policies within Nationalist ranks. Supported by pro-Nazi elements of the Kuomintang right wing and advised on military strategy by the German military mission, Generalissimo Chiang disregarded the evidence of disaffection provided by adverse press criticism and the pleadings of China's intelligentsia. Moreover, he ignored the warnings implicit in the rebellious movements from 1931 onward that an outraged nationalism was again becoming a revolutionary force, even among the Chinese military.

In particular, Chiang seemed unaware or unconcerned that "anti-imperialism" had struck deep roots among Chang Hsueh-liang's Northeastern (Manchurian) forces, long exiled from their home-land in Manchuria and now facing the Communists in the North-west. The military situation was similar to that of 1933, when the Nineteenth Route Army flanked the Communist base from the east, in Fukien; but the political climate had notably changed.

The Communists had established their headquarters in Paoan, deep in the arid mountains of northwestern Shensi. While in Kiangsi, their poverty-stricken leaders had placed the revolution-ary emphasis on antifeudalism (the equivalent of Sun Yat-sen's Principle of the People's Livelihood) and won some support, but not enough to rouse the nation. Social radicalism would have to cede place to a stronger revolutionary urge for Mao Tse-tung's men to be able to counter Chiang Kai-shek's superior military force and advance toward political power.

The new force had already made its appearance. Since the Mukden Incident of September, 1931, the increasing danger inher-ent in each surge forward of the Japanese had caused a commen-surate welling up of Chinese nationalism. The Communist task was to harness this powerful force for their revolution. In this they were helped by the deterioration in the European situation that had led Moscow to shift its world strategy.

The Chinese Communists by 1936 had been enjoined officially to work for a new coalition of forces against the common foreign enemy. The Seventh (1935) Comintern Congress directed member Communist parties "to *strive* in the future by every means to *estab-lish* a united front on a national as well as an international scale." More particularly, in the words of the pertinent Comintern resolu-tion, "in China, the extension of the Soviet movement and the strengthening of the fighting power of the Red Army must be combined with the development of the people's anti-imperialist movement all over the country."

Chinese delegate Wang Ming (Ch'en Shao-yü) faithfully echoed the Comintern thesis. China, he said, was passing through an un-precedented crisis, and the only way to save the country was by mobilization of the entire Chinese nation, employing anti-imperialist national front tactics, for the sacred national-revolutionary struggle against Japanese imperialism. When Mao Tse-tung admitted in

1936 that the failure to join forces with the Nineteenth Route Army in 1933 had been an error, he spoke with the benefit of the Comintern's 1935 directive.

From their base at Paoan, the Communists established secret contacts with Chang Hsueh-liang in the spring of 1936. During the summer, the new liaison was developed to such an extent that Communist representatives took up regular residence at Sian, Chang's headquarters. Chiang Kai-shek almost certainly anticipated winning a double victory by his next bandit-suppression campaign: not only were the Reds to be wiped out, but Chang Hsueh-liang's military strength would probably be finally eliminated as a major factor in Chinese domestic politics. Unknown to Chiang, however, the Northeasterners had already been subverted.

By the fall of 1936 there had been a new concentration of Red forces. Hsu Hsiang-ch'ien's Fourth Army Corps had moved north in October, 1936, and joined Mao's forces in the new base area. Ho Lung, leading the Second Army Corps, left his base area on the Hunan-Hupeh border and in October, 1936, also combined with the Communist forces in Northwest China. The Communists at that time commanded approximately eighty thousand "regulars," and numerous militiamen besides. They still had far fewer rifles than troops. But they were obviously more than a "remnant" force. In fact, their army was nearly as strong as the one which started out from Kiangsi on its Long March two years before.

In that same October, when the Communist forces had completed their concentration in the Northwest, Chiang Kai-shek visited Sian to confer with Chang Hsueh-liang about the sixth bandit-suppression campaign. Marshal Chang Hsueh-liang confronted him with proposals that he stop the civil war, establish a united national front, enter upon an alliance with the Soviet Union, and undertake a program of resistance against Japan. Chiang brusquely rejected the propositions and returned to his field headquarters at Loyang, on the Lunghai Railway farther east, to continue preparations for "annihilation" of his domestic enemies. In Shanghai seven prominent leaders of the patriotic National Salvation League were arrested. The German-Japanese Anti-Comintern Pact, signed on November 25, 1936, meanwhile loomed up in international affairs like an ominous augury of war. And in Kansu Province the Reds inflicted heavy losses on Chiang Kai-shek's crack First Army.

On December 7 Generalissimo Chiang returned to Sian and informed Deputy Commander-in-Chief of Bandit-Suppression Chang

Hsueh-liang and General Yang Hu-ch'eng, commander of the Shensi forces, that the sixth bandit-suppression campaign was about to be launched: the orders to attack would be published on December 12. On December 11 Chang Hsueh-liang, Yang Hu-ch'eng, and various division commanders met and laid their own plans. On the critical day, December 12, they arrested Chiang Kai-shek. Then they addressed a circular telegram to the Nanking Government and the nation. The first demands of their eight-point program were for reorganization of the National Government on a coalition basis and the immediate cessation of civil war in favor of a general policy of armed resistance to Japan.

Nanking was shaken to its foundations. Minister of War Ho Ying-ch'in proposed to launch a punitive expedition against Sian employing bombers that had been concentrated for use in the bandit-suppression campaign. General Ho's plan would seem to have been framed without excessive solicitude for what might happen during the air bombardment to the Generalissimo, now a prisoner in the target area. Wang Ching-wei, in Germany recuperating from an assassination attempt of the previous year (and from political frustration), made contact with Ho Ying-ch'in and started for home. It was evident that he considered this to be an opportunity to take over leadership of the National Government.

The wish of the more radical Sian insurgents was to kill their captive. But politics plays strange tricks. Chiang Kai-shek, who had helped wreck the Kuomintang-Communist partnership in 1927 and brought death to so many Communists, was now saved by international Communism. The instrument was Chou En-lai, who had narrowly escaped death in Shanghai during Chiang's purge of 1927. The eight-point program offered by dissident Nationalists Chang Hsueh-liang and Yang Hu-ch'eng fitted the Comintern's 1935 directive exactly in its major aspects, and the Chinese Communists promptly came forward in support of that program and in favor of a national united front that would include Chiang's Kuomintang Government. On December 15 Chou En-lai, ably seconded by Red Army Chief of Staff Yeh Chien-ying and former Party secretary general Ch'in Pang-hsien (Po Ku), arrived in Sian.

From December 17 to 24 Chang Hsueh-liang, Yang Hu-ch'eng, and Chou En-lai negotiated with Generalissimo Chiang to get his acceptance of the eight-point program. W. H. Donald, T. V. Soong, and even Mme Chiang Kai-shek arrived by plane from Nanking and participated in the discussions. On December 24 Chiang accepted the conditions providing for resistance against Japan and guaranteeing no renewal of the civil war, and he was released on Christmas Day. Minister of War Ho Ying-ch'in's projected punitive expedition was canceled; and Wang Ching-wei, still on the high seas, altered his itinerary to end in Shanghai what was to have been his triumphal return to Nanking. Still in that fateful December of 1936, the Red Army occupied Yenan, south of Paoan in Shensi Province.

The Sian incident vitally affected several prominent personalities. Chang Hsueh-liang, who had served Chiang Kai-shek so well in 1928 and 1930, displaying a quixotism unusual in a Chinese politician, accompanied the Generalissimo back to Nanking and in January, 1937, was condemned to ten years' imprisonment for his offense. He was then given a special pardon and placed in the custody of the Chairman of the Military Affairs Commission, Chiang Kai-shek himself. At the Generalissimo's death thirty-eight years later, Chang still lived, on Formosa, under Nationalist surveillance. Yang Hu-ch'eng was murdered in a prison camp at Chungking in 1949 when the National Government left to take refuge in Formosa. The Sian agreement for a cessation of the civil war and resumption of Kuomintang-Communist cooperation affected yet another political figure. In April, 1937, the Generalissimo's son, Chiang Ching-kuo, returned home from the Soviet Union with his Russian wife after an absence of twelve years. It had been ten years between Kuomintang-Communist coalitions.

The Li Li-san line, which in 1930 had pushed Mao Tse-tung and Chu Teh to fruitless attacks on urban centers, had been a failure. Subsequent Communist efforts to build up a revolutionary movement based primarily upon a rural antifeudalism had achieved some notable successes but in 1936 faced a growing threat from disciplined troops possessing superior armament and a well-contrived strategy. Chiang Kai-shek, with the help of his German military advisers, might in other political circumstances have had his way.

But a renascent Chinese nationalism had intervened to interrupt the military process. Just as General Ts'ai O of Yunnan had rallied the nation by rebelling against Yuan Shih-k'ai's imperial ambitions in 1916, so Nationalist forces led variously by Feng Yü-hsiang, Li Tsung-jen and Pai Ch'ung-hsi of Kwangsi, and Ch'en Ming-shu and Ts'ai T'ing-k'ai of Fukien, in a series of insurrections had prepared the way for the 1936 coup. The revolutionary force of nationalism had compelled a *volte-face* by Chiang Kai-shek in his domestic and foreign policies. The Communists were once more officially linked to a national strategy of resistance to a foreign enemy and were thus protected, for the time being, from the domestic police power. In their first coalition both the Communists and Nationalists had made good use of the powerful drive of anti-imperialism. China's political future would in good part depend upon which party in the second Communist-Nationalist coalition would prove able to exploit that same drive more successfully.

OUTBREAK OF SECOND SINO-JAPANESE WAR; CHINESE "UNITED FRONT"

The Japanese had watched closely the startling developments that followed Chiang's kidnapping. The Kwantung Army, in a statement of December 28, 1936, made the Japanese position clear:

If the [Chinese] Central Government crushes the Communist Party within its country and adopts a far-sighted policy based on joint defence against Communism, the Kwantung Army will gladly come to its aid. If, on the other hand, the Chinese Government should compromise with the Communist Party and kindred elements and accept Communism and a policy of anti-Japanese resistance, the Kwantung Army will, as it had announced in the past, devise whatever measures it deems necessary for the defence of Manchoukuo and the preservation of peace throughout East Asia.

By the Amau Declaration of 1934 Japan had in effect claimed an exclusive protectorate over China; one of Foreign Minister Hirota's Three Principles of 1935 proposed that China and Japan collaborate in fighting Communism; from the time of the signature of the Anti-Comintern Pact in 1936, Japan had tried to draw China into an "alliance." Now the Japanese Army had plainly indicated a martial alternative.

Although Nanking studiously refrained from announcing, after Chiang's return to freedom, that the price for his life had been a reversal of its foreign policy, it soon became evident that such was the case. The sixth bandit-suppression campaign was never launched, and a *de facto* truce in the civil war took effect. The agreement at Sian had been only in principle, and it had been oral. Negotiations now began, some quietly, some openly, regarding concrete measures to implement a strategy of resistance to Japan's expansionism.

The Kuomintang Central Executive Committee convened at Nanking on February 15, 1937. It had before it a telegram of February

10 from the Communist Central Committee proposing, among other things, the cessation of all civil wars and the concentration of national strength against foreign aggressors, and accelerated preparations for armed resistance against Japan. The message pledged that, if the Kuomintang would accept the proposals, the Communists would (1) suspend all armed activities throughout the nation aimed at the overthrow of the National Government and (2) change the titles of the Soviet Government to Special Area Government of the Republic of China and of the Red Army to Chinese National Revolutionary Army. This Army would then be placed under the immediate direction of the National Government at Nanking. There were several other points; but the first two, offering recognition of the civil and military authority of Nanking, were patently the most important.

The Japanese exerted the utmost pressure to check the new political trend. Their ultimate goal was still the achievement of Hirota's three-point program: (1) the thorough suppression of anti-Japanese thoughts and activities in China; (2) conclusion of a Sino-Japanese anti-Communist military pact; and (3) achievement of "economic cooperation" between Japan, Manchoukuo, and China, with a special position provided for North China. The National Government knew the price it would have to pay—China's subordination to Japan's predominant position. The Government's independence of action would be lost in the contemplated relationship. If only for purely selfish reasons, the Nationalist leaders could not afford to accept the program.

Major General Kita Seiichi, sometime Section Chief of the Tokyo General Staff who had been newly assigned to Nanking as military attaché, in March visited Chinese military figures in a tour of Honan, Shantung, and North China. Lieutenant General Tashiro Kanichiro, commander of the Japanese North China forces, had several contacts with Sung Che-yuan, the harassed chairman of the Hopei-Chahar Political Council. At Nanking, Japanese Ambassador Kawagoe pressed Foreign Minister Wang Ch'ung-hui hard on the matter of "cooperation." Japanese military men met variously together at Tientsin and Shanghai; there was much coming and going of Chinese officials. In particular, discussions between the Nationalists and Communists continued, with Nationalist officials negotiating in Northern Shensi with the Communists and Chou En-lai visiting Chiang Kai-shek in Kuling.

At the end of April Kawagoe returned to Japan for important

conferences. In Tokyo, on May 10, he made a detailed report on Sino-Japanese relations to War Minister Sugiyama, Navy Minister Yonai, and Foreign Minister Sato. A few days earlier, on May 7, Sugiyama had denied in a meeting with the Chinese Ambassador to Washington, C. T. Wang, that Japan planned an invasion of China; but Sato, in a press conference about the same time, had displayed pessimism regarding the future of Sino-Japanese relations.

There was, naturally, no direct disclosure of what transpired at the May 10 meeting, but Kawagoe's report presumably proved decisive. It was announced that Japan was sending three divisions to the mainland—one to Manchoukuo, one to the Jehol-China border, and one to Tsingtao. And, in an address to prefectural governors summoned to Tokyo for an emergency conference on May 19, Sugiyama said that China's "over-confidence" was causing it to adopt an attitude "insulting to Japan." There was danger, he said, that China might soon adopt measures "designed to balk our peaceful expansion at its very source." Sato, for his part, told the Tokyo Free Trade Association on May 24 that, if Japan's honor and prestige were injured, it would have no alternative but to go to war.

The tension mounted. In North China Sung Che-yuan, caught between Nanking and the Japanese, retreated to his home town in Loling, Shantung, in an effort to dodge the mounting pressures. In distant Northwest China, Chiang Ching-kuo was negotiating, according to the Japanese, with Chou En-lai for a reorganization of the Chinese Communist Party with a view to according it legal status.

But it was in Japan that the most portentous change occurred. There, on June 5, a new Cabinet headed by Prince Konoye Fumimaro superseded that of General Hayashi Senjuro. Sugiyama remained as War Minister and Yonai as Navy Minister, but Hirota Koko returned as Foreign Minister instead of Sato. In addition to his diplomatic duties, Hirota was to head the National Planning Board. On that same June 5, the *Miyako Shimbun* quoted the new Foreign Minister as stating that the Three Principles he had advanced for improving Sino-Japanese relations were a mere abstract expression, and no longer practicable, as those relations had advanced from the period of endeavor to an epoch when concrete questions should be solved. In North China, Lieutenant General Katsuki Kiyochi replaced Lieutenant General Tashiro as commander of the Japanese forces.

At Lushan, Chiang Kai-shek's summer capital, there was unusual activity. The political debris of the December Sian incident had been swept aside with the transfer of Chang Hsueh-liang's North-eastern forces from Shensi and Kansu to Honan and Anhwei provinces, where they were being reorganized into the National Army. Chang Hsueh-liang was in Chiang Kai-shek's personal custody; Yang Hu-ch'eng, his partner in the episode, had finally been appointed a special envoy to study military conditions abroad, and he sailed from Shanghai at the end of June. Important conferences had already taken place between Chiang Kai-shek and various prominent military figures, and a whole series of conferences was scheduled for the period July 15 to August 14 at Lushan. On July 4 a special training course for fourteen thousand selected Army personnel began at Lushan. Among those present at the summer conferences were Communists Mao Tse-tung, Chu Teh, and Chou En-lai.

Wednesday, July 7, was a balmy summer's day at Peiping, with no feeling of special urgency in the air. That night Japanese troops on maneuvers knocked at the closed gates of the small walled town of Wanping, not far from Peiping's own walls, to demand entry; one of their soldiers was missing, they said, and they wanted to look for him. The officer in charge of the Wanping military force rejected the demand, the Japanese opened fire, and the Chinese troops fired back.

That came to be known as the Lukouchiao Incident. Even as in the Mukden Incident of September, 1931, the situation was at first viewed by the Chinese as negotiable. In fact, the Hopei-Chahar Political Council was reported to have signed an agreement expressing China's apologies for the affair, promising to withdraw Chinese troops from the area of conflict—and, more importantly, promising action against Blue Shirts (Nanking's fascist-type body), Communists, and other "public organizations inimical to good Sino-Japanese relations." Those concessions would have given Japan, at least in North China, the essence of Hirota's third point. But Nanking promptly announced that it would not recognize any local agreements made without its sanction.

Sung Che-yuan finally left Loling and arrived in Tientsin on July 12 to attempt a settlement of this latest of numerous "incidents." "Agreements" were reached only to be followed by new clashes. In reality, the Second Sino-Japanese War had begun. The fighting could not be stopped, for the Chinese nation had been told that it would be asked to retreat no farther, and Japan had decided to force the issue. Japanese forces were now pouring into China.

In Peiping Sung Che-yuan's Twenty-ninth Army men dug trenches in the streets—not so much for a final desperate street-by-street battle against enemy troops that might storm the city walls as to guard against any sortie by Japanese troops stationed in the old Legation Quarter. And when a cavalry squad approached from that direction, the Chinese at the barricades opened fire. The "enemy" turned out to be American Marines (the only mounted Marines in the Corps were stationed in Peiping), but how were the Chinese to know that they were not Japanese? One Marine was wounded, and the rest took shelter in a side street until the misunderstanding was cleared up. That was the only blood shed in the ancient capital itself.

Elsewhere in North China, meanwhile, the situation was rapidly worsening. On July 25 Japanese troops advancing from Tientsin took the railway station Yangtsun, half-way to Peiping, after a brisk fight. On the twenty-sixth, General Katsuki demanded withdrawal of General Feng Chih-an's 37th Division unit from Lukouchiao by noon next day. On the night of July 28 Sung Che-yuan and two of his captains led 37th Division forces out of Peiping.

At Nanyuan, just south of Peiping, Chinese troops were caught in an ambush and slaughtered. And for several days Japanese bombers were active in the skies over the Western Hills, the site of many Taoist and Buddhist temples and of gracious summer homes of foreigners, on Peiping's blue horizon. The sounds of battle became dim and then faded away. On August 8 the denizens of the Legation Quarter stood on the ancient Tatar Wall and watched the Japanese forces enter Peiping. The old capital had seen many conquerors before, and now the Japanese had come.

In September came the formal announcement, as the fruit of lengthy negotiations between Chou En-lai and Chiang Kai-shek, of the formation of the second Kuomintang-Communist united front. The Chinese war for national survival had begun.

The Chinese Communist Party, upon entering the new coalition, had, nevertheless, not abandoned its aim of introducing socialism and, ultimately, communism into China. Nor, in fact, did it pretend to do so; it purported to have done no more than change its tactics to fit the exigencies of China's perilous position. Thus Mao Tse-tung's public announcement of September 22, 1937, on "Urgent Tasks of the Chinese Revolution Since the Formation of the Kuomintang-Chinese Communist Party United Front" asserted that the "reunion of the two parties is about to usher in a new era in the Chinese revolution." In his view, the united front corresponded to the demand of the Chinese people, but it had to be more than a simple alliance of the two political parties; it had to be a truly nation-wide united front, based upon "mobilization for a war of resistance on a national scale" and governed by common policies.

And the common policies? Mao explained that they should be Sun Yat-sen's Three People's Principles and the "Ten Great Policies for Anti-Japanese Resistance and National Salvation" proposed on August 15 by the Communist Party. For Communism and the Three People's Principles were not incompatible:

Communism is to be implemented in a future stage of the revolutionary development. Communists do not wishfully envisage the realization of Communism at present, but are striving for the realization of the historically determined principles of national revolution and democratic revolution.

Those two latter principles, Mao held, were identical with Dr. Sun's corresponding principles:

The Chinese Communist Party has never ceased its firm resistance to imperialism; this is the principle of nationalism. The Soviet system of people's representative councils is nothing else than the principle of democracy and the agrarian revolution is without a doubt the principle of people's livelihood.[4]

The Chinese Communist leadership, in short, envisaged a mass upsurge of the Chinese people in a national war of resistance against Japan. It doubtless anticipated that, in the course of the war, the Kuomintang and the Communist Party would vie for the allegiance of the nation in a process which today would be called "competitive co-existence." To attain the united front with the National Government, the Communist Party had actually agreed to renounce its aim of overthrowing the Kuomintang by force, to abandon sovietization and abolish its Soviet Government, and to discontinue the policy of land confiscation. The designation "Red Army" was likewise abolished, and the Communist forces were reorganized as the Eighth Route Army of the National Revolutionary Army—and brought nominally under control of the Central Government's Military Affairs Commission.

In its outward aspect the arrangement seemingly envisaged what was essentially a return to the Kuomintang-Communist partnership of 1924–27, in which two alien forces had been bound together by a common purpose. The Kuomintang manifesto issued in September, 1937, on the historic occasion of formal reconciliation was responsive to the proprieties of the situation: "We should earnestly strive to unite, so that as a united nation we may safeguard the continued existence of the Republic"; and "the Government will gladly accept the services of any political organization provided it is sincerely working for the nation's salvation, and is willing under the banner of our national revolution to join with us in our struggle against aggression."

Both parties were thus in nominal accord regarding their objectives. But Confucius himself had advised, over two millennia before, that the first thing to be done in administering government is "to rectify names." He explained to his incredulous interlocutor: "If names be not correct, language is not in accordance with the truth of things. If language be not in accordance with the truth of things, affairs cannot be carried on to success." The Nationalists and Communists might both pay lip service to Sun Yat-sen's Three People's Principles, but it was entirely clear, and had been since 1927, that they gave widely different interpretations to those principles of "nationalism," "democracy," and the People's Livelihood.

In 1937 the Communists entered upon a renewal of the old alliance with their eyes wide open, alert to lessons they had learned in the past. There were three major differences in their 1937 situation, as compared to the position they had occupied in the 1924–27 coalition. For one thing, the Communist Party was much stronger, having been steeled in fire, than it had been in the earlier period. For another, the Communists now commanded their own armed forces, and they did not intend to give them up—regardless of the September agreement. Finally, in the Northern Expedition of 1926–27 the major enemy had been the Chinese warlords, and the dynamism of anti-imperialism had not been given full play. Now the nation looked on Japan as the major threat to its existence. The Communists knew that the domestic struggle would be won by the party which most ably captured and exploited the force of anti-imperialism—Chinese nationalism.

Both parties to the Kuomintang-Communist coalition thus entered upon the relationship with bitter memories of old deceits and bloody conflict, and with strong mental reservations. For the Communists, the liaison was a *mariage de convenance* dictated by considerations of international politics as determined by the Comintern and by Chinese power factors, as well as by the exigencies of Sino-

Japanese relations. For Chiang Kai-shek, the new union with the Communists was nothing more or less than a shotgun wedding. While facing the Japanese, Nationalists and Communists alike would give earnest thought to a future day of domestic reckoning.

7 THE SECOND SINO-JAPANESE WAR

THE OUTBREAK of hostilities in China had an immediate impact on international affairs. On July 16, 1937, Secretary of State Cordell Hull enunciated various high principles of international conduct, including the customary reference to equality of commercial treatment, and on August 10 *informally* offered to Japan the good offices of the United States—without eliciting a Japanese response. On October 6 the State Department announced that it considered Japan's action in China to be contrary to the Nine-Power Treaty of 1922 and the 1928 Kellogg-Briand Pact. The day before President Roosevelt had made an address in which he recommended "quarantine" to halt the spreading "epidemic of world lawlessness." His anathema was directed against aggressors generally, but its applicability to Japan was clear.

But the United States had rejected effective intervention when Japan invaded Manchuria in 1931, and no action was taken now to implement the half-hearted lead in the direction of "quarantine." Nor did Washington impose sanctions. American merchants continued to sell shiploads of steel scrap to Japan. And the United States offered no material aid to China in its struggle. By the Neutrality Acts of 1935 and 1937, the American Government confirmed its policy of nonintervention.

Germany occupied an anomalous position: allied to Japan by the Anti-Comintern Pact, it was giving military aid to China when the war broke out. Through German Ambassador Trautmann, Hitler's government endeavored for some time to mediate between the two warring countries and restore peace, and the German military mission under General von Falkenhausen remained at Nanking. Under pressure from Japan, however, the military mission was withdrawn by Hitler's orders in the spring of 1938 (except for a few men who chose to remain in private capacity).

The great-power contest in China at that stage was waged chiefly between Japan and the USSR. Both of the Far Eastern powers knew that China was less a combatant in the struggle than the prize. After Japan's occupation of Manchuria, and with the rise of Nazi power in Europe, the USSR had made a tactical retreat on its Eastern front. It had liquidated its Manchurian position by selling the Chinese Eastern Railway to Japan in 1935. But the Soviet Union had built up its Far Eastern position generally, and it had signified where it would make a stand by signing a mutual assistance pact with the Mongolian People's Republic in March, 1936.

International forces in East Asia were thus taking on new alignments, which converged inexorably toward conflict. The results of the impending struggles would shape the world pattern of power relations as well as the future China.

FIRST STAGE: "SPECIAL UNDECLARED WAR," 1937–38

Sometime after the hostilities began, Reuter's correspondent Frank Oliver, observing that neither China nor Japan had actually declared war, asked a Japanese military man to define the existing legal situation. This, said the Japanese, was a "special undeclared war."

One country, however, recognized the imbroglio for the crucial war it was. That was the Soviet Union. It had been quick to react to the radically changed situation. On August 21, prior to the formalization of the Kuomintang-Communist entente (but in all logic immediately related to it), the USSR and China signed a nonaggression pact. The Soviet Union, which had been forced to retreat in Manchuria, was returning to confront the potential enemy in another sector of the wide-flung Far Eastern front.

The signing of the pact was followed by an extension of Soviet credits for the purchase of war matériel. The munitions were transported laboriously overland, through Central Asia; they were paid for in time by cargos of Chinese tungsten, wool, and tea, shipped by the same route. The first Soviet credits, negotiated in 1938, were for $100 million; another credit, arranged in July, 1939, was for $150 million. China thus received tens of thousands of tons of needed munitions from the USSR—and the USSR received repayment later, when it stood in sore need of supplies itself.

Moscow dispatched five air wings of Soviet planes and pilots to help in the Chinese defense. Since the German military mission had departed, the USSR also assigned military advisers and technicians to the National Government. At its peak the Soviet military mission numbered some five hundred men, including such outstanding figures as Generals Grigori K. Zhukov and Vasili I. Chuikov (the later defender of Stalingrad). But Chiang Kai-shek did not consult the Soviet advisers on strategic problems as he had the Germans, and their talents were left largely unused. The top Soviet personnel, therefore, soon departed. Soviet planes played a more important role, helping to protect Hankow, Chungking, Chengtu, and Lanchow against Japanese air raids. Soviet fliers fought several important air battles against the Japanese and contributed notably to the Chinese defense.

Moscow's relationship with Sheng Shih-ts'ai in Central Asia, established back in 1934, now proved its usefulness. With the outbreak of war in East Asia, the Soviet Union further buttressed its deep flank by entering upon close relations with Sheng and stationing a reinforced brigade of Soviet troops (disarmingly designated the "8th Regiment") in Chinese uniforms, at Hami, the eastern gateway to Sinkiang. Those moves blocked any Japanese thrust westward into Central Asia. The Soviet Union had not been led by simple altruism to aid China and support the Chinese front. Moscow had good reason for sustaining the enfeebled Nationalist war effort, for the logic of the 1936 German-Japanese Anti-Comintern Pact pointed to an ultimate assault on the Soviet Union. Both Tokyo and Moscow knew that greater battles were still to come.

In the Sino-Japanese War itself Japan had been winning almost uninterrupted victories. Following the Lukouchiao Incident, the Japanese had rapidly rolled up first Sung Che-yuan's Twenty-ninth Army, and then other provincial forces. They faced only a modest task: they operated from a base position, built up over recent years, inside the Wall; and they were opposed by troops which, although brave, were supplied with no heavy artillery or planes by Nanking and were commanded by men without either experience or much knowledge of modern warfare. Besides, some of the traditional diseases of Chinese warlordism would persist—the urge "to maintain strength intact" (that is, to avoid military losses for fear of political effacement), unilateralism and self-seeking, and defection by some to the enemy.

The Japanese proceeded by a well-conceived plan, undertaking first to consolidate their military position in North China. They thrust westward toward Suiyuan Province and quickly broke through the strategic Nankow Pass when the defending general, the old-style politico-militarist Liu Ju-ming, disposed his troops better to cover his retreat than to block the enemy. Nankow was lost, and Kalgan fell on August 27. The Japanese forces went on to an easy conquest of Tatung, commanding the gateway into Shansi Province, because Yen Hsi-shan's relative, General Li Fu-ying, was chiefly interested in preserving his strength and abandoned the fortress town without a fight. Li Fu-ying was executed by order of Yen Hsi-shan himself, but the defense of mountainous Shansi had been breached.

Fu Tso-yi, the old Yen Hsi-shan man who had labored for some years both to combat the separatist tendencies of Teh Wang's Mongols and to strengthen Suiyuan's defenses, had been ordered into Shansi at the beginning of the war to buttress that mountain fastness. His task was now made doubly difficult. Fu Tso-yi had left the defense of eastern Suiyuan to a weak rear-guard force commanded by Ma Chan-shan, Hero of the Nonni River, and to two other subordinate commanders. Teh Wang and his Mongolian Military Government joined in the Japanese drive into Suiyuan. His Mongolian army and a Manchoukuo force, stiffened by a small Japanese cadre, completed the conquest of Suiyuan Province, taking Kweisui on October 13 and pushing easily on to Paotow. And in December the Japanese established at Kweisui (which was given back its old Mongol name Huhehot) a Mongolian Federated Autonomous Government. The senior Mongol Prince, Yun Wang, became first Chairman. When Yun Wang died in 1938, Teh Wang succeeded to the position.

While the Japanese were driving toward Tatung, the front south of Peiping had been quiet, and the Chinese had concentrated along a line well north of Paoting, Sung Che-yuan's new headquarters. With the occupation of Kalgan and Tatung, the Japanese re-deployed for a two-pronged drive into Shansi, southward from Tatung and southward likewise along the Ping-Han rail line in a wide flanking movement. They struck at Chochow, where Sun Lien-chung had concentrated fifty thousand troops, accompanying their movement with a flank attack. Fu Tso-yi had held Chochow under siege for nearly one hundred days a decade earlier, but now Sun Lien-chung put up one brisk fight and then speedily withdrew to Paoting to escape encirclement.

The Chinese resisted desperately at Paoting, but on September 24 the city fell to the attackers. The Japanese continued rapidly southward along the rail line to the strategic rail junction of Shihchiachuang and then drove into Shansi province itself.

Their approach from the east met only weak opposition. But the drive southward from Tatung ran into unexpectedly heavy resistance from a Communist force holding the strategic pass of Pinghsingkuan in the inner section of the Great Wall. That was the Communists' first brush with the enemy against whom they had declared war in 1932, and they acquitted themselves creditably. But, with that resistance overcome, the Japanese drive southward against the forces of Yen Hsi-shan and Fu Tso-yi gained momentum, and the Japanese pincers closed on the provincial capital, Taiyuan. It fell on November 9.

The Japanese also thrust southward from Tientsin, along the Tsin-Pu rail line, and they increased the threat to Shantung by making a naval landing at Tsingtao in mid-August. The northern column quickly reached the frontier of Shantung, took Tehchow on October 3, and then stopped. There ensued a long period of military inactivity on the Shantung front, pending the outcome of developments elsewhere.

Fighting had begun at Shanghai on August 13. A major incidental tragedy marked the second day of the fighting, when two disabled Chinese planes accidently dropped two separate bombs in refugee-congested streets of the International Settlement killing over 1,800 people and wounding as many more. But the Chinese forces in the Shanghai sector put up a bitter, stubborn fight and held their entrenched positions until their flank was turned in early November by a surprise Japanese landing in Hangchow Bay; then they pulled back. The Japanese captured Shanghai and rolled on toward Nanking.

The National Government announced the removal of government offices to Chungking, on the upper Yangtze in remote Szechwan. The capital fell in mid-December, with the attendant Japanese atrocities, looting, and general violence winning the label "the rape of Nanking" for the event. The National Government had moved out in advance to Wuhan, its home in its earlier revolutionary stage.

Quiet had long reigned on the Shantung front, accompanied by rumors questioning the attitude of Shantung Chairman Han Fu-chü, the man who had betrayed Feng Yü-hsiang and built up an empire out of the ruins left by Chang Tsung-ch'ang. In Tokyo, War Minister Sugiyama observed at the beginning of October that General Han was "still sitting on the fence and maintaining an ambiguous attitude." In view of persistent reports that he was negotiating with the enemy, Han felt compelled to make a public denial of the attributed equivocation. And on October 10, the customary day for expressing patriotic sentiments, he instructed his officers to resist the Japanese to the end.

Shantung's fate was naturally not settled in public negotiations. With the Shanghai-Nanking campaign over, the Japanese undertook to shatter the Chinese line extending from Haichow on the seacoast along the Lunghai Railway to the strategic Tungkuan Pass at the entrance to China's Northwest. In the latter part of December, they launched a pincers operation from Tehchow, in the north, and Tsingtao, on the coast to the southeast, against the Shantung provincial capital, Tsinan.

The Chinese forces at Tsingtao burned the town and withdrew. Han Fu-chü commanded some seventy thousand soldiers, popularly regarded as among the best in China. But he gave up Tsinan on December 25 with hardly a fight—the Japanese suffered an estimated 120 killed and wounded—and concentrated his troops near Tsining, to the southwest. On January 5 he gave up Tsining. Chiang Kai-shek sternly ordered him not to retreat without orders. But Han's forces continued their withdrawal, exposing the key point of Hsuchow to Japanese attack.

Li Tsung-jen, so long opposed to Chiang Kai-shek on grounds of both domestic and foreign policy, had been placed in command of the Hsuchow front. By order of Chiang, Li arrested Han Fu-chü on January 11 and sent him to Hankow for trial. Han and nine other high-ranking officers were executed at Hankow on January 24. At the time, Han was charged with retreat in disobedience of orders. After the war, an official version of the affair asserted that he had actually plotted with the Japanese to withdraw his forces deep into the hinterland and there coordinate his moves with the Japanese advance to bring about the downfall of the National Government. The truth will probably never be known. But it was quite evident that Han Fu-chü had enough guilt to hang him.

The battle for Hsuchow thus began with the Chinese flank

thinned. The Chinese had nevertheless concentrated some thirty divisions in southern Shantung, and the attackers evidently faced a contest not unlike that which had taken place at Shanghai. The battle for Hsuchow began on March 24 with an attack on Taierhchuang, a small walled town northeast of Hsuchow; the Japanese claimed occupation of the town on March 31. But battle-scarred Li Tsung-jen had laid a trap, and now he sprang it, counter-attacking heavily. By April 9 the Chinese were able to announce a smashing victory over the enemy. The Chinese claim that two famous Japanese divisions had been wiped out, with seven thousand dead, was exaggerated, but there was no doubt that the defenders had scored, and that the Japanese had suffered a severe reverse.

War Minister Sugiyama now took over command of the Northern Army from Terauchi, and the Yangtze Expeditionary Force under General Hata moved up from the south. The latter force crossed the Hwai River in early May and moved on Yungcheng, southwest of Hsuchow. A force of the Northern Army moved southward from Tsining to cut the Lunghai line west of Hsuchow. The two forces then effected junction west of Hsuchow and took the town on May 19. But the Japanese columns had been unable to encircle Hsuchow solidly with the forces at their disposal; most of the Chinese units escaped annihilation and moved westward into Honan. The Japanese, for their part, drove westward along the Lunghai line.

Famed Doihara, commanding a heavily outnumbered Japanese unit, was in desperate straits near Lanfeng. But with the timely arrival of the heavy Japanese columns, and the subsequent relief of Doihara, the attackers took Lanfeng on May 24 and rolled on to capture oft-battered Kaifeng.

The Japanese had clearly planned to continue westward to the strategic railway junction of Chengchow, where they could join with the column already at Hsinhsiang for a drive south on Hankow —and perhaps westward against Tungkuan as well. But the Chinese, who had upon occasion used scorched-earth tactics, now acted drastically: they opened the Yellow River dikes and flooded the entire countryside.

The cost in Chinese peasant lives and property was tremendous. The outcry was so great that Chinese officialdom retreated behind the charge, maintained to this day, that the Japanese had done the deed. But the action, far from bringing any conceivable benefit to the Japanese, threw their entire strategy awry, to the *military* benefit of the Chinese. There is little doubt that the Chinese, who were in military control of the region where the first break occurred, had breached the dikes.

The Japanese were forced to change their plans and shift the direction of their attack. Except for mopping-up operations, North China became quiet. The scene of action shifted back to the Yangtze.

Re-deployed, the Japanese began to advance westward along the Yangtze in a combined land and naval operation in June, 1938. They took Anking on June 12 and went on to confront the barrier offered by the Matang boom, fortified and equipped in accordance with the plans of the German military experts, who considered it impregnable. The Chinese commanding general abandoned the position without firing a shell from its modern artillery. He and several subordinates were later executed, but the Japanese had Matang.

They took the similarly important Lion Hill defenses, guarding Kiukiang farther upriver, by the simple but apparently unexpected expedient of crossing Poyang Lake in small craft and taking the fortifications from the rear. Kiukiang fell on July 26.

Further advance was slowed by the deadly summer heat of the middle Yangtze area, and by the dysentery and cholera endemic to the region. But in September the Japanese pressed closer to Hankow, and took various Hupeh towns north of the Yangtze by the end of the month. Hsinyang, a critical rail town on the Ping-Han line to the north, fell to a subterfuge on October 12. The Wuhan position was now untenable. After firing the town and the Japanese Concession in particular, the Chinese retreated; Hankow was taken on October 25, 1938, Wuchang and Hanyang on the following day. The Japanese then pushed on to capture Yochow, the gateway to Hunan Province, on November 12. The Chinese command at Changsha thereupon panicked and on November 15 set fire to the town, which burned to ashes. No Japanese troops appeared; the Chinese command had taken at face value an unconfirmed rumor that the Japanese were at the nearby village of Hsinho, whereas a troop of Japanese cavalry had briefly appeared at Hsinchiangho on the Chinese front line south of Yochow.

The Japanese were pushing the Chinese armies back from the seacoast. On October 12 a force of some thirty thousand men under Lieutenant General Furusho landed at Bias Bay, 175 kilometers southeast of Canton. The Chinese had theoretically long been prepared for an enemy attack against the "capital" of South China, but the Japanese landing met little opposition. Proceeding by four routes and supported by naval units advancing up the Pearl River, the Japanese forces occupied Canton on October 21. The Emperor's brother, Prince Chichibu, had participated in the action and now returned to Tokyo to inform his sovereign of an easy victory.

With the capture of the Wuhan cities, there ensued a prolonged period of relative peace. The Japanese undertook no further major military operations in China for six years. The Chinese Government sat in Chungking. According to Japanese figures, as of October, 1938, the Chinese had suffered some eight hundred thousand dead in battle, as compared with about fifty thousand Japanese killed. The figures, though open to challenge, were at least suggestive of the reality. And the Japanese claim to be in occupation of about 1,500,000 square kilometers with a population of 170 million was not far from the mark, taking into account the fact that the Japanese occupancy was one of points and lines.

The Chinese armies were cut off from the main seaports. They retained only one thin rail connection with the sea through French Indo-China and had lost the use of the Burma Road, offering an outlet to the south, when the British closed it to traffic in response to a Japanese demand. Overland, they were served by Soviet supplies carried laboriously by motor caravan from Kazakhstan, in Central Asia, to Lanchow, Kansu Province, 1,700 miles to the east. The Japanese had achieved the nearly complete strategic isolation of the enemy forces.

The Japanese strategy hinged on the belief that the Nationalists, in view of their perilous position, would be compelled to accept Tokyo's peace terms. In the fall of 1938, after the Nationalist defeat in the Wuhan sector, they made a new attempt to get a negotiated settlement, this time using the veteran revolutionary, Wang Ching-wei. Wang seemingly believed that the Anti-Comintern Pact powers were destined to win the impending struggle. Now he proceeded to Chungking with the mission of converting his old-time opponent, Chiang Kai-shek, to acceptance of the Japanese terms, which he carried.

Wang failed in his mission, left Chungking on December 18 ostensibly for Kunming, and kept on going to reach Hanoi, in Indo-China. Japan's terms were made public by Prince Konoye on December 22. He proposed, along familiar Japanese lines, that China should undergo a "rebirth" and participate in a new economic order for East Asia. This was, in embryo, the concept of Greater East Asia Co-Prosperity Sphere—another brain child of the sometime Kwantung Army staff officer, Ishihara Kanji.

In a long statement of December 26, Chiang Kai-shek rejected the Japanese proposals, saying:

> We must understand that the rebirth of China is taken by the Japanese to mean destruction of an independent China and creation of an enslaved China. The so-called new order is to be created after China has been reduced to a slave nation and linked up with made-in-Japan Manchoukuo. The aim of the Japanese is to control China militarily under the pretext of anti-Communism, to eliminate Chinese culture under the cloak of protection of Oriental culture and to expel European and American influences from the Far East under the pretext of breaking down economic walls. . . .
>
> Japanese magazines openly advocated that Japan, Manchoukuo and China under the "East Asia bloc" should form a patriarchal system with Japan as the patriarch and Manchoukuo and China as his children. In other words, the former will be the governor and the latter the governed slaves.

In their proposed plan for a Greater East Asia, the Japanese had left no room for Chinese independence, or politicians of the caliber of Chiang Kai-shek. He would not surrender on those terms. In Hanoi, in January, 1939, Wang Ching-wei was the target of an assassination attempt that failed only because of mistaken identity: the assassin killed his close associate, Tseng Chung-ming, instead. Wang joined the Japanese.

The Nationalists were holding out, and the Chinese armies remained in being. In March of 1938 a quasi-representative People's Political Council had been set up. The one-party Kuomintang dictatorship continued, but hope was held out for more democracy to come. The April, 1938, Kuomintang Congress had formulated a "Program of Armed Resistance and National Reconstruction," and it was accepted by both the Kuomintang and the Communists as a common wartime platform. Moreover, although most of China's productive capacity had been lost, Moscow had clearly indicated the strength of its intentions, and Soviet aid was coming in. Finally, the Japanese had halted their pursuit of the Nationalist forces. At the end of 1938 the situation appeared favorable to a consolidation and strengthening of the Chinese nation. In fact, the period proved to be the country's finest hour. Subsequently, there followed years of political and economic decay, particularly in the Nationalist camp.

One of the considerations in Chiang's decision not to surrender
—but also not to exhaust himself by fighting if he could help it—
was his firm conviction that Japan would eventually collide with
a third power and that China's war would be won for it by that
outside agency. This conviction, incidentally, both sapped the
Nationalist war effort and tended to corrupt the relationship between the Nationalists and the Communists.

Chiang Kai-shek had needed no more than a native shrewdness
to guess that the Japanese were preparing for a bigger adversary
than China. Japan's two potential antagonists were neighboring
Russia and the challenging Occidental naval power, the United
States. In 1938, even before the fall of Hankow, Japan undertook
to test the strength of Soviet Far Eastern defenses.

On July 20, 1938, the Japanese Ambassador in Moscow demanded the withdrawal of Soviet forces from a region near Lake
Khasan, where the borders of Korea, the Soviet Union, and China
meet, on the grounds that the territory in point belonged to Manchoukuo. The Soviet Union produced a map accompanying a treaty
signed with China in 1886 to support their contention that the
land was theirs. At the end of the month, the Japanese attacked
with the powerful 19th Division and took the hill known as
Changkufeng.

The Japanese victory had been won against border-guard forces.
The Soviet command responded to the Japanese action by bringing
up artillery, tanks, aviation, and elements of the First Primorye
Army; a heavy Soviet counterattack, on August 6, took back the
disputed ground. The battle ended on August 11 with Changkufeng in Soviet possession.

There was more to come. In mid-May of the following year Japanese forces suddenly attacked Mongol border guards at Nomonhan
on the Outer Mongolian frontier in the vicinity of Buir Nor, again
with initial success. Moscow then warned that, by virtue of its
mutual-defense treaty with the Mongolian People's Republic, it
regarded the Mongolian border in the same light as its own. At the
beginning of July, the Japanese advanced with some thirty thousand
troops supported by artillery, tanks, and planes. They were met by
Soviet forces fighting side-by-side with the Mongols. The battle
was joined.

General Zhukov, who had found too little to do in China, was now put in charge of the joint Soviet-Mongol operations, and he immediately began to reinforce. On August 20 the Mongol-Soviet forces took the offensive and by the end of the month had achieved a decisive victory over the Japanese. The Russo-German nonaggression pact was signed on August 23, 1939, while the struggle was still in progress. In mid-September, Moscow and Tokyo agreed to a cease-fire and the creation of a border-demarcation commission. Both sides had suffered heavy losses in the field, but the *status quo ante* had been restored, and it was the Japanese who had met political defeat.

The 1938 and 1939 battles at Changkufeng and Nomonhan almost certainly influenced, in an important way, Japan's subsequent strategic decisions. The Japanese empire builders discovered that the Soviet Union was prepared to resist on both its own and the Outer Mongolian frontiers. Moreover, Germany had embarked upon war in Europe without previously consulting or even notifying its Oriental ally. Tokyo was shocked into a realization that Berlin was not going to prove a "sincere" partner in the enterprise of empire-building and that Japan's plans might be subject to betrayal from within the Anti-Comintern relationship.

Japan was consequently impelled to make its decisions without reliance on Nazi aid. After the outbreak of the war in 1937, it had established a Mongolian Federated Autonomous Government in Inner Mongolia, a "Provisional Government" at Peiping, and then, in March, 1938, had set up a "Reformed Government of the Republic of China" at Nanking. In March, 1940, Wang Ching-wei came out to head a reorganized Reformed National Government, still based at Nanking. In theory, that government wielded political authority over Japanese-occupied China proper; in practice, Japanese jealousies kept even Peiping outside Nanking's authority, and Wang's "National Government" remained, like the other Japanese-sponsored regimes, a puppet organization. It was consequently unable to command substantial Chinese popular support.

The Japanese were still concerned with the evolution of their grand strategy. In April, 1941, they took the significant step of signing a nonaggression pact with the Soviet Union. They had decided to strike southward. But a fatal flaw had already been discovered in the German-Japanese military combination—failure to coordinate national strategies.

Still another important consideration entered into Tokyo's strategic decision: relations with the United States were becoming increasingly strained over the question of China. In January, 1940, the United States Government began, if belatedly, to restrict the shipment of certain critical war supplies to Japan. Decreased supplies of scrap iron would eventually have pinched Japan; the reduction of petroleum shipments really hurt, for the Japanese Navy depended upon oil for fuel.

The die was cast at a Japanese Imperial Staff conference of July 2, 1941, ten days after Germany's surprise attack on the Soviet Union. There it was decided that Japan would proceed with its program for the establishment of a Greater East Asia Co-Prosperity Sphere (of progressive economic integration), would press for a solution of the China affair and would "proceed with the southward movement to secure the basis for self-sufficiency and self-defense [that is, would attack the Anglo-American-Dutch positions]. The Northern problem [that is, the problem of dominating the USSR] will be dealt with in accordance with changes in the situation." [1]

In September, 1940, after the fall of France, Japan had occupied northern Indo-China; now, on July 21, 1941, it occupied the southern part. On July 26 the United States froze Japanese assets in the United States and embargoed petroleum exports to Japan. The hour of crisis approached.

As Secretary of State Cordell Hull worked at the crucial peace-or-war negotiations with the Japanese envoys at Washington in November, 1941, he came under increasing political pressure. At the critical juncture, when the immediate American aim was at least to secure a delay of the impending clash with Japan, Hull proposed to offer Japan a *modus vivendi*, effective for an initial period of three months, during which Japan was to make no further advances, immediately withdraw its forces from southern Indo-China and reduce the remaining Japanese garrison in Indo-China, in return for which the United States would relax the trade restrictions imposed on Japanese imports and exports and unfreeze Japanese assets.

But Hull communicated the project to the Chinese Ambassador as well as to the British and Netherlands envoys. He has recorded a sequel: "The reaction to the *modus vivendi* from China was violent. Chiang Kai-shek himself sent cables of protest to Churchill and to his brother-in-law in Washington, T. V. Soong, asking the latter to hand the message to Secretaries Stimson [Secretary of War] and Knox [Secretary of the Navy]."

A cable arrived from Churchill, "obviously influenced by Chiang Kai-shek's cable to him." So, Hull said: "After talking this over again with the Far East experts of the State Department, I came to the conclusion that we should cancel out the *modus vivendi*." The note Hull actually handed the Japanese Ambassadors on November 26 proposed, among other things, that Japan should withdraw all military, naval, air and police forces from China and Indo-China; and it proposed further: "The Government of the United States and the Government of Japan will not support—militarily, politically, economically—any government or regime in China other than the National Government of China with capital temporarily at Chungking."[2]

Acceptance of the American proposals would have required Japan to abandon all of the mainland gains, including Manchoukuo in its entirety, won since the Mukden Incident of 1931. There was no room left for negotiation. The Japanese decision of July 2, which had been confirmed and crystallized in a new Imperial Conference of September 6, was already being implemented. On December 7 there came the surprise Japanese attack on Pearl Harbor and American, British, and Dutch positions in the Pacific. On the following day, China formally declared war on Japan—and, for good measure, on Germany and Italy as well.

Stalin had won a vitally important political campaign by diverting the Japanese thrust away from the Soviet Far East and toward the Anglo-American-Dutch positions in the Pacific, in quite the opposite direction. Hard-pressed at Moscow and Stalingrad, the Soviets could now safely reduce their military aid to China: Nationalist China, with the help of Chiang Kai-shek's first major political coup in Washington, had become an ally of the United States.

Japan would still endeavor, through its puppet Governments at Nanking and Hsinking, and by application of military and political pressure, to get the National Government to accept a Sino-Japanese alliance as the logical solution of its difficulties. The Soviet Union would watch the effects of the "imperialist war" on China's social structure, in line with its theory that major wars stimulate revolutionary trends. The United States, driven by the urge to "win the war and get it over with," and with its range of action limited by its concern for political legitimacy, was ill prepared psychologically to project its view beyond the Chungking National

Government with which it had official diplomatic relations. As it had been bound to the former Peking government for as long as the *tuchüns* lasted, so now was it wedded politically to the Kuomintang regime.

The American strategic aim in the Asian war theater was to "keep China in the war, and so to strengthen her that she might exact a constantly growing price from the Japanese invader." [3] A China-Burma-India (CBI) Theater of War was created in January, 1942, with Chiang Kai-shek Commander-in-Chief of the China Theater. This was logical. Lieutenant General Joseph W. Stilwell, a good soldier with deep knowledge of China, was made United States commander of the CBI Theater and given concurrently the post of Chiang's Chief of Staff—on a level with the Chinese soldier-politician Chief of Staff, Ho Ying-ch'in. This appointment had a fundamental fault: Stilwell was being called upon to serve two masters, and one was sure to be dissatisfied.

Stilwell had great faith in the Chinese soldier's worth as a fighting man—if properly fed, paid, trained, equipped, and led. He first tried to influence the war in Asia by leading a Chinese force into Burma in early 1942, in an effort to stop the Japanese advance there. But his men, together with the defending British forces, were thrust back into a bitter retreat. He gave a simple explanation for the reverse: "We took a hell of a beating." The Chinese performance on that occasion had not measured up to hopes. Stilwell attacked the problem of strengthening the Chinese Army.

He faced major difficulties. Chiang Kai-shek's war aims differed vastly from those of the United States. Nor did he propose to achieve victory in the same manner. He aimed at China's aggrandizement in the international sphere and at maintaining Kuomintang domination of the domestic scene, particularly in the postwar period. And he proposed to utilize the United States to achieve success on both the foreign and domestic fronts.

The National Government moved without delay: on December 30 it asked the American and British Governments for loans of $500 million apiece. Chiang Kai-shek also wanted vast quantities of military supplies and the participation of strong allied forces in the war in Asia; but, in view of the difficult situation in both Europe and the South Pacific, the CBI Theater was accorded only a low priority. China was called upon to look in good measure still to its own resources. Stilwell, for his part, proposed not only to train and equip the Chinese troops and get them into battle but to reorganize the National Army's command structure, so the troops could be given adequate generalship. However, Chiang Kai-shek refused to permit any basic changes in the command structure. Stilwell, who proposed a new Burma offensive for the spring of 1943, began training thirty Chinese divisions—but under obvious handicaps.

The Stilwell difficulty was compounded by the presence on the scene of a fervent air-power advocate. Claire Chennault, retired from the United States Army, had gone to China and organized the American Volunteer Corps (the "Flying Tigers") at a time when the American Government was upholding its "neutral" position. With the outbreak of war in the Pacific, Chennault was given command of the USAF China Air Task Force. Wedded to the doctrine of air supremacy, he by-passed Stilwell, his theater commander, in a campaign to win acceptance for his theories. He found a ready listener in Chiang Kai-shek.

Relations between the Nationalists and Communists were a factor in the situation. Their mutual antagonism became strongly crystallized with America's appearance on the scene. As had been the case with Soviet military supplies, all American aid went to the National Government, which did not share that aid with the Communist armies—even for the purpose of fighting the Japanese.

Beginning right after Pearl Harbor, Chiang Kai-shek evinced a pronounced reluctance to take the field against a foreign enemy locked in a death struggle with the United States and Britain: barbarians were at last fighting barbarians, and it was China's cue to preserve its own strength, which Chiang viewed as being that of the Nationalist regime. He would permit no abridgment of that principle. In the course of the civil wars, he had sometimes listened to the advice of Generals von Seeckt and von Falkhenhausen on strategy. He gave little consideration to recommendations from Soviet advisers, and from American military men who came later, on the manner in which his armies could best engage the Japanese.

Chiang acted to serve strictly Nationalist objectives. The Nationalist strategy was thus his own personal creation, and the command structure of the Nationalist Army remained weakened by corruption and favoritism, but it remained bound to Chiang by feudal loyalties. The army rank and file were maltreated, ill-fed conscripts lacking the essential elements of military and political discipline.

A large proportion of the Nationalist conscripts, often to be seen in Chinese wartime towns roped together to prevent escape, died *even before reaching their assigned units.* Thousands of others, deprived of basic medical care and even their rations by grafting superiors, died of neglect later. It was not until 1944 that steps began to be taken to correct the situation. As a consequence, the army's generalship was bad, and troop morale was worse. The Nationalist armies sat tight in defensive positions and hoarded their new American weapons for eventual use against the domestic opposition. From 1941 to 1944 China's war against Japan was largely in suspense as far as Chungking was concerned. But a strong military cordon was set up around the Chinese Communist base in Northwest China.

And if the Nationalists were reluctant to engage the Japanese enemy, they did not hesitate to maneuver to obtain political benefits from the difficulties of friendly states. In 1942, when the Soviets were engaged in a death struggle at Stalingrad, the Nationalists took advantage of the occasion to coax Sheng Shih-ts'ai away from his ties with Moscow—and then took steps to oust Soviet influence from Sinkiang.

The Soviets were caused to withdraw their advisers, together with the 8th Regiment stationed at Hami. Later, the Nationalists would be forced to pay, in long-range interests, for having so shortsightedly seized upon a quick profit. And Sheng, after briefly occupying the sinecure of Minister of Agriculture and Forestry in Chungking, would be forced off the political stage.

It was not only in Sinkiang and against the Soviet Union that the National Government played that brand of Machiavellian politics. In the summer of 1943 it concentrated troops on the Tibetan border preparatory to an invasion aimed at bending the Lhasa government to its will. However, presumably at American suggestion, the project was shelved.

The Nationalist pursuit of gain carried over into the market place. A flourishing trade was carried on between Chungking and other Nationalist points and the Japanese-held downriver ports, notably Shanghai. The Nationalists contended that this benefitted the Allied cause by draining away the economic strength of Japan, even though they received such items as silk stockings and fountain pens in exchange for tungsten and foodstuffs.

In the meantime, Chungking's demands on the American Government were incessant and seemingly limitless. Nevertheless, all of Stilwell's exhortations and pleadings during 1943 could not get the Nationalists to pull their weight in the war against Japan. The proposed 1943 Burma campaign never got started.

The end of 1943 was a turning point. In November President Roosevelt, Prime Minister Churchill, and Generalissimo Chiang Kai-shek conferred at Cairo on the prosecution of the war. Chiang obtained from his allies a promise of the return to China of Manchuria and of Formosa and the Pescadores. And he won a specific war commitment for a joint allied action, Operation Buccaneer, in the Burma Theater, with the British charged with undertaking an amphibious landing in the Bay of Bengal.

Upon leaving Cairo, however, Roosevelt and Churchill went to Tehran to meet with Stalin, and there learned that Russia was prepared to enter the war against Japan when the war with Germany was over. The Tehran Conference put a different complexion on matters: (1) it brought the shift of greater emphasis to Operation Overlord, the Normandy landing scheduled for the following spring; and (2) it reduced the importance of China in the over-all war picture. The Chinese Nationalists had not made an active war theater of China, the naval war in the Pacific was now going well, and the major war role that China had been booked to play was discovered unnecessary for performance of the final act. Largely through Churchill's urging, Operation Buccaneer was cancelled.

Angered, Chiang Kai-shek demanded what was in effect a consolation prize. In a communication to President Roosevelt he asked that, in order "to assure the Chinese people and army of your serious concern in the Chinese theater of war," the United States Government should extend a billion dollar loan to China, supply double the number of planes previously agreed upon, and increase the airlift of supplies into China to at least twenty thousand tons monthly by February, 1944.

Chiang Kai-shek did not get the billion dollars. Following this clash, Roosevelt became chillier toward his Chinese ally and adopted a new firmness in dealing with him. China ended 1943 having alienated the Soviet Union, having damaged its relationship with the United States, and without having achieved any major successes against the Japanese arms. By virtue of the October, 1943, Moscow Declaration, China had been recognized, chiefly on American insistence, as one of the four "great powers" that would mold the postwar world. In 1943, also, Britain and the United States at long last relinquished their extraterritorial rights in China. But those gains could hardly compensate for the substantial losses incurred. And the year ahead was destined to prove a hard one.

THIRD STAGE: GROWING DIVISIONS, 1944–45

The unsatisfactory course of Chungking's foreign relations was paralleled by a pronounced deterioration in the domestic Nationalist-Communist alliance. Wartime collaboration had failed to bridge the animosity between the two factions. Instead of working together, each was obviously working toward its own ends, and mutual distrust developed into outright hostility.

The National Government had cause to suspect Communist motives; and the Communists, in the light of history, had no more reason to trust the *bona fides* of their ancient adversary. Even in 1938, when the two Chinese forces had seemed to seal a compact as comrades-in-arms, the relationship began to decay. That very year, Chiang Kai-shek assumed the post of *Tsung-ts'ai* or "leader," a position held only once before in Kuomintang history, by Sun Yat-sen as *Tsung-li*. Chiang's autocratic leadership was no longer contested in the Nationalist camp, but it was disputed by the Communists. The issue was pointed up by the Communist refusal to relinquish territorial and military controls to the Central Government, as promised in 1937, until the Kuomintang gave up its one-party dictatorship. The war had enforced a temporary public truce, but both sides prepared for the next stage of contest.

The Communists regarded the war as both imposing the task of fighting the Japanese and offering the opportunity for development of their own strength through training, experience, and the consolidation of concrete gains. They organized a vast political network, carried on guerrilla activities behind the Japanese lines, and in "Free China" consolidated their bases. They had substituted a Shen-Kan-Ning (Shensi-Kansu-Ningsia) Border Government for the "dissolved" Soviet Government; in January, 1938, they added a Chin-Ch'a-Chi (Shansi-Chahar-Hopei) Border Government to their holdings. Subsequently, they went on to create others. In their unremitting work to expand their military and political power, they did not narrowly weigh strength in terms of arms alone. Their political authority, in North China especially, visibly began to expand immediately after the outbreak of war.

The Nationalists could see what was happening and undertook countermeasures. They themselves won no victories in guerrilla operations against the Japanese, for their "guerrillas," once sent into occupied territory, with lamentable regularity defected to the enemy. In 1938, even while still at Hankow, however, they dissolved a number of quasi-Communist organizations and sought to check Communist-motivated activities. From Chungking, in 1939, they began to form a military cordon around the Communist-held Shen-Kan-Ning region. Relations between the two camps grew worse.

The Communist strategy of building up political and military strength was implicitly legitimized by the agreement for a joint war effort against Japan. The Nationalist *domestic* strategy was designed to achieve first the containment, then the defeat, of the Communist forces. With China at war, the Communist strategy offered a far better prospect for winning popular support.

An early clash betrayed the deep animosity between the two erstwhile allies. The Communists had created the New Fourth Army (Communist-led, although not technically a part of the Communist military organization) and moved it close to Shanghai. The Army's presence so close to China's greatest seaport contributed, of course, to the national war effort; but it also clearly placed the Communists in an advantageous position with respect to postwar developments, no matter how distant. Moreover, Chekiang was Chiang Kai-shek's home province. In October, 1940, the Nationalists ordered the New Fourth Army to withdraw north of the Yangtze.

Such a move, besides leaving a vacuum in the occupied territory, entailed a perilous passage across the Yangtze River under Japanese guns. The Communist leadership protested the order; the Nationalist command was insistent. While arguing, the wary Communists secretly began moving their troops out of the area. They had succeeded in withdrawing the bulk of their forces across the Yangtze by early January, when the Nationalists, not the Japanese, fell upon the New Fourth Headquarters unit and the accompanying rear guard and almost wiped them out. Chief of Staff Hsiang Ying was killed and Army Commander Yeh T'ing wounded and taken prisoner; the Communists suffered several thousand casualties.

The "New Fourth Incident" aroused public opinion and attracted unfavorable foreign attention. The USSR suspended arms deliveries. Under compulsion to repair the damage, Chiang Kai-shek on March 6 sent the People's Political Council a long message in which he analyzed the relationship between the Government and the CCP, charged the Communists with bad faith, and then said:

I need scarcely assert that our Government is solely concerned with leading the nation against the Japanese invaders and extirpating the traitors,
and is utterly without any notion of again taking up arms to "suppress the
Communists." It desires never again to hear of that ill-omened term
which now has a place only in Chinese history. Let them obey orders,
give up their attacks on their comrades-in-arms and cease all their
provocative acts; the Government will then treat them with all possible
consideration.

But, "can two walk together, if they be not agreed?" The Communists were not convinced by Chiang's fair-sounding words; nor
did they become more amenable than before to his authority.
Chiang had ordered the New Fourth Army dissolved after the
January clash. The Communist high command kept it in being,
replacing the captive Army Commander with Ch'en Yi; Liu Shao-ch'i
became the New Fourth Army's political commissar.

Chiang Kai-shek was quoted as saying privately in 1941: "The
Japanese are a disease of the skin. The Communists are a disease
of the heart." Said Mao Tse-tung, at about the same time: "If any
people's revolutionary force wishes to avoid extermination by
Chiang Kai-shek . . . it has no alternative but to wage a tit-for-tat
struggle against his counter-revolutionary policies." From January,
1941, onward, the Nationalist-Communist wartime "collaboration"
progressively weakened.

Publicly Chiang maintained that civil war between Nationalists
and Communists was a thing of the past. As late as September,
1943, addressing the Kuomintang Central Executive Committee, he
stated categorically: "I am of the opinion that first of all we should
clearly recognize that the Chinese Communist problem is a purely
political problem and should be solved by political means." But
he was clearly preparing for a military resolution of the problem.
And the Communists were well aware of his intent.

In 1944 China reaped the fruits of internal discord. By February
of that year, five hundred thousand Nationalist troops faced the
Chinese Communists in Northwest China. General Stilwell con-
sidered it unlikely that the two Chinese antagonists would come
to blows before the end of the war with Japan, but he once again
reminded the United States Chief of Staff, General George C.
Marshall, that the factional quarrel was hindering the war effort.
The danger of the situation was evidenced by the query of the
Nationalist Chief of Ordnance, General Yü Ta-wei, whether the
American Lend-Lease arms might be employed against the Com-

munists. "[United States General] Hearn was understood . . . to
have replied that the Chinese could not successfully explain such
an action to the people of the United States." [4]

The Japanese had long been inactive in the China theater, thus
permitting the Chinese to indulge in domestic politics as usual—a
development doubtless taken into account by Japanese strategists.
But Japan was now being hit by American air raids from Chinese
bases. General Chennault had contended that if the United States
concentrated on building up his 14th Air Force, he would bring
Japan to its knees even without the aid of other armed forces.
Stilwell had contended that the plan could be no stronger than the
ground forces available to defend the air fields. Chiang Kai-shek
and his lobbyists in Washington had sided with Chennault.

The Japanese proved Stilwell right. In April, 1944, they launched
Operation Ichi-Go, a vast sweep by sixteen divisions through Central and East China. They were opposed by at least three or four
times as many Nationalist troops. But Chiang had rejected, for
political reasons, the reorganization of his army that Stilwell had
proposed. The Nationalist forces, despite their overwhelming nu-
merical superiority, were easily scattered by the Japanese attackers.
Only at Hengyang, in southern Hunan, did they stage a good fight.
There General Hsueh Yueh, not of Chiang's "household," held out
for forty days against heavy odds—with Chungking refusing support. More significant still was what had happened in Honan
Province: when the Japanese struck, the long-suffering Chinese
population rose up and helped butcher the demoralized Nationalist
troops.

The East China airfields, constructed with so much backbreaking
labor, and at considerable American expense, were overrun by
the enemy. As the Americans abandoned them, one by one, they
blew up the expensive equipment and valuable stores brought in,
ton by ton, by American planes over "The Hump" of the eastern
spur of the Himalayas. By mid-September, 1944, Operation Ichi-Go
had achieved its objectives. But Stilwell won no credit with the
Generalissimo for being right.

The Roosevelt Administration, at the inception of the Sino-
American war alliance, had been more than willing to take the
National Government at its own evaluation. But the Nationalists'
stubborn refusal to engage the Japanese enemy, their endeavor to
milk the United States of vast sums, and Chungking's continued

preoccupation with domestic politics had disillusioned Washington. The Department of the Army's official war history described the shift:

After the conferences at Cairo and Tehran in December 1943, President Roosevelt's attitude toward China changed greatly. The Generalissimo's conduct at Cairo, the Soviet promise to enter the war against Japan, the Generalissimo's linking his request for a loan of $1,000,000,000 with the cancellation of the Andamans operation (BUCCANEER), Chinese insistence on making the Americans literally pay to fight in China, the contrast between Stilwell's defeating the Japanese *18th Division* with three Chinese divisions and the Generalissimo's reluctance to engage the weakened *56th* [Japanese Division] with twelve Chinese divisions, all played their part in the President's appraisal of Chiang Kai-shek as a soldier and as a statesman. The President's messages to the Generalissimo grew steadily harsher in tone, culminating in a threat to cut off lend-lease if the Generalissimo continued his refusal to attempt to break the blockade of China.[5]

The Nationalist debacle in the summer of 1944, and Chiang Kai-shek's subsequent threat to withdraw the Nationalist expeditionary force that had been committed to operations in North Burma, crystallized the American reappraisal. President Roosevelt in early July proposed that Stilwell, hamstrung as Chiang Kai-shek's Joint Chief of Staff, should be made Field Commander of the Chinese Army. In a message delivered to Chiang on September 19, the President applied heavy pressure:

I have urged time and again in recent months that you take drastic action to resist the disaster which has been moving closer to China and to you. Now, when you have not yet placed General Stilwell in command of all forces in China, we are faced with the loss of a critical area in east China with possible catastrophic consequences. . . .
Even though we are rolling the enemy back in defeat all over the world this will not help the situation in China for a considerable time. . . . Only drastic and immediate action on your part alone can be in time to preserve the fruits of your long years of struggle and the efforts we have been able to make to support you. Otherwise political and military considerations alike are going to be swallowed in military disaster.[6]

The President's recommendation was strong:

I am certain that the only thing you can now do in an attempt to prevent the Jap from achieving his objectives in China is to reinforce your Salween armies immediately and press their offensive, while at once placing General Stilwell in unrestricted command of all your forces.

The Generalissimo had previously expressed willingness for Stilwell to be appointed commander of the Chinese armed forces, but he undoubtedly thought of any such assignment as purely nominal and never intended to relinquish his own supreme authority. He was now greatly angered—and, since his wrath could not reach the American President, it was directed at Stilwell. Underlying his anger was the knowledge that the Americans at this critical juncture thought to equip and use Communist forces against the Japanese.

There were personality factors involved. Stilwell knew China and the Chinese well, but he was not one who suffered military malingering gladly, and the frustrations he experienced in his efforts to get Chiang's forces to take the field against the common enemy wore his patience thin. And the Generalissimo, who never brooked opposition to his political scheming from his entourage, wanted none from a foreigner who, as he well knew, had been only a colonel a short time before.

Through his two brothers-in-law, H. H. Kung in Washington and T. V. Soong in Chungking, who worked respectively on Harry Hopkins and General Patrick J. Hurley, Chiang Kai-shek maneuvered to make it appear that Stilwell's recall was essential for the good of Sino-American relations.[7] In a message of October 18, President Roosevelt acceded to Chiang's request for the recall. Chiang had obtained vengeance for his wounded *amour propre*.

In his message Chiang had proposed a "replacement" for Stilwell, but here Roosevelt refused satisfaction, saying: "I do not feel that an American should in the present situation assume responsibility in a command position for the operations of Chinese forces in China." He added that the China-Burma-India Theater would now be separated into two war theaters "so far as American interests are concerned"—the China Theater and the India-Burma Theater. He stated that he would make Lieutenant General Albert C. Wedemeyer available to serve as Chiang's Chief of Staff, if acceptable, and would then also make Wedemeyer Commander of United States Forces in the China Theater. The Department of the Army's official war history summed up:

With receipt of the President's message in Chungking, the Generalissimo's victory was an accomplished fact, though not of the dimensions at which he and his advisers had aimed. Stilwell was now on orders to return to the United States, but there was no American to take the responsibility for whatever might happen in China. In retrospect, the Generalissimo's triumph acquires an aspect it probably did not wear at the time. It was the last diplomatic victory he was to win for many years.[8]

Pyrrhus' victory in the battle of Asculum was far less costly than Chiang Kai-shek's in Washington, which lost him the opportunity to have the Nationalist Army remade at American expense into an effective, modern fighting machine.

The war was developing favorably for the United Nations in both Europe and the Pacific, with the USSR committed to attack Japan after the European phase was over. China's aid was clearly not required for allied victory, even in the Pacific. Japan had suffered heavily in the Pacific theater in 1944 and was weakening. Pressures on the Nationalists to take the field against the Japanese were relaxed. The United States turned to the obviously pressing task of patching up Kuomintang-Communist relations, to the end that renewed Chinese civil war should be avoided and a strong and united China be ready to replace a defeated Japan in the East Asian balance of power.

This effort had already begun. Chiang Kai-shek had informed Vice President Wallace, during the latter's visit to Chungking in June, 1944, that he would be happy to have President Roosevelt's assistance in settling the Communist problem; the President had accordingly assigned Major General Patrick J. Hurley to Chungking as his personal representative to the Generalissimo.

Hurley arrived in Chungking in September, 1944, charged with two mediation assignments: to restore harmony in the already ragged relations between Stilwell and the Generalissimo, and, in Hurley's own words, "to unify all the military forces in China for the purpose of defeating Japan." In the case of Stilwell, he had accepted T. V. Soong's position that the Stilwell-Chiang breach was irreparable and that Stilwell should be replaced. In December, 1944, when Ambassador Clarence E. Gauss resigned shortly after Stilwell's departure, Hurley became American Ambassador to China. His second task remained to be accomplished.

In the fateful September of that year, the Communists had proposed to the People's Political Council at Chungking that the Kuomintang one-party dictatorship be immediately terminated and a democratic coalition government established. The official American record noted the subsequent course of events:

General Hurley reported in December 1944 that with the consent, advice and direction of the Generalissimo and members of his Cabinet and on the invitation of leaders of the Communist Party, he had begun discussions with the Communist Party and Communist military leaders for the purpose of effecting an agreement to regroup, coordinate and unite the military forces of China for the defeat of Japan. He continued: "The defeat of Japan is, of course, the primary objective, but we should all understand that if an agreement is not reached between the two great military establishments of China, civil war will in all probability ensue." [9]

Hurley at the same time credited Chiang Kai-shek with a political attitude that possibly reflected recent chastening:

He [Chiang] now feels that he can reach a settlement with the Communist Party without foreign entanglements. When I first arrived, it was thought that civil war after the close of the present war or perhaps before that time was inevitable. Chiang Kai-shek is now convinced that by agreement with the Communist Party of China he can (1) unite the military forces of China against Japan, and (2) avoid civil strife in China.

Here the reputed conviction of Chiang Kai-shek, the wishes of the United States Government, and the aspirations of the Chinese nation converged. But the country's intelligentsia and liberal politicians alike were becoming increasingly convinced that a peaceful solution of China's domestic problems depended primarily upon two related actions: termination of the Kuomintang "period of tutelage" and the granting of legal status to other political parties with simultaneous introduction of representative multi-party government. Finally, after so many years of civil and foreign wars, there was a prevailing desire that there should be promptly undertaken, after the war, the long-promised national reconstruction through industrial development and the fundamental rehabilitation of agriculture.

The crux of the problem was distribution of domestic power. The Kuomintang's one-party dictatorship had its sanction in an attendant obligation to convey "political tutelage" to the nation so that representative government could be instituted; in actuality, there had been no training of the people in the practice, functions, or theory of representative government. The Kuomintang was now dominated by its right wing, epitomized by the C-C Clique; its prime concern was the amplification and consolidation, not the curtailment, of its authority. Yet, the Kuomintang itself had decreed in June, 1929, that the period of tutelage (that is, the one-party dictatorship) should end in 1935.

The Chinese Communist Party was Revolution embodied. Its own ambition was disclosed in the Constitution of the Soviet Republic of November, 1931, establishing "a state based on the democratic dictatorship of the workers and peasants." Speaking in January, 1940, "On the New Democracy," Mao Tse-tung purported that the Communists intended to establish "a new democratic republic," based still upon a bourgeois-democratic revolution, as their first step. But Mao at that time spoke with acute comprehension of the lessons learned during the Communists' Kiangsi experience, and within the context of a working "united front" with the Kuomintang, entered into for temporary, wartime purposes. In his same exposition, he stated that it was "inevitable that this [bourgeois-democratic] revolution [would] become a part of the proletarian-socialist world revolution," and that the second step of the Chinese revolution was to go forward toward a socialist society.

The two political parties, respectively ultraconservative and ultraradical, were natural antagonists. Only foreign aggression had succeeded in bringing them together again—and their coalition had fallen far short of amalgamation or even cooperation. The persistence of the underlying antagonism, and the resulting interference with China's war effort, had defied the best efforts of American military and political representatives since the beginning of the war in the Pacific.

YALTA; WAR'S END

More than Chinese domestic problems loomed up for postwar consideration. Wartime alliances of incompatible states always have a way of breaking up when the emergency touching national survival has passed, and the American-Soviet alliance, even as the Kuomintang-Communist coalition, bore full promise of following that pattern. The United States was politically conservative, the staunch supporter of international legitimacy and the *status quo,* while the Soviet Union represented Revolution. This difference would not by itself suffice to bring conflict between the two; but the convergence of their political interests in the West Pacific made a collision almost certain. The United States, borne forward by the momentum of its war effort, had projected its influence into the heart of China. The Soviet Union, when relieved of the demands of the European war theater upon its immediate attention and energies, would naturally resume the historic Russian march to the East—if the way was open.

The Yalta Pact of February, 1945, setting forth the conditions under which the Soviet Union would enter the war against Japan, sowed extra seeds of conflict in the Far East, for a harvest to be reaped after the war was won. In accordance with the doctrine of visiting vengeance upon the defeated enemy even for the misdeeds of his ancestors, the Pact provided for the restoration of "the former rights of Russia violated by the treacherous attack of Japan in 1904," and more. After extended negotiations at Moscow by T. V. Soong, with the United States giving an occasional nudge from the side, the National Government assented to the provisions of the Yalta Pact in the Sino-Soviet treaty of August 14, 1945.

By the authority of those two international acts, the Soviet Union obtained: (1) Karafuto (the southern half of Sakhalin Island); (2) the Kurile Islands; (3) recognition of unspecified Soviet "pre-eminent interests" in the commercial port of Dairen and resur-rection of the Russian lease of Port Arthur as a naval base; and (4) establishment of joint Soviet-Chinese control over the Chinese Eastern and South Manchurian Railways.

In their zeal to get the military bargain they sought, the Amer-ican negotiators of the Yalta Pact overlooked some cogent historical facts. For one thing, in the Russo-Japanese War of 1904–5 Wash-ington's sympathies had been openly on the side of Japan; and the Portsmouth Peace Conference, which brought Japan such gains as southern Sakhalin and transfer of the lease to China's Liaotung Peninsula, was held under American auspices. President Theodore Roosevelt had personally exercised his good offices to get both sides to accept the peace treaty in its final form. In short, the United States was in an important sense an accessory to the 1905 Treaty of Portsmouth.

Moreover, the Soviet Government's 1919 and 1920 renunciations of Tsarist rights and interests in China had been defined and formalized by the Sino-Soviet agreement of May 31, 1924, thus implicitly adding another denial of the existence of any Soviet claim to either the Liaotung Peninsula in its entirety or Port Arthur in particular. The Tsarist lease of Port Arthur as a naval base, even had it been left undisturbed by the Treaty of Portsmouth, would have expired in 1923.

As for the Chinese Eastern Railway, in which the Soviet Union enjoyed joint managerial rights for a limited period of years under the same 1924 treaty, Moscow had *sold* its rights in that railway to Japan in 1935. The South Manchurian Railway, for its part, was a mammoth enterprise embracing many subsidiary parts. It was by 1945 mainly a Japanese creation, built around the trunk line ceded by Russia in 1905. And the Japanese title to the Kurile island chain had been confirmed in a political trade between Japan and Russia in 1875, when the two expanding powers adjusted their common frontiers in the West Pacific.

Seldom in modern times has political horse-trading been based on such scanty rationale—or, one might add, undertaken with less regard for possible long-term consequences. Not only did the United States ride roughshod over Chinese interests; it neglected its own.

The secret Yalta agreement regarding the Far East was drafted by President Roosevelt and Stalin. Prime Minister Churchill signed for the British Government but later recorded a particular qualification:

I must make it clear that though on behalf of Great Britain I joined in the agreement, neither I nor Eden took any part in making it. It was regarded as an American affair and was certainly of prime interest to their military operations. It was not for us to claim to shape it. Anyhow we were not consulted but only asked to approve. This we did.[10]

The official American version states, with regard to Yalta, that "at no point did President Roosevelt consider that he was compromising vital Chinese interests." [11] Nevertheless, however pure its motives, the United States Government had in fact proposed, and pressured the Chinese Government to accept, cession to the Soviet Union of various "rights" that had already passed out of existence. One of the world's foremost champions of "legitimacy" this time chose the way of political expediency, manufacturing "rights" to serve as a *quid pro quo* for Soviet entry into the war in the Pacific.

The question of whether it was necessary, or desirable, to offer Stalin a high price in February, 1945, for Soviet participation in the Pacific war after Germany had been defeated is now academic. It is proper to observe, however, that the rationalization offered for the trade was poor in logic and that American computations should have included long-term postwar factors as well as immediate military requirements. Manchuria's historic role—in the Sino-Japanese War of 1894-95, the Russo-Japanese War of 1904-5, the Japanese Twenty-one Demands of 1915, the Siberian intervention of 1918-22, and the Japanese drive for empire in 1931-45—should have alerted statesmen to the Yalta agreement's potentialities as a source of trouble in the period of fundamental readjustment that would inevitably follow the war. For the United States, as a sea power with major interests in the West Pacific, to aid the Soviet Union in extending its sovereignty over southern Sakhalin and the Kuriles could only reflect a disastrous underestimation of Japan's strategic importance and a calamitous refusal to abandon the wartime make-believe that Nationalist China could and would assume the postwar responsibilities of a great power.

Certain American misjudgments of Asian developments began to drive their roots deeper as the war neared its end. Ambassador Hurley had been informed in Moscow by Soviet Foreign Minister Vyacheslav M. Molotov in September, 1944, that "the so-called Chinese Communists are not in fact Communists at all." On April 15, 1945, after the Yalta Pact was signed, Hurley passed through Moscow again, and this time met with both Molotov and Marshal Stalin. He gave the two Soviet leaders his analysis of the situation in China (having been there a total of seven months), generously adding an exposition of American policy toward China.

Hurley received Stalin's assurance of support for the American policy, which, as expounded by Hurley, in essence comprised "the policy of endorsement of Chinese aspirations to establish for herself a united, free, and democratic government and for the unification of all armed forces in China in order to bring about the defeat of Japan." [12] Stalin was then still waiting for the Chungking Government's signature on a treaty confirming the Yalta Pact's provisions regarding China and could hardly have failed to endorse the policy as described. Stalin went further and "spoke favorably of Chiang Kai-shek." Hurley was clearly impressed.

It would be fruitless speculation to try to penetrate the shadows surrounding the dead Soviet leader, to plumb his intent and his hidden meanings. Stalin's reputation for Oriental craftiness nevertheless was such that any horse-trading Yankee who accepted his statements at face value, without a collateral appraisal, would surely have been guilty of the utmost naiveté. The American Embassy at Moscow, after Hurley reported so optimistically to the State Department on his April 15 conversation with Stalin, in fact felt it necessary to add its own analysis of that same conversation, in a message that ended with a warning:

It would be tragic if our natural anxiety for the support of the Soviet Union at this juncture, coupled with Stalin's use of words which mean all things to all people and his cautious affability, were to lead us into an undue reliance on Soviet aid or even Soviet acquiescence in the achievement of our long term objectives in China. [13]

The Moscow Embassy was closer to the mark. In all logic, it had to be inferred that the Stalin-Molotov generalities were qualified by certain specific corollaries, such as the prerequisite of a reformed and friendly China. The National Government had seized upon the opportunity to lever Soviet influence unceremoniously out of Sinkiang in 1942; that the Soviets had remembered was indicated by their rejection, in 1943, of Sino-American efforts to arrange for the transshipment of American war supplies to China via the Soviet Union and Sinkiang. A victorious Soviet Union was unlikely to entertain willingly, in the postwar period, fresh Chinese Nationalist hostility toward Soviet interests. Stalin had only told Hurley, in their April interview, that the Soviet Union had in times past befriended Chiang Kai-shek. He did not inform the American envoy how Chiang had repaid the Soviet Union or what would be expected of the Nationalists if they desired Soviet friendship again.

That information was better obtained from current articles in Soviet periodicals, as from one that was published the very day of Hurley's interview with Stalin. After calling attention to the forces in China opposing democratization of the political regime, the writer said: "One thing is clear: unless urgent measures for the democratization of the political life of the country and the creation of national unity are carried out, China cannot occupy the place in the comity of democratic nations that she ought." [14]

It was, moreover, noteworthy that the Chinese Communists had adopted no pose of being simple patriots concerned only with war and agriculture and not with the national future. Even in their propaganda, the Communists did not pretend that they were mere "agrarian democrats," as asserted by Chiang Kai-shek in his meeting of June, 1944, with Vice President Wallace. Mao Tse-tung spoke in an established pattern when, addressing the Seventh Communist Party Congress at Yenan on April 24, 1945, on the subject "Coalition Government," he explicitly dealt with the question of Communist orientation:

We Communists never conceal or disguise our political aims. Our future, or ultimate, program is to advance China into the realm of socialism and communism; this has been settled and cannot be doubted. The very name of our party and our Marxian world outlook definitely points to this boundlessly bright direction of our highest idea.[15]

Mao Tse-tung had made his position clear long before. Replying to an American journalist's question in September, 1939, as to whether the Communists had become "mere reformists," as asserted by some, or were still "anti-imperialist and antifeudal," Mao had answered: "We are always social revolutionaries; we are never reformists." [16]

Nor did Communist Chairman Mao, in opting for coalition government, quite veil the Communist estimate of the situation. At the time he spoke, the Communist Shensi-Kansu-Ningsia Border Region was flanked by the Japanese to the north and east and by Nationalist forces on the south. Mao probably expressed a real apprehension when he said that renewed civil war would "drag China to her former dependent, unfree, undemocratic, disunited, poor, and weak state." All objective circumstances seemed to indicate that, given Nationalist troop strength and armament, *and* massive American aid, the way of civil war would be hard, bitter, and long.

Mao Tse-tung described an ideal alternative course: "to unite the entire nation, to abolish the dictatorship, to effect democratic reform, to consolidate and expand the anti-Japanese forces, to beat the Japanese aggressors completely, and to build up a new, independent, free, democratic, united, and prosperous China." [17]

There was no doubt as to which of the two alternatives was desired by the Chinese nation in the spring of 1945, as the war in Europe neared its end and victory over Japan came into sight. Mao was cleverly appealing to the deepest desires of the people, who, like the war-weary Russians in 1917, wanted peace above all else. But that did not mean that Mao assumed a peaceful solution was assured.

The Communist concept of coalition government obviously provided no place for either the existing Kuomintang one-party "tutelage" system or Chiang Kai-shek's personal dictatorship. On the other hand, there was no place provided for the Communist Party in the Kuomintang monopoly of government. Both adversaries possessed strong armies, this fact giving grave emphasis to the well-defined polarization of forces in China.

The balance of political power, the sanction to determine the final outcome, lay with the Chinese people—with the academicians, students, and writers, who shaped opinion; with the petty bourgeoisie and the peasants, who bore proportionately the heaviest burden of taxes; and with the minor officials of the country's vast bureaucracy. In April, 1945, the issue was still open. Mao reported the political deadlock to his Party's Seventh Congress: there had been negotiations, but "all our proposals were rejected by the

Kuomintang government, which was unwilling not only to end the one-party rule and to set up a coalition government, but also to effect any urgently needed democratic reform."

Mao Tse-tung was not one to foster illusions among his followers. He warned that, "after the realization of international peace, the struggles between the anti-fascist masses and remnant fascist forces, between democratic and anti-democratic forces, will go on in most parts of the world," and he defined the Party's short-term tasks:

All Chinese Communists and all who sympathise with the ideas of Communism must struggle to achieve the objective of the present stage; they must struggle against foreign and feudal oppression and for the deliverance of the Chinese people from their tragic fate of colonialism, semi-colonialism and semi-feudalism, and for the establishment of a new-democratic China under proletarian leadership and with the liberation of the peasantry as its main task, i.e. a China of the revolutionary Three People's Principles of Dr. Sun Yat-sen, a China independent and free, democratic and united, prosperous and powerful.[18]

There should have been no doubt, by that time, of the Chinese Communists' revolutionary aims. And the Nationalists and Communists alike, in the light of the sanguinary prewar civil strife and their wartime conflicts, were, in fact, free of major illusions about each other. Some Americans may have been poorly informed and wide of the mark in their estimates of the significance of Chinese political developments; Chiang Kai-shek and Mao Tse-tung were not.

Hurley had been energetically pursuing mediation efforts since arriving in China the preceding September but had thus far failed to bring the Government and the Communists together. Since the pressures of eight years of war had failed to weld the contending factions into a durable agreement, the long-awaited advent of peace was almost certain to find China still divided domestically. Articles and speeches emitted on the July 7 anniversary of the beginning of the war expressed old hopes, but a chilling sense of realities made itself felt in the conventional texts.

On August 6 and 9, respectively, the United States dropped A-bombs on Hiroshima and Nagasaki; the Soviet Union entered the war in the Pacific on August 8. Hostilities ended on August 14. The victory against Japan had been won by an alien deus ex machina as Chiang Kai-shek had anticipated from the first.

That was the day that the Sino-Soviet agreements incorporating the Yalta Pact's basic provisions respecting China were signed.

National Government circles, surprisingly enough, were evidently not displeased with the over-all arrangements. The Nationalist chieftains apparently felt that China's somewhat battered relations with the USSR had been rehabilitated, albeit for a price; and, moreover, that the Soviet Union had been debarred from infringement upon China's territorial sovereignty in Manchuria (occupied by Soviet troops in action against the Japanese) and Sinkiang (where a Turki rebellion against Chinese rule had begun in 1944). Chungking seems further to have believed that Moscow had been estopped from rendering aid to the Chinese Communists; and the Nationalists would actually be found implying, in their propaganda, that the Soviet Union had committed itself to siding with the Nationalists *against* the Communists in the postwar period. Any such interpretation required a misreading of the August 14 treaty of alliance. Nationalist judgments at the end of the war were, in any event, strongly influenced by the anticipation of continued American aid. Chungking entered the postwar period, therefore, with an essentially mistaken reading of the demands of the hour in China.

8 KUOMINTANG-COMMUNIST STRUGGLE: FINAL STAGE

W HEN the Second World War ended, the challenges confronting the National Government loomed large. There were some two million Japanese military and civilians to be repatriated, with Japanese governmental, industrial, commercial, and personal property in China to be taken into custody and preserved for an international accounting. The United States and Britain had relinquished their extraterritorial rights in China during the war, thus creating new problems for Chinese law and administration. The capital had to be moved back from Chungking to Nanking, which the government had left seven years before. Manchuria, lost fourteen years earlier, beckoned to the resources and energies of the Chinese governmental apparatus. A new administration had to be set up for Formosa, ruled by Japan since 1895. After thirty years of internal disorders and eight years of international war, the problem of national economic reconstruction was still waiting to be solved. And finally, there was the task of settling differences with the Communists, who had contended for power with the Kuomintang since 1924, when the two parties started out together in Canton to carve out their political fortunes.

V-J DAY: MILITARY AND POLITICAL FORCES

As far as relations with the Communists were concerned, there could be no return to the *status quo ante bellum*. In April, 1945, Mao Tse-tung had put both the Nationalists and foreign countries on notice that the Communists would not accept a continuation of the Kuomintang's one-party dictatorship. Their proposal was for "coalition government."

The Communists had put very little sugar-coating on their basic proposals for political reorganization. They were patently ready to consider coalition government because they believed that such a solution of the country's political conflict, and the political opportunities deriving from it, would further their own cause. Mao Tse-tung's proposal that the Kuomintang Government be transformed into a coalition regime therefore may well have reflected a real initial Communist willingness to reach a political settlement, to see if it were possible to achieve a more broadly based government instead of resuming the civil war.

The Communists had experienced no change of heart or theory. The rationale for their proposal was entirely practical. China's articulate middle group, whose shift of allegiance to one side or the other could prove of critical importance in the period immediately ahead, was weary of war and would oppose any political party that even *gave the appearance* of being warlike. The Democratic League, a combination of middle-of-the-road parties, strongly supported the Communist proposal for a coalition government. The Communists consequently had nothing to lose by opening with this gambit. They could exploit a double advantage in standing for a peaceful settlement of China's domestic dispute. If such settlement were attained, they would have gone a long way toward their goal by political means; if their proposal was rejected, they still stood to gain valuable popular support by playing the role of supporters of the peace arrayed against a war party.

Evidently, if China chose civil war for the solution of its postwar problems, the Government party would still have a hard road to travel. Mao Tse-tung in his opening address to the April Party Congress had sketched the Communist strength: a Communist Party of 1,210,000 members, (Communist) Liberated Areas with a population of 95,500,000, and an army of 910,000 regulars and 2,200,000 militia.

Compared to some 80,000 Red troops commanded by Mao Tse-tung, Chu Teh, P'eng Teh-huai, Ho Lung, Hsu Hsiang-ch'ien and others in 1936, the new figures reflected a substantial increase in Communist strength. True, the Nationalists and their American allies had a lower estimate of Communist strength (as we shall see below). Tests on the field of battle, however, later demonstrated that the Nationalists, in particular, had overestimated their own powers—and underestimated those of the enemy.

The official Communist organ at Chungking, the *Hsin Hua Jih Pao* (New China Daily News), set forth Communist troop strength by areas:

Area	Regular Army	Militia
North China	470,286	1,615,000
Central China	343,982	580,000
South China	20,730	5,000
Shensi-Kansu-Ningsia	80,540	
Total	915,538	2,200,000

The Communists had effectively exploited the Sino-Japanese War for the build-up and toughening of their military forces and expansion of their political influence. And, during the eight years of war, they had won a potentially decisive contest: they had identified themselves with anti-imperialism, the chief wartime drive of the people. The momentum of this drive remained. If China's civil strife were resumed, the Communists would be found psychologically well equipped for it.

From a strictly military viewpoint the Nationalists enjoyed marked initial advantages. According to an official American estimate, the National Government at the time of Japan's formal surrender in September "possessed an estimated five to one superiority in combat troops and in rifles, a practical monopoly of heavy equipment and transport, and an unopposed air arm." [1] The American figures (almost certainly derived from Nationalist sources) credited the Communists with only 600,000 regulars and 400,000 militia and the Government with 3,000,000 combat troops. This estimate probably overrated the Nationalist combat forces. Moreover, the Nationalist Army's command was still riddled with the Generalissimo's political favorites and subject as always to his inveterate habit of interference in field operations. If the Nationalists started with certain advantages, the Communists could count some of their own —even on the Nationalist side. Nevertheless, in rough terms, the American estimate reflected the disparity between Nationalist and Communist military strengths, particularly the clear Nationalist predominance in heavy arms.

Another advantage probably weighed even heavier in Generalissimo Chiang Kai-shek's calculations. On August 10 the War Department at Washington instructed General Wedemeyer, as Commander of United States Forces in the China Theater (and still Chiang Kai-shek's Chief of Staff), to continue aid to the National Government, so that it could accept the Japanese surrender and reoccupy all areas held by Japanese troops in China. The order bore a qualifying injunction: there should be no infringement of the basic principle that the United States Government would not support the National Government in a civil war. The order carried an implicit contradiction. As subsequent events demonstrated, American association with and aid to the National Government in military affairs inevitably meant involvement in the Chinese civil war.

The first report of Japanese readiness to surrender came on August 10. Two clashing military orders were issued in China the following day. Generalissimo Chiang, from his headquarters in Chungking, instructed Communist Commander-in-Chief Chu Teh that the Communist forces should maintain their existing positions, refrain from accepting Japanese surrenders, and await orders. From Yenan, Chu Teh ordered that "all anti-Japanese forces of the various Liberated Areas" should accept the enemy's surrender in their vicinity, take over enemy arms, and occupy and administer towns and communications previously held by both Japanese and "puppet" troops.

The unresolved Chinese domestic issue thus gave rise to an open clash of wills on the very eve of peace. The Communists unhesitatingly took up the challenge. On August 13, 1945, the Yenan party organ, the *Chieh Fang Jih Pao* (Liberation Daily), editorially defined "The Urgent Present Task" in language that was only thinly veiled. It was in effect a call to arms, beginning: "At this turning point in history, our Chinese people should clearly recognize that the urgent present task is firmly and undeviatingly to press on to the objective of their own liberation." This statement was technically qualified by a reference to the large number of Japanese troops awaiting disarmament, but even the qualification was given an unusual twist by a summons for enlistments in the Communist armed forces and by the admonition that, for the military tasks ahead, old guerrilla tactics should be abandoned in favor of troop concentration, with unified command in the higher echelon. The editorial emphasized the following point especially: "From the countryside to the towns, from guerrilla warfare to mobile warfare —this is the shift anticipated in our [Communist] Party's Seventh Congress. With the sudden change in this situation, this must now quickly be realized." The *Chieh Fang Jih Pao* was obviously talking about something other than the Sino-Japanese War.

The editorial exhorted the newspaper's readers to study the changed line and thus indicated its official nature. That "line" proposed that, since a national democratic coalition government had not yet been established, the army and people of the Liberated Areas bore the responsibility for "liberating" places occupied by the enemy. "Bravely advance," enjoined the editorial, "thoroughly to wipe out the Japanese aggressors!" The trained reader could appreciate that the Communist-Kuomintang issue was again being joined and that radical new developments were impending.

An open break was temporarily averted by a fresh exchange of messages. On August 14 Chiang Kai-shek invited Mao Tse-tung to visit Chungking for a joint discussion of "state affairs." Mao replied most briefly on the sixteenth, stating only that Chu Teh was "setting forth the ideas of our side" in a message of the same date and that, "after you have indicated your ideas, I will consider the question of meeting you."

Chu Teh's telegram of August 16 was long and detailed, and blunt to a degree that any Chinese would recognize as calculated rudeness. It surveyed the course of the Sino-Japanese War, compared Communist achievements with the Nationalist record on the battlefield, and charged that "your government and troops have heretofore adopted a policy of looking on with hands in sleeves, sitting to await victory, preserving strength, preparing for civil war." Commander in Chief Chu said that the Communists were "exceptionally dissatisfied" with wartime developments, including the rejection by Chiang and his government of all moves to establish a democratic coalition government: he warned that "the danger of civil war is unprecedently grave" and laid down six defiant "demands." In sum, Chu Teh demanded full Communist participation in postwar political and military arrangements, including those for disarming the Japanese and for administration of recovered areas.

The final demand reflected the tone of Chu's message and pointed up the major issues outstanding between the Kuomintang and Communist factions:

It is requested that you at once discard one-party government and call a conference of all parties, establish a democratic coalition government, discharge grafting officers and corrupt officials and all reactionary elements, punish traitors, discard special-service [secret police] organs, recognize the position of all parties and all groups (the Chinese Communist Party and all democratic parties have, up to the present, been considered illegal by your government), abolish all reactionary laws and regulations oppressive of the people's freedom, recognize the popularly-elected governments and anti-Japanese forces of the Liberated Areas, withdraw the troops surrounding the Liberated Areas, release political prisoners, effect economic reforms and all other kinds of democratic reforms.[2]

At the end of his message Chu Teh categorically rejected Chiang Kai-shek's order of August 11. There was left no doubt that the Communists had no intention of backing down. (With the publication in 1960 of the fourth volume of Mao Tse-tung's *Selected Works*, it was disclosed that the telegram bearing Chu Teh's signature had been written by Mao Tse-tung himself.)

An important event occurred the day after Japan's surrender on August 14: General Douglas MacArthur, as Supreme Commander of the Allied Powers (SCAP) in the Pacific, issued his General Order No. 1, which, among other things, designated Generalissimo Chiang Kai-shek as the agency for accepting the Japanese surrender in China (excluding Manchuria), Formosa, and Indo-China north of the 16th parallel. The order gave *prima facie* support to the National Government's claim to be the sole legitimate agency in China, and it must be presumed to have influenced the next moves in the internecine struggle.

Chiang now sent Mao a telegram couched in conciliatory terms. He said that Chu Teh's telegram had apparently been phrased without full understanding of the arrangements for Japanese surrender. The procedure, he said, had been fixed by the allied army headquarters for all military theaters, and all were bound to act accordingly. He ended his message by urgently, and this time warmly, repeating his previous invitation. After another exchange, Chiang invited Mao a third time; and it was conveyed to Mao that his safety in Chungking would be guaranteed. On August 24, in a telegram strikingly different in phraseology from Chu Teh's message of August 16, Chairman Mao accepted.

On August 27, Nationalist General Chang Chih-chung and Ambassador Hurley left by plane for Yenan. Upon departing, Hurley said: "In going now to Yenan, I have received the agreement and full approval of Chairman Chiang [Kai-shek] and respond to the invitation of Chinese Communist Party Chairman Mao Tse-tung." The next day he escorted Mao Tse-tung and his colleagues to Chungking.

In his statement of April, 1945, "On Coalition Government," Mao Tse-tung had warned the British and American Governments in particular "to pay serious attention to the voice of the overwhelming majority of the Chinese people, so that their foreign policy may not go against the will of the Chinese people." On the day of the Hurley party's return to Chungking, the Communist organ *Hsin Hua Jih Pao* carried an editorial on "Postwar China and the United States." Warning that the time was past for supporting, anywhere, reactionary antidemocratic regimes hated by a nation's people, it said:

A strong democratic China is essential to guarantee peace, prevent the renaissance of Japanese fascist aggression, and for the happiness and prosperity of all countries on the shores of the Pacific Ocean. If China is permitted to remain in a condition of poverty, disorder, and nondemocracy, this will not only be a disaster for the Chinese people but doubtless will be unfortunate for the whole Far East and even the world. . . . We believe, thinking of the American people's interest, that the time has come when they should seriously consider this common truth.

The Communist reaction to the Sino-Soviet agreements of August 14 was revealing. The actual texts of those agreements were not made public until August 27, but on August 17 the Communist organ at Chungking led off with an editorial, declaring that only by an alliance of the two nations could the safety of the Pacific area be guaranteed and only thus would it be possible to prevent the recurrence of Japanese fascist aggression. It further contended that this international consolidation was closely related to domestic democracy. Thus:

The clock of history sounds, the world has set off on a new track, the people's era has come. . . . The world tide of democracy is not to be resisted, the War of Resistance against Japanese fascist aggression has been victorious, but the struggle for thorough obliteration of the last vestiges of fascism is still not ended. The achievement of the Sino-Soviet Treaty of Friendship and Alliance is a victory for the will of the Chinese people. In a great era still to come, this great victory will necessarily have strengthened the confidence of the Chinese people to seize freedom and democracy.

Communist ardor did not cool when the actual texts of the August 14 agreements finally became available. In a fresh editorial *Hsin Hua Jih Pao* held that these agreements settled many outstanding Sino-Soviet problems, strengthened traditional Sino-Soviet friendship, fixed a pillar of peace for the Far East, and shattered anti-Soviet and anti-Communist plots of "Japanese robbers, Chinese traitors, and remnant fascist bastards"; and concluded: "Dawn is heralded for the dark continent of Asia."

The Nationalist-Communist negotiations at Chungking thus began with both sides bracing for civil contest. The United States, because of its wartime military relationship and Hurley's efforts at mediation, was deeply involved.

In due course, Hurley announced a measure of success. Shortly before September 22, when he departed for the United States for consultation, he reported to Washington that the two sides had agreed on five points, the first being "that they will collaborate for the establishment of a democratic government in China for the reconstruction of China and the prevention of civil war." Further, it was agreed that both parties would support the doctrines of Sun Yat-sen and the leadership of Chiang Kai-shek as President of the Republic; and the Communists agreed that "they will recognize the Kuomintang as the dominant party in control of the government and will cooperate with that party during the period of transition from the present form of government to a democratic regime."

The accord had a bearing on some fundamental political issues. Ambassador Hurley noted, however, that agreement was still lacking on (1) the right claimed by the Communists to appoint Communist governors "or" (and?) mayors in certain provinces, and (2) the number of Communist troops to be included in the national peacetime army. The Communists had first held out for forty-eight Communist divisions in a national army of eighty to a hundred divisions, but they were preparing to consider the Government's counterproposal that they be allotted twenty. That gap appeared bridgeable. But in the background there loomed the thorny, potentially explosive issues of the disposition of existing military forces and American military aid to the National Government.

Chairman Mao Tse-tung, who was still in Chungking, in an interview with the Reuters correspondent expressed the Communist Party's agreement to over-all nationalization of the country's armed forces, provided that there was democratization of the State. The qualification was crucial, for China's government was still far from being democratized. Moreover, as the leaders talked at Chungking, elsewhere rapid troop movements were being directed toward seizure of the political power formerly exercised by the Japanese over "Occupied China."

THE GATHERING STORM, AND AMERICAN INVOLVEMENT

The main lines of postwar troop movements were northward and eastward. On V-J Day, the Communists controlled most of the North China countryside and had a strong head start over the

Nationalists in the race for towns. As a result of the War Department's order of August 10, however, United States armed forces in the China Theater quickly airlifted three Nationalist armies to key positions in North and East China and then provided ships for the northward movement by sea of large numbers of Nationalist troops. A total of 400,000–500,000 Nationalist troops were soon moved by American transport to new positions. In addition, 53,000 United States Marines landed in North China to occupy Peiping, Tientsin, the Kailan coal mines, and the Peiping-Shanhaikuan railway system.

American military aid was thus extensively utilized to hold political authority in trust for the Chungking Government, pending the arrival of Government forces. The initial Communist advantage of position was overcome. The United States maintained that it was "non-involved" in Chinese domestic affairs. Aid given exclusively to one side in a two-sided conflict, however, in practice results automatically in involvement. The Nationalists had a natural appreciation of the truism; so did the Communists.

The Soviet Red Army in occupation of Manchuria was also expected to wait upon the arrival of Nationalist military units and transfer political authority solely to Chungking's representatives. In addition, the Japanese forces in North China were ordered by SCAP to hold their positions and to surrender only to Nationalist authority. In various sectors, and particularly in Shantung and Shansi Provinces, Japanese units were later used in offensive operations against the Communists.

In early October the Communists accepted the Nationalist proposal that they should contribute a maximum of twenty divisions to the projected National Army. On October 11 the Nationalists issued a statement summarizing a Nationalist-Communist agreement of the day before, China's "Double Tenth" holiday. There was substantial agreement in principle, but major differences still persisted over such critical practical issues as the procedure for troop reorganization, the organization of government in the Communist-controlled Liberated Areas, and Communist participation in accepting Japanese troop surrenders. In short, there had been essentially no progress since Hurley's report of September 22.

The struggle for power was focused in the North. Nationalist political slogans heavily emphasized acquisition, without delay, of rich industrialized Manchuria: "China will survive or perish with the Northeast!" To take over and hold so valuable a piece of territory Chiang Kai-shek proposed to use nothing less than his elite forces that had been trained and equipped by the United States. On V-J Day those forces were mostly in Yunnan Province, Burma, and India, so there was a delay while the Nationalists waited for their crack troops to be air- and sea-lifted thousands of miles to Manchuria.

While Nationalist troops were riding in style in American planes and LST's to North China, tens of thousands of Communist troops were rapidly being deployed on foot. The "One-eyed Dragon," Communist General Liu Po-ch'eng, straddled the Ping-Han Railway with a hundred thousand men. His power was supported by Ch'en Yi's New Fourth Army, which, with a strength of about two hundred thousand, was heavily concentrated in Shantung and controlled the Tsin-Pu Railway. These two armies threatened to keep north-south rail communications broken, preventing the consolidation of Nationalist forces in the Yangtze Valley with those in North China.

The Soviet forces commanded by Marshal Rodion Ya. Malinovsky still occupied Manchuria. The National Government had early ordered the establishment at Changchun (Hsinking), the seat of the Soviet Army's headquarters, of a Northeast Headquarters of the Military Affairs Commission and the redivision of Manchuria into nine provinces. By October 15 some two hundred Nationalist officials had assembled at Changchun. General Tu Yü-ming was appointed Commander-in-Chief of the Nationalist forces for the Northeast (Manchuria).

The Communists also had their eyes on Manchuria. They were determined that the postwar situation there would be different. One of their official organs had already made the Communist thinking plain: "A fascist dictatorial rule and feudal remnants will not be permitted again to enter one step into the four Northeastern Provinces! . . . The four Northeastern Provinces are located in the area of contact of several important States. They are a pivot for welfare, and also a pillar for peace." [3] (The term "four Northeastern Provinces" here includes Jehol.)

In September Lin Feng had gone from Yenan to Manchuria to lay down the political line and perform the necessary spadework. Upon their arrival the Communists would find there the military man Chou Pao-chung, returned from the Soviet Union in August in the train of the Soviet forces that struck at the Japanese. Chou Pao-chung had promptly started reorganizing the feeble underground Anti-Japanese Allied Army into the People's Self-Defence Army.

In September also Communist General Lin Piao (a graduate of Chiang Kai-shek's Whampoa Military Academy) began moving Communist forces by both land and sea into the Northeast from North China and Chahar Province. By November Communist forces in Manchuria numbered 130,000. The People's Self-Defence Army now became the Northeastern Democratic Allied Army with Lin Piao as Commander in Chief and Chou Pao-chung a Deputy Commander. Ships of United States Vice Admiral Barbey's Seventh Amphibious Force tried to land Nationalist troops at Dairen but the Soviet High Command blocked the landing; in the next try, the Manchurian ports of Hulutao and Yingkow were found already in Chinese Communist hands. The Nationalists were finally unloaded at Chinwangtao, where U.S. Marines were in control.

Chiang Kai-shek was concentrating forces in North China for the advance into Manchuria. With armed clashes between Communist and Nationalist forces already occurring, the Communists became increasingly resentful of American participation in Nationalist military movements. In October Communist Chief of Staff Yeh Chienying, speaking for Chu Teh, protested that American military movements constituted intentional interference in China's domestic affairs.

By early November it was obvious that the Nationalist takeover of Manchuria would be a much more arduous undertaking than the recovery, with American help, of North China. It was equally evident that the transfer of authority from the Soviet Army to the National Government could not be accomplished within the ninety-day time-limit originally set, which was due to expire on November 15. The Nationalists were confronted with a dilemma: they ardently desired the Soviet departure; but, since there were Communist but no Nationalist troops in Manchuria at this juncture, Soviet evacuation would mean a Communist takeover. It was decided in Sino-Soviet discussions at Changchun to fix December 3 as the new date for the withdrawal of Soviet forces from Manchuria.

General Wedemeyer was still making his professional military advice available to the Generalissimo. On November 14, 1945, he informed Washington that the Nationalists were completely unprepared to occupy Manchuria against Communist opposition; he had recommended to Chiang Kai-shek that, prior to an advance into Manchuria, the areas south of the Great Wall should be consolidated and land communications lines in those areas secured.

Chiang Kai-shek had by now deployed six armies along the Great

Wall. On November 15, one day after Wedemeyer's report to Washington, the Nationalists attacked. The following day they took Shanhaikuan at the sea end of the Great Wall and then continued north into the Liaosi corridor. The contest for Manchuria had been taken to the battlefield.

The Communist armies at that time possessed neither manpower nor fire power adequate to withstand the heavy American equipment and disciplined strength of the American-trained Nationalist divisions, and they offered no more than light resistance. Advancing rapidly, the Nationalist forces took the port of Hulutao on November 22 and Chinchow four days later. On November 25 Communist leader Chou En-lai flew back from Chungking to Yenan, where Mao Tse-tung had preceded him. The Communists clearly considered further negotiations to be pointless.

At this time, on November 26, General Patrick J. Hurley dramatically submitted his resignation as Ambassador to China. He damned the State Department and its personnel as he went, but it is reasonable to assume that his sudden exit was not unrelated to the rapidly deteriorating situation in China. The developing Chinese civil war did not brook protracted attempts to soothe the disaffected envoy, and on the following day President Truman announced both the acceptance of Hurley's resignation and the appointment of General George C. Marshall as his special representative to China.

The President's instructions of December 15 made it clear that General Marshall's mission would be essentially to take up the task of mediation where Hurley had left off: he and Secretary of State Byrnes were "both anxious that the unification of China by peaceful, democratic methods be achieved as soon as possible." And the President also stated: "Specifically, I desire that you endeavor to persuade the Chinese Government to call a national conference of representatives of the major political elements to bring about the unification of China and, concurrently, to effect a cessation of hostilities, particularly in North China." [4]

The Nationalist drive into Manchuria was continuing toward Mukden without serious difficulty; but it would have been impolitic to ignore the American President's peace mission. The United States had completed shipment to the National Government of equipment for thirty-nine divisions and eight-and-one-third air wings by December; and, with the Communists barred from taking Japanese surrenders, the Nationalists had acquired the arms of all Japanese formations disarmed in China proper, numbering 1,200,000 men. Chiang's military position looked outwardly strong.

With Marshall's arrival on the China scene, the political situation took a new turn. President Truman's December 15 instruction to Marshall had envisaged the convocation of a national conference. The Kuomintang-CCP agreement of October 10 had provided for the holding of a Political Consultative Conference (PCC) "to which all parties and nonpartisan leaders will be invited, to exchange views on national affairs and discuss questions relating to peaceful national reconstruction and the convocation of the National Assembly." On December 31, therefore, it was announced that the Generalissimo had decided to convoke the Political Consultative Conference at Chungking on January 10, 1946.

"The Committee of Three"—General Marshall, Nationalist General Chang Chih-chung, and Communist General Chou En-lai—held its first meeting on January 7, 1946. Three days later, the Committee agreed on the cessation, effective January 13, of all hostilities in China. An Executive Headquarters at Peking, commanding truce teams for field investigations, was to implement the agreement. The PCC, made up of representatives of the Kuomintang (KMT), CCP, Democratic League, Youth Party, and nonaffiliated delegates, began its meetings the same day in Chungking.

The Political Consultative Conference met for a full three weeks. The final session of January 31 brought agreement on government organization, a program for peaceful national reconstruction, military problems, a National Assembly, and the 1936 draft Constitution. The PCC decisions were followed, on February 25, by an agreement between the Nationalists and Communists for military reorganization and integration of the Communist forces into a reduced National Army to be made up, at the end of eighteen months, of fifty Nationalist and ten Communist divisions.

The Marshall mission appeared to have succeeded. The agreements and accompanying declarations had introduced, at least for the moment, a strong note of conciliation into the political situation. In Manchuria, immediately after the truce agreement of January 10, the Soviet Headquarters had made provisions for the movement and takeover of authority by Nationalist officials. On January 15 Nationalist troops moved by rail from Sinmin to Huangkutun, just outside Mukden, to await the Soviet withdrawal. The door seemed open to Nationalist authority in the Northeast.

But more massive developments were already imposing their

imprint on events in China. The United States had blocked Soviet participation in the military occupation of Japan; there were growing American-Soviet differences not only regarding the future of Korea but of Europe as well. In that uneasy international situation, Chiang appeared determined to push ahead in Manchuria. Although "there was no implication or indication in the meetings of the Committee of Three that Manchuria was not included within the scope of the cessation of hostilities order,"[5] the National Government refused to permit the extension of the truce machinery to Manchuria. Chiang's move could only deepen Moscow's suspicion, which probably had existed from the beginning, that Manchuria was an arena of potential conflict between the Soviet Union and the United States and that "American imperialism" aimed at using the Nationalist forces as an instrument for attacking Soviet interests in that area. Chiang Kai-shek's Manchuria policy now began to threaten the ultimate success of the Marshall Mission.

The Soviet Union was as ready as Chiang to play power politics. In response to a fresh request from the National Government, the USSR had postponed withdrawal of its troops from Manchuria a second time, from December 3 to February 1. Now, as the February deadline drew near, the Soviets alleged that the Manchurian winter had caused transport difficulties that would enforce a delay in their scheduled troop evacuation until March 1. And on January 26 Moscow informed Chungking that Japanese enterprises in Manchuria that had rendered services to the Japanese Army were regarded by the Soviet Union as "war booty." The Soviets also proposed joint Sino-Soviet control over former Japanese enterprises in Manchuria.

On February 11 the American Government made representations at Chungking and Moscow regarding the disposition and control of Manchurian industrial enterprises. This evidently encouraged the Nationalists to stiffen their attitude towards Moscow. Beginning February 22, student demonstrations in Chungking (spreading to Shanghai) called upon the Soviet Union "loyally to observe the Sino-Soviet treaty of friendship" and exhorted the Chinese people "decisively to preserve intact the territory and sovereignty of the Northeast." The indications were that the demonstrations were officially inspired.

Presumably to counter the unfavorable popular reaction to Soviet policies, Marshal Malinovsky's Chief of Staff issued a lengthy statement on February 26 regarding the matter. He said that Soviet troops had in fact begun their withdrawal on January 15, that the withdrawal was continuing, and that a large number had already left Manchuria. The reason for the slight delay was that the Chinese (Nationalist) troops had been excessively slow in reaching the areas where Soviet troops were stationed. "Because of this, under a variety of conditions, the Soviet Headquarters could not but delay troop withdrawal." The spokesman concluded with an assurance: "The Headquarters of the Soviet Army has determined that the withdrawal of the Soviet forces from Manchuria will be completed before the withdrawal of the American Army from China, and in this period cannot in any event be delayed." [6] A connection between Soviet actions and American policy in China was now admitted, if only by implication.

The Chinese Communist attitude on the Manchurian question had at the same time hardened. In a press conference at Yenan on February 13, 1946, a spokesman for the CCP's Central Committee set forth the Communist policy regarding the Northeast in sharper detail: (1) "democratic personages" and other non-Kuomintang personnel should participate in Manchuria's political reorganization; (2) existing anti-Japanese "democratic military forces" should be recognized and consolidated; (3) "democratic autonomous governmental authorities" of Manchurian hsien should be recognized; (4) the Government should limit to a specific number the troops sent to Manchuria for the takeover of sovereignty, (5) any incorporation by the Government of Northeastern puppet troops, or utilization of North China puppet forces, for takeover of authority in the Northeast, should cease.[7]

The grave nature of Kuomintang-Communist differences was here made clear. The growing Communist toughness reflected neither desperation nor foolhardiness. The Soviet troops had disarmed the Manchoukuo Army, numbering at least 320,000 men, and the Communists had begun, as soon as their first skeleton units arrived, recruiting the well-trained Manchoukuo soldiers. Nor would the new Communist formations be pinched for want of equipment. There were large Japanese stockpiles of equipment and munitions in Manchuria. The Soviet forces apparently left behind no heavy military equipment, but the Communists certainly came into possession of some light Japanese ordnance and munitions. A Nationalist source put that windfall at a round six hundred thousand tons.

Thus the Communists had found in Manchuria both the men and matériel needed to develop a war machine fit to challenge the

Nationalists, and they had wasted no opportunities. On February 13 the Yenan spokesman announced that the Northeastern Democratic Army then comprised an organized force of nearly three hundred thousand men, not counting the Peace Preservation Corps (militia) and police. It was from a position of some strength that the Communist side defined the issue for Manchuria: was the problem one for political or for military solution?

The Soviet garrison troops remaining in Mukden began to withdraw on March 9, southward to Dairen and northward to Changchun. It was only on March 11, the day that Marshall left Chungking for consultation in Washington, that Chiang Kai-shek finally agreed *in principle* that truce teams might enter Manchuria. The last Soviet troops left Mukden the next day. On March 15, seven months after V-J Day, the Nationalist Fifty-second Army formally occupied Mukden.

POLITICAL BREAKDOWN

The political reconciliation achieved earlier had already begun to fall apart. The KMT Central Executive Committee had convened at Chungking on March 1 to pass on the PCC resolutions, and on the fifteenth the session passed a resolution proposing "consideration" and "improved procedures" regarding the PCC decisions. On the seventeenth, the meeting adjourned. The net result of the Kuomintang conference was nominal approval but practical subversion of the PCC agreements.

In a meeting at Yenan on March 21 between Communist and Nationalist representatives, the Communists demanded prompt and complete fulfilment of the PCC agreements, but the meeting ended fruitlessly. The Communists, however, were not waiting to carry their point by logic. The evidence indicated that, from March 15 at the latest, *both* sides were committed to the assumption that their differences would be settled on the field of battle. Both sides, and especially the Communists, continued to seek political benefit from the American mediation and to convince the nation of the rights and wrongs of the matter. Thereafter a number of military developments inexorably shaped the future.

The truce was still technically in effect. The Committee of Three on March 27 finally agreed on the dispatch of truce teams to Manchuria in implementation of Chiang Kai-shek's commitment; Executive Headquarters teams would at long last, on April 8, arrive in the Northeast. There was now a welter of movement in Manchuria, including Japanese civilian repatriation, Soviet evacuation northward, and Nationalist and Communist troop actions.

In mid-March, the Nationalists had only about 137,000 troops available in Manchuria and Jehol Province. If one accepts the Communists' figures, their troops already outnumbered the Nationalists in the disputed area by more than two to one, though they were notably inferior in equipment. The general shape of the coming struggle for Manchuria was already foreshadowed; Government forces were mainly deployed around the major towns and along communications lines, whereas the Communists were deployed at great depth throughout the countryside. The Nationalists had thus far enjoyed superior transport facilities for their movement; but the Communists, through well-coordinated and energetic action, had succeeded in canceling out some of the Nationalist advantages in transport and matériel.

On March 17, following the Nationalist occupation of Mukden, a Communist force attacked Ssuping, a strategic railway junction halfway between Mukden and Changchun. They took it the next day. The Communists thus controlled a roadblock against an advance on Changchun from the south. On March 22 the Soviet Ambassador to China informed the National Government that the Soviet forces would complete their withdrawal from Manchuria by the end of April at the latest. The Nationalists, with four armies in the Mukden area and five more moving up from inside the Wall, deployed heavy forces northward and southward from Mukden. And on April 5 the American-trained and -equipped New First Army reached the Ssuping sector, now occupied by a strong Communist force. Events were moving rapidly. On April 14 the Soviet garrison evacuated Changchun, leaving it in the hands of four thousand Nationalist troops, who had been recently air-lifted into the area, and some two thousand Manchoukuo Peace Preservation forces enlisted by the Nationalists. A Communist force under Chou Pao-chung attacked Changchun the same night and captured the city on April 18.

It was on that same day that General Marshall returned to China. During his absence Nationalist and Communist actions had brought a serious deterioration in the over-all political situation. He thus found the truce disintegrating. General Sun Li-jen's New First Army had begun an all-out attack against the Communist position at Ssuping on April 16. The Communist forces had had a month to dig themselves in and resisted stubbornly. The Soviet forces were now rolling rapidly westward out of Manchuria, but it was the Chinese Communists who, behind the Ssuping roadblock, were occupying the evacuated territory. From Moscow it was finally announced that the Soviet troops (originally numbering some three hundred thousand) had completed their withdrawal from Manchuria on May 3. Behind them, the Chinese Communists were found to be in full control of North Manchuria, beyond immediate challenge, and of much of the rest of China's Northeast besides. Chungking had got the desired Soviet withdrawal but had failed to gather the fruits of the victory.

Conditions in North and Central China worsened alongside the crisis in Manchuria. But it was the Manchurian situation that dominated the national scene, exacerbating all relations between Right and Left. It was becoming evident that, unless the problems posed by Manchuria could be solved, the peace would be lost.

"In conversations with National Government leaders General Marshall endeavored to emphasize the seriousness of the situation." He noted the distrust present on both sides and various Nationalist actions that had enabled the Communist Party to challenge the Government's good faith. The official American record shows also that Marshall made another critical point in those conversations:

He said that the Kuomintang had had an opportunity to have peace in Manchuria but had not utilized the opportunity, and concluded that the Chinese Communists were now taking advantage of the existing situation and were becoming stronger daily, thus placing the National Government in a very dangerous military position with over-extended lines and a constantly increasing dispersion of forces.[8]

The Generalissimo insisted "that he would accept nothing less than complete National Government sovereignty in Manchuria."[9] The negotiations between mediator Marshall and Chiang Kai-shek and Chou En-lai regarding the Manchurian issue foundered on the hard rock of the Generalissimo's obduracy.

The fighting at Ssuping had now developed into the bloodiest battle of the postwar period. It was the first major positional engagement that had been fought between Communists and Nationalists since 1934, and its outcome meant much to both sides. For the Nationalists, Ssuping in Communist hands endangered any Nationalist advance to the north and had to be taken. For the Communists, Ssuping was the rear-guard shield for their forces engaged in consolidating positions occupied upon the evacuation of Soviet forces.

On May 20, after more than a full month's fighting, the Nationalists succeeded in taking the position. The Government had been forced to commit a total of seven divisions, probably 70,000 men, to the operation. According to a Nationalist version the Communists had engaged 110,000 troops in defense of the position. The Nationalists won at Ssuping, but the Communist capacity to stand and fight tenaciously when necessary was a portent for the future. And the Communists had achieved their objective: they now were strongly entrenched in North Manchuria.

Following the Communist occupation of Changchun in April, the Nationalists had demanded its surrender; Marshall supported the demand. After losing Ssuping, the Communists on May 22 evacuated Changchun, announcing that they did so in the interests of peace. On May 25 Chiang Kai-shek went to Mukden to attend, at some distance, the re-entry into Changchun of Nationalist forces under Cheng Tung-kuo. The Nationalist forces prepared to advance from Changchun eastward against Kirin.

With the Nationalist military position in Manchuria apparently improved, the Generalissimo made certain proposals on May 24 for the restoration of peace. His terms maintained the essence of the Nationalist position and would have required demonstrations of good faith from the Communist side, but they contained no offer to halt or restrict Nationalist military actions. They were terms that the Communists would have accepted only if they thought they were losing.

The Nationalists, exploiting their latest military success, continued on to take Kirin and Hsiaofengman (the site of Manchuria's biggest hydroelectric plant); and, fanning out from Changchun, they advanced northward. At the beginning of June, the 91st Division crossed over to the north bank of the Sungari River; on June 4 it reached Shuangcheng, halfway between the Sungari and Harbin.

But while the Nationalists had been speeding to the north and east after their occupation of Changchun, the Communists had gone into action in Southern Manchuria, now lightly defended, and in Jehol Province. Communist forces captured the steel center of Anshan on May 26, and followed up this victory with the occupation of Haicheng and Tashihchiao. The Nationalist defeat at Haicheng was sharpened by the defection there of the 184th (Yunnan)

Division to the Communist side. It was a portent for the future. The port of Yingkow held under the Communist attack, but to the west, in Jehol, Communist arms swept the Nationalists from the Chihfeng-Yehposhou railway line. While all this was going on, in Shantung the Communist New Fourth Army made substantial gains and surrounded Tsinan.

Reinforced Government troops recovered the lost towns in South Manchuria. But recent developments seemingly brought a slight softening of the Generalissimo's opposition to further political discussions. He returned to Nanking on June 3 and once more became accessible to Marshall for negotiations, as he had not been for ten critical days.

Chiang now consented to a ten-day truce in Manchuria, during which period, he stipulated, Nationalist-Communist agreement should be achieved in three major areas of differences: "(1) detailed arrangements to govern a complete termination of hostilities in Manchuria; (2) definite detailed arrangements, with time limits, for the complete resumption of communications in North China; and (3) a basis for carrying out without further delay the agreement for military reorganization of February 25." [10] Chou En-lai requested that the negotiators be granted more time to accomplish those truly herculean labors, and Chiang finally agreed to extend the truce period to fifteen days. It was on this basis that a truce for Manchuria became effective at noon, June 7, 1946.

In view of the magnitude of the task at hand, a fortnight was all too little time. Nationalist troops stopped their advance north of the Sungari River, but the tensions and fighting continued in both Manchuria and China proper. The military developments reflected increasing exacerbation of a virtually irretrievable political situation. It was on June 17, when ten of the truce period's fifteen days had passed, that Chiang Kai-shek presented to Marshall, for transmittal to Chou En-lai, his conditions for peace. Chiang's proposals would have required withdrawal of Communist forces from various strategic points in Shantung (the stronghold of the Communist New Fourth Army), the Communist evacuation of Jehol and Chahar provinces by September 1, and the Nationalist occupation of major Communist-held Manchurian positions.

It was hardly to be expected that the Communists would surrender such important military advantages without at least a political *quid pro quo;* Chou En-lai replied that the conditions were unacceptable. The Generalissimo then extended the truce period

through June 30 and presented two additional demands: (1) that
the Communists withdraw from the Tsinan-Tsingtao railway line
(in Shantung) before August 1 and (2) that the procedure requiring unanimous vote in the Committee of Three and Executive
Headquarters should be revised before June 30.

The Communists conceded that the American representatives
should have the deciding vote on field teams and in Executive
Headquarters on procedural matters regarding the cessation of hostilities and in the interpretation and execution of agreements. On
June 26 the Committee of Three further agreed that the terms of
the January 10 truce should govern in Manchuria as in the rest of
China, and formulated a "Directive for the Termination of Hostilities in Manchuria."

Chiang Kai-shek had stipulated, however, that settlements of
individual issues would be inoperative in the absence of agreement
of *all* major issues. The Communists, in the tense last-minute negotiations during the June truce, refused to accept the Government's
proposals for troop disposition and army reorganization without
commitments from the Government regarding the character of the
civil organization to be set up subsequently. Further, although the
Communists were prepared to withdraw their troops from certain
points and areas, they insisted on the stipulation that Nationalist
forces should not thereupon occupy those places.

Patiently General Marshall went back and forth between Chiang
Kai-shek and Chou En-lai. June 30, the final day of the Manchurian
truce, arrived with Marshall endeavoring to wring some concessions
from the Generalissimo:

General Marshall pointed out to the Generalissimo that statements issued
by his military leaders indicated that the Government was washing its
hands of any democratic procedure and was pursuing a dictatorial policy
of military force . . . General Marshall informed the Generalissimo that
in his opinion an extension of the existing form of partial truce would
probably result in violent ruptures due to the tense and explosive situation, the bitterness of the commanders in the field, and the strong desire
of Government military leaders to settle matters by force, for which the
National Government plans were complete and fairly well known to the
Communist Party.[11]

The Nationalist Minister of Information, P'eng Hsueh-p'ei, announced on June 30 that the truce had expired without a satisfactory agreement, but that the Government had asked General Marshall to continue mediation for the purpose of reaching a peaceful
settlement. On the same day the spokesman for the Communist

delegation at Nanking praised the energy of General Marshall and lauded the concessions made by the Communist side; he blamed the Government for the current impasse, asserting that Nationalist military movements contradicted the words of Minister P'eng Hsueh-p'ei. The Communist Party, he said, still wanted peace and was opposed to civil war. But the issue of political power had been directly joined, and there remained no common ground for political negotiation. Reconciliation of the opposing points of view had proved impossible. The Marshall Mission, charged with stopping the trend to civil war and achieving the peaceful unification of China, had failed.

"THIRD REVOLUTIONARY CIVIL WAR": FIRST YEAR

The failure of the Marshall mission opened the gates to full-scale civil war. Nationalist chieftain Chiang Kai-shek clearly felt strong because of the American help he was receiving. Up to V-J Day, the United States had authorized $1,515,700,000 in Lend-Lease aid and financial credits to the National Government; it had, moreover, paid Chiang handsomely for the construction of airfields and other war facilities on Chinese soil and for the board and lodging of American troops stationed in China. Mainly through such American gener-osity, the National Government came out of the Sino-Japanese War with foreign-exchange holdings totaling some $900 million—far more than it had possessed when the war began.

The Japanese occupation had left no widespread material devas-tation in its wake. Excepting the Japanese campaign of 1944, there had been no large-scale military operations in China after 1938. The Communist campaigning had been a guerrilla warfare of harass-ments and attacks on Japanese communications and small garrisons. American bombings had been directed at Japanese cities, not at towns in occupied China (except for ineffectual airraids on Mukden and Anshan in Manchuria). Coal, iron, and electric-power produc-tion had actually increased under the Japanese occupation, espe-cially in Manchuria. Yet the United Nations Relief and Reha-bilitation Administration (UNRRA) came to China's aid with $658,400,000 (of which the American contribution was $474,000,-000), and by the end of 1945 had delivered three hundred thousand tons of supplies to China.

When the Nationalists had returned to East China after V-J Day, they had not only recovered Chinese Government property appropriated by the Japanese-sponsored Wang Ching-wei regime, but they had inherited as war booty substantial Japanese enterprises. Moreover, the ruling group's "Four Families" (those of Chiang Kai-shek, Ch'en Li-fu, H. H. K'ung, and T. V. Soong) had strengthened their hold on the Government's economic machinery during the period of exile in West China. The regime's "bureaucratic capitalism," under which the Central Government monopolized China's larger and more profitable economic undertakings, had come to be operated even more than before for the benefit of the dominant "dynasty," and, as a result, the foreign bank accounts of prominent Kuomintang officials fattened.

Corruption infected the political administration, and from there the rot was transmitted to the military machine. Political and economic forces weighed as heavily in the civil war scales as men under arms. When Kuomintang rule was confined to a half-dozen poor provinces in West China, the growth of Nationalist venality and maladministration was restrained by geographical factors. But with the triumphal Nationalist return to East China such restraints were left behind. The restoration of Nationalist rule over Japanese-occupied territory was accompanied by one of the biggest carpet-bagging operations in history.

The areas of major Japanese investment and development, Formosa and Manchuria, were the hardest hit. Formosa had been under Japanese rule for half a century, and legal title had not passed to China with Japan's defeat. The Nationalists, in occupying that rich island, should properly have acted as custodians of its considerable accumulated wealth and rendered accounting of their stewardship to the United Nations. Instead, there was unabashed and unbridled looting, with so little consideration for the rights of Formosa's inhabitants, most of whom were Chinese, that widespread resentment was soon aroused.

As the Nationalists looted Formosa, so the Russians plundered Manchuria. Manchuria, thanks to earlier Russian and Japanese investments, was the most highly industrialized part of China; it also produced valuable agricultural surpluses. As the lawful occupying force in Manchuria, the Soviet Army had the over-all responsibility for safeguarding public and private property until authority could be transferred to the responsible Chinese representatives. Instead, the gold discovered in Manchoukuo banks was confiscated. Large amounts of property and commodities were purchased with "Red Army notes," with the notes left behind for redemption by the successor government. The Soviet forces also stripped Manchuria of valuable industrial components worth nearly $900 million. And the ultimate loss from those removals, which often affected key installations, was several times greater. Chinese looters added to the damage.

By the time the Nationalists arrived in Manchuria, therefore, the area's economy had already suffered heavily. The losses were now compounded. Friction developed between the Nationalist Commander in Chief, General Tu Yü-ming, and Chiang's proconsul for civil affairs, General Hsiung Shih-hui, as each strove to acquire more power. Other Nationalist generals concentrated on the flesh-pots of the chief Manchurian centers and in the acquisition of Japanese real estate or personal property; in fact, the latter interest tended more and more to eclipse their military responsibilities.

The activities of Nationalist military and civilian officials were paralleled by feverish small-scale looting by a veritable swarm of carpetbaggers from inside the Wall. The roofs, paneling, and plumbing of residences and office buildings disappeared, the tools of workshops and equipment of hospitals were looted to be vended on the streets, and Chinese gangs stripped Japanese civilians of the last possessions they bore on their backs as they made their way to the sea for repatriation. As the accumulated wealth of decades was rapidly dissipated, increased suffering and disillusionment came to the people of Manchuria. The military and political affairs of the area suffered accordingly from neglect. One of Napoleon's War Maxims, "Nothing will disorganize an army more completely than pillage," was validated.

The Generalissimo's power drive was another important factor in the equation. The Manchurians, harboring as strong a provincialism as that of any other Chinese group, naturally desired to participate in the running of their own affairs. At the end of the war they hoped that the National Government would treat them as fellow Chinese who had suffered under alien conquerors and would respect their political rights. Instead, the Nationalists castigated the Manchurians as "collaborators," denied them a voice in government of the area, and ignored them in disposing of Manchuria's great wealth. Determined to rule Manchuria, Chiang Kai-shek seemingly disregarded the possibility that the Manchurians, if alienated by the Nationalists, might side with the Nationalists' enemies.

The United States was also in the picture. It had continued aid to the National Government after V-J Day, and, by authority of a Presidential order of February 25, 1946, a United States Military Advisory Group to China was established "to assist and advise the Chinese Government in the development of modern armed forces." The Export-Import Bank made $82,800,000 in credits available to the Nationalists after V-J Day and in April, 1946, earmarked an additional $500,000,000 for China. On June 14, 1946, the United States Government extended $51,700,000 in long-term credit to the National Government, covering the delivery of "civilian type" equipment and supplies in the Lend-Lease "pipe-line" on V-J Day.

In spite of all the wealth and goods made available to the National Government, by July, 1946, the economic situation in China had seriously deteriorated. UNRRA supplies were often diverted to fatten the accounts of Chinese officials, or else rusted or rotted in warehouses. The Government emitted more and more paper money to meet increased military expenditures, and the inflation of commodity prices kept pace. By maintaining an artificial official rate of foreign exchange, the National Government depressed exports and stimulated a flood of imports—many of them useless for the exigent task of strengthening the Chinese economy. The Government's foreign-exchange reserves had declined radically. So had the Kuomintang regime's stock of good will among China's politically conscious middle-of-the-road groups: they had not thought of the War of Resistance as being fought for the ultimate benefit of carpetbaggers.

The political situation contained elements distinctly unfavorable to the Nationalists. Middle-of-the-road Chinese had become increasingly critical of the American mediation, contending that such intercession and American material aid to the Nanking regime must inevitably embolden the reactionary wing of the Kuomintang and thereby frustrate attempts to adjust the country's domestic affairs on the basis of strictly Chinese interests. The nation generally had come to favor a political settlement of the Kuomintang-Communist dispute that would provide a broader base for government. This demand was closer to the Communist than to the Nationalist position.

If the political and economic situation was bad when the Communists' "Third Revolutionary Civil War" began in July, 1946, the military situation was worse, apparently, than assumed by the American Government. According to the official United States *China White Paper*, the Government forces in mid-1946 numbered about three million men, and the Communists some six hundred thousand regulars and four hundred thousand irregulars. These figures, however, were merely a restatement of the *White Paper's* estimate of relative troop strengths in September, *1945*. If they had been correct, they would have reflected a stagnant situation instead of one in which the Communists were rapidly expanding their forces by new recruitment, particularly in Manchuria. It is now evident that Washington overestimated the Nationalist and underestimated the Communist troop strength as it stood at the end of the truce period. This meant that American policy was operating on the basis of erroneous premises.

The Communist attitude toward the United States hardened perceptibly after the truce expired. On the July 7 anniversary of the outbreak of the Sino-Japanese War, the CCP's Central Committee issued a statement bitterly attacking American policy. The Communist declaration charged that American military, economic, and financial aid to the National Government was designed to support the "reactionary clique" in dictatorship and civil war and called upon the United States "to cease armed intervention in our country's internal affairs," to stop fostering civil war, to stop sending military supplies and military advisers, and to withdraw immediately all military forces from China.

Although the truce had expired, Chou En-lai remained in Nanking for the time being. General Marshall also stayed on, and was joined in July by the new American Ambassador, Dr. J. Leighton Stuart. They met and negotiated with both Chou En-lai and Chiang Kai-shek. But it was too late for peace. The Nationalist armies had gone into action in North China about mid-July and were winning victories; at the same time the Generalissimo's demands were becoming ever more harsh. The civil war had been resumed in earnest. Significantly, it was in July, 1946, that the Communists renamed their military forces the People's Liberation Army (PLA).

The coffin-lid was nailed down on American mediation on August 30 when the United States sold to the National Government, at bargain prices, war surplus with a procurement value of $900 million. Although stocked originally for the use of the American armed forces, the supplies were designated as "civilian-type." General Marshall went to some pains to explain to Chou En-lai that the supplies did not include combat material but (in the words of the *China White Paper*) "consisted of machinery, motor vehicles, communications equipment, rations, medical supplies and various other

items which would be of considerable value in the rehabilitation
of the Chinese economy." The United States Government could
hardly expect the Chinese Communists to rest assured, however,
that the Nationalists would not use military trucks and communications equipment in the war that was being fought.

The same document recorded the reality of the situation: "With
respect to United States military aid programs General Marshall
was being placed in the untenable position of mediating on the one
hand between the two Chinese groups while on the other the United
States Government was continuing to supply arms and ammunition to
one of the two groups, namely, the National Government." Recognizing the dilemma, Washington in August suspended "certain portions
of these programs which might have a bearing on the continued prosecution of hostilities in China." In late September shipments of combat items from "war surplus" depots in the Pacific area were also
suspended. But the American ban was partially lifted on October 22
to permit delivery of "civilian type items for the Chinese Air Force."
It was entirely rescinded in May, 1947.

That was the setting in which the trial by arms was being undertaken. The Nationalist advances looked good on the map. Government forces had extended their control notably in Hopei Province
and along the Lunghai and Tsingtao-Tsinan rail lines. In October
they occupied Kalgan, the gateway to Chahar Province, and cleared
much of Jehol Province. In Manchuria the Nationalists fanned out
to the southeast from Mukden and took Antung, a town on the Yalu
River that divides Manchuria from Korea. From the Changchun
base area they extended their positions north and northwestward,
and it was evident that they planned to drive on Harbin soon.

The progress of the Government forces had been deceptively
easy. Even as they advanced, however, weaknesses showed up in
the military situation that should have disturbed the Nationalist
high command. The Communist forces were using the tactics of
mobile warfare, and the Nationalist armies were unable to force
them into positional warfare for a decision. The Nationalists, taking
town after town, became more extended. As they thinned out their
forces to spread them over their gains, the Communists began
appearing in strength in wide areas behind the "front."

The political contest entered a new stage on November 15, when
the Nanking Government convened the long-projected National
Assembly that was to provide the basis for constitutional government in China. The Communists and the Democratic League boy-

cotted the meeting; it was essentially a Kuomintang affair, providing a built-in majority for any measures proposed by the ruling Nanking hierarchy. Chou En-lai stated: "The door of negotiation has by now been slammed by the single hand of the Kuomintang authorities." He boarded an American plane on November 19 and flew back to Yenan, never to return to the negotiators' table. Thereafter the Communists insisted on two prerequisites for any resumption of talks: dissolution of the "illegal" National Assembly and restoration, on the basis of the January 10 truce order, of the military positions existing as of January 13, 1946. Those conditions were never met.

On December 18, 1946, President Truman issued a long statement describing American postwar policy toward China. He reported withdrawal of the Marines from North China in September, and the reduction of American armed strength in China to less than 12,000 as compared with 113,000 a year before. The President maintained what had become a transparent fiction: "We are pledged not to interfere in the internal affairs of China. Our position is clear. While avoiding involvement in their civil strife, we will persevere with our policy of helping the Chinese people to bring about peace and economic recovery in their country." On January 29 the Department of State announced American withdrawal from the Committee of Three and from the Peiping Executive Headquarters. The American mediation was officially ended; the American involvement continued, as shown by the continued presence of the United States Navy in Tsingtao and of the Military Advisory Group at Nanking.

During the winter of 1946, Communist strength was growing in the Manchurian countryside; the Government forces were over-extended along fragile lines of communication. The Nationalist strategists were unworried, declaring that it was "too cold" for the Communists to fight in Manchuria's winter. To protect their political and economic gains, they constructed elaborate pillbox and barbed-wire systems around the Nationalist towns and settled back into the military posture pithily described by the Chinese as "sitting the enemy to death."

Before the Nationalists could safely undertake the contemplated big push against Harbin, scheduled for the spring of 1947, they faced the tedious but not difficult task of cleaning up a Communist pocket in the Chang Pai mountains on their eastern flank. They had already concentrated forces for the operation when in January the

Communists unexpectedly launched the first of a series of offensives from North Manchuria.

The drive was a sudden probing thrust by three PLA columns across the frozen Sungari north of Changchun. The Nationalists counterattacked, the PLA forces retired and were back across the Sungari at the end of a fortnight. The drive had not proved dangerous to Nationalist strongpoints, but it surprised the Nationalist command and introduced a new element of uncertainty into the situation.

A second PLA offensive launched on February 21 repeated the January pattern, but with greater force and over a wider area. The Nationalists brought up reinforcements and mauled two PLA Divisions. The Communists once more retreated back across the Sungari. This time the Communists had used a small number of tanks and light artillery pieces.

It was now evident that "normal expectations" were obsolete where PLA timetables were concerned. No sooner had their second drive ended than the Communists on March 8 launched a diversionary thrust in a new sector on the Sungari River line. Other PLA forces pushed forward near Tungliao in Western Manchuria; and in the Kirin area they recaptured several district towns lost earlier. In mid-March the drive ended.

Presumably, the March offensive had achieved its objectives. The Communist position in eastern Manchuria, instead of being brought under Nationalist attack, had actually been strengthened. The Nationalists now retained only a small bridgehead on the Sungari's north bank. Their war plans had been thrown off badly and talk of the "imminent" capture of Harbin declined noticeably. The PLA's spring offensive had forced a reconsideration of Nationalist strategy in the Manchurian theater.

As the PLA's third spring drive ended in Manchuria, a large Government force of seventy-five thousand men occupied the former Communist capital of Yenan with great fanfare. The primitive Shensi town was empty when the Nationalist force arrived, the Communists having withdrawn well in advance. In the meantime, however, the PLA had expanded its control in neighboring Shansi to four fifths of the total area. Shansi Chairman Yen Hsi-shan bitterly characterized the Nationalist operation as "trading a fat cow for a lean horse."

In May of 1947, Lin Piao's PLA command took the wraps off newly created units equipped with Japanese weapons and unloosed the biggest drive up to that date in Manchuria. This time both Mongol and Korean units were included in the PLA columns. The offensive was again triggered by a single thrust from the Sungari River but developed some ten days later into an advance by four columns in central Manchuria. A Nationalist report put the PLA forces at 270,000 men.

The PLA advanced rapidly southward through the thinly held countryside, sweeping town after town into their bag. With the Communists deep in the rear, the Nationalists abandoned their small remaining bridgehead on the north bank of the Sungari and outposts north of the Changchun-Kirin line. Changchun and Kirin were isolated and their garrisons immobilized. The Nationalist Seventy-first Army was defeated in the Changchun sector, lost two more battalions in retreat, finally came to rest at Ssuping and was surrounded. The PLA pressed on the Mukden defense perimeter. In a supporting offensive, Communist forces advanced from the Jehol-Liaosi border area shortly after mid-May against Nationalist positions in Jehol; a sixth Communist force struck at the beginning of June in the southern Liao region, which lay between Mukden and their rear.

The Government forces, compelled to strengthen their Mukden sector, withdrew from the chief points of southeastern Manchuria. They then began to recover their balance and moved from the north and south to relieve the Ssuping garrison. The Communist besiegers of Ssuping withdrew from the battlefield. The PLA's fifth Manchurian offensive was over at the end of June, with the Communist forces withdrawing on all fronts. Totting up the balance, a Communist source claimed the capture of forty-two towns in the offensive, and held that the military situation had been restored to what it was before the Nationalist occupation, in May, 1946, of Ssuping, Changchun, and Kirin. The claim was essentially correct.

The *over-all* Nationalist condition was even worse than it had been a year earlier. Changchun, Kirin, and Mukden were left isolated from each other, with the connecting rail lines badly wrecked. The Communist offensive of May–June, 1947, had advanced the Communist lines about 150 miles to the south. It had also achieved the vital strategic objective of severing the inner lines of rail communication between the main elements of the Nationalist garrison force. By this offensive the Communists had seized the initiative in Manchuria. They would retain it thereafter, to the end of the civil war.

The Nationalists had suffered heavy losses in territory, personnel, equipment, and morale; the Communists had made corresponding gains. With social and economic conditions in China proper deteriorating rapidly and the Government's political and military strength being drained by heavy demands, any tangible possibility of a Nationalist victory in the Manchurian theater had vanished. Although the Nationalists had partially redressed their shattered position, in the light of what had happened to rail communications it was now fully obvious that China's Northeast could become a gigantic strategic trap for the Nationalist forces. The jaws of the trap had, in fact, begun visibly to close.

Chiang Kai-shek nevertheless chose to play the game out. On July 4, 1947, the National Government declared the Communists to be in a state of rebellion. The Nationalist military headquarters was renamed, as of old, the Bandit-Suppression Headquarters. At the end of August the Generalissimo shifted his Manchurian command structure, replacing Hsiung Shih-hui with Chief of Supreme Staff Ch'en Ch'eng and Tu Yü-ming by Lieutenant General Cheng Tung-kuo—both of the new generals being more competent by far than their predecessors. Chiang also reinforced Manchuria with troops from North China. This did not restore the situation in the Northeast, and it drained the North China reserves, although the consequences of this action would not be perceived until some time later.

In North China some half-million Government troops had expanded Nationalist control in Shantung Province, which had been so long dominated by the Communist New Fourth Army. But that success, like the earlier capture of Yenan, was not quite real; it was achieved chiefly because the Communists had avoided positional battles against the Government's North China forces and had instead moved in strength southward into Central China, where the Government had virtually no forces. In August veteran Liu Po-ch'eng spearheaded the strategic Communist movement by thrusting from Hopei across the Lunghai line. Ch'en Yi moved troops from Shantung into southern Hopei to fill the gap left by Liu. Those two PLA generals were consolidating a position of great importance, as would be revealed in late 1948.

Nationalist gains in Shantung had been offset further by losses

in the west. In Hopei Province the Communists had cut the northern section of the Ping-Han Railway and succeeded in joining together the Shansi-Hopei-Shantung-Honan and Shansi-Chahar-Hopei
Liberated Areas. Shihchiachuang had been isolated and the ring
around Taiyuan drawn closer. At the end of the year the PLA
effectively controlled all of Hopei and Shansi Provinces except the
Taiyuan fortress area and the narrow corridor extending from
Tientsin along the Ping-Sui Railway. That long, tenuous ribbon
running through hostile territory was perilously controlled by the
troops of General Fu Tso-yi, seated in Peking.

On July 9, 1947, President Truman gave General Wedemeyer a
new mission: "You will proceed to China without delay for the
purpose of making an appraisal of the political, economic, psychological and military situations—current and projected." On September 19 Wedemeyer submitted his comprehensive report, later published in the *China White Paper*. Key sentences in the report aptly
described the China scene. Political: "On one side is the Kuomintang, whose reactionary leadership, repression and corruption have
caused a loss of popular faith in the Government. On the other side,
bound ideologically to the Soviet Union, are the Chinese Communists, whose eventual aim is admittedly a Communist state in
China. . . . Reactionary influences continue to mold important
policies even though the Generalissimo remains the principal de-
terminative force in the Government." Economic: "Under the impact of civil strife and inflation, the Chinese economy is disintegrating." Military: "The overall military position of the National
Government has deteriorated in the past several months and the
current military situation favors Communist forces."

"Throughout strife-torn China there is a passionate longing for
peace, an early, lasting peace," concluded Wedemeyer. In mid-1947
it was evident that the Chinese people were nearing final disillusionment with the Nanking regime and were becoming receptive
to a radical change on the grounds that "nothing could be worse
than the Kuomintang." On October 28, 1947, the Government outlawed the Democratic League and thus alienated more scholars
and intellectuals. Exploitation of the petty bourgeoisie by currency
manipulation and the siphoning-off of American aid to corrupt ends
were now leading even the merchant class to feel sympathy for the
peasants marching under the Red banner and for the revolutionary
intellectuals who demanded an end to venal and impotent government. The Nationalists stood in imminent danger of losing the

Mandate of Heaven; they had not heeded the ancient warning of Mencius to princes: "Heaven hears as our people hear; Heaven sees as our people see."

In his analysis of the military situation in China, General Wedemeyer noted that, "although the Nationalist Army has a preponderance of force, the tactical initiative rests with the Communists." Actually, in September, 1947, the People's Liberation Army possessed not only tactical but the strategic initiative. It was ready to go into the counteroffensive.

The Nanking regime had some appreciation of its difficult position but patently counted on American aid, not domestic reforms, to save it in any extremity. Upon withdrawing from North China the United States Marines had abandoned over 6,500 tons of ammunition to the Nationalists; excess American Army stocks of unknown procurement value located in West China had been transferred to them under the bulk sale agreement of August, 1946; and in June, 1947, the United States sold the Nationalists 130 million rounds of rifle ammunition at ten percent of procurement cost. But the Nationalists wanted still more aid.

When it was proposed in Washington that the United States provide a fund of $300 million in aid to China, Nanking leaders characterized this as "a drop in the bucket" and on November 15 suggested the alternative figure of $3 billion, to be provided over a period of three years. Mme Chiang Kai-shek flew to Washington to plead the Nationalist case, but she won no major increase in the proposed program. However, in December the United States Government sold Nanking 150 C-46 transport planes at $2,500 each, and signed another agreement with the Nationalists transferring 131 naval vessels (procurement cost, $141,300,000) to Chiang's government.

The military situation was not waiting upon American aid. The Wedemeyer report was dated September 19. On September 20, after a breather of two-and-a-half months, the Communists in Manchuria launched a new offensive with an attack from Jehol against the Liaosi corridor. By the end of the month Nationalist communications through the corridor were totally severed. General Cheng Tung-kuo succeeded in reopening the corridor by October 10, but the Nationalist Forty-ninth Army was nearly wiped out in the action. The Communists had meanwhile attacked at various points between Mukden and Changchun. The rail line between the two points, which the Nationalists had advertised would reopen to traffic on October 10, was returned to a state of ruin.

Heavy fighting took place north of Mukden, but the Government forces under Liao Yao-hsiang, one of Nanking's most capable commanders, held their ground; the Nationalists began to rally along the Mukden-Ssuping line. The PLA shifted its weight and attacked on the Changchun-Kirin front, netting several more towns. The sudden advent of the Manchurian winter about October 20 marked the end of the PLA offensive; the subsequent recovery of several towns by the Nationalists, and the re-establishment of contact with Kirin on November 13, were mere routine.

The Nationalist high command had by this time abandoned any idea of offensive action or even of combat in the open field. The Government units dug even deeper into their clusters of concrete pillboxes. By their latest offensive the Communists had both tightened up the isolation of the Nationalist strongholds from each other and further blocked the possible exits out of Manchuria. They were now prepared to challenge the Nationalists in positional warfare.

In mid-December the PLA interposed a massive block against Mukden's western defenses. By December 23 five PLA columns, supported by artillery and employing siege warfare tactics, had been placed in position facing the Mukden fortress quadrilateral along a front stretching from Sinmin on the west to Faku on the north. The final stage of the Manchurian campaign had begun.

The American accounting gave the Nationalists an over-all strength of 2,700,000 troops at the end of 1947, an increase of 100,000 over their reputed total at the beginning of the year. The official American figure of 1,150,000 Communist troops at the end of 1947, on the other hand, was a mere 250,000 increase over Mao Tse-tung's April, *1945* claim *for regulars alone;* it seemed inadequate to explain what had happened to Mao's claimed 2,200,000 militia, and to account for recruitment from ex-Manchoukuo Army elements and additions of defected Nationalist forces. Speaking on December 25, 1947, Mao Tse-tung himself claimed 2,000,000 PLA troops.

In any event, the Nationalist military position was much bleaker than indicated by the bare figures for troop strength. In Central China the Communists had built up a heavy concentration of strength that offset the improved Government posture in North

China. In Manchuria the Nationalists had now been cut down and isolated into three separate localities centering respectively on Mukden, Changchun, and Kirin. A Nationalist source recorded Government strength in Manchuria as being 418,000 men in December, 1947, compared with no more than 300,000 Communists. But Wedemeyer had remarked in his report: "Chinese [Nationalist] information on Communist supply, equipment, casualties, and manpower is completely unreliable and inaccurate." Besides, Manchuria's land communications with North China had been lost, and the Nationalist garrison could be supplied only by laborious and inadequate air-lift. The state of the Nationalist position in that theater was comparable to the predicament of the German forces before Stalingrad in early 1943.

Reporting on December 25, 1947, to the CCP Central Committee, Mao Tse-tung exuded confidence: "The Chinese people's revolutionary war has now reached a turning point." The PLA had assumed the offensive and was now carrying the war into Nationalist-controlled areas. The Chiang Kai-shek band had launched civil war in 1946, Mao said, thinking themselves strong and able to rely on the United States, and believing further that " 'the war between the United States and the Soviet Union is inevitable' " and that " 'the outbreak of a third world war is inevitable.' " He described the PLA's military tactics for defeating the Nationalists, saying that those tactics were known to both Chiang Kai-shek and his American military advisers—but that there was nothing that would save "the Chiang Kai-shek bandits" from defeat.[12]

In his New Year's message the Generalissimo made no shift; he said that the annihilation of the regular "bandit" formations could be accomplished within a year, although it would take one or two years more to mop up the "scattered bandits" in China as a whole. In Manchuria, he indicated, the Government would continue as before.

It seemed a bad omen for Nanking when in January, 1948, disaffected Party chieftains led by Feng Yü-hsiang and Li Chi-shen formed a Kuomintang Revolutionary Committee in Hong Kong. The echoes of Chiang's New Year's message had, in fact, hardly died away when, on January 5, the Communists launched a new offensive in Manchuria. A PLA drive from the north was coordinated with action by the Communist force blocking Mukden from the west and south, creating a pincers operation designed to push Mukden's outer defense lines back and strengthen the roadblocks on the Nationalist garrison's lines of retreat via the Liaosi corridor and the port of Yingkow.

With the PLA columns advancing rapidly, Chiang Kai-shek conferred with his commanders in Mukden. A new military command under the capable General Fan Han-chieh was established to defend the Liaosi corridor. On February 1, in yet another shift in the Manchurian high command, General Wei Li-huang became Commander-in-Chief of a new Northeastern Bandit-Suppression Headquarters. The circumstances attending his inauguration were inauspicious. The Communist drive had already netted important points west of Mukden; south of Mukden, Anshan was isolated; in early February the heavy PLA concentration north of Chinchow checked the forward movement of Fan Han-chieh's divisions.

By mid-February PLA strength on the western and southern flanks of the Mukden quadrilateral comprised ten columns numbering about two hundred thousand men, and the build-up was continuing. Mukden asked Peiping for reinforcements, and troops were air-lifted from Kirin and Changchun. The PLA strategist Lin Piao, reacting to the weakening of the Kirin and Changchun garrisons, shifted his weight northward and again put battle-scarred Ssuping under siege.

In November, 1947, Washington had instructed Major General David Barr that, as senior officer of the United States Army Advisory Group at Nanking, he might make his advice available to the Generalissimo on an "informal and confidential basis." So, in early March, 1948, when the Communists had withdrawn their main forces from the immediate vicinity of Mukden and Changchun, Barr advised Chiang Kai-shek to take the opportunity to make a progressive withdrawal of Nationalist forces from Manchuria. It seemed to Barr that the Communist movement offered a chance for the Nationalists to escape. Chiang "was aghast at the proposal," Barr reported, "stating that no circumstances would induce him to consider such a plan."

At the end of March Ambassador Stuart reported to Secretary of State Marshall:

Demoralization and deterioration of situation . . . have continued at an accelerated pace. There is an increased feeling of helplessness in government circles as elsewhere and a fervent searching for some means of bringing a stop to civil war and economic and political uncertainties resulting from it. There is an increasing realization, shared even by the Generalissimo, that military victory over Communists is impossible and that some other solution must be reached if Communist-domination [*sic*] of all China is to be avoided. . . .[13]

In an address a week later to the National Assembly, Generalissimo Chiang Kai-shek predicted that the Communist forces south of the Yangtze would be annihilated within six months; and he affirmed that China's economic situation (rampantly inflationary in fact) was "not only stable, but more solid than it had ever been before." On April 19 the National Assembly gave the Generalissimo a vote of confidence by electing him President by an overwhelming majority. It was, of course, his own Assembly.

While the National Assembly deliberated at Nanking, the United States Congress on April 2 passed the China Aid Act providing another $463 million for the National Government. But a series of portentous events soon shook China. In March PLA commander P'eng Teh-huai had gone into action in Shensi, destroyed several Government brigades, and cut off the Nationalist line of retreat from Yenan. The Government had thereupon air-lifted twenty-three thousand troops from the Kaifeng-Loyang sector to Sian in an effort to retrieve the situation. In the heavy fighting that had followed, the Communists had inflicted heavy losses on the Government forces in central Shensi. Two Nationalist divisions had been almost totally wiped out northwest of Sian, and many Nationalist troops had simply defected to the enemy. In mid-April the Communists had retaken Yenan, wiping out Nanking's widely heralded success of 1947.

The Nationalist transfer of troops from the Loyang-Kaifeng area to reinforce the Sian command had seriously weakened the Government position on the Lunghai line. The Communists next took Loyang, thus cutting the Nationalists in the Chengchow-Kaifeng sector off from Hu Tsung-nan's powerful force in southern Shensi. PLA commanders Ch'en Yi, Liu Po-ch'eng, and Ch'en Keng then massed some two hundred thousand men against the Government's two hundred fifty thousand in the Chengchow-Kaifeng sector and launched a general attack at the beginning of June. They occupied Kaifeng, the capital of Honan Province, on June 19, capturing huge stocks of military supplies. The psychological shock to the nation's morale was an even greater gain.

Manchuria had heretofore been the main war theater. But the Kaifeng battle, in which the Communists had overwhelmed the Nationalists in large-scale positional fighting, was an unmistakable sign that the insurgents would soon be fighting on Nanking's very doorstep in Central China. The Communist evacuation of Kaifeng within a week was obviously no Government "victory." The PLA strategy, as shown by the abandonment of Yenan in 1947, placed no value on territory: the Communists, as Mao had explained clearly, aimed at maintaining their mobility—and destroying the enemy forces.

KUOMINTANG ARMAGEDDON

The PLA forces in Manchuria took a full half year to regroup and re-equip after the long winter offensive. Their armament by now included much American equipment, including artillery, captured from the Nationalists. They began to deploy early in September. On September 12, an attack by some thirty thousand PLA troops set off heavy fighting in the Liaosi corridor, the only Nationalist escape route by land from Manchuria.

Disaster now piled on disaster for the Nationalists. At Tsinan, in Shantung, the Nationalists lost some eighty thousand troops, with all their equipment, in a battle lasting from September 14 to 24 in which part of the garrison defected to the enemy. Generalissimo Chiang Kai-shek assumed personal charge of the Nationalist forces in Manchuria at the beginning of October and, according to General Barr, directed battle operations from Peiping, "without the assistance of his Supreme Staff whom he failed to keep informed as to what was taking place."

Too late by at least half a year, Chiang Kai-shek finally tried to evacuate the Manchurian garrison. At the port of Hulutao, where the Nationalists had concentrated eleven divisions to help open the Liaosi corridor, a part of the Yunnan Ninety-third Army defected to the Communists as soon as it was put in movement; the remainder of the Hulutao force was left unused by a command fearful of its loyalty. Cut off at Chinchow, a short distance away, the Nationalist garrison, comprising eight divisions and five regiments, capitulated on October 15. Again huge stockpiles of American military stores were lost. At Changchun the Yunnan Sixtieth Army defected to the Communists on October 17, then helped the PLA forces to overcome the American-equipped New Seventh Army in the same sector the following day. Both Northeastern field commander Cheng Tung-kuo and General Fan Han-chieh were made prisoners.

With staff work completely snarled, the bulk of the Mukden

garrison, comprising the New First, New Third, and New Sixth armies and elements of other units tried to cut its way out of the Communist encirclement. But PLA General Lin Piao had massed overwhelming strength in General Liao Yao-hsiang's path; on October 27 he struck hard at the Nationalist columns, then about midway between Mukden and Chinchow.

The Nationalist Fifty-third Army and the 207th (Youth) division, back in Mukden, made no effort to help. General Tu Yü-ming, appointed to take Cheng Tung-kuo's place, General Wei Li-huang, and such others as could, fled from Mukden by plane. By October 30 Liao Yao-hsiang's entire force had been wiped out or taken prisoner. On November 1 the Fifty-third Army and the 207th Division surrendered Mukden. The only Nationalist troops that escaped the debacle were a few thousand soldiers of the Fifty-second Army who had been in the southern sector and succeeded in reaching the port of Yingkow; they were evacuated by ship. The Manchurian fighting of 1948 had cost the Nationalists well over four hundred thousand troops with all their armament and mountains of American military supplies. When the Communists took Yingkow on November 5 and the Nationalists abandoned the Hulutao beachhead, all of Manchuria had been lost. In view of the clear meaning of the Nationalist defeats at Tsinan and in Manchuria, the United States Navy at this juncture withdrew from Tsingtao.

One of the great battles of modern history, the Battle of the Hwai-Hai, took place immediately afterwards in Central China; and it was here that Chiang Kai-shek's military power received its *coup de grâce*. The Communist commanders were once more Ch'en Yi, Liu Po-ch'eng, and Ch'en Keng, with Ch'en Yi in over-all command. The chief Nationalist field commanders were Generals Ch'iu Ching-ch'uan and Huang Po-t'ao, both of whom had figured in the Chengchow-Kaifeng campaigning, under the over-all command of General Liu Chih. Chiang Kai-shek's second son, Chiang Wei-kuo, led the Government's treasured Armored Corps. In due course Tu Yü-ming joined the Nationalist command centered at the railway junction of Hsuchow. But once again the Generalissimo himself, from Nanking, directed Nationalist military operations.

The tremendous battle of annihilation began on November 7 along the eastern section of the Lunghai line with half a million men deployed on each side. The Communist command employed the strategy that had served so well in Manchuria, methodically cutting communications around a vast battlefield extending from the Lunghai Railway to the Hwai River (hence the designation Battle of the Hwai-Hai) and chopping the defending force into segments to be dispatched piecemeal. Chiang Kai-shek sent in reinforcements, but to no avail; they were likewise blocked and surrounded. When the great sixty-five-day battle ended on January 12, 1949, the Nationalists had lost five army groups, seven other full divisions, the Armored Corps, and miscellaneous units besides— approximately 550,000 men. Generals Huang Po-t'ao and Ch'iu Ching-ch'uan had been killed in battle, Tu Yü-ming and General Huang Wei, commander of the powerful Twelfth Army Group, were prisoners. Generals Liu Chih and Chiang Wei-kuo, however, had escaped from Hsuchow by plane.

By that crushing defeat the Nationalists lost the last of their thirty-nine American-equipped divisions. The Communists had won an enormous war booty; and they had eliminated the last tough military elements that should have formed the Nationalist defense bulwark at either the Hwai River or the Yangtze. The way to Nanking was now open to the Communists.

The economic situation had been deteriorating rapidly since midsummer. In August the Shanghai wholesale commodity price index was over three million times higher than the immediate prewar level. Prices had increased by forty-five times in the first seven months of 1948; the black market rate for American dollar notes had risen by more than fifty times in the same period. Economic chaos reigned in the Nationalist-held towns, blockaded as most of them were (except in South China) from the Communist-held countryside that was their normal source of food supply.

The United States Economic Cooperation Administration (ECA), established to implement the China Aid Act, set up a system for feeding nearly 13 million people in seven major cities and undertook to provide raw cotton, petroleum, and cotton cloth to industry and the citizenry. The effort unfortunately was indeed but "a drop in the bucket." On August 19, when the exchange rate stood at about one United States dollar to 12 million yuan, the National Government effected its last big currency "reform": the Chinese dollar (yuan) was converted to a new "gold yuan," to be guaranteed and held stable at one United States dollar to four gold yuan. All persons, Chinese and foreigners alike, were required to deliver their holdings of gold, silver, and foreign currency to the Government. The currency conversion was to be completed November 20.

JAPAN'S MAINLAND
AGGRESSION AND
CHINESE CIVIL
STRIFE

 Japanese occupation

autonomous province or
region

de facto independent

Communist control

OCTOBER, 1934

DECEMBER, 1936

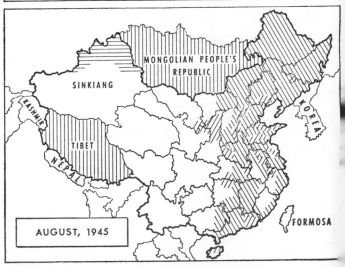

AUGUST, 1945

JULY, 1947

NOVEMBER 7, 1948

APRIL 20, 1949

The Japanese mainland advance, beginning with the occupation of Manchuria in 1931, did not result in an immediate cessation of China's civil wars. In particular, the National Government pursued its "bandit-suppression" campaigns against the Communists and continued simultaneously to extend authority over previously autonomous (if nominally "Nationalist") provinces. The Sian Incident of 1936 and the War of Resistance against Japan that began in 1937, however, radically changed the situation, so that now a unified Nationalist force stood side-by-side with the Communists in a common front against the Japanese aggressor. At the same time, each camp prepared as well for a renewal of the domestic contest when, in the postwar period, the country should once more be free of the foreign invader. The civil war thus was resumed, almost inevitably, in 1946. It reached its end with the Communist victory over the Nationalists in 1949.

Long before the Hwai-Hai battle was over, the Government's new "stable" currency began to slide, then plummeted. With the gold yuan went the last savings of the middle class, and also the last scant measure of trust the petty bourgeoisie had kept for Chiang Kai-shek's rule. In his 1949 New Year's address to the nation, the Generalissimo dropped the familiar appelation of "bandits" and said: "If the Communists are sincerely desirous of peace, and clearly give such indication, the Government will be only too glad to discuss with them the means to end the war." But at that moment nothing remained of his legions on the vast Hwai-Hai battleground except a rear-guard force of about one hundred fifty thousand men, surrounded and doomed to be wiped out.

On January 8, 1949, the National Government requested the intervention of the American, British, French, and Soviet governments. The note to Washington stated:

The Chinese Government wishes hereby to assure the United States Government of its sincere desire for a peaceful settlement with the Chinese Communist Party and particularly avail itself of this opportunity to ascertain in [sic] the views of the United States Government on this subject. The Chinese Government will welcome any suggestion by the United States Government which may lead to an early restoration of peace in China. The Chinese Government further signifies its readiness, through the possible intermediary of the United States Government, to initiate negotiations with the Chinese Communist Party with a view to attaining the end stated above.[14]

There could now be no return to anything even approximating the power position envisaged in the PCC agreements of January, 1946. The Communists on January 14 listed eight harsh conditions for a political settlement: in sum, the Kuomintang legal system was to be abolished and all authority of the "Kuomintang reactionary government" was to be taken over by a democratic coalition government. The British and American governments rejected Nanking's plea for intervention on January 15, Moscow did the same on January 17. On January 21, 1949, dictator President Chiang Kai-shek went through the ceremony of handing authority over to the Vice President who had been elected with him the preceding April, General Li Tsung-jen. Chiang thus "retired" from the Presidency. It was announced from Peiping the following day that General Fu Tso-yi had capitulated, on terms, to the Communists; another two hundred fifty thousand men and all of North China except Suiyuan Province and the Taiyuan pocket had been lost to the Communists.

Major General David Barr, reporting to Washington on his mission to the National Government, summarized the military factors resulting in the Nationalist defeat:

Many pages could be written covering the reasons for the failure of the Nationalist strategy. I believe that the Government committed its first politico-military blunder when it concentrated its efforts after V-J Day on the purely military reoccupation of the former Japanese areas, giving little consideration to long established regional sentiments or to creation of efficient local administrations which could attract wide popular support in the liberated areas. Moreover, the Nationalist Army was burdened with an unsound strategy which was conceived by a politically influenced and military inept high command. Instead of being content with consolidating North China, the Army was given the concurrent mission of seizing control of Manchuria, a task beyond its logistic capabilities. The Government, attempting to do too much with too little, found its armies scattered along thousands of miles of railroads, the possession of which was vital in view of the fact that these armies were supplied from bases in central China. In order to hold the railroads, it was also necessary to hold the large cities through which they passed. As time went on, the troops degenerated from field armies, capable of offensive combat, to garrison and lines of communications troops with an inevitable loss of offensive spirit. Communist military strength, popular support, and tactical skill were seriously under-estimated from the start. . . . The Nationalists, with their limited resources, steadily lost ground against an opponent who not only shaped his strategy around available human and material resources but also capitalized skillfully on the Government's strategic and tactical blunders and economic vulnerability.[15]

The outcome of the civil war had been decided, in short, by something besides fire power. On November 16, 1948, after the fall of Manchuria, Barr put the matter succinctly:

I am convinced that the military situation has deteriorated to the point where only the active participation of United States troops could effect a remedy. . . . Military matériel and economic aid in my opinion is [sic] less important to the salvation of China than other factors. No battle has been lost since my arrival due to lack of ammunition or equipment. Their [the Nationalists'] military debacles in my opinion can all be attributed to the world's worst leadership and many other morale destroying factors that can lead to a complete loss of will to fight. The complete ineptness of high military leaders and the widespread corruption and dishonesty throughout the Armed Forces, could, in some measure, have been controlled and directed had the above authority and facilities been available. Chinese leaders lack the moral courage to issue and enforce an unpopular decision.[16]

As Baron Antoine Jomini, famed nineteenth century strategist, said: "Iron weighs at least as much as gold in the scale of military strength." The struggle between the Nationalists and Communists had of course extended far beyond the battlefield. The Nationalists had been defeated militarily, true; but it was when they lost the loyalties of the intelligentsia and the "little people" of the towns, and when the agricultural countryside rose in revolt against long neglect and oppression, that the Nationalists finally lost the nation.

The denouement of the civil war, seen as the curtain came down on Nationalist rule over China, was a drab continuation of what had gone before. Hoping to salvage something from the wreckage, the Kwangsi men, Acting President Li Tsung-jen and Pai Ch'ung-hsi, commanding the forces in central China, proposed to rehabilitate Nationalist power south of the Yangtze. For Chiang Kai-shek, whose "retirement" was more nominal than real, the most dangerous enemy was always the nearest competitor. In this case the nearest competitors were Li and Pai. Should they succeed, Chiang would be left isolated without chance of ever again playing an important role in China's affairs; so he acted to break the power of Li Tsung-jen. Still "the Generalissimo," Chiang continued from his native home in Fenghwa in Chekiang Province to issue directives and orders to Government officials and to countermand military orders issued by Acting President Li in his last-hour effort. Chiang had already caused the removal to Formosa of both the Nationalist Government's gold stocks and a substantial number of Government troops and their equipment. He now harassed Li Tsung-jen from the flank.

A Nationalist delegation headed by Chang Chih-chung, closely associated with Chiang Kai-shek since Whampoa Academy days, arrived in Peiping on April 1 to negotiate a peace settlement with the victorious Communists. The Communist position at this stage was so strong as to leave little room for a compromise settlement. The Communists imposed an April 20 deadline for conclusion of the negotiations; the day arrived without agreement and the People's Liberation Army crossed the Yangtze.

Nanking fell on April 22, and a dreary parade of collapses followed: Taiyuan, with 77,000 men, surrendered on April 24; Wuhan on May 17, Sian May 20, Nanchang May 23, and Shanghai on May 27. On September 19 six Nationalist army commanders and nine divisional commanders surrendered at the head of their troops in southern Shensi. Suiyuan Province capitulated on September 20. All of Sinkiang went over to the Communist side on September 29. The new Central People's Government of the Chinese People's

Republic had most of China's territory under its jurisdiction when it was formally installed at Peking (as the Communists promptly renamed Peiping) on October 1, 1949.

The National Government had fled from Nanking to Canton in April, then went on to the wartime capital of Chungking. Chiang Kai-shek announced that he was going to join it there; Li Tsung-jen, alert to the probability that Chiang planned still to manipulate the situation against him personally, withdrew from the scene on the eve of Chiang's arrival, made a stopover in his native Kwangsi Province, then proceeded to Hong Kong and the United States. Behind him, the Generalissimo moved the peripatetic Government to Chengtu, the capital of Szechwan. But this was only in preparation for the ultimate flight. In December, 1949, the rump National Government went into exile on Formosa. After twenty-one years the Kuomintang dictatorship of China had ended.

PART III

THE COMMUNIST ERA
IN CHINA

9 THE NEW REGIME

THE CHINESE Communist regime established at Peking in October, 1949, was confronted with tremendous problems both at home and abroad. In the domestic sphere it was necessary to consolidate political power, to get the economy running again, and then to embark upon the long-term program of political and economic development promised to the nation ever since the 1911 Revolution. In the field of foreign affairs China, which had never made close friends, was now assured of strong enemies. As the history of the French and the Russian revolutions show, a social revolution has traditionally attracted strong animosities. In the circumstances it was strategically desirable for China to enlist the support of some powerful international agency against the hostile forces surrounding it.

There was no question as to the Peking regime's political nature and international orientation. The "coalition" government was dominated by the Chinese Communist Party, which was avowedly both Communist and revolutionary. The party had been a member in good standing of the Comintern from 1922 until the Comintern's dissolution in 1943. The Chinese Communists wore the badge of Communist orthodoxy and were openly committed to a pro-Soviet policy. The United States, by siding with the Nationalists in the civil war, had helped to solidify the Communists in that position.

CHINESE COMMUNIST IDEOLOGY

The Greek poet put it clearly: "Snub-nosed are the Immortals, and black, the Ethiops say. But no, the Thracians answer, red-haired and with eyes of gray." The Chinese gods are Chinese. It was so in the past, and equally so in 1949. The practical significance of this observation was indicated earlier by Mao Tse-tung when he said: "Russian history created the Russian system; . . . Chinese history will create the Chinese system." Mao did not propose to follow Soviet Russian patterns blindly and unswervingly.

For a reliable guide to the actions of the Chinese Communist Party during the period of its rule, it is essential to look into the wellsprings of Chinese Communism. If the Chinese could be expected to act as if they were identical twins of the Russians, we might learn their behavior patterns the more easily. But it must by definition be quite different if Chinese characteristics dominate Peking's thinking and make *Chinese* Communism into something different from the Russian prototype. It is this writer's proposition that the Chinese Communists are Chinese first and Communists only second. In other words, instead of being a corpus inherited from Marx and Engels via Lenin and Stalin, the Chinese Communist doctrine is shaped by China's past. Both "Communism" and "China," of course, are important factors in the composition called "Chinese Communism"; but the Chinese element is the more important.

The "Chineseness" of Chinese Communism comes from a number of basic factors. The Chinese language itself is one. Language, as the vehicle of thought, has an important influence on the form of thought itself, and this is particularly true in the case of thinking in Chinese. The language, fundamentally different in construction from any Occidental language, literally enforces a different type of thinking. One encounters, therefore, grave difficulties in translating accurately from other languages into Chinese, or vice versa. The introduction of new concepts into Chinese is like putting new wine into old bottles; the wine is often somewhat changed, if not spoiled. And past political concepts deeply influence contemporary thought. Two of those are of particular relevance here.

The first concept revolves around the belief in the existence of a universal truth. This was a basic principle of Confucianism, which was established as a State religion in the Han Dynasty and constituted the basis for autocratic rule. During the two millennia

characterized by the Confucian pattern, orthodoxy indeed took
only one form. Nevertheless, the Chinese were capable of holding
other "truths" with equal fervor. What was heterodoxy before might
become present orthodoxy, but it would still be Chinese. Even
political revolution was expressed inevitably in a Chinese (that is,
"orthodox") manner. In sum, Confucianism was not the only possible expression of Chinese "universal truth." A wide variety of
other ideologies might be equally "compatible with the Chinese
nature."

The second basic concept that permeated Chinese thinking
through the millennia is that of universal empire. The *Shu Ching*
(Book of History) records a document entitled "Hung Fan," attributed to the end of the Shang period (about 1100 B.C.), that
incorporated a plan for the whole of civilization as seen at that
time, including the objectives of government. The concept of *Ta
T'ung,* or universalism, which provided the theme for K'ang Yu-
wei's *Ta T'ung Shu,* had a long tradition behind it. The Chinese
concept of civilization was of a "middle kingdom," namely China,
surrounded by concentric rings of barbarians and vassals. There
was only one civilization worthy of the name—the Chinese. The
evidence indicates that the men who came to power in Peking in
1949 were true sons of the Middle Kingdom and felt as did their
forebears that Chinese culture in its totality was superior to all
others. To that philosophic constant there is now added the messianic
conviction that the Chinese, as a "leading" cultural group, are destined to guide the world's "oppressed" peoples, and especially their
fellow Asians, into a New Era—to be determined by Maoism.

It is, therefore, useful to look to other possible indications of
"Chineseness" in Peking's ideology. There have been many other
influences operating besides Confucianism, the Kuomintang's nationalism, and pure Marxism. Mao Tse-tung's reference to a "Hundred Schools of Thought" provides a lead, and one might profitably
examine earlier expressions of Chinese "socialistic" philosophy,
beginning with that of the Legalist School of the late Chou period.

Legalism derived from the philosophy of Shang Yang, of the
fourth century B.C. Lord Shang, as he was called, strongly opposed
the political ideals of the feudal order and the following of historical precedents, that is, he was opposed to the ideals of Confucianism. Instead, he proposed that the State be governed by an
absolute autocrat exercising a harsh law.

Shang Yang's concepts were brought to their full philosophic

flowering by Han Fei Tzu, and adopted by Han Fei Tzu's contemporary Li Ssu, the minister who helped Ch'in Shih Huang-ti
both to create the empire and to establish uniformity within it.
It was under Li Ssu's direction that Shih Huang-ti attempted to destroy the old feudal civilization by executing or exiling opponents of
the regime, burning the classics cited by scholars in support of
the ancient order, and burying alive scholars who ventured to dissent. The laws of other predecessor feudal states were suppressed,
and Ch'in codes enforced throughout the empire. Also under Li Ssu
there was standardization of the Chinese script, strict literary cen-
sorship, and an effort to centralize education—for thought control.

The Ch'in system was a centrally planned military economy with
state stockpiling, a government monopoly of resources, state control
of commerce, and vast public-works projects. Han Fei Tzu said:
"The intelligent ruler carries out his regulations as would Heaven,
and handles men as if he were a divine being." The Ch'in reign
was characterized by mass mobilizations, enforced mass migrations,
and vast labor corvées for the construction of imperial highways
and irrigation projects and for the completion of the Great Wall.
One hundred twenty thousand aristocratic families, for example,
were transported to Shensi after having been gathered from all
parts of China, thus destroying the landlord elements of the noble
clans. Tradition has it that a million men died making the Wall.
Shih Huang-ti and his minister Li Ssu believed that the empire
they had built would last ten thousand years.

The Ch'in concept of a centralized Chinese empire of universal
authority lasted as long as the dynastic system. So, too, despite
the superimposing of "Confucian" forms on the state in Han times,
did some political practices of Ch'in Legalism. It is quite evident
that some elements of the Ch'in spirit persisted even *after* China's
"Confucian" era ended.

Some non-Confucian but quite "Chinese" ideas made their appearance in Wang Mang's short-lived "New Dynasty" of 9–23 A.D.
Wang Mang's concepts were suggestive of some of the elements
of Mao Tse-tung's "New Democracy." One of the New Dynasty
principles was that "the land shall belong to the state, the slave
shall belong to himself." Wang Mang attacked the agrarian problem by dividing up large land holdings, reducing land rents, and
issuing low interest loans to the peasants. He established monopo-
listic control of the production and sale of certain commodities,
specifically salt, wine, iron, and wood. He also effected monopo-

listic control over water supply, currency, and copper smelting. Socialism thus was launched eighteen hundred years before Marx and Engels.

Wang An-shih, as minister under the Emperor Shen Tsung, reintroduced socialistic forms in the eleventh century, when China was being threatened by barbarian invasions. Wang An-shih tried to increase the military potential of his country. The peasantry was oppressed and overtaxed, and he sought to bring them relief. He instituted free and universal education, with changes in the examination system, and set up public granaries for use in time of dearth. But Wang An-shih's program, too, attacked the vested interests of his time, and his enemies turned against him and forced him from office. The socialist thought of Wang An-shih was rejected as had been the pure totalitarianism of Shang Yang and the socialism of Wang Mang—for the time being.

Finally, there had been the great T'aip'ing Rebellion. Here, too, a Chinese revolutionary movement tried to establish a new universal truth. The T'aip'ings, being anti-Manchu, were in one respect nationalists. But the movement arose primarily out of popular peasant misery and discontent, and the T'aip'ing ideology proposed radical social and economic reforms, especially in agriculture. Although the rebels failed to achieve their goals, they nevertheless confirmed that the phenomena offered by Wang Mang and Wang An-shih were not isolated aberrations of the Chinese character, but might reflect something much deeper, namely, an urge toward a type of social organization that, while possessing parallels in both Occidental socialism and Occidental totalitarianism, was basically Chinese *sui generis*.

The Chinese Communists have naturally made no overt acknowledgment of a debt to "imperialists" such as Shang Yang or Wang Mang. They purport to have descended, rather, from the T'aip'ing peasant revolutionaries and to hold deep sympathy for the Boxers' antiforeignism.

More immediately, however, their philosophy in 1949 was the end-result of a quarter century of their own experience, much of it bitter. The Chinese Communist Party had come close to extinction at the time of the 1927 break with the Kuomintang. The party leaders had been faced with a real problem of survival. Mao's primary strategic opponent was Chiang Kai-shek. Chiang Kai-shek was a student of the mid-nineteenth century political general Tseng Kuo-fan, who combined political conservatism with military orthodoxy. Mao Tse-tung was a student of the much earlier strategist, Confucius' contemporary Sun Tzu, who has influenced generations of military men down to the present. Sun Tzu said: "To fight and conquer in all your battles is not supreme excellence; supreme excellence consists in breaking the enemy's resistance without fighting," and: "Know the enemy and yourself, and in a hundred battles [you'll suffer] no defeat."

Mao developed his canny military philosophy during the long struggle with Japan, as can be seen particularly in his 1938 essay "On Protracted War." In that monograph he started from the joint premises that China's war was "progressive and righteous," and that Japan was "a moribund imperialism in a period of decline" with insufficient manpower and in an unfavorable international position. Mao conceded that there existed a disproportion of forces but held that the intrinsic factors making for a strong Japan and weak China were relative rather than absolute. He therefore foresaw three stages in China's protracted war: (1) the enemy's strategic offensive, and China's strategic defensive; (2) the enemy's strategic defensive, and China's preparation for a counteroffensive; and (3) China's strategic counteroffensive and the enemy's strategic retreat.

America's entry into the war against Japan made it unnecessary for China itself to undertake the strategic counteroffensive: Mao Tse-tung instead implemented his strategy to the full against his domestic enemy, the Nationalists, with striking success. As Ch'in Shih Huang-ti succeeded to the hegemons of the Warring States, so Mao Tse-tung inherited China from the ever-bickering Nationalist generals.

In the meantime, however, because he believed that "war cannot be divorced from politics for a single moment," Mao had been evolving his political strategy as well. And in his 1940 discourse "On the New Democracy" Mao sketched, in bold strokes, the shape of China's future. "In the historical course of the Chinese revolution two steps must be taken: first, the democratic revolution, and secondly, the socialist revolution." According to Mao, "the Chinese revolution is a part of the world revolution"; this referred not to the old bourgeois world revolution but to a new "socialist world revolution." The first stage of the Chinese revolution, constituting a new type of bourgeois-democratic revolution, would not bring about the evolution of a capitalistic society under the Chinese bourgeoisie's dictatorship; it would, instead, achieve "the establishment

of a new-democratic society under the joint dictatorship of all
Chinese revolutionary classes headed by the Chinese proletariat."

Speaking "On Coalition Government" at the Seventh CCP Congress in April–June, 1945 (that is, before the end of the second
World War), Mao spelled out his political thought in more detail.
He held that, when the Japanese invaders were defeated, there
should be convened a national assembly "on a broad democratic
basis" to establish a democratic government, a coalition embracing
all parties, groups, and non-party elements, "to build a new China."
The Kuomintang dictatorship should be abolished; and China
should not endeavor to build "a state along the old-type democratic
lines entirely ruled by the liberal bourgeois dictatorship. . . . We
want to set up a political system based on the united front and the
alliance of all democratic classes."

Mao's words on that occasion did not fully reveal the role intended for the CCP. But during the long years following 1927, the
CCP, under Mao's leadership, had expounded in considerable detail its military, political, and economic theory. So when victory in
the civil struggle came in 1949, the Communists knew what they
proposed to do. They possessed a body of philosophy, experience,
and established tactics ready for use in both domestic and foreign
affairs. They had available for their use likewise the rich experience of the Communist Party of the Soviet Union and the revealing
history of the transformation of Russia into the Soviet Union, on
which they would draw heavily—especially, in the first eight years
of their rule.

In the period from 1937 to 1949 it was necessary to win the allegiance of the critical middle group of China's influential bourgeoisie, who traditionally provided China's bureaucratic and managerial skills. In times of dynastic overthrow in the past, Confucian
bureaucrats had ordinarily chosen to remain at their posts and serve
the victors, even if they had been "barbarian" Kidani, Mongol, or
Manchu warriors. Through coalition government, to which the Communists were committed, Peking saw a means for mobilizing vital
support for the tasks ahead.

The Communists had given themselves all the latitude of choice
they needed. Much earlier Mao had spoken of a united front to
comprise four classes and had made it clear that some groups were
beyond the pale. And even as regards the four classes, it was only
the "democratic elements" who were acceptable to polite Communist society. For approval one had to be a "democrat," as defined

by the Chinese Communist Party. Writing on June 30, 1949, "On the People's Democratic Dictatorship," Mao Tse-tung made the position clearer still. He announced flatly that China would follow the course dictated by experience and employ a "people's democratic dictatorship" as its form of government. "That is, the right of reactionaries to voice their opinions must be abolished, and only the people are allowed to have the right of voicing their opinions."

In Confucian China, under a ruling hierarchy comprising Heaven, the Son of Heaven (the emperor), and the Ministers of the State, there existed four classes of subjects: gentry, farmers, artisans, and merchants. Mao now set up, under the rule of himself and his Communist comrades, Marxism-Leninism-Maoism to take the place of Confucianism and established a new division of "people" into four categories: workers, peasants, petty bourgeoisie, and national bourgeoisie. Outside the pale were three disenfranchised groups (the "non-people" who had the obligations of citizenship but none of the rights) comprising the landlords, bureaucratic capitalists, and "the Kuomintang reactionaries and their henchmen representing these classes." Those non-people were, by Mao's dictum, to be suppressed. This disenfranchisement had precedent in recent Chinese history. The Manifesto of the First Kuomintang Congress of 1924 also denied the privileges of citizenship to those opposed to the Revolutionary State: "Only those who are loyal to the Revolution, and opposed to Imperialism, will enjoy the benefits of the Revolution."

At the time of Mao's June 30 pronouncement, the Communists had effectively seized power but still lacked legitimacy. This lack they proposed to remedy by convoking a Chinese People's Political Consultative Conference (CPPCC), representing a united front of all the "people." The Conference met at Peiping from September 21 to 29 and adopted three basic documents: the Common Program of general principles, to act as an interim Constitution pending adoption of a permanent document; the Organic Law of the Central People's Government, to provide the interim governmental structure; and the Organic Law of the CPPCC.

In Communist legal theory, the CPPCC itself was the source of supreme power, possessing both a constituent and legislative function as representative of the nation. It was with the sanction of the CPPCC, therefore, that on October 1, 1949, the Central People's Government of the Chinese People's Republic was formally established in Peking. By no stretch of the imagination could the new regime be termed a creation of the Kremlin. It was Chinese.

THE APPARATUS OF GOVERNMENT

The Chinese Communist political system was laid initially on a base different from that of the Soviet system. In Russia, the Bolsheviks had established a dictatorship of the proletariat; in China, Mao decreed that a people's democratic dictatorship would rule. The Bolsheviks had been harsh in their treatment of aristocrats, bureaucrats, and intellectuals who had belonged to the Tsarist regime. The Chinese Communist Party, contrariwise, deliberately decided that non-Communist parties and individuals could constitute acceptable instruments for its rule of China. The CCP was viewed as a party of proletarians in alliance with the peasantry; but for its rule, in the so-called democratic revolution, it proposed to utilize a broad united front of "democratic elements" of all classes of the "people."

With the establishment of the new regime, political personalities were blurred: the collective of the CCP Politburo had replaced the individual on the Chinese political stage. By his infallibility Mao Tse-tung indeed reminded one of the Son of Heaven; but other personalities were largely submerged in the anonymity of The Apparatus. Moreover, the collective was nominally extended to include other political groupings. In the civil war proper, China's "democratic parties" had not played a fighting role; nevertheless, in the political struggle that had led the Chinese center to shift allegiance to the Communist side, the minor parties had performed an important function.

Most important of the various parties to appear during the war was the Democratic League. First organized after the New Fourth Incident of 1941 as a federation of small political groups, both Right and Left in complexion, the Democratic League took the present name in 1944 and began to play an important role as a middle-of-the-road group. Its leader was Chang Lan, the President of Chengtu University. But the right-wing elements separated from it in the postwar period: the Youth Party deserted as early as October, 1945, and part of the National Socialist Party (organized by Chang Chün-mai in 1931) entered the Kuomintang camp in November, 1946. In October, 1947, when the National Government outlawed the Democratic League as allegedly accessory to the "bandits," the League sided categorically with the Communists.

The Kuomintang Revolutionary Committee, organized on January 1, 1948, by Li Chi-shen and Feng Yü-hsiang, provided an organization through which disaffected Kuomintang members could express their political aspirations. The passage over to the Communist side of many prominent Kuomintang leaders in 1949 effectively marked the beginning of the end for Chiang Kai-shek's rightwing clique. For the great majority of the Kuomintang membership did not follow Chiang to Formosa. Those who decided to remain on the mainland, together with Li Chi-shen, and work with the Communists, included such figures as Soong Ch'ing-ling (Mme Sun Yat-sen), the sister of Mme Chiang Kai-shek; hard-fighting military men like Fu Tso-yi, Wei Li-huang, Ch'eng Ch'ien, and the long-time Dean of the Central Military Academy, Chang Chih-chung; Nationalists of the out-and-out warlord type, as Liu Wen-hui of Szechwan and Lung Yun of Yunnan; oldtime diplomats, and a plethora of academicians and scholars. Many of the prominent figures who remained behind took up government posts.

Some of the most important Nationalists to leave China still did not follow Chiang to Formosa. The leading representatives of three of the so-called Four Families, namely, T. V. Soong, H. H. K'ung, and Ch'en Li-fu, chose the United States as their new country of residence, not Formosa. So did Sun Fo, son of Sun Yat-sen, and others. Acting President Li Tsung-jen arrived in December, 1949; and in 1954 American-educated K. C. Wu, the governor of Formosa itself, broke away from the regime that had become a One-Family oligarchy instead of a Four-Family hierarchy. The gathering on Formosa had not resulted in a clean separation of the elite governing class of China into the sheep and the goats.

In Peking the Communist Party leadership remolded the "democratic parties" into fit instruments for the Communist rule. The several parties were assigned the respective social groups from which they might recruit. The Kuomintang Revolutionary Committee naturally became the refuge for former Kuomintang members and ex-officials and was subsequently employed in campaigns to entice both individual members of the Kuomintang and the entire Nationalist regime on Formosa to come over to Peking. It served the immediate organizational purpose well enough; but it made no headway toward subverting Chiang's new island regime.

The Democratic League, biggest of the democratic parties, was broken up into its original constituent elements—obviously to render it impotent so that it could be readily manipulated by the Communists. The League as such became active in the cultural and educational fields. Its member parties were assigned other social groups as their particular spheres of activity; one "party" was to recruit college professors, a second to take in middle- and primary-school teachers, a third was given the function of corralling former private businessmen.

In this way the democratic parties were charged with performing various functions which, if hardly related to the activities of political parties of the Occidental type, were integral parts of the Chinese power structure. They provided legitimacy, and window-dressing, for the regime. In more practical terms they were something in the nature of isolation wards for leading members of different social groups who, deemed unsuitable for CCP membership because they might infect that pure organization, nevertheless could not safely be left to go their own way since they might provide focuses for troublesome dissent.

In a more positive aspect, the democratic parties were to assist the CCP line, educating and guiding the people the way the CCP wanted them to go, mobilizing their enthusiasms and energies for the work of "socialist construction." They had limited functions and were destined to have a limited lifetime. The National Salvation Association, for one, was disbanded at an early date on the grounds that its purpose of national salvation with respect to the Japanese had been accomplished. The existence of the democratic parties was not planned to extend beyond the period of "contructing socialism," for they had no function to perform in the "classless" society of the future. As in Orwell's *Animal Farm* it was discovered that "all animals are equal, but some are more equal than others," so in China the CCP was "more equal" than its pretended associates. The democratic parties were but pale satellites to it. They had no more power than did the parliamentarians during the warlord era or minor parties under the Kuomintang's one-party dictatorship. Thus it happened that, from the institution of the Republic in 1912 to the present time, a multiparty parliamentarian democracy has never been tried in China.

Mass organizations were created for all walks of life after the pattern of the democratic parties. Some of them had honest backgrounds as free agencies, but all alike came to be servants of the all-powerful State. Among these were the All-China Federation of Trade Unions, All-China Federation of Democratic Women, All-China Students Federation, All-China Federation of Democratic Youth, and, of course, a Sino-Soviet Friendship Association. All were governed by the principle of democratic centralism; all were made effective appendages of the CCP by lateral contacts at all levels, starting at the top. The honorary chairman of the All-China Federation of Trade Unions, for example, was Liu Shao-ch'i, the Chairman Communist functionary Lai Jo-yü. As might be expected, the "labor" organization's function was no longer to look simply to the benefit of labor but, apart from dealing with labor-management contracts and handling labor welfare, to indoctrinate labor, increase production, and carry out state policies.

Other mass organizations were provided to which the urban street dweller, the village handicraftsman, and the peasant in the countryside would respectively belong. In China today there exist no secret societies, no nonofficial associations, and no private relationships—at least in so far as the Communist rulers have had their way. Practically everybody instead has been called upon to belong to several interlocking organizations in which all that any member does is publicly known. The result has been not identification but atomization: the right to a private personality has been lost, and the State's domination over the individual has been made nearly complete. The Chinese Communists, like the Legalists, believe in absolute social control.

The Chinese Communist Party had long been a tightly knit organization. In 1949, when it won national power, the CCP was in a position different from that of the victorious Bolsheviks in 1917. It was a seasoned, disciplined organization with twenty-eight full years of experience in military and political affairs. It had fought, and ruled, on a major scale. The top men had long worked together and were hardened by adversity. Mao Tse-tung, founding member of the CCP, was chairman of the Party's Central Committee; Chu Teh, founder of the Red Army, was commander-in-chief of the People's Liberation Army; Chou En-lai, Chiang Kai-shek's political commissar at the Whampoa Military Academy, had become premier of the Central People's Government; Liu Shao-ch'i, Moscow-trained labor organizer, was second only to Mao as a party theoretician. Other big names followed theirs in the membership of the Central Committee, those of Ch'en Yun, Teng Hsiao-p'ing, Liu Po-ch'eng, Lin Piao, P'eng Teh-huai, Ch'en Yi, P'eng Chen, and several scores of others. They were all veterans. In the twenty-eight years of CCP history up to 1949 there had been no wholesale purges of leadership such as had occurred in the Communist Party of the Soviet Union. During that period some, such as Li Li-san and Ch'en Shao-yü (Wang Ming), had indeed been ousted from leadership; however, only three leading figures had fallen by the wayside and been expelled from the Party: Ch'en Tu-hsiu, T'an P'ing-shan, and Chang Kuo-tao. And T'an P'ing-shan was rehabilitated after the Communist victory. The CCP leadership had been a stable one.

The Central People's Government, which is the *alter ego* of the CCP, came into being fully equipped with the police power necessary for maintenance of authority and control. Whereas in the spring of 1929 the fledgling Red Army had some ten thousand men, at the end of 1949 the People's Liberation Army, swollen by former Nationalist forces, numbered perhaps five million.

Besides Commander in Chief Chu Teh, other military men under him were credited with notable accomplishments on the field of battle. In 1949 such able generals as Lin Piao, Ch'en Yi, P'eng Teh-huai, Liu Po-ch'eng, Ho Lung, Ch'en Keng, and Nieh Jung-chen commanded vast armies in the field. At that time there was still much mopping-up and consolidation to do on the mainland. A large Nationalist Army had escaped to Formosa and would be a threat until annihilated, and there still remained the not inconsiderable task of absorbing or disbanding the hundreds of thousands of Nationalist troops who had changed sides or surrendered. Finally, the history of dynasties, and of the Republic itself, warned that individual military men might endeavor, if moved by personal ambition, to carve out semi-independent domains under their own rule.

A notable feature of the new government at Peking was the People's Revolutionary Military Council (which continued in being until 1954). Under that Council, which functioned independently of the Government Administration Council, the country was divided into six big military administrative districts: Northeast, Northwest, Southwest, East, South-Central, and North. In each district, one of the leading Communist generals had prime authority to accomplish the remaining military tasks, to consolidate political power, and to maintain order during the period of "land reform" immediately ahead.

The central government established in October, 1949, was clearly an interim apparatus, to be replaced by a more permanent structure after the period of initial consolidation. It comprised four main branches. There was the Central People's Government Council, with legislative, executive, and judicial powers. The Government Administration Council, the equivalent of a cabinet, with various appended committees, was the highest administrative body of the land. The People's Revolutionary Military Council, headed by Mao

Tse-tung as chairman and having seven vice chairmen, exercised direct control of the armies during the quasi-military period still in being. Finally, as complementary to the executive organs and definitely subsidiary to them in spirit as well as in law, there were the Procurator General's Office and the Supreme People's Court.

Local government comprised everything else, from provinces on down. From the beginning, however, changes from the old order loomed in the offing. For one thing, although the tempting offers of the early CCP Congresses of the right of self-determination for national minorities was withdrawn, a sop to the nationalism of non-Chinese peoples was given in the form of a grant of autonomy—and the establishment of autonomous areas ranging in size from *hsien* (county) to several "regions" which comprised hundreds of thousands of square miles. In 1949, however, it remained to be seen just how much of the substance of autonomy would actually be enjoyed by the minorities.

Another distinctive feature was discernible in the early phase of the Communist regime: where the imperial system reached down only as far as the *hsien,* the Communist governmental structure penetrated to the lowest limits—to the *hsiang* (township) and village in the countryside, and to the ward and street in towns. And whereas the Kuomintang "period of tutelage" for the training of the nation in the ways of government had lasted from 1928 to 1948, and even then had never borne more than the most barren fruit, the Communists began immediately to develop on a nation-wide scale, in accordance with the provisions of the Common Program, so-called "people's all-circles' representatives conferences" in preparation for the National People's Congress that was to introduce representative government to China. It was evident that the Communists intended to use a different timetable from that of the Kuomintang in instituting the form of government envisaged by their program.

In 1954, with the convening of the National People's Congress and the adoption of a Constitution, the whole governmental structure was formalized. The Congress superseded the Chinese People's Political Consultative Conference as the highest organ of state power. In theory, it is scheduled to meet yearly; but it is too big and unwieldy a body to function in the manner of Western representative bodies (there were 1,226 delegates elected to the 1954 Congress), and between the infrequent sessions its full authority is exercised by the Standing Committee, comprising a chairman, thir-

teen vice-chairmen, a secretary general, and thirty-five ordinary
members. Liu Shao-ch'i, the first chairman, was succeeded by Chu
Teh in 1959.

Reflecting the new Constitution and the consolidation of power
that had been effected by 1954, the Central People's Government
was tightened up. The Government Administrative Council was replaced by a State Council having regular cabinet form, with Chou
En-lai still as Premier. The Government Council was abolished, and
its powers divided between the Standing Committee of the Congress and the State Council. The People's Revolutionary Military
Council was divided in two, with the part in immediate control of
the armed forces becoming a regular Ministry of Defense in the
State Council, and a large group (over one hundred) of high-ranking military men being organized in 1958 into a separate National
Defense Council headed by the Chairman of the Republic—from
1959 on, Liu Shao-ch'i. The National Defense Council was presumed
to have functions related to over-all military planning; however,
since a number of its members were obviously simply enjoying honor-
able military sinecures, and many were ex-Nationalist generals, it
must be concluded that the Council was not charged with the evolution of grand strategy. The nation's top-level military planning
was almost certainly the function of two other military organs,
namely the PLA General Staff and the shadowy Military Affairs
Committee of the CCP Central Committee. Lo Jui-ch'ing replaced
Huang K'e-ch'eng as Chief of General Staff in 1959. Mao Tse-tung
himself was the titular chairman of the Military Affairs Committee,
but its effective head was ex officio the Minister of National De-
fense(always a high Party man), from 1959 Lin Piao.

Finally, there was inaugurated a new institution, the Supreme
State Conference, in the form of ad hoc meetings between the
chiefs of various state organs for the purpose of coordinating, at the
top level, the work of the different branches of government. Again
the omnipresent Chairman of the Republic headed the group. For
at the peak of the governmental structure stood the Chairman of
the Chinese People's Republic. On an adjoining height was the
other position of supreme power, that of the Chairman of the Central Committee of the Chinese Communist Party, Mao Tse-tung.

At the beginning of the Communist period China possessed a
stout organizational skeleton prepared for the tasks ahead. However, decades of foreign and civil wars had worn down the country's strength. Before embarking on the path of socialism, Mao Tse-

tung and his fellows undertook to consolidate their political and economic position.

PERIOD OF CONSOLIDATION: 1949–1952

In his essay of June 30, 1949, Mao Tse-tung had revealed the key to his strategy. China, he said, could not look to imperialist powers for help; only the revolutionary Soviet Union would be prepared to provide the assistance that would make China's sinews strong. Consequently, China would lean to the side of the Soviet Union.

On October 1, the day it was formally inaugurated at Peking, the new regime communicated with the consular representatives stationed there, inviting recognition and the establishment of regular diplomatic relations. The Soviet Union, which had maintained "correct" relations with the National Government to the last, recognized the new regime the following day and had its ambassador in the capital within a week.

It was not unexpected, given both his political philosophy and the international situation as he saw it in the crystal ball of Marxism, that Mao Tse-tung went to Moscow in December to negotiate details of a new relationship between the two Communist states. Mao desired to borrow strength from the USSR for China's use in both foreign and domestic affairs during its period of weakness. In February and March, 1950, the two nations signed a treaty of political and military alliance and subsidiary economic agreements (to be discussed in detail below). Doubtless he hoped for still more economic aid than he got by that first *démarche*, but he had made a beginning. Besides, the Chinese obtained certain important political commitments at Moscow. Mao left for home knowing in general terms how much assistance China could count on for both its anti-imperialist policy and its work of economic rehabilitation.

In June, 1950, Mao Tse-tung offered his people an estimate: the period of reconstruction would take about three years. On the basis of this estimate, it could be assumed that the first stage of the Communist rule would last roughly through 1952. The date was to prove significant. This would be a period for the consolidation of control.

As of October, 1949, the Communist regime saw itself still confronted with four immediate enemies, namely, Kuomintang military remnants, Kuomintang "bureaucratic capitalism" (comprising the holdings of the state and the Four Families, including ex-Japanese properties), "feudalism," and imperialism (that is, foreign influence in China).

At the end of 1949 Kuomintang elements, including both military forces and agents, were still in being in West China, Sinkiang, on the island of Hainan, and on Formosa and a number of off-shore islands. No more than mopping-up operations were needed in most sectors. The Communists attacked Hainan in an amphibious operation in March, failed, but returned and took it in April, 1950. In May they occupied the Chusan islands lying off the mouth of the Yangtze. In May, also, Chiang Kai-shek, who had two months earlier resumed the reins of power on Formosa, announced that he would be ready to attack the mainland in two years' time. Chiang, however, was without any significant support left on mainland China. In May and June the Chinese Communists worked at concentrating a force evidently to be used against Formosa, and the end of the Nationalists seemed in sight.

The attack on the second enemy, bureaucratic capitalism, was speedily completed. The material manifestation of that enemy was the National Government's properties. They were inherited directly by the Communists. There were tremendous stocks of military supplies, state enterprises, and other state property, including the bulk of material aid given Nanking by the United States. Whatever was left behind of the wealth of the leading "enemy" Nationalists who had fled the country was confiscated. Much of that wealth had already been sent abroad and found safe haven in foreign bank accounts, stocks and bonds, and personal possessions. Nevertheless, anything that the Communists were able to seize in that category represented a clear profit. Similarly, the Japanese properties in China —industries, railways, real estate, and military supplies—had never been turned over to an international accounting by the Nationalists and thus came into Communist hands.

Bureaucratic capitalism no longer existed in China; that particular enemy had been eliminated through a metamorphosis into *state* capitalism. A collateral development was taking place. Beginning in October, 1951, and lasting for eight months, the Communists waged a "five-anti" campaign in the ranks of the national bourgeoisie—a class that had the status of "people." The drive was directed against five sins against the state attributed to the Chinese mercantile group: bribery, tax evasion, fraud, theft of state property, and theft of state economic secrets.

The first three of the anti-social actions were certainly not new sins of the national bourgeoisie; but the last one, in particular, was a mark of the new order in which the divulging of any information deemed important by the regime would be regarded as a crime against the state. The campaign for extirpation of these social sins was carried out by procedures that were to become standard. During the first months of Communist control, cadres had made inquiries, investigated, checked business books; then there came accusations and public accusation meetings, the judgments of people's tribunals, demands for confessions and recantations, and the imposition of fines and penalties. The "cleansing" was effective in more ways than one: the state netted from the operation an estimated $1,250 million. The national bourgeoisie had been disciplined. Moreover, although Mao's division of the "people" into four classes had envisaged a role for private capital in a mixed Chinese economy, the "five-anti" campaign of 1951–52 was a big step in the direction of the takeover of private enterprise.

During the 1949–52 period, the attack on feudalism was vigorously pressed home. Feudalism, by Mao's interpretation, was landlordism. The landlords of China were not possessors of great estates: their holdings were on the average only about forty acres. But they lived, in the market town or the county seat, on the rentals from their lands and had consequently been cast among the damned as "non-people."

In their Yenan period the Communists had exercised moderation with respect to the landlords, but that reflected wartime exigencies. There had been, however, a tell-tale straw in the wind: after V-J Day, they had begun large-scale confiscation of both landlord and rich-peasant holdings. But they still had to win the civil war, and soon there was a partial shift toward restraint. With the conquest of Manchuria in 1948, however, "land reform"—which meant confiscation of landlord holdings and division of the land among the peasantry—went forward.

In the Land Reform Law of June 28, 1950, the Communists spelled out the initial stage of their land program. It provided that land, draft animals, farm implements, surplus grain, and surplus housing of landlords should be confiscated. Landlords might retain other property, including cash and investments, and they were to get an equal share of land and the means of agricultural production during the process of redistribution of land. There was one qualification: landlords who were "enemies of the people" were ineligible.

Agricultural tenants fell into three strata—rich peasants, middle peasants, poor peasants and farm laborers. There was to be a leveling down (of rich peasants) and a leveling up (for the poor peasants and farm laborers). The common pool of real property was fed also by another stream, that of "requisitioned" rural land belonging to ancestral shrines, temples, monasteries, churches, schools, and other institutions.

China's land reform was carried through in accordance with practical precedents already established and with the Reform Law of 1950. The procedure was harsh, and often bloody. Previously Communist cadres had gone into the agricultural villages, made inquiries, entered the peasants' homes, and checked on old grievances. When their preliminary investigations had been completed, they had formed peasants' associations, which were to constitute an instrument of prime importance during the land-reform period. Led by the Communist cadres, the associations staged accusation meetings at which the landlords' past "crimes against the people" were proclaimed. People's tribunals were set up to try the alleged evildoers—in public, as urged by the Communist activists. The accused was often condemned to death and his entire property confiscated. Several million people are reported to have been killed in the course of the "land reform"; and, just as thoroughly as Ch'in Shih Huang-ti had wiped out the aristocratic families of his time, so Communist China liquidated the landed gentry as a class. The peasant class of the country had been made to participate and to accept responsibility in the whole process. The new government had incidentally been projected throughout the countryside.

As a consequence, an equalization of land tenure among the remaining agricultural population left each farm family (averaging five mouths) in possession of about two and one-half acres of cultivable land. Signs of other impending events were the establishment of mutual-aid teams (in which peasants combined to help each other in busy agricultural seasons) and the introduction of "agricultural producers cooperatives" (in which peasants pooled their land and other property for *joint* ownership and exploitation). In short, land reform had led up to the next stage of the agricultural program—collectivization.

While Kuomintang remnants, bureaucratic capitalism, and the landlord class were wiped out as social groups, the Communist Party's own membership was subjected to a cleansing. Where there had been 1,210,000 members in April, 1945, there were 5,800,000 in 1950. Many of the newcomers were careerists; many more might have been usable in time of war but were unsuited for the politically more complicated tasks of peace.

The Party had found it necessary to carry out a "rectification movement" in 1942–44 to rid the membership of "bad" habits. In 1951 it found itself confronted with the same need, and (shortly before it launched the "five-anti" attack on the national bourgeoisie) undertook new rectification by means of a "three-anti" campaign. The attack focused on waste, corruption, and bureaucratism on the part of the membership and resulted in a broad purge of undesirable (and undesired) elements and a disciplining of those remaining. (Another "three-anti" campaign was launched in 1953, with the new objective of eliminating "commandism," bureaucratism, and "violation of laws and discipline.") The party apparatus was tightened up accordingly.

The attack on the foreign enemy, imperialism, met little real resistance: that enemy had abandoned most of the field long before. The Nationalists had already won part of the victory by their recovery of tariff autonomy, various territorial concessions in China, and by the final abolition of extraterritoriality in 1943. The unequal treaties were a thing of the past, and Japan's influence in China had been shattered with V-J Day. The only country that still possessed anything in the nature of special interests was the Soviet Union, China's ally, with its rights in Dairen and Port Arthur and rights of joint operation of the Manchurian railway system. This situation could only have been galling to the Chinese. They quickly won concessions from the Soviet side. It was agreed in the February-March negotiations of 1950 that, by the end of 1952, the Soviet Union should return to China, without compensation, all of its rights in the Manchurian railway system. The special position that Moscow had gained in Dairen and Port Arthur by virtue of the August, 1945, treaty with the Nationalists was to be abandoned upon the signature of a peace treaty with Japan—but also not later than the end of 1952. (After the beginning of the Korean War, that time limit was extended temporarily, but restitution was actually accomplished in 1955.)

The March agreements also provided for the establishment of three new Sino-Soviet joint-stock companies, one to operate three airlines between China and the Soviet Union, a second to exploit petroleum resources in Sinkiang Province, and the third for the survey and the exploitation of nonferrous mineral resources in

Sinkiang. There remained no other political infringement of China's jealously cherished "sovereign independence."

Positive gains to China flowed from the alliance. In readily measurable terms, there was a $300 million Soviet credit, to be expended over five years and repaid over ten. More valuable still, if less tangible, was the extension of Soviet technical aid, in the form of expert advisers, blueprints, and invaluable experience. Finally, China won the incalculable benefit of having a guaranteed trade channel. The young USSR in the 1920s, because of its isolation from "friendly" markets, had suffered considerable disadvantage both in procurement of desired goods and in disposal of its products, which it frequently had to dump on the world markets. Communist China, on the contrary, was assured of a source of supply and a parallel market.

In addition, Article 4 of the treaty of alliance provided for consultation regarding international affairs of common interest. This meant that China, in the international sphere, would in effect stand side-by-side with its giant Eurasian neighbor. In so far as Moscow was willing, Peking was in an advantageous position to wield an authority and a force borrowed from the Soviet Union. It had obtained a "derived power" far in excess of what it held in its own right.

There were, of course, relics of other "imperialistic" foreign influence in China, in the form of business and missionary enterprises, banks, shipping companies, and foreign consular establishments scattered throughout the country. *Even those weak and inoffensive remnants were not acceptable to the Chinese ideologues.* They hated blindly everything that smacked of the ignoble in China's past. They had "leaned to one side," as Mao put it, partly for the purpose of getting Soviet support for a war on "imperialism." They meant to make use of that support.

The CCP's basic intent in that regard had been set forth in 1931, when the Provisional Soviet Government was established in Kiangsi: it proposed by expulsion and confiscation to rid China entirely of foreign economic and political power. In 1949–50 it launched a general attack and proceeded to uproot and destroy the few enfeebled remnants of *non-Soviet* foreign rights and interests still left in China. The Economic Cooperation Administration supplies that the United States Government had shipped to the country for relief distribution were confiscated. The Communists fomented labor troubles against foreign enterprises, shackled their activities, and milked them dry before driving them out of business. Christian churches were compelled to cut all foreign ties, and the activities of foreign missionaries were so curtailed that they were forced to give up their religious work, and many were jailed. Curbs were applied to foreign journalists, and then they lost their accreditation. The United States Information Agency was caused to stop operations. And, just as the churches were wrested from foreign control, so were schools, charitable institutions, and hospitals which had been supported by foreign funds.

By 1952 the privileged position of "imperialism" in China had been completely wiped out. Moreover, incidental to their elimination of "enemies," the Communists confiscated considerable wealth. The British lost an investment valued at $800 million; the Americans, whose investments were much smaller, did not lose as much, unless one took into consideration the material aid given the Nationalists. The Japanese, of course, sustained the greatest loss of all; but, as a vanquished power, they had in any event lost forty percent of their empire.

The position of foreign investment capital in China had been destroyed. And the treaty ports that had been the center of foreign activities suffered corresponding shock. The metropolis of Shanghai, once so great a world seaport and commercial center, but so hateful to Chinese nationalists for what it symbolized, was deliberately strangled to near-death by the new regime.

From 1950 to 1952 China had made a remarkably clean sweep of "enemies," domestic and foreign. The localized efforts had been crowned by substantial accomplishments with respect to consolidation of its frontiers, for national aggrandizement and national security. After the mopping-up of isolated pockets of Nationalist resistance and the extension of Communist authority to the shores of the China Sea, there remained only the question of Formosa and the Pescadores, occupied by the remnant Nationalists. But all other gains in the 1949–52 period were heavily outweighed by two major accomplishments with respect to China's frontiers.

In the first place, the Peking regime restored Chinese control over Tibet, which had evaded Chinese authority since the beginning of the Republic. The matter was accomplished with dispatch. In October, 1949, Peking announced its intention of "liberating" Tibet, and the tenth Panchen Lama, nurtured by the Nationalists to achieve just that, voiced his wholehearted support for the venture. Liu Po-ch'eng, in charge of the Southwest Military Administrative

District, was charged with accomplishing the task and began to move troops in October, 1950.

The denouement was revealing. Tibet appealed to the United Nations for help. It won no support, however, from the Great Powers which upon occasion had stood for self-determination and the independence of peoples. The resolution asking for UN intercession on behalf of Tibet was put forward by little El Salvador. Naturally, Moscow supported Peking's assertion of right to rule Tibet. The Chinese Nationalists voiced as firmly as the Communists the claim to an unqualified Chinese sovereignty over Tibet. The United States was governed by a past acceptance of the Chinese claim and bound besides by its liaison with the Nationalists. Britain also was committed to past legal positions. Under the circumstances, the Western delegations seemed happy to defer to the country then having primary interest in the fate of Tibet—India. And India asserted that it had reason to hope that a satisfactory political settlement could be worked out.

Tibet, therefore, found no help. It could only bow to the inevitable. The Tibetan garrison at Chamdo, on the eastern marches, had already suffered a crushing defeat at the hands of Liu Poch'eng's well-armed legions. Lhasa agreed to "negotiate" and sent a delegation to Peking to surrender. In the agreement signed in May, 1951, the Chinese Communists rendered lip service to Tibet's right to "regional autonomy." But the critical provisions covered basic functions of Tibet's government, its foreign affairs, and its armed forces. Tibet was categorically incorporated within the framework of the Chinese Communist state; it was stripped of the power to handle its own foreign affairs; and its armed forces were to be amalgamated with the People's Liberation Army.

Communist China acted also to consolidate its national defense system in another area, Korea. The course of the Korean War will be treated at greater length in a later consideration of China's foreign relations. It may be noted at this point, however, that the strategic importance of Korea had been amply proved in the past by such historical events as the first Sino-Japanese War and the Russo-Japanese War. The so-called "Cold War" between the United States and the Communist camp had begun in 1947 and, although American troops had evacuated South Korea in 1949 (the year of the Communist victory in China), American armed forces remained in Japan, and the American interest in South Korea continued to make itself felt. A prime factor leading to the Korean War was undoubtedly Chinese hostility to the American "presence" in South Korea.

It is not only probable but to be accepted as beyond reasonable doubt that Mao Tse-tung and Stalin discussed the question of Korea during the course of Mao's visit to Moscow. It must also be assumed that they determined upon their joint strategy at that time, in accordance with the spirit of that provision of the new treaty of alliance that provided for mutual consultation in such circumstances.

In view of the events that followed the North Korean attack of June, the Chinese intervention of October, 1950, was a logical development. That intervention brought, first, a restoration of the military *status quo ante* and, second, an effective stalemate even before the end of 1952. The truce of mid-1953 was the natural sequel.

Just as the campaigns against domestic enemies had exercised a significant influence on the consolidation process then in course in China, so, too, did the Korean War. It brought in its train a further strengthening of domestic controls, particularly through the operation of the "Resist America, Aid Korea" campaign. There were intensive drives for the collection of "patriotic" donations, and another large amount of treasure was thus squeezed from the Chinese population. In 1951–52, coincident with the aforementioned "five-anti" drive but related more immediately to the Korean War, there was a national scourging of "counter-revolutionaries," with the execution of some hundreds of thousands of alleged antagonists of the new order. (The drive was repeated in 1955—the year of the first Formosa Strait crisis.) The war also resulted in the re-equipping of the hard core of the People's Liberation Army, and its further hardening in battle against a foreign foe. Furthermore, even as Japan had won enhanced prestige in Asia by its defeats of China in 1895 and Russia in 1905, so Communist China won renown and a somewhat apprehensive respect among Asian observers by reason of the visible evidence of its military prowess, as exhibited against the United Nations and, more particularly, against the United States.

By 1952, the end of the three-year period of rehabilitation anticipated by Mao Tse-tung, Peking had stabilized the currency, restored the wrecked communications system, brought industry and agriculture nearly back to the prewar level, extended and consolidated its machinery of domestic police control over the en-

tire country, and eliminated the three domestic "enemies" who had
existed in 1949. The regime had got rid of much domestic corruption and economic waste and had confiscated a vast quantity
of capital. It had, moreover, redistributed the country's agricultural
land.

Its accomplishments in the foreign field were equally impressive.
The Peking regime had ousted "imperialism" and special rights and
interests (and most individual foreigners who represented them)
from China. It had extended its authority over an important segment of "lost territory" and maintained North Korea as a security
buffer.

At the end of 1952, with those accomplishments under its belt,
China prepared to advance from the "New Democracy" stage to
"the transition to socialism."

THE FIRST FIVE-YEAR PLAN, 1953–1957

In 1953 the Communist regime turned to the long-pending task
of national economic reconstruction. According to Sun Yat-sen's
view, the basic purpose of the projected modernization of China's
economy was to raise the abysmally low living standard of the
Chinese nation. The Communist orientation was based unequivocally upon considerations of national power. Peking's initial decision
entailed sacrificing the well-being of a generation of Chinese and
by-passing the building of a light industry in favor of the prior
construction of a national *heavy* industry, the more quickly (it was
thought) to make China strong.

Although the country possessed great natural resources, an ac-
curate picture of them had not been given by previous surveys
of its mineral deposits. But the iron-ore reserves, even if of low iron
content, were considerable, and the country had vast coal deposits,
including good coking coal. There were verified petroleum deposits in Kansu, Sinkiang, and Tsinghai. The country was rich in
antimony and manganese. Other industrial minerals were believed
to exist in quantity in little-explored regions, such as Sinkiang and
Tibet, and the methodical prospecting in progress promised to turn
up valuable new deposits. The raw materials for industrialization
were at hand.

The situation was generally favorable. The national economy had
been largely rehabilitated; 1950, 1951, and 1952 had been good crop
years. There was internal peace, and the component elements for

economic progress. The base on which it was proposed to erect the imposing new structure, however, was debilitated, comprising an antiquated economy that was primarily agricultural. Even with repairs completed, China's industry was still in only a rudimentary stage of development and incapable of providing the goods required for the equipment of a heavy industry. Most heavy industry was concentrated in Manchuria, owing to the earlier efforts of Russian and Japanese entrepreneurs.

In late 1952 it was announced that China was embarking upon its first Five-Year Plan in 1953. However, *no plan was made public at the time.* The reason for Peking's reticence was a fundamental one. China was short of both capital and skilled manpower. In free enterprise systems capital is obtained variously from savings of the bourgeoisie, from foreign trade surpluses, foreign loans, and foreign investments, and even from the expenditures of foreign diplomatic and military establishments and foreign tourists. From this listing the immediate obstacle that was faced by Communist China is apparent. China had expropriated "bureaucratic capital" and landlord holdings. It had mopped up a large proportion of the wealth of the bourgeoisie. The field of private enterprise had been radically reduced and was growing smaller still. There was neither room nor incentive for capital savings.

Foreign investments in China had likewise been expropriated, and the investors physically expelled, these actions reflecting the CCP's devil theory of imperialism. In the "bad" old days, annual income from foreign loans, investments, and expenditures had been about $80 million. Overseas Chinese remittances had averaged another $100 million. In the past, foreign trade, oriented chiefly toward Britain, Japan and the United States, had offered China opportunities to dispose profitably of its coal, antimony, tungsten, tung-oil, sheep-casings, eggs, and rugs. There had been little export of industrial products, for there had been little industry.

Now China had the expropriated wealth, but there would be little more coming in from the source of that wealth: the Communists had nearly killed the goose that laid those particular golden eggs. Foreign loans and credits would have to come, if at all, from the Communist bloc, not from the United States. Trade, also, in view of the doctrine of "leaning to one side" and the expulsion of foreign traders from China, would have to be reoriented toward the Communist bloc, with prices more often to be fixed according to a pinched view of bloc demand than on the basis of a "comradely" willingness to meet China's bottomless needs.

Under the circumstances, it was evident that the primary reliance for capital for industrialization and "economic reconstruction" would be on the country's poverty-stricken agriculture.

China was also short of trained personnel. Skilled labor for industry and communications was available in only limited amount, owing to the small size of the national industry and to the fact that foreign enterprises in China had regularly used their own nationals to fill top technical and management positions. In part, also, because of the lingering Confucian tradition that directed ambitious youth to aim for either the bureaucracy or the polite, scholarly profession of teaching in the humanities, there was no big reservoir of young engineers, technicians, and industrial managers aspiring to replace Japanese and other foreigners. For some years China would have to rely on outside aid also for trained personnel. Moreover, there were three obstacles to the efficient use of existing personnel, domestic or foreign: lack of both an adequate statistical system and planning experience; the general application of the slogan "politics in command," with its implication that practical considerations should give way to the political; and the arrogant disdain on the part of the "pure" revolutionary for the sober calculations of mere "experts."

It was because China's existing deficiencies could not be adjusted to any conceivable plan of important dimensions that the first Five-Year Plan was not set forth in detail when announced at the end of 1952. It waited upon the USSR's commitment to further aid. Whether Mao Tse-tung had gone to Moscow in 1950 hoping for aid in the order of $20 billion requested by Sun Yat-sen from the victorious Allies in 1919 for China's economic reconstruction will probably never be known, but it is safe to hazard that he desired more than the $300 million he got (at one percent). That credit was already half exhausted by the end of 1952; it was obviously nothing with which to start a five-year plan.

In the latter part of 1952 Chou En-lai led to Moscow an important delegation. Among its tasks was the negotiation of additional aid. In September, 1953, the delegation reaped the fruits of its protracted efforts. Moscow promised to help China build 141 industrial plants. This agreement did not involve any new Soviet credit: the aid was to be paid for currently in Chinese goods. Later, when Bulganin and Khrushchev visited Peking in October, 1954, to participate in the celebration of the fifth anniversary of the establishment of the Communist regime at Peking, a supplementary accord was negotiated: the Soviet Union agreed to help build fifteen additional industrial enterprises. The terms of repayment varied slightly from those of 1953: apart from partial payment in current Chinese deliveries, a Soviet credit of $130 million was provided. The sum of $430 million, comprising the amounts involved by the 1950 and 1954 agreements, constitutes the total of long-term Soviet economic credits known to have been extended China in the first Five-Year Plan.

Another arrangement was also made at the October, 1954, meeting. China had evidently been discontented with even the limited qualification of its national sovereignty found in the existence of the three joint-stock companies operated by itself and the USSR. So on October 21, 1954, at Chinese request, the companies for the exploitation of petroleum and nonferrous metals and the operation of China-USSR airlines were dissolved. All of the companies' property went to China, with payment to the USSR for its share to be made in the form of Chinese goods over a period of several years.

This new financial obligation was assumed by China in addition to the above-mentioned $430 million. Added to it also was an unknown sum owed the Soviet Union for military equipment supplied during the Korean War. Finally, it is to be noted that in the first Communist decade China sent over 6,500 students to the USSR to study, and their expenses, together with those of Soviet technicians working on construction projects in China, constituted a charge against Chinese income. China was piling up debits, mortgaging the future in order to implement its first Five-Year Plan. And the first payment for the 1950 Soviet credit came due in 1954.

The outlines of the Five-Year Plan (if not the details) had already been made known to the nation. The general line laid down by the Party in 1952 was that China would achieve socialist transformation of its economy by three Five-Year Plans, that is, by 1967; it would become a world economic power by the end of the century—2000 A.D. In February, 1955, after two years of patchwork effort, and particularly after obtaining the new Soviet commitments of 1953 and 1954, the detailed blueprint of the plan was completed. The plan was made public by State Planning Commission chief Li Fu-ch'un in July. It put the stress strongly on the development of heavy industry, to the relative neglect of both light industry and agriculture. This was in accord with Mao Tse-tung's earlier dictum: China should leap over the intermediate stage of constructing light industry.

The inner meaning of the decision was plain: light industry

would provide little in consumer goods for either workers or peasants—who would thus be left with limited incentives. As in the early Soviet five-year plans, agriculture was to be squeezed to produce the surplus for capital investment. But the experience of the Soviet Union with respect to the role of economic incentives was to be disregarded: the "revolutionary spirit," and the Party's assumed genius for the control of the human mind, were to take the place of crass economic rewards.

Li Fu-ch'un's report made it quite evident that the Soviet contribution would constitute the backbone of industrial construction in the Five-Year Plan. The USSR was aiding with the erection of iron and steel enterprises, nonferrous metallurgical plants, power plants, plants for machine building, and with the construction of motor vehicles and tractors. It was to provide much of the equipment for such plants, and for coal mining, petroleum processing, and chemical works.

The whole project had to be viewed against the background of the hard fact that China's population was discovered in 1953, the first year of the plan, to be 583 million, which was about 100 million more than previous maximum estimates. And it was increasing at the net rate of 12–15 million annually. During the five-year period in point there would come into being an additional 60–75 million people to be fed, clothed, and housed.

Evidently China proposed to follow the economic example of contemporary Russia, not the Russia of 1928. This it proposed to do even though the demographic factors were vastly different and it was starting far behind the USSR of 1928, even in absolute figures. The Soviet capital investment rate in its first Five-Year Plan (1928–32) was lower than China's, and a lesser proportion was devoted to industry. Hard though it had pinched the people with respect to consumer goods, the Soviet Union put 14.1 percent capital investment into consumer-goods industries in 1928–32; China, in its first Five-Year Plan, invested only 11.2 percent in that field. It was, moreover, to be noted that the Chinese figures represented *gross* investment, that is, no allowance was made for depreciation. It was therefore doubtful whether the recorded "capital investment" in light industry in the final accounting covered much more than plant upkeep. Finally, whereas the first Soviet plan allotted 19.4 percent of the total for capital investment in agriculture, forestry, and water conservation, the Peking regime provided only 7.6 percent.

Another point of comparison is appropriate. Both civil war and foreign interventions had long been over when the Soviet Union embarked upon the implementation of its plan in 1928; but, in the case of China, the Korean War continued into 1953, the Indo-China War into 1954, and the existence of a joint Nationalist-American threat in the Formosa Strait region, combined with China's compulsive urge to become a great power and oust "imperialists" from all Asia, resulted in a continued high rate of expenditure for military purposes.

China was also notably weaker than the USSR of 1928 in terms of its communications system. Because of its greater need, China in its 1953–57 plan indeed put an investment in transportation, posts, and telecommunications comparable (in percentage) to that of the first Soviet plan. A total of 4,084 kilometers of new railway line was constructed. Even here, however, there was less gain than indicated by the bare figures. Some of the new lines were extensive rather than intensive in their function. Sun Yat-sen had dreamed of a transcontinental rail line that would connect a grand new port on the China Sea with Europe via arid Central Asia. The Communists, largely out of strategic considerations, undertook to build just such a transcontinental line, to connect Lanchow in Kansu Province with the Soviet Turk-Sib system at the Sinkiang border. Other rail lines, constructed in West China, were economically less productive than would have been the case if like mileage had been built in the densely populated areas of East China. But Peking, obsessed by its urge for empire, served political considerations first.

The Chinese nation thus was driven to the task, which was defined as being the extraction of the last ounce of productive capacities from both the industrial plant and what was once called the Good Earth—but had now come to be regarded as a somewhat refractory element to be beaten into line. The Chinese workers were called upon to "storm" the plant machinery, to undertake "socialist emulation" contests, to meet ever higher "norms." Peasants were urged in the same direction, the Communist cadres whipping both on with the promise that two or three years of effort would suffice to bring about substantially better days, and also always with the implicit threat that those who proved "uncooperative" would naturally be regarded as "counterrevolutionaries."

Serious maladjustments made their appearance by 1956. In a situation where the worker got less blame for breaking machinery by overloading it than for failing to achieve his "norm," plant breakdowns become more frequent. Where quantity was the primary consideration, products were often of lamentably poor quality. By reason of inadequate initial planning, and frequent changes of plan, there was a growing shortage of construction materials, industrial raw materials, and fuel (especially coal), because each sector of industry competed with the others for the needed supplies. Communication problems were growing, for an advancing industrialization put ever heavier loads on the already inadequate system for the movement of both raw materials and finished products. Not least important, worker enthusiasm lagged in both agriculture and industry: the Chinese nation had, after all, been promised a virtual paradise in about three years, and rewards had not been forthcoming in the anticipated dimensions. The "revolutionary spirit" was not proving a lasting incentive.

Certain corrections were undertaken in 1956. Through Anastas I. Mikoyan, who came to China in April, the USSR undertook to build fifty-five more industrial plants, supplying equipment, designer services, and other technical aid, in the total value of $625 million, with payment through current trade deliveries. In 1956 also, a minor adjustment was made by shifting the ratio of investment in heavy as compared to light industry from 8:1 to 7:1, but this still could hardly do more than cover plant depreciation in the light industry sector.

Nor was the state light industry deficit being made up by increased production by private industry. Instead, as announced in January, 1956, the nation's private industry had been "basically" liquidated. At the beginning of the Five-Year Plan, the economy possessed four major sectors: state, joint state-private, cooperative, and private. Now the Peking regime had deliberately dispatched the national bourgeoisie the way of "bureaucratic capitalism" and foreign entrepreneurs. Only three sectors of the national economy were left.

The results of the 1953–57 Plan were impressive. The annual rate of increase in the gross national product for the Five-Year Plan period is computed to have been 7 percent; between the arbitrary base year 1952 and 1957, industrial output had expanded at the annual average rate of 13–14 percent. Steel production increased from 1952 to 1957 by a total of some 325 percent, coal production by upwards of 200 percent. But the achievements in agriculture were notably less impressive. The 1952 production of grain (with the category including sweet potatoes, but not soy beans) had been

154 million tons; in 1957 production was 185 million tons. Agriculture, in sum, although subjected to ever increasing demands, was advancing at a much slower pace than industry.

There had been important changes in agriculture during those five years. "Land reform" had, of course, been viewed as only a step on the way to socialized agriculture. Liu Shao-ch'i, speaking in June, 1950, on the projected Agrarian Reform Law, set forth the basic aim as being "to set free the rural productive forces from the shackles of the feudal ownership system of the landlord class, in order to develop agricultural production and thus pave the way for New China's industrialization." After the completion of the expropriation of landlords' holdings and the division of land, in early 1953, a drive was launched to carry agriculture into the next stage. It was proclaimed that small individual land holdings were not suitable for mechanized farming. Collectivization, it was said, would lead to the economy of large farms and mechanized farming, with intensive irrigation and the extensive use of chemical fertilizers.

Collectivization proceeded through three stages. First, there was organization of mutual-aid teams. Next, primary Agricultural Producers Cooperatives were formed by pooling land, farm implements, and labor, organized on a joint ownership basis. The respective owners drew dividends according to their investment as well as labor, and they might withdraw from the undertaking with their property if they chose. Later came the so-called higher-stage Agricultural Producers Cooperatives, in which the property was held in common rather than on a joint ownership basis. In this arrangement members no longer received dividends from their capital investment and might not withdraw the property they had contributed to the common holding. This form of agricultural enterprise was essentially the true collective, rather than the cooperative.

Speaking in July, 1955, on the question of agricultural cooperation, Mao Tse-tung noted the basic program: by 1957, one half of China's 110 million peasant families were to be organized in cooperatives or collectives; by the end of 1960 the other one half would also be so organized, and socialist transformation, including mechanization of agriculture, was to be completed by the end of 1967.

When Mao spoke, some 17 million households had joined the cooperatives. In that same speech, however, he called for a speedup of collectivization. The Party went into action, and by the end of December 50 million more households had been collectivized.

The next month it was revealed in a draft plan for the twelve-year development of China's agriculture that the full socialist stage of collectivization was to be completed not by 1967 but by 1958.

China's agriculture was being called upon to increase food production at the same time that it was undergoing radical transformation. The load was heavy. In prewar days China was a net importer of grain, getting about one percent of its annual requirements abroad. In the postwar period grain imports had been stopped, and China became instead a net exporter of grain, to help settle its foreign trade accounts.

The population increase was a major factor. Assuming a yearly minimum population increase of 12 million, there had to be a 10.4 percent increase in food output between 1953 and 1957 just to keep food consumption at a level. It had, moreover, been discovered that the collective farmer was beginning to consume more of the grain that he produced than he had before collectivization. This was only natural. The ownership of the food supply was now collective, rather than individual, and the urge to make sparing use of available supplies had been correspondingly reduced. As early as 1953, the "planned purchase" of some agricultural products and grain rationing had been instituted. In 1955 strict controls were established over food consumption, and in August a comprehensive monopoly purchase and marketing plan was inaugurated. A national food rationing system was introduced on November 1.

Other factors entered the picture. In the first place, there had been a shift from food crops to industrial crops. In the second place, in the absence of a breakdown of the "grain" category, it was patently difficult to be sure that sweet potatoes and coarser grains had not displaced in substantial measure such superior food grains as wheat and rice. Furthermore, China's international debit payments as of 1957 were increasing, rather than decreasing.

At the end of 1957 it was clear that agriculture was falling behind the demands of industry, the nation's consumption needs, and the requirements of China's international debit position. There was a spreading scissors gap between agriculture and industry. The United Nations *Economic Survey of Asia and the Far East, 1961* described the situation clearly: "During the first 5-year plan period, the gross value of industrial production increased at an annual average rate of 18 per cent, and that of agricultural production by 4.5 per cent; this meant that the plan target was attained in agriculture and exceeded (by 20 per cent) in industry." The same report noted, however, that owing to the transfer of some agricultural effort to the production of industrial raw materials, the annual rate of growth for food output during the period was only 2.6 percent. In short, the food production growth rate had barely kept ahead of population growth (about 2 percent). The situation consequently called for an "agonizing reappraisal" of China's program for economic reconstruction.

10 PEKING AT THE CROSSROADS

THE DEVELOPMENTS inside China should be viewed, and weighed, against the background of developments in the international field. By its own avowal, China was part and parcel of the movement of proletarian internationalism opposed to "imperialism."

Peking's strategy in international affairs had been spelled out early. From the end of the Marshall mediation and the resumption of the civil war, the Communists had progressively burned a number of political bridges behind them. The Cold War was already well in course as victory in the civil war loomed upon the horizon in 1949. In his basic policy statement of June 30, "On the People's Democratic Dictatorship," Mao Tse-tung asserted that it was impossible, while imperialism lasted, for a true people's revolution in any country to win and consolidate its victory without "assistance in various forms from the international revolutionary forces," and he held that "one must lean either to imperialism or Socialism. . . . Neutrality is merely a camouflage; a third road does not exist." He was thus found in agreement with the contemporary Cominform doctrine that there was no room for neutralism.

The militancy of the Chinese Communist Party was authoritatively expressed in November of the same year by theoretician Liu Shao-ch'i. At the opening session of the Australasian Trade Unions Conference in Peking, Liu expounded the doctrine that revolution in other countries of Asia—and he specifically included Burma, India, and the Philippines, which had already won their independence from colonialism—would inevitably follow the Chinese pattern of armed revolt. The essence of Liu's thesis regarding the form

Asian "struggles for liberation" should take is to be found in his fourth point:

"When and where possible it is necessary to establish a national People's Liberation Army, powerful and good for fighting and led by the Communist Party. . . . And the armed struggle is the main form of struggle for many colonial and semi-colonial peoples. These are the basic roads taken by the Chinese people in achieving victory inside the country. . . . These roads can also be the pattern . . . for peoples of other colonial and semi-colonial countries.[1]

This was not an isolated aberration on the part of a maverick Communist theoretician. The prodigal son Li Li-san, whose adherence to the concept of urban uprisings had in 1930 led to bloody disasters for the Communist arms, in a 1949 article held that, in colonial and semi-colonial feudalistic countries such as China had been,

The working class definitely cannot fundamentally better its status and livelihood, not to speak of winning the revolutionary victory like that of today, without building a revolutionary army under its own leadership and waging a revolutionary war against the rule of imperialism and its lackeys with the support of the broad masses of the people.[2]

COMMUNIST CHINA'S FOREIGN AFFAIRS, 1949–1955

The Chinese Communist Party's foreign policy in its first phase was unequivocally revolutionary. It had been determined for the period immediately ahead with regard to three distinctly different sectors—the Communist bloc, the "imperialist" powers, and the "unliberated" (and presumed benighted) ex-colonial but non-Communist countries of Asia. China would collaborate with the first sector, carry on a protracted war against the second, and have neither war nor peace with the third group until they had seen the light and undertaken a Communist revolution to overthrow the "bourgeois dictatorships" that were their governments. Just as Trotsky expected world revolution to follow on the heels of the Russian Revolution of 1917, so Mao Tse-tung anticipated that the Chinese Communist victory would be followed by similar upheavals in other parts of Asia.

China's foreign strategy was not long in taking concrete form. The Sino-Soviet agreements of February and March had shown a clear focus on Manchuria and Japan. China's Communist leaders, like the Nationalists, would view the Northeast as the powerhouse of the nation, with primary significance for the country's future. The Soviet Union, for its part, had for twenty years been gradually shifting its economic center of gravity eastward, closer to Asia, and the movement had received a strong stimulus from the Second World War. In that east-west belt of Asia of which Manchuria is the Far Eastern and most powerful segment, the two great powers had combined in alliance. The fulcrum of the 1950 Sino-Soviet Axis was Manchuria, which would almost inevitably play a leading role in any war in Northeast Asia. The prime objective of Axis policy would naturally be Japan, especially since the United States had set itself up there militarily.

The Peking-Moscow Axis soon revealed its line of attack. Chinese and Soviet press treatment of the subject of Formosa and of American relations with the Nationalists followed a common pattern from December, 1949, onward. Peking's anti-American propaganda was broadened to include General MacArthur's administration of Japan, American relations with the Philippines, American military aid to the French in Indo-China, and the alleged organization of an American espionage apparatus for subversive activities in China.[3]

Japan, contended the propagandists, was being converted into a permanent American base, to constitute the central sector of an offensive line extending from the Aleutians to Japan, the Ryukyus, and South Korea. Soviet forces had been withdrawn from Korea in December, 1948, American forces in June, 1949. Peking charged that the Mutual Defense Assistance agreement signed between the United States and the Seoul government in January, 1950, gave the United States military bases in South Korea and made the peninsula a part of the aforementioned offensive military line. The Chinese people were being conditioned to feel that, beyond the Nationalists, there stood another, more powerful enemy.

During the spring of 1950 a menacing concentration of PLA forces had been built up in the Chekiang-Fukien coastal sector, and it was the current estimate of the American Government that the Nationalist regime's days were numbered. Peking could be expected, however, to coordinate any move in the Formosa Strait with Communist actions planned for other sectors.

Stalin was still alive, and the accepted Asian Communist doctrine of the period was evidently the concept of armed uprising advocated by Liu Shao-ch'i and Li Li-san. A logical place to implement the doctrine was in Korea, which remained divided at the 38th parallel—with neither the Democratic People's Republic in the

north nor Syngman Rhee's Republic of Korea in the south content
with the existing state of affairs.

The elections of May 30, 1950, sponsored by the United Nations
and limited by necessity to South Korea, set off a spate of denuncia-
tions and proclamations in North Korea. An editorial carried by the
Pyongyang *Labor News* in mid-June stated: "The Korean people
cannot watch the Fatherland continue along the way of division,
but will decisively employ the people's own strength to settle the
fate of the Fatherland." [4]

On June 25, 1950, the North Korean Army struck across the 38th
parallel. Imperial Japan had proposed to Tsarist Russia a half
century earlier that the 38th parallel should be taken as a dividing
line of their respective spheres of influence, but St. Petersburg had
been unwilling to accept such a division. Similarly, it appeared that
in 1950 Moscow and Peking were not content to have South Korea
an American sphere of influence.

The North Korean aggression was followed closely by two critical
American moves: military intervention in Korea under the United
Nations banner and interposition of the United States Seventh Fleet
in the Formosa Strait. The second American move, which bore no
UN sanction, was avowedly for the purpose of protecting the flank
of American armed forces in a dangerous, uncertain military situation by keeping Formosa out of Communist hands. It blocked any
attack by the People's Liberation Army on Formosa. As a result
the rump Nationalist regime, which previously had been hardly
breathing, acquired a new lease on life.

If events in Korea and the Formosa Strait were linked in American eyes, the Chinese saw them no differently, only from the opposite
side. Current talk of substantial demobilization of PLA forces was
stopped. As developments in Korea began to tip in favor of the UN
forces, there appeared clear signs of a Chinese intention to intervene. Speaking in Peking on Army Day, August 1, PLA chief
Chu Teh said: "We Chinese people recognize that the [North]
Korean people's struggle is entirely just. We definitely come to the
relief of the Korean people, and definitely oppose the American
Government's aggression against Korea!" [5] The original Chinese
for the phrase "come to the relief" ordinarily signifies "come to the
relief of troops in difficulty." To the initiated the usage meant more
than a mere manifestation of Chu Teh's sympathy: it promised concrete action.

The Chinese reactions became sharper still after the UN landing of September 15 at Inchon, behind the North Korean lines. Soon there were indications that an important policy decision had been reached. On September 24 Kuo Mo-jo as chairman of the Chinese World Peace Salvation Society addressed a gathering of fifty thousand youths in Peking and gave an alert: "We should, in the name of the progressive youth of the whole world, oppose American imperialism's aggression [in Korea] and *use practical actions* to come forward to support the Korean People's *just struggle*." (Italics added.) [6] Then, on September 29, the Chinese Aliens Association of North Korea sent the Peking Government and Mao Tse-tung a telegram, stating in part:

We desire, under the brave and enlightened leadership of yourself and the Central People's Government, to manifest a spirit of internationalism and patriotism and directly to support the Korean people's war of liberation, and to overwhelm the common public enemy of the two countries China and Korea—the American imperialists—in order to protect our Fatherland and to protect Korea, and to fight to protect world peace.[7]

These were clear Communist calls to fight a "just war" (which, in Mao Tse-tung's theory, is one that *ought* to be fought), and a "war of liberation"—such as Liu Shao-ch'i had proposed would have to be fought by colonial and "semi-colonial" countries of Asia. Public bodies began to send in petitions "demanding" that the Central People's Government act to prevent violation of Chinese territory (that is, according to Peking's repeated charges, by American planes).

The Chinese and Soviet ratifications of the February 14 treaty of alliance and five subsidiary agreements were formally exchanged at Peking on September 30, 1950. October 1 was a day pregnant with significance. At 12 o'clock noon General MacArthur issued a surrender order to the North Korean forces: "Lay down your arms and cease hostilities under such military supervisions as I may direct." South Korean forces crossed the 38th parallel. In a speech at Peking, where the first anniversary of the Chinese People's Republic was being celebrated, Chou En-lai referred pointedly to the Sino-Soviet alliance and warned that, if the "American aggressors" were to deem the peace-loving Chinese to be weak,

Then they will again make the same serious error as the Kuomintang reactionary party. . . . The Chinese people definitely cannot tolerate foreign aggression, and cannot allow imperialists recklessly to aggress against their own neighbor and disregard it [the aggression]. Whoever might plot to expel China's nearly 500 million people from the United

Nations, and whoever would wipe out and destroy the interests of this quarter part of the human race and foolishly think to settle arbitrarily any Eastern question directly related to China, then he will certainly break his head and spill his blood.[8]

On October 3 Chou En-lai informed the Indian Ambassador that China would intervene in Korea if UN forces crossed the 38th parallel.

At that point anyone who remained unalerted' to at least the possibility of Chinese intervention in the Korean War had either ignored the usual publicity media and official pronouncements or, in what D. W. Brogan has called "the illusion of omnipotence," disdained to consider that the Chinese nation would dare to challenge the United States. Actually, however, a news item published in the New York *Times* as early as August 17 had reported that Mao Tse-tung and Soviet Foreign Minister Molotov had agreed in the course of conversations at Peking that China would send troops into Korea if UN forces crossed the 38th parallel.

The United States 1st Cavalry Division crossed the 38th parallel on or about October 7, and the combined UN forces drove rapidly toward the Korea-Manchuria border. On October 25 China intervened militarily in the Korean War. The Chinese forces, now using *against Americans* some of the American arms and equipment they had captured from the Nationalists, were successful in restoring the military situation to essentially what it had been before the attack of June 25. The North Koreans were saved from loss of territory and from the need to surrender. The Chinese, in defense of what they deemed their national security, had maintained the Korean buffer before Manchuria. After a long and frustrating stalemate, an armistice was signed in July, 1953, and the opposing forces were left still facing each other roughly along the line of the 38th parallel.

The Korean War crystallized Sino-American relations in a mold of mutual hostility. The angry sentiment was compounded by a similar clash of Chinese and American policies in Southeast Asia, where the United States supported the French in their colonial war in Indo-China and the Chinese gave aid to the revolutionary Vietminh. Dominating the whole question of Sino-American relations was a conflict over the status of Formosa that had been seriously aggravated by developments subsequent to June, 1950.

President Truman's Executive Order of June 27, 1950, had stated that "the determination of the future status of Formosa must await the restoration of security in the Pacific, a peace settlement with Japan, or consideration by the UN." The Democratic Administration seemingly proposed to "neutralize" the island and shelve the issue of its legal status for the duration of the emergency in Korea. But, after the Chinese intervention in the Korean War, an American military mission arrived in Formosa on May 1, 1951, to help rehabilitate the Nationalist military establishment. The Japan peace treaty signed at San Francisco in September, 1951, detached Formosa from the Japanese Empire, but passed title to no one, and thus left the intent of the Cairo Declaration unfulfilled. By this time Formosa was already viewed as being a link in the American "island defense chain" in the West Pacific; the United States had acquired a vested interest in maintenance of the political *status quo* of that island and its neighbor archipelago, the Pescadores.

On February 2, 1953, President Eisenhower had obeyed the tenet of a new political myth assuming the potency of Chiang Kai-shek's anti-Communism and "unleashed" the Chinese Nationalists, so that they might at will attack the mainland. By that act, the neutralization of Formosa was voided and the United States became automatically involved in the civil war of its protégé, Generalissimo Chiang Kai-shek. Chiang made no military move after the February, 1953, "unleashing," even though, with the Chinese Communists then engaged in a war against sixteen member States of the United Nations on the Korean Peninsula, optimum conditions for a Nationalist attack had prevailed. The Nationalist chieftain instead limited himself to welcoming the de-neutralization of Formosa; but he made a revealing remark: "Our plan for fighting communism and regaining the mainland will necessarily form . . . an important link in the general plan of the free world to combat world-wide Communist aggression." In other words, his strategy was to wait for a third world war.

On July 20, 1953, as the Korean truce neared, Chiang urged the negotiation of a West Pacific security pact to include Formosa and all other countries bordering China. And in November, when Korea's Syngman Rhee visited Chiang in Taipei, the two bellicose statesmen issued a communiqué bidding the free countries of Asia (presumably excluding India, Burma, and Indonesia, all of whom had recognized the Peking Government) to form a united anti-Communist front, and other "freedom-loving nations" (certainly the United States in particular) to back them.

A move had been made in that direction when the United States on October 1, 1953, after the Korean truce, signed a mutual security pact with the Seoul Government. Beginning with Secretary of State John Foster Dulles's speech of January 12, 1954, the Washington Administration undertook the serial exposition of the new doctrine of "massive retaliation," which, according to Dulles, was already effective for the Far East in particular. Agreements signed in July ended the fighting, and the French colonial rule, in Indo-China. In September, 1954, the United States, Britain, France, Australia, and New Zealand joined with three Asian nations—the Philippines, Thailand, and Pakistan—to form a joint defense system, SEATO, for Southeast Asia. Then, on December 2, 1954, the United States signed a bilateral alliance with the Nationalist regime on Formosa.

In an address to the United States Congress on July 28, 1954, South Korean President Syngman Rhee had bluntly proposed that the United States go to war in Asia. On October 10 Chiang Kai-shek had asserted that preparations for liberation of the mainland were nearly complete and that the fighting should start within the visible future. The "massive retaliation" doctrine launched in January had taken on a more positive aspect. Chinese Communist and Nationalist military actions already in course around a number of Chinese offshore islands held the clear danger of developing in a manner that would involve the United States.

Such a development soon occurred: the Chinese Communists on January 18, 1955, occupied the minor offshore island of Yikiangshan and then turned to threaten the Tachen Islands, 200 miles north of Formosa. On January 24 President Eisenhower told Congress that a situation was developing in the Formosa Strait that "seriously imperils the peace and our security" and asked for authority "to engage in whatever operations may be required" for the defense of Formosa. Congress precipitately gave the President the desired authority in a joint resolution signed into law on January 29, and the Senate shortly afterwards approved the treaty of alliance with the Nationalists.

The plan for creation of a solid united anti-Communist front in the West Pacific was still to be realized. It had been able to make no headway against Syngman Rhee's implacable hostility toward Japan, and Japan's own wariness. And the boundary line governing SEATO's jurisdiction had carefully been drawn immediately north of the Philippines archipelago: "controversial" Formosa was not included in the SEATO area.

At the SEATO conference in Bangkok in early February, 1955,

when the United States stood on the brink of war with China, Secretary of State Dulles argued strongly that, in the event of hostilities, the "three fronts" comprising Japan–South Korea, Formosa, and Southeast Asia should be linked together. He failed to win agreement. Chiang Kai-shek saw the stage all set for his war of liberation, but the play did not go on. World opinion, as manifested inside the United Nations and out, stood in solid opposition—and the United States and Formosa were discovered to be isolated.

In 1955 Peking, in service of its "anti-imperialism," remained firmly fixed in an anti-American position; Washington, serving "anti-Communism" with similar fervor, had openly assumed an anti-Chinese stance. The two were alike heavily committed to mutual animosity.

The establishment of the American "first line of defense" in the China Sea by means of a series of military alliances offered a much greater threat to China's security than the continued existence of "bourgeois nationalist" governments in the Asian neighborhood. And China, as has been seen in the preceding chapter, had in 1953 turned to the herculean task of becoming an industrial power. The Liu Shao-ch'i strategy for foreign affairs had been found wanting.

"BANDUNG SPIRIT" AND "HUNDRED FLOWERS," 1955–1957

The whole strategy of the Sino-Soviet alliance vis-à-vis the Asian "revolution" took on a new aspect. Much water had gone over the dam since theoretician Liu Shao-ch'i in 1949 had proposed violent revolution for all "unliberated" countries of Asia. The thinking in Peking and Moscow had shifted radically after the Korean aggression promptly brought a consolidation of world opinion—including, most importantly, Asian opinion—against the adventure. The major change of course was presumably decided upon at Moscow in August–September, 1952, during the month-long negotiations between Soviet leaders and the Chinese delegation headed by Premier Chou En-lai and Deputy Chief of Staff Su Yü. The Moscow discussions almost certainly dealt with various crucial questions of grand strategy in Asia. China and the Soviet Union were moving to develop the full meaning of the 1950 alliance.

The joint Sino-Soviet appraisal of the new exigencies, and opportunities, inherent in the world situation was reflected in Stalin's monograph on "Economic Problems of Socialism in the U.S.S.R.," published on October 2, 1952, and Malenkov's concurrent report to the Nineteenth Communist Party Congress at Moscow, both of which underscored the concept of "peaceful coexistence." Stalin argued in his analysis that the most important consequence of the Second World War was the disintegration of the single universal world market and its replacement by "two parallel world markets . . . counterposed to one another." In his report Georgi M. Malenkov, Secretary of the Party Central Committee, gave global application to the concept. He held that "the colonial system of imperialism is actually disintegrating as a result of the war and the new surge of the national liberation struggle in the colonial and dependent countries." He asserted: "We are confident that in peaceful competition with capitalism the socialist economic system will prove its superiority over the capitalist economic system more and more strikingly with each passing year"; and he called for the welding together of a worldwide peace front and for a policy of "international cooperation and promotion of business relations with all countries." [9]

Stalin's death the following March facilitated the further evolution of what was evidently an altered world strategy. Communist moves toward compromise brought the Korean truce to the eve of realization and were also to bring about a truce in Indo-China. The new Communist strategy, in all logic reflecting close Sino-Soviet agreement, patently envisaged a damping down of military actions, a *détente*, to permit broader exploitation of the political potentialities of the situation.

Mao Tse-tung's "non-neutrality" of 1949 and the Cominform's twin concept of a bipolar world divided into two antagonistic camps were now shelved. The spirit of Asian nationalism had proved stronger than the discontents engendered by economic misery, and it was found necessary to harness the stronger motive force for revolution. Peking and Moscow propaganda would no longer attack "bourgeois" Asian and Arab statesmen as "tools of imperialism," nor would the Communist bloc demand that uncommitted countries make a definite choice between it and "the imperialist camp." The 1952 Congress had effectively marked the end, at least for the time being, of the Communist policy of waging guerrilla warfare against non-Communist Asian regimes that commanded the resources of Asian nationalism. The Korean and Indo-China truces of 1953 and 1954 cleared the deck for implementation of a new Sino-Soviet strategy tailored to the political realities of contemporary Asia.

The clearest expression of the contemporary spirit and will of Asia came at the Bandung Conference of twenty-nine Asian and African nations, meeting in April, 1955, at the peak of the first Formosa Strait crisis. SEATO's three Asian members—the Philippines, Thailand, and Pakistan—were represented. So were China, Japan, and the nations of the Middle East (except Israel). Formosa, North Korea, and South Korea were not. The Cold War did not determine the conference's political climate. The Bandung Conference's final communiqué of April 24 noted the "general desire for economic cooperation among the participating countries on the basis of mutual interest and respect for national sovereignty." It recorded the intent of the several Governments "to work for closer cultural cooperation . . . developed in the larger context of world cooperation." The conference strongly endorsed human rights and self-determination, holding that "colonialism in all its manifestations is an evil which should speedily be brought to an end." It also stood for universal UN membership and universal disarmament. Finally, the twenty-nine nations laid down ten principles designed to promote world peace and cooperation.

Indian Prime Minister Jawaharlal Nehru, in his concluding address to the meeting, voiced what was obviously a general sentiment, and made clear the practical application of the Bandung spirit to the great powers' world strategy. He said:

The countries assembled in the conference are not banded against anyone. We send our greetings to the great countries of Europe and America. We want to be friends with them and cooperate with them. But Europe and America are in the habit of thinking that their quarrels are the world's quarrels and, therefore, the world must submit to them this way or that way.

Why should we be dragged into their quarrels and wars? I hope we shall keep away from those quarrels. Are we copies of Europeans, Americans or Russians? We are Asians or Africans and none else. For anyone to tell us that we have to be camp followers of Russia or America or any country in Europe is not very creditable to our new dignity, our new independence, our new freedom, our new spirit.[10]

Nehru was plainly saying: "Let Occidentals fight Occidentals." Asians would stay apart from nuclear wars and cultivate their own gardens. It is in the light of the Bandung Conference that certain events of 1955 should be judged. In May of that year the Soviet Union and the Eastern European satellites agreed at Warsaw that they would not "interfere in the internal affairs of each other"— which was the purport of one of the ten operating principles adopted

at Bandung the month before. In June Tito and Moscow were reconciled on the basis of the doctrine of "different forms of Socialist
development," that is, by Soviet recognition of Yugoslavia's right of
self-determination—a right also emphasized at Bandung. And when
President Eisenhower attended the Geneva "summit" meeting with
Soviet leaders that same summer, the United States slipped, for the
moment, into the pattern of "peaceful coexistence." Soviet Premier
Nikolai A. Bulganin and Party chief Nikita S. Khrushchev rounded
off the year with a journey to South Asia that was something like a
triumphal tour.

The polished Communist strategy was revealed at the Twentieth
Communist Party Congress at Moscow in February, 1956. Khrushchev there offered a judgment:

The new period in world history, predicted by Lenin, when the peoples
of the East play an active part in deciding the destinies of the whole
world and have become a new and mighty factor in international relations, has arrived. . . . International relations have spread beyond the
bounds of relations among countries inhabited chiefly by peoples of the
White race and are beginning to become genuinely world-wide relations.[11]

Khrushchev said that the Communist countries were not rich,
but poor, having had to make their way up with difficulty from a
low level of economic well-being. They therefore could not afford
to make gifts, but they could and would extend credits at low rates
of interest and exchange certain products of their own for those of
underdeveloped countries. The Soviet Union, he said, would seek
to extend and strengthen friendship and cooperation with the
countries of the East.

According to the 1928 Program of the Communist International:

Colonies and semi-colonies . . . represent the *world rural district* in
relation to the industrial countries, which represent the *world city*. Consequently the problem of organizing socialist world economy, of properly
combining industry with agriculture is, to a large extent, the problem of
the relation towards the former colonies of imperialism. . . .

In view of the existence of centres of socialism represented by Soviet
Republics of growing economic power, the colonies which break away
from imperialism economically gravitate towards and gradually combine
with the industrial centres of world socialism. . . . Every assistance
[must] be rendered to the economic, political and cultural growth of the
formerly oppressed "territories," "dominions" and "colonies," with the
object of transferring them to socialist lines.

Communist leader Khrushchev, speaking over a quarter of a century later, in effect proclaimed to his followers that the clock of history had struck.

War damage to the Soviet economy had been speedily repaired, and the country had gone on to new achievements in the field of economic production. Along with the evolution of new political relationships among the Soviet Union, Eastern Europe, and China, bloc national planning had been projected into intra-bloc dimensions *for its European sector* and coordinated, with the institution of a measure of international division of labor. By the beginning of 1956, when Khrushchev spoke, the Communist bloc had laid the foundation for international economic cooperation as an institution and was ready for business with the ex-colonial areas of Asia.

In this complex the Soviet Union bore the features of the "world city." The underdeveloped countries of Asia, from China through the "arc of free Asia" to the Middle East, still neatly fitted the description of "world rural district." These Asian states were predominantly agrarian and their peoples poverty-stricken; yet populations were growing at an explosive rate. The international market for raw materials was weak, at a time when most of the underdeveloped countries depended upon the export of only one or two primary products for their foreign exchange. The capital resources required for rapid economic betterment were generally lacking. In sum, the poor nations of the earth were being hard put even to maintain their *status quo* of economic misery. They needed technical assistance, capital credits, and markets for their products to be able to achieve economic betterment. This was "the revolution of rising expectations."

The Soviet Union had comprehended that situation and embarked upon an endeavor to effect something like an amalgam of the Russian and Asian revolutions. Economic elements were to make up the chief instrument to be employed in this enterprise. Associated with the USSR in the undertaking was its Asian ally, China.

Beginning with 1955, China's trade and aid program reflected that strategy. Its trade had already been largely reoriented toward the Communist bloc and away from the sea powers. It still exported tungsten, wolfram, tung oil, hog bristles, and feathers. But where China had before been a net importer of grain and flour, it now exported important quantities of foodstuffs—rice, soy beans, wheat, animal products, and vegetable oil, as well as the usual tea. There had also been a great change in the composition of imports. The overwhelming proportion of imports were of machinery, machine tools, industrial equipment, and petroleum products; luxury items and everything unessential had been crossed off the list. In the period 1935–37 only 10 percent of China's imports comprised machines and hand tools; in 1954, 88.5 percent of the imports were of instruments of production.

The extent of the foreign-trade shift to the Communist bloc (accelerated by the impact of the UN embargo laid down in the course of the Korean War) may be shown by percentages: in 1950 trade with the bloc accounted for 26 percent; in 1951 it was 61 percent, in 1953 (the last year of the Korean War) 75 percent, and in 1954 rose to 80.55 percent. And China's total trade was growing. In 1955 exports and imports totaled nearly $4.7 billion.

On their face the figures looked favorable. Nevertheless, it should be remembered that China was doing some buying on credit and paying for imports in the main with agricultural products. The 1955 figures showed a big trade deficit, reflecting its use of credit. Beginning in 1956, with debts coming due, the country was called upon to export more than it imported. Total trade dropped in 1956 and fell still more in 1957. This development occurred shortly after the adoption of the "Bandung spirit" strategy, which had led China, apparently bemused by the favorable domestic credit situation it had early enjoyed, not only to issue credit to target Asian countries, in accordance with the trade-and-aid strategy, but to make outright grants. Peking proposed, in effect, to outdo the Soviet Union: China would vie with the United States by sometimes giving aid gratis to the underdeveloped countries of Asia and the Middle East. So China traded outside the bloc with both Japan and Western Europe, and with India, Burma, and Ceylon. In addition, in the best style of international charity, it made outright grants to various countries whose populations could hardly be deemed worse off than the Chinese: to North Korea, North Vietnam, and the Mongolian People's Republic, where the USSR already had launched programs; to Cambodia and Nepal; and even to Hungary and Egypt.

As early as 1956, however, the leaders at Peking had noted signs of malfunctioning in the economy. They undertook minor adjustments of the economic program and turned as well to a consideration of the factor of national morale. A strong need had developed for improving relations between the Party and the people so that the collaboration should be more fruitful. This need was felt in relations with peasants and workers, but more particularly in the matter of getting a more enthusiastic participation by China's intellectuals in the huge task of national construction. During the course of the Five-Year Plan many intellectuals, badgered by the Party cadres, had become unresponsive and even negative in their reactions to the Communist program. Corrective measures were imperative.

As a domestic counterpart to the Bandung strategy in foreign affairs, Peking began to promote a thaw in the country's intellectual life. The Soviet "de-Stalinization" move at the February, 1956, Congress, signifying a relaxation of strict Communist controls in the Soviet scene, fitted in nicely with the Chinese program. In May, at a Supreme State Conference, Mao Tse-tung launched the theme: "Let a hundred flowers bloom, and a hundred schools of thought contend." By his selection of metaphor, Mao suggested that the freedom of philosophical discussion that had prevailed back in the feudal period, when the Hundred Schools of Philosophy had flourished, was being restored. Propaganda chief Lu Ting-yi enlarged upon the concept in an address to Peking intellectuals. The full sense of the two statements was that the country's thinkers should consider themselves freed from some of the restrictions the over-zealous cadres had fixed upon their intellectual questing. It was evidently hoped that a wide variety of flowers would bloom to enrich the Communist garden.

In the latter part of 1956, the Polish and Hungarian uprisings caused still greater restlessness in the international Communist movement. Mao Tse-tung, speaking to the Central Committee plenum in November, 1956, nevertheless went on to project the concept of freedom of thinking in the field of literature and the arts into the political sphere.

The Hundred Flowers suavely invoked by Mao Tse-tung and Lu Ting-yi were slow in making their appearance. There is a strong tradition of Chinese distrust of pronouncements by officialdom, regardless of its political complexion. The intellectuals remained impassive. In the spring of 1957, the last year of the first Five-Year Plan, Peking strangely made a strong effort to call forth the desired reaction. Party organs and cadres prodded leading non-Party officials and intellectuals to "bloom" with criticism of Communist policies and practices.

By June articulate elements of the Chinese society had swung into the spirit of the Hundred Flowers concept and began to voice violently anti-Communist sentiments. As their fervor heightened, the Party released the text of a confidential talk given by Mao Tse-tung in February "On the Correct Handling of Contradictions among the People." Admittedly, Mao's speech had been amended since that earlier date, so the world will probably never know just how far the Chinese Communist leader had shifted his position to meet the developments of June. As published, however, Mao's essay held that "the days of national disunity and turmoil which the people detested have gone forever." That did not mean that there were no longer any contradictions in Chinese society. "We are confronted by two types of social contradictions—contradictions between ourselves and the enemy, and contradictions among the people." The two types were totally different in nature.

Mao Tse-tung went on to amplify his thought in terms easy to understand. "Certain contradictions do exist between the government and the masses." Contradictions between the working class (identified with the government) and the national bourgeoisie fell under the general rule. If the national bourgeoisie would not accept resolution of contradictions as being in principle nonantagonistic, that is, would not accept criticism and "education," then the contradictions could become antagonistic. And the function of the people's dictatorship was to suppress reactionary classes and solve (by force) "contradictions both between ourselves and the enemy within the country." The people did indeed enjoy democratic freedoms. "But this freedom is freedom with leadership and this democracy is democracy under centralized guidance, not anarchy. Anarchy does not conform to the interests or wishes of the people."

A party rectification campaign, initiated by a directive of late April, was transformed into a general counter-offensive against all so-called rightists. Clearly caught off balance by the virulence of the criticism it had evoked, Peking now said that its original purpose had been to discover "poisonous weeds." A number of important "democratic personages" lost their positions in the government, and the position of the "national bourgeois" remnants was undermined accordingly. Undermined too was the remaining confidence of the intelligentsia in the good faith of the Communist regime.

The effective period of freedom had lasted just six weeks, rather

less than one-half the Emperor Kuang Hsu's Hundred Days of
Reform. In the latter part of 1957 the Party undertook a rectification campaign to induce right thinking in the minds of the people.
In theory, the Hundred Flowers policy continued, but it was much
circumscribed. It was also no longer effective: the Chinese intellectuals had learned, once again, to remain quiet.

Occurring at the same time as the Hundred Flowers episode, a
clash had developed between the Central People's Government
and the national minorities. From 1952 to 1956 Peking propaganda
had periodically attacked "Great Han chauvinism," that feeling of
Chinese superiority to "barbarian tribes" that had been so characteristic of Chinese rule of non-Chinese people in the past. Such
chauvinism, Peking said, would be no more. But by 1956 the
Mongols, Turki, and Tibetans had begun to demand loudly that
they should be given the substance as well as the name of autonomy. By 1957 there had developed a real movement of opposition
to Chinese rule in certain areas where the Chinese were in a distinct
minority. The movement took on its greatest force in Sinkiang.

While the "poisonous weeds" that had made their unwelcome
appearance in Peking's intellectual garden were being uprooted,
there was only fitful skirmishing against the minority autonomy
movements. Then, in December, 1957, the Chairman of the Sin-
kiang-Uighur Autonomous Region, Saifudin, let loose with heavy
guns on those Turki peoples who demanded that they be given the
promised autonomous rule. Saifudin spoke no more of Great Han
chauvinism but dwelt instead with the theme of "local nationalism,"
which he characterized as "the most dangerous ideological trend
of the present time." Remarking that some of those narrow nationalists wanted Sinkiang renamed the Uighuristan Republic and that
"ultranationalists" even worked for the expulsion of all Hans from
the area, Saifudin said that there was no need to talk about "seces-
sion" or "independence": Sinkiang was an indivisible part of China.

The following February, Nationalities Affairs Commission Vice
Chairman Wang Feng, in a long report made at Peking, gave an
even broader, blunter treatment of the subject. He said that the
question was "Nationalism or socialism?" Wang Feng himself gave
the answer: there would be socialism under the leadership of the
Chinese Communist Party. The "local nationalism" of China's minority peoples was ruthlessly crushed as a heterodox deviation.

So China approached the end of 1957, and the end of its first
Five-Year Plan, beset by numerous problems, both political and

economic. The subject minority peoples had demonstrated a preference for independence over the benefits of Chinese rule—as in imperial days. The Hundred Flowers approach had brought forth no new magic formulas for solution of the national problems within the framework of Communism, but violent attacks on first principles and the Party itself.

Certain interim decisions had been made with respect to domestic political affairs with the aim of steadying the situation. But the political depended in the long run on the economic factor, and fundamental economic problems, graver in their aspect, were still waiting to be solved. The agricultural system had not been made substantially stronger through reorganization, for it had simultaneously been starved of capital and of rewards. It was consequently failing both domestic industry and foreign trade. China's exports for 1957 were discovered to have dropped to $2.28 billion from a high of $2.35 billion the year before. It was a sign of the times.

This meant, incidentally, that China was unable to exploit as effectively as the USSR the Bandung Spirit strategy in foreign affairs: it could not use raw materials and manufactured goods to compete for influence abroad when it was in need of those same materials for the building up of its home economy. China needed either more material, financial, and technical aid or a change in the Sino-Soviet grand strategy—or both.

THE "GREAT LEAP FORWARD," 1958

An occasion was provided in late 1957 for China to attempt to obtain a change in policy, and a greatly increased amount of long-term aid, from its Soviet ally. In November Moscow celebrated the fortieth anniversary of the Bolshevik Revolution, and the leading lights of the Communist world attended. Mao Tse-tung made his second pilgrimage to Moscow.

The celebration had been given a booming prelude by the firing of the first operational Soviet intercontinental ballistic missile (ICBM) and the launching of the first sputnik. Mao Tse-tung made his famous speech centered on the theme "The East Wind is prevailing over the West Wind." And he magnanimously said: "The socialist camp should have a leader, and that leader is the Soviet Union."

It is necessary to view Mao Tse-tung's observations in the context of his military philosophy. It was his strong conviction that, if an army wins an advantage over its opponent, it should drive the advantage home. Mao did not look upon the Soviet Union simply as a spiritual or ideological leader but as a leader in the struggle with imperialism. And in that struggle one of the functions of the leading nation should be to provide both the vanguard forces and the service of supply to guarantee victory. In the light of subsequent events, it seems highly probable that Mao proposed to Khrushchev a return to Liu Shao-ch'i's (and Mao's) strategy of 1949, namely, that the Communist camp should go over to the offensive against "the failing capitalist world" and further, as a corollary, that there should be at least partial remission of China's outstanding obligations to the USSR and a substantial diversion of Soviet aid from countries such as India and Burma to China itself. In Peking's secret thoughts, the securing of massive economic aid would have been the primary consideration.

The representatives of the twelve Communist countries of the bloc, all in attendance at Moscow, met in conference on that occasion. The declaration issued at the end of their deliberations provided an answer to the presumed Chinese *démarche:* it was on the 1956 line of peaceful coexistence and economic cooperation. In sum, the Soviet Union did not propose to renounce a strategy favorable to it for a strategy favorable first and foremost to China and possibly gravely detrimental to the USSR. China signed the declaration, for it was not in a position to do anything else; but there was no reason to assume that Mao was convinced at heart of the superior merit of the Soviet "dialectic."

The problem now facing Peking was which way to turn. In making his political report to the Eighth CCP National Congress in 1956, Liu Shao-ch'i had remarked the "tremendous successes" to date of the first Five-Year Plan and proceeded to outline the basic tasks of the Second Five-Year Plan (1958–62). There would be, he said, a continuation of "industrial construction centered on heavy industry," extension of the system of collective ownership and "ownership by the whole people," a corresponding development of transport and commerce, personnel training, and the strengthening of scientific research, strengthening of national defense, and a raising of the level of material and cultural well-being of the people "on the basis of the growth of industrial and agricultural production."

By 1962, according to Liu's forecasts, steel production would rise from the 4.2 million metric tons planned for 1957 to between 10.5 and 12 million tons; coal production would go up to 190–210 million tons. He assured his listeners that there would be a relatively high rate of development of light industry. Some 8,000–9,000 kilometers of new railway line would be constructed. The gross national product should be about 50 percent greater than at the end of the first plan. Average wages of workers would increase 25–30 percent, the *total* income of peasants the same.

Liu dealt somewhat obliquely with the question of agriculture, but his meaning was clear to those who could read between the lines. He noted that agriculture faced "immense tasks" with respect to the increase of production. He acknowledged that cooperative agriculture was being advanced largely without farm machinery and went on to say: "The mechanization of agriculture in our country can only be brought about in a proper and gradual way, following the industrialization of the country and in accordance with different farming conditions in different localities." The efforts of the Agricultural Producers Cooperatives and the peasants would bring increased crop yields. The goals were to be attained by increased water-conservancy work, more manure to the land (Liu made no mention of any greater availability of chemical fertilizers), soil improvement, better seed selection, the introduction of new types of farm *tools*, the raising of the multiple-crop index, the improving of agricultural techniques, the prevention of plant diseases, and the eradication of insect pests. From Liu's account it was evident that the projected capital investment in agriculture would remain small; the peasant would be expected to do most of the planned work with his bare hands, and a few antediluvian tools.

The Congress drew up general proposals for the Second Five-Year Plan, which in theory was to bring China two thirds of the way to its goal of achieving an integrated, socialized, basic industry by 1967, but no definite targets had been fixed as of the end of 1957. As a result of a capital investment of $20.7 billion during the first plan period, China could count some outstanding accomplishments. Industrial production had increased at the average rate of 19.2 percent yearly, to make a total increase of 141 percent over the five years. Of the 211 projects to be built with Soviet aid, 68 had been completed; 27 of those planned for construction with Eastern European aid had also been finished. There had been continued enlargement of the steel and coal-mining plants in Manchuria. But whereas that area produced 90 percent of the steel and pig-iron and 50 percent of the coal in 1952, there had been a progressive shift inland of the industrial center of gravity, with the erection of new major iron-steel complexes at Paotow in Inner Mongolia and at Wuhan, and a greater exploitation of coal resources inside the Wall. The exploitation of petroleum fields was being pressed in Kansu, the Tsaidam area of Tsinghai, and at Tushantzu and Karamai in the Sinkiang-Uighur Autonomous Region. The old textile-manufacturing centers in the former treaty ports had been revived, while new mills had gone up in inland cotton-growing areas of Hopei, Shensi, and Honan provinces. The extension of the railway system, crowned by the bridging for the first time of the mighty Yangtze at Wuhan, had been supplemented by the construction of highways.

The accomplishments in industrialization and the nonagricultural branches of the economy were tantalizingly impressive. But a critical gap had developed between agricultural production on the one hand and the demands of industry and foreign trade on the other. Since Mao Tse-tung had obtained no further Soviet commitment of gratis aid when at Moscow in November, the issue was now categorically before the Communist leaders: should China endeavor to "go it alone" at the same headlong speed by making a greater effort, or should it slow down for a period of adjustment and consolidation? It is evident that there were some misgivings in the Chinese leadership at the period when the decision had to be made; the debate between the moderates and the radicals (who doubtless termed themselves the "true revolutionaries") must have been vigorous and prolonged.

But Mao Tse-tung, as Wang Mang two millennia earlier and K'ang Yu-wei at the end of the nineteenth century, was a man in a hurry. To renounce the program would have been to cede the race for the "disputed zone" of the underdeveloped countries to the Soviet Union. It would have meant acquiescence in a delay of frustrating years in China's march toward great-power status. From what followed, it became evident that the radicals had won out. China would endeavor to lift itself by its own bootstraps.

At the February, 1958, meeting of the National Peoples Congress a call went out for the performance of "a great leap forward" in economic developments during the next three years. For 1958 alone there were projected increases in steel production of 19 percent, coal 17 percent, and electric power 18 percent. Nor did the February figures stand: where the steel production target in that month was 6.2 million metric tons, by August it had been increased to 10.7 million metric tons (about twice the production figure for 1957). And where the National Peoples Congress foresaw an increase in industrial production of 14.6 percent for 1958, the New China News Agency in March boosted the percentage of anticipated increase to 33 percent.

In the second session of the Eighth CCP Congress, held in May, the Party was mobilized for action in support of the new program. Party cadres set out immediately to whip the people into the proposed great leap. A campaign was launched to set up, in the villages, small workshops and simple steel furnaces built in the traditional native style. By the end of June Hopei Province alone was reputed to have established half a million factories and workshops. By October it was reported that 600,000 of the "backyard furnaces" had been put into operation. Visitors to China reported the great activity night and day of a nation plunged into the construction and operation of factories, furnaces, irrigation projects, and a multitude of other enterprises. Millions of Chinese who were peasants by day were now forced to be industrial workers at night, and the eight-hour workday upon which the Chinese Communist Party had hopefully fixed its sights back in 1931 when the Provisional Soviet Government of China was established, was now stretched to fourteen, sixteen, and even more hours.

The year of the Great Leap Forward also saw the introduction of agricultural communes. The beginning came in April with the establishment of a commune, significantly named "Sputnik," in Honan Province. Soon afterward it was reported there was a "spontaneous" demand on the part of the peasantry for the establishment of communes throughout China. A drive began for the merging of Agricultural Producers Cooperatives into substantially larger units to provide "unified management" with respect not only to agriculture but to industry, commerce, education, social activities, and military affairs in China's countryside.

There were certain notable features to this development. Payment was to be partly by cash wages and partly by free distribution of necessities, including food. There were to be communal dormitories and mess halls. Communal nurseries were also part of the scheme, for it was proposed that there should be massive mobilization of women's labor. Another outstanding feature was the mobilization of the nation's peasant manpower on a paramilitary basis.

The rationale behind this movement was that the Agricultural Producers Cooperatives were too small to undertake big "collective" enterprises such as works of irrigation and other construction. Moreover, larger units were deemed to be more efficient in terms of management. It had been determined at the aforementioned 1956 National Peoples Congress that there should be a greater decentralization of economic activities with more autonomy for individual enterprises. The highly centralized control of industries by the ministries at Peking had been discovered to foster inefficiency and inflexibility (that is, bureaucracy). If intensive centralization of control had proved bad, contrariwise decentralization must be better. So China undertook decentralization, returning control of some enterprises to local government. (It is to be noted that decentralization was undertaken at about the same time in the Soviet Union.)

Soberer reasoning would have suggested that the Communists, in pursuit of the principle of decentralization, should have refrained at this time from combining the collective farms into huge agricultural undertakings that demanded skilled personnel and fine coordination for efficiency. Peking's rulers had, however, shown time and again that their logic was vulnerable to "revolutionary" slogans. Moreover, there still existed the factor that had caused a reduction of agricultural surplus for export in 1957, under conditions where the gross production for that year had apparently increased: the peasants had been eating more of the fruits of "their" labor.

A decisive way to check that particular development and to extract a larger share of agricultural production for the uses of the state was to dispossess the peasant of his collective property and impose a regimentation that would facilitate strict rationing. The rationale now offered was that land, draft animals, farm equipment and tools had become the property of the "whole people," and this meant that the peasant was not entitled to divert to his own uses any of the products of that national holding without the consent of the "whole people," that is to say, the regime at Peking. The Chinese Legalist School some two thousand years earlier had advocated a similar regimentation. The peasant had been returned to a condition he had not known since the end of the true feudal period back at the beginning of the Empire. By the total mobilization designed to increase the state's control over the national labor pool, he had been deprived of choice with respect to economic activity, working conditions, place of residence, and even family husbandry.

In August the Party Politburo met and announced a decision that obviously had been made at the top level some time before. All China was now ordered to adopt a communal system, to introduce it was said, the "ownership of the whole people." In one of the most revolutionary social movements in human history the 740,000 Agricultural Producers Cooperatives were amalgamated into 26,425 rural communes. Further amalgamation brought the figure to approximately 24,000 in 1959. Each commune finally comprised an average of 10,000 acres that, with some 5,000 households, commanded an effective labor force of at least 10,000, or one able-bodied worker per acre.

In connection with this tremendous upheaval, various techniques were introduced in order to make intensive use of agricultural labor. Party cadres, acting under instructions from the top, directed close planting of crops, following the rather too simple thought that, if a given quantity of agricultural product could be obtained from a field planted with a crop in rows a given distance apart, twice that amount could be obtained if the distance between rows were reduced by half. Party workers fostered deep plowing. This was achieved by anchoring a winch on one side of the field, attaching it by cables to a plow on the other side, and then by winding up the winch; the result was the plowing of the soil to depths of two feet and more. Since sparrows ate grain, a campaign was launched to kill all sparrows. Here there was a massive mobilization of manpower, for the process employed consisted of keeping the sparrows in flight by noise and movements from the ground until they fell exhausted, whereupon they were pounced upon and killed. When the final accounting was made, it was claimed a billion sparrows had been liquidated. In line with the mobilization of 100 million peasants between October, 1957, and June, 1958 (agriculture's slack season) for work on irrigation projects, the masses of peasants were driven to perform new miracles of hydraulic engineering. All this work was done with the crudest of tools and implements and, be it said, with the crudest of management procedures. All was in accordance with the concepts adopted by the Party's May, 1958, Congress and embodied in the slogan "Walking on two legs," an expression signifying a combination of the use of modern methods and of ancient Chinese practices.

On October 1 the official *Ren Min Ri Bao* (People's Daily) made a proud claim: "With the great leap forward in production, communism has already begun to push forth sprouts in our actual life." China was entering the stage of "communism" in the Marxian process before the Soviet Union! On the following day, Foreign Trade Minister Yeh Chi-chuang, in his annual review, predicted that the country's foreign trade volume in 1958 would be 14 percent higher than in the year before—because of the increased import and *export* of machinery.

These claims were only forerunners to a final trumpet blast. At the end of the year Peking announced tremendous production increases. Agricultural production was up approximately 100 percent over the year before, with the output of grain and cotton both doubled. Production of iron and steel had doubled. The output of machine tools was said to have trebled. Oil output had increased 50 percent, electric power 40 percent. The Communist statisticians were not content to limit themselves to reporting actual production; they claimed discovery of a great wealth of natural resources for future exploitation: owing to prospecting by the peasants, they said, China's iron-ore reserves had been revealed as being not 11 billion but 100 billion tons.

There was no denying that a tremendous upheaval had taken place in China. But the exact dimensions and significance of what had happened remained for the moment unclear.

RETREATS OF 1959–1960: LESS THAN COMMUNISM

Again, reference to the Russian experience is enlightening. The Russian Revolution of 1917 had occurred because the army, largely composed of peasants, was war-weary and land-hungry. The Bolsheviks were able to capture the revolution from the moderates because they effectively broadcast the promise of land to the *muzhiks* and peace to the people (who were 85 percent peasants, just as in the China of the first half of the twentieth century). Lenin, speaking to the Third Comintern Congress in 1921, explained the success of the October Revolution:

It was because ten million workers and peasants were under arms and refused to fight any more. They followed us because we threw out the slogan of "immediate peace at any price." But we did not owe our triumph to that fact alone. *We won because instead of applying our own agrarian programme, we adopted that of the Social Revolutionaries.* [Italics added.]

When Sun Yat-sen evolved the Three People's Principles under Borodin's tutelage, he had an effective slogan in his war cry "Land to the tiller!" Mao Tse-tung, building up his army and the Revolution on the foundation of peasant distress, made use of the same promise, and Chiang Kai-shek's armies finally refused to fight any more.

In the Russian experience, Preobrazhensky had initially proposed "feudal exploitation" of the peasantry for the financing of rapid industrialization. Stalin eventually adopted that idea, but it had been rejected in Lenin's time in favor of the New Economic Policy (NEP), introduced in 1921. NEP represented a retreat from the stage of "war communism," with restoration of free trading, confirmation of private ownership of the land by the peasants, use of wage incentives, and the offering of inducements to foreign capital. This had been necessitated by the calamitous drop in agricultural production in particular: the grain harvest of 1922 was down 37½ percent from the prewar level. NEP brought production back up, from 50 million metric tons in 1922 to 73 million tons in 1928 (as compared with 80 million tons in 1913), the beginning of the First Five-Year Plan. By 1927 also, $100 million of foreign capital had been invested in the Soviet Union. Then, with the undertaking of agricultural collectivization in 1929, crops fell off, there was a heavy slaughter of livestock, economic dislocation, and starvation that reduced Russia's population by 3 million.

The Soviets had waited twelve years before they undertook collectivization of agriculture; the Chinese Communists began to develop collectives three years after coming to power and launched upon communization in six years. The Soviet experiment continues, but it cannot even yet be deemed to have brought in rich fruits. Lenin, in offering his justification for the application of NEP to agriculture, touched on the heart of the matter:

It is essential to wake up the activity of the small farmer, to give him an incentive, to stimulate his work. Of course, freedom of trade means the growth of capitalism. One cannot escape from that. . . . Is it possible to restore, to a certain extent, freedom of trade for the benefit of small farmers, without striking at the roots of the political power of the proletariat? It is possible because it is merely a question of degree.

In China the agricultural problem was aggravated by the First Five-Year Plan's pronounced emphasis on heavy industry. It was proposed that capital funds for industrialization should be squeezed from the peasantry, but the margin of "surplus" was exceedingly small. The per capita income in 1928 in the Soviet Union, which was far from being a rich nation, was $270 a year. In China in 1953 it was $30–40 and by 1957 was reported to have reached $63. Even assuming the reliability of the figure showing an advance in average yearly income, the people's living standard was still too low to permit much paring back, and, with or without paring, the joint demands of growing industrial activity and a growing trade-and-aid program could not be satisfied. Peking had boasted of great gains, and it was apparent that some increase in production had been achieved. But it was also evident, even as the amazing figures were announced, that not all had gone well with the revolution in China's countryside.

Right after the 1958 harvest Peking had taken note of peasant unrest and various shortcomings in connection with the Great Leap Forward. The utilization of labor had brought truly onerous working conditions. In the past the Chinese peasant, for all his assiduous care of his little plot of land, had enjoyed certain unengaged periods during the working year: peasant men had averaged about 200 days, and peasant women 100 days of work under the old system. Under the conditions of the Great Leap, however, the peasants were not even given enough time for sleep. There was consequently an increasing exhaustion of the labor force, a spread of illness and absenteeism. There being no increase in pay (or other compensation) for the increase in work load, morale also declined.

The drive to make the peasants eat in common mess halls, where they got both inadequate food and faulty service, had a further deleterious effect on morale. There was injury to both family and individual well-being. And there was actual loss of labor hours besides, as workers were forced to line up and wait in turn for food.

In connection with the drive to find metals to feed the furnaces, the peasant was forced to give up his kitchen utensils, the hinges of his doors, and any other metal bits and pieces that appeared to be loose. As doubtless had been foreseen, this increased the pressure on the peasant to eat in the common mess halls. An additional thrust toward communal living came in the destruction of private dwellings in some agricultural villages for the purpose of constructing those common dormitories in which the peasantry were to live together as one happy family. The double aim was to destroy family ties and to tighten the regimentation. With the tearing down of village dwellings (ordinarily built with mud walls and thatched roofs), however, there was a shortage of building materials for the larger "modern" structures, nor was manpower available for all the new construction work. Finally, the attack on the family aroused a general sullen resistance. The drive toward communal living slowed down.

Another failing was discovered in the careless use of farm tools, animals, and supplies. Since those properties no longer belonged

to the peasant either as an individual or as a member of a collectivized group, but to the "whole people," why should the peasant care?
And there was a growing discontent regarding wages and other
returns received for labor. A general work slowdown began, such
as had been experienced previously in roughly similar circumstances
in the Soviet Union.

Another factor entered in. During the 1953–57 period there had
been a great drive to bring more acreage under cultivation. It was
discovered in due course that the presumed "virgin" lands were
truly waste lands, uneconomic for cultivation by the native methods
still being employed. In 1958, as a consequence, there was a swing
in the other direction, with reduction of the cultivated area from
about 280 million to some 250 million acres, the emphasis now
being put on intensive cultivation of the better land and an effort
to increase the output of a given unit of land in the growing season.
Decline of the livestock population (especially hogs) had however
resulted in a reduction of the amount of natural fertilizer available,
while the use of chemical fertilizer had increased from only 295,000
tons in 1952 to an estimated 1,650,000 tons in 1957 (compared with
a target of 5,156,000 tons, including imports). The failure of the
over-burdened soil to meet Peking's inflated expectations had left
agriculture with an additional deficiency in the non-use, for all the
farm labor available, of some marginal lands.

The various malfunctionings in agriculture naturally did not entirely escape the Party's attention, and at the beginning of November the Politburo met at Chengchow, in the heart of the central
plains region, to consider the situation. Following that meeting the
Central Committee met in Wuhan. From that larger conference
there came the so-called Wuhan Resolution of December 10. The
main feature of the Resolution was a shift of emphasis from the
communal back to the collective aspect. The Wuhan Resolution
gave its rationale in the following words: "Once the commune is
brought under public ownership all losses will have to be borne by
the State, and however large the losses the State would have to
maintain the members' consumption at the same level."

This meant that the Peking regime had discovered that it was
disadvantageous for the state to undertake at that juncture to offer
supplies "to each according to his needs." Commune members were
again going to be made responsible for their own basic support.
The Resolution backed away from the proud boast of three months

before that China was about to enter the Marxian stage of communism and talked of hard struggles still ahead: "We should not declare that peoples' communes will enter communism immediately. . . . This distorts and vulgarizes the great ideal of communism, strengthens the petit-bourgeois trend toward equalitarianism, and adversely affects socialist construction." Where "equalitarianism" had a short time before been the essence of the ideal held out to the peasantry, now it was damned as petty bourgeois.

The Resolution proposed an increased emphasis on money wages in relation to free supply. This was a return to the incentive doctrine. It was, moreover, proposed that peasants' homes, personal property, personal savings, and vegetable patches be returned to them. The peasants would be permitted to engage in side activities, which was something in the nature of a return to NEP measures in order to stimulate production. As for the mess halls, it was ruled that the peasants might eat at home if they chose.

New directives were issued regarding utilization of the labor force. During slack seasons the maximum engagement should be eight hours work and two hours study; during busy seasons, the work period should not exceed twelve hours per day. Each worker should have at least eight hours sleep and four hours for his meals and recreation.

Finally, commune industry was thereafter to be related primarily to agriculture. The significance of this was immediately clear: the peasant was no longer to be charged with carrying on industrial activities which might be deemed supplementary to the great steel plants of Anshan and Paotow. Of course, by December, 1958, practically every available bit of steel scrap—and much other metal that by no stretch of the imagination could qualify for a smelting plant—had been collected and consigned to the backyard furnaces.

The Central Committee shouldered no blame with respect to the evident shortcomings of the communes. The cadres were blamed, accused of being "dizzy with success and . . . unwilling to do the patient work of persuading the masses." It was charged that they had exaggerated or invented successes, and leading personnel were admonished that they "must keep close to objective reality." The December 10 Resolution provided for the dispatch into the countryside of tidying-up commissions which were charged with investigating the operation of the communes. They were directed besides to "mobilize the masses to purge those cadres who showed a bad style of work." Some ten thousand such investigators went to work in each province. Mao Tse-tung and Liu Shao-ch'i went on tours of investigation. Corrections of the excesses began.

From December, 1958, to August, 1959, there was extensive reappraisal of the communes with various adjustments of detail. Then, in August, the Central Committee met at Lushan in northern Kiangsi. Long before it convened, the people of China had been experiencing hunger despite the boasted doubling of food production in the preceding year. The truth could no longer be hidden, and it was now announced that the grain production in 1958 had not in fact been 375 million tons as claimed, but only 250 million tons; that the steel production had not been 11 million tons, but only 8. In particular, it was admitted that 3 million tons of "steel" turned out by the backyard furnaces had proved useless.

On July 21, a short time before the Central Committee meeting, Soviet Premier Nikita S. Khrushchev spoke at Plawace in Poland on the question of agricultural collectivization—which he insisted should be voluntary. On that occasion he made a comment on early communal organization in Russia that was interpreted as having reference to the existing situation in China:

> Communes were organized, though there were not the appropriate material nor political conditions—I am thinking about the consciousness of the peasant masses. A situation arose in which all wanted to live well and at the same time contribute as little work as possible to the common cause. . . .
> Nothing issued from many such communes.

But the Chinese comrades hadn't needed to wait on Khrushchev's information. Stalin, speaking to the Seventeenth Congress of the Communist Party of the Soviet Union in 1934, had set forth in some detail the reasons for the failure of the agricultural communes in the Soviet Union—for those who might be interested.

It was against that background that the Communist leadership next undertook measures of fundamental adjustment. An effective reorganization of the agricultural communes was launched on the basis of a system of "three levels of ownership." The first level was that of the commune proper, usually having the same boundaries as a *hsiang* (township). The commune remained in over-all control of all activity, including capital accumulation, ownership of larger items of machinery, equipment, and the major means of transportation, and the general allocation of labor.

The next level of ownership was that of the production brigade, which was essentially the old "higher APC," or collective. The Lushan Resolution put effective ownership of subsidiary industries, draft animals, and tools here, whereas in the beginning all ownership had been placed in the commune itself. The production brigades were made responsible for the entire productive process.

Finally, there was ownership at the level of the production team, which was the former primary APC, or cooperative, approximately equivalent to the old agricultural village. This unit remained subject to the direction of the production brigade, but it had immediate custody and limited ownership and control of and, of course, responsibility for tools, farm animals, and workshops related to the fields actually cultivated. The Communist leadership had discovered the desirability of having individual peasants, not the "whole people," responsible for the carrying out of agricultural processes.

After the harvesting of the 1959 crop there was a further adjustment of wages: a maximum of 40 percent, and usually only 30 percent, of the peasant's income would be in the form of supplies, and 60–70 percent in cash wages. Nor did all receive equal compensation. A graduated scale of rewards was established, fixed not only in accordance with work output, but with reference as well to political attitudes.

The significance of the whole development was that there had been an increased transfer of responsibility for the care of movable farm property and for the raising of crops back to the peasantry, and incentives had been built into the structure of the communes. No longer would the peasant be compensated according to his need.

Peking had backed away from its extravagant claims and extreme measures, and the Great Leap was checked, but serious economic dislocation remained. The final accounting was still to be made. The "corrected" figure of 250 million tons of grain for 1958 was, of course, exactly two thirds of the earlier claim of 375 million tons. The figures were in convenient round numbers, and the mathematical coincidence made them suspect at first glance. Expert opinion has computed the 1958 grain production to have been actually about 190 million tons. This represented an advance over the 185 million tons produced in 1957, but the cost had been tremendous.

The target figure for grain output in 1959 was at first exuberantly fixed at 525 million tons; in the "morning-after" stage, it was cut down to 275 million. At the end of 1959 Peking asserted that the country had produced 270 million tons in the past year, thus exceeding the alleged production of 1958 by 20 million tons. Weather conditions during the crop season had been bad, and the claim was undoubtedly spurious, as indicated by domestic food-supply conditions and the country's export position. The figure had probably been sent out into the glaring light of day because the regime could not bear to admit no advance; the actual figure is believed to have been some 180 million tons.

The year 1959 was not an unqualified failure: steel production went up to about 10 million tons. The output of pig iron and coal substantially increased, and there was a notable increase in power output. But there was only a slight advance in the manufacture of cotton cloth, reflecting agriculture's failure to provide more raw cotton. Raw-cotton production actually dropped somewhat in 1959. And the home production of chemical fertilizer merely topped, for the first time, a million tons—insignificant in the light of agriculture's needs. Agriculture continued to be the critical sector in the economy.

No figures were issued for 1960 production in agriculture, but it is known that grain output dropped even further that year, to approximately 155 million tons, that is, to the level of 1952, the "year of recovery." In November the People's Daily made a revealing comment on the general state of affairs: "A rough estimate shows that if people's food needs are to be met adequately China's grain output should be at least double its present level. If the population's clothing needs are to be met adequately cotton output should be at least trebled." [12] Most revealing of all, perhaps, was the circumstance that Peking was forced to ask the Soviet Union to grant China postponement of payment of $300 million due on its trade account for 1960; then, in early 1961, it entered the world market to buy grain and contracted for the purchase of some 10 million tons of food grains for current and future delivery from Canada, Australia, Argentina, France, and even Burma.

Peking continued to blame the existing situation in the main on natural calamities and in part on the all-too-human weaknesses of its own cadres. In fact, the cause of the agricultural failure was complex, ranging from the psychological factor to the ecological. There was widespread neglect of the fields at critical periods because of the directing of legions of peasant-workers to nonagricultural tasks; the care and storage of harvested grain was often faulty, with resultant waste. The overloaded transportation system, given the additional task of feeding the backyard furnaces with raw materials and hauling away the nearly worthless product, was unable properly to serve agriculture. The vaunted deep-plowing turned up unfertile soil in areas where the top soil was thin—and there are many such areas in China. The digging of numerous wells in semi-arid areas resulted in lowering the water table. Vast irrigation projects, hastily planned, caused water shortages in some areas due to diversions farther upstream: there was, after all, only so much water. Elsewhere, faulty irrigation measures induced waterlogging and salinity. After the killing of the sparrows for their eating of grain, it was discovered that they had eaten bugs, too, and with the disappearance of the sparrows insect pests flourished. Peking reversed itself and directed that sparrows should *not* be killed, but the sparrows were already dead.

Finally there was that incalculable factor of morale to which Mao Tse-tung had paid so much attention back in the days when he was fighting a guerrilla warfare against the Nationalists and the Japanese. The Communist ideologues in their far-reaching subjectivism had thought that their machinery had given them control of the mind and spirit of man. They had been too hasty in their conclusion.

In the final accounting, the economic dislocations introduced by the Great Leap had seriously reduced the vitality of the entire agricultural sector. In the political field, consequently, the Great Leap introduced an element of major disillusionment of the Chinese people with their leadership—and with Mao Tse-tung in particular. It had moreover engendered new tensions, and dissensions, within the CCP leadership, where unifying factors had theretofore proved so strong.

11 SHIFT IN PEKING'S FOREIGN POLICY

CHINA'S undertaking of the "liberation" of Tibet at the same time that it plunged into the Korean War against the United Nations was a measure of the strategic boldness of Mao Tse-tung and his associates. The Chinese strategy and tactics were beyond the experience of most Western political leaders. NATO's chieftain, the United States, had projected the encircling operation into Southeast Asia and the West Pacific to contain the USSR and Communist China in another continent. The contest between Communism and anti-Communism has been viewed in the United States as being the vital factor in world affairs, and as being primarily a military matter. The American military structures of NATO, CENTO, SEATO, and bilateral alliances were built on the foundation of nuclear power, ICBMs, and future space ships. Divisions and naval units were deployed, air forces tensed in a state of constant alert. The governing concept was the apolitical one of the Maginot Line.

There was a basic weakness here. Many Western political leaders, habituated to cultural dominance, had taken it for granted that the Orient was inherently sympathetic to what the West stood for. They believed in their hearts that men such as Syngman Rhee and Chiang Kai-shek were closer to them, and to democracy, than to their fellow-nationals and Asian values. They neglected the facts of history. For four centuries the Western maritime powers roamed the Eastern seas almost at will, breaking down political barriers to erect a vast structure of Asian colonialism. If the meeting of East and West in Asia had resulted in something like an amalgamation of Oriental and Occidental cultures, the presumption of East-West sympathy might have a certain validity today. But there has been no such joining together: Kipling's "East is East, and West is West" still reflects the actuality. With Asian colonialism effectively ended, the Orient now confronts the Occident as a political equal in circumstances where cultural accommodation is conspicuously absent.

Mao Tse-tung's strategic concepts, if Communist, were Asian, not Occidental. His stress was on the political factor first and foremost; the military element played a secondary role, except at critical junctures. His was not the ancient China, politically disjointed and culturally somnolent, of the era of Western predominance, but a renascent nation of revolutionary turbulence. China's twentieth-century nationalism had crystallized into its current virulent anti-imperialism, which it viewed as being a common Asian cause; and it saw itself as the rightful leader of a "protracted war" against the imperialist enemy. A major front in that protracted struggle lay in the China Sea.

SECOND FORMOSA STRAIT CRISIS, 1958

The first Formosa Strait crisis of 1955 had subsided not because of a settlement of differences between the United States and China but with a freezing of Washington's and Peking's mutually antagonistic positions. In August, 1955, as a result of a *démarche* by Chou En-lai from the Bandung Conference, Sino-American talks began on the ambassadorial level at Geneva. If their concern was "the relaxation of tensions," there was no meeting of minds from the beginning. Ambassador U. Alexis Johnson sought to get Peking to renounce the use of force in the Formosa Strait; Ambassador Wang Ping-nan demanded the withdrawal of American forces from the same area. Naturally, no progress was made.

In the meantime, the American build-up of Nationalist strength continued; and Peking, for its part, continued to try to get Taipei to engage in direct talks for Formosa's "peaceful liberation"—the way Tibet was "liberated." Peking's wooing during 1956 and 1957 bore no fruit. Quemoy and Matsu had been only lightly garrisoned in 1955; by 1958 the situation had changed radically, with substantial Nationalist troop strength and military supplies concentrated on the islands. Moreover, twenty American military advisers were stationed on Quemoy, where none had been present in 1955.

The Nationalists became more open regarding the offensive character of their offshore island position. The chief political officer of the Quemoy command was quoted in July, 1957, as stating that the island was being changed from a defense outpost to a forward command post and prepared for use as a stepping-stone to the mainland. The Nationalists made regular use of Quemoy and Matsu as bases for commando attacks against the mainland and the landing of subversive agents. For years Nationalist reconnaissance aircraft had regularly flown over China's southeastern provinces photographing air fields and other military objectives. Transport planes, employing high-level fighter cover, had as regularly distributed propaganda leaflets over the mainland. Peking had quite obviously chafed at such activities.

At the beginning of August discussions had taken place at Peking between Khrushchev and Mao Tse-tung, with Marshals Malinovsky and P'eng Teh-huai also in attendance. In a joint communiqué issued on August 3 the Communist chieftains paid the usual lip service to the peace policy and then said: "The two parties exchanged views fully on a series of major questions confronting the two countries in Asia and Europe in the present international situation and reached unanimous agreement on the measures to be taken to safeguard peace." It may be assumed that their conference had touched on the situation in the West Pacific.

In the period after 1955 the Communists had built up their strength opposite Quemoy until it numbered approximately two hundred thousand troops. They had stationed a large number of Soviet-built fighter and bomber planes within striking range of Formosa, and their small navy had recently been strengthened by deliveries of Soviet motor torpedo-boats to give it a modest representation in coastal waters. The Nationalist military strength on Quemoy alone was between eighty and one hundred thousand men. The Nationalist navy, comprising about ninety American-supplied vessels of all types, far outweighed the Communist fleet.

On the mainland the Chinese nation was being spurred to greater production efforts and herded into the agricultural communes. The appearance on the horizon of a hated enemy at that juncture would have been advantageous from the government's point of view, as it would clearly have had the incidental effect of reducing resistance to its revolutionary program. That consideration may indeed have been a factor in Peking's military decision.

It is probable, however, that Peking's chief aims lay elsewhere. Its maximum objective may have been to subjugate the offshore island garrisons and by that heavy blow to bring down the Nationalist regime on Formosa. A logical minimum objective would have been to impose a political defeat on Formosa and the United States. The Chinese objectives were matched by standing American aims. The governing American desideratum was the restoration of Chiang Kai-shek's control of the mainland; at the minimum, the United States desired to contain Communist China and to protect the Nationalists on Formosa.

On August 24, the Communists launched a heavy shelling of Quemoy; the bombardment continued to the accompaniment of calls on the Nationalist garrison to surrender. The struggle had begun.

The United States intervened, rushing planes, ships, and United States Marines to the area. The American Navy began to escort Nationalist convoys carrying supplies to Quemoy, and American Air Force planes flew alongside Nationalist planes in protective cover missions for air drops over the island. The Nationalists were patently elated at the prospect that American military forces would come to grips with the Communists.[1]

But the critical moment passed quickly. The general political pattern of 1955 was repeated. Canadian Prime Minister Diefenbaker suggested that the UN should intervene in the "threatening" Formosa Strait situation. On the same day, September 6, Premier Chou En-lai broadcast a statement charging the Chiang regime with use of the offshore islands as bases from which to harass the mainland—but proposing at the same time the resumption of talks at the ambassadorial level "for the defense of peace." To the undisguised dismay of the Nationalists, Washington promptly took up the suggestion. Khrushchev's message of September 8 to President Eisenhower stating that "an attack on the People's Republic of China . . . is an attack on the Soviet Union" came after the peak of the danger had already been passed.

There followed a series of involved maneuvers. The ambassadorial talks resumed. According to newspaper columnist Marguerite Higgins, the United States made it clear in those talks that it would not deliver over the offshore islands but had at the same time conveyed to Peking, through other channels, the intelligence "that it would respond to a Communist ceasefire by persuading the Nationalists to forego the use of Quemoy and Matsu as bases for attacks against the mainland."[2] Peking Defense Minister P'eng Teh-huai on October 6 ordered a one-week cease-fire, and the United States promptly stopped escorting the Nationalist convoys. At the end of the truce period, P'eng extended it another two weeks, magnanimously saying that this was to enable Chinese "compatriots" on Quemoy to obtain needed civilian and military supplies and "strengthen their entrenchment."

Secretary Dulles visited Formosa a week later in an effort to obtain an agreement with Chiang Kai-shek. On October 23, after three days of negotiation, there was issued a joint communiqué recognizing that "under the present circumstances the defense of the Quemoys, together with the Matsus, is closely related to the defense of Taiwan and Penghu [the Pescadores]." This acknowledgement concerned the American side in particular. The Nationalist regime, on the other hand, committed itself to the proposition that "the principal means of successfully achieving its mission ['the restoration of freedom to its people on the mainland'] is the implementation of Dr. Sun Yat-sen's Three People's Principles *and not the use of force.*" (Italics added.)

There was thus to be no withdrawal of the Nationalist offshore-island garrisons; instead, the United States had pledged itself to their support—at least "under the present circumstances." Peking had manifested its presence by breaking its unilateral cease-fire on October 20, the day of Dulles' arrival on Formosa, charging (apparently correctly) that an American naval vessel had been part of a Nationalist convoy the night before. On October 25, the Communists played their trump card by announcing that they were unilaterally imposing an alternate-day cease-fire for Quemoy: the initiative, they said in effect, was neither Washington's nor Taipei's but theirs. The United States was boxed in: the Nationalists had forced it to accept the principle that Quemoy and Matsu fell within the Formosa defense perimeter, and the Communists had abetted the Nationalist move to prevent any withdrawal of the Nationalist garrisons.

The second Formosa Strait crisis faded out in November. For Taipei both credit and debit were to be counted. In credit, there had been a notable increase of American aid. In the three weeks after the beginning of the crisis, $90 million worth of military supplies were sent to Formosa. By the end of the fiscal year 1959, it was currently estimated, the military aid might total $300 million. But there was a big debit. As a result of American pressure, the Nationalists had to cease using the offshore islands to harass the mainland. Quemoy and Matsu had also been "neutralized." Peking had not achieved its presumed maximum objectives, and had betrayed certain military limitations—at least, in the presence of American military might. In terms of its minimum objectives, however, it could count substantial credit. Except for occasional long-range (and high-altitude) reconnaissance flights, there was a cessation of Nationalist air activities, including leaflet drops, over the mainland. Commando raids from the offshore islands stopped. The effective half cease-fire was controlled from Peking.

The effects of the 1958 Formosa Strait crisis on Formosa's relationship to the mainland were therefore substantial. In the first place, the Nationalists had publicly acknowledged that they had no practical prospect of returning to the mainland unless there was a revolt there similar to the Hungarian uprising of 1956. The October 23 Nationalist-American communiqué had had the effect of freezing the political situation: the fate of Formosa and the Pescadores had been solidly linked to the future of Quemoy and Matsu.

On the mainland of China, in the meantime, the "war crisis," heavily charged with politics though it was, had doubtless considerably facilitated the Communist rulers' further regimentation of the Chinese people.

CHINA'S WORLD POSITION, AND THE TIBETAN AFFAIR

During 1958, while China was undertaking the Great Leap in domestic affairs and challenging the United States in the Formosa Strait, there were a number of developments in its foreign relations that, if seeming at first to bear little relation to each other, finally fell into a pattern to indicate a new trend in Peking's foreign policy.

China began the year with a flourish in the trade-and-aid field. It was exporting Diesel engines to Egypt and Syria, had contracted to supply rubber tires to such a variety of countries as Finland, Rumania, Syria, Burma, and Ceylon. It was also supplying, according to reports, complete machinery sets for knitting-mills and soap factories in Indonesia, Burma, and Egypt. It signed a pact with Yemen, where Soviet technicians were already present, granting a loan of some $16,380,000 for the construction of a highway and several light-industry plants, with China to supply technicians and skilled workers for the construction. It offered a $20 million loan for long-term industrial purposes to Indonesia, to which the USSR had extended a $100 million credit in 1956. China's foreign trade had fallen off in 1957 as it had in 1956. But Foreign Trade Minister Yeh Chi-chuang, with his prediction of a 14 percent increase, had indicated the belief that the Great Leap Forward would reverse the downward trend. China would storm world markets just as it stormed its industrial plants and rice-fields at home.

The year's trade pattern began to take on some new aspects. Britain and other W stern European countries had in May 1957 put trade with China on the same basis as trade with the Soviet Union. And in 1958 various countries of Western Europe, as well as the Soviet bloc countries such as Czechoslovakia, Poland, and Rumania, substantially increased their China trade. China's commerce with its major trading partner, the Soviet Union, however, dropped during the same year.

Japan had led the way in breaching the UN trade embargo laid down against China in 1951. Trade with Japan by 1955 had reached the value of $155 million. Developments up to early 1958 had seemed to promise further expansion of trade relations between the two near neighbors. The Japanese were constrained to exercise caution, for the mainstay of their trade was with the United States, and they also had a profitable commerce with Formosa. But Japanese businessmen viewed the potentialities of the China trade with sympathy and interest. Agreements had virtually been concluded between the two countries for a substantially increased trade in 1958 and for an exchange of Chinese iron ore, coal, and rice, for Japanese steel products during 1958–62 to the value of nearly $300 million, when in May Peking suddenly broke off the negotiations because of a minor flag incident, which they would never have noticed had they been interested in reaching an agreement.

Other sour notes began to creep into China's relations with its Asian neighbors, with whom it was supposed to be living in a spirit of "economic cooperation." In the year of the Great Leap Peking began to dump products of its light industry on the South and Southeast Asia market. The exports included not only cameras and bicycles but also textiles, sugar, cement, and even footwear.

These Chinese sales at cut-throat rates were undoubtedly designed to obtain badly needed supplies of foreign exchange with which to pay for imports of machinery and other capital equipment from the bloc countries and Western Europe. The immediate impact was felt, however, by manufacturers in Hong Kong, Japan, and India who had been making assiduous efforts to develop markets in that region for themselves. The countries concerned naturally considered possible countermeasures. At the Colombo Plan economic conference held at Singapore at the end of October, it was

charged that China's state-owned industry was selling textiles at
cut-rate prices in an apparent effort to capture the market. From
8.4 million square yards in 1954, China's textile exports to Indonesia
had grown to 100 million square yards in 1957; and where China
had no part of the Hong Kong market in gray cotton-goods in 1953,
by 1957 it had won 84 percent of that market. In the first ten
months of 1958, China's exports to Hong Kong reached the value
of $190 million, as compared with a total of $119 million for all
1954. By 1958 also, some 70–80 percent of all cement used in Hong
Kong was imported from China, which was winning a near-mo-
nopoly of the market by underselling local and Japanese producers.

Singapore, Malaya, and Hong Kong took steps to protect their
markets against the flood of Chinese goods. Peking had aroused an
unfavorable reaction by trying to make a "great leap" in the foreign-
trade field. And, in the end, its foreign trade for the year only
totaled $3.9 billion: it may have sold more goods in some areas but
at bargain prices it received less for them. And, after all, it was its
trade with the Soviet Union that counted most.

In early 1959 a straw in the wind significantly pointed up a new
direction. In the preceding October, presumably reading the preliminary estimates of the staggering results of the Great Leap Forward, China had concluded an agreement with Finland for the
delivery of 20,000 tons of sugar, beginning the following March.
Through its sales Finland had accumulated a credit of some $27.5
million in China, and was naturally desirous of getting some return.
But at the beginning of March, 1959, Peking canceled the contract,
on the grounds that it lacked the means to fulfill it. Nevertheless,
China substantially increased its trade with both the Soviet bloc
and Western Europe in 1959, while its trade with Asia was cut in
half. It finished the year with a $4.4 billion total for exports and
imports.

But one feature of the situation had become glaringly clear:
China was supporting its foreign trade with consumer goods and
raw materials needed at home. This was a sure way to create serious
domestic shortages, as had been discovered much earlier when
heavy Chinese exports of grain, soy beans, and vegetable fats to
the Soviet Union had quickly brought stringency of supplies of
those items for the Chinese people. Peking argued that the exports
constituted only a minute percentage of the whole of China's production; but the hard fact was that, with the rapid population
growth, even if it had used *all* of its production for domestic pur-

poses, China would still have been short; and any exports aggravated the deficits.

The reason for China's 1958 break with Japan suggests itself: in
the preliminary negotiations China had committed itself beyond its
power to deliver. The political factor also entered in. Besides "economic cooperation," China was committed to abide by the concept
of "peaceful coexistence." The *Panch Shila,* or Five Principles, of
peaceful coexistence had had their origin in the Sino-Indian agreement of April, 1954, and been publicly proclaimed by Nehru and
Chou En-lai upon the occasion of their meeting at New Delhi the
following June. And *Panch Shila* became, effectively, the Bandung
Spirit. Put into Marxist phrasing, it constituted the essence of the
Communist world strategy proclaimed at the Twentieth Congress
of the Communist Party of the Soviet Union in 1956.

In 1959, however, developments in Tibet caused an open rift
between Peking and New Delhi. In the 1954 agreement Peking had
given India no commitment regarding Tibetan autonomy; instead,
India recognized that Tibet was an integral part of China. India
also agreed to withdraw the military contingents it had maintained,
under the old order, at the trading points Yatung and Gyantse and
to transfer to China all Indian state property in Tibet, comprising
the telegraph, telephone, and postal systems, and trade-route rest-
houses. The two countries, thereafter, would each have the right
to maintain trade agencies at three specified points in the territory
of the other; and trade and pilgrim traffic would be confined to six
specified routes. The last relics of the British imperial influence in
Tibet had been liquidated.

The Chinese had been constructing two military highways into
Tibet from the east, one from Tsinghai and the other from Chamdo.
Both were completed in 1954. A third, from Yehchung in Sinkiang
to Gartok in Tibet, opened to traffic in October, 1957; it cut across
Ladakh, or eastern Kashmir, that is, Indian territory. The Chinese
were then in a position to deal swiftly with any movement of
Tibetan opposition.

Peking continued to abide by the letter of the provision for autonomy contained in the 1951 agreement with Tibet. In April, 1956,
a Preparatory Committee for the Tibetan Autonomous Region had
been established at Lhasa. Its chairman was the Dalai Lama himself, and the first vice chairman his traditional enemy, the Panchen
Lama. In the meantime, CCP cadres swarmed into Tibet, the PLA
undertook development of agricultural programs as it had in Sin-

kiang, Chinese geologists explored the countryside, and Peking's men began to introduce the approved "socialist" education.

In eastern Tibet, the influx of hungry Chinese immigrants had in 1956 sparked a minor tribal revolt. The PLA was present in force and easily suppressed the uprising. The immigration continued, and the Tibetan resistance became more general, with some groups moving westward before the advancing Chinese flood. Among the Tibetan migrants was a tribe known as the Khampas, who finally came to rest near the Tibet-Nepal border. In April, 1958, Peking complained to Kathmandu regarding an alleged movement of arms from Nepal into southern Tibet.

The Khampas were tough fighters who frequently carried on a part-time occupation as highwaymen. They were not a politically sophisticated group. It is, therefore, logical to suspect that it may have been outside instigation, perhaps Nationalist, that led the un-enlightened Khampas in July to demand that Chinese authority be withdrawn from Tibet.

The Chinese military commander at Lhasa requested the Dalai Lama to send forces to suppress the rebels. The Dalai professed his inability to comply. Then, in March, 1959, the world was startled by the news of a revolt that burst forth in Lhasa itself. On March 12 the Dalai's Cabinet, the Kashag, unilaterally denounced the 1951 agreement between China and Tibet and declared Tibetan independence.

On March 17 the Dalai Lama fled his capital. Two days later, Khampas and armed monks rose up against the Chinese military power. The whole adventure was a hopeless undertaking, either conceived by the politically naive Dalai or by interested anti-Communist partisans, possibly provoked by the politically astute Chinese Communists themselves. The strong Chinese garrison, now maintained by three military highways and strategically placed military airfields, put down the uprising in two days. The Chinese then proceeded to do what they had doubtless been itching to do for some time: they effected a thoroughgoing purge of rebellious elements in Tibet, focusing their action where theocratic power lay —in the lamaseries. According to one report, some sixty-five thousand anti-Chinese Tibetans were killed.

The Dalai Lama had been the bulwark of resistance to the rapid Sinicization of Tibet, for he was able to cite the limits to Chinese action provided in the 1951 treaty. But after the Kashag's denunciation of the treaty and the Dalai's flight from Lhasa, on March 28

Peking decreed the dissolution of his government and handed over interim governing authority to the Preparatory Committee. With the Dalai gone, the Committee came under the control of the puppet Panchen Lama.

It was only on March 31 that the Dalai Lama crossed the border of Tibet into India for refuge. It has been widely assumed that the Dalai made his escape in spite of the best Chinese efforts. But logic suggests that it would have been awkward for China to do away arbitrarily with either the Dalai Lama or his power while he remained in Lhasa, whereas his departure notably facilitated the carrying forward of the Chinese program. It seems probable that Peking was only too glad to have the Dalai depart. Chou En-lai gave a revealing—one might even say exultant—interpretation of events at a banquet given in honor of the Panchen Lama in Peking on April 14: "The obstinate Tibetan reactionaries have chosen the way of treason against the people and the country. In destroying themselves they have created conditions extremely favorable for the democratization of Tibet." Tibet, predicted Chou, would now rapidly progress toward autonomy under the leadership of the Panchen Lama.

The Tibetan theocratic rule formerly headed by the Dalai Lama was ended. On the basis of historical example, it was easy to foresee the country's future course. Tibet would follow in the way of Sinkiang, Inner Mongolia, and Manchuria: it would be amalgamated irrevocably into China, in ethnological and cultural as well as political and economic terms.

This development was of prime importance to the country on the south, India. Imperial British policy had envisaged the maintenance of a Tibetan autonomy that would keep Tibet as a buffer between China and India. India's protests in 1950 against Chinese armed action in Tibet and its statements in the spring of 1959 showed that Prime Minister Jawaharlal Nehru's government likewise saw the strategic advantages of maintaining Tibet's autonomous status. But India had not been prepared to make the matter an issue, in its national interest, before the United Nations in 1950; and from 1954 onward, Nehru and Krishna Menon had chosen to believe that Peking was sincerely committed to the *Panch Shila*.

In 1959 the political situation had changed before the Indians' very eyes. Chinese power was solidly established in Tibet, the "Roof of the World," which towers strategically over the subcontinent that is India. The Tibetan plateau had been converted into a staging ground for Chinese political and military power. Increased Chinese pressures against the northern Indian border, and more especially against the petty border principalities of Nepal, Bhutan, and Sikkim, could be readily foreseen. The flight of the Dalai Lama had marked the end to both Tibet's autonomy and its buffer function.

Sino-Indian tensions began to build up along the border immediately after the Dalai Lama's flight, and it soon became apparent that Peking challenged the border itself. After a number of clashes between border patrols, the nature of the Chinese challenge became clear: Peking denied the validity of the McMahon Line, drawn in accord with provisions in the Simla Convention of 1914, and claimed some forty thousand square miles of India's Northeast Frontier Agency.

This can hardly have come as a complete surprise to the Indian Government, since the Communists' position and their maps were practically identical with those of the Chinese Nationalists. The Indian public was shocked to learn, however, that the Chinese had actually constructed their Yehchung-Gartok road across the eastern end of Ladakh, and were thus in physical possession of some twelve thousand square miles of Kashmiri territory. Nehru's government admitted that it had known of the matter earlier, but said that it had desired to spare public opinion. In September, 1959, New Delhi published a White Paper setting forth its correspondence with Peking on the matter. But Chinese troops were garrisoned in Ladakh, and Chinese military truck caravans continued to thread their way over the highways from China into Tibet, in concrete evidence of the changes that had been wrought on the Roof of the World.

There were two interesting consequences to the developments of 1959. The Chinese crushing of Tibetan nationalism probably did not surprise Asians: they knew from history that any Chinese regime commanding the necessary strength would have done the same. But the Chinese action gave a concrete demonstration that Peking now actually commanded such strength. Then, when Peking went on to thrust with newborn Chinese forcefulness against the Indian frontier, in obvious violation of the spirit of peaceful coexistence, the neighboring Asian countries realized that traditional Chinese imperialism had returned, if with new trappings, and an old fear coursed through them.

Effects of the events in the high Himalayas were felt farther afield, in the area of Sino-Soviet relations. The Soviet Union, with a confirmed interest in Afghanistan, had shown a keen interest in developments in neighboring Pakistan and India. As the Sino-Indian border dispute worsened during the course of 1959, Moscow surprisingly assumed a "neutral" attitude. Then, after a visit to the United States in the "Camp David spirit" of peaceful coexistence, Khrushchev, with no more than the briefest of stops at Moscow, flew on to Peking to see the Chinese oligarchy on what bore the appearance of pressing business.

The occasion was the celebration of the tenth anniversary of the establishment of the Communist regime in Peking. But the gravamen of Khrushchev's speech was of another matter. Patently speaking as an international Communist, he said:

We, on our part, must do everything possible to preclude war as a means for settling outstanding questions.

We must . . . correctly understand the present situation, and this certainly does not mean that since we are strong we should test the stability of the capitalist system by force. This would be wrong.

The question when this or that country will embark on the Socialist road is to be decided by the people themselves. This principle is the holy of holies for us.

What Khrushchev said sounded as if the Chinese had been urging war with India as a means of bringing Communism into power in that country (and incidentally effecting a readjustment of India's northern borders to China's benefit). Under the circumstances, it is interesting to consider Nehru's observation before the Indian Parliament in November: "I doubt that there is any country that cares more for peace than the Soviet Union. I doubt that there is any country that cares less for peace than China." New factors, the Indian one included, had evidently entered into the Sino-Soviet relationship.

THE PEKING-MOSCOW AXIS, 1958–1960

After the Polish and Hungarian uprisings of 1956, there had been profound soul-searching in Peking. In December the Chinese Politburo finally produced an essay, "More on the Historical Experience of the Proletarian Dictatorship," in which Mao's theory of contradictions was extended to acknowledge the existence of contradictions between socialist countries and also between Com-

munist parties. It was explained, however, that "this type of contradiction is not basic; it is not the result of a fundamental clash of
interests between classes, but of conflicts beween right and wrong
opinions or of a partial contradiction of interests." As was only
natural, the Politburo argued that the solution of those "nonantagonistic" contradictions must "first and foremost be subordinated to
the over-all interests of the struggle against the enemy."

Chou En-lai visited Eastern Europe in early 1957, when the
western section of the Soviet bloc was still suffering from the impact of the Polish and Hungarian revolts, to plead for bloc solidarity behind the USSR. Referring to current reports of Sino-Soviet
differences, he said that "our differences are of secondary importance."

Chou was hewing to the Mao line: the Sino-Soviet differences
were "nonantagonistic contradictions" and hence susceptible of
solution by the process of discussion and negotiation. But this left
open the issue suggested by the old observation: "Orthodoxy is
my doxy; heterodoxy is another man's doxy." History is replete
with instances of "minor" differences in the field of ideology, religious and secular, that have in due course become primary, or, as
Mao would put it, "antagonistic."

In the first 1937 exposition of his theory of contradictions, Mao
had provided for a nearly endless shifting of evaluations, and of
contradictions: "Processes change, old processes and contradictions
disappear, new processes and new contradictions emerge, and the
methods of resolving contradictions differ accordingly." If that
meant anything at all, it meant that the "doxy," or Truth, would
itself change according to changing circumstances. The international "ally" of today might become the enemy of tomorrow. Proof
of the theory was shown in the experience of Communist China's
domestic development, where the concept envisaged the progressive elimination of groups and classes by attacking them as "antagonistic" where they had been "nonantagonistic" before, with the
survival of only one supreme power. In the foreign field the aspiration, although not voiced, was to have China recover the
position of a nonpareil "Middle Kingdom," predominant and strong
beyond the need of allies. The strategic objective might be limited
in its first application to Asia, but it was obviously susceptible of
extension.

It would therefore appear that Mao Tse-tung, looking at the
world situation in the latter part of 1957, arrived at a fuller ap-

preciation of the real strength of the forces with which China would have to contend. American military and economic aid spread over the world in the postwar period was measured in the tens of billions of dollars ($100 billion through 1962), a large proportion of which was issued gratis. Although Khrushchev had said in 1956 that the Soviet Union was too poor to give free aid to other countries, in actuality the USSR had become, in relation to the underdeveloped countries, a "have" nation, with surplus capital, machinery and other capital goods, and technicians, available for export. China, in contrast, was a "have-not" nation, itself underdeveloped, short of both capital and technical skills, its people poverty-stricken.

How could China compete in the foreign trade-and-aid contest? As of the end of 1957, a major scissors gap had developed between industrial and agricultural output. Industrial production had increased in gross value at the average annual rate of 18 percent during the Five-Year Plan period, agricultural production only at the average rate of 4.5 percent. The country depended heavily upon agriculture not only for the supply of raw materials for light industry but for export products to pay for imports—and to service the national debt. And its debt to the Soviet Union, including obligations incurred in the course of the Korean War and through liquidation of the last Soviet economic enterprises in China, by this time totaled $2.4 billion. "Democratic personage" Lung Yun, ex-warlord of Yunnan, had addressed himself to that matter during the Hundred Flowers period. He remarked that it would take the country over ten years to repay its loans from the USSR, and put out the (inspired?) thesis that it was unreasonable for China to bear all of the expense of the Korean War. He had gone on to raise the issue of compensation by the USSR for machinery removed from Manchurian industrial establishments during the postwar occupation.

Lung Yun was publicly denounced for his "absurd views," but his argument may well have been aired for the consideration of Moscow. If that was so, it clearly did no good. During his November visit to Moscow Mao Tse-tung must have learned that the bill was still to be paid. The time had not yet come for a socialist sharing of its wealth by the USSR.

By demanding political equality in the 1950–54 period and getting it, as a corollary China was accorded economic equality, or, in harsher terms, the right to no more of the Communist bloc's goods than it could produce by its own efforts. This was doubtless one factor that entered into the calculations of the representatives of the eleven other Communist parties when they met with Mao Tse-tung in Moscow in November, 1957. So the November Declaration held to the established Bandung Spirit line. It was, however, notable that, while asserting that "the socialist states are united in a single commonwealth by the fact that they are taking the common socialist road," the Declaration at the same time made a qualification: "The forms of the transition of different countries from capitalism to socialism may vary." Mao could hardly object: hadn't he said essentially the same thing?

Voted down in the Communist bloc councils, China next undertook its fantastic Great Leap Forward. The Peking regime's proud boast in October that China was entering the stage of Marxian communism was an indication of the forcefulness with which it would have pursued its policies inside the bloc and out had the Great Leap actually succeeded. That was not to be: by the end of the year China's rulers knew that their radical venture had failed in its aim of leaping over a generation of toil by a single great effort. As a consequence, in December came Peking's retraction of the implicit claim that China was ahead of—and superior to—the Soviet Union.

Having discovered that it was impossible to work miracles by the manipulation of the human Chinese mass alone, Peking desperately needed massive Soviet aid for continuation of the Second Five-Year Plan. Moscow was not prepared to underwrite Chinese industrialization, population growth, and aggrandizement. Nevertheless, the Soviet strategists were farsighted men. They had a continuing need of keeping China in the bloc, if under control. The Chinese recantation of December came first. Then, in February, 1959, Moscow signed a new agreement with Peking for the provision of $1.25 billion worth of goods for expenditure over the period of the Second and Third Five-Year Plans (1958–67) in connection with the construction of seventy-eight new industrial projects. Technically this was merely an agreement for the exchange of goods, not a long-term credit. It had to be repaid by the Chinese in current deliveries.

The differences of opinion between Peking and Moscow had been resolved not in accordance with Mao Tse-tung's theoretical formulas but through Moscow's exercise of superior economic strength. The argument as such remained in being.

Khrushchev, speaking at the Twenty-first Party Congress at Moscow just *before* the signing of the new economic agreement with Peking, made a comment directly applicable to the agricultural communes as originally set up by the Chinese. He said: "Egalitarian communism would lead to the eating away of accumulated means and would make impossible further successful developments of the economy and expanded production." This was a clear reminder to the Chinese comrades that they lacked the adequacy of consumer goods that Soviet theorists had been contending was a prerequisite for a communistic society.

The Chinese Communist Party made no theoretical concessions. Beginning in 1958 and continuing in 1959, Peking's news media first held Mao Tse-tung up as a "great Prophet" and then as "one of the most outstanding Marxist-Leninist revolutionaries, statesmen, and theoreticians of our age." Finally the burgeoning thought was put forward in all its boldness: Mao Tse-tung's writings, and his thought, *were* Marxism-Leninism; and, according to the contention of the *People's Daily* of early 1960, Mao had Sinicised Marxism-Leninism. The significance of the argument was that the Chinese Communist Party, under Mao's leadership, was claiming that Mao's thought had special virtues for Asia. This was a challenge to Moscow's ideological leadership and a challenge to the exclusive right of the Communist Party of the Soviet Union to leadership of revolutions in underdeveloped countries, including those in Africa and in Latin America. The CCP's aim was evidently the establishment of an Asian Comintern of which the leader would be China.

The 1959 drop in agricultural production suggested to the Chinese leaders how great a price they would have to pay for the economic dislocations brought about by the frenzy of 1958. Mystical slogans no longer bore convincing promise of quick successes. With a brashness that could hardly be believed, the Chinese ideologues returned to their attack on the Soviet strategic position. The campaign was launched in an essay entitled "Long Live Leninism!" published in the authoritative Party journal *Hongqi* (Red Flag), in April, 1960, on the occasion of the ninetieth anniversary of Lenin's birthday. In that essay the Chinese Party presented its own doxy as orthodoxy. It cited the principle of the Paris commune according to Marx: "The proletariat should use revolutionary means to seize State power, smash the military and bureaucratic machine of the bourgeoisie and establish the proletarian dictatorship to replace the bourgeois dictatorship." This meant that the bourgeois nationalist governments of South and Southeast Asia should be overthrown in favor of Communist dictatorships. Peking quoted the Moscow declaration of 1957 to the effect that "the revisionists tried to kill the revolutionary spirit of Marxism, to undermine faith in socialism among the working class and the working people in general." Then the editorial continued:

At the present time, the Socialist Soviet Union clearly holds the upper hand in the development of new technics [e.g., space satellites and the ICBM]. . . .

If . . . we lose our vigilance against the danger of the imperialists launching a war, do not arouse the people of all countries to rise up against imperialism, but tie the hands of the people, then imperialism can prepare for war just as it pleases and the inevitable result will be an increase in the danger of the imperialists launching a war.

That appeared to be an argument in favor of pre-emptive military action. Peking obviously believed that, since the Soviet Union had the upper hand, it should drive the advantage home. And, according to the *Red Flag* version, the venture could not have other than a happy outcome even if this meant general war, for it argued that the experience of the Russian and Chinese revolutions showed that, should the imperialists launch a war, "on the debris of a dead imperialism, the victorious people would create very swiftly a civilization thousands of times higher than the capitalist system, and a truly beautiful future for themselves."

But the Russians have known the Chinese intimately since Mongol times and in recent decades have suffered political losses owing to deceptions practiced on them by such "friends" as Chiang Kai-shek, Feng Yü-hsiang, and Sheng Shih-ts'ai. Borodin, making his weary way homeward from the 1927 Comintern debacle in China, remarked to the American journalist Anna Louise Strong: "When the next Chinese general comes to Moscow and shouts, 'Hail to the World Revolution,' better send at once for the G.P.U. [state security forces]. All that any of them want is rifles." [3] Quite clearly the Soviets were not swayed by the loveliness of the Chinese vision presented in 1960. Moscow girded its loins and met the Chinese stand initially by publishing on June 10, the fortieth anniversary of the appearance of Lenin's *Left-wing Communism— an Infantile Disorder*, an article attacking the "present day Leftism in the Communist movement" that opposed the policy of collaboration with non-Communist, bourgeois groups. The selection of that particular date was pointedly suggestive.

Then, at a gathering of the clans in Bucharest on the occasion of the Rumanian Party Congress, Khrushchev shed his gloves and hit hard at the Chinese argument. Speaking on June 21, the Soviet leader said that "only madmen and maniacs can now call for another war," with its "fatal consequences." Some of Lenin's propositions (which had been cited by the Chinese) were evolved decades ago when things were very different. One could not "mechanically" repeat Lenin on imperialism "and go on asserting that imperialist wars are inevitable until socialism triumphs throughout the world." Khrushchev argued in his turn that "no world war is needed for the triumph of socialist ideas throughout the world. These ideas will get the upper hand in the peaceful competition between the countries of socialism and capitalism."

The leader of the Chinese delegation to the Bucharest conference, P'eng Chen, nominally took his stand on the 1957 Declaration, but he gave an interpretation that was Chinese, holding that "the aggressive and predatory nature of imperialism will never change" and that "U.S. imperialism is the arch enemy of world peace." War could be held off, he contended, "only by continually strengthening the forces of the people in countries of the socialist camp, the liberation movements of the Asian, African, and Latin American peoples, and the revolutionary struggle of the people in various capitalist countries and by relying on their alliance in the resolute struggle against U.S. imperialism and its lackeys so as to isolate U.S. imperialism to the greatest extent." P'eng condemned not Moscow and Khrushchev but "modern revisionists, represented by the Tito clique." The Chinese phrase "pointing at the mulberry and cursing the locust" indicates the device the Chinese delegate was using: in pointing to the "Titoist revisionists" he was really damning Moscow and the Communist ideologue Khrushchev himself.

There was a real schism in the Communist camp. Moscow was called upon to take action if it was not content to see a steady attrition of its strength as a consequence of the Chinese campaign. What ensued must be viewed as a masterpiece of Soviet generalship. Moscow did not rely simply upon a reconvening of the twelve Communist and Workers parties which had formulated the 1957 Declaration. It convened, instead, presumably with the acquiescence of Peking—but how could Peking object?—a conference of eighty-one Communist and Workers parties. The delegations met in Moscow in November but sat well into December before they were able to agree upon a joint statement.

The Chinese delegation was a strong one, led by Liu Shao-ch'i.

Others on the delegation included P'eng Chen, propaganda chief Lu Ting-yi, and CCP General Secretary Teng Hsiao-p'ing. Mao Tse-tung was not present, and his prestige was not committed. The Soviet Union in the end won a decisive victory over its Chinese opponent, but China left its imprint upon the final document. The statement indicated basic continuation of the peaceful coexistence line with a variation that reflected the Chinese pressure. It held that the principal characteristic of our time is that "the world socialist system is becoming the decisive factor in the development of society," whereas "the world capitalist system is going through an intense process of disintegration and decay." It took oblique note of China's claim of two years earlier to be entering a stage of communism in the statement: "The Soviet Union is the first country in history to be blazing a trail to communism for all mankind." As for the moot question of peace or war:

The time has come when the attempts of the imperialist aggressors to start a world war can be curbed. World war can be prevented by the joint efforts of the world socialist camp, the international working class, the national-liberation movement, all the countries opposing war and all peace-loving forces.

The signatories thus still stood for a united front of Communist and bourgeois forces. Then, remarking that "the complete collapse of colonialism is imminent," the statement introduced a new element:

The Communist Party which guide themselves by the Marxist-Leninist doctrine have always been against the export of revolution. *At the same time they fight resolutely against imperialist export of counterrevolution.* They consider it their internationalist duty to call on the peoples of all countries to unite, to rally all their internal forces, to act vigorously and, relying on the might of the world socialist system, to prevent or firmly resist imperialist interference in the affairs of any people who have risen in revolution. [Italics added.]

This last provision offered clear evidence that the Chinese argument had had an effect on the Soviet position and had made it more radical. The Soviet position regarding over-all strategy, including the factors of aid to, and collaboration with, bourgeois nationalists, had been maintained; but the Communist countries were called upon to take a stronger stand against any "imperialist" intervention in favor of "counterrevolutionary" forces. This doctrine was clearly applicable in the "disputed zone" generally and Southeast Asia in particular.

Shortly afterward, in early January, Khrushchev in an address to party workers in Moscow sharpened some of the passages of the December statement. Characterizing it as "one of the most brilliant pages" in the history of the world Communist movement, he offered balm to Peking: "The CPSU is overflowing with an unwavering resolve to strengthen its bonds of eternal friendship with the CCP and the great Chinese people." By Khrushchev's interpretation the statement reaffirmed the allegiance of the Communist parties to the 1957 Declaration. He said that it would be "profoundly wrong" to argue that world war is an indispensable condition for the further intensification of the general crisis of capitalism. Khrushchev did not say so, but it was entirely obvious that the party which must have argued thus could only have been the Chinese.

At that time China had still not issued (and has not yet done so) figures for its agricultural production in 1960, but it was already known that the combination of economic dislocation and unfavorable weather had brought a sharp drop in grain output. Khrushchev could not refrain from making his basic point regarding the prerequisites for communism even clearer than before. For the building of communism, he said, "it is necessary for people to be able to eat well, dress well and have housing and other material and cultural conditions." China was a long way from possessing such prerequisites. Borodin had pointed a generation earlier to the same relationship between consumption goods and social organization: "The only Communism possible in China today," he said, "is the Communism of poverty, a lot of people eating rice with chopsticks out of an almost empty bowl." [4] China, in 1961, was still deep in poverty.

BEHIND THE "INEVITABILITY OF WAR" ARGUMENT

The whole Sino-Soviet debate of 1960 had a certain unreal quality to it. There was a tendency to attribute this to the fact that Communists were talking with Communists, on fine, quasi-mystical points of their peculiar dogma. But it would be sounder to regard the ideological debate as an elaborate smokescreen that hid a clash of national interests that was both real and of vital importance to the contending parties.

The surface argument regarding the "inevitability of war" deserves passing consideration on its intrinsic merits. China's entering the lists in defense of Lenin's decades-old thesis was, of course, not without ulterior motives: the Chinese were not being as reckless of consequences to themselves as it might have seemed at first glance. Any new world war would be fought chiefly between the nuclear powers, and, in a life-and-death struggle where everything depended upon early obliteration of the nuclear enemy, they would hardly be inclined in the beginning (and probably decisive) phases of the war to waste either time or nuclear missiles on secondary targets, such as China. The United States and USSR, in short, would first engage in mutual destruction; and there might not be much nuclear warfare after that phase of the fighting was over. Granted that China would be prepared to sit out that phase of the struggle, it might then be left to inherit the earth—for Maoist Communism. It seems hardly likely that Peking presented this line of reasoning to Moscow, but the Soviet strategists, being acquainted with Chinese ways from of old, would have been able to fathom the thought behind the "idealistic" attitude. And, it is hardly likely that they would view with other than a jaundiced eye a proposition requiring possible sacrifice of the Russian people for the benefit of the Chinese.

The visible part of the argument, however, was like the peak of an iceberg: the substantive matters of the Sino-Soviet dispute, like the bulk of the iceberg, were located beneath the surface. The Chinese are great bargainers and inclined to playing one force against another (which is, in fact, the essence of Mao's tactics at home and abroad). It seems entirely possible that, for one thing, Peking referred to the dangers of war, and exaggerated them, to support its request to its Soviet ally for nuclear weapons. The Chinese Communists may have argued, as the Nationalists contend to the United States, that with modern equipment in their hands they could "go it alone" in an Asian war, to achieve their policy objectives, with little or no inconvenience to their ally.

Peking had upon occasion manifested its interest in possessing nuclear armaments. In early 1958 Foreign Minister Ch'en Yi forecast that China would in due course obtain such arms. In September, 1958, with Soviet aid, China had brought its first atomic reactor (a 10,000 kw. heavy-water research plant) into operation. But, to all indications, the USSR had given no nuclear weapons to China for the "inevitable war."

The Chinese argument, however, had more practical political aspects than those referring to nuclear arms. Clearly implicit in the

Chinese argument and the Soviet responses was Peking's desire that the Soviet Union renounce support of "bourgeois" governments through the trade-and-aid strategy in favor of channeling greatly increased amounts of aid, preferably gratis, to "loyal," "socialist" China.

The argument would have denied the validity of the Bandung principle of "economic cooperation," to which China had subscribed earlier, and would have required a reversal of the "aid" programs China itself had undertaken from 1955 onward. The Peking regime would have had no practical difficulty in reconciling itself to a reversal of course that would bring such prompt relief from the drain on its national resources, but it wanted the Soviet reversal as well. Otherwise the field would have been abandoned to Soviet and American exploitation alone.

The Chinese were under a "dialectical" compulsion to supply their argument with theoretical justification, and did so. The evidence indicates that China argued for more active and direct support of Asian, African, and Latin American revolutions, in accordance with Liu Shao-ch'i's 1949 thesis. That support should be in the form of political organizers, military technicians, perhaps armed volunteers, equipment, matériel, and money. If this was in direct contravention of the Bandung principle prohibiting interference in the internal affairs of other countries, why, had not Mao himself said that "old processes and contradictions disappear, new processes and new contradictions emerge"? The change would work to China's positive benefit, for, being located in the Asian field and purporting to have evolved a formula for revolution that was especially efficacious in underdeveloped countries, it would expect to fill the role of directing Communist revolutionary movements. The Soviet Union's role would be limited to providing the material supplies for China's use in that connection.

Moscow knew how to debate most effectively. Quite apart from its mobilization of the support of world Communist parties (in which it had predominant influence by reason of past and present ties), it commanded economic power that could hurt China badly. In August, 1960, well before the November congress, the Latvian Party organ, *Soviet Latvia*, published an article by Party theoretician S. Titarenko in which he raised the question whether a country in the position of China would be able to build socialism if it were to find itself "in an isolated position—not able to rely on the cooperation and mutual aid of all other Socialist countries."

In the same month Soviet advisers and technicians (of whom 10,800, according to Soong Ch'ing-ling, had worked in China during the ten years 1950–59 on the various enterprises Moscow had agreed to build) left by the trainload for home, taking their blueprints with them.

In a long article published in the *Peking Review* of August 23, state planning chief Li Fu-ch'un gave what was inferentially China's answer: "Modern revisionists since 1958 have launched movements in an effort to isolate us but they will only isolate themselves." Those were brave words; but they were foolish, reflecting at best an inflated estimate of China's power to bend Moscow to its will. China had renounced its use of the traditional device of "using barbarians to control barbarians" when it chose in 1949 to adopt a categorically hostile stand vis-à-vis the "imperialists" and "lean" to the side of the Soviet Union: it had thereby lost contact with possible counterweights to the USSR. The Soviet Union had access to the greater leverage: besides withdrawing its experts, it evidently reduced its exports to China, including presumably both new industrial equipment and spare parts for Soviet-made machinery.

China was heavily dependent upon the USSR for supplies of heavy military equipment, to the use of which its armed forces had been converted. It was also vulnerable to pressure from the Soviet Union as regards petroleum. Exploitation of the country's oil resources had hardly begun under the Nationalists. Domestic production of crude petroleum, 1.46 million tons in 1957, was raised to 3.7 million tons in 1959. The 1960 production reached 5.5 million tons, thus exceeding the target figure of 5.2 million tons. Most of China's production, however, except for production from shale in Manchuria, was located in remote sections of the country's Northwest. And 5.5 million tons was well under the country's current (1960) needs, which were estimated at 7–8 million tons for a meager annual consumption of three imperial gallons per capita (as compared with an Indian consumption of five gallons per capita).

The Soviet Union had been supplying the required petroleum imports. It had also supplied the machinery and technicians for the exploitation of China's oil fields: liquidation of the Sinkiang joint-stock petroleum company in 1954 had not liquidated China's need for modern oil-well and refinery equipment nor its need for technical skills. In the oil fields, China had won its independence only on paper. The departure of Soviet technicians from China's oil enterprises could easily prove this fact.

The trade figures for 1960 incontrovertibly and painfully confirmed China's vulnerability: its foreign trade that year dropped $400 million below the 1959 figure and included a decrease of $100 million in imports from the Communist bloc. Its trade with the USSR was down 19 percent, with a 23 percent decline in exports and 14 percent drop in imports. Although in 1959 China had been the USSR's leading trade partner, in 1960 it ranked behind East Germany and Czechoslovakia.

China was in grave trouble. Peking undoubtedly recognized this situation even *before* the 1960 meeting of the eighty-one Communist and Workers parties. On the occasion of China's October 1 anniversary Chou En-lai expressed China's "deep gratitude" to the USSR for aid rendered. Moscow sent a telegram felicitating Peking on the anniversary. On October 22, presumably after an extensive appraisal of China's agricultural, industrial, and foreign-affairs prospects, Mao Tse-tung, Liu Shao-ch'i, Chou En-lai, and Marshal Chu Teh sent a joint reply in which they characterized the USSR as the leader of the Communist world, held that the Sino-Soviet relationship was one of "monolithic solidarity," and spoke hopefully of the prospects for world peace.

In its October issue *Red Flag* carried an editorial article vastly different in tone from its April piece. In a voice of the same authority as before, the journal now declared that revolution could be neither exported nor imported and that no Marxist-Leninist party proposed that socialist countries should spread revolution by means of war. Peking had evidently recognized that it could not hold the position it had taken up. The Chinese doubtless put forward stout arguments in the Communist conclave that followed, but they quite appreciated that it was they, and not the Soviet Union, that stood in grave danger of being isolated. They had prepared their line of strategic retreat in advance, however, and in the end signed the December statement together with the other eighty "comrade" parties.

Despite the signature of what should have been a treaty of peace, the conflict carried over into 1961 and 1962. Peking had acknowledged a battle lost, but not the war. The agreement in any event had not covered differences that, even if unmentioned, were nevertheless vital. Peking's propagandists therefore continued to attack the "Yugoslav revisionists," and Moscow railed at "Albanian dogmatists," until the next big Communist meeting took place, in the Twenty-second Congress of the Communist Party of the Soviet Union in October, 1961.

The overt Albanian position was similar to the Chinese in three important respects: Albania wanted more Soviet aid to come to it, instead of going to "bourgeois nationalists"; it desired a more radical Communist bloc policy against "imperialism"; and it maintained (for its own special reasons) an anti-Yugoslav stand.

Khrushchev came to the Twenty-second Congress with his position of leadership so strong that he was able to complete the process of de-Stalinization that had begun in 1956 by successfully carrying his attack to the "anti-Party group." He thus confounded the observers, perhaps including certain Chinese, who had thought they perceived a Khrushchev retreat at the Twenty-first Congress of 1959. The Soviet leader went further and leveled a direct attack on the Albanian party leaders—and thus on the Chinese—as dogmatists, saying, with reference to the strategic course laid down at the Twentieth Congress of 1956, that the Soviets could not yield on the question of principle "either to the Albanian leaders or to anyone else."

China supported Albania. Chou En-lai first protested the public debate of a question of Communist relationships, which he contended had best be dealt with as a family affair, and then left the halls of the Congress altogether. Moscow had an answer for that also: in December the USSR and its Eastern European satellites broke off diplomatic *and economic* relations with Albania, thus throwing Albania into the Chinese lap for support at a time when China, which had loaned Albania $125 million the preceding April, was unable to pay its own bills.

In the final accounting, the item that showed the greatest divergency between the Soviet and the Chinese points of view was that of the Soviet Draft Party Program as adopted by the Twenty-second Congress to carry the Soviet economy and society into the stage of communism by the target date 1980. The concept governing the deliberations of the 1959 Congress had been that all socialist countries would enter the stage of communism at approximately the same time. The 1960 Moscow statement, with reference to socialist development, noted the need for paying "due regard to the historical peculiarities of each country." The 1961 program was designed for the USSR alone, although the pattern would fit the Eastern European Communist countries equally well. It was based on

Khrushchev's concept of having, as a prerequisite, adequate supplies of consumer goods. It envisaged a society widely divergent not only from Chinese capacities but from Chinese ideals. Mao was hoist on his own petard.

Soviet theoretician S. Strumilin had given a preview of the Party's blueprint in an article on "The World Twenty Years from Now," published in the Soviet organ *Kommunist* of September, 1961. Saying, in the section entitled "Everything for Man," that the Soviet Communist Party aimed at assuring a higher standard of living for the USSR than that enjoyed by any capitalist country, Strumilin held that work was to become both lighter and more interesting: "It is ceasing to be merely a means of survival and is turning into a genuinely creative process and a source of joy." Khrushchev hewed to that line, saying: "Our party's policy is pervaded with the great communist idea: Everything in the name of man, for the benefit of man!" He went on to stress that, in order to move from socialism to communism, time and certain conditions were required. He sketched the prerequisites, in terms of creation of a material and technological base and the evolution of a high level of political consciousness in the nation. China did not command those prerequisites.

The practical significance of the issue was pointed up by Zvonimir Kristl, writing in the Yugoslav journal *Vjestnik* (Herald) in January, 1962, on "Economic Conflicts." Kristl professed to give the substance of a talk by the Deputy Secretary General of the Italian Communist Party, Luigi Longo, before the December plenum of the Italian Party's Central Committee. According to Longo, it was not a question of coexistence, of war or peace, or even of roads of transition from capitalism to socialism, that was in dispute; rather, it was the question of transition from *socialism* to *communism*, that is, a question of the pace of development of the Chinese economy. Longo expressed the view (in the words of Kristl) that the CCP leadership "confronts the developed socialist countries with the request that they interrupt their progress, placing all their advantages at the disposal of the underdeveloped socialist countries so that the latter may catch up with them, and then proceed, all together, towards communism."

According to Kristl's account, the fundamental aim of the Chinese leadership in international relations "consists in wresting by forcible means from the other socialist countries, above all, decisive assistance in accelerating this rate of speed [of national development]." The Chinese leadership proposed to achieve its ends in the international sphere, he said, by promoting a deterioration in the international situation that would lead the USSR to aid and strengthen China *in its own interest* and by challenging Moscow's primacy in the Communist bloc. Stating this thesis in even balder terms, it meant that Peking was demanding that the Communist bloc supply China with the economic sinews it needed to wrest leadership from the Soviet Union in the world's disputed zone— the underdeveloped countries in Asia, Africa, and Latin America.

In April, 1962, the National People's Congress sat in session in Peking to view the disarray of the Chinese economy and foreign relations. Grain production in 1961 had been only about 165 million tons. The 1961 import of grain had totaled 6 million tons. Raw cotton production was down 12 percent from the year before. In 1962 the country would need 9 million tons of petroleum products. Confronting the Chinese leaders were unsolved problems of production and distribution. In theory, the year 1963 would see the beginning of China's Third Five-Year Plan. It is now known, from secret PLA documents made public by the State Department in August, 1963, that the regime's bungling and the resulting economic distress had given rise to widespread unrest; even military units had become disaffected. The delegates met in a spirit of due sobriety. No strident paeans of support for "loyal Albania" were voiced at the Congress; the tirades against "revisionist Yugoslavia" were muted. As the Congress neared its end, a Soviet economic delegation, headed by minister of Foreign Trade Nikolai S. Patolichev, arrived in Peking to talk business. China had once more bowed to the force of the superior Soviet economic position. Mao's men had not changed their minds, but they would have to wait until they grew stronger. In the meantime, they would nurse their frustration and anger; and, they were to be stung by an additional goad—hunger.

12 THE GREAT PROLETARIAN CULTURAL REVOLUTION

THE APRIL, 1962, National People's Congress offered a revealing commentary on the state of affairs in China. The regime still gave no detailed accounting for 1960–61 production in either agriculture or industry. There was no question why: a true picture would have shown the regime at a distinct disadvantage. Where a few short years before the CCP had proposed, first, that the Chinese Revolution should be taken as a political model for other countries groaning under colonial or semi-colonial (including bourgeois nationalist) rule and, next, that underdeveloped countries desiring to make rapid economic progress would be well advised to follow the bold and shining Chinese example, now actual performance did not support the proposition.

The economic achievements up to 1958, in the face of grave setbacks and difficulties, had been considerable, but the agricultural base had proved too weak to support an industrialization program of Great Leap proportions and velocity. The national weakness was found in the imbalance between a nearly stationary agricultural production and an industrialization process that had outrun finances, markets, and supplies of raw materials.

The initial urge to press forward with industrialization was understandable: China had a long way to go to become a major economic power with the capacity of meeting its people's growing needs—and of supporting a modern military establishment. In the first decade of the Peking regime's effort, when it was following the Soviet pattern of economic development, with the construction of new plants for the production of everything from steel to cement, the output of heavy industry in particular had shot upwards. Sample UN figures inferentially based upon Peking's own statistics indicate roughly the character of that advance:

Product	Production (million tons)		
	1952	1957	1959
Coal	63.6	130.0	348.0
Pig iron	1.9	5.94	20.5
Steel	1.35	5.35	13.35

The semi-official figures for 1959 were patently inflated, and can only be taken for their suggestive value. Steel production for that year has been more realistically estimated to have been about ten million tons, and coal under 300 million tons. Moreover, steel production, after climbing to about fifteen million tons in 1960 (the claimed output was over eighteen million tons), is thought to have fallen below ten million tons in 1962; and coal production, after climbing in 1960, fell back in 1962 to an estimated 240 million tons. Those gyrations resulted from dislocations induced by the attempted Great Leap, and in part doubtless also reflected the breakdown in Sino-Soviet economic cooperation.

The Congress in effect decided to tighten the collective Chinese belt and return to the way of relative economic sobriety. The central figure in the deliberations was now the "moderate" Chou En-lai. Chou paid formal tribute to the Great Leap, but also remarked that the nation had suffered "serious natural calamities" during the three years 1959–61. He outlined "Ten Tasks for the Adjustment of the Economy in 1962" in which were discovered not only the outlines for future effort but also indications of past error: (1) "Strive to increase agricultural production, first of all the production of grain, cotton and oil-bearing crops"; (3) "continue to retrench the front of capital construction and to use material, equipment and manpower where they are most urgently needed"; (4) reduce the urban population "by persuading first of all those workers and functionaries who came from rural areas to return to rural productive work and strengthen the agricultural front"; (7) "work energetically to fulfill foreign trade tasks"; (10) "continue to improve the work of planning to insure an all-round balance between the branches of the national economy in the order of *agriculture, light industry and heavy industry*." [1] [Italics added.]

The reversal of economic priorities to give agriculture first place was a radical departure of prime importance: it highlighted the danger of a breakdown in the national food supply. By its Great Leap extravaganza, the Peking leadership may have retarded China's economic development by as much as a decade. To resume the upsurge in industrialization, to restore a vigorous foreign trade, and to buttress the national position in international relations, China needed a strengthening of the agricultural base. But since such a program demanded innovation, substantial capital investment, the introduction of additional managerial and technological skills, and the expansion of transport facilities besides, China would clearly need, at a minimum, the entire period of the next five-year plan to construct an agricultural base strong enough to support its growing industrial superstructure—and thus a vigorous foreign policy. The problem was: what procedures, added to China's material and human resources, best promised the attainment of that goal?

At that juncture, the Peking regime still seemed bent on leading the nation along the way of the "three Red banners" it had adopted as battle standards—the general line of constructing socialism, the Great Leap Forward, and the communes. It showed a determination that the country should still press forward in the economic field, "walking on two legs." The shift of emphasis from heavy industry to agriculture could logically have been taken as an indication that the sobriety that had marked the economic effort since 1959 would continue. But the Great Leap advocates would seize upon the very fact that economic rationalization had brought about a measure of recovery as warranting a return to Great Leap concepts. And then, even earlier, a schism had begun to develop within the outwardly monolithic Party under the stresses of intra-Party differences regarding national policies. The year 1962 marked the beginning of an entirely new stage in Chinese Communist history.

RETURN TO "CLASS STRUGGLE"

CCP Chairman Mao Tse-tung was the ultimate divisive force. In the attempted Great Leap Forward of 1958, Mao had shown himself to be not a revolutionary materialist of the Marxist-Leninist stamp but a Utopian idealist, a dreamer of dreams who would be ready to undertake great national ventures *that might be wholly impracticable*. It was in the light of the massive failure of that great voluntarist effort of 1958, and the demonstration of his fallibility, that Mao was forced by those who considered themselves his revolutionary peers to abdicate as chairman of the Chinese People's Republic in favor of Liu Shao-ch'i, hardheaded organization man, who undertook to govern China with greater reference to practical than ideological considerations.

The real confrontation had occurred at the Lushan Party Central Committee gathering of August, 1959. P'eng Teh-huai's challenge to the dethroned Mao was basic: he charged that the procedures adopted during the Great Leap Forward constituted adventurism. And P'eng was supported by others. Mao had met that particular challenge by threatening that if his proposals were rejected he would retreat to the agricultural countryside, raise a new peasant army, and wage civil war. Faced with this major threat to Party unity and the very heart of the Communist authority, the Central Committee had bowed to Mao's will.

Liu Shao-ch'i, who had been described officially as Mao's "closest comrade in arms" when he took over the position of chairman of the Chinese People's Republic in April, 1959, was to all outward appearances a wholehearted supporter not only of the Party Chairman but also of the doctrine of permanent revolution and of the Great Leap Forward. However, faced by the exigent national need of restoring the badly damaged economy to the semblance of a working order, the Peking regime under Liu's leadership had progressively thrust the voluntarist "Reds" into the background after 1960, and gave first place in its councils to the "experts" instead. The bureaucrats were again given a loose rein, to enable them to solve the problems pressing upon the nation; and there was widespread recourse to material incentives to spur production. Liu, if he talked radically, was enough of an organization man to be a pragmatist in practice. But in Mao's eyes, such pragmatism was tantamount to a reversion to capitalism.

In an important sense Liu, cloaked now with both the prestige and the authority of the position of head of state, had come by 1962 to overshadow, to a degree, Mao Tse-tung. Liu had begun to compete, if only in the natural course of events, with Party Chairman Mao for leadership of the Chinese Revolution. But Mao had won a negative victory at the bitter Lushan conference: the Central Committee had refrained from official condemnation of the Great Leap Forward strategy, and thus the concept of Chairman Mao's infallibility had been maintained. This circumstance facilitated moves undertaken shortly thereafter to build up the Maoist personality cult to truly heroic proportions. And there was another element of victory in 1959 that offset, to a degree, the 1958 defeat: Mao had succeeded in ousting his challenger, P'eng Teh-huai, from the position of Minister of National Defense, and in replacing him by Lin Piao.

Lin was a man of solid achievement in the field of revolutionary military affairs. He had demonstrated masterly generalship in both the war against Japan and the Third Revolutionary Civil War that followed. After taking over his new position, he began to demonstrate an exceptional devotion to the Thought of Mao Tse-tung, particularly as it might be applied in the People's Liberation Army. For those who remembered Mao's axiom that "Power grows out of the barrel of a gun," it was perhaps an augur of the future when Lin in 1961 began to step up political work in the Army.

There now appeared signs that the chief Party effort was not, after all, to be concentrated on the economic problem. At the Party Central Committee plenum of September, 1962, a new "rectification" movement was launched, aimed at "socialist education." The Third Five-Year Plan did not get off the ground in 1963 as first projected (it was not formally launched until 1966). The National People's Congress and the 9th CCP Congress, both scheduled to be held that year, did not convene. Party Chairman Mao clearly believed that the time was not auspicious. In May, 1963, he warned of the danger of a counterrevolutionary restoration if the class struggle and the drives for production and scientific experimentation were neglected. The "socialist education" program was stepped up. With the country still distant from its national goals, Mao was thrusting it into a new disruptive adventure. He planned a resumption of the "class struggle" in the form of an attack on domestic "revisionism," thus to eliminate degenerate "capitalistic" elements now reappearing under the NEP. Underlying this program, by later evidence, was his determination to recover full control over the course of the Chinese Revolution.

The next year, 1964, saw the opening moves of what eventually came to be identified as the Great Proletarian Cultural Revolution (GPCR). The Party's ideological journal, *Hongqi* (Red Flag), under the editorship of Mao's longtime secretary-associate Ch'en Po-ta, on January 1 proclaimed a program of intensified class struggle and socialist education. Soon after, there was acceleration of the campaign for emulation of the PLA. A *People's Daily* editorial of

February 1 put the essence of the concept in its title, "Learn from the Experience of the People's Liberation Army in Political and Ideological Work." At this time, the PLA was being bent by Lin Piao toward full and unswerving loyalty to the Thought of Mao Tse-tung, and to the idea of a nation in arms ready to wage guerrilla warfare against a foreign foe, in the manner of Yenan days. This was carrying Great Leap voluntarism over into the field of military affairs. Mao seemingly harked back increasingly to the idealized Yenan period (when, for one thing, his wartime authority was beyond challenge). Speaking in 1919 in somewhat similar circumstances, Lenin had made a point that seemed applicable to the Chinese scene: "The whole of the opposition's error lies in this, that they, being bound to this *partizanshchina* [guerrillaism] by traditions of a heroism that will never be forgotten, will not understand that those days are over."

But Mao, as regards the employment of the armed forces, had a purpose beyond national defense: he proposed to use the military to reassert his will over the Party. The PLA was to be "a party within the Party," to serve Mao's personal ends.

The Party proceeded with the socialist-education program, but results were meager, and Mao's suspicions of the bona fides of the administrators of the program doubtless deepened. The pace of the movement quickened. On July 1, 1964, Peking Mayor P'eng Chen, powerful Politburo figure who had served variously as political commissar under Lin Piao in Manchuria during the civil war and as deputy director of the CCP organization bureau under Liu Shao-ch'i, launched a "Cultural Revolution," designed to effect the rectification of thinking and attitudes in cultural circles. Then, in December, Premier Chou En-lai called for the radical transformation of all ideology which was not consistent with China's economic base and with socialism, and for the elimination of capitalism and the bourgeoisie. There was a precedent for his summons: in 1957, during the "anti-rightist" phase of the Hundred Flowers campaign, Teng Hsiao-p'ing, the Party's secretary general, had brought up the "fundamental question" of eliminating the bourgeoisie as a class. It was one of Mao's standing objectives.

In 1965, China was confronted by two major problems. Early in the year, the United States carried its war against the Vietnamese revolutionaries into North Vietnam, by sea and air, and a few short months afterwards it introduced massive combat forces into South Vietnam, thus ripping the camouflage off its military intervention in support of the Saigon regime. This raised for Peking the issue of national defense. (See Chapter 13, below.)

The second problem was economic. It had been duly announced that in 1966 the nation would undertake its Third Five-Year Plan (by reason of the attempted Great Leap Forward, the Second had of course been aborted). Given the country's low rate of capital accumulation, coupled with weak technology and a weak agriculture, however, Peking faced the exigent question: *how* could the country mount a major program of economic construction, especially when, by its foreign policies, it had cut itself off from the chief sources of foreign aid? Mao chose in effect to deny the validity of either issue.

There was a psychic factor of considerable importance operating in the equation. In the post-Great Leap period, the new powers and privileges granted the intellectual elite tended to carry over from the economic and administrative fields into that of politics. Using an old device of indirection, certain Chinese intellectuals began to write essays and critiques which, nominally based on historical episodes, could be taken to have reference to analogous circumstances in the present. The American writer Anna Louise Strong, in one of her newsletters from Peking, would in due course report that in the "hard years" 1959–61 a number of "right opportunists" in the Party caused the publication of over a hundred articles "sneering at all party policies such as 'big leap' communes and intellectuals doing manual labor." [2]

It can confidently be assumed that those deviations from what Mao Tse-tung considered orthodoxy did not escape his attention. At a secret extraordinary meeting of the CCP Central Committee in September, 1965, Mao demanded an intensification of warfare on "reactionary" and "revisionary" ideology. The majority of that body, reputedly under the leadership of the Party's Peking committee headed by P'eng Chen, rejected the proposition, undoubtedly thus compounding, on the one hand, Mao's congenital dislike of "liberals," elites, and bureaucrats, and, on the other, increasing his suspicion that there existed a plot against him, The Leader, and his Thought.

It was suggestive of the state of political affairs within the Party leadership that, in addressing a conference of Party propaganda cadres that same September, P'eng Chen should have stated, in substance, "that everyone in the face of truth was equal, that everyone should be given freedom to speak, and that even if the Chairman is wrong, then he too must be criticised." [3] Mao's opposition had become bolder.

In defeat, Mao Tse-tung retreated to Shanghai. This was, however, only a tactical move: in November, 1965, the first blows were leveled at opponents of Mao and Maoism.

THE GREAT PROLETARIAN CULTURAL REVOLUTION

The first casualty of Mao's new "struggle" may have been Chief of General Staff Lo Jui-ch'ing. He was a proponent of military professionalism (as opposed to the "guerrillaism" currently being espoused by Mao and Lin Piao), and his advocacy of a strong stand against foreign "enemies" was in opposition to Mao's own position, which if verbally bold was cautious in actuality. Lo disappeared from sight in late November. The official reason for his disgrace was disclosed only much later, when he was publicly condemned as an associate of P'eng Teh-huai and Huang K'e-ch'eng.

The first *open* attack came in the field of literature. Wu Han, sometime historian and university professor, had been deputy mayor of Peking since 1952. His 1961 play, "Hai Jui Dismissed from Office," told the story of an upright official (of the Ming Dynasty) who had acted in behalf of the people according to his conscience—and had been dismissed by the emperor. In November, 1965, the young super-Maoist (and Mme. Mao's reputed son-in-law) Yao Wen-yuan brought Wu Han under attack in the Shanghai newspaper *Wen Hui Pao*—which would act as the vehicle for numerous later expositions of Maoist doctrine. In essence, Yao charged that Wu's treatment of his theme was counterrevolutionary. A year and a half later it was disclosed that Yao Wen-yuan's article had been written "under the direct guidance of Comrade Chiang Ching," [4] Mao Tse-tung's wife. The situation developed until, in March, 1966, Mao Tse-tung directly condemned Wu Han —and the Peking municipal Party committee for defending him.

The action took on the full dimensions of one of Mao's celebrated "movements" when, on April 18, 1966, the PLA journal *Jiefangjun Bao* (Liberation Army Daily) called for "cultural revolution"— and quickly received the support of Premier Chou En-lai. For the moment, the intellectual community and the system of higher education appeared to be the chief target area. Still in April, however, the Communist Youth League was shelved, and the first Red Guard detachments were organized. In May, Teng T'o, secretary of the Peking municipal Party committee, came under attack for alleged ties to Wu Han and for "singing the same tune as . . . Khrushchev"—that is, he was charged with revisionism.[5] But his real offense was that he had been critical of Mao Tse-tung and Maoist policies—at home and abroad.

By this time, Mayor P'eng Chen was clearly in the line of fire. P'eng, who had been mayor of Peking for a full fifteen years and headed the Peking municipal Party committee, was actually toppled from power soon after. He had faithfully followed the Maoist line, having supported both the drive for rapid collectivization at home and the drive against the Soviet "revisionist" policy of "peaceful coexistence" abroad. The news of his dismissal was made public in Peking on June 3, and on the following day the *People's Daily* carried an editorial warning:

Anyone who opposes Chairman Mao Tse-tung, opposes Mao Tse-tung's thoughts, opposes the party central leadership, opposes the proletariat's dictatorship, opposes the correct way of Socialism, whoever that may be, however high may be the position and however old his standing, he will be struck down by the entire party and by the entire people.[6]

Promptly after the ousting of P'eng, the case against Wu Han, Teng T'o, and another man, Liao Mo-sha, won the press name of "The Gangster Den of the Village of Three Families," and the charges were pressed home, with Yao Wen-yuan leading the attack. Teng T'o, as the prime culprit, was alleged to have followed the line of right opportunists who were "slandering the party line for Socialist construction as forced and claimed China's only way out is to learn from the Soviet revisionist clique and practice revisionism in China." [7]

The purge was now extended to the country as a whole, with various provincial officials brought under fire on the basis of the central charge that they had opposed Mao Tse-tung's Thought. The *Red Flag* warned, as had Mao three years earlier, that there was the danger of a "bourgeois" counterrevolution—unless steps were taken to prevent it. In mid-month, speaking to a Rumanian delegation led by Party leader Nicolae Ceausescu, Premier Chou En-lai described the sweeping character of the new Maoist "class struggle." "The main cutting edge of this cultural revolution," he said, "is turned against a handful of bad elements that are waging dirty anti-Communist activity under the cover of a false communism. It is directed against a handful of antiparty, antisocialist and counterrevolutionary bourgeois intellectuals." [8] In a significant move Peking now closed the schools, thus making provision for a supply of the raw material for a new "mass movement" in the field of ideological affairs. Throughout the country, students undertook to browbeat and humiliate their "bourgeois" professors. Was not the bourgeoisie to be destroyed as a class?

More directly, the Wu Han affair swept up individuals charged with supervision of the ideological purity of the nation. Chou Yang, the Party ideological watchdog who had hounded various prominent intellectuals from public life for their alleged heterodoxy, was thrust from his position as deputy director of the Party's propaganda department. Department director Lu Ting-yi fell from grace at about the same time. Chou and Lu had failed to repress the veiled literary criticism of Mao Tse-tung.

Lu was replaced by T'ao Chu, who had once been political commissar in Lin Piao's Fourth Field Army. His ideological qualifications seemed impeccable: he was a doughty champion of the Great Leap Forward, and he energetically supported the program—close to Chiang Ch'ing's heart—to replace the old classic drama by works on contemporary "revolutionary" themes. Another sign that the leftists in Mao's entourage were increasing in influence came in July, with the identification of Ch'en Po-ta as "leader of the group in charge of the cultural revolution under the party's Central Committee." [9]

The lines of intra-Party conflict were being drawn. Liu Shao-ch'i moved to convene the CCP Central Committee (which had not sat in plenary session for four years) before Mao Tse-tung and Lin Piao had fully mobilized their forces. But Secretary General Teng Hsiao-p'ing withdrew his support from the enterprise, and the move was thwarted. Then, in August, *Mao* convened the eleventh plenum of the Central Committee—and packed the gallery with non-member supporters. The majority was thus faced with a threatening display, and saw military chieftain Lin Piao at Mao's side.

The intimidated Central Committee formally launched the Great Proletarian Cultural Revolution (GPCR) by means of a sixteen-point program adopted August 8. The first point undertook to define the movement:

The Great Proletarian Cultural Revolution now unfolding is a great revolution that touches people to their very souls and constitutes a new stage in the development of the socialist revolution in our country, a deeper and more extensive stage. . . . At present, our objective is to struggle

against and crush those persons in authority who are taking the capitalist road, to criticize and repudiate the reactionary bourgeois academic
"authorities" and the ideology of the bourgeoisie and all other exploiting classes and to transform education, literature and art and all other
parts of the superstructure that do not correspond to the socialist economic base, so as to facilitate the consolidation and development of the
socialist system.[10]

Further definition was discovered scattered throughout the document. It was stated *inter alia* that the chief resistance to the Cultural Revolution came from "those in authority *who have wormed
their way into the Party and are taking the capitalist road.*" [Italics
added.] It was proposed that "all those in authority who are taking
the capitalist road" should be dismissed, thus to "make possible the
recapture of the leadership for the proletarian revolutionaries."
"Don't be afraid of disorder," came the charge; and, "firmly rely on
the revolutionary Left." A dictum that naturally had its greatest
appeal to the faction voted down by the majority the year before
was set forth: "sometimes the truth is with the minority." And
there was the suggestion of a new political structure envisaged as
arising from the movement: cultural revolutionary groups, committees, "and other organizational forms created by the masses"
were described as being "organs of power of the Proletarian Cultural Revolution." A key point displayed the essential spirit attending the new order: "It is necessary to institute a system of general
elections, *like that of the Paris Commune,* for electing members
to the cultural revolutionary groups and committees and delegates
to the cultural revolutionary congresses." [Italics added.]

The spirit of Mao was manifested also in the voluntarist justification: "The aim of the Great Proletarian Cultural Revolution is to
revolutionize people's ideology and as a consequence to achieve
greater, faster, better and more economical results in all fields of
work. If the masses are fully aroused and proper arrangements are
made, it is possible to carry on both the Cultural Revolution and
production without one hampering the other, while guaranteeing
high quality in all our work. The Great Proletarian Cultural Revolution is a powerful motive force for the development of the great
productive forces in our country."

Mao's GPCR indeed had in it idealistic elements of opposition to
a bureaucracy that, as in other countries, had waxed somewhat fat
and conservative. He proposed to revive the spirit of revolution and
provide steeled, inspired cadres to constitute the "revolutionary
succession"; and he proposed in the process to further the remaking

of Chinese Man. There was nevertheless also present a more mundane, more coldly Machiavellian purpose, namely, to destroy the opposition that had endeavored, for what it found good reason, to thwart his policies in domestic and foreign affairs.

In political terms, this meant that the Maoist minority faction had set out to defy the will of, and to destroy, the majority that had opposed it in the Party Central Committee. This move was in violation of the governing CCP operating concepts, which nominally proposed the maintenance of solidarity and discipline within the Party, the subordination of the nation to the Party's will (viewed as being the true expression of the will of the proletariat), and the upholding of the prestige of the Party, the government, and the nation's leadership. Citation of a single source suffices to exemplify the doctrine theretofore applicable:

In the political life of our people, how should right be distinguished from wrong in one's words and actions? . . . we consider that, broadly speaking, the criteria should be as follows:
(1) Words and actions should help to unite, and not divide, the people of our various nationalities.
(2) They should be beneficial, and not harmful, to socialist transformation and socialist construction.
(3) They should help to consolidate, and not undermine or weaken, the people's democratic dictatorship.
(4) They should help to consolidate, and not undermine or weaken, democratic centralism.
(5) They should help to strengthen, and not discard or weaken, the leadership of the Communist Party.
(6) They should be beneficial, and not harmful, to international socialist unity and the unity of the peace-loving people of the world. Of these six criteria, the most important are the socialist path and the leadership of the Party.

So spoke Mao Tse-tung in his 1957 discourse on "The Correct Handling of Contradictions among the People," as published in the Little Red Book, *Quotations from Chairman Mao Tse-tung.*[11]

It had indeed been previously agreed that the minority might turn out to be right, but as an operating principle the minority had been called upon to obey the decision of the majority, with which the "legal" sanction resided. Now Mao had set out to overthrow the rule of the majority. Back at the time of the Hundred Flowers, the "democratic personage" Chang Po-chün had ventured the observation that 500,000,000 Chinese were slaves, eight million (the Party members) were Puritans, and one was a god. Before, all Old Comrades had been deemed worthy of respect, if only for their past revolutionary accomplishments; now only one was sacrosanct —Mao Tse-tung. The threat to Party unity that had been evaded in 1959 returned and became reality, by Mao's initiative, in 1966. Coincident with the proclamation of the Great Proletarian Cultural Revolution, the Red Guard formations appeared on the political stage. And in addressing a Red Guard rally in early November, Lin Piao called for "extensive democracy."

With the masses charged with assaulting the Party that had previously been viewed as the embodiment of the popular will, the prestige and authority not only of the Party leadership but also of the working cadres was automatically diminished. Mao Tse-tung had begun the destruction of the CCP as China had known it. He proposed to create instead a new power base, and a new hierarchy. What had begun as a clash in Great Leap times between "Red" and "expert," and had led to factional conflict over national policy during the ensuing reconstruction period, had been transformed, under Mao's leadership, into an intra-Party struggle for power.

This circumstance was given public confirmation when, on November 23, the inspired Red Guards put up posters charging that Liu Shao-ch'i, head of the Chinese state since 1959 and long viewed as Mao's probable successor, was an enemy of Mao Tse-tung. Associated with him in that infamy was Teng Hsiao-p'ing, secretary general of the CCP. Shortly afterward, the rationale behind the purge was given even more explicit expression. At a rally held in Peking at the beginning of December, it was announced that Mao's wife, Chiang Ch'ing, sometime movie actress, had been elevated to the position of consultant to the PLA Political Department. The Peking radio, reporting on the event, said that Chiang Ch'ing had asserted that the new Peking municipal Party committee was antirevolutionary and anti-Maoist, and had demanded that those opponents of Mao should "be wiped out once and for all." [12]

FLOODTIDE IN THE GPCR

The GPCR lasted formally (not counting its devious prelude) for a full two and a half years, from August, 1966 to April, 1969. The Red Guards were Mao's first chosen instrument. They were told that they should "dare to be violent" and that "to rebel is good," and were directed first against old influences, particularly the "four olds": old ideas, culture, habits, and customs. Some eleven million youthful Red Guards received their inspiration in a series of eight great mass meetings held at Peking. There they were reviewed by, and saw, Chou En-lai, Lin Piao, and the Great Leader himself—Mao Tse-tung. In the capital and other urban centers of China they stormed the streets, private residences, public buildings. There was something in the phenomenon reminiscent of Bakunin's contention that it was through revolutionary destruction of the old world that democracy would be able to create a new world. In his words, "The urge for destruction is at the same time a creative passion."

For the moment, the young iconoclasts did not evidence much "creative passion," excepting in such incidental matters as vesting old streets with new, revolutionary names. They roamed the country, "exchanging revolutionary experiences," at the expense of the state—and of the population. But, although given a semblance of organization by the Maoist faction that had conceived them, they remained immature, inexperienced, and in large measure undisciplined; moreover, their inspirers had not yet confided to them the real identity of the ultimate enemy, or fixed stable procedures for them to follow. It was also discovered that, allegedly by design of the "capital-roaders in power" but no doubt in part naturally, the movement soon was rent by growing factionalism: all indeed waved Mao's Little Red Book and mouthed the proper revolutionary phrases, but they were otherwise far from being of one mind or one objective. In November, the Red Guards were ordered to return to their homes. But they had tasted of forbidden fruit, and had come to think that indeed "to rebel is good." The orders to cease and desist were repeated in December, and then in February; but the students remained in the field.

In December, 1966, a new force entered the arena—the "revolutionary rebels." These were an older generation of workers in shops and factories, and they took the GPCR into the industrial sector of the economy. Then, in a New Year's editorial of January 1, 1967, the *People's Daily* called for a general attack on the countryside as well as on industry. This was the so-called January Revolution, employing the slogan "Bombard the Headquarters," and purposing "the seizure of power from below." The Revolutionary Rebels, however, in turn became bogged down in the same factionalism that had assailed the Red Guards; moreover, it became entirely clear that the call to the workers to labor for revolutionary idealism alone was not a compelling one. There were widespread labor disorders, with the chief unity evidenced in demands for higher wages and better working conditions. The Maoists complained that the enemy was using a vile "economism" in order to thwart the revolutionary purpose.

Within the Maoist camp itself, a clash of policies and personalities had made its appearance. T'ao Chu, so rapidly risen to power, had in mid-December been the first top leader to denounce openly Liu Shao-ch'i as an enemy of Mao Tse-tung. Less than a month later, he was himself identified in Red Guard "big character" posters as a "bourgeois" supporter of the man he had condemned.

Liu Shao-ch'i, still operating under the quasi-anonymity conferred upon him by the polemical designation of "top Party person in authority following the capitalist road," possessed a notable power of resistance that derived from his control of personal loyalties and a vast bureaucracy. Given the strength of the opposition and the weakness of his own political instrumentalities, Mao Tse-tung now called upon the PLA to join the revolution. His decision was formalized in an eight-point directive issued on January 28, 1967, by the Party's Military Affairs Commission. The Army was called upon to support the revolutionary aim of "seizing power" —and at the same time to maintain a semblance of order. One of the main developments to arise out of the new situation was the establishment of military control commissions, to act as governing bodies in the place of the Party and government structures being destroyed. Given the inherent difficulty of differentiating (without guidelines) between true and false "revolutionaries," the PLA proved more concerned with order than with revolution, and was soon directed again to remain neutral with respect to struggles between competing "Maoists"—and all contestants arrogated to themselves that categorization.

That tactical zigzag was only the first of several to occur in 1967. A Shanghai Commune, patterned on the Paris Commune of nearly a century before, was established on February 5. It was stated that the Paris Commune would be the pattern for all China, and one was projected for Peking. But the development of autonomous, "democratic" governments throughout the country, each authorized to follow its own will, would obviously have brought into being a multiple challenge to the authority of the central government—and of Mao himself. Minister of Public Security Hsieh Fu-chih warned of the danger of the development of "federalism," and on February 28 the Shanghai experiment was abandoned.

By this time, there had begun what came to be called "the February adverse current"—the widespread reversal, by those in power, of the "revolutionary verdicts" of the leftists. But this was only a temporary setback for the revolutionaries. In March and April, there was a new swing to the left, with attacks on personages as high as four vice premiers charged respectively with administration of economics, finance, agriculture, and foreign affairs. In a striking display of the character of the movement, a Peking mass meeting of 200,000 persons on April 10 watched Red Guard activists "drag out" and denounce a number of once-respected personages: P'eng Chen, Lu Ting-yi, former State Planning Commission chairman Po Yi-po, and former Minister of Higher Education Chiang Nan-hsiang. As the news account related it, "They were not allowed to walk out"; they were "dragged out to be shown to the people from a stage dominated by a life-sized statue of Chairman Mao." [13] Lo Jui-ch'ing was not among those present; it was later reported that, about mid-March, he had committed suicide—an action denounced in wall posters as "an act of defiance" against the CCP.[14]

Under the battering of those bent on fulfilling Mao Tse-tung's exhortation to "seize power," the CCP structure was being shattered at all levels. The same destructive force desolated governmental organs, especially in the provinces, *hsien* and *hsiang*. "Revolutionary committees" born of a "triple alliance"—of the revolutionary masses, the PLA, and Party cadres of certified revolutionary bent— were projected to take the place of the Party committees. Information emanating from Peking indicated that Mao Tse-tung proposed to provide the Chinese state with a fundamentally changed structure and entirely new institutions.[15]

For the time being the Army, as the sole disciplined force remaining intact, was charged with a large share of administering the country, with maintaining communications (in circumstances where the Red Guards were filling the trains to ride around the countryside), and with sustaining agricultural processes under conditions where the GPCR continuously threatened to overflow from towns to countryside and disrupt the planting, care, and reaping of the crops on which the nation depended for sustenance. On top of all this, the PLA was further charged with propagating "the thought of Mao Tse-tung and the revolutionary proletarian line" among the peasants.[16] It still retained, of course, its prime function of national defense.

The disorders spread, and in the natural course of events antagonisms built up between the PLA and Mao's revolutionaries. It was a sign of the times when, on June 6, there was posted a notification signed by the State Council, the CCP Central Committee, the central Cultural Revolution Group, and the Military Affairs Committee of the Central Committee prohibiting violence, destruction, arbitrary arrests, requisitions in homes and offices, and theft—aberrations now found widespread throughout the countryside. Again the PLA was charged with carrying out the directive, but it was still not authorized to use force to do so.

By this time, the country had begun to show signs of fragmenting under the impact of the Maoist "revolution." Various provinces manifested, in different ways, alienation from the Peking line. The PLA itself was beginning to show signs of acute discontent as its duties became increasingly onerous because of the growth of factionalism and violence among the many "Maoist" groups.

One region severely shaken by conflict was Hupeh Province, which now was the scene of an incident that proved a major turning point in the GPCR. On July 14, an investigating team headed by Hsieh Fu-chih, who had just become head of the Peking revolutionary committee, and *Red Flag* deputy editor Wang Li, arrived in Wuhan for the purpose of bringing unity to powerful Party, military, and rival "revolutionary" factions warring for power. When Hsieh and Wang endeavored to impose a settlement favoring the extremist rebels as against the conservatives, they were assailed, beaten, and put under detention at the military headquarters, commanded by Ch'en Tsai-tao. It was only after Premier Chou En-lai personally went to the scene that the two emissaries were released and were able to return to Peking. *Then,* there followed prolonged —if restrained—military action accompanied by political measures that resulted in the dissolution of the insurgency. Ch'en Tsai-tao finally went to Peking in response to Mao's orders, was condemned for his deviations, and was dismissed from the post of commander of the Wuhan military district. His lieutenants also lost their posts.[17]

Red Flag gave the official explanation of what had happened: ". . . . a handful of powerholders in the army and the party taking the capitalist road in the Wuhan region united together and suppressed proletarian revolutionaries. We must throw these reactionary powerholders in the party and the army into the garbage heap." [18] To achieve this "dragging out" of the "handful of powerholders" in the PLA, the Maoist leadership authorized the arming of selected Red Guard and Revolutionary Rebel units. More violence was thereby released—and total anarchy came closer.

In September, Mao Tse-tung made a tour of inspection of five north, central, and eastern provinces. His trip was patently designed to give him a firsthand impression of local conditions, and probably to consolidate his support where it was strongest. The radical faction of Mao's entourage, the Cultural Revolution Group in particular, was behind the proposal that the purge should be carried into the military establishment. But the Wuhan events demonstrated that the country's one remaining viable political institution, the PLA, was itself now threatened with internal disruption. Mao and his revolutionary cohorts were compelled to pull back, for fear of civil war.

On September 5, Chiang Ch'ing gave a talk at Peking in which she notably damped down her own revolutionism. She denounced Maoist revolutionaries for attacking PLA personalities as powerholders following the capitalist road, and for seizures of arms from the military; she disclosed that the Party's Central Committee had now authorized the PLA to strike back, and if necessary to fire upon revolutionaries who might seek to capture arms. The past year, she said, was "the time to light the fire of revolution"; but now, "there is a wind that tries to knock over all the revolutionary committees already approved by the Central Committee." [19]

Defense Minister Lin Piao spoke on behalf of Mao Tse-tung at the celebration, on October 1, 1967, of Communist China's national day. He proclaimed that a "tremendous victory" had been won in the Cultural Revolution. Various prominent personalities were missing from the group of those who stood approved, on that occasion, in the presence of Great Helmsman Mao. Absent were Liu Shao-ch'i, Teng Hsiao-p'ing, P'eng Chen, Lo Jui-ch'ing, Vice Premier T'an Chen-lin, CCP Propaganda Department chief T'ao Chu, Acting Propaganda Department chief Wang Li, Inner Mongolian leader Ulanfu, Marshals Liu Po-ch'eng and Ho Lung, and First Secretary for the Southwest Li Ching-ch'uan. It was easy to perceive the significance of Lin's triumphal announcement. If emphasis of the point were needed, it was perhaps to be found in the report that the unfortunate Party leader of 1930 who had long been out of favor, Li Li-san, had recently taken his own life; and in the further intelligence that the members of "The Gangster Den of the Village of Three Families," Wu Han, Teng T'o, and Liao Mo-sha, had also committed suicide—by impressive coincidence, all three on the same day, September 26, 1967.

The Red Guards and Revolutionary Rebels remained out of control and riven by factionalism. The CCP Military Affairs Committee at this juncture issued a directive to the PLA to organize and send special forces into schools, factories, and countryside to suppress internal strife and unite the warring factions—and to rehabilitate the authority of administrative and executive personnel who had been buffeted by the GPCR. As a supporting measure, a joint instruction from the several organs headed respectively by top leaders Mao Tse-tung, Chou En-lai, Lin Piao, and Ch'en Po-ta and Chiang Ch'ing stressed the need to combat self-interest and promote "great revolutionary alliances." Again the radicals were being curbed. It was currently reported that the central Cultural Revolution Group had shrunk in size from fourteen members to a possible six, and it was suggested that the decline in the group's power had resulted from its attempt to extend the purge into the military: one of those purged was Wang Li, of Wuhan Incident fame, who was reputed to have been responsible for the appearance in July of the slogan "Drag out the small handful of powerholders in the army." [20] Two other deputy editors of Red Flag who were associated with Wang in that venture, both of them members of the Cultural Revolution Group, shared his fate. And Minister of Security Hsieh Fu-chih now called upon the Red Guards to renounce the "myth" that new institutions providing for elections like those of the Paris Commune would be evolved.[21]

Mao Tse-tung came forward with one of his "latest instructions," designed to justify the shift in line from revolutionism to pragmatism. He held that "the situation in the Great Proletarian Cultural Revolution throughout the country is not just good, but excellent," and that the movement had culminated in a "big victory," [22] but the purport of his directive was clear: the time had come for consolidation, not a continuation of the "revolutionary" disorders. Emphasis was now placed on the task of rebuilding the Party. Peking called for the rehabilitation of officials who had been denounced in the course of the GPCR—excepting "incorrigible" enemies of Mao Tse-tung.[23] By late 1967, the moderates had returned temporarily to authority—even as after the Great Leap of 1958.

Loyalty to Mao had become the final touchstone. The Shanghai Wen Hui Pao, in an article entitled "We Will Infinitely Adore President Mao," made new accusations against Liu Shao-ch'i and Teng Hsiao-p'ing: they had been violently opposed to the cult of personality. "But," the article contended, "in order to lead a great revolutionary movement, there are needed a great political

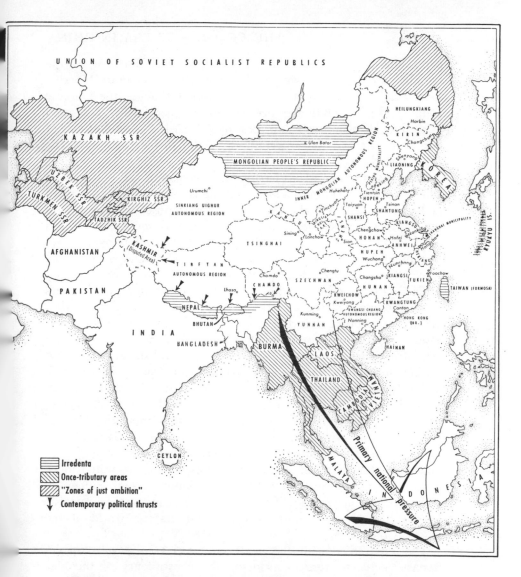

CHINA UNDER THE COMMUNIST REGIME (1971)
showing the principal administrative divisions (provincial level).

The surrounding areas, according to the Chinese Communists, are (*a*) ir-
redenta, subject to recovery; (*b*) once-tributary areas, deemed to fall
properly within China's sphere of influence; and (*c*) "zones of just ambition," determined by past Mongol or Manchu rule or conquests and
ethnological relationships.

Outlines from *China: Provisional Atlas of Communist Administrative Units*,
prepared by Central Intelligence Agency (Washington, D.C., 1959).

party and a wise and prestigious leader. Mao Tse-tung is the founder of our party as well as the greatest contemporary Marxist-Leninist. To Mao Tse-tung and his radiant thought the Chinese people and all revolutionary peoples vow respect, fidelity, adoration as well as an infinite worship. President Mao is the reddest sun of our heart: here is the cry emitted by the revolutionaries of the entire world." [24]

In theory, the Maoist leadership was overcoming all obstacles. A 1968 New Year's editorial announced the coming birth of a purified and transformed CCP charged with fostering, in collaboration with the PLA, a new society where "uninterrupted revolution" would reign.[25] On the other hand, some of the leftist revolutionaries were beginning to feel that the much-touted revolution was being betrayed—by the revolutionary leadership itself. In a contemporary article entitled "Whither China?" a leftist group in Hunan (Mao's home province) stated that the masses had concluded that, after all the commotion, everything remained the same as before, and asserted that people found it difficult to understand why Mao had ceased his advocacy of the Paris Commune and instead promoted the revolutionary committees, in which revolutionary mass organizations played a role secondary to those of the PLA and rehabilitated Party cadres. The article characterized the revolutionary committees as "bourgeois reformist," and said that "the fruit of revolution has been . . . reaped by the capitalist class." [26] The article called for eventual consideration of the possibility of winning outright victory in one or more provinces as an initial move toward overthrowing the revolutionary committees and the central governmental apparatus: "Let the new bureaucratic bourgeoisie tremble . . . the China of tomorrow will be the world of the [Paris] Commune."

The "contradiction" in the situation was clear: if Mao's "revolutionary" activists were to make up the constituency of the new CCP, anarchy threatened to prevail in both the political and economic sectors, and the PLA by itself could not hold the situation together—and would probably give up trying. If, on the other hand, the experienced pragmatists were to be returned to authority in politics and the economy, the "revolution" would end up where it began—which was of course what leftist Red Guards and Revolutionary Rebels feared might happen.

The struggle was being fought out at the very top of the Communist hierarchy. In March, Chief of General Staff Yang Ch'eng-wu, a Lin Piao man, was dismissed from his post. The political commissar of the Air Force, General Yu Li-chin, and the commander of the Peking garrison, General Fu Ch'ung-pi, were both arrested. The charge against them, reputedly leveled by Lin Piao himself, was that they were "two-faced counterrevolutionaries" who had campaigned against Hsieh Fu-chih in his capacity of head of the Peking revolutionary committee. The developments brought out into the open the fact that there now existed a factional struggle *within* the Maoist faction, between the radical Cultural Revolution Group led by Ch'en Po-ta and Chiang Ch'ing, the governmental group under Chou En-lai, and the PLA headed by Lin Piao.

GPCR: PROLETARIAN OR PRAETORIAN?

The May 1 celebration brought a sign of the way the factional struggle for domination within the Maoist group was going. Now the central Cultural Revolution Group seemingly had only five members left: Ch'en Po-ta, K'ang Sheng, Chiang Ch'ing, Shanghai leader Chang Ch'un-ch'iao, and ideologue Yao Wen-yuan. That extremist faction was in decline. Provincial military and civilian leaders who had come to Peking for the May 1 occasion remained there for much of the month. The Maoist leadership was presumably taking advantage of their presence to work out solutions for the problems facing the country. The indications were that the final decision had been reached to restore the Party to a commanding position, and in the meantime to give the military the guiding role in the revolutionary committees. On June 1, Huang Yung-sheng was formally appointed to the post of chief of general staff vacated by Yang Ch'eng-wu. Huang, a former subordinate of Lin Piao, had headed the Canton military region since 1955. As chairman of the Kwangtung revolutionary committee, he had proved able to sustain Red Guard attacks leveled at him in 1967. Coincident with his entry upon his new duties, there began a vigorous damping down of the disorders, with the charge that "spies and traitors" had infiltrated the revolutionary committees. Executions of "counterrevolutionaries," which had been taking place with increasing frequency in 1968, were notably stepped up.

The Red Guard students had on various previous occasions been instructed to return to their studies, but had failed to do so. Now, in July, it was announced that higher education was to be resumed for at least two disciplines, science and engineering. There was an interesting aspect to this development: evidently the plan provided limited practical schooling in the indicated disciplinary area only for workers having several years of labor experience; and after their advanced training they were to return to farms and factories. Significantly, the doors of higher education were not for the moment being reopened to admit the regular college students who had departed the classroom to participate in the Cultural Revolution.

The radicals did not permit the struggle to go by default. On July 21, Yao Wen-yuan's *Wen Hui Pao* editorialized that the moment had come to accomplish great historical reform, by overturning earth and sky in the administrative, cultural, industrial, and artistic domains, thus to accomplish one hundred percent the tasks of the GPCR. But Mao Tse-tung, who had veered erratically for months from left to right and back again in his "latest instructions," had at last been forced to a final commitment against revolutionary chaos. On July 28, meeting with five student leaders of different factions involved in bitter fighting at Peking's Tsinghua University, Mao effectively charged them with betraying his trust that they could lead his revolution. An official "propaganda team" was dispatched to Tsinghua, *imposed* a settlement on the fractious students, and duly received a gift of mangoes from Chairman Mao. The symbolic act wrote *finis* to the Red Guard revolution; its creator had come out in favor of law and order. At the end of July, a joint editorial of the *People's Daily*, *Red Flag*, and *Liberation Army Daily* called upon the PLA to support firmly the new revolutionary committees and protect them from class enemies—which were identified as being either of the right or of the extreme left.

The "extensive democracy" once extolled by Lin Piao had already been relabeled "ultra-democracy," deemed bad. There now issued a condemnation of "polycentrism," with an accompanying demand for obedience to a sole center, that is, to Mao Tse-tung and his immediate lieutenants. The *People's Daily*, in observing the second anniversary of the formal launching of the GPCR, made the situation explicit: "The proletarian headquarters [Mao Tse-tung and Lin Piao] is the sole leading center of the whole party, of the whole army, of the whole country and the broad popular masses. . . . There may not be a second one." [27] And the Army paper two days later stated that it was necessary to give effect to instructions and appeals "whether they are understood or are momentarily not understood. . . . Revolutionaries must never act according to their own sweet will." [28] This was a far cry from the slogans of two years earlier exhorting the people "Don't be afraid of disorder" and directing the Party leadership to "firmly rely on the revolutionary left." The vision of the Paris Commune receded even farther into the background.

It was announced on September 7 that revolutionary committees had been organized for Sinkiang and Tibet. Such organs had now been set up in all twenty-nine province-level administrative divisions. It was notable that the dominant elements in those committees were the representatives not of Mao's "revolutionary masses" but of the PLA and moderate cadres. On October 1, national day, the character of the new leadership group itself became apparent with the listing of the fourteen personalities present on the reviewing stand at the Gate of Heavenly Peace. Nominally representative of the Maoist revolutionaries, the PLA, and the Old Cadre bureaucracy, the group comprised Mao Tse-tung, Lin Piao, Chou En-lai, Ch'en Po-ta, K'ang Sheng, Chiang Ch'ing, chairman of the Shanghai revolutionary committee Chang Ch'un-ch'iao, Yao Wen-yuan of the same committee, Minister of Security Hsieh Fu-chih, Chief of General Staff Huang Yung-sheng, Air Force chief Wu Fa-hsien, commander of the Peking garrison Wang Tung-hsing, Deputy Chief of General Staff Wen Yü-ch'eng, and Yeh Chün (wife of Lin Piao). The military component was patently strong.

From October 13 to October 31, the CCP Central Committee sat in its twelfth enlarged plenum. Besides the regular and alternate members, commanding elements of the revolutionary committees and of the PLA, as well as all members of the Cultural Revolution Group, were also in attendance. However, Mao's revolutionary "little generals" were conspicuous by their absence, and the plenum was marked by a sobriety befitting the circumstances. The GPCR was *pro forma* held up as a political revolution of the proletariat against the bourgeoisie and other exploiting classes. The session also now officially proclaimed that the bourgeois headquarters headed by CPR Chairman Liu Shao-ch'i, "China's Khrushchev" and "the top Party powerholder following the capitalist road," had been smashed, and that he was to be expelled from all posts both inside *and outside* the Party. The Old Comrade who had written the tract on "How to Be a Good Communist" had been damned as a renegade revisionist.

The plenum purported to believe that there still was "a handful of counterrevolutionaries hiding among the masses," and it issued a clarion call to "march forward . . . and seize all-round victory."

But *Red Flag* now characterized the GPCR as being a movement for *consolidation* of the Party. It was entirely evident that the CCP plenum had been charged, for all the propaganda, with terminating the GPCR.

The particular aim of the "cultural revolution" of creating a new revolutionary-succession generation had been frustrated. The GPCR had wrought havoc in the field of education. Over sixty top figures in higher education, including the Minister of Education, had been purged even as of the end of 1966. Primary and secondary schools had been nominally reopened in February, 1967, one of the dates on which the Peking authorities had urged students to return to their classrooms; but, with the old order discarded, and the academicians under unrelenting attack, no answers had yet been forthcoming for the problems of providing new curricula, textbooks, or even teachers. Out of anarchy, there had to come a new order—but only Mao Tse-tung could safely describe its shape.

Some trends were visible. The school program had been shortened to nine years, instead of the previous twelve, for primary and higher education. Higher education was thereafter to be for manual workers, who would attend technical institutes for three years, and then return to labor in the industrial or agricultural sectors. And worker-soldier-peasant teams were being assigned to govern the processes of education.

Mao Tse-tung had always distrusted the "bourgeois" intelligentsia. In the GPCR, he had tried by fire the generation of youth indoctrinated under strictly Communist auspices, found it wanting, and in his innate populism turned once more to the workers and peasants. That was the symbolic message conveyed by the gift of mangoes. The official publicity media issued appropriate interpretations. A Kirin newspaper remarked that the Red Guards had played "a certain role" in the Cultural Revolution, but said that the selfishness and fanaticism manifested by the intellectuals proved "that they cannot lead the revolution"; a Kiangsi newspaper editorialized that China's educated youth "have always run counter to Mao Tse-tung's thought"; and in mid-October the Wuhan radio station reported that the provincial revolutionary committee had announced that "intellectuals should all go to the mountains and rural areas." [29] The students refused to return to the classrooms? Hundreds of thousands of the youth of the classes of 1966 and 1967—the elements that had answered Mao's bidding to become the backbone of the GPCR—were now dispatched to lifetime work assignments on farms and reclamation projects, and into factories and mines. Their academic careers had ended.

As upon historic occasions in the past, the intellectuals of China had been degraded and consigned to a subordinate role. There was a clear residual danger in the situation: coincident with the inculcation of contempt for the authority of the CCP, there had been a major alienation of intellectuals from the Communist rule. Would they thereafter serve the regime as loyally and ardently, as *productively*, as before? Might they not instead become a source of dissidence, a seedbed of infectious future discontents, in Chinese society?

Those questions arose in a social situation much changed since the Great Leap effort of 1958, and since the beginning of the "cultural revolution" in particular. The GPCR had notoriously been attended by widespread social disorders, which had brought serious deterioration of the social fabric and left deep-rooted indiscipline in their wake. A suggestion of the scale and violence of those disorders was given in the report of author Edgar Snow, writing against the background of an interview with Premier Chou En-lai, that there had been "hundreds of thousands" of casualties in the factional fighting before the PLA finally resorted to force to restore order.[30] The force had quite sufficed to bring an end to chaos; but in the GPCR there had been a resurrection, to some degree, of Chinese individualism.

The political area offered a bleak picture. According to the official version, the basic work of construction of a new Party organization had been completed; however, the CCP had been too seriously battered for full rehabilitation in short order. The GPCR had reduced the authority and prestige of the Party, of the government, and of individuals—including Mao Tse-tung himself. The Chinese youths who had ardently supported Mao's revolutionism were disillusioned, and had to be considered a possible source of future discontent. The Party membership had notably changed in character. Of a total of 172 regular and alternate members of the Party Central Committee, ninety-three had in one way or another been either purged or badly battered in the GPCR; twenty-three of the country's province-level Party leaders had been hit one way or another. The "revolutionary alliance" had been designed as an equilateral structure, but twenty-one of the twenty-nine new provincial-level revolutionary committees were headed by military men; and the revolutionaries generally were overshadowed by the PLA and the old guard CCP cadres.

The composition of the new command structure was not a good indication of the over-all situation. The military had notably enhanced their role in Chinese society, given the police, administrative, and productive functions they had performed during the GPCR—and to an important degree performed still. Mao's standing dictum that the Party commanded the gun, and that the gun should never be permitted to command the Party, still stood in theory. But the hard fact was that, as of the effective end of the GPCR in October, 1968, the Army dominated the China scene.

美帝国主义对中国的军事包围（示意图）

钦 哲 绘

图例

1 美国驻军　2 海军基地　3 空军基地　4 导弹基地　5 航空母舰　6 核潜艇

CHINESE COMMUNIST MAP DEPICTING "MILITARY
ENCIRCLEMENT OF CHINA BY U.S. IMPERIALISM"

13 "REVOLUTIONARY DIPLOMACY"

M ODERN Chinese rulers have proved congenitally unable completely to divorce themselves from the thought patterns of emperors who governed China when it was dominant in Asia, and all the rest of the known world was inhabited by "barbarians." Ethnocentrism, combined with the political calculation that the existence of a menace against the country's borders tends to distract the people from some of their native grievances and unify the nation, has caused Chinese governments from the time of the Boxer Rebellion onward to keep at least one foreign "enemy" in being. A series of Republican governments led the country into clashes with Germans, British, Russians, and Japanese, sometimes for what must be viewed as less than ample reason, often in circumstances where China's chances of achieving victory were slight—unless it were able to manipulate another power into collision with the "chief enemy." Yuan Shih-k'ai, Chang Tso-lin, and Chiang Kai-shek were variously anti-Japanese, anti-British, and anti-Russian. Mao Tsetung added the United States to the list of "enemies"; but he was no innovator with respect to the basic spirit of Chinese nationalism. Nor did his assumption that his Thought had universal application free him from parochialism in some of his judgments on world affairs.

There have, however, been differences in the foreign policy of China under Communist rule, reflecting changed circumstances and the appearance of new factors. For one thing, Communist China, being unified, has commanded greater real power with respect to the outside world than any of its predecessor Republican governments, and thus could entertain practical aspirations of playing a more important role in world affairs. Second, Mao Tse-tung had evolved a world view which he and his supporters believed to incorporate final Truth, and to have universal application. And, finally, the world scene had changed radically.

URGE TO POWER

World War II had brought an effective end to colonialism as an institution employed for the governance of the politically weak and underdeveloped countries of Asia, Africa, and Latin America. But the discarding of the institution did not immediately bring about the termination of the struggle among the strong to exercise a dominating influence over the destinies of the weak. Lenin had held that the end of colonialism would mark the beginning of the end of imperialism, and the nations of the post-World War II Communist bloc aspired to win the developing nations over to their side. There was opposition from the non-Communist sector, and in particular from the United States, which since World War II has viewed any expansion of "Communist" (or revolutionary) influence as something in the nature of a threat to "the free world" (equated, very simply, with the non-Communist sector). And the United States shouldered the worldwide "commitment" to war against the presumed threat. This strategic objective was deemed, upon occasion, to require the deployment of American economic or military power to influence elements of the "free world" to act in the way Washington thought they should. Thus the competition between "anti-imperialism" and "anti-Communism," in so far as it was not displayed as a direct confrontation of the superpowers, tended naturally to center in the Third World.

The ex-colonial and other underdeveloped countries of course have minds and aspirations of their own—although this does not always seem to have been clearly recognized by others. With political independence won, they became less interested in political ideologies than in social progress, and began to experience that economic hunger so graphically described as "the revolution of rising expectations." Alfred T. Mahan, writing on *The Problem of Asia* in 1900 (the year of the Boxer Rebellion), contemplated the stirring of ancient civilizations and said that the coming confrontation of the Eastern and Western cultures would necessarily lead either to amalgamation or to conflict, and that the Occident was not free to reject the issue:

If with wealth, numbers and opportunity, a people cannot so organize their strength as to hold their own, it is not practical to expect that those to whom wealth and opportunity are lacking, but who have organizing faculty and willingness to fight, will not under the pressure of need enter upon an inheritance which need will persuade themselves is ethically their due.

The Chinese are such a nation "to whom wealth and opportunity are lacking." They possess "organizing faculty and willingness to fight," and their present leaders have had no difficulty in persuading themselves that a larger share of the world's wealth is "ethically their due." It comes naturally to them to identify their cause with that of the Third World.

There has been no amalgamation of Eastern and Western cultures; instead, there exists a wide gulf of political misunderstanding, even mutual incomprehensibility, between them. The gulf is being currently deepened as the realization grows that the *economic* gap between the rich, industrialized countries and the poor, "developing" countries is getting progressively wider, not narrower. The contemporary trend is toward the second of Mahan's alternatives: intercultural conflict threatens to grow.

It was in the light of that radically changed and changing world situation that Mao Tse-tung evolved his concept of the role China should play in power politics. A half century before, K'ang Yu-wei had translated the Confucian concept of universalism into modern terms in a work that envisaged the obliteration of boundaries between states and races, and the leveling of the whole, for an amalgamation of the human race. Mao believes in the inevitability of a world revolution which would have essentially the same effect—excepting that the final political forms would be "communist," as *he* interprets the term.

Mao's "universalist" theory, however, has an important content of Chinese elements. China's political and economic urges, as he has given them expression, are strongly reinforced by the nation's inherent feeling of cultural superiority, which in its obverse form acts as a natural urge to national aggrandizement. And Mao, the conqueror of the Nationalists and (by the Maoist legend) of the Japanese besides, has had the confidence that comes with great accomplishment: he has felt that the mobilized power of the Chinese nation can perform miracles. He has been ready strategically to press China's international fortunes to the limit—while tactically avoiding the critical point of danger.

For China's enhanced strength as a unified nation has not brought it into the class of the *great* powers: it remains only a second-class power. If the spirit is willing to contemplate the extension of Chinese influence into far corners of a revolutionary world, the flesh is weak. In distant Africa and Latin America, China competes at a distinct disadvantage against the vastly superior economic and political power of the United States and the USSR; it is better able to make its weight felt on its periphery, in South and Southeast Asia. Here the urge to revolutionary empire is fortified by the feeling, drilled into all Chinese since the beginning of the Republic, that all territory ever included in the vast Manchu Empire rightfully belongs to China—even if ceded by treaty in the past to other countries.

The Nationalists, in their day, were bold in advancing their claim to territories that had long since passed out of China's hands. From the standpoint of international law, past possession by itself constitutes no real case for recovery, but irredentism makes sense to the Chinese. It could therefore be taken for granted that, for all of the soothing words about "peaceful coexistence" that issued after the 1955 Bandung Conference, Peking had no intention of relaxing *permanently* its claims to various territories on its periphery.

The general rule applies quite naturally to Outer Mongolia. Also, since countries such as Korea, Annam, and Burma (in part) were once vassals of the empire, Peking would aim at bringing them back under the Chinese aegis. And since Bhutan, Sikkim, and Nepal had close ties to Tibet before, and their peoples are related to the Tibetans by blood, the present rulers at Peking, even as other former occupants of the Chinese capital, would assume it entirely proper that they should return to the Chinese family of nations.

At the end of World War II, the Nationalists asked Moscow to restore Outer Mongolia to China, without success. The 1949 change of rule in China made no difference, one way or the other. Harrison E. Salisbury, of the New York *Times*, reports that he was told by Premier Tsedenbal that one of the first things Mao Tse-tung did upon coming to power was to ask Stalin to return the Mongolian People's Republic to Chinese suzerainty.[1] As was to have been expected, Stalin again rejected the bold petition. Mao made the same proposal to Khrushchev in 1954, only to get another refusal. And if the Outer Mongolians, feeling a sentiment of comradely Asian nationalism well up in their breasts, were by chance somewhat receptive in the beginning to the thought that they might draw closer to the Communist Han Chinese, that amiable sentiment quite obviously dried up as they observed, over the years, the course of events in "autonomous" Sinkiang, Tibet, and Inner Mongolia under Peking's iron rule. Within a decade after the advent of the Communists to power in Peking, the Mongols had patently become quite reconciled to their lot in spite of drawbacks connected with Soviet "protection." Yet none could doubt that the Mao regime continued to feel a fierce urge to "liberate" that Mongol people which had become so benighted as no longer to desire Chinese rule.

It was only natural that the conflict with India should remain in being: "bourgeois" India, according to Maoist thinking, was destined, as stated by Liu Shao-ch'i in 1949, to experience a revolution in the Chinese pattern—and in the meantime it had a relationship with China that contained strong elements of "antagonistic contradiction." The brandishing of spears over the disputed Aksai Chin plateau of Ladakh, across which China in 1957 had constructed its military highway connecting Sinkiang and Tibet, continued in 1962.

Some of the belligerent gestures represented political bargaining. China wished to obtain title to the 12,000 square miles of Ladakh, which it occupied militarily, in exchange for its claim to 40,000 square miles in India's Northeast Frontier Agency, south of the McMahon Line. New Delhi exploited to the utmost Peking's loss of credit in the international sphere, infiltrated its troops into the barren, sparsely-held Aksai Chin region, and in July announced that it had recovered and consolidated control over 3,500 square miles of the disputed Ladakh area. In military operations that flared up in October and were terminated by Peking's unilateral decision in November, India was defeated on both fronts. China restored the *status quo ante* in Ladakh, *without* negotiations, voluntarily withdrew to the McMahon Line in the east, and went on to turn the Indian political flank by border negotiations with Pakistan. In those negotiations it achieved its objective, a Sino-Pakistani border settlement.

China thus was left in full control of its Yehchung-Gartok highway across the Aksai Chin plateau, with its strategic position consolidated in that sector. The general situation in South Asia, comprising in the main India and Pakistan, remained in flux. There were strong possibilities, even the probability, of a deterioration of economic and social conditions in India, or the exacerbation of underlying Indian-Pakistani animosities. The Chinese leadership would see no reason to renounce its hopes for profit in that sector of its periphery.

The clashes with India had their parallels elsewhere. Indonesia had been one of the first non-Communist countries to recognize the new Peking regime. China had traded with it since 1953, and the trade balance increased from $2 million that first year to a volume of $53 million in 1957. Indonesian leader Achmed Sukarno was following a strongly anticolonial policy, and his "guided democracy" was of a nature that might logically have been expected to find modest favor in Peking's eyes. There was, however, the factor of political alignment: Indonesia was receiving important quantities of military and economic aid, on a commercial basis, from the Soviet Union.

In 1959 there was a clash between Peking and Jakarta arising out of the Sukarno government's application of restrictions on both the residence and the business activities of aliens in Indonesia. The nearly three million Chinese, who practically monopolized rural retail trade, were the chief target group. The two countries in 1955 had signed a treaty providing that Chinese nationals living under Indonesian jurisdiction should give up their dual nationality and choose one citizenship or the other within two years after ratification. Indonesia had still not ratified the treaty by 1959. Peking's own recent treatment of aliens in China had hardly been marked by a cosmopolitan liberalism, but in the present instance it chose to assume a distinctly nationalistic stance and protested against the "persecution" of Chinese in Indonesia and organized the usual mass meetings of "popular indignation." The Indonesian authorities merely tightened up the restrictions they had imposed.

This time, China was without recourse: Indonesia was out of reach. In the end Peking surrendered, and in December, 1960, the two countries signed a protocol for implementation of the 1955 treaty. Sino-Indonesian relations were again on a "friendly" basis. They could not be expected to remain that way permanently, for the two were competitors for power in the "Nan Yang" (Southern Seas), viewed by Chinese as something in the nature of a southern projection of China. In the final analysis, the basic power interests of the two are antagonistic.

Japan, lying just across the Yellow Sea and nearly touching strategic Korea, was yet another potential contender for power in the Asian arena, a circumstance recognized implicitly in the Sino-

Soviet alliance of 1950. The existence of a large reservoir of Japanese sympathy for the Chinese experiment, Japan's undisguised interest in trade with the mainland, and the growth of anti-American sentiment in various segments of the Japanese population seemingly led Peking to believe that the Liberal-Democratic government of Japan could be toppled without too great difficulty, and Japan thus be brought closer to revolution—and the service of Chinese purposes as envisaged long before by Sun Yat-sen. Coincident with the Great Leap, there was a distinct radicalization of Peking's foreign policy. The country at the time—for all of the extravagant claims regarding Great Leap accomplishments—was experiencing a shortage of export goods; and the Tokyo government refused to sanction the long-term credits being demanded by the Chinese. With one of the factors clearly a plain inability to deliver on contracts, China in 1958 broke off trade relations with its Japanese neighbor.

Peking had committed a major error: the move could do no important harm to Japan, which was economically in a much stronger position than China and which, politically and militarily, was in the enviable position of being allied to the United States. Furthermore, as in the past, Japan had the added option of drawing closer to Russia—even if Moscow were allied to Peking. Soviet-Japanese relations in the immediate postwar period had been understandably bad, and had worsened as the United States moved to make Japan into a hostile *American* bastion in the West Pacific. But Peking's decision to manifest hostility toward Japan at the same time that it was mounting a quarrel with the Soviet Union led to a new departure on the part of Moscow: early in 1960, it began to hold out to Tokyo the vision of an Eastern Siberia undergoing rapid development and in need of Japanese goods and capital. Japan was consequently brought to a fuller appreciation of the bargaining leverage it commanded in its middle position between the United States, China, and the USSR.

The withdrawal of Soviet technicians and aid from China in the summer of 1960 might well have been taken as an earnest of Moscow's readiness to limit its help to a China that had become overly obstreperous. The Japanese appear gradually to have become convinced that the opportunity offered was of major importance. In 1962, Japanese interests signed an agreement to construct nearly $100 million worth of ships on a Soviet order, and a Japanese trade mission that visited the USSR in August of the same year won other

big trade orders. By now, the Soviet trade effort was overshadow-
ing that of the Chinese similarly in India, Indonesia, and the
Mongolian People's Republic. China's own trade with Japan had
been resumed in 1960, but its exchanges with the Communist bloc
in general and the USSR in particular had by the year 1962 gone
into a steep decline.

Operating with an economy in fundamental imbalance, and hard
hit by the agricultural failures of 1959–61, China faced substantial
difficulties in maintaining its foreign commerce. In 1961, its foreign-
trade volume dropped some 25 percent; and, instead of exporting
agricultural products to pay for imports of industrial goods, it imported nearly six million tons of grain that year. It was not only
to the USSR that China failed to deliver according to agreement:
even earlier, there had been breaches of contract for shipments to
countries such as Pakistan, Egypt, and Ceylon. Trade with Czechoslovakia dropped 65 percent from the 1960 figure, partly by reason
of Prague's calculated policy of reducing exports to China in order
to check further buildup of that country's outstanding debit
balance. Even so, China failed to deliver shipments of pork contracted by the Sino-Czech trade agreement for 1962, with the result
that by midsummer Czechoslovakia was experiencing a serious
meat shortage.

China's ally, the Soviet Union, seemed no longer prepared, as it
had been in the past, to extend commercial credits. In the spring
of 1963, Peking and Moscow signed the usual trade protocol covering the exchange of goods during the current year. Reading between the lines of the brief announcement, it was easy to deduce
that China won no new credits in the negotiations. By this time,
making a virtue of necessity, Peking in its propaganda was stressing
the virtues of self-reliance.

Mao Tse-tung at this juncture had to be viewed as a man of
multiple frustrations. China's agriculture, instead of leaping into
a glorious new stage of development under the spur of Maoist
voluntarism, had suffered widespread collapse. Industry had slowed
down, instead of making a great leap forward. Then there was
frustration of the national purpose in the revolutionary course
Peking had followed since 1958 in foreign affairs, whether with
respect to the Formosa Strait and Japan, or in China's relations
with such important Asian countries as India and Indonesia. With
the retreat of the Soviet Union from its supporting position in 1960,
China effectively stood isolated in a hostile world; and in 1961 the

Eastfoto

Eastfoto

The Great Proletarian Cultural Revolution initially evoked wild enthusiasm
in the younger generation of intellectuals, and in the romantic guise of
Red Guards they undertook first to assail the "four olds" and then to "bombard the headquarters" where the Party opposition to Mao Tse-tung resided.
By mid-1967 the Cultural Revolution threatened national chaos. The Army
was finally loosed on the rebels, and the students who had refused to return
to the classrooms were in 1968 exiled instead to work in factories and the
agricultural countryside. But the Party opposition had been purged.

Wide World Photos

Eastfoto

ANTI-AMERICAN
PARADE IN SUPPORT
OF NORTH VIETNAM,
WUHAN, 1966

ANTI-AMERICAN SKIT IN
ANTI-BURMESE
DEMONSTRATION, PEKING,
1967

PRESIDENT
RICHARD M. NIXON
AND PREMIER
CHOU EN-LAI,
PEKING, 1972

Compix of UPI

Anti-foreignism was one expression of the Cultural Revolution. Many states were targets, but the Soviet Union and the United States in particular seemed a close tie for the position of China's "Enemy No. 1." Hostility against the USSR was damped down in 1969; and in 1972 détente was introduced into the Sino-American relationship.

American military intervention had begun in Vietnam, on China's critical southern boundary.

Pragmatic consideration of the difficult situation would have counseled caution with respect to China's only ally, and perhaps some compromise for a rapprochement. But the logic of Mao's doctrine of self-reliance was inexorable: China could get along without the Soviet Union, too.

DRIVE FOR LEADERSHIP OF THE DISPOSSESSED

The background for the Chinese decision to "go it alone" was complex, and included important ideological elements. It will be remembered that, beginning in 1957, Mao Tse-tung had endeavored to get the Soviet Union to confront the United States on the issue of world revolution, even at the risk of war. Speaking in May, 1971, Premier Chou En-lai gave some confirmation of this in a revealing if measured survey of the background of the Sino-Soviet dispute. He said that the Chinese side had endeavored at the 1957 Moscow conference to dissuade Khrushchev from proceeding too far along the road of revisionism—described by the reporter as "the Chinese Communists' term for the Soviet policy of coexistence with capitalist states and for what the Chinese view as a revival of capitalism in the Soviet Union." [2] Then, in 1959, Chou continued, Khrushchev had torn up existing agreements for "atomic energy cooperation" (that is, for Soviet assistance to China in the development of atomic weapons). Chou mentioned also, as other grievances, Khrushchev's 1959 meeting with American President Eisenhower to woo the United States in "the so-called spirit of Camp David," and the Soviet withdrawal of aid in 1960.

The critical developments would appear to have come in 1962. In a welcoming speech of June 17, 1962, to a visiting North Korean delegation, Politburo member P'eng Chen expressed what was to have been taken as the official Peking standpoint: "The U.S. imperialist aggressors must get out of South Korea, get out of Taiwan, get out of Japan, get out of South Vietnam, get out of Laos, get out of Thailand, and get out of the whole area of Asia, Africa, and Latin America." His thesis was a bellicose elaboration of the concept expressed by the Congress of the Toilers of the Far East in 1922—or by Sun Yat-sen in his Kobe speech of 1924. The P'eng Chen statement was indicative of a Chinese determination to continue to pursue an "antagonistic" confrontation with the United

States, and as a corollary to carry on with the attacks against Moscow's policy of "peaceful coexistence."

Peking gave a demonstration of its own readiness to take limited risks by its military operations in October and November of 1962 against India, backed up though India was by the British Commonwealth and, ultimately, the United States. Chou En-lai in his 1971 analysis also included Moscow's disapproval of China's action in that episode, and the Soviet sympathy shown for the Indian position, as another factor in creating the Sino-Soviet split. Chou did not remark the circumstance, but Moscow had that year "failed" Peking in another respect. It was while the Sino-Indian conflict was in course that the Soviet Union and the United States approached the brink of nuclear war in the Cuban missile crisis; Moscow bowed to the American threat and withdrew its offending missiles from Cuban soil. Moscow had been tried and, in Peking's revolutionary scales, was found wanting. Peking charged that the Soviet retreat constituted "capitulationism." It is evident that, after the Cuban missile crisis, the Chinese Communists abandoned any idea that Moscow would accede to Mao's demand that the Soviet Union should renounce "peaceful coexistence" with the United States in favor of revolutionary action; they chose instead to challenge the Soviets for revolutionary leadership in a world in which imperialism was presumed to be headed for quick ruin.

Other countries, and other Communist parties, would soon become embroiled in the Sino-Soviet dispute. Through delegations attending a series of European Communist party congresses held between November, 1962, and January, 1963, Peking undertook its campaign to wrest control of the world Communist movement from Moscow. The arguments dealt with the familiar ideological topics and trod familiar ground, with the introduction of new case histories in the form of the Sino-Indian and Soviet-American crises. In his report of December, 1962, to the Supreme Soviet, Khrushchev took cognizance of the Chinese criticism of Soviet behavior in the Cuban missile crisis and asked what would have happened if Moscow, instead of showing "proper restraint" during that critical period, "had heeded the prompting of the 'ultrarevolutionary' loudmouths?" He answered his own question: thermonuclear war, with its dire consequences. Later in his speech he made a pointed charge: "Some dogmatists have taken to Trotskyite positions and are seeking to push the Soviet Union and other socialist countries onto the path of unleashing a world war." [3]

The Chinese were not deterred. And although Moscow in February, 1963, proposed that the two Communist *parties* engage in bilateral talks for a resolution of differences, and Peking in due course accepted the invitation, the signs were not propitious. On May 12, just three days after Peking had agreed that the interparty talks should be convened on July 5 in Moscow, CPR Chairman Liu Shao-ch'i, on ending a state visit to Hanoi, declared that the current Marxist-Leninist polemics centered on the question of "whether the people of the world should carry out revolutions or not and whether proletarian parties should lead the world's people in revolutions or not." [4] Patently, both the CCP and the CPSU were "proletarian parties."

Both sides sent capable, top-ranking representatives to the party meeting of July designed to iron out the Sino-Soviet differences. Teng Hsiao-p'ing and P'eng Chen headed the Chinese delegation, ideologue Mikhail A. Suslov led the Soviet group. But the conference had already been compromised by the Chinese Party's issuance on June 14 of a long letter outlining hard-line positions. Peking stood for a purist, "Leninist" belief in the inevitability of war, rejected the united-front concept in domestic struggles in favor of Communist-led revolutions, disagreed fundamentally with Moscow on the possibility of a peaceful transition from capitalism to socialism and even on the process of transition from socialism to communism, and held to its demand that the socialist countries (meaning the Soviet Union) should assist the "revolutionary struggles" of the oppressed *classes and nations* of the world.

Moscow, Washington, and London were at that moment engaged in negotiations aimed at a limited ban on nuclear testing. Moscow had its options: detente with the United States and crisis with China, or vice versa? Given the military ordeals the Russians had experienced since 1917, the cautious foreign-policy line followed with major consistency from Stalin's advent to power onwards, *and* the compelling logic in favor of the current Soviet strategy of peaceful coexistence and economic cooperation-cum-competition, the choice was dictated.

Moscow refused to surrender to the Chinese position, and the inter-party conference adjourned. Moscow went on to enter upon the limited test-ban treaty with Britain and the country regarded by Mao as "the greatest imperialist of them all," the United States.

It was now obvious that, for so long as the respective leaderships of the Chinese and Soviet parties continued in power, they would work at cross-purposes, and remain in competition. Since the parties were effectively the governments in China and the Soviet Union, this meant that the party confrontation would in the final analysis be a confrontation between the two nations. The formal conversion of the inter-party dispute into a larger conflict actually followed close upon the heels of the July party conference. Peking charged that the Soviet leaders had "begun to collude with U.S. imperialism" against China. This was a matter of inter-*state* relations. And since the campaign against the USSR was of Mao Tse-tung's designing, his prestige automatically became committed to the anti-Soviet line. To all intents and purposes, he was now as anti-Soviet as Chiang Kai-shek.

A feature of Peking's changed strategy was the concept of the "intermediate zone," enunciated in January, 1964. Mao Tse-tung still held to the thought that this was a bipolar world, with American imperialism at one pole and the revolutionary socialists at the other, but where in 1949 he had held that all belonged in either one camp or the other, now the governing concept discovered in between a vast intermediate zone, comprising two major groupings: (1) industrialized states oppressed by the United States, and (2) the dispossessed and oppressed nations of the world. In a modified revival of the "united front" concept of 1935, Peking found it fitting that all those opposed to the United States should collaborate for the destruction of the common enemy. There was as yet no explicit exclusion of the Soviet Union from such a crusade.

At the moment when the new doctrine was proclaimed, Premier Chou En-lai and Foreign Minister Ch'en Yi (of New Fourth Army fame) were at the head of a large delegation in Africa, where they strove to further the program in a two-month tour. They showed themselves too revolutionary for the success of their program. Chou purported to see African revolution on the horizon; his "bourgeois" hosts wanted none of it. He made critical comments that offended King Hassan of Morocco and Emperor Haile Selassie of Ethiopia, after both of them had been his hosts. Then the party was forced to cancel scheduled visits to Uganda, Kenya, and Tanganyika because of the outbreak of military disorders in those countries. In the end, the visit won China the recognition of several African countries; but the revolutionary "anti-imperialist" cause was not advanced.

As regards the moot question of how the transition to socialism was to be effected, Peking held to its established position, as set forth by *Red Flag* in March: "Violent revolution is a universal law of proletarian revolution." And the editors forecast that, "In advocating the parliamentary road, Khrushchev and his followers can only meet the same fate as that of the revisionists of the Second International." [5]

Momentarily, after Khrushchev was ousted from power in October, there seemed to be the suggestion that Peking might be prepared to make some shift in its foreign policy. Chou En-lai proclaimed that China was "willing to coexist peacefully with the United States," and he went on to express hope for an improvement of relations with the USSR.[6] It would have been logical to conclude from this statement that the Chinese regime proposed to seize upon the opportunity offered by Khrushchev's passing from power to abandon the confrontation doctrine in favor of the principle of peaceful coexistence.

PEACEFUL COEXISTENCE OR WORLD REVOLUTION?

If that thought was actually behind Premier Chou's statement, it must have been killed before it flowered. Chou headed a Chinese delegation that attended the November 7 anniversary celebration in Moscow, but there was no reconciliation with the new Soviet leaders, Premier Alexei N. Kosygin and Party chieftain Leonid I. Brezhnev, who proved no readier than Nikita S. Khrushchev to accept Mao's revolutionary doctrine. The next Chinese move was one of open challenge: on January 24, 1965, Premier Chou launched the idea that there should be organized a "revolutionary" United Nations of Afro-Asian states. Indonesia had just withdrawn from the UN, and Peking clearly hoped that this event meant, at last, the turning of the tide toward revolution.

The hopes were vain. India had recently moved to smash the pro-Peking faction of the Indian Communist Party, and in the Mongolian People's Republic Premier Tsedenbal purged pro-Chinese elements from the Mongolian People's Revolutionary Party. Almost coincident with the issuance of a joint statement by Chou En-lai and Indonesian Foreign Minister Subandrio at Peking condemning the alleged inadequacies of the UN, the tiny African country of Burundi, which Peking had used as a base for subversive activities in neighboring states, abruptly suspended diplomatic relations with China and ordered the Chinese mission to leave the country within two days.

And if there had been hopes in Peking that the election of Lyndon B. Johnson to the American presidency would halt any move toward escalation of the war in Vietnam, as promised by Johnson in his campaign speeches, those hopes were soon dashed. In August, 1964, the United States had suddenly bombed North Vietnam in "retaliation" for the dubious "Tonkin Bay incident." In February, 1965, soon after Chou En-lai had proposed the formation of an Afro-Asian United Nations, the United States began sustained bombing of North Vietnam. The war had been escalated to the near vicinity of China's borders. Peking was automatically called upon to assess its world strategy: should Mao's twin "anti-revisionist" and "anti-imperialist" campaigns *both* be continued? The Maoist theory of contradictions held that there could be only one principal contradiction at a time. Which was now China's prime antagonist—the Soviet Union or the United States?

At that time, it was being argued strongly by Moscow's camp that there should be a restoration of Communist international unity in order to confront the United States with solid support for the Vietnamese revolutionaries. On the face of it this seemed to be in accord with Maoist doctrine, and high Chinese officials made statements in favor of a strong stand against American actions in Southeast Asia. In a *Red Flag* article in May, Chief of General Staff Lo Jui-ch'ing held that an "active defense" against the United States was "the only correct strategy," and urged that "first priority" be accorded to the psychological preparation of the Chinese people for war—even nuclear war.[7] In May also, Peking Mayor P'eng Chen proclaimed, in the course of a visit to Indonesia, that the principal contradiction was between "imperialism headed by the United States" and the "oppressed" nations of Asia, Africa, and Latin America. His position was based upon the interpretation that, by its actions in Southeast Asia, the United States was showing itself to be China's chief antagonist.

If the P'eng Chen identification of the "principal contradiction" was correct, the accepted tactics called for subordination of the quarrel with the Soviet Union and a major endeavor to create and support a united front of sympathetic Asian, African, and Latin American nations. The date for the new Afro-Asian conference, booked to be held in Algiers, had been fixed for the end of June. Peking still sought to exclude the Soviet Union from the gathering. In the course of a preliminary tour to Cairo and Algiers that spring, Chou En-lai stopped at Tirana, and in a speech there reversed his line of the previous October with regard to U.S.-China relations and brought forward a revolutionary touchstone he obviously hoped would be used at the coming conference:

Peaceful coexistence with American imperialism is totally excluded. Does one oppose American imperialism, yes or no? Does one oppose in truth or does one do so only in appearance? This is the principal criterion of distinction between Marxist-Leninists and the modern revisionists.[8]

It was evident that Peking was standing by its anti-American policy; it was equally clear that the Chinese leadership held to the position that Moscow could redeem itself only by adopting the same strategy.

Premier Chou made no gains in his new trip to Africa. Presumably acting by Mao's instructions, he felt compelled to proclaim again that conditions in Africa favored revolution. East African countries he had been scheduled to visit thereupon closed their doors to him. The Kenyan Minister of Health and Housing expressed what seemed to be a growing feeling when he said that Kenyans had not fought the British in order to bring in the Chinese to take over the country.[9] A Maoist "People's Front of East Africa" called upon "the broad masses of the Kenya people" to condemn President Kenyatta's "African socialism" as a new front for "imperialist colonialist capitalism," [10] but the Kenya government was unshaken.

The spirit of the first Afro-Asian conference, that of 1955 in Bandung, was crumbling under the insistence of Peking that the Afro-Asian nations, when they met again, should follow the Chinese revolutionary line. With the ousting of the Ben Bella government in the projected meeting site, Algiers, the conference was postponed; but any prospect for unity in a common cause had already been wrecked by the Chinese. The Mao regime had found none to join an Afro-Asian International headed by China, none to join it in a crusade against the great powers. Indeed, its own motives had come under suspicion. In December, 1965, the Tunisian Minister for Foreign Affairs denounced what he called China's "imperialism" and "expansionist aims."

During this time, the American assault on the revolutionary forces in Vietnam had been increasing in intensity and scale: not only had the bombing of North Vietnam taken on a "strategic" character, but U.S. combat forces had been introduced into the warfare in South Vietnam. In the debates within the Peking leadership with respect to the strategy to be followed, Liu Shao-ch'i, P'eng Chen, and Chief of General Staff Lo Jui-ch'ing were reported to have taken the position that China should participate in the projected united-front action in support of the Vietnamese revolutionary forces; Mao Tse-tung and his lieutenant Lin Piao argued in opposition to that proposal, and held that China could and should avoid direct involvement in the revolutionary struggle against the Americans in Southeast Asia.

That Mao's faction had won the argument was indicated when, on September 3, there was published an essay by Lin Piao entitled "Long Live the Victory of People's War!" in which the author developed the thesis that revolutionaries should depend upon their own resources, and not upon outside help, for victory. And what of Peking's argument vis-à-vis Moscow that socialist states should assist revolutionaries in other countries, and that those who refused to take such risks were cowardly revisionists? Practical political considerations, it appeared, sometimes should be permitted to prevail over principle. It had been made evident that Mao Tse-tung had supported the doctrinal position in point chiefly with the aim of combating Soviet influence and winning preeminence for China in the Third World.

There was soon to be a testing of the Maoist prescription for "violent revolution" and an emphasizing of the Lin Piao thesis. All indications were that Peking pinned high hopes on revolutionary developments in Indonesia, with its large Communist Party commanded by a man who was sympathetic to the Maoist policy line. When the military staged a coup at Jakarta on October 1, the Indonesian Communists were quick to come out in support of the action. Consequently, when the coup was put down, the victors wreaked a part of their vengeful wrath on the Indonesian Communist Party, which was effectively destroyed.

Those events demonstrated that Mao's prescription for active revolution instead of Khrushchevian parliamentarianism did *not* have an absolute value, and that when the prescription failed (in this case, true, far from China's borders) China could not offer salvation. The meaning of the Lin Piao doctrine became crystal-clear: expect advice from Peking, but not active intervention. Peking's drive for leadership of the dispossessed of the earth had run aground on the rocks of reality: in circumstances where the PLA was not to be equipped with modern artillery, tanks, air force, and missiles, but would instead have to function as a "people's army," it could act effectively only at home, in the Yenan pattern.

Confirmation of China's inability to influence major events outside its borders came in the Indian-Pakistan dispute that broke out in mid-1965. Peking struck poses and even issued an ultimatum to New Delhi regarding an alleged Indian violation of the Sikkim-Tibetan frontier, but in the end the matter was settled without reference to Chinese wishes—at Tashkent, through *Soviet* mediation.

Even before this last development, the accumulation of failures in the field of foreign affairs, combined with the problem of adjusting China's economy, had brought about the administering of the rebuff to Mao Tse-tung at the CCP Central Committee meeting of September, 1965—and in his undertaking the sweeping movement against his Opposition that came to be called the Great Proletarian Cultural Revolution. The new development inevitably had its impact in the field of foreign affairs. Where Mao's opposition to Soviet "revisionism" had almost certainly helped push him into the launching of a campaign against that evil as discovered on the home front, now, in a continuation of the cycle, his drive against domestic "revisionists" would cause him to demand an even purer brand of revolution abroad.

While Mao was concentrating on the critical preliminary moves directed toward the Great Purge, the country's foreign affairs showed no discernible change in pattern. In April, 1966, CPR Chairman Liu Shao-ch'i made a ceremonial visit to Afghanistan, the recipient of some $1 billion in American and Soviet aid since 1950. The Afghans entertained their distinguished visitor with native dances and expert horsemanship, but moved no closer to the Middle Kingdom. About the same time, an African leader showed that he had been deliberating upon some of the hidden aspects of Peking's revolutionary foreign policy. President Felix Houphouet-Boigny of the Ivory Coast observed that the Chinese were unable, for different reasons, to expand into either Siberia or South and Southeast Asia, and warned that "Africa, underpopulated Africa, is their long-term goal and we must be alive to the danger." Holding that the Chinese would spread over the continent unless African governments and peoples were alert to the situation, he said: "It will take time—decades, perhaps centuries—but what is a century to a people like the Chinese?" [11]

In midyear, after Mao's campaign against China's intellectuals had gotten well under way, the *Liberation Army Daily* published a doctrinal guide for revolutionary literary workers. Criticizing the philosophy of survival in the nuclear age, the guide condemned the Soviet leadership for endeavoring to find a means of coexisting with the West without war, and denounced any dealings with the "imperialist" United States in particular. The doctrine called for an unremitting struggle until the last revisionist and last capitalist might have been erased from the face of the planet.[12] And the communiqué issued by the CCP Central Committee in August, as the GPCR was formally inaugurated, was equally uncompromising in its language. It held on the one hand that the struggle against Soviet "modern revisionism" was to be carried through to the end, and on the other it condemned "U.S. imperialism" as "the most ferocious common enemy of the peoples of the whole world" and called for creation of the "broadest possible international united front" (always excepting revisionists) against "U.S. imperialism and its lackeys." [13] According to the communiqué, "We are now in a new era of world revolution. All political forces are undergoing a process of great upheaval, great division and great reorganization. The revolutionary movement of the people in all countries, and particularly in Asia, Africa and Latin America, is surging vigorously forward." From this time onward, during the course of the GPCR, Peking would extend its approval to foreign revolutionaries only in so far as they professed the Maoist faith and followed the current Chinese doctrine of violent revolution. The liberal interpretation of the united-front concept was for the time being in the discard. Peking was "anti-bourgeois" as well as "anti-imperialist" and "anti-revisionist."

ANARCHY AND FOREIGN POLICY

Soon after the inauguration of the GPCR in August, 1966, the Red Guards undertook to carry their revolutionary concepts into the Foreign Ministry, with the aim of revolutionizing both ministry operations and foreign policy, and that organ remained embroiled until September of the following year. In the beginning Foreign Minister Ch'en Yi resisted the invasion of his establishment, but the Red Guards had other ready targets at hand, namely, the diplomatic missions located in Peking. It was not long before "popular demonstrations" began to be mounted against the embassies.

The Soviet mission was made the first target, coming under attack at the end of August and again in October. In October, too, "mass demonstrations" in which, according to Moscow's report, some 2,000,000 Chinese participated were staged along the Sino-Soviet border (particularly, on the Manchurian—Soviet Far Eastern frontier) in support of Chinese claims to certain territories, once "Chinese," now located in the Soviet Union. There was no reason to assume that those "popular" demonstrations were spontaneous in origin.

At the time of the January (1967) Revolution, the revolutionaries marked up a success that could only have whetted their appetites. Maoists in the Portuguese colony of Macao, seizing upon an excuse offered by a minor matter of administrative procedure, in December had whipped up demonstrations and riots in which eight persons were killed. Peking intervened politically in support of the Chinese, who now made sweeping demands on the colonial authority, and on January 29, 1967, the Portuguese signed agreements not only providing for compensation to injured parties but effectively ceding some of their sovereign rights in Macao. This was a victory over "imperialism."

By this time, Red Guard actions against the foreign missions located in Peking were increasing in fury. East European diplomats in the capital, as "revisionists," were now being harassed, and sometimes assaulted. At the end of January, Red Guards beat two members of the Czechoslovak mission, attacked the car of the Hungarian ambassador, and staged a demonstration against the Yugoslav mission. The Soviet embassy evacuated staff dependents early in February, and when British Chargé d'Affaires Donald Hopson and French Ambassador Lucien Paye endeavored to intervene as Soviet women and children were forced to crawl under portraits of Mao Tse-tung and Stalin in the face of a menacing Red Guard mob at the airport they were themselves manhandled. Ulan Bator demanded that the security of its mission be assured, whereupon the Foreign Ministry on February 9 gave the Maoist rationale for the Red Guard disregard of the established principles of diplomatic courtesy and privilege, reputedly stating that "diplomatic immunity is a product of bourgeois institutions, and countries conducting a revolution do not recognize bourgeois norms." [14] It was reported that Czech, East German, and Yugoslav protests elicited similar responses.

The atmosphere in Peking at this time was highly reminiscent of the xenophobia of the Boxers and the siege of the legations of over half a century before. The Maoist leadership presumably felt that it was desirable as a matter of political tactics to keep the nation aware of foreign "enemies" during the period of domestic turmoil, in order to facilitate mobilization of the masses in support of the domestic program at hand.

There was a paradoxical aspect to the matter. Foreigners resident in China, normally enjoying only limited freedom of movement, now were forbidden to peruse Red Guard wall posters, under suspicion of espionage.[15] Diplomatic missions were also limited in their movements and their functioning. Later in the GPCR, they would be prohibited from acquiring or reading provincial periodicals, or from having access to other newspapers than the official *People's Daily* and the *Kuang Ming Jih Pao*.[16] If the Peking leadership disdained to observe "bourgeois" norms of behavior at home, however, it nevertheless insisted on the "right" of Chinese residing abroad to propagandize Mao's Thoughts and the doctrines of the GPCR, and was prompt to complain when the freedom was denied. Hsieh Fu-chih, speaking at a Peking rally in support of activists in Hong Kong, gave expression to the governing concept: "All activities carried out by our compatriots in Hongkong in studying, propagating, applying and defending Mao Tse-tung's thought are their absolute, sacred and inviolable right." [17]

A temporary subsidence of the assaults on foreign diplomatic missions came with the setback suffered by the Red Guard extremists in February; but when the leftist faction regained the initiative in the following month, radicalism was soon again the order of the day in Peking's relations with the embassies. The relationship with India had never been fully mended after 1962, and in mid-June Peking charged that the first and second secretaries of the Indian embassy had been guilty of espionage, and asserted that they would be brought to judgment, stripped of diplomatic immunity, before a Chinese court, prior to being permitted to leave the country. They were in fact "tried" before an assembled crowd of thousands, sentenced to deportation, and beaten by Red Guards at the airport en route home. Other embassy personnel who tried to aid them were also assaulted. In New Delhi, the Indian government took retaliatory action against two secretaries of the Chinese embassy, and Indian demonstrators attacked the embassy and assaulted staff members. At the end of the month, the *New China News Agency* hailed the peasant uprising in the Naxalbari region of West Bengal, and proclaimed that "the appearance in India of the armed peasant struggle directed by the Indian Communist

Party marks a new stage of the vigorous struggle of the Indian people against the reactionary dominance; it foreshadows the approach of a great people's revolution, of which the principal form is armed struggle, in India." [18] Relations between the two countries deteriorated further.

In late June a serious strain developed in Sino-Burmese relations, theretofore viewed as being a nearly ideal example of good relations between Asian states having different social systems. When, in response to prompting from the Chinese embassy, Chinese schoolchildren began flaunting Mao badges and Maoist propaganda was widely circulated, the Burmese government prohibited the wearing of insignia of other than recognized Burmese organizations. The schoolchildren persisted, and rioting Burmese in Rangoon and elsewhere killed upwards of a hundred Chinese (Peking put the number of dead at "several hundreds"). In retaliation for the Burmese mob actions, which included an attack on the Chinese embassy, Red Guards staged demonstrations against the Burmese embassy at Peking, and the Peking press denounced the Ne Win regime as a "fascist military dictatorship" and proclaimed its support for the White Flag Burmese Communist Party in its war of liberation.

But the pro-Peking faction in the White Flag Party had in the meantime, almost certainly under Peking's urging, purged the moderate (and therefore presumed pro-Soviet) faction of the Burmese Party as "revisionist," and the fanatical fervor with which they now waged their "struggle" alienated support the Party had previously enjoyed in the villages and among Burmese intellectuals. A year and a half later, owing to their political errors and the energetic action Ne Win's army took against them, the pro-Mao White Flags had been much reduced in strength—and were far from their announced goal of "liberating" Burma from Ne Win's rule.[19]

When Prague in July rejected Peking's request that Chinese students should be permitted to return to Czechoslovakia, Peking filed a formal note of protest, and Red Guards on the same day demonstrated against the Czech embassy and plastered the embassy walls with insults. China's Mongolian neighbors, who had before so fruitlessly requested the protection appropriate to foreign missions, were among those who suffered Red Guard blows. In early August, the chauffeur of the Mongolian ambassador refused a portrait of Mao Tse-tung thrust in through the car window by Red Guards. He was dragged from the car, and the car set on fire. Then the Red Guards proceeded to the Mongolian embassy, painted anti-Mongol slogans on its walls, and finally invaded the premises and assaulted five of the embassy staff.

Relations between Peking and Jakarta had been strained since the failure of the attempted coup of 1965. On August 5, Red Guards demonstrated in front of the Indonesian embassy; on the same day, Indonesians assaulted the Chinese embassy at Jakarta. Matters were advanced one stage further when, at the beginning of September, Indonesia suspended commercial exchanges between the two countries. On September 15, Foreign Minister Adam Malik announced that, since the Indonesian embassy in Peking no longer enjoyed the protection requisite for its proper functioning, the entire staff was being withdrawn. On October 1, Indonesian students leveled another attack against the Chinese embassy in Jakarta, this time sacking it. These events led to the virtual rupture of relations between the two countries, which repatriated the last members of their respective embassy staffs at the end of October. Peking sought to gain a measure of revenge by extolling the actions of armed rebels against the Suharto regime; but President Suharto effectively continued the military suppression of rebel bands in West Borneo and the arrest of suspected pro-Communists throughout the country.

Still in September, after Tunisia had detained a Chinese table-tennis instructor and an embassy official, and Peking had charged President Bourguiba with "siding with American imperialism" and betraying the interests of the Tunisian and all Arab peoples, China closed its embassy in Tunisia. During that turbulent summer of 1967, Peking also had trouble with Ceylon, Nepal, Kenya, Bulgaria, and others besides. Peking's insistence on the right of its citizens residing abroad to proselytize in behalf of Mao Tse-tung led Prince Sihanouk of Cambodia, long a friend of the Peking regime, to denounce such interference in Cambodian internal affairs, and brought him to the verge of withdrawing the entire embassy staff from Peking. He was dissuaded by the personal intervention of Chou En-lai, who gave assurances that the objectionable practices would cease. When Japanese Premier Sato Eisaku paid an official visit to Taiwan, the *People's Daily* denounced the action as part of a vast conspiracy concocted by the American imperialists and Soviet revisionists to lay the foundations of a "military alliance of Northeast Asia" directed against China,[20] and Peking proceeded to expel three of the nine Japanese newsmen resident in the capital.

Peking also undertook at this time to pressure North Vietnam into choosing definitively between "revolutionary" China and the "revisionist" Soviet Union. On the occasion of the arrival of an economic delegation from Hanoi on July 20, the *People's Daily* quoted Foreign Minister Ch'en Yi: "The struggle between the two lines on the Vietnam question is the concentrated expression of the acuteness of the international class struggle. To oppose imperialism, it is imperative to oppose the counter-revolutionary line of the Soviet revisionist ruling group. There is no middle road in the struggle between the two lines." [21] Peking failed to bend Hanoi to its purpose. However, it held that the general worsening of China's foreign relations was to be attributed to the "international conspiracy" headed by the United States and the Soviet Union.

The United States was of course out of reach of the Red Guards. It was the fate of the USSR and Great Britain to suffer the most serious attacks on their diplomatic establishments during that trying period. On August 14, fresh demonstrations were mounted against the Soviet embassy, and three days later the Red Guards invaded the consular section of the mission and destroyed official files. Moscow delivered a stiff protest regarding the matter, and about this time Marshal Ivan Yakubovski, first vice minister of defense and commander in chief of the Warsaw Pact forces, made a personal trip to Khabarovsk and alerted the Soviet Far Eastern forces to the need of reinforcing "their vigilance and their combat readiness." He took the occasion to recall past military exploits of Soviet forces in Northeast Asia, from the battle of Nomonhan to the victory of 1945.

Developments had taken on a menacing aspect for the British when, seizing upon the circumstance that the Hong Kong police had intervened to prevent Red Guard sympathizers from pursuing their violent aims to the utmost, Peking in mid-May demanded that the British should cease the use of police to check leftist mob action, release and compensate arrested leftists, and apologize. The demands were backed up by a series of strikes and other labor troubles in Hong Kong, but the British stood firm. They dispatched the aircraft carrier *Bulwark*, which arrived with heavy helicopters ostentatiously displayed on the deck. The *New China News Agency* condemned this "flagrant deployment of force" and called upon Hong Kong Chinese to "launch a vigorous attack against the wicked British imperialists." [22] A week later, the *People's Daily* urged the inhabitants of Hong Kong to continue their struggle against the British until victory was achieved. "The British imperialists fight like a beast caught in a trap and will not live long." [23]

Peking had presumably been encouraged by the victory won over the Portuguese colony of Macao in January, and perhaps by a recollection of the British surrender of its concessions at Hankow and Kiukiang under the application, in 1927, of the "revolutionary diplomacy" of Foreign Minister Eugene Ch'en. But there were factors in the equation that would have suggested caution to the Chinese. For one thing, the American aircraft carrier *Hancock* joined the *Bulwark,* bringing the number of warships anchored in Hong Kong harbor to six. Moreover, China in 1966 had earned some $600 million in its trade with Hong Kong for the benefit of its scanty foreign-exchange reserves. To "liberate" Hong Kong in 1967 would have been costly in more ways than one.

The next development sprang from the Hong Kong government's suspension of three pro-Communist Chinese newspapers. On August 20, Peking delivered an ultimatum: the British would be required, within forty-eight hours, to cancel the suspension of the newspapers and to release a number of Chinese journalists then being detained or under sentence. The *People's Daily* announced that Hong Kong was Chinese territory, and that it "must return to the domain of the motherland." [24] Promptly after expiry of the deadline without satisfaction of the ultimatum, on the night of August 22–23, Red Guards attacked the premises of the British embassy at Peking, penetrated into the interior to the accompaniment of cries of "Kill! Kill!," burned the chancery to the ground, and then assaulted and beat embassy personnel, including Chargé d'Affaires Hopson and two British women.

The British in their turn delivered a strong note of protest against the Chinese violation of the established principles of international intercourse. Seemingly recognizing that employment of such "revolutionary tactics" had become too hazardous, the Peking leadership pulled back: on September 3, Chou En-lai announced that Red Guards might indeed demonstrate against, but not invade, foreign embassies. Not long after, the restriction was made still tighter. On October 30, the government and the CCP Central Committee issued a joint directive which, remarking that foreigners resided in China with the knowledge and under the protection of the government, proclaimed that severe punishment would be imposed upon any who might stage *unauthorized* demonstrations against foreign diplomatic missions.

There was still no immediate relaxation of Sino-British tensions, for Chinese prestige was involved. In September, following a pattern used against the American consulate general at Peking in 1950, the Chinese confiscated the Shanghai office of the British Diplomatic Mission in China (from 1851 to 1949, the British consulate general). The rationale offered was that the office had served as a "base of aggression" against China for over a century and had been taken over "to satisfy the public demand and for the needs of Shanghai's urban development." [25]

But those developments in China's foreign relations were to the accompaniment of the growing tensions *within* China that had taken dramatic form with the military revolt at Wuhan. The province of Kwangtung, off which Hong Kong lay, was one of the areas hardest hit by disorders—which were put down by the PLA. In late November, after the British had agreed to six minor conditions governing administration of the common border between Hong Kong and Kwangtung, the situation eased. The crisis was over. But it was estimated that China had lost approximately $100 million in foreign exchange from Hong Kong that year. China had lost more than it gained by its practice of revolutionary diplomacy against Hong Kong.

A diminution of China's antiforeign activities coincided with the manifestation of increased concern for domestic stability. The incidents involving the Soviet and British embassies had occurred at the height of the travail of the Foreign Ministry, which for about two weeks in mid-August was effectively dominated by extremist elements. Now Ch'en Yi had been restored to full authority, and the October 30 order had spelled out the policy shift. The disorders that had swirled about diplomatic missions in the capital ceased, and there was a gradual return to customary diplomatic protocol.

During 1966 and 1967, five countries—Indonesia and four African states—had suspended diplomatic relations with China. The damage done to relations with a large number of other countries through the exercise of Peking's fanatical "revolutionary diplomacy" had been severe. China's foreign affairs were in a shambles, its prestige at a new low. A shift toward a more pragmatic, more conventional, course was dictated by national considerations—and was being undertaken. On September 5, 1967, Peking signed an agreement with Tanzania and Zambia for construction of a railway linking the two countries, with China to supply an important credit in that connection. On November 8, China and Ceylon signed a trade and payments protocol to govern commercial exchanges in the coming year.

A critical development of early 1968 made China's international position safer than it had been at any time since 1965: at the end of March, President Johnson announced the deescalation of U.S. bombing operations over North Vietnam, and this development was followed by the opening of quadrilateral peace talks at Paris. That initial "winding down" of the Vietnam War substantially lessened the threat to China's national security.

The trend toward *détente* continued. For all of Peking's condemnation of the Sato government's allegedly iniquitous foreign policy, China and Japan, on March 6, 1968, signed a new agreement for trade exchanges in the current year. In May, it was announced that China had agreed with Guinea and Mali to assist in the construction of a railway from Bamako in Mali to connect with an existing railway in Guinea, thus giving Mali access to the sea. That same month, Canadian Prime Minister Trudeau announced that he favored any measures, including the extension of Canadian recognition "on suitable terms," which might bring closer relations between the two countries and thus "contribute to international order and stability." [26] In foreign affairs, China was beginning to assume a new, more attractive appearance.

Maoist doctrine had viewed armed struggle as being a basic element in achieving social change; it assumed further that the Chinese revolutionary pattern was suited to all underdeveloped countries, either for the ousting of colonial authority or for the overthrow of "bourgeois" power. Communist "revisionists" who rejected that dogma were *ipso facto* guilty of collusion with imperialism—and, as renegades, were worse than the bourgeoisie. But the attempt made in the course of the GPCR to prove the validity of that doctrine had failed beyond any reasonable doubt. There had been nothing left for Peking to do but to change its foreign-policy line. Communist and revolutionary countries alike had rejected Maoism as universal doctrine; it was viewed as purely a *Chinese* product—and the GPCR had only crystallized the conviction.

14 END OF THE MAOIST ERA

W HERE Mao Tse-tung in 1945 had exhorted his followers not to indulge in wastefulness and extravagance but to "treasure our manpower and material resources," in the Great Proletarian Cultural Revolution (GPCR) he had once again, in the pattern of the Great Leap, led the nation to waste both. He had effectively demolished the basic concept that the Party embodied the "proletarian consciousness" and should be viewed—and respected— as the repository of the Proletarian Truth. In his theory the masses possessed the ultimate wisdom, and Mao was endeavoring in various ways to put the theory to practical use; but now it was only The Leader who might authoritatively voice the masses' political "decisions." As of the fall of 1968, the way of establishing a new, viable political order threatened to be hard and long. The issue before the nation's political leaders was: where there was distrust of the value of a Leninist party form, could a better, Maoist form be evolved? And could the revolutionary committees govern effectively at local levels?

CELEBRATION, AND DEMISE, OF THE GPCR

After the CCP Central Committee plenum of October called a halt to revolutionary turmoil, the next logical step was the holding of a new Party Congress, to mark the rehabilitation of the Party, to judge the fruits of the GPCR, and to point out the path of the future. The Party was now also clearly charged with reasserting its authority over the Army. Seven years overdue, the Ninth Party Congress convened in Peking on April 1, 1969.

It was remarkable that, at a Party congress nominally celebrating "unity" and "victory," there were no guest delegations present. The reasons were fairly obvious. For one thing, this congress had as a prime purpose the rehabilitation of the Party after a bitter interne-cine struggle: the "unity" would patently have shown imperfections. For another, attendance of delegations from foreign parties would have been unimpressive, for Peking had been notably unsuccessful in prying other Communist parties away from loyalty to the Soviet line and into the "revolutionary" Maoist camp. By its extravagances, Peking had alienated much of the support it had built up during 1953–57, when it was following a policy of sobriety and pragmatism in foreign affairs. Its foreign policy was a shambles; Peking could flaunt no victories there. Worse, it would have been hard put to sub-stantiate its claims to victory even at home—in either the political or economic sector. China had suffered serious setbacks in all fields as a result of the Great Proletarian Cultural Revolution.

This was a rubber-stamp congress. Hsieh Fu-chih, speaking to the Peking revolutionary committee in January, 1968, had said that delegates to the new congress would be named from the "central level" on down, in order to "insure that the rebels among party members will be in the majority." [1] Refinement of the thought was indicated in a *Red Flag* editorial of mid-October. "Blind faith in elections," said that organ, constituted a conservative line of thought, and persons apt at study and application of Mao's Thought should be "selected" rather than elected to top posts in the Party or-ganization.[2] The pattern of the Paris Commune was now quite ignored; what is more, the Communist principle of "democratic centralism" had been stood on its head. And one could see that only a half of the hallowed Maoist "mass line" was left: the concept "to the masses" indeed remained, but the corollary "from the masses" had been renounced in political practice.

True to that prescription, the membership of the Ninth Congress was in fact not elected in the manner prescribed by the Party con-stitution, but "selected." There was a skimped agenda: the delegates had only to approve a new Party constitution, adopt Vice Chairman Lin Piao's political report, and elect a new Party central committee.

The hand-picked congress performed its assigned functions. The GPCR was given the ultimate sanction in Lin Piao's statement that it had been "personally initiated and led by our great leader Chair-man Mao," and was described as having been necessary "for con-solidating the dictatorship of the proletariat, preventing capitalist restoration and building socialism." [3] Lin characterized the GPCR as "a great revolution in the realm of the superstructure" carried out "under conditions of dictatorship of the proletariat." The rationale adduced in support of the thesis was hardly convincing. The main purpose of that part of the exposition was clearly designed to portray the shortcomings of the post-Stalin Soviet leadership, which had allegedly "turned the world's first state of the dictatorship of the proletariat into a dark fascist state of the dictatorship of the bourgeoisie." China was different; there, Chairman Mao had put forward "the theory of continuing the revolution under the dictatorship of the proletariat."

Lin set forth in detail "counterrevolutionary plots" attributed to "Liu Shao-ch'i and his gang," who had allegedly "always wantonly opposed Chairman Mao's proletarian revolutionary line." But there was a didactic purpose as well: the new revolutionary committees "must put the living study of Mao Tsetung Thought above all work and place Mao Tsetung Thought in command of everything." The policies of the GPCR were redefined, and now redirected toward the promotion of production. With respect to consolidation and building of the Party, Lin set up a standard of discipline different from that formerly embodied in either the Party constitution or Mao's own works: "Whoever opposes Chairman Mao, whoever opposes Mao Tsetung Thought, at any time or under any circumstances, will be condemned and punished by the whole Party and the whole nation."

Lin's stress was nevertheless on moderation, with prescription of reeducation for the old (bourgeois) intellectuals and leniency for those persons who had committed errors "characteristic of the capitalist-roader in power [Liu Shao-ch'i]" but who had repented. He was reticent on economic matters, but called for a consolidation of the economic base of socialism, "so as to insure that the country continues to advance in giant strides along the road to socialism." Treatment of the revolutionary committees was equally sketchy: Lin seemed to suggest that they would continue to function as the governing apparatus—without, however, defining their relationship to the CCP structure. Citing Mao as source, Lin voiced another thought, which had a distinctly martial ring: "the main component of the state is the army."

It was possible to make certain tentative deductions from Lin's glossing over economic and organizational issues, in conjunction with his reference to the Army's importance. The Party-rehabilitation process had not yet been completed; and the development of the country's economy had been slowed by the GPCR. It was to be anticipated that the (PLA) would still be called upon, as in the past two years, to play a major role in both political and economic processes. The sum total spelled more regimentation for the social structure.

The new Party constitution, duly approved, was notably shorter than that of 1956, and less precise. The Thought of Mao Tse-tung was enshrined as the governing doctrine. But the document was ambiguous with respect to the role of the Party; and it contained only the vaguest of Party programs, summarily set forth as being "the complete overthrow of the bourgeoisie and all other exploiting classes, the establishment of the dictatorship of the proletariat in place of the dictatorship of the bourgeoisie and the triumph of socialism over capitalism. The ultimate aim of the Party is the realization of communism." The document was also unspecific regarding the organization and administration of the Party. The process for the exercise of suffrage was indicated by the provision that leading bodies of the Party should be "elected," at all levels, "through democratic consultation." The structure of the operational apparatus received no further definition than the following:

Under the leadership of the Chairman [Mao], the Vice Chairman [Lin Piao] and the Standing Committee of the Political Bureau of the Central Committee, a number of necessary organs, which are compact and efficient, shall be set up to attend to the day-to-day work of the Party, the government and the army in a centralized way.

The 1969 constitution was essentially a sanction for the exercise of personal rule by the Party Chairman. In the final analysis, one thing was clear: the CCP had now departed radically from the Leninist pattern offered by the Communist Party of the Soviet Union.

As noted above, the GPCR had devastated the ranks of the Eighth Central Committee: those purged included twelve Politburo members, seven deputy premiers, and forty-two Cabinet ministers and vice ministers. The Congress proceeded to form a new Central Committee, the list of candidates having been "worked out after full consultation." The new organ was bigger than the previous committee. Of its 279 regular members, only 53 had been members of the Eighth Central Committee; 112 were to be classified as military men. The Party secretariat (formerly headed by Teng Hsiao-p'ing) was abolished; but the committee proceeded to set up a Politburo dominated by thé five-man standing committee comprising Mao,

Lin, Chou En-lai, and Cultural Revolution Group members Ch'en Po-ta and K'ang Sheng.

The veteran revolutionary Liu Shao-ch'i was duly condemned, as had been Lavrenti P. Beria in the USSR in 1953, for having allegedly plotted the restoration of capitalism. Lin Piao vilified him as "an old-line counterrevolutionary, renegade, hidden traitor and scab." Liu could legally have been removed from his post as chairman of the Republic only by action of the National People's Congress; but he had been *politically* and effectively purged de facto. There was a significant negative factor in the proceedings: although many old revolutionaries had come under Maoist attack during the GPCR, none besides Liu was officially damned as "renegade" and "traitor" for the Party history. The ghosts of the many other Old Comrades who had been purged sat in on the proceedings; but Mao's men were now striving to restore unity, and the concentration of attention on Liu Shao-ch'i was indicative of political compromise. Even so, Mao's personal victory seemed . . . adequate.

The announced original purpose of the GPCR had been to "seize power from below," in order to lay the foundations for a proletarian order patterned after the Paris Commune; the factionalism of the "revolutionary masses," however, had in the end brought power into the hands of the military. Nor did the new Central Committee provide much in the way of a guarantee for the "revolutionary succession" envisaged by Mao: 80 percent of the Ninth Central Committee were pre-Long March (1934) Party members, as against 84 percent in the Eighth Committee. None of the new Committee members had risen out of the Red Guard movement.

The fragmentation of authority that resulted from the GPCR had to a degree been perpetuated by the concentration of ultimate authority in the hands of the Leader and his immediate associates. The Party's "bureaucratic" control functions had been reduced, with corresponding *de*centralization of operational authority. And there was an added element of possible instability: how to provide for political continuity when Mao Tse-tung might disappear from the scene? For with the Party itself convicted of past major deviationism, the "revolutionary succession" generation tried and found wanting, and the principle of collective leadership cast into the discard, little remained besides the leadership concept.

In the course of the GPCR, Lin Piao the soldier and Chou En-lai the statesman had supplied such political cohesion as persisted.

The Party constitution described Lin as having "most loyally and resolutely carried out and defended Chairman Mao Tse-tung's proletarian revolutionary line," and then purported to give the answer to the succession problem: "Comrade Lin Piao is Comrade Mao Tse-tung's close comrade in arms and successor." But the constitution did not stipulate *how,* and in what *capacity,* Lin would succeed Mao the Great Helmsman.

In whatever legal theory that existed in China, it was the National People's Congress that constituted the supreme authority, not the CCP—or Mao. The Third NPC had not sat since 1964–65, and thus was well over its stipulated age of four years. A new NPC was obviously required, to give something in the nature of final sanction and form to the concepts set forth by the Party congress, and also, in particular, to approve a revised national constitution. The problems of convening such a congress, with attendant necessity of obtaining a consensus on the provisions for a new state constitution, were manifestly immense. The Ninth CCP Congress had marked the end of a stage in the Party power struggle; it had not resolved all major personal and power differences.

This became manifest when the Ninth CCP Central Committee met in its second plenum at Lushan August 23 to September 6, 1970. There Lin Piao, supported by Ch'en Po-ta and several top military men came out in favor of maintaining, in the draft for a revised constitution, provision for the post of state chairman—this in the face of Mao's express proposal to eliminate that position. *Lin, Ch'en, et al. had violated Lin's own precept—that opposition to Chairman Mao, "at any time or under any circumstances," was proscribed.* In a summary of talks made by the Chairman in the course of a provincial tour from mid-August to September 12 of 1971, Mao was quoted as saying that those persons who had mobilized the generals and launched their surprise attack at Lushan by their behavior showed that "they had some aim in mind. . . . In my view, behind their surprise attack and underground activity lay purpose, organization and a programme. Their programme was to appoint a state chairman. . . ." [4] Mao suspected a plot against his hegemonic authority.

At the time, however, there was no outward sign of conflict within the leadership. The PLA was successful in gradually restoring order, and the joint 1971 New Year's Day editorial published by the *People's Daily, Red Flag*, and *Liberation Army Daily* proclaimed that the first year of "the great 1970s" had seen a "new upsurge of socialist revolution and socialist construction." Announcing that the Third Five-Year Plan (1966–70) had been "successfully fulfilled" (while not offering any statistics in support of the claim), it hailed 1971 as the first year of the Fourth Five-Year Plan for developing the national economy. There was the conventional quotation from Chairman Mao to justify the program: "The Chinese people should have a great and far-reaching plan and strive to change China's economic and scientific and cultural backwardness within several decades and enable it rapidly to reach advanced world levels." The editors viewed the situation optimistically: "The dictatorship of the proletariat in our country is more consolidated than ever. The revolutionary spirit of our people is soaring. Our great socialistist motherland is flourishing."

However, a joint editorial issued by the leading metropolitan periodicals for the fiftieth anniversary of the founding of the CCP, July 1, 1971, seemed to put the goal of creation of a simon-pure proletarian power into a more distant future. It said that it would be an illusion to believe "that one, two or even three cultural revolutions would suffice to assure the definitive victory of socialism in China," and alerted the nation: "We still have to carry on a prolonged and complex struggle in order to consolidate the dictatorship of the proletariat." [5] Nevertheless, return to normal Party dominance seemed promised when, on August 26, Peking announced the formation of the last four province-level Party committees. If the work of reconstruction of the Party at the *hsien* and lower levels still remained to be achieved, the superstructure at least appeared to have been completed. The power balance was similar to that which had been discovered in the revolutionary committees: of 158 leading figures in the twenty-nine province-level committees, 59.5 percent were military men, 34.8 percent were civilian cadres, and only 5.7 percent were representatives of the "masses." [6]

THE PROLETARIAN DICTATORSHIP IN DISORDER

It was notable, however, that the country's leaders had still not fixed a date for the election (or selection) of the new National People's Congress. Then, in September, a strange series of events occurred. In the early morning of September 13, there was the mysterious crash of a Chinese military plane in the Mongolian People's Republic, with all nine persons aboard killed. From September 13 to 15, all civilian and military aircraft in China were grounded, and military personnel on leave were instructed to rejoin their units. Something of a serious nature had happened.

An amazing story gradually unfolded. In March, 1971, Lin Piao, Ch'en Po-ta, and others had drawn up a project for a revolutionary coup designated "571" (homonym, in the Chinese, for "military uprising"). The purported document gave a striking description of the situation prevailing under the Maoist rule:

Lively political discords in the country; symptoms of danger everywhere; the dictator loses more and more the support of the people; the situation within the governing group is undetermined; the struggle for power, intrigues and internal dissensions have reached their peak . . . The clique of dogmatists is made up of tyrants. They have concentrated the military power, but they have enemies on all sides. They puff themselves up like turkeys and overestimate their forces.[7]

As regards Mao Tse-tung, that same document offered criticism:

Consider the history of these last ten years. Is there to be found a single man whom he [Mao] has elevated good and high without condemning him later to political death? What political force would be able to collaborate with him in constant fashion? He has led his companions at arms and his intimate friends, who are incidentally not many, to folly. He is a suspicious and cruel man. When he clashes with someone, he does not stop until he has finished off his adversary, then he casts the blame on others. The truth is that one after another people become his victims; all serve him as scapegoats.

Then Lin (reputedly) set forth the issue:

There are two possible strategies. Either we prepare ourselves and annihilate them, or the enemy easily (while we wait) will open his jaws to devour us. Finding ourselves before a danger so direct, whether we are ready or not, we must act.[8]

The plot, now allegedly contemplating the assassination of Chairman Mao,[9] was activated on September 8, But it was betrayed to Premier Chou En-lai by Lin's daughter, Lin Tou-tou, and the plotters, their plan wrecked, attempted to escape. Those who died in the plane crash in Mongolia included Minister of National Defense Lin Piao, his wife Yeh Ch'ün, and his son Lin Li-kuo. Associated with Lin Piao in the plot, it was charged, were Chief of General Staff Huang Yung-sheng, Commander of the Air Force Wu Fa-hsien, First Political Commissar of the Navy Li Tso-p'eng, and Director of the General Logistics Department Ch'iu Hui-tso. Those four military men, and Yeh Ch'ün, were the same five dignitaries who reputedly supported the Lin-Ch'en Po-ta effort at the Lushan plenum to retain the constitutional provision for a state chairman. The four military men, and Ch'en were promptly taken into custody—and relieved of all posts.

The ultimate test of the leadership concept had come. On the basis of his theory of contradictions, Mao's determination of the orthodoxy of the moment had led to his discarding of his "close comrade in arms" Liu Shao-ch'i, and to the demonstration that dozens of other Old Comrades were weak and unreliable vessels. Now Lin Piao, his "close comrade in arms and successor," seemingly had also failed him. The stark question stood forth: who would fill the position of Pontifex Maximus when Mao Tse-tung might be gone? It was apparent that not even Mao had been able to supply the answer. To fix the succession, in the manner of the emperors of old, had proven beyond his powers.

In the last quarter of 1971, after the abrupt exit of Lin Piao from the scene, the Chinese propaganda agencies put added stress on the matter of political controls. A joint editorial carried by the *People's Daily, Red Flag,* and *Liberation Army Daily* on December 1 held that the main factors to be emphasized in the strengthening of Party leadership were: (1) strengthening of the Maoist concept that the CCP was "the core of leadership of the whole Chinese people"; (2) the thoroughgoing implementation of education in ideology and the political line; (3) strengthening of Party unity; (4) the strengthening of Party discipline; and (5) the practice of Marxism-Leninism, not revisionism. Given Chairman Mao's substantial contribution to both popular and Party *indiscipline* and *disunity,* and to national factionalism, it was noteworthy that the Chairman was now quoted as being against all those evils.

It was moreover granted that the GPCR had adversely affected the economy. Under the urging of the GPCR radical faction, national planning had been discarded, workers in factories had swept management aside in outbursts of anarchistic decision-making, the transportation system had been disrupted, and—according to reports carried by the provincial press—egalitarianism in the countryside had had adverse effects on labor productivity. Now it was established as requisite to implement the principle of "from each according to his ability, to each according to his work," and to permit commune members to engage in private sideline activities (e.g. the cultivation of private plots and the carrying on of handicraft enterprises), thus to stimulate the initiative of "the masses" and the better to advance them along the road to socialism.

In the formal educational apparatus and out, new stress was placed on the study of Marxism, Leninism, and the Thought of Mao Tse-tung—that is, on political indoctrination. Here, too, it was the Maoist line, which advocated the downgrading of academic elitism in favor of political indoctrination of the urban and (especially) rural "masses," that dominated. If there was some pious philosophizing, as in the Party organ *Red Flag*, that socialism did not mean either egalitarianism or uniformity, no evenhandedness was evident in practice in the field of education. But there was a changed factor in the ideological equation: the prestige of Mao Tse-tung the Omniscient Leader had suffered a severe blow, in institutional terms, by reason of the disastrous outcome of the "Great Leap" undertaken at his instigation in 1958; further, the effort to build up his personality cult in the course of the GPCR had been counterproductive, given the disorders attendant upon that last great "movement": could a man who would dream up and sanction an operation so destructive for Party, government, and the economy really be all-knowing? Mao's yearning for what Robert Jay Lifton has termed "revolutionary immortality" was being frustrated. But there were those who would still endeavor to exploit his ebbing forces for their personal benefit, in power terms.

The year 1972 was a poor one in agriculture: it was announced that the harvest had been some 10 million tons under that for 1971 (when the claimed grain production was 250 million tons). And the rate of increase in industrial production had slowed down. On January 1, 1973, the customary New Year's Day editorial still stressed the importance of strengthening the Party leadership. Interestingly enough, where Lin Piao and Ch'en Po-ta had theretofore been condemned as ultra-Leftists, now the line shifted: their sin had been that they were ultra-Leftists in appearance but ultra-Rightists in reality. In the first half of 1973, the campaign against alleged "ultra-Rightists," identified as "swindlers like Liu Shao-ch'i," was accompanied by an interesting—and significant—political development: a number of prominent political figures purged during the GPCR as "capitalist-roaders" were rehabilitated. Among those who made their reappearance was the sometime CCP Secretary General, Teng Hsiao-p'ing, who resurfaced in April. And the pattern was repeated at the provincial level, where various cadres returned to positions of influence in the local Party organizations. The trends were definitely toward diminution of the role of the PLA, and enhancement of the prestige and effectiveness of the

Party. If it was necessary to rehabilitate former dissidents to achieve those two ends, why, Mao was prepared to accept the inevitable— for the moment.

"GREAT ORDER," AND "CLASS STRUGGLE"

The changes in the domestic balance of power were reflected in, and legitimized by, the Tenth CCP Congress held August 24–28, 1973. As was the Ninth before it, the Tenth Congress was designed to recover a measure of prestige for the battered Party, to restore some political stability, and to legitimize the *faits accomplis*. Where the Ninth had approved the purge of Liu Shao-ch'i and others as vile "capitalist-roaders," the Tenth gave its imprimatur to the purge of Lin Piao—damned also as a rightest who had deceitfully posed as a leftist.

Mao Tse-tung attended the Party Congress, and presided, but did not speak. It was left to Chou En-lai to report on the state of the nation and to outline the tasks ahead. Chou dutifully gave primacy to the matter of criticizing Lin Piao, whom he charged with having launched an armed courterrevolutionary plot. There had been in the course of a half century, Chou reported, ten important struggles in the CCP between the two lines, and "The collapse of the Lin Piao anti-party clique does not mean the end of the two-line struggle within the Party." Citing various "contradictions" discovered in Chinese society, Chou said that "For a long time to come, there will still be two-line struggles within the Party, reflecting those contradictions, and such struggles will occur, ten, twenty, or thirty times. Lin Piaos will appear again, and so will persons like Liu Shao-ch'i, P'eng Teh-huai and Kao Kang." [10]

But the Congress had another function: to sanction the rehabilitation of various Party functionaries who had been disgraced and condemned during the GPCR as Rightists and reactionaries. Prominent among those restored to positions of authority was Teng Hsiao-p'ing. The exigent need for this move was obvious: with Chou En-lai in failing health (it was not publicly revealed at the time, but in 1972 he was discovered to have cancer), there was good reason to enlist the services of so powerful an organization man as Teng, to perform yeoman's service to help keep the government functioning effectively in the difficult political conditions prevailing after the GPCR—and the purge of Lin Piao. Others were also reenlisted to assist in the task, among them sometime Vice Premier T'an Chen-lin, the president of the Sino-Japanese Friendship Association, Liao Ch'eng-chih, and the Mongol Ulanfu. After the Congress adjourned, another once-prominent figure returned to the turbulent public life of Mao's China—sometime Politburo member Li Ching-ch'uan. But there were also newcomers to political eminence. Among the new members of the 21-man CCP Politburo were two who had been elected to the Party's Central Committee only at the Ninth Congress —the youthful Shanghai activist Wang Hung-wen and Hua Kuo-feng, a Shansi man who had of recent years held political posts in Mao's native province of Hunan.[11] Surprisingly enough, Wang Hung-wen also became a member of the Politburo's Standing Committee and was named second Party vice chairman (of five), next in rank after Premier Chou En-lai himself—and thus seemingly booked for the succession to the Party chairmanship should Chairman Mao and Premier Chou die before him, as was logically a strong probability. But there was a potential contender for the position, too, in the person of Chang Ch'un-ch'iao, the Party's Secretary General.

The CCP had experienced new internal strains, and reduced political stature, due to the Lin Piao affair. Once more, in Premier Chou's treatment of the matter, it was envisaged that the Party should resume its former dominant role of exercising centralized leadership: it should exercise overall direction in seven major sectors: industry, agriculture, commerce, culture and education, the Army, government, as well as the Party. As regards economic affairs, Chou characterized Lin as a bourgeois careerist who, together with Ch'en Po-ta, had contended that the main task after the Ninth Congress of 1969 had been to develop production. Chou held that, "'taking agriculture as the foundation and industry as the leading factor,' China should implement the general line of 'going all out, aiming high and achieving greater, faster, better and more economical results in building socialism, grasp revolution and promote production.'"[12] Industry should learn from the example of Taching, agriculture from Tachai. In furthering the national purposes, Party members should conscientiously study Marxism, including the works of Chairman Mao, and adhere firmly to dialectical materialism and fight against idealism and metaphysics.

In the light of subsequent events, it was perhaps of more than usual interest that the report on the revision of the Party Constitution was given by the new second Vice Chairman, Wang Hung-wen. Wang emphasized the importance of abiding by the Maoist principle of "the three do's and three don'ts": "Practise Marxism, and not revisionism; unite, and don't split; be open and aboveboard, and don't intrigue and conspire." [13] He asserted that "We must strengthen the Party's centralized leadership. . . . But at the same time, it is necessary to give full play to the role of the revolutionary committees, the other sectors and organizations at all levels." Continuing the self-contradictory Maoist line, he said that "Party committees at all levels must, on the basis of Chairman Mao's revolutionary line, achieve unity in thinking, policy, plan, command and action." He extolled the GPCR; and he voiced a warning: "Revisionism remains the main danger today." [14]

The new Party constitution adopted on August 28 to replace the 1969 document (that which had named Lin Piao successor to Mao Tse-tung) actually provided *inter alia* as in 1969 that the organizational principle of the Party was democratic centralism; but again the "democracy" had its own peculiar flavor: elections to the leading organs of the Party at all levels should be "through democratic consultation in accordance with the requirements for successors to the cause of the proletarian revolution and the principle of combining the old, the middle-aged and the young." Once more, after a period of disorder, there was a renewed stress on order: "The whole Party must observe unified discipline: the individual is subordinate to the organization, the minority is subordinate to the majority, the lower level is subordinate to the higher level, and the entire Party is subordinate to the Central Committee." [15]

With respect to foreign affairs, Premier Chou in his report had voiced strong condemnation of both the United States and the Soviet Union, but he reserved his most violent criticisms for the latter. True, "The Sino-Soviet controversy on matters of principle should not hinder the normalization of relations between the two states on the basis of the Five Principles of Peaceful Coexistence." Nevertheless, it was evident that Chou found it basically impossible to distinguish, in any meaningful way, State-to-State relations from philosophical debate on Marxist theory. He employed an ancient Chinese saying to mark a shift in the Chinese line: where Peking had been announcing to all and sundry that the USSR was about to attack the PRC, Chou now said that the West wanted indeed "to urge the Soviet revisionists eastward to divert the peril towards China," but, "At present, the Soviet revisionists are 'making a feint to the east while attacking in the west,' and stepping up their contention in Europe and their expansion in the Mediterranean, the

Indian Ocean and every place their hands can reach." The Maoist attempt to alarm the United States and its West European allies was plain to see. This was not a simple dispute about the interpretation of modern-day Marxism.

The new Party Constitution set forth the Party's world view in general terms:

The Communist Party of China upholds proletarian internationalism and opposes great-power chauvinism; it firmly unites with the genuine Marxist-Leninist Parties and organizations the world over, unites with the proletariat, the oppressed peoples and nations of the whole world and fights together with them to oppose the hegemonism of the two super-powers—the United States and the Soviet Union—to overthrow imperialism, modern revisionism and all reaction, and to abolish the exploitation of man by man over the globe, so that all mankind will be emancipated.

This was of the essence of Mao Tse-tung's apocalyptic world view—for all the ceremonial genuflections before the doctrine of "peaceful coexistence."

ABORTED SUCCESSION: TWO LINES

The Tenth Congress did not in fact resolve the conflict at the top between the "two lines." Instead, it exacerbated that conflict. Mao Tse-tung and his immediate cohorts still occupied commanding positions; the revolutionary urge was still running strongly in their ranks, and they were unreconciled to a "bourgeois" stability. But the critical problems facing the nation demanded practical approaches. The modernization of industry was proceeding at a slow tempo; agriculture was still backward and hardly keeping pace with the demands of industry for such elements as raw cotton and the demands of the growing population for food; and the educational establishment had been crippled by the Maoist demand that it be molded to the pattern and purposes of the vaunted "proletarian dictatorship." For those problems, the voluntarist element of the Thought of Mao Tse-tung was unable to supply real answers. The conditions against which Lin Piao had reputedly been ready to rebel remained in being.

With the disappearance and disgrace of Lin Piao, the PLA had been left without either Minister of Defense or Chief of General Staff. The Tenth Party Congress did not repair that deficit. The importance of the military, considerably enhanced during the GPCR, had been somewhat reduced. The outstanding PLA figure was now

PEKING, APRIL 4, 1976. MEMORIAL WREATHS HONORING CHOU EN-LAI FESTOON THE MOMUMENT TO THE HEROES OF THE PEOPLE, TIEN AN MEN SQUARE.

CANTON, OCTOBER 25, 1976. POPULAR CELE-BRATION OF PURGE OF "THE GANG OF FOUR." CARICATURE FIGURES, LEFT TO RIGHT: YAO WEN-YUAN, WANG HUNG-WEN, CHANG CH'UN-CH'IAO, CHIANG CH'ING.

he year 1976 witnessed revolutionary developments in the factional struggle over the suc-ession in China. In April, after the death of Premier Chou En-lai, by Mao's initiative Vice remier Teng Hsiao-p'ing was purged and Hua Kuo-feng was appointed to the premier-iip. But, after the death of Chairman Mao in September, the radical leadership was purged its turn.

Wide World Photos

PEKING, OCTOBER 25, 1976. RALLY OF A MILLION ARMYMEN AND CIVILIANS IN CELEBRATION OF HUA KUO-FENG'S ACCESSION TO PARTY POWER AND OF THE PURGE OF "THE GANG OF FOUR."

Wide World Photos

PEKING, SEPTEMBER 10, 1977. THE NEW PARTY/STATE LEADERSHIP PAYS HOMAGE TO THE EMBALMED CHAIRMAN IN THE MAO TE-TUNG MAUSOLEUM. FROM LEFT TO RIGHT: CCP CHAIRMAN HUA KUO-FENG, VICE CHAIRMEN YEH CHIEN-YING, TENG HSIAO-P'ING, LI HSIEN-NIEN, WANG TUNG-HSING.

PEKING, 1977. NIGHT VIEW OF MAO TSE-TUNG MAUSOLEUM.   Wide World Photos

With the purge of the radical faction, the governing apparatus headed by Hua Kuo-feng promptly altered course in domestic policy and returned to a pragmatic line. Twice-purged Teng Hsiao-p'ing shortly reappeared, to participate in a new ruling hierarchy of five which drew authority for domestic and foreign policy alike from the Thought of deceased Chairman Mao Tse-tung.

Yeh Chien-ying, Old Comrade of Long March days, currently occupying the position of vice chairman of the CCP military commission and fourth Party vice chairman—after Wang Hung-wen and
K'ang Sheng. This was in a situation where the succession struggle
—nominally and "legally" settled by the Ninth Party Congress—had
been automatically set in motion again with the death and political
disgrace of Lin Piao. If Chou En-lai as first vice chairman ranked
next to Chairman Mao Tse-tung in the Party hierarchy, it was to be
remarked that he had constituted a stabilizing, i.e. "pragmatic,"
force in government during the GPCR. Would the radicals be
reconciled to his accession to supreme power? Second Vice Chairman Wang Hung-wen had risen as a meteor within the Party
hierarchy—patently as a favorite of Chairman Mao. In the Politburo, he would find support in Chiang Ch'ing—and also in Yao
Wen-yuan, another Politburo member (and another Shanghai man)
who during the GPCR had served faithfully as mouthpiece for
Mao's revolutionism. If the design of the Tenth Congress was to
introduce a new period of "great order" after a period of "great
disorder," in the Maoist cycle, the design was faulty.

At the end of 1973, Peking with manifest calculation transferred
to new assignments various commanders of Military Regions who
had won power during the GPCR. The Lin Piao political structure
was being dismantled. It appeared that civilian authority had re-
established dominance over the military, in accordance with the
Maoist dictum that "The Party commands the gun, and the gun
must never be allowed to command the Party."

But the Party was not at peace with itself. It was not long before
the Maoist faction resumed the "class struggle." that interminable
contention between the "two lines"—Mao's "proletarian revolutionary" line and the "bourgeois revisionist" line. Shortly after the Tenth
CCP Congress, the Chinese media (controlled in main by the radicals) launched a new campaign—this time an attack on Confucius. The ancient philosopher was charged with favoring slavery.
But the Confucian school was opposed in the third century B.C., the
argument ran, by Legalists such as Hsun Tzu and his disciple Han
Fei Tzu, representing the progressives of the feudal class. By the
Maoist interpretation, "The struggle between the Confucian School
and the Legalist school . . . was an expression of the class struggle
on the ideological front at that time." [16]

This new campaign was shortly given modern application: it was
broadened to include Lin Piao, as an "ultra-Rightist," who was

"truly a faithful disciple of Confucius," and "an agent of the land-lord class and the bourgeoisie." [17] And the quoted editorial re-marked in passing that Lin Piao's attack on Ch'in Shih Huang-ti, the Legalist emperor who had unified China and founded the Ch'in Dynasty in 221 B.C., "was in fact a disguised and sinister attack on the dictatorship of the proletariat." The thesis was expanded to give favorable place to the Legalist doctrines of Shang Yang,[18] who "opposed the idea of 'following the ancient way,'" opposed the ancient rites and music, and, among other things, proposed agri-cultural reform and encouraged military achievement. On Feb-ruary 2, 1974, the *People's Daily* called editorially for carrying the "p'i-Lin p'i-K'ung" (criticize Lin and Confucius) campaign on to the end. And the second 1974 issue of *Red Flag*, the Party organ, likewise contained an editorial calling for amplification and deepen-ing of the "p'i-Lin p'i-K'ung" movement. One of the charges against Confucius, that he had said it was necessary "to cause extinct states to be reborn, to raise up again disinherited noble families, to restore to positions those who have entered the shadows," was strongly suggestive, in part, of Chou En-lai more than Lin Piao: had it not been Premier Chou who had engineered the return to power, via the Tenth Congress, of such "capitalist-roaders" as Teng Hsiao-p'ing et al.?

And there was a further parallel to be noted: the treatment accorded Ch'in Shih Huang as having overturned the feudal system and then introducing various progressive measures readily evoked in the public mind the image of the great modern revolutionary, Mao Tse-tung. That Ch'in Shih Huang had been the complete auto-crat, the "dictator" *par excellence,* did not seem to deter Mao's sup-porters from playing on the image; Ch'in Shih Huang-ti had been The Leader who ruthlessly destroyed The Old and introduced "new things"—if hardly anything that could logically be equated with "*socialist new things.*"

The "p'i-Lin p'i-K'ung" campaign was patently a political device invented by the radicals with the aim of advancing their cause in the power struggle with the pragmatists. It continued during the year 1974. But it was all too obviously an artificial political ploy: Confucius had been dead for nearly two and a half millennia; and Lin Piao had conclusively departed the earthly sphere. The radicals had no warrant in the decisions of the Tenth Congress for speeding up their political vehicle, the "Cultural Revolution" that would keep "politics in command," other than such support as Mao Tse-tung could and would give them. And Mao's powers were patently waning. Efforts on the part of the radical faction to build up momentum behind their attack on those who inferentially supported the "reactionary" program propagated by Confucious and Lin Piao of "Restrain oneself and return to the rites [e.g. the rules— discipline]" failed to make headway; the not-so-subtle endeavors to identify Chou En-lai with Confucious also failed. For the time being, the leadership issue remained dormant.

It was the personality, and the spirit, of Chou En-lai that dominated the brief Fourth National People's Congress, meeting January 13–17, 1975—a full decade after the convening of the Third Congress. Significantly, Mao Tse-tung did not attend—although he was quite well enough at that time to receive Franz-Joseph Strauss, Chairman of the Christian Social Union of West Germany. The rubber-stamp gathering performed its assigned tasks with dispatch. A new state constitution was adopted that followed the prevailing line by stipulating in the Preamble that China should build socialism independently, through self-reliance; should strengthen its unity "with the socialist countries [no differentiations made] and all oppressed people and oppressed nations" and "oppose the hegemonism of the superpowers." [19]

When it came to specifics, there were interesting emphases. In the realm of power, "The People's Republic of China is a socialist state of the dictatorship of the proletariat led by the working class and based on the alliance of workers and peasants" (Art. 1). But the workers and peasants had guidance: "The Communist Party of China is the core of leadership of the whole Chinese people . . ." (Art. 2). And so did the ultimate state authority: "The National People's Congress is the highest organ of state power under the leadership of the Communist Party of China" (Art. 16). In the domestic field, "democratic centralism" was to govern; the aim was to create a political situation "in which there are both centralism and democracy, both discipline and freedom, both unity of will and personal ease of mind and liveliness . . ." (Art. 13). If this was suggestive of a Maoist contradiction, a more clear-cut trend was confirmed in the provision of Article 12 that "Culture and education, literature and art, physical education, health work and scientific research work, must all serve proletarian politics. . . ." And the constitution provided that State organs and personnel must "firmly put proletarian politics in command . . . " (Art. 11) All this was on the ideological line of the Maoist radicals.

But the appointment of Marshal Yeh Chien-ying to the post of Minister of Defense—vacant since the Lin Piao episode of 1971—evidenced the strength of conservative military elements in the Chou En-lai scheme of things. Moreover, the constitutional provisions regarding economic matters showed a clear trend away from Maoist radicalism; there, pragmatism reigned. That same pragmatism impregnated Chou En-lai's "Report on the Work of the Government." He gave ritualistic obeisance to the movement to criticize Lin Piao and Confucius, repeated the unremitting Chinese charge that the two superpowers "are the biggest international oppressors and exploiters today, and they are the source of a new world war," and held that "The third world is the main force in combating colonialism, imperialism and hegemonism"—and China belonged to that world. But his main stress was on the need to work hard to increase economic production, and the need for successful completion in 1975 of the Fourth Five-Year Plan. Referring to past economic programs, he envisaged the construction of "an independent and relatively comprehensive industrial and economic system . . . before 1980," and the accomplishment of "the comprehensive modernization of agriculture, industry, national defence and science and technology before the end of the century, so that our national economy will be advancing in the front ranks of the world."

The master pragmatist Teng Hsiao-p'ing, having recovered less than two years before from his purging, had been Vice Chairman of the CCP Central Committee, and member of the Standing Committee of the Politburo, at the Central Committee's second plenum, held just before the NPC itself. Now, at the NPC, he became the highest-ranking of twelve Vice Premiers; thus, he stood first in line to succeed ailing Premier Chou En-lai. It seemed certain that the arrangement had the sanction of Chou, but whether it also had the blessing of Mao Tse-tung appeared distinctly more problematical.

In sum total, the Fourth NPC, while paying lip-service to Mao Tse-tung and his Thought, appeared to provide a fresh concentration of national effort in the economic field, and plans for an orderly succession. But the "contradictions" evidenced by the constitution, and by Chang Ch'un-ch'iao's report on the revision of that document and Chou En-lai's political report, constituted clear indication that the conflict between the "two lines" had not been definitively resolved.

Chou En-lai's illness contributed to the buildup of a political crisis. If Teng Hsiao-p'ing was patently, and quasi-legally, booked to be Chou's successor, Teng the pragmatist had strong enemies— in particular the radical faction. Signs of an impending clash appeared in the field of education. In the post-GPCR period, the stress had been on enrollment of workers, peasants, and soldiers into the PRC's enfeebled institutions of higher learning—with "practical experience" and political motivation the determining qualifications for entrance rather than scholarship. The quality of the graduate had suffered along with the quality of education, to the detriment of China's science and technology, not to mention the fine arts. In the latter part of 1975, charges were circulated—and sent to Mao Tse-tung—that existing educational policies had resulted in a decline in academic standards. The matter became a public issue in December with the appearance of articles in Peking's official publications charging that there were those who proposed to reverse the revolution in education. The joining of the issue was inevitable: the radical faction considered that the matter of first priority was the training of a generation of revolutionary successors to power in the current Maoist mold of political *and economic* orthodoxy, and the faction decried reference to scholarship as a standard; but in the eyes of the opposition, the decline of academic standards threatened China's advance to power—and for them this was of prime concern.

The clash over educational policies was only one manifestation of the larger struggle, that over the succession to power. The death of Chou En-lai on January 8, 1976, removed his steadying influence and sparked a series of political quakes. Vice Premier Teng Hsiao-p'ing presided over the memorial service held on January 15; but he did not succeed to the premiership as anticipated. Instead, on February 7 there came the surprising announcement that Minister of Public Security Hua Kuo-feng, a little-known figure, had been made Acting Premier, and there appeared wall posters attacking an allegedly "unrepentant capitalist-roader" who had said that "It doesn't matter whether the cat is black or white, so long as it catches mice"—Teng Hsiao-p'ing! Publicity organs stepped up the campaign against those who were "blowing the Right deviationist wind to reverse previous verdicts," and would "negate the principle of taking class struggle as the key link" by advocating putting "unity and stability" and "develop the national economy" on the same level of principle, thus making those three Maoist "instructions" the key link to all work.[20] The transparently disguised "capitalist roader" in point was soon pinned with another cognomen—"China's Khrushchev." The leader of the attack against Teng, it appeared, was GPCR activist Chiang Ch'ing, Mao's wife.

The development climaxed on April 4, the Ch'ing Ming festival. On that date great masses of people crowded into the T'ien An Men Square in Peking and in an outwardly spontaneous outpouring of sentiment piled up great heaps of wreaths and placards to commemorate the deceased Chou En-lai. Some of the placards were political in character; in particular, there were reported attacks on Chiang Ch'ing—and, worse, assertions that the era of Ch'in Shih Huang had ended. Overnight, the police removed the wreaths *and* placards, and on the following day there was rioting in the square. On April 7, "On the proposal of our great leader Chairman Mao," the Party Politburo dismissed Teng Hsiao-p'ing from all posts "both inside and outside the Party" (but not from his Party membership) and apponted Hua Kuo-feng First Vice Chairman of the CCP Central Committee and Premier of the Government. No matter that the Politburo lacked the legal authority to dismiss Teng from the post of Vice Premier or to make Hua Premier: had not Chairman Mao proposed such action? The press coverage of the dismissal of Teng (e.g., a *People's Daily* editorial of April 10) left no doubt that Teng had been ousted by Mao Tse-tung's decision. Chou En-lai's carefully arranged succession plans, which envisaged the accession of pragmatists to power for the benefit of China's economy and polity alike, had been thrown awry.

Certain events that followed in the year might well have been taken by the Chinese nation as bad omens. There came an official announcement in June that Chairman Mao Tse-tung would no longer receive foreign visitors. On July 6, death came to Chu Teh, founder of the Red Army and chairman of the Standing Committee of the NPC. There had been a serious earthquake in Yunnan Province in May; now, at the end of July, a devastating earthquake hit North China. Its epicenter was the important mining town of Tangshan, which was effectively destroyed, with heavy loss of life. This was followed, in August, by yet another quake in northern Szechwan. Those imbued with traditional Chinese superstition might well have concluded that the natural disasters presaged political calamity. And, in fact, on September 9 CCP Chairman Mao Tse-tung died.

Mao had indubitably won an unassailable place in history as a great revolutionary who had changed the face of China. He and his comrades-in-arms had overthrown a corrupt, anachronistic regime that had been insensible to the needs of the people. They had wiped out the oppressive "feudalistic" system of land tenure, introduced a far greater measure of social egalitarianism (liberating women from their many remaining social disabilities in the process), rehabilitated the economy, and constructed a system of economic distribution that was far better designed than the old to meet the needs of the nation.

Under Mao's leadership, there had come better hygiene, a lower death rate, and a vast reduction in both crime and corruption. With planning, the nation had progressed, waxed stronger, and prospered —relatively. In the manner of the T'aip'ing rebels, Mao had assailed old evils, including the perennial bane of bureaucracy. He had demonstrated a truly giant imagination in conception, and great boldness in execution, of national plans. Mao Tse-tung will go down in history as one of the great earthshakers.

And yet, in his declining years Mao had manifested a revolutionary impatience and a tendency to give loose rein to some of the more millenarian—and more unsound—elements of his philosophical compound. A narrow ethnocentrism of the sort upon occasion termed by the Communists themselves "Great Han chauvinism," combined with a sadly warped estimate of world trends, brought him to lead the nation into protracted warfare against Soviet "revisionism" (in due course termed "social imperialism"); an anarchistic voluntarism led him into the excesses of the Great Leap Forward, and hatred of pragmatism and bureaucracy caused him to launch the Great Proletarian Cultural Revolution—to purge Party elements that opposed his policies. Overwhelmed finally by that autocratic belief in his own omniscience and omnipotence that governed the ancient emperors, so that he finally found an ideal prototype for himself in Ch'in Shih Huang-ti, Mao Tse-tung had first rendered the concept of "democratic centralism" meaningless and then committed the ultimate error of destroying the "socialist legality" that was the Party's mainstay.

Reference to a historical parallel is suggestive in this regard. In December, 1956, after de-Stalinization, the *People's Daily* in an editorial entitled "More on the Historical Experience of the Dictatorship of the Proletariat" set forth an authoritative treatment of Stalin's role. The editor(s) judged that the Soviet leader had made a great contribution to the progress of the USSR and to the development of international Communism, but held further that he had also made some serious mistakes in both domestic and foreign policies. The editorial continued: "His arbitrary method of work impaired to a certain extent the principle of democratic centralism both in the life of the Party and in the state system of the Soviet Union, and led to a partial disruption of socialist legality. . . . In suppressing counterrevolutionaries, Stalin . . . wronged many loyal Communists and honest citizens." In tackling certain concrete questions with regard to relations with brother countries and parties, Stalin "showed a tendency toward great-nation chauvinism and himself lacked a spirit of equality. . . . Sometimes he even intervened mistakenly, and with many grave consequences, in the internal affairs of certain brother countries and parties." [21]

The editor(s) had an explanation for Stalin's having fallen into error. It was complex:

. . . . the decisive factor is man's ideological condition. A series of victories and the eulogies which Stalin received in the latter part of his life turned his head. He deviated partly, but grossly, from the dialectical materialist way of thinking and fell into subjectivism. He began to put blind faith into personal wisdom and authority; he would not investigate and study complicated conditions seriously or listen carefully to the opinions of his comrades and the voice of the masses. As a result, some of the policies and measures he adopted were often at variance with objective reality. He often stubbornly persisted in carrying out these mistaken measures over long periods and was unable to correct his mistakes in time.

And, said the editor(s), "One of the gravest consequences of Stalin's mistakes was the growth of doctrinairism."

It is highly improbable that the editors of the *People's Daily* thought in 1956 (which can perhaps properly be taken as the last year of Mao's pragmatic stage) that their judgments would come home to roost in two short decades; but this, to a remarkable degree and in unexpected ways, had happened. Mao Tse-tung, by the time of his death in 1976, had quite discredited both his personality cult and his "uninterrupted revolution"; he had unwittingly laid the foundation for a Chinese Communist "revisionism," that is, for the introduction of political forms and processes of which illuminist Mao would have strongly disapproved. And this unhappy fate for his Thought would in large measure be of Mao's own making. In his later years Mao had aspired to be equated with Ch'in Shih Huang-ti, who had assaulted the conservative, "stable" Confucian philosophy and unified Chinese society on the basis of Legalist concept; but the irony of it all was that, even as Ch'in Shih

Huang-ti's Legalism would be thrust back by a renascent (and revised) Confucianism, so some of the more "revolutionary" elements of Mao's philosophy were destined to be discarded by the pragmatists of the Party that he had helped to create. For those elements, too, were often "at variance with objective reality."

Mao Tse-tung indeed fulfilled what must have been one of his lifelong ambitions, namely to outlive Chiang Kai-shek (d. 1975). It was perhaps Mao's misfortune, however, in terms of the credit that will be accorded him by posterity, that he also outlived so long the period of his fundamental pragmatism.

For Mao Tse-tung left a flawed legacy. One of the purposes of the Cultural Revolution from 1964 onwards had been to bring into being "socialist man" motivated not by acquisitiveness and ambition but by revolutionary fervor and a pervasive sense of social responsibility. The GPCR's purpose had been to crown that aim: it would have rid China of the bourgeois spirit and proletarianized the nation.

Again it is instructive to hark back to antiquity. One reason that it proved possible to weld Confucianism and Legalism together to provide China with an imperial philosophy was that the two philosophies had certain elements in common. The concepts of conformity and authority were two such elements. Confucius said: "In the Book of Poetry there are three hundred poems. But the essence of them can be covered by one sentence: 'Have no depraved thoughts.'" The Legalists also felt the high desirability of the subject people's having "no depraved thoughts," particularly in a political sense, and so too did Mao Tse-tung.

Legalism, Confucianism, and Maoism were also similar in their dogmatic assumption that Chinese Truth is universal truth. Maoism, if decked out in modern garb, has in it important elements of the older Chinese philosophies. But there are also radical departures. Where Confucianism designed that the political universe should be kept in stable balance, Maoism has proposed "uninterrupted revolution" through manipulation of "contradictions" to achieve progressive political ends. In practice this meant the pitting of one force against another, one social group against another, in a stimulation of popular antagonisms by virtue of which one group unwanted by the Communist Party would be eliminated until the ideal homogenous classless society would have been brought into being. Finally, during the Great Proletarian Cultural Revolution, Mao undertook to mobilize supporters of his doctrine against those *within* the Party who opposed his voluntarist undertakings in the fields of both politics and economics, and thus fostered factionalism. An intra-Party struggle for power upon the death of Mao consequently became not just a possibility, but a probability.

The Maoist political tactics implanted a basically destructive element in Chinese society. In his 1957 thinking "On the Correct Handling of Contradictions Among the People," Mao said of the people's democratic dictatorship: "Its first function is to suppress the reactionary classes and elements and those exploiters in the country who range themselves against the socialist revolution, to suppress all who try to wreck our socialist construction." The Maoist approach to the task of "struggle" (against designated "enemies") relied heavily upon the tactics of attacking one objective at a time, and, once that task was accomplished, then selecting another target. Mao even provided a dialectical rationale to govern such shifts, in his work "On Practice":

When a certain objective process has already advanced and changed from one stage to another, [the true revolutionary leader must] be adept at making himself and all his fellow revolutionaries advance and revise their subjective ideas accordingly, that is to say, he must propose new revolutionary tasks and new working programs corresponding to changes in the new situation.

"Truth" thus was viewed as changing with evolution of the political situation, and those citizens accorded an approved categorization today for tactical reasons might be damned as "enemies" tomorrow. The doctrine demanded that the people continually be "persuaded" of that protean truth. But this involved the surmounting of a truly major obstacle: how could the regime cause the Chinese mass man to believe with equal faith and enthusiasm one thing today and its opposite tomorrow, especially when the persuasion, given the implicit threat behind it, was in the final analysis coercive? The problem was one of creating a mind so attuned to CCP dialectics, as defined by Mao Tse-tung the Leader, that it would react to Mao's postulated changing situation as if by reflex, and in mass. Man was to become robot.

The chief instrument available to the Maoists for their purpose was education (in all its aspects), which they regarded, as had the rulers of old, as a means of social control. The educational process basically followed the thought of Mao Tse-tung, who had early set forth pungent views on the subject. In his statement of February,

1942, "On Correcting Unorthodox Tendencies in Learning, the Party, and Literature and Art," he defined a basic term:

What is knowledge? From ancient times down to the present, there have been only two types of knowledge: one type is knowledge of the struggle in production; the other is knowledge of the class struggle, in which is included knowledge of the national struggle. What knowledge is there aside from this? There is none.

That harsh circumscribing of the role of knowledge provided little place for art and literature. Speaking in May of the same year to a forum at Yenan on literature and art, Mao was cruelly narrow in his definition of the function of fine arts:

Art for art's sake, art which transcends class or party, art which stands as a bystander to, or independent of politics, does not in actual fact exist. . . .

Proletarian literature and art are one part of the entire proletarian revolutionary cause. . . .

We not only do not recognize abstract and eternal political standards, but also do not recognize such standards for art.

Our demand . . . is a unity of politics and art, a unity of content and form, and a unity of revolutionary political content and an artistic form of as high a standard as possible.[22]

The primary aim was a remolding of Chinese intellectual life and the Chinese mind, with destruction of the old loyalties of the traditional "five relationships" (sovereign-minister, father-son, husband-wife, brothers, friends) in favor of *one* loyalty—that to the Party/State, supposed to represent "the whole people." The Common Program of 1949 clearly indicated a design for the service of national political objectives in the stipulation that the purpose of education was "the raising of the cultural level of the people, the training of personnel for national construction work, the eradicating of feudal, compradore, and fascist ideology, and the developing of the ideology of service to the people."

Formal education thus was "planned study in the Marxist spirit," designed to induce conformity. The teaching staff, with allowances made for older professors taken over from the precedent system (who, however, had to undergo thought reform), was fitted to the Maoist mold. Students were subjected to the same formative process through criticism, self-criticism, denunciation of their fellows, demands for conversion, and finally confession, just as if one were an errant landlord.

After Liberation, the new education placed heavy emphasis on engineering, science, and technical training; it was aimed at providing personnel for the staffing of a new, industrialized China. At the same time there was a heavy downgrading of the humanities. The quantitative advance was partially vitiated by the arbitrary selection of educational goals.

Political indoctrination courses were prominent in all curricula, in line with the concept that education was basically for the service of proletarian politics. The worker-citizen was expected to become both "Red and expert." But in education as in industry and agriculture, the governing concept was "politics in command," and this factor ultimately exercised a critical influence. In the late 1950s half-study-half-work programs were instituted in the universities, and regular work-study schools were organized in the provinces. Students and professors were regularly dispatched to the fields and factories to perform manual labor alongside the regular workers. The intellectual was to acquire the viewpoint of the laboring masses. The governing slogan in that regard was "Intellectualize the proletariat; proletarianize the intelligentsia!"

Individualism, whether as idiosyncrasy or creativity, was automatically ruled out. But if the purpose of that approach to education was to achieve a very considerable molding of Chinese minds, the net result was inevitably a reduction of intellectual mobility and an increase of ideological rigidity. Whereas the new jobs requiring a middle-range education were far fewer than the tens of millions of Chinese currently being given education on that level, there was an evident urgent need for brains of the first order in all walks of life; yet, the new learning process had the effect of leveling down the intellectual peaks. The thinking process became increasingly barren.

It was partly in an effort to overcome that drawback and evoke ideas sorely needed by the strictly conformist Party that the Hundred Flowers invitation was issued. And criticism in due course ensued—in force and volume. But the critics, when sharply put down after attacking the Communist order of things that had brought about the sterility, withdrew within themselves once more and remained silent during the Great Leap while the Communist cadres committed egregious errors in the fields of both agriculture and industry. However, the unregenerate behavior of the older men during the Hundred Flowers period can only have confirmed the

Communist leaders in their original judgment that the "bourgeois" intellectuals were incorrigible.

The process of thought reform reached its ultimate definition in the Cultural Revolution that was launched in 1964 and was metamorphosed in 1966 into the Great Proletarian Cultural Revolution. In that latest effort to discredit "bourgeois" ideology (and incidentally heretical "modern revisionism") and to remake the minds of the intellectuals and indeed of the entire nation, existing educational structures, from professorial staff to curricula, were battered out of recognition. Many academicians were attacked for their teaching, and dismissed; "bourgeois" textbooks were destroyed. The GPCR, at first diverted from "sensitive" research areas, in due course smashed its way into the Academia Sinica, China's academy of sciences. It penetrated such organs as the Scientific and Technological Commission, charged with programming the development of weapons for China's military establishment. The Revolution was universal.

If the destruction came easily to the inspired Red Guards, reconstruction was more difficult. The drive was against bourgeois "liberalism," anathema to Mao Tse-tung because it condoned the harboring of deviant views, and against intellectual elitism as such. But if the existing staff of teachers was humbled and discredited, would they be prepared to resume their teaching functions, as if nothing had happened, when the storm had passed? The answer was given in the spring of 1967 when the government ordered the schools to open again: many teachers, not to mention the Red Guard students, failed to put in an appearance. There were other practical questions. Would Chinese education be stronger if limited to the slavish mouthing of Maoist phrases? How far, after all, would the Thought go toward replacing textbooks on either the social sciences or technological subjects? Maoism alone obviously would not meet all needs for new knowledge; and, with the general discarding of existing scholarship, the production of scholarly works *without* specific Maoist sanction would be scanty.

The projection of the Maoist populist educational doctrine into the post-GPCR period proved the point—to the satisfaction of organization men such as Chou En-lai and Teng Hsiao-p'ing, and of military men such as Yeh Chien-ying. The attack by the Maoists on educators for concerning themselves with theory and pure science instead of emphasizing practical knowledge (such as possessed by peasants and workers) and applied science, the insistence that higher education should be governed by the concepts put forward by workers and peasants, the condemnation of borrowing of foreign technical knowledge as constituting "slavish devotion to things foreign," all brought about a general perversion of the Chinese educational process. It is not too much to say that two generations of college students were wasted in the years of 1966–76. And prominent in the development of the policy of wastage were supporters of Mao Tsetung, and in particular Chiang Ch'ing and Yao Wen-yuan.

The cost to the national enterprise was high. Agriculture remained in large measure backward, deprived of the mechanical advances promised earlier by the Chinese leadership. Industrialization was retarded, by the stress put on the doctrine of "self-reliance," to the extent that potentially useful foreign scientific knowledge was neglected. And this, combined with Chairman Mao's primitive contention that man, not weapons, is decisive in modern warfare, gave rise to a deficiency that was to prove decisive in the power struggle in Peking: the Chinese military finally reached the conclusion that the defense establishment was dangerously inferior to those of potential major enemies in all *but* manpower, and that P'eng Teh-huai was right in 1959 when he argued in favor of acquiring advanced weaponry. In circumstances where prominent figures of the Communist era, even as most other influential Chinese leaders of the twentieth century, have yearned to have China attain to a position of wealth and power in the world, that conviction finally gained too many adherants for the Maoist populists to overcome. The advance of the PLA to prominence during the period of the GPCR gave military chieftains a new solidarity, and a new sense of their critical importance—a sense strengthened by the belief that existing policies were blocking the road to military modernization. If the attempts at the Ninth and Tenth Party Congresses to reduce the power of the military, taken in conjunction with the purge of Lin Piao and some of his prominent lieutenants, represented an effort again to subordinate the Army to the Party, Mao Tse-tung's own anti-Party policies weakened the effort—and created a sense of common purpose among prominent military men.

Thus, the seeming social calm that followed the purge of Lin Piao had been deceptive. It can be roughly estimated that the Party's claim to possess virtues entitling it to a special position of leadership carried general conviction through 1957. The Hundred Flowers episode, however, capped by the stupendous bungle of the

Great Leap, probably marked a turning point of sorts for the Chinese people, who possess abundant earthy political sophistication. And when, in the course of the GPCR, Mao led the attack on many of the country's highest leaders and on the sacrosanct Party itself, leaving only himself omniscient, all-virtuous, and inviolate, what would remain of the body of faith that had been built up? People would once more put their faith in, and accord their respect to, power; and the PLA commanded *organized* power.

The Chinese had been taught that the only good—and the only safety—was to be a Maoist; and so they appeared outwardly to be. They conformed. But there was the social habit of conformity in Confucian times, too, and it was best to assume that there was ache in some of the old scars and disabilities, that certain aspects of the current scene might in some respects reflect the weird and disturbing phenomenon of mass play-acting without belief, what the Chinese of old called "outward conformity, inner alienation."

It was therefore premature to conclude, as some observers did, that the Maoist experiment had succeeded in molding the mass mind, to the end that all men should react automatically and in uniformity in accord with a shifting but unerring pattern as conceived by The Leader. The "bourgeois" intelligentsia that played such an important role in China's past had been purged indeed, and a pervasive intellectual sterility had begun to afflict the nation, but it remained to be seen whether "proletarian intellectuals" any more than their elitist predecessors would limit their thinking to the bounds fixed by the Dogma; or how, if they were to do so, China could attain its national—and international—goals.[23]

15 CHINA AFTER MAO

IN MARXIST THEORY, the proletarian revolution is to liberate man from class oppression and economic exploitation—and coincidentally to liberate the human spirit. In March, 1971, the editorial departments of the *People's Daily*, *Red Flag*, and *Liberation Army Daily* issued a joint piece entitled "Long Live the Victory of the Dictatorship of the Proletariat!" in commemoration of the Paris Commune of a century earlier. They quoted Marx: the Commune of 1871 was "the dawn of the great social revolution which will liberate mankind from the regime of classes forever." Nevertheless, in an important sense the Chinese reality denied the Marxist dream. The Paris Commune, after all, had not been founded on the concept of the dictatorship of the proletariat; and by Mao's own proclaimed philosophic concept, the people's will (the *narodnaya volya* of the Russian nineteenth-century populists) should govern. But the political structure that had emerged from the Cultural Revolution was far from being one designed for the expression of the popular will; it was instead one that regimented, to an extent uncomfortably suggestive of Legalist theory, both the bodies and the minds of the citizenry. The aspirations, and the will, of the nation—and particularly of the intelligentsia, the bureaucrats, and the military alike —had been better expressed in the practical concept voiced by Premier Chou En-lai at the Fourth National People's Congress in 1975. Chou was now dead; but so, too, in September, 1976, was Mao Tse-tung.

PRAGMATISTS TO POWER

After the purge in April 1976 of Teng Hsiao-p'ing, the avowedly true Maoist believers had carried on a campaign of denigration of the disgraced Vice Premier, now associating him in obloquy with Liu Shao-ch'i and Lin Piao, and with other unnamed "capitalist-roaders" still in power. The oft-reiterated refrain was that Teng had long opposed the Chairman's proletarian revolutionary line, collaborating with Liu Shao-ch'i to promote revisionism even before the Great Proletarian Cultural Revolution. The villainous Teng, it was charged, instead of giving priority to the class struggle had wanted to effect an overall rectification of practices and procedures that would reinforce regulations and discipline, give industrial command to expert administrators, stress scientific technology, introduce material incentives, and even make use of imported technology, for the devolpment of the Chinese economy. This was of course a denial of Mao Tse-tung's revolutionary philosophy as developed during the Great Proletarian Cultural Revolution that had given birth to the "socialist new things" linked to Mao's voluntarism.

Mao's disappearance from public view in June had bereft the radical faction of a major element of support, and the campaign against alleged "capitalist-roaders" had faltered. The radicals suffered a new setback with the Tangshan earthquake: the magnitude of the disaster made their polemics sound trivial in comparison. Then had come Mao's demise. The adjurations contained in the official announcement of his death were within the framework of recent polemical conventions:

We must carry on the cause left behind by Chairman Mao and persist in taking class struggle as the key link, keep to the Party's basic line and persevere in continuing the revolution under the dictatorship of the proletariat. . . .

We must . . . deepen the criticism of Teng Hsiao-p'ing, continue the struggle to repulse the Right deviationist attempt at reversing correct verdicts, consolidate and develop the victories of the Great Proletarian Cultural Revolution, enthusiastically support the socialist new things, restrict bourgeois right and further consolidate the dictatorship of the proletariat in our country. We should continue to unfold the three great revolutionary movements of class struggle, the struggle for production and scientific experiment, build our country independently and with the initiative in our own hands, through self-reliance, hard struggle, diligence and thrift, and go all out, aim higher and achieve greater, faster, better and more economical results in building socialism.[1]

The announcement, issued jointly by top organs of both Party and Government, recounted how Mao had led the Party to wage protracted and complex intra-Party struggles to defeat Right and Left opportunist lines pursued by various Party figures—including defeat of "the counter-revolutionary revisionist line of Liu Shao-chi, Lin Piao and Teng Hsiao-ping. . . ."

On October 1, the anniversary of the establishment of the CPR, the *People's Daily* carried an editorial exhorting the nation to follow Mao's proletarian revolutionary line. The editorial paid nominal tribute to the need for damping down factionalism, the need for Party unity, by citing the Maoist "three do's and three don'ts" dictum that had been given emphasis at the "unity" Tenth CCP Congress of 1973. That the writers of the editorial were not prepared to renounce their drive on the designated prime "capitalist-roader," however, was indicated in their directive on the demands of the current situation. Stigmatizing as "poisonous weeds" three down-to-earth official studies prepared under the direction of Teng Hsiao-p'ing—"On the General Programme for All Work of the Party and the Country," "Some Problems Concerning the Work of Science and Technology," and "Some Problems in Accelerating Industrial Development"—the editors held that it was imperative to "carry the struggle to criticize Teng Hsiao-ping and repulse the Right deviationist attempt at reversing correct verdicts through to the end, consolidate and develop the victories of the Great Cultural Revolution and consolidate the dictatorship of the proletariat." [2]

On October 6, four leaders of the radical faction, all members of the Politburo and all close associates of Mao in his declining years, were arrested. They were Wang Hung-wen, youthful CCP Vice Chairman: Vice Premier Chang Ch'un-ch'iao, who had been a contender for the premiership; Chiang Ch'ing, Mao's widow, who had wielded such a devastating influence on the arts in the course of the GPCR; and Yao Wen-yuan, the Shanghai journalist-polemicist. On the next day, October 7, the CCP Politburo appointed Hua Kuo-feng to the position of Party Chairman, in succession to the Great Helmsman himself.

Confirmation of Hua's appointment (as irregular as his acquisition of the post of premier) and of the arrests came only later. It was on October 21 that the New China News Agency gave official confirmation of both actions. As regards the arrested personalities, now dubbed "the Gang of Four," it was charged that they had planned a coup d'état for the seizure of Party and State power. The theme was developed, and expanded upon with variations, over the succeeding months. What might be assumed to be the final, official version of the alleged political conspiracy of the Gang of Four was finally set forth (at great length) in Premier Hua Kuo-feng's Political Report of August 12, 1977, to the Eleventh CCP Congress.

Hua held that the struggle with the "anti-Party" Gang of Four was the eleventh major struggle, in the Party's history, between the two political lines.[3] The Gang had promoted "an ultra-Right counter-revolutionary revisionist line." Their political deviationism had of course not escaped the attention of the prescient Leader, but for all of Mao's admonitions the culprits had failed to mend their ways. Mao was thus being ex post facto dissociated from the current wrongdoers—the losers.

One of the outstanding offenses of the Four was to conspire against Premier Chou En-lai by criticizing "the Duke of Chou" and "the big Confucian of our time." Other targets had been Vice Chairman Yeh Chien-ying "and many other leading comrades in the Party, the government and the army at the central and local levels." On September 11, after the death of Mao, acting without the knowledge or authorization of the Central Committee, they "notified" the provinces, municipalities, and autonomous regions that those units should report to them for instructions on important questions. They distributed arms in Shanghai for armed rebellion. "Still more sinister" was their forgery of what they claimed to be Mao's deathbed injunction, "Act upon the principles laid down." The Four, said Hua, had hoped to reverse the course of history and restore capitalism in China. He got down to particulars:

Chang Chun-chiao has been a Kuomintang secret agent, Chiang Ch'ing is a renegade, Yao Wen-yuan an alien class element, and Wang Hung-wen a new bourgeois element. The "gang of four" are a sinister clique formed of old and new counter-revolutionaries who sneaked into our Party. They are typical representatives within our Party of landlords, rich peasants, counter-revolutionaries and bad elements as well as of the old and new bourgeoisie, and they embody the desire of class enemies at home and abroad to restore capitalism in China.

Thus the radicals, who had played such a prominent role in attacking "capitalist-roaders" in the Party, were now themselves transmogrified into ultra-Rightists who had breached Mao's revolutionary line, stirred up factionalism in violation of his "three do's and three don'ts" injunction, and plotted to usurp power. The purge of their followers began with the arrest of the Four, and was ex-

tended to all sectors—Party, government, and Army—in Peking
and in the provinces. One of the chief foci of purge action was
naturally Shanghai, the home base of the Gang. And, significantly,
the population rejoiced with an enthusiasm that seemed notably
more real than had been the case in many of the "popular celebra-
tions" of recent years. The radicals had alienated in large measure
their potential popular support. So it was that the pragmatists,
headed by the man who had been thought of a short time before as
Mao's man—Premier Hua Kuo-feng—and commanding PLA support personified by Defense Minister Yeh Chien-ying, were able to
purge ultra-Maoists so readily in Mao's name and in service of his
revolutionary Thought.

The purge of the Gang of Four and their immediate supporters
effectively introduced a period of reassessment and change in the
nation's policies. The dimensions and urgency of various problems
confronting the nation tended to sanction, even dictate, the practical
rather than the romantic "metaphysical" approach of the radical
ideologues. A year later, political, industrial, and educational leaders would be found characterizing the decade of political anarchy
and economic turmoil that had ended in 1976 as "Ten lost years!" [4]
To restore political order, and recover economic momentum, was a
task of truly forbidding proportions. The restoration of Party unity
and discipline was high in the order of priorities; it was essential to
redefine the relationship between the Center and the localities,
between the Party and the masses. In government, it was requisite
to strengthen the bureaucracy, in order that it should be able to administer the vast country more effectively, in everything from running the railroads to formulating—and implementing—the nation's
Five-Year Plans for economic development. The economic factor
inexorably acted to reinforce the new regime's pragmatic thinking
in the political field. One of the charges against the Gang of Four
was that, in pursuit of their ideological fantasies, they had disrupted
industrial production and thwarted initiation of the country's Fifth
Five-Year Plan. It was held that where Mao's concept as voiced in
1949 envisaged the transformation of China from an agricultural
to an industrial country, so that it should become "a great socialist
state," and Premier Chou En-lai in his address to the Fourth National People's Congress in 1975 had set forth the tasks of mod-
ernizing agriculture, industry, national defense and science and
technology before the end of the century, so that China's national
economy would rank among the world's leaders, the Four had op-

posed the projected socialist modernization. According to a writer
in the *Peking Review,* they had "sabotaged the socialist revolution
and socialist construction and opposed building China into a modern, strong socialist country." [5] Why? The Four had argued that,
when China might be modernized, there would be, as had allegedly
happened in the Soviet Union, the restoration of capitalism. But
also, they proposed to disrupt production in order to further their
political design of usurping Party and state power.

There was yet another major charge leveled against the radicals—
one of the easiest to establish, but one of the most delicate to handle
given Mao Tse-tung's own patent connection with the matter. That
was the allegation that the Four had corrupted the arts and debased
the educational process, all to the national detriment. The responsibility, and guilt, of the radical Maoists in that field were outstanding and notorious. They were the ones who had deprecated discipline
and learning, condemned the elitism of academicians, and given
political indoctrination priority over both pure science and technological training. The impact of their influence in that particular area
was indicated by the results of a test given university *graduates* engaged in scientific and technical work in Shanghai, as reported in
October, 1977: 68 percent failed in mathematics, 70 percent in
physics, and 76 percent in chemistry. [6] In circumstances where
China sorely needed modern skills and technology, native and
foreign, for its modernization, the radicals—with Mao's support—
had truly inflicted major injury on the national enterprise.

For an ideological nation depending heavily upon the Truth for
its guidance, it was of course necessary to provide appropriate
rationale for the shifts in line. The thinking of the victors had
crystallized long before, and rationalization followed fast on the
heels of their political victory. Here the utilization made in the
Soviet Union of "Marxism-Leninism" as final standard provided useful precedent—even if Mao Tse-tung had not himself shown the
way. The man who had purported during his lifetime to be the final
authority on revolution, even on the course to be followed by revolution until the whole world should be communized, was destined
to serve after his demise as unassailable authority for orthodoxy
respecting discipline and order. Even in the funeral oration, Hua
Kuo-feng had fixed the general course: China should hold high the
Red Banner of Mao Tse-tung Thought. More concrete "Maoist"
guidelines for the future were soon produced. On December 25,
1976, at the second national conference on Learning from Tachai

in Agriculture, Chairman Hua again routinely castigated the Gang of Four for their sins, which included both the causing of "great ideological and political confusion and enormous economic losses," and presented the nation with four major tasks for 1977: the first, and main, task for the Party was to expand the mass movement to expose and criticize the Gang of Four; next came the matter of strengthening the Party; third, there should be promotion of learning from Tachai in agriculture and Taching in industry; and, finally, there should be stepped-up study of the works of Marx, Engels, Lenin, Stalin, and Chairman Mao.

With a simple substitution of the name of Lin Piao for "the Gang of Four," those four propositions could all be found in Premier Chou En-lai's report to the Tenth CCP Congress of 1973. But the proposition for the study of Mao's works was to be duly given a more specific definition. The next day, December 26 (Mao's birthday), there was published the defunct Chairman's April 1956 talk before the Party Politburo "On the Ten Major Relationships." The document had a revealing sidelight. It had first been given publicity, unofficially, via a 1967 Chinese-language volume, *Mao Tse-tung ssu-hsiang wan-sui!* (Long Live the Thought of Mao Tsetung!). It was now discovered by an American scholar who had included the original version, in English translation, in a book he had edited, that the 1976 version departed in important respects from the earlier text.[7] Notoriously, Mao Tse-tung had stood ever ready to rewrite history to suit his political convenience. It now appeared that Mao in turn was perhaps to be subjected to "reinterpretation" upon occasion, so that he would the better serve as exemplar.

The Mao speaking "On the Ten Major Relationships" (as edited) is Mao at his most pragmatic. In the first four Relationships, Mao soberly treated economic matters.[8] Here Mao stood for giving priority to the development of agriculture and light industry, which, he argued, would lead to the greater and faster development of heavy industry. In speaking of the relationship between economic construction and defense, he similarly proposed that there be a reduction of military and administrative expenditures in favor of increased investment in economic construction—in order that there could be "more progress in defense construction." As regards the relationship between the state, the production units, and the producers, he held that with increase in labor productivity there should be a gradual improvement in the working conditions and collective welfare of the workers. "With the growth of our economy as a whole, wages should be appropriately adjusted." Similarly, as regards the peasantry (then concentrated in large measure, it will be recalled, on cooperatives—not communes), he took the stand that "Except in case of extraordinary natural disasters, we must see to it that, given increased agricultural production, 90 per cent of the cooperative members get some increase in their income and the other 10 per cent break even each year, and if the latter's income should fall, ways must be found to solve the problem in good time."

In the political field, Mao stood for stimulating initiative of local authorities by granting increased local independence but proposed at the same time that the unified leadership of the central authorities be strengthened. That seemed like a Maoist contradiction, but Mao clarified the matter to a degree by holding that there should be definition of the areas of prime concern to the central authorities, and those where authority was to be exercised primarily by localities, from provinces down to townships. Mao was quoted, not surprisingly, as opting categorically for maintenance and strengthening of the dictatorship of the proletariat for the fight against counterrevolutionaries and imperialists and for the construction of socialism. But as regards the struggle against counterrevolutionaries, and against political error, Mao in 1956 showed himself more liberal than at the beginning of the 1950s—when a large number of "counterrevolutionaries" had been executed: now, China should follow the policy of "learning from past mistakes to avoid future ones and curing the sickness to save the patient."

As regards relations with other countries, Mao was shown at his most pragmatic—with respect to matters that might be beneficial to China. "Our policy is to learn from the strong points of all nations and all countries," he said, "learning all that is genuinely good in the political, economic, scientific and technological fields and in literature and art." That approach should be used as regards learning from the experience of the USSR and other socialist countries; it should also govern relations with nonsocialist countries: "We must firmly reject and criticize all the decadent bourgeois systems, ideologies and ways of life of foreign countries. But this should in no way prevent us from learning the advanced sciences and technologies of capitalist countries and whatever is scientific in the management of their enterprises." In conclusion Mao displayed the spirit that moved him: "We must do our best to mobilize all positive factors, both inside and outside the Party, both at home and abroad, both direct and indirect, and build China into a powerful socialist country."

As of the end of 1976, a new trend was distinctly visible in the realm of ideology; a new spirit could be sensed in the area of education and the arts. Where under the influence of the radicals political indoctrination had been given precedence over knowledge and skills, with perversion of the "both Red and expert" theme into "Red above all," now there was a retreat from that mode of "socialist education," accompanied by an advance of the spirit of liberalism. From November onward, a progressive debate was waged with respect to education, art, and culture in general. A New China News Agency article of early December charged that the Gang had "enforced a fascist dictatorship over literary and art circles." [9] And Mao Tse-tung's 1956 thinking, as well as the thrust of Premier Hua's December 25 speech, were both reflected in the prediction of the *People's Daily* on December 30 that: "With the smashing of the 'gang of Four,' the revolutionary line of President Mao in art and literature will be applied still better. Proletarian art and literature are flourishing like a hundred flowers, and a new springtime of a Thousand Flowers is being manifested." [10]

Quite evidently, the concept that made worker-peasant judgments and capacities supreme in culture was to be discarded. In the academic world, a restoration of professional men to positions of authority was foreshadowed; in art and literature, new freedom was promised; and, in its world outlook, the new Chinese educational establishment was to show distinctly less of the xenophobic urge to focus the gaze at home, and a new readiness to borrow foreign knowledge and skills. If memory of the purge of "rightists" of those who expressed their thought too freely in response to Mao's 1956 invitation to "Let a hundred flowers bloom" would tend naturally to inhibit somewhat the venting of unorthodox views in the new era, there was nevertheless solid evidence of the presence of urges to raise academic standards, to achieve more creative expression in art and literature (even if subject to some political limitations), to give a richer content to media presentations, and, finally, to have such exchanges with other countries—socialist, capitalist, or "bourgeois"—as might promise to make Chinese society the richer. The PRC was abandoning the radical Maoist doctrine of "self-reliance" that it had adopted effectively in 1960.

In April, 1977, again as edited under the calculating supervision of the new regime in Peking, Volume 5 of Mao's *Selected Works* was issued. It contained the Chairman's works for the full period of Mao's pragmatism after establishment of the Communist regime in Peking—that is, 1949–57. Those and other Maoist works would effectively serve the future purposes of the new leadership of China.

With the holding on July 16–21 of the third plenary of the Tenth CCP Central Committee, the situation crystalized. A press communiqué of July 22 summed up its stunning accomplishments. The Committee had unanimously elected Hua Kuo-feng as Party Chairman (thus confirming the Politburo action of the preceding October 7), and as chairman of the Party's Military Commission. Where the Central Committee had unanimously agreed to purge Teng Hsiao-p'ing in April, 1976, it now unanimously agreed that he should be reinstated to his posts as member of the Central Committee, member of the Politburo and of its Standing Committee, Vice Chairman of the Central Committee, Vice Chairman of the Party's Military Commission, Vice Premier, and chief of staff of the PLA. The Central Committee judged "entirely correct" the actions taken by the Politburo, under Hua's leadership, against the Gang of Four—"a fantastic victory for the Great Proletarian Cultural Revolution, for the Thought of Mao Tse-tung and for the revolutionary proletarian line of Chairman Mao." [11] Listing once more the Gang's "criminal activities," which allegedly included a plot first to overthrow Chou En-lai and an attempt later to overthrow Hua Kuo-feng, and which aimed "to transform our dictatorship of the proletariat into a fascist dictatorship of the bourgeoisie and to restore China to its former condition of a semi-colonial and semi-feudal country," the Committee voted, always unanimously, to oust the Four from the Party. The victory of the pragmatists was thus completed.

Finally, from August 12 to August 18, 1977, the CCP held its Eleventh Congress, in Peking—before the expiry of the 10th Central Committee's stipulated lifetime of five years, given the political crisis the country had just passed through. Chairman Hua Kuo-feng's long Political Report was devoted for the most part to analysis of the "eleventh struggle" the Party had just experienced. In pronouncing his tribute to Mao Tse-tung at the funeral service for the Chairman on September 18, 1976, Hua had said that the GPCR, launched and directed by Mao, had shattered the plots of Liu Shao-ch'i, Lin Piao, *and Teng Hsiao-p'ing;* it had subjected their counterrevolutionary revisionist confederation to criticism and re-

covered a part of the powers they had usurped in the state apparatus, "thus assuring the victorious progression of our country along
the way of Marxism-Leninism." Now, significantly, Hua said that
one of the crimes of the Gang of Four was that, "Defying Chairman
Mao's instructions and going their own way, they attacked Comrade
Teng Hsiao-p'ing and brought false charges against him." [12] And
in fact the Eleventh Congress completed the rehabilitation of the
twice-purged Teng: he now occupied the position of Party Vice
Chairman, ranking immediately behind 79-year-old Marshal Yeh
Chien-ying. Behind Teng were two more Vice Chairmen: Vice Premier Li Hsien-nien, who had been a close collaborator of Chou
En-lai, and Wang Tung-hsing, formerly Vice Minister of Public
Security under Hua Kuo-feng. Each of those two powerful figures
had special qualifications. Li was a prominent specialist in economic
affairs—of a distinctly nonradical bent. Wang, who had become a
full member of the Politburo at the Tenth Congress, headed the
"8341 Unit," a military detachment charged with guarding the
Chungnan Hai area in Peking, where the country's top leaders reside. Bodyguard for Mao Tse-tung during the Long March of the
1930s, Wang was reported to have made the arrest of the Gang of
Four at Peking the previous October.[13]

There was further piquant interest in the circumstance that Lo
Jui-ch'ing, sometime Chief of General Staff and close associate of
Liu Shao-ch'i, purged early in the GPCR and reported a suicide
(see above, page 411), had reappeared on the eve of Army Day
(August 1) in 1975, and now was listed as a member of the new
Central Committee. That his resurrection was of more than sym-
bolic significance was discovered on the occasion of the official
dedication of Mao Tse-tung's mausoleum on September 9, 1977.
There, Lo was identified by the New China News Agency as "a
leading member" of the CCP's military commission.

In the new Politburo (now expanded to 23 members, plus three
alternates), in fact, the military again commanded strong representation. Eleven of the 26 men had military backgrounds. The signs of
the times were clear enough: Where the PRC for a full decade—
that marking Mao Tse-tung's ebbing years—had been governed erratically by policies evolved in good part by the Gang of Four
operating with Mao's sanction, it was now going to be ruled by a
Collective of Five hard-headed organization men, with the PLA in
support. And if lip-service would be given to the doctrine of "democratic centralism" (as there had been before in Party history), it

was now quite evident that there would be much more centralism than the "democracy" of the sort fostered by the radicals over the preceding decade.

In his Political Report to the Congress, after treating at length the sins of the Gang of Four, Chairman-Premier Hua dealt with "The Situation and Our Tasks." Where at the end of the previous year he had set forth *four* major undertakings for 1977, now he laid down eight "musts," with extensive argumentation, as follows: [14]

First. We must carry the great struggle to expose and criticize the "gang of four" through to the end. . . .
Second. We must do a good job of Party consolidation and rectification and strengthen Party building. . . .
Third. We must do a good job of consolidating and building up our Party's leading bodies at all levels. . . .
Fourth. We must grasp revolution, promote production and push the national economy forward. . . .
Fifth. We must make a success of the revolution in cultural and educational spheres and strive to develop socialist culture and education. . . .
Sixth. We must strengthen the people's state apparatus. . . .
Seventh. We must promote democracy and strengthen democratic centralism. . . .
Eighth. We must implement the policy of overall consideration and all-round arrangement.

True, much of this was the familiar litany of the Ninth and Tenth Congresses. And yet, the same spirit of sobriety was brought to permeate the new constitution adopted by the Congress. Longer than either the brief document formulated in 1969 or the constitution of 1973, it was introduced by a General Programme which, while reiterating certain established revolutionary dogma, nevertheless emanated the spirit of political discipline and economic constructiveness.[15] It indeed stressed even as the two preceding congresses the Party's need to observe discipline and strengthen its unity; but it added "oppose the assertion of independence from the Party and oppose anarchism." And where, in the chapter governing organization, the 1973 constitution had provided that election to leading bodies of the Party at all levels should be "through democratic consultation," the parallel provision in the 1977 document was for election "by secret ballot after democratic consultation." Significantly, one of the "main tasks" now proposed for the primary Party organizations was: "to promote inner-Party democracy, practise criticism and self-criticism, expose and get rid of shortcomings and mistakes in work, and wage struggles against violations of the law and breaches of discipline, against corruption and waste, and against bureaucracy and all other undesirable tendencies. . . ." The last half of that provision embodied new constitutional doctrine. In his long "Report on the Revision of the Party Constitution," Yeh Chien-ying set forth in detail the philosophy behind the work of revision, stating in summary that "The draft of the revised Party Constitution, holding high the great banner of Chairman Mao, fully embodies his teachings on Party building and the theory and line of continuing the revolution under the dictatorship of the proletariat, and reflects the fruits of victory in the great struggle to smash the 'gang of four.'" [16]

The new Party constitution in truth formalized the end of one era in China, and the beginning of another. The departure from the political stage of Mao, Chou En-lai, Chu Teh, and other Long March veterans had divested the Party of much of its revolutionary aura, but some of that generation, such as Yeh Chien-ying and Teng Hsiao-p'ing remained behind to help Hua Kuo-feng accomplish the transfer of authority to the successor generation in orderly fashion, so that the nation might with unity of purpose attack the task of making China into a prosperous and powerful state. The credit—and the responsibility—would be attributed to Mao Tse-tung, but to Mao the pragmatist rather than Mao in the messianic role he had played at the end of his life. But the real credit for the new "great order" established in the land one short year after the death of Party Chairman Mao Tse-tung belonged to the hard-headed organization men of the Party, Army, and government —the "bureaucrats" so despised by the Gang of Four and their followers—who had early perceived that, for the national good, it was essential to establish categorical bounds for the Great Proletarian Cultural Revolution; they had prevailed in the end. The national purpose given expression by Premier Chou En-lai at the Fourth National People's Congress in January 1975 was to be implemented.

Political indoctrination and "class struggle" for the perfection of Chinese Man were to be downgraded. It was a mark of the changing times when, in October, 1977, eleven years after the GPCR had first dislocated the processes of higher education, Peking ruled that the universities should reestablish entrance examinations for admission, and that those universities and colleges possessing the facilities to do so should provide, beginning in the current school year, postgraduate courses for training of specialized research workers.[17]

This was a fundamental reversal of the Maoist approach to education. But it was only one part of the new pattern, in which the stress would be put on Chou En-lai's "four modernizations": of agriculture, industry, national defense, and science and technology. In other words, the main effort thenceforth would be directed toward the practical problems of political reorganization within a design of stability and order, of economic modernization, and of the development of a military force fitted for possible war against "superpowers." The course of Mao Tse-tung's "uninterrupted revolution" had been interrupted, to the end that the nation might concentrate more effectively on the arduous task of making China into a powerful socialist state, in political, economic and military terms, before the end of the century.

REVOLUTIONARY LINE IN FOREIGN AFFAIRS

The program set forth by Hua Kuo-feng in August, 1977 was notable for an omission: there were no "musts" stipulated for the field of China's foreign relations. This was not to say that there had been no mention of foreign affairs in the year since Mao Tse-tung had died. There had been; but statements had in general fallen into the pattern dictated by the oft-repeated principle: follow Chairman Mao's revolutionary line in foreign affairs. All logic suggests that, from the death of Mao Tse-tung to the holding of the Eleventh CCP Congress nearly a year later, the new leadership was concentrating its efforts in the field of domestic affairs, and that no major reappraisal of foreign policy had yet been undertaken.

Typical of the foreign policy statements was that contained in the December 2, 1976, Announcement by the CCP Central Committee and its Military Commission, the NPC Standing Committee and the State Council, as follows:

The revolutionary line and policies in foreign affairs personally laid down by Chairman Mao Tse-tung for us are a beacon illuminating the triumphant advance in our country's external affairs. We will continue to implement unswervingly Chairman Mao's revolutionary line and policies in foreign affairs, and adhere to proletarian internationalism. We will never seek hegemony or be a super power. We will unite with all genuine Marxist-Leninist Parties and organizations the world over and carry the struggle against modern revisionism through to the end and wage a common struggle for the realization of communism and the emancipation of all mankind. We will strengthen our unity with the international proletariat, the oppressed nations and oppressed people the world over and the people of the Third World countries, and with all countries subjected to aggression, subversion, interference, control and bullying by imperialism or social imperialism, and in so doing, form a broad united front against imperialism particularly against the hegemonism of the two super powers, the Soviet Union and the United States. We will unswervingly establish or develop relations with all countries on the basis of the Five Principles of Peaceful Coexistence.[18]

The third plenary session of the 10th CCP Central Committee, when it met in July, 1977, followed that general line, if with differences of nuance. So did the Party's new constitution, as adopted on August 18, 1977, in a foreign policy statement contained in the introductory "General Programme." [19] And Chairman Hua, while not adducing a "must" in that general connection, had not neglected the field of foreign affairs. He was on the established Maoist line in asserting that "the main trend in the international situation is that countries want independence, nations want liberation and the people want revolution." He was orthodox in his estimate that the two superpowers, the United States and the Soviet Union, both strove to dominate the world, were found in contention everywhere, and that war was consequently inevitable—"either a war between them or a revolution by the people, and there cannot be any lasting peace."

But Hua was somewhat more direct than had been Mao, in recent years, in setting forth Peking's Machiavellian rationale for endeavoring to exploit, to China's benefit, the rivalry between the two superpowers. He chose to put his concept in modern, Leninist terms:

Historical experience has repeatedly shown that victory in a revolution depends chiefly on the people's own strength, but at the same time it is necessary to win over as many allies as possible. Lenin said: "The more powerful enemy can be vanquished only by exerting the utmost effort, and most thoroughly, carefully, attentatively and skilfully making use *without fail* of every, even the smallest, "rift" among the enemies, of every antagonism of interest among the bourgeoisie within the various countries and among the various groups or types of bourgeoisie within the various countries, and also by taking advantage of every, even the smallest, opportunity of gaining a mass ally, even though this ally be temporary, vacillating, unstable, unreliable and conditional. Those who fail to understand this, fail to understand even a particle of Marxism, or of scientific modern Socialism *in general*." [20]

Chairman Hua described that principle as of "enormous and immediate significance" in the present struggle of the people of the world against hegemonism. The Chinese listener was able to identify without undue difficulty the "mass ally" China should try to gain, however "temporary," in its endeavor to exploit every "rift" among enemies. And Hua remained on the established line by holding that China belonged to the Third World of developing countries and supported Second World countries (the industrialized states apart from the United States and the USSR) "in their struggle against control, intimidation and bullying by the superpowers." And the PRC's direct relations with those superpowers? Relations with the United States would continue to improve, provided that the principles set forth in the Shanghai Communiqué of 1972 were carried out in the spirit of that Communiqué. But when and how Taiwan shall be liberated "is entirely China's internal affair. . . . " As regards the USSR, "we have always held that China and the Soviet Union should maintain normal state relations on the basis of the Five Principles of Peaceful Coexistence." But it was the fault of the Soviet leadership that no progress had been made in the negotiations on the Sino-Soviet border question; and it was that leadership that had been trying to force China to change the Marxist-Leninist line laid down by Chairman Mao. If the Soviet leadership desired to improve Sino-Soviet state relations, they should prove it "by concrete deeds." In summing up, Hua reiterated the essence of the argument set forth in the authoritative Announcement of December 2 of the previous year.

This all was indeed the Maoist "revolutionary line"—posthumous Maoism—in foreign affairs. Is that line so logical, in terms of the rewards that it offers, that it will stand? For years Mao Tse-tung had regularly proclaimed that "There is disorder under Heaven, and the situation is excellent." The meaning of his seemingly self-contradictory thesis was entirely clear: world disorder was operating to China's advantage. But is that premise correct? And, if not, will not the Maoist world strategy threaten failure—and lead the new pragmatic leadership in Peking to change the nation's foreign policy, even as its domestic policy, to meet changing world conditions, and thus to operate at a greater profit to the People's Republic of China? If first premises are faulty, the policy based on them must fail; and sensible men would then undertake a revision of their calculations.

Consideration of the matter in some historical depth is in order. An occurrence in 1968 far from China's borders seems to have contributed substantially to bringing about a shift in Peking's strategy. On August 20–21, there was the startling intervention in Czechoslovakia by the USSR and four other Warsaw Pact powers. A warning letter the five had sent previously to the Czechoslovak Communist Party set forth a significant rationale: "We cannot agree to have hostile forces push your country away from the road of socialism and create danger of Czechoslovakia being severed from the socialist community. . . . The frontiers of the socialist world have moved . . . to the Elbe and the Bohemian Forest. We shall never agree to these historic gains of socialism . . . being placed in jeopardy." [21] The Brezhnev Doctrine of "limited sovereignty" had been born, and if it were judged warrant for taking action against unorthodoxy in Czechoslovakia, it was in logic equally applicable to China. In any event, Moscow's military action against the deviant Communist state was by itself an indication that, in some peacetime circumstances, the Soviet Union might be prepared to employ its armed forces elsewhere outside its borders.

China and Albania joined in condemning what Tirana termed the "barbarous aggression of the Soviet revisionists and their valets against the Czechoslovak Government and people." But Soviet economic strength and massive military power were hard facts which would figure in any realistic geopolitical calculation. And when *Pravda* on November 25 issued a call to arms against the external and internal enemies of Communism, defined respectively as the imperialists and "right-wing and left-wing opportunists and splitters who are undermining the Communist and workers' movement," [22] the reference to China was unmistakable.

The long CCP Central Committee plenum held in the latter part of October can be taken as marking the beginning of Peking's return to the Bandung policy of "peaceful coexistence" and "economic cooperation." But the next year, 1969, proved decisive. In the spring and summer, there were dangerous clashes on the Sino-Soviet frontier, and by August the Soviet Union had constructed a system of new missile sites along the border and deployed heavy military forces. There was talk of war. Also in the summer came President Nixon's enunciation of the "Nixon [Guam] Doctrine," built around the concept that the United States was a West Pacific power and determined to remain in Asia.

And there was the Nixon Doctrine corollary providing for "Vietnamization" of the Indo-China War—with the implied proposition that, over the longer term, there should be the "Asianization of America's Asian wars: Asians should supply the ground forces for such actions. It is pertinent to remark here that the device of using others to fight one's wars is not unknown to the Asians, and particularly the Chinese. Chiang Kai-shek during his mainland rule regularly endeavored to maneuver one great power against another for China's gain,[23] and in the postwar period looked to the United States for aid against his domestic enemies, the Communists. The rulers at Peking are quite as faithful followers of the Chinese imperial adage, "use barbarians to control barbarians," as have been the Nationalists at Nanking and Taipei; and Moscow for one has charged that the Mao regime sought to embroil others—and particularly the USSR—in war, for its own anticipated profit.

From 1960 onward, it had become increasingly clear that Peking, under Mao Tse-tung's leadership, had decided to wage protracted political warfare simultaneously against both the United States, as the last of the Occidental sea powers present, and the Soviet Union, as an alien ("non-Asian") intruder into the Far East, with the aim of establishing China's predominance in Asia. Two important assumptions seemingly entered into the strategic decision: first, that the confrontation between the United States and the USSR would continue, and that they would cancel each other out—perhaps annihilate each other in a nuclear collision; second, that Japan was not a prime mover in the power complex, and that China could either win it over or overcome it.

But by 1969 the trend in American-Soviet relations was toward a relaxation instead of a heightening of tensions, whereas the confrontation between China and the United States remained in being; meanwhile, the danger of a hard punitive strike by the Soviet Union against China appeared to be growing. In a meeting of the CCP Politburo at Peking on May 18, according to a later (October 28) report by the *Tokyo Shimbun*, Lin Piao warned that, "if natural disasters or war occur or Chairman Mao dies, there will be political crises and 700 million people might be thrown into confusion." One element of his warning was more pointed: "If a war breaks out, people will take the side of the counterrevolutionaries and may point their guns at us." That particular hypothetical eventuality would appear to have been Lin's chief concern.

The USSR had dealt Chinese military forces a sharp blow in the second of a pair of "incidents" that had occurred in March on the frozen Ussuri River, dividing Manchuria and the Soviet Far East, and border tensions had mounted in the months that followed. The Soviet deployment of heavy forces facing China, and the increasing severity of the Soviet military responses to provocative Chinese actions, viewed against the background of the Czechoslovak episode, could only have convinced Peking that the limits of safety had been reached, and that one of its basic premises was incorrect. The Sino-Soviet quarrel was *nominally* only between the two Communist Parties, with normal state-to-state relations, by official Peking acknowledgment, in theory entirely feasible. In September, one month after another serious clash had occurred on the Sino-Soviet border in Central Asia, Premiers Alexei I. Kosygin and Chou En-lai met at the Peking airport for an hours-long exchange of views, and diplomatic negotiations regarding matters of common interest began in October. Border clashes ceased.

Mao Tse-tung's personal prestige was involved in the Sino-Soviet dispute: the campaign against Soviet "revisionism" was, after all, his own brainchild; the "contradiction" in the relationship continued. The ancient Chinese theoretician Sun Tzu, in discussing offensive strategy, held that "what is of supreme importance in war is to attack the enemy's strategy"; and "next best is to disrupt his alliances." Peking still damned both "U.S. imperialism" and "Soviet revisionist social imperialism" (as the alleged Soviet heterodoxy was designated after the Czechoslovak affair), and professed to see revolutionary promise on the horizon. The *People's Daily* and *Red Flag* in a joint 1970 New Year's day editorial held that "the old world shakes under the tempest, volcanoes erupt one after the other, and crowns fall one by one. One finds no longer a single 'peaceful oasis' on earth for imperialism." [24] The editors held that "Soviet revisionist social imperialism can neither redress the debacle of the entire imperialist system or save itself from the ruin. The pretended 'Brezhnev doctrine' is basically no more than a variant of dying neo-colonialism."

But Peking was at the same time, in line with its changed policy, presenting an amiable countenance toward almost everyone else. Its ambassadors resumed their posts, and the fence-mending process began. North Korea's relations with Peking had seriously deteriorated during the GPCR; in early April, Premier Chou En-lai made a personal visit to Pyongyang, and the breach was healed. [25] At a banquet tendered the visitor on that occasion, Premier Chou and Premier Kim Il Sung pledged their unity, "sealed by blood," in the common struggle against the United States and Japan. [26]

Relations between Peking and Hanoi had shown signs of strain because of Chinese interference with Soviet arms shipments via

China to North Vietnam, and because of Peking's displeasure at Hanoi's agreement in 1968 to engage in peace talks with the United States at Paris. Beginning in late 1969, however, Peking started to depict Hanoi as an ideological comrade-in-arms,[27] and the American–South Vietnamese incursion into Cambodia at the end of April, 1970, drove the two Communist neighbors into a close embrace.

There was rapprochement with others than close neighbors. Yugoslavia, which had recognized the Chinese Communist regime in October, 1949, had been viewed by the "orthodox" Peking leadership as so impossibly "revisionist" that there was no exchange of ambassadors until 1955—and then they were withdrawn in 1958.

For a decade, Peking reviled Yugoslavia as a "running dog of imperialism." However, the Soviet incursion of 1968 into Czechoslovakia make a difference. In April, 1970, after twelve years of bitter dispute, China and Yugoslavia agreed again to exchange ambassadors.

In Burma, in the first eight months of 1969, the army had suffered 380 casualties fighting the White Flag Communists that Peking had proposed should overthrow the "fascist" Ne Win regime. But General Ne Win in November publicly acknowledged Burmese error with respect to the anti-Chinese riots of 1967, and indicated a readiness to resume relations with Peking. The process was slow, and was attended by the waging of successful Burmese military campaigns against the Communists and the Karen rebels in 1970, with the result that the rebels "were reduced from thousands operating efficiently under the direction of the clandestine Burmese Communist Party to hundreds hardly daring to come out of hiding in the jungle." [28] In October of that year, Rangoon named a new ambassador to Peking; and on August 8, 1971, General Ne Win arrived in Peking by the invitation of the Chinese government and was greeted by Premier Chou En-lai, who declared at a banquet given in honor of the distinguished visitor that Sino-Burmese relations had "returned to normal" over the course of the past two years.[29]

Nor were Peking's efforts limited to patching up old relationships. Prime Minister Trudeau's May, 1968, suggestion of Canada's readiness to establish diplomatic relations with China had been a straw in the wind. With Peking's return to the Bandung line in foreign policy, it won diplomatic recognition from fourteen other countries between October, 1970 (Canada), and October 1971 (Belgium). This striking achievement within the confines of conventional diplomacy was in good measure responsible for Peking's decisive victory of October, 1971, in the United Nations: in the voting on the Chinese representation issue, Peking was overwhelmingly accepted as the legitimate ruler of China, and the clients of Washington, the Nationalists, were forced to vacate the China seat.

Even before this, there had been a development which had led other countries, of East and West, and especially China's neighbors, to undertake reappraisals of their Asia policies. Mao Tse-tung had told Edgar Snow in December 1970 that he would welcome a visit by President Nixon to Peking, since it was with the American President that outstanding problems in Sino-American relations would have to be solved.[30]

Lin Piao, by the evidence, disagreed with the project for a *démarche* toward the United States, favoring instead a rapprochement with the Soviet Union. Mao had come to entertain a visceral hatred for the Soviet leadership, because it denied his omniscience and refused to accept his orthodoxy; and Lin had dared, as regards a major item of foreign affairs even as with respect to a prime domestic issue, to challenge the wisdom of the course fixed by the imperial Mao.

So it happened that, introduced by the quaint and unforgettable ping-pong gambit in Peking's "people-to-people diplomacy," and by Washington's lifting of its 21-year embargo on the China trade, American Presidential Adviser Henry A. Kissinger made his secret visit to the People's Republic of China and, on July 15, 1971, President Nixon announced his forthcoming visit to Peking. Lin Piao died in that plane crash a little less than two months later. The Mao strategy vis-à-vis the United States crystallized with the Nixon visit of February, 1972: détente was introduced into what had previously been viewed, in Washington's geopolitical jargon, as an "adversary relationship." By virtue of the joint Shanghai communiqué of February 27, the two parties voiced their adherance to the doctrine of peaceful coexistence.

However, the détente was still strictly limited: major issues dividing the two remained in being. In general terms, the United States was the world's foremost capitalist power, while Peking professed its devotion to the concept of proletarian internationalism, and condemned "American imperialism." And, more particularly, there was no agreement between the two with respect to the future of Taiwan, nestling under the protective American wing by virtue of the mutual-defense treaty of December, 1954. There seemed indeed to be superficial agreement between the two parties to the Shanghai communiqué that Taiwan and the Chinese mainland were two parts of one whole. However, there was no attendant agreement respecting the procedures to be followed in achieving a reconciliation of the political opposites—the Chinese Nationalists and the Chinese Communists. And it naturally did not fit in with the Maoist strategic concepts that, in May, 1972, President Nixon also made a visit to Moscow—and inaugurated détente with the USSR even as with the PRC. Mao did not acclaim that particular development in international affairs as "excellent."

PROLETARIAN DICTATORSHIP IN A MULTIPOLAR WORLD

This suggests the actuality: the Sino-American relationship was not to be viewed as strictly bilateral: two other major powers were in the play—Japan and the USSR. An original aim of the 1950 Sino-Soviet alliance had been to pry Japan loose from the American embrace. The alliance was evidently viewed, by Moscow at any rate, as being more political and economic than military. The relationship between the United States and Japan, in contrast, had since 1951 in particular been determined basically by the military provisions of the governing agreement, and by the important trade between the two countries. Following the announcement of the Nixon Doctrine in the summer of 1969, the American-Japanese relationship had been given an even more martial interpretation. On the occasion of the visit of Premier Sato Eisaku to Washington in November, he and President Nixon issued a joint communiqué, proposing in essence that Japan would collaborate with the United States for the maintenance of peace and order in Asia. When President Ford, in enunciating the "Pacific Doctrine" in December, 1975, cited the American partnership with Japan as "a pillar of our strategy" (in the Pacific), he was standing firmly on the established line.

The termination of the American intervention in Vietnam by virtue of the Paris accords of January, 1973 was naturally hailed by Peking as a victory of revolutionary forces over those of "imperialism." That it constituted a victory for the revolutionaries was indeed beyond challenge; but that the outcome of the long struggle was a vindication of Maoist strategy and tactics was a proposition that would not have been granted by the Hanoi leadership, which had come to depend much more upon Soviet material aid—and, seemingly, political inspiration too—than on the Chinese offerings. There was always in the background of Vietnamese thinking deep-rooted recollections of traditional examples of Chinese imperialism.

The American withdrawal from Vietnam was accompanied by other evidence of the debility of "imperialism." It was in 1973 that President Nixon proffered American "leadership" to Western Europe, only to have the offer spurned. And in 1973 also, with the Yom Kippur War in the Middle East, the OPEC countries showed their strength by imposing an oil boycott on the United States and some of its associates—the while other American "allies" refused to follow Washington's strategy. The American dominance of the world scene had been short-lived; the United States was now demoted, in Maoist estimation, to the position of a secondary enemy, the while the USSR was accorded the role of "principal enemy of the moment."

Again Chinese domestic developments found their relationships in the international sphere. In April, 1974, one year after the United States had withdrawn its military forces from Southeast Asia and thus gave confirmation that it was truly the American intent, as indicated in the Nixon Doctrine, to reduce its military presence on the Asian mainland, Vice Premier Teng Hsiao-p'ing, speaking at the United Nations, set forth a revised Chinese strategic doctrine. He held that, "As a result of the emergence of social imperialism, the socialist camp which existed for a time after World War II is no longer in existence. Owing to the law of uneven development of capitalism, the Western imperialist bloc, too, is disintegrating." [31] The world, Teng said, was now divided into three: there was the First World, comprising the "imperialist" United States and the "social imperialist" Soviet Union. The First World exploited, and was opposed by, a Third World of developing nations; in between there was the Second World of industrialized states, in varying degrees controlled or threatened by one or the other of the superpowers. The superpowers contended between themselves for world hegemony, and there was no reconciling the "contradiction" between them: "Either they will fight each other, or the people will rise in revolution."

The latest expression of the Maoist world view retained as an essential element that concept of irreconcilable bipolar conflict between the United States and the Soviet Union that had governed in Washington during the Cold War era. But the Maoist embellishment effectively denied allies to either the United States or the Soviet Union: those sometime elements of the "imperialist bloc" and the "socialist camp" allied to one power or the other now were lumped together in a Second World which, by the Maoist doctrine of tactical expediency, should naturally be won over, if possible, to the side of the Third World—to fight against *both* superpowers. Since the envisaged struggle would patently take on the character of a "protracted war," Teng advised that Third World countries (even as China) should struggle for economic as well as political independence (Peking's well-advertised economic "self-reliance"), with due regard for the special importance of achieving economic cooperation among themselves. And where did the PRC fit into the picture? Teng had the answer to fit the revised doctrine: "China is a socialist country, and a developing country as well. China belongs to the Third World. . . . China is not a superpower, nor will she ever seek to be one."

The total victory won in March–May 1975 by the revolutionary forces in Indochina can only have confirmed Mao Tse-tung in the belief that, in the analysis presented by Teng to the United Nations in 1974 (undoubtedly with the full approval of the Chairman), the nation's grand strategy was on the right line. And that, by the evidence, was the "revolutionary international line of Chairman Mao" which, according to Hua Kuo-feng's report to the Eleventh CCP Congress of 1977, would be followed by the new regime at Peking. But there were international influences that effectively challenged Mao's claim to hold the key to the future. Given the basic assumption that Chinese strategy is self-serving in nature (if sometimes mistaken in its assumptions), a survey of certain elements of the changing world scene is suggestive.

What of Peking's long-term drive to wrest leadership of the world Communist movement from Moscow and have the Maoist interpretation of Marxism/Leninism accepted as universal Truth for revolutionaries? The meeting of European Communist parties in East Berlin in June, 1976 proclaimed effectively that there exists no one universal Communist doctrine, that each national Party has the right to determine its own Truth. If Moscow can no longer regard itself as the seat of Communist orthodoxy, neither can Peking. More, where the PRC by its new state Constitution of January, 1975 asserted that the nation has consolidated the dictatorship of the proletariat, the Communist representatives meeting in East Berlin renounced the concept of proletarian dictatorship per se.

In practice, the nominal Chinese adherance to international radicalism has not inhibited Peking from taking steps dictated by a political expediency calculated to embarrass China's designated "enemies" and bring it profit. Josip Broz Tito of Yugoslavia had vowed never to visit the People's Republic of China while Mao Tsetung lived, and he held to his word. But on August 30, 1977, almost one year after the death of the Great Helmsman, Tito began a state visit to Peking; and, where during Mao's lifetime he had been castigated as the prime Communist "revisionist," he was now accorded a warm welcome.

At an official banquet in Tito's honor his host, Premier Hua Kuofeng, spoke with approval of the Yugoslav policy of nonalignment, noting how the nonaligned movement was currently "playing an ever greater role in international affairs." [32] But that policy, it was to be noted, was inherently contradictory of the Chinese Third World strategy, and put Yugoslavia in competition. Premier Hua asserted *pro forma* that the two superpowers were locked in fierce rivalry for world hegemony, and held that their continued rivalry "is bound to lead to a world war some day." But Tito, while lauding China's revolutionary accomplishments and giving praise to Chairman Mao Tse-tung's achievements, was not led to express full agreement. He held that the international situation was very complex, burdened with serious problems, "and the fact that they are not being resolved gives rise to our concern." [33] He opted for the *relaxation* of international tensions, and the development of cooperation —for peaceful coexistence. "Much to our regret, we cannot say today that peace has been secured. . . . However, the war is not inevitable, either." And for the last words of his toast, and thus of his speech, Tito chose "to the broad co-operation and understanding in the world."

According to a Yugoslav source, agreement was reached on a program of economic, technical, scientific and cultural cooperation, and for a quadrupling of commercial exchanges (modest indeed) between the two countries in the course of 1978.[34] Such an agreement between the Chinese "proletarian dictatorship" and Tito's regime, condemned by Mao Tse-tung for its economic as much as for its political "revisionism," could not have come during Mao's lifetime. But now there was evidence that Peking was genuinely interested in the working of Yugoslavia's unorthodox system of socialist self-management of factories, schools, and villages—a system bearing a resemblance to some of the Chinese communal endeavors, which however had not worked out as well.

Although the Tito visit did not immediately bring out a resumption of formal relations between the Chinese Communist Party and the Yugoslav Communist League, the Sino-Yugoslav rapprochement naturally did not go unobserved in the country that over the years had shown itself to be closest to the Maoist line in international affairs, Albania. The Hoxha regime had already been alienated, to a degree, from its previous sympathies by Peking's policy of drawing closer to the United States. On July 7, an editorial in the Party organ *Zeri I Popullit* had denounced as "opportunist" and "anti-Leninist" the Maoist doctrine of Three Worlds; and the Albanian Communist Party had also criticized the policy of characterizing the USSR as "principal enemy" in favor of the United States. Now, on September 2, in the midst of Tito's visit, the Albanian Embassy in Peking circulated among other embassies and foreign-press correspondents a pamphlet reproducing a *Zeri I Popullit* editorial of September 13, 1963—denouncing the contemporary visit of Soviet leader Nikita S. Khrushchev to Belgrade. The first of three principal conclusions drawn by the editorial was that, by uniting with the Tito clique, the revisionist group of Moscow "has compromised itself even more profoundly with the camp of enemies of Marxism-Leninism, of socialism and of peace, and has sunk even more into the quagmire of treason" [35] The parallel discovered in Peking's hosting of Tito was plain to see.

In his banquet speech, Premier Hua had taken the occasion to state that, in the international field, China would adhere to "proletarian internationalism and Chairman Mao's thesis differentiating the three worlds. . . . " Now, on September 2, the same day the Albanian Embassy went into action, the *Peking Review* published extensixe extracts from an article carried by the Japanese magazine *Theory and Practice* extolling the differentiation theory of Three Worlds. Remarking the circumstance that, in leading the Chinese revolution, Mao Tse-tung had exploited contradictions among imperialist powers and within the Chinese ruling classes alike, the article pointedly quoted Lenin to the some effect as had Chairman Hua at the Eleventh Party Congress on the desirability of exploiting conflicts of interest among one's enemies. Then came what had to be viewed as Peking's answer, even if voiced in Japanese, to the Albanians: "Labelling as capitulation the Marxist-Leninist concept of making use of the contradictions among imperialist countries to the advantage of the revolution is a slander which resembles Trotsky's attacks on Lenin when the latter concluded the Treaty of Brest-Litovsk with German imperialism by making use of the contradictions among imperialist countries. This proves that such abuse is hurled from enemy trenches."

The Chinese Communist Party thus stood ideologically isolated from the great majority of other Communist parties—even the Albanians, not to mention the Soviet, Yugoslav, Japanese, Mongolian, and Vietnamese. It was also found isolated as regards particular revolutionary movements. By the Maoist strategic concepts, developments between the Third and First Worlds were to determine humanity's future. Had China then earned preeminent prestige and influence for itself in the Third World? It had not. The Third World in 1977, after Mao's passing, was no more ready for a unified undertaking to overcome the First World of "imperialism" and "social imperialism" than it was in either 1965, when Lin Piao expounded the doctrine of the People's War, or in 1974, when Teng Hsiao-p'ing portrayed the Third World as antagonist of the First World.

In practice, insofar as Peking had desired to establish contacts with and to influence Third countries, it found it incumbent to deal with established, largely conservative, governments—and to forgo revolution. In those circumstances, given the limitations experienced with respect to Chinese economic power, China's ventures in the Third World had made little progress in the face of competition from the United States, Japan, and the Soviet Union—not to mention the European Economic Community. For the hard, unrevolutionary fact was that Third World governments at this stage of world history were more interested in obtaining economic benefit, and making economic progress, than they were in making revolution—Maoist slogans to the contrary notwithstanding.

What then of Peking's other primary assumption in its grand strategy, namely that war between the United States and the Soviet Union is inevitable—with the secondary, unvoiced assumption that China as bystander will stand to gain major profit from such a war? There is indeed a chance that the basic thesis may prove correct: there is as yet no discernible advance from détente to true entente and cooperation between Moscow and Washington. But two factors operate against realization of the Maoist proposition: (1) with the growth of nationalism *pari passu* with the proliferation of nation-states, and with the exacerbation of numerous national and international problems having no relationship to the Communist–anti-Communist confrontation, the world's bipolar aspect has been eclipsed by a multipolar aspect of diminished ideological content;

and (2) in that world the United States and the Soviet Union find it increasingly useful and jointly beneficial, on particular occasions, to cooperate toward solving dangerous world problems. As regards the second part of the Maoist proposition, namely that China could remain apart from a major war, which would involve not only the United States and the USSR but inevitably American and Soviet allies *in Asia as well as in Europe,* this must be viewed as Maoist romanticism in pure form. And the pragmatists in power in Peking in 1977 in all probability appreciated that the scenario was too far removed from at least short-range practicality to form the basis for an effective grand strategy.

In China's home continent, Asia, major changes were in course as Peking pondered its strategy. For one thing, biopolarism had disappeared from that world sector, too. The United States, for all of its professions of unwavering interest in Asia, was distracted by other pressing, competing concerns—in the Middle East, Africa, Latin America, and Western Europe. SEATO was dead, the United States had scheduled the withdrawal of its ground forces from South Korea, and its ties with Japan had loosened. Where the Chinese had in the past endeavored to harness variously the Soviet Union and the United States to its chariot, it aimed similarly to entice the Japanese into a collaboration profitable to the PRC; but, having to concentrate their efforts, so far as Japan was concerned, in the economic field, they operated at a disadvantage: they could not offer profits of the magnitude the Japanese could find elsewhere.

Japan had embarked upon a course of increased independence from the United States—but not for the purpose of becoming allied to China. North Korea, Indochina, and the Mongolian People's Republic alike reject the relationship of satellite to the sometime Middle Kingdom; they've experienced such status before. The Association of Southeast Asian Nations (ASEAN), India, and Pakistan are all governed by considerations of their own national interests —which do not coincide with those of the People's Republic of China. Peking heads no revolutionary force—anywhere. Its brand of "proletarian internationalism" has no market.

China itself in the post-Mao era is interested first and foremost in more prosaic, but also more exigent, matters in the field of economics: it has abandoned the "metaphysical" voluntarism of Mao Tse-tung and the Gang of Four in favor of discipline and hard work—and profitable exchanges with the outside world. The "great order" at home cannot be related logically or effectively to a "great disorder under Heaven." To accomplish the economic tasks it has set itself at home, China is compelled to adopt a course of sobriety abroad. As it committed itself at the 1955 Bandung Conference— and time and time again subsequently—it must engage in an essential measure of peaceful coexistence and economic cooperation.

Where Mao Tse-tung proposed that the world should be remade in the Maoist design, the pragmatists who came to power after Mao's passing will probably in time reject his millenarianism as being as impractical for China's foreign affairs as for the nation's domestic affairs. For want of a better doctrine, China can be expected to follow the Maoist line in international affairs *outwardly* for some time to come. But that will be on the surface of things. Insofar as the Third World does not show signs of rising in revolt against the superpowers in service of Maoist doctrine, and the United States and the Soviet Union fail to fulfill the Maoist prophecy that they will "inevitably" fall upon each other in a war of mutual destruction, China will be caused by purely practical considerations to adopt a less dogmatic, more flexible, grand strategy. In line with Maoist dialectics, the PRC has zigzagged before in its foreign policy; it will probably do so again. For in the final analysis, a viable Chinese foreign policy must give due heed to the manifold and compelling needs of the nation's 900 million people.

NOTES

INTRODUCTION: "CONFUCIAN" CHINA

1. Brooks Adams, *America's Economic Supremacy* (New York, 1900), pp. 42–43.

1. DECAY OF THE DYNASTIC PRINCIPLE

1. U.S. Dept. of State, *Papers Relating to the Foreign Relations of the United States*, 1900, pp. 94–95. Hereinafter cited as *Foreign Relations*.

2. U.S. Dept. of State, *United States Relations with China* (Washington, D.C., 1949), p. 417. Hereinafter cited as *China White Paper*.

3. Sergei I. Witte, *The Memoirs of Count Witte*; trans. by Abraham Yarmolinsky (New York, 1921), pp. 121–22.

4. Text in Victor A. Yakhontoff, *Russia and the Soviet Union in the Far East* (New York, 1931), p. 371.

5. C. T. Liang, *The Chinese Revolution of 1911* (Institute of Asian Studies, St. John's University; Jamaica, N.Y., 1962), p. 33.

6. *Foreign Relations*, 1912, pp. 64–65.

2. THE REVOLUTION THAT FAILED

1. *Foreign Relations*, 1915, p. 58.

2. *Ibid.*, 1915, pp. 76–77.

3. *China White Paper*, p. 8.

3. THE BIRTH OF MODERN CHINESE NATIONALISM

1. Quoted in Chow Tse-tsung, *The May Fourth Movement* (Cambridge, Mass., 1960), p. 46.

2. *Foreign Relations, Russia*, 1918, II, 328–29. See also Far Eastern Republic, *Japanese Intervention in the Russian Far East* (Washington, D.C., 1922), p. 13; and William S. Graves, *America's Siberian Adventure* (New York, 1931), p. 161.

3. *Foreign Relations, Russia*, 1919, p. 359. The Big Five defined their policy objectives as follows: "To restore peace within Russia by enabling the Russian people to resume control of their own affairs . . . and to

restore peace along its frontiers by arranging for the settlement of disputes . . . through the peaceful arbitration of the League of Nations." (*Ibid.*)

4. REVOLUTIONARIES AGAINST THE WARLORDS

1. Lenin, *Selected Works* (New York, 1937), IV, 307.
2. *Hsin Ch'ing Nien* (New Youth), April 1, 1917.
3. *I-i Sezd Narodov Vostoka* (1st Congress of the Peoples of the East), stenographic record (Petrograd, 1920), p. 13.
4. *Foreign Relations*, 1921, pp. 41–43.
5. Communist International, *The First Congress of the Toilers of the Far East* (Petrograd, 1922), pp. 229–30, 234.
6. From translated text, see Conrad Brandt, Benjamin Schwartz, and John K. Fairbank, *A Documentary History of Chinese Communism* (Cambridge, Mass., 1952), p. 63.
7. *Foreign Relations*, 1922, p. 722.
8. *Ibid.*, 1923, Vol. I, p. 562.
9. Quoted in Lyon Sharman, *Sun Yat-sen, His Life and Its Meaning* (New York, 1934), p. 304.
10. George E. Sokolsky, "The Kuomintang," in *China Yearbook, 1928* (Tientsin, 1929), p. 1370.

5. "FIRST PACIFICATION, THEN RESISTANCE"

1. Feng Yü-hsiang, *Wo So Jen Shih Ti Chiang Chieh Shih* (The Chiang Kai-shek I Knew) (Shanghai, 1949), p. 18.
2. League of Nations, *Report of the Commission of Inquiry, Appeal by the Chinese Government* (Geneva, 1932), p. 29.
3. Japan, Foreign Office, *Relations of Japan with Manchuria and Mongolia, Document B*, revised ed. (Tokyo [?], 1932), pp. 26–27.

6. THE RESURGENCE OF CHINESE NATIONALISM

1. Mao Tse-tung, "A Single Spark Can Start a Prairie Fire," in his *Selected Works* (London, 1954), I, 116–28.
2. Yang Chien, "Communist Menace in China," *Central China Post* (Hankow), July 20, 1931.
3. *Central China Post*, November 25, 1931.
4. Conrad Brandt, Benjamin Schwartz, and John K. Fairbank, *A Documentary History of Chinese Communism* (Cambridge, Mass., 1942), pp. 253–54.

7. THE SECOND SINO-JAPANESE WAR

1. Togo Shigenori, *The Cause of Japan* (New York, 1956), p. 80.
2. Cordell Hull, *Memoirs* (New York, 1948), II, 1073, 1077, 1081–82.
3. Henry L. Stimson and McGeorge Bundy, *On Active Service in Peace and War* (New York, 1948), p. 528.
4. Charles F. Romanus and Riley Sunderland, *United States Army in World War II—China-Burma-India Theater—Stilwell's Command Problems* (Washington, D.C., 1956), p. 303.
5. *Ibid.*, pp. 450–51.

6. *Ibid.*, pp. 445–46.

7. Herbert Feis, *The China Tangle* (Princeton, N.J., 1953), pp. 185–99.

8. Romanus and Sunderland, p. 469.

9. *China White Paper*, p. 73.

10. Winston Churchill, *The Second World War*, Vol. VI: *Triumph and Tragedy* (Boston, 1953), p. 390.

11. *China White Paper*, p. 115.

12. *Ibid.*, p. 95.

13. *Ibid.*, pp. 96–97.

14. V. Avarin, "Whither China?," *War and the Working Class*, April 15, 1945, pp. 15–19.

15. Mao Tse-tung, *Selected Works* (Bombay, 1956), IV, 274.

16. Edgar Snow, "The Chinese Communists and Wars on Two Continents," *China Weekly Review*, January 13, 1940, p. 246.

17. Conrad Brandt, Benjamin Schwartz, and John K. Fairbank, *A Documentary History of Chinese Communism* (Cambridge, Mass., 1942), p. 301.

18. Mao Tse-tung, *Selected Works*, IV, 275.

8. KUOMINTANG-COMMUNIST STRUGGLE: FINAL STAGE

1. *China White Paper*, p. 311.

2. *Ta Kung Pao* (L'Impartial [Chungking]), August 21, 1945.

3. *Hsin Hua Jih Pao* (New China Daily [Chungking]), August 24, 1945.

4. *China White Paper*, p. 605.

5. *Ibid.*, p. 145.

6. *Hsin Hua Jih Pao* (Huaiyin), March 1, 1946.

7. *Wei Tung Pei Ti Ho P'ing Min Chu Erh Tou Cheng* (Fighting for Peace and Democracy of the Northeast) (n.p., n.d.), pp. 5–6.

8. *China White Paper*, p. 151.

9. *Ibid.*, pp. 149, 153.

10. *Ibid.*, p. 158.

11. *Ibid.*, p. 169.

12. Mao Tse-tung, "The Present Situation and Our Tasks," in his *Selected Works* (Peking, 1961), IV, 157–76. But compare Chinese text in *Hua Ch'iao Jih Pao* (Overseas Chinese Daily [New York]), January 12–14, 1948, for different shades of meaning.

13. *China White Paper*, pp. 845–46.

14. *Ibid.*, p. 923.

15. *Ibid.*, pp. 336–37.

16. *Ibid.*, pp. 358–59.

10. PEKING AT THE CROSSROADS

1. *Hsin Hua Yueh Pao* (New China Monthly [Peking]), December 15, 1949, p. 441.

2. Li Li-san, "Trade Union Work and Movement in China," *China Digest* (Peking), December 14, 1949, p. 19.

3. *Ren Min Ri Bao* (People's Daily [Peking]), February 14, March 14, March 21, March 23, April 2, 1950.

4. Quoted in *Ren Min Ri Bao,* June 15, 1950.

5. *Ren Min Ri Bao,* August 2, 1950.

6. *Ibid.,* October 2, 1950.

7. *Ibid.,* October 3, 1950.

8. *Ibid.,* October 1, 1950.

9. From translation in Leo Gruliow, ed., *Current Soviet Policies* (New York, 1953), pp. 1–10, 99–124.

10. *Economic Review* (New Delhi), May 1, 1955.

11. From translation in *Current Digest of the Soviet Press,* Vol. VIII, No. 4, *Pravda,* February 15, 1956.

12. Quoted by New York *Times,* November 10, 1960.

11. SHIFT IN PEKING'S FOREIGN POLICY

1. New York *Times,* September 9, 1958.

2. New York *Herald Tribune,* September 18, 1958.

3. Anna Louise Strong, *China's Millions* (New York, 1928), p. 53.

4. Henry Wei, *China and Soviet Russia* (Princeton, 1956), p. 42, quoting T'ang Leang-li, *Foundations of Modern China* (London, 1928), p. 168.

12. THE GREAT PROLETARIAN CULTURAL REVOLUTION

1. "Press Communiqué on the National People's Congress," *Peking Review,* No. 16 (April 20, 1962), pp. 5–7.

2. New York *Times,* July 17, 1966.

3. Philip Bridgham, "Mao's 'Cultural Revolution': Origin and Development, Part 2," in Richard Baum and Louise Bennett, eds., *China in Ferment: Perspectives on the Cultural Revolution* (Englewood Cliffs, N.J., 1971), p. 107, citing information supplied by a defector who had had access to secret Party documents.

4. Charles Mohr, New York *Times,* May 30, 1967. If the "guidance" was Chiang Ch'ing's, the immediate inspiration for the attack was evidently Mao's, as see William P. Dorrill, "Power, Policy, and Ideology," in Thomas W. Robinson, ed., *The Cultural Revolution in China* (Berkeley-Los Angeles-London, 1971), p. 81.

5. Seymour Topping, New York *Times,* May 9, 1966.

6. Seymour Topping, *ibid.,* June 4, 1966.

7. David Oancia, Toronto *Globe and Mail,* in the New York *Times,* June 3, 1966.

8. Henry Kamm, New York *Times,* June 19, 1966.

9. New York *Times,* July 11, 1966.

10. From text in Baum and Bennett, eds., *China in Ferment,* pp. 99–106.

11. *Quotations from Chairman Mao Tse-tung* (Peking, 1966), pp. 48–49.

12. New York *Times,* December 5, 1966; see also David Oancia, Toronto *Globe and Mail,* in the New York *Times,* December 6, 1966.

13. David Oancia, Toronto *Globe and Mail,* in the New York *Times,* April 14, 1967.

14. New York *Times,* May 24, 1967.

15. "Accalmi à Pékin," *Le Monde,* March 10, 1967.
16. *Le Monde,* February 28, 1967.
17. For an extended treatment of this development, see Thomas W. Robinson, "The Wuhan Incident: Local Strife and Provincial Rebellion during the Cultural Revolution," *The China Quarterly,* July–September, 1971, pp. 413–38.
18. New York *Times,* July 31, 1967.
19. Tillman Durdin, *ibid.,* September 22, 1967.
20. Charles Mohr, *ibid.,* October 28, 1967.
21. *Le Monde,* November 3, 1967.
22. Charles Mohr, New York *Times,* November 13, 1967.
23. New York *Times,* November 12, 1967.
24. *Le Monde,* November 3, 1967.
25. *Ibid.,* January 3, 1968.
26. Charles Mohr, New York *Times,* June 14, 1968.
27. *Le Monde,* September 8–9, 1968.
28. *Ibid.*
29. Charles Mohr, New York *Times,* October 20, 1968.
30. Edgar Snow, "The Army and the Party," *The New Republic,* May 22, 1971, pp. 9–12.

13. "REVOLUTIONARY DIPLOMACY"
1. Harrison E. Salisbury, "Image and Reality in Indochina," *Foreign Affairs,* April, 1971, pp. 387–88.
2. Audrey Topping, New York *Times,* May 21, 1971.
3. From text in Alexander Dallin, ed., *Diversity in International Communism: A Documentary Record, 1961–1963* (New York-London, 1963), pp. 670–95.
4. Robert Trumbull, New York *Times,* May 17, 1963.
5. New York *Times,* March 31, 1964.
6. *Ibid.,* October 29, 1964.
7. Max Frankel, *ibid.,* May 13, 1965.
8. Jean Baby, *La grande controverse sino-sovietique (1956–1966)* (Paris, 1966), p. 216.
9. Editorial, "China Too Far Too Fast?" *Christian Science Monitor,* June 12, 1965. See also Joseph Fellows, New York *Times,* June 3, 1965, on the Kenyan reaction to Chinese revolutionism.
10. John Chamberlain, New York *Journal American,* October 26, 1965.
11. Drew Middleton, New York *Times,* April 10, 1966.
12. David Oancia, Toronto *Globe and Mail,* in the New York *Times,* July 16, 1966.
13. From text in the New York *Times,* August 14, 1966.
14. *Keesing's Contemporary Archives,* p. 22047.
15. *Le Monde,* May 27, 1967.
16. Tillman Durdin, New York *Times,* April 14, 1968.
17. Quoted by Peter Van Ness, *Revolution and Chinese Foreign Policy: Peking's Support for Wars of National Liberation* (Berkeley-Los Angeles, 1970), p. 217.

18. *Le Monde,* July 2–3, 1967.
19. See in this connection Joseph Lelyveld, New York *Times,* November 1, 1968.
20. *Le Monde,* September 12, 1967.
21. New York *Times,* July 22, 1967.
22. *Le Monde,* June 1, 1967; New York *Times,* June 4, 1967.
23. *Le Monde,* July 6, 1967.
24. Charles Mohr, New York *Times,* August 21, 1967.
25. *Le Monde,* September 15, 1967.
26. New York *Times,* May 12, 1968.

14. END OF THE MAOIST ERA
1. Tillman Durdin, New York *Times,* January 14, 1968.
2. Charles Mohr, *ibid.,* October 17, 1968.
3. All quotations from the report as published in an English-language version in *Peking Review,* April 30, 1969, pp. 16–35.
4. Stuart Schram (ed. and Introduction), *Chairman Mao Talks to the People—Talks and Letters 1956–1971,* translated by John Chinnery and Tieyun. New York: Pantheon Books, 1974, "Summary of Chairman Mao's Talks with Responsible Comrade at Various Places During His Provincial Tour," pp. 290–99.
5. *Le Monde,* July 2, 1971.
6. Tillman Durdin, New York *Times,* August 29, 1971.
7. A. Bovine, "Recheniia, kotorye, nichego ne reshli" (Resolutions that have resolved nothing), in translation in *Problemes Politiques et Sociaux,* Série Extrême Orient, October 26, 1973, pp. 37–39.
8. *Ibid.* Be it noted that this project "571" has appeared in different versions. For one derived from a Nationalist source, see Michael Y. M. Kau, ed., *The Lin Piao Affair: Power Politics and Military Coup* (White Plains, N.Y.: 1975), pp. 81–90.
9. As stated by Premier Chou En-lai, "Report to the Tenth National Congress of the Communist Party of China, August 24, 1973," *Peking Review,* September 7, 1975, pp. 17–25.
10. *Ibid.*
11. *Problemes Politiques et Sociaux,* Série Extrême Orient, October 28, 1973, p. 22.
12. Text in *Peking Review,* September 7, 1973, pp. 17–25.
13. Quotes from *Peking Review,* September 7, 1973, pp. 29–33.
14. From text in *ibid.,* pp. 29–33.
15. Text in *ibid.,* pp. 26–29.
16. Yang Jung-kao, "Confucius—A Thinker Who Stubbornly Upheld the Slave System," *Peking Review,* October 12, 1973, pp. 5–10.
17. Editorial, "Deepening Criticism of Lin Piao Through Repudiating Confucius," *Peking Review,* February 1, 1974, pp. 3–4.
18. See, for example, Yang Jung-kuo, "Struggle Between Two Lines in the Ideological Sphere During the Spring and Autumn Period and the Warring States Period," *Peking Review,* February 22, 1974, pp. 4–7.
19. All quotations from *Peking Review,* January 24, 1975.

20. "Quarterly Chronicle and Documentation," *The China Quarterly*, June 1976, pp. 428–29.

21. From text in Center for International Affairs and East Asian Research Center, Harvard University, *Communist China 1955–1959: Policy Documents with Analysis* (Cambridge, Mass., 1962), pp. 257–72.

22. Conrad Brandt, Benjamin Schwartz, and John K. Fairbank, *A Documentary History of Chinese Communism* (Cambridge, Mass., 1952), pp. 414–18.

23. For a revealing analysis of Chinese popular reactions in the Hundred Flowers period, see Lucien Bodard, *La Chine du cauchemar*, Paris, 1961. For a survey of the situation as it appeared at the beginning of the GPCR, see Harrison E. Salisbury, New York *Times*, August 16, 1966; for an analysis of the end results, see Ross Terrill, "The 800,000,000," *The Atlantic*, Part I, November, 1971, pp. 90–120 *passim;* Part II, January, 1972, pp. 39–62. For a consideration of the effects of the Cultural Revolution on Chinese scientific work, see John Gardner, "The Gang of Four and Chinese Science," *The Bulletin of the Atomic Scientists*, September 1977, pp. 24–30.

15. CHINA AFTER MAO

1. From text in "Quarterly Chronicle and Documentation," *The China Quarterly*, December 1976, pp. 875–78.

2. *Peking Review*, October 8, 1976, quoted in "Quarterly Chronicle and Documentation," *The China Quarterly*, March, 1977, p. 191.

3. For text of Hua's speech, see *Peking Review*, August 26, 1977, pp. 23–57, of which pp. 25–39 were devoted to the "11th Struggle."

4. Harrison Salisbury, New York *Times*, November 5, 1977.

5. Chi Wei, "How the 'Gang of Four' Opposed Socialist Modernization," *Peking Review*, March 11, 1977, pp. 6–9. See also in this connection Jen Ping, " 'Gang of Four': A Scourge of the Nation," *ibid.*, Nov. 26, 1976, pp. 12–14.

6. New York *Times*, October 25, 1977.

7. Stuart R. Schram, "Chairman Hua Edits Mao's Literary Heritage: 'On the 10 Great Relationships,' " *The China Quarterly*, March 1977, pp. 126–35. Professor Schram's book is *Chairman Mao Talks to the People: Talks and Letters 1956–1971* (New York: 1974).

8. For text of "On the Ten Major Relationships," as derived from *Peking Review*, January 1, 1977, see "Quarterly Chronicle and Documentation," *The China Quarterly*, March, 1977, pp. 221–38.

9. Fox Butterfield, The New York *Times*, December 7, 1976.

10. Alain Jacob, *Le Monde*, January 1, 1977; see also same author, *ibid.*, January 31, 1977.

11. From text given in *Le Monde*, July 24–25, 1977.

12. Hua Kuo-feng, "Political Report to the 11th National Congress of the Communist Party of China, *Peking Review*, August 25, 1977, pp. 23–57.

13. Fox Butterfield, New York *Times*, September 22, 1977.

14. See Peking Review, August 25, 1977, particularly pp. 44–56.

15. For text, see *Peking Review*, September 2, 1977, pp. 16–22.

16. *Ibid.*, pp. 23–37.

17. Fox Butterfield, New York *Times*, October 22, 1977. See also in this general connection Harrison Salisbury, *ibid.*

18. "Quarterly Chronicle and Documentation," *The China Quarterly*, March 1977, p. 205.

19. *Peking Review*, September 2, 1977, p. 17.

20. *Ibid.*, pp. 41–42.

21. *Keesings Contemporary Archives*, p. 22887.

22. Henry Kamm, New York *Times*, November 26, 1968.

23. There is a piquant interest in the fact that the fledgling Communist regime in Kiangsi, in its 1932 "declaration of war" on Japan, charged that the Nationalist regime hoped to foment world war in order to gain, in a clash of the great imperialist powers, a solution for China's problem of division. See Wang Chien-min, *Chung-kuo kung-ch'an-tang shih-kao* [Draft History of the Chinese Communist Party] (Taipei, 1965), III, 24–25, for text.

24. *Le Monde*, January 3, 1970.

25. See, for the process, Tillman Durdin, New York *Times*, March 4; *ibid.*, April 5; and Takashi Oka, *ibid.*, April 8, 1970.

26. *Le Monde*, April 7, 1970.

27. Charles Mohr, New York *Times*, December 28, 1969; for earlier signs of warming, see Tillman Durdin, *ibid.*, September 29, 1969.

28. Henry Kamm, New York *Times*, August 31, 1970.

29. *Le Monde*, August 8–9, 1971.

30. Edgar Snow, *The Long Revolution* (New York, 1972), pp. 172–73. See for interesting sidelights on political maneuvers laying the groundwork for the Nixon visit of 1971.

31. *Peking Review*, April 12, 1974; from text in "Quarterly Chronicle and Documentation," *China Quarterly*, July/September 1974, pp. 641–42.

32. "At the Banquet in Honour of President Tito—Chairman Hua Kuo-feng's Speech," *Peking Review*, September 2, 1977, pp. 8–10. See *ibid.*, August 19, 1977, p. 47, for a brief laudatory consideration of how Yugoslavia, in pursuit of its nonalignment policy, had established commercial relations with nearly 90 developing countries and had engaged in mixed commissions for economic cooperation with many of them—an accomplishment Peking must have envied.

33. "President Tito's Speech," *ibid.*, pp. 10–13.

34. *Le Monde*, September 6, 1977.

35. *Le Monde*, September 4–5, 1977.

BIBLIOGRAPHICAL NOTE

The present volume has been presented, as befits its general character, with a bare minimum of source references. A due respect for the concern of the reader nevertheless makes it desirable to give a general report on source materials. No effort will be made to give a comprehensive bibliography on the subject of China. The work by Charles O. Hucker, *China: A Critical Bibliography* (Tucson, Ariz., 1962), has already fulfilled that function, and John K. Fairbank's section on "Suggested Reading" in his book *The United States and China* (3d ed.; Cambridge, 1971), admirably complements the more formal bibliography with his critical evaluations. Finally, Allan B. Cole in his pamphlet *Forty Years of Chinese Communism: Selected Readings with Commentary* (Washington, D.C., 1962), gives even fuller treatment of sources for the later period of Chinese revolutionary history. The present bibliographical note proposes, in a more limited manner, to indicate some useful sources for different aspects of China's history from the Boxer Rebellion down to the present. In these circumstances, of course, omission of a particular title does not constitute anything in the nature of an invidious selection. This note is by no manner of means exhaustive.

GENERAL INTRODUCTION

The work compiled by Wm. Theodore de Bary, Wing-tsit Chan, and Burton Watson, *Sources of Chinese Tradition* (New York, 1960), presents an annotated selection of philosophical concepts which have gone to make up the Chinese mind. Without some appreciation of that ideological background, attempts to interpret contemporary Chinese politics and policies must often fail. Two books, that by Franz H. Michael and George E. Taylor, *A History of the Far East in Modern Times* (New York, 1956), and John K. Fairbank's aforementioned *The United States and China*, are especially useful for their general treatments of Republican China as it emerged from the Confucian order. The volume by Ssu-yü Teng and John K. Fairbank, *China's Response to the West: A Documentary Survey 1839–1923* (Cambridge, 1954), shows the ancient civilization's struggle to readjust to the new forces bearing down upon it.

THE CHANGING ORDER

J. O. P. Bland and E. Backhouse, in the work *China under the Empress Dowager* (Philadelphia, 1910), give a picture of imperial life and politics and bring the story down nearly to the Revolution that overthrew the Confucian order. Arthur H. Smith, in *China in Convulsion* (2 vols.; New York, 1901), gave a contemporary account of the Boxer Rebellion against a background analysis of the events that gave rise to Chinese antiforeignism. Another missionary (and well-known Sinologue), W. A. P. Martin, presented an eyewitness account of developments at the focal point of the Rebellion, the nation's capital, in *The Siege in Pekin: China against the World* (New York, 1900). Commanding much wider resources, Victor Purcell has made a recent study of the Boxer Rebellion, in political context, in *The Boxer Uprising: A Background Study* (Cambridge, Eng., 1963). The book edited and with an introduction by Mary Clabaugh Wright, *China in Revolution: The First Phase, 1900–1913* (New Haven, 1968), offers a series of essays on different aspects of the modern Chinese revolution in its formative period. Jerome Ch'en's biography *Yuan Shih-k'ai (1859–1916)* (Stanford, Calif., 1961), has a direct bearing upon pivotal historical developments from the time of Yuan Shih-k'ai's advent in Korea (1882) down to his death in 1916. At several critical junctures, Yuan Shih-k'ai effectively made history. Similarly, the work edited by Arthur W. Hummel, *Eminent Chinese of the Ch'ing Period (1644–1912)* (2 vols.; Washington, D.C., 1943), constitutes a veritable mine of information for the history in which his subject persons played their parts.

Reginald F. Johnston's *Twilight in the Forbidden City* (London, 1934), written against the background of his service as tutor to the last Manchu Emperor, Hsuan T'ung (P'u Yi), during the latter's residence in the Imperial Palace at Peking in the post-Revolution period, offers valuable material for limited aspects of the "warlord era" that began with Yuan Shih-k'ai's death. For the warlord era in general, Li Chien-nung's book, *The Political History of China, 1840–1928*, translated and edited by Ssu-yü Teng and Jeremy Ingalls (Princeton, N.J., 1956), is a good source, if not as well organized as it might have been. The work compiled by Kao Yin-tsu, *Chung Hua Min Kuo Ta Shih Chi* [A Record of Major Events of the Chinese Republic] (Taipei, 1957), offers a chronological record of important political events from January, 1912, onward and becomes more detailed as it progresses into the period of Nationalist prominence. It is inadequate for treatment of events initiated by "bandits" or foreign "enemies." For the period from 1912 onward, however, the *China Year Book*, British-edited (for years, by H. G. W. Woodhead) and published variously in London, Tientsin, and Shanghai, is a source of political information the value of which increased progressively down through the years until it ceased its being in the war year 1939. And in 1917 there was launched *Millard's Review*, in due course metamorphosed into the *China Weekly Review*, which for two decades, most of the time under the able editorship of J. B. Powell, recorded and commented intelligently upon the tangled developments of China.

NATIONALIST PERIOD

The Nationalist period—and the Communist period—can be arbitrarily taken to have begun in 1919, during the warlord era. Chow Tse-tsung's work, *The May Fourth Movement: Intellectual Revolution in Modern China* (Cambridge, 1960), shows why this is so. An intimate story of the politics involved in organizing nationalism into a force that was able to overthrow the *tuchün* regime at Peking and set up a new power center at Nanking is told by T'ang Leang-li in *The Inner History of the Chinese Revolution* (London, 1930). Ch'ien Tuan-sheng, writing on *The Government and Politics of China* (Cambridge, 1950), treats the old order and the new in China, but especially the constitutional and administrative systems of the Republic, with heavy stress on the period of Kuomintang rule. George E. Sokolsky contributed two long essays on "The Kuomintang" to *China Year Book, 1928*, and *China Year Book, 1929–30*, setting forth much detailed background on the history of the Nationalist movement. And F. F. Liu has written *A Military History of Modern China* (Princeton, N.J., 1956), that is highly useful for the study of the National Government in its military aspects.

Nationalist history, however, is more one of personalities than of institutions. Harold Z. Schiffrin, *Sun Yat-sen and the Origins of the 1911 Revolution* (Berkeley, 1968), offers a perceptive treatment of the role of the man popularly viewed as the outstanding Chinese revolutionary of the first quarter of the century. C. Martin Wilbur's scholarly *Sun Yat-sen, Frustrated Patriot* (New York, 1976), intensively researched, makes a rich contribution to our understanding of the part Sun played in the making of Republican China. Chün-tu Hsueh, in *Huang Hsing and the Chinese Revolution* (Stanford, 1961), brings further balance into a picture that had been distorted by official worship of Sun Yat-sen. For the period after the Nationalists came to power, two outstanding figures are competently treated in James E. Sheridan, *Chinese Warlord: The Career of Feng Yü-hsiang* (Stanford, 1966), and Donald G. Gillin, *Warlord: Yen Hsi-shan in Shansi Province, 1911–1949* (Princeton, 1967). A definitive biography of the man who dominated the political landscape from 1928 to 1949, Chiang Kai-shek, is yet to be written. Of the existing biographies, however, Hollington K. Tong's *Chiang Kai-shek—Soldier and Statesman* (2 vols.; Shanghai, 1937), and S. I. Hsiung's *The Life of Chiang Kai-shek* (London, 1948), are useful for the subject. A certain partisanship of the portrayals is easily counterbalanced by such works as Feng Yü-hsiang, *Wo So Jen Shih Ti Chiang Kai-shek* [The Chiang Kai-shek I Knew], and Yin Shih (pseud.), *Li-Chiang Kuan Hsi Yü Chung Kuo* [*The Li* [*Tsung-jen*]-*Chiang* [*Kai-shek*] *Relations and China*] (Kowloon, 1954). And Chiang Kai-shek has himself disclosed the nature of his thinking in the realm of political economy in his book *China's Destiny* (first published in 1943, but made available in English, with notes and commentary by Philip Jaffe, New York, 1947). The work edited by Howard L. Boorman and Richard C. Howard, *Biographical Dictionary of Republican China* (4 vols., New York, 1968–71), presents, as did the Hummel volumes for the Manchu period, a wealth of valuable information with respect to individual actors in the drama of the 1912–49 period.

CHINESE COMMUNISM

As noted above, the Communist movement developed side-by-side with the Nationalist movement in China; in a sense, they reflected each other. Various works jostle with each other for attention in this field. Covering the whole period from 1919 to 1957 (the end of the first Five-Year Plan), there is the Soviet work by A. S. Perevertailo, as chief editor, and his co-editors V. I. Glunin, K. V. Kukushkin, and V. N. Nikiforov, *Ocherki istorii Kitaya v noveishee vremya* [Sketches of the History of China in the Contemporary Period] (Moscow, 1959). Despite an unabashed sympathy with the revolutionary events portrayed, the book provides a comprehensive account not as yet available in English. A shorter companion volume is that by V. Nikiforov, G. Erenburg, and M. Yur'ev, *Narodnaya revolyutsiya v Kitae: ocherk istorii bor'by i pobedy Kitaiskogo naroda* [The People's Revolution in China: A Sketch of the History of the Struggle and Victory of the Chinese People] (Moscow, 1950), which treats more cursorily revolutionary developments between 1925 and 1949 in particular. Harold R. Isaacs, in *The Tragedy of the Chinese Revolution* (rev. ed.; New York, 1961), covers in detail the period of Kuomintang-Communist collaboration that ended with the breakup at the Yangtze in 1927 and projects the account swiftly down to the Communist victory of 1949. B. G. Sapozhnikov, in *Pervaya grazhdanskaya revolyutsionnaya voina v Kitae 1924–1927 g.g.* [The First Revolutionary Civil War in China of 1924–1927] (Moscow, 1954), gives a parallel account of a scantier—and different—sort. Victor H. Yakhontoff, in *The Chinese Soviets* (New York, 1934), depicted the reviving Communist power at a time when some foreign governments were prepared to accept the National Government's report that the Communists were only "Red bandits." Edgar Snow's *Red Star over China* (New York, 1938), convinced some of the skeptics that the revolutionaries, then once more joined with the National Government in resistance to the Japanese aggressor, were more than peasant robbers. Agnes Smedley's book *The Great Road—The Life and Times of Chu Teh* (New York, 1956), being for the most part Chu Teh's personal account as told to the author, is a substantial contribution to the literature on the Communist movement in China. Unfortunately, that part of the manuscript dealing with the Long March was apparently lost in the long years before publication occurred, leaving a major gap in the story. The party role of Chu Teh's partner in revolution, Mao Tse-tung, is ably treated by Benjamin I. Schwartz in *Chinese Communism and the Rise of Mao* (Cambridge, 1951). But it is the two-volume autobiographical work by Chang Kuo-tao, one of the founding members of the CCP who defected from Mao's camp in 1938, *The Rise of the Chinese Communist Party* (Vol. I, *1921–1927*, Wichita, 1971; Vol. II, *1928–1938*, Wichita, 1972), that offers the richest source of information on the tortured developments within the Party from its founding down to the time of its second united front with the Nationalists. Unabashedly partisan, and so detailed as sometimes to raise incredulous eyebrows, it possesses unique importance as an "inside story" by one of the prime movers of the early Chinese Communist movement.

NATIONALIST-COMMUNIST WARTIME COALITION

The relations between the Nationalists and Communists during wartime have been relatively neglected, but a number of works offer pieces readily fitted together. The official Department of the Army history by Charles F. Romanus and Riley Sunderland, *The United States in World War II, China-Burma-India Theater*, in three volumes—*Stilwell's Mission to China* (Washington, D.C., 1953); *Stilwell's Command Problems* (Washington, D.C., 1956); and *Time Runs Out in CBI* (Washington, D.C., 1959)—offers an incontrovertible account of the Nationalists' failure to pull their share of the load in the wartime alliance with the United States, with the first two volumes the more valuable. The role played by Lieutenant General Joseph W. Stilwell in the troubled American-Nationalist-Communist wartime triangle in China, once the subject of hot American domestic controversy, has been expertly and probably definitively treated by Barbara W. Tuchman in her *Stilwell and the American Experience in China, 1911–45* (New York, 1971). Vivid colors are added to the general record of the period by several journalistic accounts, outstanding among them being the books by Theodore H. White and Annalee Jacoby, *Thunder Out of China* (New York, 1946), and Ilona Ralf Sues, *Shark's Fins and Millet* (New York, 1945). Chalmers A. Johnson, using mostly Japanese sources, in *Peasant Nationalism and Communist Power* (Stanford, Calif., 1962) records how the Communists were building up their military and political strength under the same wartime conditions that led the Nationalists ever deeper into political corruption and military weakness. Carsun Chang writes on the efforts of the minor (and unarmed) middle-of-the-road political groups to find a solution to China's political problems in *The Third Force in China* (New York, 1952). General L.-M. Chassin, in *L'ascension de Mao Tse-tung, 1921–1945* (Paris, 1953), portrayed the growth of Communist power under leadership of the man who would bring Chiang Kai-shek to defeat —and deny the validity of the "third force" concept.

FINAL NATIONALIST-COMMUNIST STRUGGLE

In another book, *La conquête de la Chine par Mao Tse-tung (1945–1949)* (Paris, 1952), General Chassin recounts how Mao Tse-tung accomplished the final military destruction of his Nationalist foe. Well worth reading in conjunction with this volume is the work of V. I. Glunin, *Tret'ya grazhdanskaya revolyutsionnaya voina v Kitae* [Third Revolutionary Civil War in China] (Moscow, 1958). The American military man Robert B. Rigg, who experienced capture by the Communists near one of Manchuria's battlefields, described the leadership, organization, and tactics of the People's Liberation Army, as it existed in the late civil-war period, in *Red China's Fighting Hordes* (Harrisburg, Pa., 1951). A. Doak Barnett, in his collection of reports, written originally from the field, entitled *China on the Eve of Communist Takeover* (New York, 1963), describes conditions which led many Chinese finally to conclude that "Nothing could be worse than the Kuomintang." Derke Bodde, in *Peking Diary: A Year of Revolution* (New York, 1950), contributes a picture of Peking in the months before and after Communist occupation in January, 1949. C. Patrick Fitzgerald, in *Revolution in China* (London, 1952), skillfully shows how the shift of the middle group of the Chinese nation from allegiance to the Nationalists to the side of the Communists determined the final outcome of the long struggle. Kuo P'ing-chia, under the title *China: New Age and New Outlook* (New York, 1956), using a deeper historical background than Fitzgerald, endeavors to weigh the significance of the revolutionary change. Using a powerful journalistic style, Jack Belden, in *China Shakes the World* (New York, 1949), pictured the tremendous changes then being wrought. And the French diplomat-scholar Jacques Guillermaz presents, in *A History of the Chinese Communist Party 1921–1949* (New York, 1972), an overall, authoritative survey of the development of the Chinese Communist revolution, including both the political and military elements, from its humble beginnings down to the striking victory over the Nationalists in 1949.

The nature of periodical material for the periods of both the Sino-Japanese War and the subsequent civil war changed as compared with the preceding period. Some periodicals naturally went out of existence— or into Japanese service. The outstanding newspaper *Ta Kung Pao* [L'Impartial], however, once of Tientsin, with the advent of war moved to Chungking and continued under wartime conditions to present solid news and a liberal, middle-of-the-road viewpoint. The *Hsin Hua Jih Pao* [New China Daily] (Chungking, and later Huaiyin) and the *Chieh Fang Jih Pao* [Liberation Daily] (Yenan) were openly and avowedly Communist but offered information not available elsewhere. The periodicals of the Institute of Pacific Relations, *Pacific Affairs* and *Far Eastern Survey*, published much valuable information and analysis regarding Chinese (and other Asian) developments, from the mid-1920s onward, for the whole period under consideration. Additional material for that same troubled era has recently been coming out in the pages of the magazine *Ch'un Ch'iu* [Spring and Autumn] (Hong Kong). Established only in 1957, after the Communist victory, it has from the beginning published essays and monographs on events and personalities of the entire Republican period; the quality of the contributions tends naturally to be somewhat uneven, but the source is of first-rate importance for its intimate accounts of obscure events. As regards the Communist aspect of the political developments in China for the three decades of Nationalist-Communist competition that ended with the Nationalist Armageddon of 1949, the handbook produced by the joint efforts of Conrad Brandt, Benjamin Schwartz, and John K. Fairbank, *A Documentary History of Chinese Communism* (Cambridge, 1952), offers a discerning selection of extracts from important documents, with critical commentary.

THE COMMUNIST ERA

The Nationalists in exile on Formosa have received only limited treatment. Fred W. Riggs, in *Formosa under Chinese Nationalist Rule* (New York, 1952), gave an objective and in main generous account of the Nationalists in their refuge. But the world is more interested in what is happening on the mainland. For the ideological background, Mao Tse-tung's *Selected Works*, published in various editions (with the official version comprising that issued by the Foreign Languages Press at Peking), is of course essential. The fourth volume of that work was published in 1961. Volume V, covering what may be viewed as the most constructive period of the Maoist rule, 1949–57, issued in 1977.

There have been various accounts of developments in China after the Communist advent to power, but the outstanding feature of the landscape is the tentative character of judgments—except for outright partisans of one side or the other. The work by S. B. Thomas, *Government and Administration in Communist China* (rev. ed.; New York, 1955), was an early description of the machinery of Communist power. Peter S. H. Tang's volume, *Communist China Today: Volume I, Domestic and Foreign Policies* (rev. ed., Washington, D.C., 1961), constitutes, for all of the author's evident pro-Nationalist sympathies, a valuable description of the political machinery of the Chinese People's Republic. W. W. Rostow and others, in *The Prospects for Communist China* (New York, 1954), give a good analytical survey of the new power. Richard L. Walker, *China Under Communism: The First Five Years* (New Haven, Conn., 1955), gives a strongly critical survey of Communist China in its beginning stage of development.

Despite the excesses of the period of consolidation, China tended to win more sympathy, or at least respect, in the period 1949–57 than afterward. The year 1957 marked a distinct turning point, one aspect of which is covered by Roderick MacFarquhar in *The Hundred Flowers Campaign and the Chinese Intellectuals*, with epilogue by G. F. Hudson (New York, 1960). Mu Fu-sheng in *The Wilting of the Hundred Flowers: The Chinese Intelligentsia under Mao* (New York, 1963), considers the same political phenomenon in deep historical and cultural perspective. An interesting progression in interpretation is discovered in the case of China-born Lucien Bodard, who found the political climate much changed from one visit to the next, with his impressions recorded respectively in *La Chine de la douceur* (Paris 1957), and *La Chine du cauchemar* (Paris, 1961). In more intimate detail, writing from the standpoint of one who was a Communist official, Chow Ching-wen, in *Ten Years of Storm: The True Story of the Communist Regime* (New York, 1960), exemplifies the experience of many intellectuals who stayed to serve and, by the evidence, came to suffer bitter disillusionment.

There have been useful first-hand journalistic accounts covering the period, as those by the Canadian correspondent William Stevenson, *The Yellow Wind* (Cambridge, 1959), the writer for French newspapers Tibor Mende, *La Chine et son ombre* (Paris, 1960), and the American author Edgar Snow, *The Other Side of the River* (New York, 1962). All should be read for the valuable first-hand evidence they give—not for final judgment on the tremendous rapidly-changing development in course. The work by A. Doak Barnett, *Communist China and Asia* (New York, 1960), presents a scholarly survey of contemporary China in its domestic and foreign aspects, and Chang-t'u Hu, in his book *China: Its People Its Society Its Culture* (New Haven, Conn., 1960), presents the subject in a useful topical arrangement permitting each phase of the vast subject to be viewed in its cultural context. In *The Chinese People's Liberation Army* (New York, 1967), Samuel B. Griffith II sets forth, in political context, the history of the People's Liberation Army from its founding (as the Red Army) down to its involvement in the Great Proletarian Cultural Revolution in January 1967. John Gittings, in his own work on *The Role of the Chinese Army* (London, 1967), gives detailed treatment of the leadership, organization, and accomplishments of the PLA from the beginning of the Third Revolutionary Civil War in 1946 to the end of 1965. His and Griffith's book provide a solid basis of reference for consideration of the PLA role in the GPCR—and after.

The most recent period, that encompassing the Great Proletarian Cultural Revolution, has been treated in a number of works—and more are doubtless to come. Robert E. Elegant gives a revealing journalistic account of the whole in *Mao's Great Revolution* (New York, 1971). Both The Bulletin of the Atomic Scientists, *China After the Cultural Revolution* (New York, 1969), and Richard Baum and Louise B. Bennett (editors and contributors), *China in Ferment: Perspectives on the Cultural Revolution* (Englewood Cliffs, N.J., 1971), are compendiums of essays on various aspects of the Cultural Revolution, with the conclusions of the several writers varying from the favorable to the adversely critical. In another work of the same genre, Thomas W. Robinson (editor and contributor), *The Cultural Revolution in China* (Berkeley, 1971), there is more intensive treatment of particular aspects of the Cultural Revolution. With more specialization still, Chien Yu-shen focuses on the military in his *China's Fading Revolution: Army Dissent and Military Divisions, 1967–68* (Hong Kong, 1969); and Peter Van Ness, in *Revolution and Chinese Foreign Policy: Peking's Support for Wars of National Liberation* (Berkeley, 1970), considers a basic concept of Maoism having high importance in China's foreign policy, with Part III of his work devoted to the Cultural Revolution's foreign-affairs aspect. In *Mao's Way* (Berkeley/Los Angeles/London, 1972, 1974), Edward E. Rice makes valuable contribution to our understanding of Maoism per se, bringing the story down through the Lin Piao affair. For that fantastic episode, the compendium of documents contained in Y. M. Kau (ed.), *The Lin Piao Affair: Power Politics and Military Coup* (White Plains, 1975), is of first-rate importance. Simon Leys (pseud.), in *Chinese Shadows* (New York, 1977), presents a striking picture of the devastation wrought by Maoist messianism in the intellectual and cultural life of China. Jacques Guillermaz's successor volume, *The Chinese Communist Party in Power, 1949–1976* (Boulder, 1977), offers a comprehensive account of the accomplishments and shortcomings of the Chinese leadership in the Maoist era. Allen S. Whiting and Robert F. Dernberger, in their book *China's Future: Foreign Policy and Economic Development in the Post-Mao Era* (New York, 1977), soberly project from the situation existing upon the death of Chairman Mao to speculate on the probable course of events in the 1980's in the two fields of Chinese foreign affairs (Whiting) and economics (Dernberger), and come up with illuminating and helpful appraisals in those respects.

THE CHINESE ECONOMY

The matter comes back to the basic question of China's economy. In a situation where there is not as yet commercially available, after fourteen years, even an American map showing the new political boundaries of Communist China, the pioneering work by Theodore Shabad, *China's Changing Map: A Political and Economic Geography of the Chinese People's Republic* (New York, 1952), is of considerable value for its description of China's economic foundations. Beginning in 1953, the Communists began to work great changes in China's economy, and for study of the period the collection entitled *Communist China 1955–1959: Policy Documents with Analysis*, prepared at Harvard University under the Joint Auspices of the Center for International Affairs and the East Asian Research Center (Cambridge, 1962), with a foreword by the respective directors, Robert R. Bowie and John K. Fairbank, constitutes an invaluable handbook. Analytical studies of economic developments are given more particularly by Ygael Gluckstein, *Mao's China: Economic and Political Survey* (Boston, 1957); Choh-ming Li, *Economic Development of Communist China: Appraisal of the First Five Years of Industrialization* (Berkeley, Calif., 1959), and T. J. Hughes and D. E. T. Luard, *The Economic Development of Communist China, 1949–1960* (rev. ed.; London, 1961). A later contribution to this basic subject comes from the Swiss economist, Gilbert Etienne, who wrote *La voie chinoise* (Paris, 1962), on the basis of observations made in the course of a visit to China in 1961. Alexander Eckstein's *Communist China's Economic Growth and Foreign Trade: Implications for U.S. Foreign Policy* (New York, 1966) is a highly useful study of an area which, given the unavailability of official production statistics since the collapse of the Great Leap, must be regarded as esoteric.

SINO-SOVIET RELATIONS

Consideration of Sino-Soviet relations is not only an exciting intellectual pursuit: it is essential for any estimate of the probable destiny of China, for its political advance depends substantially upon the amount of military, political, and economic aid it can borrow from its Communist "ally." Two Soviet works, one edited by E. M. Zhukov, *Mezhdunarodnye otnosheniya na dal'nem vostoke, 1840–1949* [International Relations in the Far East, 1840–1949] (2d ed.; Moscow, 1956), and the other by M. S. Kapitsa, *Sovetsko-Kitaiskie otnosheniya* [Soviet-Chinese Relations] (Moscow, 1958), offer interesting background material for this consideration. *The Theses and Statutes of the Third (Communist) International Adopted by the Second Congress July 17th to August 7th, 1920* (Moscow, 1920); the stenographic record of *I-i Sezd Narodov vostoka* [1st Congress of the Peoples of the East] (Petrograd, 1920); and the record contained in Communist International *The First Congress of the Toilers of the Far East* (Petrograd, 1922), offer perhaps franker discussions of revolutionary purposes than those available for later meetings. The record of the Seventh World Congress of the Communist International, *Resolutions* (New York, 1935), is interesting both as comprising the decisions of the last meeting of the Comintern and as formalizing the "united front" concept employed later by, among others, the Chinese Communist Party.

O. Edmund Clubb, *China and Russia: The "Great Game"* (New York,

1971), offers a survey of the Sino-Russian relationship from beginnings
three centuries ago to the critical date October, 1969. Two good books
on the twentieth century period are those by Aitchen K. Wu, *China
and the Soviet Union* (New York, 1950), and Henry Wei, *China and
Soviet Russia* (Princeton, N.J., 1956). Victor A. Yakhontoff's book,
Russia and the Soviet Union in the Far East (New York, 1931), approaches the subject from the Russian side. Other books consider segments of that history in greater detail. Allen S. Whiting considers the
introductory period in his perceptive *Soviet Policies in China, 1917–1924*
(New York, 1954); Robert C. North stresses the 1920s, and focuses on
the Chinese Communist struggle for power, in the work *Moscow and
Chinese Communists* (rev. ed.; Stanford, Calif., 1963); Conrad Brandt,
Stalin's Failure in China, 1924–1927 (Cambridge, 1958), narrows the
range of the inquiry into developments of that period; and Charles B.
McLane brings the history down to the beginning of the "third revolutionary civil war" in *Soviet Policy and the Chinese Communists, 1931–
1946* (New York, 1958).

Max Beloff's *Soviet Policy in the Far East, 1944–1951* (London,
1953), is again a work of larger political scope, but it has its relevancy
to the subject in point. The compendium by C. Martin Wilbur and
Julie Lien-ying How, *Documents on Communism, Nationalism, and
Soviet Advisers in China, 1918–1927* (New York, 1956), comprising
documents (in English translation) seized in Chang Tso-lin's 1927 raid
on the Soviet Embassy at Peking, with the compilers' critical comments,
is a highly valuable source of information for that earlier stage of Sino-
Soviet cooperation. Howard L. Boorman, Alexander Eckstein, Philip E.
Mosely, and Benjamin I. Schwartz, in *Moscow-Peking Axis: Strengths
and Strains* (New York, 1957), treated the Sino-Soviet alliance of 1950
in its various aspects. That was before the estrangement of those allies;
Donald S. Zagoria, in *The Sino-Soviet Conflict 1956–1961* (Princeton,
N.J., 1962), considers the second half-decade of the new Sino-Russian
relationship, putting the emphasis on the ideological conflict. The thin
volume by Yugoslav Vice President Edvard Kardelj, *Socialism and War:
A Survey of the Chinese Criticism of the Policy of Coexistence,* translated
by Alec Brown (London, 1961), offers considerations largely neglected
by many other observers. The Soviet compilation under the joint editorship of I. F. Kurdyukov, V. N. Nikoforov, and A. S. Perevertailo,
Sovetsko-Kitaiskie otnosheniya 1917–1957: sbornik dokumentov [Soviet-
Chinese Relations 1917–1957: Collection of Documents] (Moscow,
1959), is a useful adjunct for use in this general connection. The book
by O. B. Borisov and B. T. Koloskov, *Soviet-Chinese Relations 1945–
1970* (Bloomington/London, 1975), making extensive use of Soviet
archival materials, offers interesting data on the Sino-Soviet relationship
not previously available. An American compilation of Soviet views,
Morris Rothenberg, *Whither China: The View From The Kremlin*
(Washington, D.C., 1977), is unnecessarily repetitive but offers valuable source material for the weighing of Soviet policy toward the People's Republic of China at the beginning of the post-Mao era in particular.

CHINA'S BORDERLANDS

Sino-Russian relations have tended in the past to manifest themselves in true aspect in the borderlands dividing the two countries. Given especially the prime importance attributed by the Nationalists to Manchuria in the postwar period, and the role the struggle there played in determining the Nationalist fate, it is of interest to note that there exist a number of Chinese works giving more details of the struggle than available in English. T'ang Yun, compiler, *Tung Pei Wen T'i Chih Chen Hsiang* [The True Nature of the Northeastern Problem] (Nanking, 1946), and an unattributed compilation, *Wei Tung Pei Ho P'ing Min Chu Erh Tou Cheng* [Fighting for Peace and Democracy for the Northeast] (n.p., n.d.), might be taken as typical partisan offerings. The Edwin W. Pauley document, *Report on Japanese Assets in Manchuria to the President of the United States* (Washington, D.C., 1946), included details of Soviet removals of industrial machinery and other social wealth from Manchuria.

Gerard M. Friters, *Outer Mongolia and Its International Position* (Baltimore, 1949), presents an entirely adequate survey of the subject in point for the pre-Communist period. Owen Lattimore, who has written various books on the Mongols and Mongolia for earlier historical periods, added up-to-date interpretation in *Nomads and Commissars: Mongolia Revisited* (New York, 1962), written on the basis of a trip to the Mongolian People's Republic in 1961. He and aides at the Johns Hopkins University also offered a study of the obscure but important province of Sinkiang, in *Pivot of Asia: Sinkiang and the Inner Asian Frontiers of China and Russia*, (Boston, 1950). That work is supplemented in the bifurcated product of Allen S. Whiting and General Sheng Shih-ts'ai, *Sinkiang: Pawn or Pivot?* (East Lansing, Mich., 1958), in which the American scholar writes history and Sheng Shih-ts'ai recounts an apologia for his rule and policies as Sinkiang *Tupan*.

SINO-AMERICAN RELATIONS

In the ultimate analysis, Americans are interested in relations between China and the United States. The subject is best studied with appropriate reference to China's own foreign policy. Werner Levi, *Modern China's Foreign Policy* (Minneapolis, Minn., 1953), offers a good general survey. Robert T. Pollard, *China's Foreign Relations, 1917–1931* (New York, 1933), confines himself to a smaller segment of the subject. R. G. Boyd, *Communist China's Foreign Policy* (New York, 1962), is an able if necessarily tentative consideration of Peking's foreign policy at the beginning of the 1960's. Approaching the matter from the other end, the work of A. Whitney Griswold, *The Far Eastern Policy of the United States* (New York, 1938), offers a general background treatment of the subject. Dorothy Borg, *American Policy and the Chinese Revolution, 1925–1928* (New York, 1947), and *The United States and the Far Eastern Crisis of 1933–1938* (Cambridge, 1964), analyzes, with close documentation, American policy at critical turning-points. Cordell Hull, *The Memoirs of Cordell Hull* (2 vols.; New York, 1948), offers important data on the three-way relationship between the United States, Japan, and China. Herbert Feis's *The China Tangle* (Princeton, N.J., 1953), based upon official State Department records, displays the contradictions within American policy toward China for the period of the war in the Pacific, 1941–45. The State Department publication, *United States Relations with China,* commonly called *China White Paper* (Washington, D.C., 1949), is an invaluable compilation of documents for the period of wartime collaboration and postwar mediation particularly. The book by Robert Blum (edited by A. Doak Barnett), *The United States and China in World Affairs* (New York, 1966), analyzes Sino-American relations from 1949 onward; Warren I. Cohen, in a broader survey, *America's Response to China: An Interpretive History of Sino-American Relations* (New York, 1971), delves into the motivations and interpretations—and misinterpretations—that have gone into the making of the American China policy. In his work *China and the Major Powers in East Asia* (Washington, D.C., 1977), A. Doak Barnett gives a penetrating analysis of the PRC's relations with the Soviet Union, Japan, and the United States in the context of what he perceives to be a new quadrilateral balance of power. The official United States Foreign Relations series for Sino-American wartime and postwar relations has issued progressively, if tardily, in recent years, and now there is needed only the publication of the last volume for 1949 (Vol. VIII, *The Far East: China*) to complete the official record to mid-century.

THE CURRENT SCENE

For study of the current scene, the observer can no longer have recourse to the *Far Eastern Survey,* which ceased publication when the American Institute of Pacific Relations was finally driven out of existence by its enemies in 1960; but it has a successor in a monthly publication, *Asian Survey.* The quarterly publication *Pacific Affairs,* formerly issued by the IPR International Secretariat at New York, is still published—but now by the University of British Columbia in Canada. Where there is no American periodical devoted particularly to consideration of current developments in China, the *China Quarterly,* published in London (with Americans among its contributors), helps admirably to fill the gap. On the other side of the globe, the quarterly *Pacific Community* (Tokyo) serves similarly as a medium for the presentation of longer-term interpretations of contemporary Asian developments. Another quarterly, *Problemy Dal'nego Vostoka* (*Problems of the Far East,* Moscow), organ of the USSR Academy of Sciences' Far Eastern Institute, offers Soviet considerations of Asian topics. And for political as well as economic matters the *Far Eastern Economic Review* (Hong Kong) is a valuable aid.

The student of Chinese affairs no longer has a wide choice of Chinese periodicals to which he might at will resort for coverage of developments in contemporary China. The pattern has changed, and newspapers have become the reflection of state policy and official propaganda. The *Ren Min Ri Bao* [People's Daily] (Peking) and the party Central Committee's

semimonthly *Hongqi* [Red Flag] (Peking) are, however, in that sense
"authoritative." So is the English-language weekly *Peking Review*
(Peking), given worldwide circulation in a variety of languages to present both journalistic items and such official documents as Peking might
want publicized. The United States Consulate General at Hong Kong,
moreover, produces, and distributes to libraries and academic institutions mimeographed translations of vast quantities of material from mainland newspapers and magazines, in the mimeographed series Survey of
the China Mainland Press, Current Background, and Extracts from China
Mainland Magazines. If the proportion of chaff to good grain in Chinese
Communist publications is great, and the bulk of the output is appall-
ingly vast, the busy scholar must nevertheless give thanks for that work
of collection and translation performed to his benefit. This is a major
source of data for more monograph studies by scholars in various disciplines and thus contributes to accomplishment of the task of discovering
the true aspect of twentieth century China.

INDEX